The Palgrave Handbook of Violence in Africa

Obert Bernard Mlambo · Ezra Chitando
Editors

# The Palgrave Handbook of Violence in Africa

Volume 1

*Editors*
Obert Bernard Mlambo
Classical Studies Section
School of Languages and Literatures
Rhodes University
Makhanda, South Africa

Ezra Chitando
Department of Philosophy
Religion and Ethics
University of Zimbabwe
Harare, Zimbabwe

ISBN 978-3-031-40753-6     ISBN 978-3-031-40754-3  (eBook)
https://doi.org/10.1007/978-3-031-40754-3

© The Editor(s) (if applicable) and The Author(s), under exclusive license to Springer Nature Switzerland AG 2024

This work is subject to copyright. All rights are solely and exclusively licensed by the Publisher, whether the whole or part of the material is concerned, specifically the rights of translation, reprinting, reuse of illustrations, recitation, broadcasting, reproduction on microfilms or in any other physical way, and transmission or information storage and retrieval, electronic adaptation, computer software, or by similar or dissimilar methodology now known or hereafter developed.
The use of general descriptive names, registered names, trademarks, service marks, etc. in this publication does not imply, even in the absence of a specific statement, that such names are exempt from the relevant protective laws and regulations and therefore free for general use.
The publisher, the authors, and the editors are safe to assume that the advice and information in this book are believed to be true and accurate at the date of publication. Neither the publisher nor the authors or the editors give a warranty, expressed or implied, with respect to the material contained herein or for any errors or omissions that may have been made. The publisher remains neutral with regard to jurisdictional claims in published maps and institutional affiliations.

Cover credit: Jürgen Schott/Alamy Stock Photo

This Palgrave Macmillan imprint is published by the registered company Springer Nature Switzerland AG
The registered company address is: Gewerbestrasse 11, 6330 Cham, Switzerland

Paper in this product is recyclable.

# Foreword

This compendium (in 2 volumes) shows that violence is not a "special practice" but that nearly every human practice can be turned into something violent. Correspondingly, this book traces the "violent turn" in human society across a great diversity of cultural settings and domains. The human is the one living being we should be most careful about since no other living species on earth causes more deaths in the human population. And with every new human practice, there is potential for new violence to emerge. The compendium is therefore also a guide for recognizing and documenting when ordinary things (including well-intended actions) turn violent. If we want to change the course of things for the better and if we want to be prepared to prevent and prosecute violence, we need to recognize it in its many possible manifestations. We need to understand its recurrent and underlying structures (for instance, in patriarchy) as this volume convincingly shows.

This collection focuses on Africa, but without entrenching the stereotype of Africa as a particularly violent place, because wherever there is violence, there are also people who seek to stop it. The many examples of ways of dealing with conflicts in non-violent ways and of turning away from violence are testimony to that. As the contributions to the book show, the human condition is never innocent and harmless—but it is not hopeless either.

Thomas Widlok<br>
University of Cologne<br>
Cologne, Germany

# Contents

**Violence in Africa: A General Introduction**     1
*Obert Bernard Mlambo and Ezra Chitando*

**Conceptualizing Violence in Africa**

**Violence in Africa: Reflecting on a Broad Concept**     23
*Ezra Chitando and Obert Bernard Mlambo*

**The Rate of Oppression (ROp): The Apartheid Studies Approach to the Study of Harm**     53
*Nyasha Mboti*

**On Systemic and Epistemic Violence in Africa**     77
*Patricia Pinky Ndlovu and Sabelo J. Ndlovu-Gatsheni*

**Technologies of Violence in Africa**     99
*Wesley Mwatwara and Obert Bernard Mlambo*

**Border Violence in Africa**     119
*Rachel Ibreck and Souhayel Weslety*

**Diaspora and the Afterlife of Violence: Eritrean National Narratives and What Goes Without Saying**     141
*Victoria Bernal*

The Chemical Violence of Colonial Encounters in Africa:
Historiographical Reflections and Theoretical Perspectives  167
*Elijah Doro*

Epistemic Violence in the Postcolony: Interrogating
the Colonial Legacy and War in Francophone African Literature  183
*Gibson Ncube*

Geographies of Violence and Informalization: The Case
of Mathare Slums in Nairobi, Kenya  203
*Maurice Omollo and Solomon Waliaula*

Through the Afrocentricity Lens: Terror, Insurgency
and Implications for Regional Integration in Southern Africa
from Cabo Delgado Province, Mozambique  221
*Daniel Nkosinathi Mlambo, Victor H. Mlambo,
and Mandla Mfundo Masuku*

## The State and Violence in Africa

Discourses on Political Violence and the Mechanics
of Legitimation in Official Commissions of Inquiry in Africa  243
*Claire-Anne Lester*

Party Politics, Violence, Impunity, and Social Injustices
in Zimbabwe (1980–2022)  265
*Vellim Nyama and Pedzisai Ruhanya*

Preventing Electoral Violence in Africa: Towards Sustainable
Peace  285
*Khabele Matlosa*

"Dirge to Slit Bodies": EndSARS, Police Brutality,
and Nigerian Dystopia in Jumoke Verissimo and James Yéku's
*Soro Soke: When Poetry Speaks Up*  307
*Ayokunmi Ojebode*

The Resource Curse and Structural Violence in Angola: A Path
for Perpetual Conflicts  329
*Jeremiah Bvirindi*

Electoral Violence in Ghana's Fourth Republic: The Case
of Party Vigilantism  347
*Emmanuel Debrah, Isaac Owusu-Mensah, Sampson Danso,
and Gilbert Arhinful Aidoo*

| | |
|---|---|
| **Investigating the Causes and Impact of Electoral Violence in Nigeria**<br>*Usman Sambo, Babayo Sule, and Mohammed Kwarah Tal* | 367 |
| **Ungoverned Space and National Security in Nigeria**<br>*Arinze Ngwube* | 387 |

## Children, Youth and Violence

| | |
|---|---|
| **Trauma, Violence, and Memory in African Child Soldier Memoirs**<br>*Stacey Hynd* | 409 |
| **Africa and Violence: The Metamorphosis and Participation of Child Soldiers in Conflict Zones**<br>*Toyin Cotties Adetiba* | 437 |
| **Youth, Violence, and Political Accumulation: Urban Militias in Zimbabwe**<br>*Simbarashe Gukurume and Godfrey Maringira* | 459 |
| **Youth, Proliferation of Small Arms and Light Weapons, and Conflicts in 21st Century Africa**<br>*Babayo Sule, Ibrahim Kawuley Mika'il, and Mohammed Kwarah Tal* | 479 |
| **Violence Against Children on the Streets in Sub–Saharan Africa: An Overview**<br>*Witness Chikoko* | 501 |
| **Violence Against Disabled Children in Botswana**<br>*Thabile Anita Samboma* | 521 |

## Nature, Religion and Cultural Violence in Africa

| | |
|---|---|
| **Violence against Nature in African Traditional Thought and Practice**<br>*Obert Bernard Mlambo and Kudzanai Melody Mlambo* | 541 |
| **Yearning for Old Time Religion in the Face of Globalization? Interpreting Fundamentalisms and Violent Extremism in Africa**<br>*Ezra Chitando* | 559 |
| **In God's Name: Violent Extremism in North East Nigeria**<br>*Jacinta Chiamaka Nwaka* | 575 |

Beyond Ethnicity: Reflections on the History and Politics
of Violence in Uganda   601
*Evarist Ngabirano*

The Intersectionality Between Violence and Poverty in Africa:
Sketching the Prevalence of Various Forms of Violence
in South Africa   619
*Rabson Hove*

Violence Against Nature in Africa: A Historical Assessment   639
*Marlino Eugénio Mubai*

Xenophobia, Afrophobia, or Promoting Xenophilia? Semantic
Explorations of Violence and Criminality in South Africa   661
*Martin Mujinga*

Enchanted Worldviews and Violence Against Persons
with Albinism in Sub-Saharan Africa   677
*Francis Benyah*

Violence Against Persons with Albinism in Malawi   699
*Jones Hamburu Mawerenga*

Globalization, Islamic Fundamentalism and Violence Through
the Youth in Kenya   721
*Susan M. Kilonzo*

## Gender and Violence in Africa

Sexual Violence Against Girls and Women in African Conflict   745
*Veronica Fynn Bruey*

The Cost of Violence Against Women in Africa   779
*Tshenolo Jennifer Madigele and Mutsawashe Chitando*

Violence against Women in Egypt: A Closer Look at Intimate
Partner Violence and Female Genital Mutilation   795
*Yasmin M. Khodary*

"Wait, Let's Talk About It": A Feminist Assessment
of the Response of the Church of the Cross Hayfield
(NELCSA) to Gender-Based Violence in Pietermaritzburg,
South Africa   819
*Lindiwe Princess Maseko*

**Breaking The Silence: Exploring the Challenges and Support Mechanisms for Male Survivors of Gender-Based Violence in Sub-Saharan Africa**   849
*Susan Monyangi Nyabena*

**Gender Violence: A Portrait of Women for Change's Fight Against Gender-Based Violence in Zambia**   865
*Nelly Mwale and Joseph Chita*

**Persisting Inequalities: An Intersectional View of Climate Change, Gender and Violence**   879
*Mary Nyasimi and Veronica Nonhlanhla Jakarasi*

**"Women's Sexuality Captured": Another Form of Gender-Based Violence (GBV) in the Swati Patriarchal Space**   893
*Sonene Nyawo*

**Changing Contexts, Changing Violence Patterns? The Case of African Diaspora Women**   909
*Nomatter Sande and Amos Muyambo*

**Adolescent Boys, Young Men, and Mental Health in Southern Africa**   925
*Mutsawashe Chitando*

**Towards a Reconstruction of Sacralized Traditions to Avert Gender-Based Violence Prevalent in Girl-Child Marriages Amongst the Akamba**   941
*Telesia Kathini Musili*

Violence, Memory and the Law in Africa

Pre-colonial and Colonial Violence in Zimbabwe: A Literary-cultural Exegesis   961
*Oliver Nyambi*

"Living in the Shadow of Death": Understandings of Political Violence and Its Aftermath in the Zimbabwean Context   979
*Chenai Matshaka and Ruth Murambadoro*

Forgetting as a Psychological Weapon? Critiquing the Call to Forget in a Zimbabwe Founded and Ruled by Violence   1001
*Collium Banda*

**Incest as Dismissal: Anthropology and Clinics of Silence**    1019
*Parfait D. Akana*

**Preventing Violent Conflict in Africa**

**Confronting Military Violence in Africa's Electoral Spaces: Law, Institutions, and Remedies**    1033
*James Tsabora*

**Managing Conflict in Africa: Challenges and Opportunities for the African Union**    1051
*Victor H. Mlambo, Ernest Toochi Aniche, and Mandla Mfundo Masuku*

**Beyond Xenophobia or Afrophobia: Strategies and Solutions**    1071
*Nomatter Sande and Martin Mujinga*

**Violent Piracy off the Coast of Nigeria: A Theoretical Analysis**    1087
*Kalu Kingsley Anele*

**Insurgency in Mozambique: Can SADC's NATO's Article 5 Treaty Address Future Insurgences in the Region**    1111
*Victor H. Mlambo, Mandla Mfundo Masuku, and Daniel Nkosinathi Mlambo*

**Mediatized Conflict: A Case of Nigerian Media Reportage of Farmer-Herder Conflict**    1133
*Ridwan Abiola Kolawole and Babatunde Raphael Ojebuyi*

**Conclusion**    1151
*Obert Bernard Mlambo and Ezra Chitando*

**Index**    1155

# Notes on Contributors

**Toyin Cotties Adetiba** is Associate Professor and Head of the Department of Political and International Studies, University of Zululand, South Africa. He has published extensively in accredited peer-reviewed journals and book chapters and co-authored a book. Adetiba is an NRF reviewer apart from reviewing for several number of accredited journals. His research interests include Political Science, International Relations, Conflict Resolution, Diplomacy, and Migration.

**Gilbert Arhinful Aidoo** is a Lecturer in the Department of Political Science at the University of Education, Ghana. His research domain includes democracy and electoral violence, terrorism, security governance, human rights, and regionalism in Africa. He has produced a few publications on democracy and electoral violence, terrorism, regionalism, and human rights in Africa.

**Parfait D. Akana** is a sociologist and anthropologist. He is founder and Executive Director of the Muntu Institute Foundation (African Humanities and Social Sciences) and teaches at the University of Yaounde II. He holds a Ph.D. in Sociology from École des Hautes Études en Sciences Sociales (Paris). He worked for CODESRIA (2014–2017) and has been Visiting Fellow for Nantes Institute of Advanced Studies (2017–2018) and Stellenbosch Institute for Advanced Study (2019). His areas of research include mental health, gender, sexual violence, digital and popular cultures. His publications include *Se mobiliser pour le football en Afrique. Une sociologie du* *supportérisme* (Muntu Institute Press, 2023), *Affects* (Muntu Institute Press, 2022), *Réflexivités africaines* (Muntu Institute Press & Jimsaan, 2021).

**Kalu Kingsley Anele** is a Lecturer in Cultural Heritage at the Preservation Research Institute, Pusan National University, South Korea.

**Ernest Toochi Aniche** Ph.D. is a Senior Lecturer and the Acting Head of theDepartment of Political Science, Federal University Otuoke, Bayelsa State, Nigeria. He earned B.Sc., M.Sc., and Ph.D. degrees from the Department of Political Science, University of Nigeria with emphasis on international relations. He belongs to various professional associations. His research interests include African regionalism, comparative regionalism, migration and border studies, conflict and peace studies, security studies, and international political economy.

**Collium Banda** is an Extraordinary Research Fellow in the Unit for Reformational Theology and the Development of the South African Society, Faculty of Theology, North-West University, South Africa, and adjunct lecturer at Theological College of Zimbabwe, Bulawayo, Zimbabwe. His research interests include African Pentecostalism, Christian doctrines in the African public space, African traditional religions, African indigenous knowledge systems, and Christianity in African contexts of suffering.

**Francis Benyah** is a Ph.D. candidate in the Study of Religions at the Åbo Akademi University, Turku, Finland. His research interests focus on pentecostal/charismatic theology and African pentecostal Christianity with a special interest in how it intersects and interacts with public life in areas such as media, politics, health, and human rights.

**Victoria Bernal** is a Cultural Anthropologist whose scholarship in political anthropology contributes to media studies, diaspora studies, gender studies, and African studies. Her work addresses questions relating to politics, digital media, migration and diaspora, war, globalization, transnationalism, civil society and activism, gender, development, and Islam. Dr. Bernal's research is particularly concerned with relations of power and inequality and the dynamic struggles of ordinary people as they confront the cruel and absurd contradictions arising from the concentration of wealth and political power locally and globally. She has carried out ethnographic research in Sudan, Tanzania, Eritrea, Silicon Valley, and cyberspace. She is the author of *Nation as Network: Diaspora, Cyberspace, and Citizenship*, and *Cultivating Workers: Peasants and Capitalism in a Sudanese Village* as well as numerous articles. She is co-editor of anthologies on *Cryptopolitics: Exposure, Concealment and Digital Media*, and *Theorizing NGOs: States, Feminisms, and Neoliberalisms*.

Professor Bernal has received fellowships from the Fulbright Foundation, the Catholic University of Leuven, Belgium, the Center for Advanced Studies in the Behavioral Sciences at Stanford, the American Philosophical Society, and the Rockefeller Foundation. She is a Professor at the University of California, Irvine where she teaches courses on Digital Media and Culture, Global Africa, Nations, States and Gender, and Security, Secrecy, and Surveillance, among others.

**Veronica Fynn Bruey** is a multi-award winner and a passionate academic-advocate. Holding six academic degrees from four continents, she has researched, taught, consulted, and presented at conferences in over 30 countries. She's authored five books, several book chapters, and journal articles. She is the founder/editor-in-chief of the *Journal of Internal Displacement*; the co-lead of Law and Society's Collaborative Research Network (CRN-11): "Displaced Peoples"; the lead of Law and Society Association's International Research Collaborative (IRC-10): "Disrupting Patriarchy and Masculinity in Africa"; and the founder of the Voice of West African Refugees in Ghana at the Buduburam Refugee Settlement in Ghana. She is also the Australian National University International Alumna of the Year, 2021, the president of the International Association for the Study of Forced Migration, and a Co-Chair of the Africa Interest Group, American Society of International Law. Currently, she is the Director of Flowers School of Global Health Sciences, and an Assistant Professor in Legal Studies at Athabasca University. Veronica is a born and bred Indigenous Liberian war survivor.

**Jeremiah Bvirindi** (Ph.D.) is the director of Evaluations and Research Solutions Africa (Pvt) Ltd (EARS-AFRICA). He is a holder of two earned doctorates, a Doctor of Philosophy in Peace, Leadership, and Governance from Africa University and a Doctor of Philosophy in Public Policy Evaluation, from the Swiss School of Management, Switzerland. He is a Lecturer at Midlands State University and Africa University (part-time) and a notable scholar who has published a number of academic papers in the field of governance, peace, and public policy effectiveness.

**Witness Chikoko** is a Senior Lecturer in the Department of Social Work, University of Zimbabwe. He is currently a Research Fellow with University of Johannesburg's Department of Social Work in South Africa. He holds a D.Phil. in Social Studies, a Master's in Social Work, a Postgraduate Diploma in Project Planning and Management, and a Bachelor degree (Honours) in Social Work, all from the University of Zimbabwe. His research interests are childhood studies and social protection.

**Joseph Chita** is a Lecturer in the Department of Religious Studies at the University of Zambia. His research interests are in religion and society, and some of his publications cut across disciplines. He is a member of the African Association for the Study of Religions (AASR), and the Association for the Study of Religion in Southern Africa (ASRSA).

**Mutsawashe Chitando** is a Ph.D. candidate in the Public Health and Health Economics Unit and Division, School of Public Health and Family Medicine, Faculty of Health Sciences, University of Cape Town, South Africa.

**Ezra Chitando** serves as Professor in Religious Studies at the University of Zimbabwe and has served as the Desmond Tutu Extraordinary Professor for Social Justice at the University of Western Cape, South Africa. He has a wide range of research and publication interests, including violence against women, political violence, and peace-building. He co-edited the volume *Justice Not Silence: Churches Facing Sexual and Gender-Based Violence*.

**Sampson Danso** is a Political Science Lecturer with the Department of Distance Education, University of Ghana, Legon and a Ph.D. candidate at the University of South Africa. His research areas are inter-party dialogue, voting patterns, and elections in Ghana.

**Emmanul Debrah** is Associate Professor in the Department of Political Science, He has published extensively in the areas of party politics, elections and democratic development.

**Elijah Doro** is an environmental historian and Research Fellow at Agder University in Norway. He has written on the environmental history of tobacco farming in Zimbabwe. His interests are histories of pollution and contamination in southern Africa and medical histories.

**Simbarashe Gukurume** is a social scientist whose work lies at the intersection of Sociology and Social Anthropology. Currently serving as a Senior Lecturer at Sol Plaatje University, he also holds a research associate position at Stellenbosch University within the Department of Sociology and Social Anthropology. Simbarashe's research interests revolve around the overarching theme of youth subjectivities and their intricate connections with various aspects of everyday life, including politics, livelihoods, and transitions. His scholarly pursuits delve into the realms of informality, religiosity, displacement, and the political expressions of youth in the midst of enduring economic and political crises. Simbarashe is a former awardee of the African Peacebuilding Network Research Fellowship (2021–2022) and the African

Humanities Programme Fellowship awarded by the American Learned Societies and the Carnegie Corporation in New York, USA.

**Rabson Hove** is a Practical Theologian. He holds a Ph.D. in Ministerial Studies from the University of KwaZulu Natal. He is a Post-Doctoral Fellow in the Research Institute for Theology and Religion (RITR) at University of South Africa (UNISA). Dr. Hove is also an ordained minister and chaplain of the Evangelical Lutheran Church in Zimbabwe (ELCZ), Diaspora His research interests include ecumenism, pastoral care, and community development.

**Stacey Hynd** gained her D.Phil. in History from the University of Oxford in 2008. She lectured at the University of Cambridge and is now Senior Lecturer in African History and Co-Director of the Centre for Imperial and Global History at Exeter. Her previous research has focused on crime, violence, the death penalty, and gender in colonial Africa, with a focus on Malawi, Kenya, and Ghana. Her current research is on the histories of child soldiering and humanitarianism in Africa.

**Rachel Ibreck** is a Senior Lecturer in Politics and International Relations at Goldsmiths, University of London. Her research interests include human rights and legal activism in atrocity, conflict, and displacement settings in Africa. She has published in academic journals including the *Journal of Intervention and Statebuilding*, the *Journal of Civil Society*, and *African Affairs*. She is author of *South Sudan's Injustice System: Law and Activism on the Frontline* (Zed Books, 2019). She is co-investigator on the Fondazione Compagnia di San Paulo research project: *Traces of Mobility, Violence and Solidarity: Reconceptualizing Cultural Heritage Through the Lens of Migration*.

**Veronica Nonhlanhla Jakarasi** is a Chartered Development Finance Analyst and the Head of Climate Finance at the Africa Enterprise Challenge Fund. She leads climate finance resources mobilization to support small and growing businesses to respond to climate change challenges and accelerate the deployment of climate-smart technologies to rural, marginalized, and vulnerable communities. She also supports SMEs to develop and implement climate-smart investment plans and prioritize climate actions. Veronica has over 15 years of experience in climate finance and diplomacy, and environment and natural resources management, having led the establishment of the Climate Change Management Department in 2014, and served as the Manager for Climate Finance and Sustainability at the Infrastructure Development Bank in Zimbabwe (IDBZ). She supports the African Group of Lead Negotiators on Mitigation issues and the Group of 77 and China on Gender and Climate

Change Issues under the UNFCCC process. She has authored different academic papers and book chapters, including on climate finance, gender, and disaster management. Veronica serves on different national and regional boards and is currently the Board Chair of the Forestry Commission in Zimbabwe.

**Yasmin M. Khodary** is Professor of Political Science at the British University in Egypt. She has been working in the development field for the past 15 years. She is the winner of the Abdelhameed Shoman Prize for Arab Researchers and the Ahmed Bahaa-eldin Research Award for Young Authors. She also won the UNDP Project-Award on Corruption Risks in Health and Education, the UNDP Project-Award on Youth Engagement, the UNDP Project-Award on Fighting Corruption and the BUE Young Investigators' Project-Award on Gender in Peacebuilding. Her fields of interest include governance, social accountability, corruption, gender and peacebuilding. Her key publications include: "Middle Eastern Women between Oppression and Resistance" in the *Journal of International Women's Studies;* "FGM in Egypt" in the *Journal of Aggression, Conflict and Peace Research;* "Assessing the Impact of Gender Equality and Empowerment in Matters of Inheritance in Egypt" in the *Journal of the Middle East and Africa;* and "Women and Peace Building in Iraq" in the *Journal of Peace Review.*

**Susan M. Kilonzo** is Associate Professor in the Department of Religion and Philosophy at Maseno University, Kenya. She is a research methodology specialist. She has held the Alexander Von Humboldt Research Fellowship in Germany. Her research and publication interests include religion and violence, gender, development, peacebuilding and method and theory.

**Ridwan Abiola Kolawole** teaches journalism and communication in the Department of Mass Communication, Fountain University, Osogbo, Nigeria. His research interest covers Applied Communication. He is a 2022–2023 Doctoral Dissertation Completion Fellow of the Next Generation of the Social Science Research Council (SSRC), New York. Kolawole is a Research Associate of the *Youth Aspirations and Resilience* project of the Partnership for African Social and Governance Research (PASGR), funded by the MasterCard Foundation.

**Claire-Anne Lester** is a Lecturer in Sociology in the Department of Sociology and Social Anthropology at Stellenbosch University, South Africa. Her research concentrates on state violence, commissions of inquiry investigating violence in the South African mining sector, critical legal theory, and political economy.

**Tshenolo Jennifer Madigele** (B.A., M.A. and Ph.D.) is a Theology Lecturer at the University of Botswana. Her teaching areas include practical theology and systematic theology. Her research interests include human sexuality, with a particular focus on the LGBTI (lesbian, gay, bisexual, transgendered and the intersexed) communities, gerontology, gender and community building, health and spirituality and both pastoral care and counselling. One of her publications is "Homes as 'Cages of Violence and Abuse for Women' During Covid-19 Pandemic: A Pastoral Care Approach to the Case of Botswana and South Africa" (Madigele and Baloyi 2022) which appeared in the journal *HTS Teologiese Studies/Theological Studies*.

**Godfrey Maringira** is Associate Professor of Anthropology at Sol Plaatje University, Kimberley, Northern Cape, South Africa. He is a National Research Foundation C2 rating. He is a senior Volkswagen Stiftung Foundation research fellow and is also a Principal Investigator of the International Development Research Center (IDRC) research on gang violence in South Africa. He is an active board member of the Social Sciences Research Council—Next Generation Social Sciences in Africa. His areas of research include armed violence in Africa with a specific focus on the military in post-colonial Africa. His 2017 *African Affairs* Journal article "Politicisation and Resistance in the Zimbabwe National Army", was awarded the Best Author Prize in 2018. In 2020 he was awarded the Benedict Vilakazi Best Author Prize, *African Studies Journal* (Routledge) for his article titled: "When Combatants Became Peaceful: Azania People Liberation Army Ex-Combatants in Post-Apartheid South Africa". He is the author of *Soldiers and the State in Zimbabwe*, Routledge, 2019.

**Lindiwe Princess Maseko** is a Ph.D. student in Gender and Religion in the School of Religion, Philosophy, and Classics, at the University of KwaZulu Natal in South Africa. Her areas of interest are reproductive health and rights, reproductive justice, and African women's identity.

**Mandla Mfundo Masuku** is an Associate Professor in the School of Built Environment and Development Studies at the University of KwaZulu-Natal. His research areas include inclusive education, food security, scholarship of teaching and learning, African studies, and gender.

**Khabele Matlosa** is a political economist and an independent policy analyst with speciality in democracy, elections, governance, conflict prevention, management and resolution, constitutionalism, human rights, migration, and socio-economic development. He has researched and written widely on these areas over the years. He possesses enormous experience working in multicultural settings with the United Nations (UN) and the African Union (AU). Through the AU, he has worked closely with Regional Economic Communities and Regional Mechanisms in Africa. He has access to networks of innovation, knowledge, practice, lobby, and advocacy cutting across various sectors in Africa including governments, civil society, private sector, political parties, media, faith-based organizations, academia and think tanks, women's groups, youth groups, and traditional governance institutions among others.

**Chenai Matshaka** is a researcher at the University of Pretoria, Centre for Mediation in Africa. She writes on transitional justice and women in mediation in Africa, as well as civil society and its role in peace processes in Africa. She has worked with diverse research institutions and Non-Governmental Organizations (NGOs) in South Africa and Zimbabwe on human rights and security, and transitional justice, as well as migration and refugee issues, all of which also form part of her research interests.

**Jones Hamburu Mawerenga** is a Lecturer in Systematic Theology, Christian Ethics, and African Theology at the University of Malawi. He holds a Ph.D. from Mzuzu University. He is the author of *The Homosexuality Debate in Malawi* (2018) and *Systematic Theology* (2019). His current research interest on the topic of discourses of albinism in Malawi was motivated by the desire to curb violent attacks and gross human rights violations against persons with albinism in the country.

**Nyasha Mboti** is the pioneer and founder of Apartheid Studies, a new interdisciplinary field of study from the Global South which utilizes the notion of "apartheid" as a paradigm by which to understand the confounding persistence and permanence of harm, oppression, and injustice. This account is articulated in *Apartheid Studies: A Manifesto* (Africa World Press, 2023). Mboti is an Associate Professor and Head of the Department of Communication Science at the University of the Free State, Bloemfontein, in South Africa. He lives in Johannesburg.

**Ibrahim Kawuley Mika'il** is a Senior Lecturer in the Department of International Relations, Institute for Transport Technology, Zaria, Kaduna State, Nigeria. He has published extensively on corruption, Nigerian political economy, and good governance. He is a leading advocate of the strategies of combating corruption in the Nigerian political system.

**Victor H. Mlambo** is a Lecturer at the University of Johannesburg, School of Public Management, Governance and Public Policy. Victor's research interests include conflict and migration studies, political geography, regionalism, and security studies.

**Obert Bernard Mlambo** is Associate Professor of Classical Studies and History, formerly based at the University of Zimbabwe, Zimbabwe. His research interests involve Roman History, Classics and Colonialism, Postcolonial Classics, and the issues of Violence, Gender, Politics, and Land in ancient Rome and Zimbabwe. Obert Mlambo now teaches Roman history in a global context at Rhodes University. He is a former Humboldt Fellow at the Institute of African Studies and Egyptology, University of Cologne, Germany, and a Guest Scholar at the Global South Studies Centre of the University of Cologne, Germany.

**Daniel Nkosinathi Mlambo** Ph.D., holds a Postgraduate Diploma in Teacher Education from the Haaga-Helia University of Applied Sciences School of Vocational Teacher Education (Finland), a Ph.D. and Master's degree in Public Administration, an Honours in International Relations, and a junior degree in Development Studies, all from the University of Zululand. His research focuses on African political economy, regional integration, governance and democracy, migration, and security studies.

**Kudzanai Melody Mlambo** is an independent scholar whose research interests include climate change, natural resources management, and food security studies.

**Marlino Eugénio Mubai** is Lecturer and Chair, Department of History, Eduardo Mondlane University, Mozambique. His research areas are warfare, environment, and society. He also explores various layers of politics, society, and culture including religion.

**Martin Mujinga** is the General Secretary of the Methodist Church in Zimbabwe and the General Secretary Elect of the Africa Methodist Council. He is also a Research Fellow of the Research Institute for Theology and Religion at the University of South Africa. Dr. Mujinga is an Adjunct Lecturer at the Midlands State University and United Theological College. His research interests are in the fields of Methodist history and theology,African spirituality, the role of religion in transforming societies, theologies of migration, women and religion, human trafficking, chaplaincy, African theology, liberation theology, political theology, Pentecostal theologies and ecotheology.

**Ruth Murambadoro** is an African feminist who writes on women, transitional justice, gender justice, and the politics of the Global South. Based at the Centre for Feminist Research, York University, her work explores the gendered nature of the post-colonial state to broaden understandings of violence perpetrated against women in Zimbabwe. She holds research affiliations with the Harriet Tubman Institute, and Wits School of Governance. Her long-term project involves working with emerging and seasoned African artists to build a digital repository (re)presenting African women's resistance in the postcolony.

**Telesia Kathini Musili** is a lecturer at the Department of Philosophy and Religious Studies, University of Nairobi, Kenya. She is also a research fellow at the University of South Africa. Her research interests revolve around the intersection of religion, ethics, media, and environment, focusing on the response to contemporary issues affecting women and society at large.

**Amos Muyambo** is a Theologian Educator and Researcher, currently affiliated to the University of Botswana in the Department of Student Welfare in the Disability Support Services. Research interests are African spirituality, gender disability. and religion and development.

**Nelly Mwale** (Ph.D.) is a Senior Lecturer in the Department of Religious Studies at the University of Zambia. Her research interests include religion in the public sphere, religion and higher education, church history, and African indigenous knowledge systems.

**Wesley Mwatwara** is Assistant Professor in Global Economic and Social History at Vrije University Amsterdam and a research associate at Walter Sisulu University. His areas of research include socio-environmental history, animal history, sustainability, and peace and conflict studies. His articles appear in journals such as the *South African Historical Journal*, *Journal of Southern African Studies*, *Kronos*, *Historia*, *Global Environments*, *Environment and History*.

**Gibson Ncube** lectures at Stellenbosch University. He has held fellowships supported by the Stellenbosch Institute for Advanced Study, the National Humanities Center (USA), and Leeds University Centre for African Studies (UK). He has published widely in the fields of comparative literature, gender, and queer studies, as well as cultural studies. He co-convened the Queer African Studies Association (2020–2022) and was the 2021 Mary Kingsley Zochonis Distinguished Lecturer (African Studies Association, UK). He currently sits on the editorial boards of the following journals: *Journal of Literary Studies*, the *Canadian Journal of African Studies*, the *Nordic Journal of African Studies* as well as *Imbizo: International Journal of African Literary* *and Comparative Studies*. He holds a C1 NRF rating. He is the author of the book *Queer Bodies in African Films* (2022).

**Patricia Pinky Ndlovu** is a Doctoral Fellow at the Chair of Sociology of Africa at the University of Bayreuth in Germany and her doctoral study is on violence and gender in the taxi industry in South Africa.

**Sabelo J. Ndlovu-Gatsheni** is Professor and Chair of Epistemologies of the Global South with Emphasis on Africa, as well as Vice-Dean of Research in the "Africa Multiple Cluster of Excellence" at the University of Bayreuth in Germany. He has published extensively on epistemic violence in Africa and is a leading advocate of decolonization.

**Evarist Ngabirano** is a Senior Lecturer and Dean of the Faculty of Humanities and Social Sciences at Mountains of the Moon University, Fort Portal, Uganda. He holds a PhD in Social Studies from Makerere University. He received the SSRC—Next Generation Social Sciences in Africa programme fellowship. His research interests focus on issues of nationalism, culture, politics, and religion.

**Arinze Ngwube** is a Lecturer in the Department of Political Science of Federal University, Oye-Ekiti State, Nigeria. He has contributed articles and book chapters on international affairs.

**Susan Monyangi Nyabena** is a Masters' student at the University of Nairobi. Her key research interests are sexual and reproductive health rights, gender equality, and transformative masculinities. She is a gender and human rights consultant at Gender Ink.

**Vellim Nyama** is a Development Practitioner who holds a Ph.D. in Human Geography from the University of the Free State in South Africa (SA). He has worked for a number of development organizations in Zimbabwe and Africa. His research interests focus on governance, participatory democracy, and peace building. He has published on the local governance process in Zimbabwe.

**Oliver Nyambi** is Associate Professor of English literature and cultural studies in the Department of English, University of the Free State in South Africa. His research focuses on crisis literatures, visual cultures of the Zimbabwean crisis, onomastics, indigenous environmentalisms, and political discourse. His latest books are *Cultures of Change in Contemporary Zimbabwe* (2021), co-edited with Tendai Mangena and Gibson Ncube, *The Zimbabwean Crisis after Mugabe* (2021), co-edited with Tendai Mangena and Gibson Ncube, and a sole-authored monograph *Life-Writing from the Margins in Zimbabwe:*

*Versions and Subversions of Crisis* (2019). His most recent book: *Contested Liberations and Transitions in Zimbabwe: (Counter)Cultures of Crisis Post-2000* is forthcoming with Brill.

**Mary Nyasimi** is a renowned scientific expert in the field of gender equality, social inclusion and climate change. Dr. Nyasimi holds a Ph.D. in Sustainability Agriculture and Ecological Anthropology from Iowa State University. With over 15 years of experience in the research and development, Mary has been actively working towards promoting policies and systems that support gender equality, social inclusion and climate change adaptation and mitigation in Africa. Her extensive knowledge and expertise make her a sought-after consultant, and she has worked with various national and international organizations. Through her work, Mary continues to be a staunch advocate for marginalized communities, particularly women, girls, youth, people with disability and indigenous people ensuring their voices are heard, and decisions impacting their lives are made with their participate and engagement.

**Sonene Nyawo** is a Senior Lecturer in the Department of Theology and Religious Studies at the University of Eswatini. She has published widely in the following areas of her research interests: new religious movements in Africa, traditional ritualization, women's fertility, climate change, religion and gender, and women and peacebuilding.

**Jacinta Chiamaka Nwaka** holds a Ph.D. in African History, from the University of Ibadan and is an Associate Professor of Peace History in the Department of History and International Studies, University of Benin, Benin City, Nigeria. She was an IDRC/UPEACE doctoral fellow (2008–2010). Dr. Nwaka was also a Post-Doctoral Fellow of the American Council of Learned Societies (ACLS) under its African Humanities Programme (AHP), and a 2016 recipient of IRG of Social Science Research Council New York under the African Peacebuilding Network (APN). She recently won the African Guest Researcher's visiting scholarship at the Nordic African Institute Uppsala Sweden. Her research interests are peace history with a focus on the intersections of religion and peace/conflict, humanitarian interventions, and women's studies.

**Ayokunmi Ojebode** is a Lecturer at SOAS, University of London, and a Fellow at the Institute for Name-Studies (INS), School of English, University of Nottingham, England. His areas of expertise are African literature, Cultural Studies, Health Humanities, and Literary Onomastics. He co-authored "Name as National Archive: Capturing of Yoruba Masculinist

Names in Tunde Kelani's Saworoide" in *The Cinema of Tunde Kelani: Aesthetics, Theatricalities and Visual Performance, Cambridge Scholars*, 2021.

**Babatunde Raphael Ojebuyi** is a Senior Faculty Member in the Department of Communication and Language Arts, University of Ibadan, where he teaches journalism, media ethics, digital media, and language use. His research focuses on these areas. Ojebuyi is the Principal Investigator of the *Youth Aspirations and Resilience* project of the Partnership for African Social and Governance Research (PASGR), funded by the MasterCard Foundation.

**Maurice Omollo** holds a Ph.D. from Kenyatta University, Kenya. He is a lecturer at the Department of Environmental Studies, Geography and Agriculture of Maasai Mara University in Kenya. Previously he taught at Kenyatta University in the Department of Geography for seven years. He is a settlement geographer with special interest in urban studies, with focus on informal settlement, and on issues including environmental, economic, and social welfare. The informality of the settlements provides an avenue towards understanding poor people's circumstances and struggles since the majority of the urban poor reside in these structures. Dr Omollo has written on the slum area of Mathare Valley of Nairobi, Kenya, touching on coping strategies relating to diverse issues that work against the residents. Currently he is involved in a study on entrepreneurial masculinity in the informal settlements of Nairobi City of Kenya.

**Isaac Owusu-Mensah** is a Senior Lecturer at the Department of Political Science, University of Ghana. He has extensive publications on various spheres of Ghanaian democracy.

**Pedzisai Ruhanya** is a lecturer at the Department of Creative Media and Communication at the University of Zimbabwe. He is also a founder and director at the Zimbabwe Democracy Institute. He holds a Ph.D. in Media and Democracy from the University of Westminster in London. He is a former Post-Doctoral Research Fellow with the University of Johannesburg's School of Media and Communication. He has more than 20 publications in peer-reviewed journals, book chapters and two co-edited books. His research interest is in the role of the media in political transitions.

**Usman Sambo** is a Senior Lecturer in the Department of Public Administration, Yobe State University Damaturu, Nigeria. He has published extensively on Nigerian governance, politics and administration in both local and international reputable journals and book publishers. He is a leading advocate of good governance and peacebuilding in Northeast Nigeria.

**Thabile Anita Samboma** is a Research Fellow under the Governance and Administration Unit at Botswana Institute for Development Policy Analysis (BIDPA). Her research interests are in policy analysis, gender, children's rights, disability, and education. She has authored several journals and a book chapter.

**Nomatter Sande** holds a Ph.D. in Religion and Social Transformation from the University of KwaZulu Natal (South Africa). Nomatter is a Practical Theologian. He is a Research Fellow at the Research Institute for Theology and Religion (RITR) in the College of Human Sciences, University of South Africa (UNISA). His research interests include disability studies, pentecostal theology, religious violence, peace, and gender.

**Babayo Sule** is a Senior Lecturer in the Department of International Relations, Federal University of Kashere Gombe State Nigeria. He has published extensively on the Nigerian electoral process, political parties, and party financing as well as conflict and peacebuilding in Nigeria and Africa. He is an advocate of peacebuilding in Northeast Nigeria, and transparent and violent-free election, as well as the liberation of Africa from neo-colonial chains.

**Mohammed Kwarah Tal** is a Lecturer in the Department of Political Science, Federal University of Kashere, Gombe State, Nigeria. He has published on political behaviour and voting culture in the Nigerian democratic process. He is an advocate of good governance and electoral integrity and transparency.

**James Tsabora** is a Senior Lecturer in Law in the Faculty of Law at the University of Zimbabwe, and senior research consultant in human rights and democratic governance, constitutionalism, rule of law, and natural resource governance.

**Solomon Waliaula** holds a Ph.D. in literature from Moi University, Kenya and is an Associate Professor in Literature and Cultural Studies at Maasai Mara University in Kenya. He is currently a Research Fellow at the Department of Anthropology and African Studies at Johannes Gutenberg University of Mainz, as well as Research Associate at University of the Witwatersrand, Department of African Literature. His research interests are in popular culture and cultural studies.

**Souhayel Weslety** is based in Sociology at the Université Tunis Carthage. He is a researcher in Migration and Political Science and a university instructor holding the Cambridge Delta. He is involved in a number of research programmes including the Fondazione Compagnia di San Paulo—funded research project *Traces of Mobility, Violence and Solidarity, Tunisian Democracy Lab* with the Friedrich Ebert Foundation and a first-of-its-kind study programme within the *Migrants* project.

# List of Figures

**Geographies of Violence and Informalization: The Case of Mathare Slums in Nairobi, Kenya**

| | | |
|---|---|---|
| Fig. 1 | The Slum Villages of Mathare Valley in Nairobi, Kenya (*Source* Extracted and modified from Data Exchange Platform for Horn of Africa [DEPHA, 2008]) | 205 |

**Preventing Electoral Violence in Africa: Towards Sustainable Peace**

| | | |
|---|---|---|
| Fig. 1 | Electoral cycle | 296 |
| Fig. 2 | Homicide rate by continent, 2017 (*Source* UNIDOC [2019: 11]) | 300 |

**Ungoverned Space and National Security in Nigeria**

| | | |
|---|---|---|
| Fig. 1 | Nigeria's security threats (*Source* Armed Conflict Location and Event Project 2021) | 399 |

**Youth, Proliferation of Small Arms and Light Weapons, and Conflicts in 21st Century Africa**

| | | |
|---|---|---|
| Fig. 1 | Youth population increase in Africa (*Source* Sow, Brookings 2018) | 483 |
| Fig. 2 | Total value of global arms trade in USD in 2018 2019 (*Source* SIPRI) | 485 |
| Fig. 3 | Flow of weapons in the Sahel 2011–2017 (*Source* DW, 2019) | 487 |

### Violence against Women in Egypt: A Closer Look at Intimate Partner Violence and Female Genital Mutilation

| | | |
|---|---|---|
| Fig. 1 | The social characteristics of the sample (education) | 801 |
| Fig. 2 | Sample distribution by age group | 801 |

### "Women's Sexuality Captured": Another Form of Gender-Based Violence (GBV) in the Swati Patriarchal Space

| | | |
|---|---|---|
| Fig. 1 | Reported abuse based on type form 2014–2018 | 896 |

### Adolescent Boys, Young Men, and Mental Health in Southern Africa

| | | |
|---|---|---|
| Fig. 1 | Social ecological model adapted to mental health in Africa (*Source* Davids et al. [2019]) | 935 |

# List of Tables

**Preventing Electoral Violence in Africa: Towards Sustainable Peace**

| | | |
|---|---|---|
| Table 1 | Pre-voting phase | 297 |
| Table 2 | Voting phase | 297 |
| Table 3 | Post-voting phase | 298 |
| Table 4 | Public trust in institutions in Africa | 299 |

**In God's Name: Violent Extremism in North East Nigeria**

| | | |
|---|---|---|
| Table 1 | Poverty index of Nigeria (CBN, 2006) | 589 |

**Violence against Women in Egypt: A Closer Look at Intimate Partner Violence and Female Genital Mutilation**

| | | |
|---|---|---|
| Table 1 | The actual distribution of inhabitants in Qalyoubia and Minia | 800 |
| Table 2 | The sample distribution according to gender and urban/rural division | 801 |
| Table 3 | IPV by gender | 804 |
| Table 4 | FGM by gender | 805 |
| Table 5 | IPV by residence | 806 |
| Table 6 | FGM by residence | 806 |
| Table 7 | IPV by wealth | 808 |
| Table 8 | FGM by wealth | 809 |
| Table 9 | IPV by education | 810 |
| Table 10 | FGM by education | 812 |

| Table 11 | The consequences of the January uprisings by gender and residence | 813 |
| Table 12 | The consequences of the 25 January uprisings by wealth | 813 |
| Table 13 | The consequences of the 25 January uprisings by education | 814 |

## "Wait, Let's Talk About It": A Feminist Assessment of the Response of the Church of the Cross Hayfield (NELCSA) to Gender-Based Violence in Pietermaritzburg, South Africa

| Table 1 | A comparison of the degree of gender-based violence affecting women and men | 840 |

## Managing Conflict in Africa: Challenges and Opportunities for the African Union

| Table 1 | Patterns of Conflict in Africa since 1975 | 1058 |

## Violent Piracy off the Coast of Nigeria: A Theoretical Analysis

| Table 1 | Actual and attempted piracy attacks, 1 January 2019–31 December 2022 | 1089 |
| Table 2 | Actual and attempted piracy incidents | 1090 |

## Mediatized Conflict: A Case of Nigerian Media Reportage of Farmer-Herder Conflict

| Table 1 | Audience perception of parties being supported by the media in relation to rating of the reportage | 1142 |
| Table 2 | Audience believability of media reportage and stakeholders held responsible | 1143 |
| Table 3 | Audience victimhood by government's attitude and efforts towards resolving the conflict | 1144 |
| Table 4 | Association between the rating of the reportage (partisan, unfair and fair) and media contribution to the escalation of the conflict | 1144 |
| Table 5 | Percentage of the audience who believe in media contribution to the escalation of the percentile | 1145 |

# Violence in Africa: A General Introduction

## Obert Bernard Mlambo and Ezra Chitando

A *Palgrave Handbook of Violence in Africa* has been desirable for some time, and hence easily justifiable. The idea of a handbook is most appropriate as it ventures across different locations, topographies, and times in Africa. A handbook is especially appropriate as it shines a light on key elements of African culture, and the cultural mechanisms for creating, sustaining, resisting, and mitigating violence in Africa.

This handbook is in 2 volumes, owing to its sheer size. Nobody engaged in thought about African history, culture, politics, and society can fail to note the enormous role violence has always played in the continent's affairs, and it is, at first sight, surprising that the idea of a handbook of violence in Africa has not already been given special consideration.

Critics might accuse us of perpetuating some sort of stereotype of Africa as a violent continent. To be clear, and for the avoidance of doubt, we do not seek to characterize Africa as the home of diverse and never-ending forms of violence. We do not wish to endorse violent images of a violent Africa. We

O. B. Mlambo (✉)
Classical Studies Section, School of Languages and Literatures, Rhodes University, Makhanda, South Africa
e-mail: obertmlambo@gmail.com

E. Chitando
Department of Philosophy, Religion and Ethics, University of Zimbabwe, Harare, Zimbabwe

do not desire to project Africa as some unique space where barbarous and hitherto unknown forms of violence are conceptualized and implemented.

Let it be understood that violence is a concrete dimension of the African historical and contemporary experience. It is not stereotypical, but rather a lived experience of encounters that define and shape existential realities. We cannot address the continent's socio-political crisis without attending to the structural, stratified, and epistemic violence that has underlain the nation-state project in Africa. As Mahmood Mamdani (2004: 3) puts it, violence is the midwife of history. Violence is part of the historical background to the Modern European state. Mamdani (2002: 12) further argues: "What horrifies the modern political sensibility is not violence per se but violence that does not make sense. And the violence that appears senseless to us is violence that is neither revolutionary nor counterrevolutionary, violence that cannot be illuminated by the story of progress. Not illuminated paradigmatically, nonrevolutionary violence appears pointless."

Violence in Africa should not, therefore, be seen as irrational and primordial. It is not "meaningless and devoid of rational basis" within the matrix of modernity and enlightenment. Since there are more than enough images available to us of a violent, burning, diseased, and dying Africa (see for example, Mbembe, 2001; Michira, 2002; Obijiofor, 2009; Manzo, 2018), we do not intend to feed "disaster journalism" (Chiwanza, 2021). We are painfully and acutely aware of the danger of a single story that Chimamanda Ngozi Adichie (2009) articulated so cogently. Nevertheless, in all its complexity (Fourie, 2015) Africa lives, Africa thrives, and Africa flourishes.

The African continent has a diversity of cultures, politics, economies, customs, institutions, religions, and beliefs. Different economic, cultural, and political landscapes, which have been subjected to numerous internal and external forces and transformations of various magnitudes, have unfolded during the ages of the continent's known history. Religions such as Christianity and Islam have had varying degrees of violent effects on Africa. The continent has also experienced, at various stages of its history, the violent and horrendous effects of the transatlantic slave trade, the intrusion of a very violent Western colonialism, and the violent struggle for independence; nor should we forget neo-colonialism and the current conditions and challenges of globalization, in which cultural and political imperialism have followed military imperialism, imposing European norms and ways of knowing onto African societies, with what may be called epistemic violence (Mlambo, 2024; see also chapters by Ndlovu and Gatsheni; Ncube; and Nyambi in this volume).

In all these changes and developments, violence has been, and is, inevitably produced and reproduced. Thus, the authors of the chapters in this handbook explore the theme of violence in the various social and historical milieux of the African continent. They train their gaze on the way violence "makes and unmakes" nations, regions, societies, borders, bodies, cultures, and social formations (cf. Scarry 1985).

Tons of books have been published that have dealt with the topic of violence in Africa, but most of these do so in an episodic manner. The majority of existing studies on violence in Africa relate more particularly to a specific theme of violence, a country or a region (for example, Tar & Onwura, 2022[1]; Kuwali, 2022[2]; Kramer, 2014[3]; Mamdani, 2009[4]; Polgreen, 2005[5]; Kriger, 1992[6]; Roesch, 1990[7]; Tim, 1989[8]; Maier, 1974[9]; Rodebeck, 1975[10]). We cannot claim to exhaust every topic of knowledge touched on in this handbook; but we believe there are advantages in a general viewpoint that takes in violence as a whole, recognizing the various aspects of violence as belonging to related rather than wholly disconnected areas of research. This handbook aims to train its lens on violence in Africa in two volumes, while attending to its various forms of expression, its psychological and cultural dimensions, mechanics, constitutive elements, patterns, progression, characteristics, and so forth. It does not merely proffer a prescriptive approach to violence but considers interpretative reflections, non-deductive data analysis, and approaches to violence in Africa at both the macro-level and the micro-level. The handbook also proffers an understanding of violence through the method of storytelling in the form of case scenarios and vignettes (Lee, 2019: 4). Telesia Musili's chapter is a case in point (see also Mwatwara and Mlambo's chapter).

Various disciplines such as sociology, anthropology, history, and the natural sciences are preoccupied with the phenomenon of violence. Nevertheless, even studies of violence focused within one area can be so diverse that it

---

[1] *The Palgrave Handbook of Small Arms and Conflicts in Africa.*
[2] *The Palgrave Handbook of Sustainable Peace and Security in Africa.*
[3] *The New Middle East: The World After the Arab Spring.*
[4] *Saviors and Survivors, Darfur, Politics and the War on Terror.*
[5] Civilians Bear Brunt of the Continuing Violence in Darfur. *New York Times*, 24 January, A3.
[6] *Zimbabwe's Guerrilla War: Peasant Voices*. Cambridge: Cambridge University Press.
[7] Renamo and the Peasantry: A View from Gaza. *Southern Africa Report* 6, 5: 21–25.
[8] Violence and Moral Knowledge: Observing Social Trauma in Sudan and Uganda. *Cambridge Anthropology* 13, 2:45–67.
[9] *Revolution and Terrorism in Mozambique*. New York: American African Affairs Association.
[10] Political Mobilisation in Guinea-Bissau. In Sam C. Sarkesian (ed.), *Revolutionary Guerrilla Warfare*, 431–451. Chicago: Precedent Publishing.

is not possible to arrive at a coherent picture of what violence signifies in specific cultural contexts. This is where the limitations of any single discipline of study are most strikingly revealed (Scott, 1985: xv). To make matters worse, such limitations abound in the absence of shared definitions of what counts as relevant, as different fields frame their own methods and approaches (Scott, 1985). This handbook seeks to overcome such limitations by bringing together academics and practitioners from various fields to contribute their expertise to scholarship on violence in Africa.

The handbook engages in important conceptual innovation with respect to the term "violence." A considerable number of chapters in this handbook pay attention to processes rather than just events of violence. Such processes are not static but caused and influenced by a wide range of forces, domestic and foreign.

The handbook also pays attention to theoretical emphases on the connections between violence and other factors such as knowledge, gender, warfare, statecraft, elections, apartheid, colonialism, regionalism, race, and technology among others. It also attends to theorized connections between violence and types of regimes that occur in Africa. In this regard the role of governments and non-state groups in targeting civilians is worth noting (Lunstrum, 2009).

Some chapters exhibit acquaintance with lesser-known parts of Africa, making uniquely revealing case studies of such micro-contexts. By paying attention to micro-level aspects of violence (e.g. microhistorical, anthropological accounts or narratives, micro-level patterns of violence etc.) such chapters have attended to important socio-cultural, economic, and political factors at a local level, contributing broadly to micro-foundational theorization of violence in Africa (Hovland, 2003; Kalyvas, 2006; Verweijen, 2015). Chapters with a macro-level focus on violence proffer a cross-national and cross-disciplinary approach, paying attention to past and present violence in Africa, and thereby setting the agenda for future research on violence, particularly in an interdisciplinary fashion.

Space limitations prevent us from accommodating all geographical areas of Africa, but this handbook breaks down barriers that previously separated scholars who worked in separate geographic compartments. Previously, seemingly impermeable boundaries separated the African continent into different regions: North Africa, Southern Africa, East and West Africa. While we do not claim that there are homogenous landscapes of violence in Africa, the handbook provides a thread that runs across these divisions, as a way to challenge narratives of separateness (Mlambo, 2022).

In this handbook we contribute to the broader question about the portrayal of violence in Africa as a whole. We forge a new type of multi-disciplinary research and transnational research involving participants from more than one field or country. In this respect we hope to contribute to the pursuit of new modes of understanding and studying violence. There is a necessary link between this new model of research and the realm of practical action, politics, and policy. Thus we hope the handbook will engage with social, cultural, political and ideological debates on the nature and practices of violence in Africa. In doing so, we hope to establish a real bridge between the academic world and the world of practice, the world of action.

The work, we hope, will be relevant and accessible to a wide public, including academics and students, non-governmental organizations and policy-making communities and bring them actively into direct dialogue wherever possible. It is a handbook whose contributors are the new generation of younger scholars, as well as practitioners and activists. We hope to bring new meanings and fresh ideas to the concept of violence, broadening its scope, and contributing to the debates that will shape Africa's common future. Therefore, this handbook would have achieved its aims if it succeeded in contributing to other fields which have given space to examine violence in Africa, namely: sociology, religion, psychology, anthropology, and others. The handbook would also have achieved its objectives if it succeeded in providing an exploration of heterogeneous landscapes of violence, probing violence's various forms, spaces of violence, temporalities, technologies of violence, military violence, race-induced violence, terrorism, electoral violence, state-sanctioned violence, the psychology of violence and the materiality of violence, among many other categories, to engender a broad appreciation of landscapes of violence in Africa.

The handbook is organized into seven parts. The first volume starts from part I to IV, while the second volume starts from part V to VII.

# 1 Part I: Conceptualizing Violence in Africa

This section attends to the many ways violence is conceptualized in an African context; for indeed, there can never be a single theory or interpretation of violence. Thus, the section explores the various ways in which violence can be conceptualized in an African context. Broadly speaking, the chapters conceptualize and frame violence in terms of various technologies. Chapters in this section explore the term "technology" as a body of knowledge about the useful arts in the construction and performance of violence. Some chapters describe the systematic appropriation of useful arts, devices, systems, tools, materials, procedures, and knowledge to commit violence, and in these chapters technology is analysed as a set of devices and a complex of industries. This includes technologies employed against nature and the environment. In talking of "technologies of violence" in this section, the chapters attend to a basic division of technology between those forms of technology which are designed and most useful for violence and violent conflict, and other forms. Among the former sort they refer to particular weapons of various kinds, as well as the "technology of repression" which includes methods of torture and incarceration (Mlambo, forthcoming).

The technology of weapons, moreover, can only exist in the presence of other support systems. The section thus highlights examples of technological systems, procedures and knowledge, including training for violent purposes (youths, rebels, recruitment of violent mobs etc.) The chapters in this section specify their conceptions of violence in terms that cater for appropriate analysis, extending and stretching the term "violence" to suit the occurrence of the phenomenon in their respective contexts (Kalyvas, 2006: 9).

**Ezra Chitando and Obert Bernard Mlambo** set the tone for this section by problematizing the concept "violence," discussing its various nuances and the conceptual terrain in a broad African context.

Debunking the myth that African scholarship is descriptive and devoid of analytical rigour, **Nyasha Mboti** unravels the apartheid studies approach—an emerging approach in conceptualizing violence from the Global South. Mboti's very novel approach to violence conceptualizes *harm* in terms of the notion of apartheid. His theory, broadly speaking, utilizes the hitherto neglected notion of apartheid as a paradigm, theoretical framework, heuristic, and methodology. He appropriates the apartheid paradigm to examine the persistence of harm and oppression in human society and human relations. He jettisons preoccupation with what the powerful and institutions do in the study of power and oppression. His independent analysis attends to the central theme of the Rate of Oppression (ROp) as a construct that defines how the oppressed experience oppression differently, at adjusted rates. In his lucid analysis, the oppressed bear the brunt of the cost of oppression and the cost of maintaining oppression, in such a way that oppression can persist indefinitely in distributed fashion and undetectably. He argues that the ultimate stage of oppression is when harm is reconstituted as merely a Rate of Oppression, and cogently explores the paradoxical scenario in which humans live with harm and in harm's way.

**Pinky Ndlovu and Sabelo J. Ndlovu-Gatsheni's** chapter "On Systemic and Epistemic Violence in Africa" is a broad and thematic/conceptual study.

They dissect violence in its various manifestations. Their chapter delves deeper into the phenomenon of violence in Africa and reveals its multifaceted character. Focusing on the systemic and epistemic violence that is always hidden, the chapter posits that overt violence has systemic and epistemic underpinnings. The chapter highlights how Africa was dragged into colonial modernity through such violent systems as mercantilism, enslavement, colonialism, racial capitalism, and heteronormative patriarchal sexism. Behind these inimical processes lurked the cognitive empire and its colonial library which operated through invasion of the mental universes of its targets and, in the process, committing epistemic violences such as theft of history, epistemicides, linguicides, and culturecides.

**Wesley Mwatwara and Obert Bernard Mlambo's** chapter "Technologies of Violence in Africa" conceptualizes violence in terms of the technologies that accompany its occurrence. In particular, they discuss the various technologies of such violence, paying attention to the increased role of the Chinese on the African continent, and the deteriorating political and economic outlook, as well as the rise of religious fundamentalism. They assess how combatants (youths, rebels, government security forces, and religious sects) have systematically appropriated various arts, devices, systems, tools, materials, procedures, and knowledge in order to commit their violence, usually on non-combatants. Thus, in investigating the dynamics of war violence in Africa, they also discuss weapons of various kinds, as well as the "technology of repression" which includes methods of torture and incarceration.

**Victoria Bernal's** "Diaspora and the Afterlife of Violence: Eritrean National Narratives and What Goes Without Saying" explores the legacies of political violence and the workings of state power in mobilizing identities around collective suffering, and the effects of political culture that reside in people in post-war time and space. The chapter conceptualizes the national narratives of the Eritrean state that celebrate sacrifice for the nation as a secondary form of violence operating on Eritreans that renders their personal losses unspeakable.

**Rachel Ibreck and Souhayel Weslety's** "Border Violence in Africa" conceptualizes the border violence of Eurocentric interventions in border management in Africa. Their chapter attends to how border violence relates to state violence, affecting migrants, refugees, and citizens. They explore the histories and meanings of borders on the African continent, referring to debates about the origins of borders in colonial interventions. Using ethnographic research methods, they offer a case study of memories and experiences of border violence.

While forms of colonial violence such as wars, coercive labour regimes, land dispossession, political repression, and racial segregation have been subject to extensive historical attention, the chemical violence of colonial encounters has largely been neglected. **Elijah Doro's** chapter argues that toxins, poisons, and chemicals constituted a significant frontier of colonial structural violence on indigenous people, landscapes, and ecosystems in Africa. The chapter conceptualizes chemical violence within the broader historiography of African history and argues for theoretical perspectives that centre it as an analytical framework.

**Gibson Ncube's chapter** "Unmasking Epistemic Violence in the Postcolony: Interrogating the Colonial Legacy and War in Francophone African Literature" juxtaposes gender and violence in Africa, focusing on the plight of the woman's body as an object of sexual abuse, and on how violence in Francophone Africa is represented in seminal literary texts and more contemporary texts. What is more, the texts he examines span different periods and cover different geopolitical zones of the African Francophone world.

Violence can be conceptualized in geographical terms, that is, it is possible to see violence by analysing patterns of violence geographically. **Maurice Omollo** and **Solomon Waliaula** in their chapter "Geographies of Violence and Informalization: The Case of Mathare Slums in Nairobi, Kenya" develop the argument that violence is a key component of the existential economy in slum settlements in Kenya. They locate this argument in a fairly well-developed discourse on African cities as inevitably informalized, partly because of the undue rigidity and unresponsiveness within formal institutions and the fact that informalization demonstrates the limits of freedom and agency in those contexts. In their chapter, they focus both on organized violation of law and order and the establishment of alternative socio-economic structures and lifestyle. They describe these as geographies of violence. Using data from fieldwork, in which they used ethnography and social survey methods, they have described and accounted for the patterns of violence in Mathare slums in Kenya.

Violence can also be conceptualized in terms of how geographical zones or regions are managed by their regional bodies, as **Daniel Nkosinathi Mlambo, Victor H. Mlambo, and Mandla Mfundo Masuku** have shown in their chapter: "Through the Afrocentricity Lens: Terror, Insurgency, and Implications for Regional Integration in Southern Africa from Cabo Delgado Province, Mozambique."

# 2 Part II: The State and Violence in Africa

This section is devoted to discussions of violence perpetrated by the state on citizens. Chapters in this section explore the concept of spaces of state-sponsored violence, understanding such spaces as fields of forces, or combat zones in which power is manufactured, applied to its intended subjects and maintained. Attention is given to situations where the state security apparatus mans and patrols spaces of violence such as streets, borderlands, and residential suburbs, imposing state power and making citizens the objects of attack, surveillance, control etc.

**Claire-Anne Lester's** chapter "Discourses on Political Violence and the Mechanics of Legitimation in Official Commissions of Inquiry in Africa" provides some clarity in conceptualizing state-sponsored violence, shedding light on how discourses on violence are connected with techniques of legitimation. It draws on various commissions held by governments to investigate violence in colonial and postcolonial Africa.

Using the retributive justice theory, **Vellim Nyama and Pedzisai** Ruhanya in their chapter "Party Politics, Violence, Impunity, and Social Injustice in Zimbabwe (1980–2022)" explore the challenges of the securocratic state, which emerged after Zimbabwe's independence in 1980. The chapter is well founded on theory and demonstrates that impunity and social injustices coupled with the breakdown of law and order at the instigation of the state through party/state conflation are key challenges that feed the sad narratives of a violent state in Zimbabwe.

**Khabele Matlosa's** chapter "Understanding Electoral Violence in Africa" explores the causes, course, and consequences of electoral violence in Africa. Anchored on conflict theory, the chapter uses the political economy approach as a framing lens through which to understand electoral violence in Africa. Through a comparative analysis, the chapter investigates five domains of electoral violence: (a) its definition, structural determinants, and proximate drivers; (b) its scope, nature, dynamics, and forms; (c) its nexus/interface with other forms of political violence; (d) its socio-economic and political impact; and (e) its prevention, management, and resolution.

**Ayokunmi Ojebode's** chapter "Dirge to Slit Bodies: EndSARS, Police Brutality, and Nigerian Dystopia in Jumoke Verissimo and James Yéku's *Soro Soke: When Poetry Speaks Up*" offers analysis of state violence in Nigeria using Nigerian literary works and documentary political activism. The chapter shows how Nigerian youths exploited social media in different Nigerian states and the diaspora, to demonstrate public outrage against the Nigerian Police Force's Special Anti-Robbery Squad (SARS) brutalities. The chapter explores imageries of violence and public encounters with police brutality underpinned by the youths' revolutionary and creative impulses.

**Jeremiah Bvirindi**'s chapter "The Resource Curse and Structural Violence in Angola: A Path for Perpetual Conflicts" examines the underlying factors behind structural violence, social disorder, and poverty in Angola. The chapter is informed by the resource curse theory, and the concepts of rent-seeking and structural violence.

In their chapter "Electoral Violence in Ghana's Fourth Republic: The Case of Party Vigilantism", **Emmanuel Debrah, Isaac Owusu-Mensah, Sampson Danso, and Gilbert Arhinful Aidoo** examine how party vigilantes' violent electoral activities permeate electoral processes in Ghana. The chapter undertakes a comprehensive discussion of how party vigilantes have carried out election violence in the electoral processes, and the effects of such violence on sustainable democracy. They examine the phenomenon of electoral violence to broadly understand and illuminate the electoral violence and party vigilantism that have shaped African democratization in recent times.

**Usman Sambo, Babayo Sule and Mohammed Kwarah Tal's** chapter "Investigating the Causes and Impact of Electoral Violence in Nigeria" scrutinises the causes and impact of electoral violence and suggests remedies for the scourge of electoral violence in Nigeria.

**Arinze Ngwube's** chapter "Ungoverned Space and National Security in Nigeria" critiques the role of the Nigerian government in providing security for its citizens, with a particular focus on the problems of ungoverned spaces in Nigeria's vast and untamed forests, water bodies, and creeks, where violent crime is rife and almost impossible to eradicate.

## 3 Part III: Children, Youth, and Violence

Young people and children have suffered from much of the violence in Africa. They are often neglected by their governments and have not received the protection necessary to cushion them from poverty, hunger, abuse, and drugs. In some war-torn regions they are recruited as soldiers. Chapters in this section examine the phenomenon of violence and how it variously affects youths and children in Africa. Some of the chapters investigate how patterns and cultures of violence affect youths and children, analysing how youths and children are both subjects and objects of violence in Africa.

**Stacey Hynd's** chapter "Trauma, Violence, and Memory in African Child Soldier Memoirs," uses the published memoirs of former child soldiers from Sierra Leone, Sudan, Uganda, Eritrea and the Democratic Republic of the Congo to explore the instrumental and discursive nexus between child soldiers, memory, violence and humanitarianism. It assesses how (former) children combatants remember and recount their experiences of war, and how these narratives can be shaped by humanitarian, literary and/or therapeutic framings. The chapter historically contextualizes the emergence of the "child soldier memoir," before analysing the narratives of recruitment, indoctrination, and violence recounted by these former child soldiers, and their attempts to rework their identities in a post-conflict environment.

**Toyin Cotties Adetiba's** chapter "Africa and Violence: The Metamorphosis and Participation of Child Soldiers in Conflict Zones" explores the metamorphosis and participation of child soldiers in conflict zones in Africa. He discusses the use of child soldiers by both state and non-state actors in Africa.

In their chapter "Youth, Violence, and Political Accumulation: Urban Militias in Harare" **Simbarashe Gukurume** and **Godfrey Maringira** examine the ways in which urban militia with political relations engage in practices of violent accumulation in the city of Harare in Zimbabwe. They problematize the "temporalities" and "materialities" of doing and understanding violence in Zimbabwe, examining the emergence and the changing practices of politically connected militia groups in Harare. Demonstrating how political violence regenerates and how it maintains a vicious cycle, they argue that being a victim of political violence is never permanent, and neither is the status of being a perpetrator.

The chapter by **Babayo Sule, Ibrahim Kawuley Mika'il and Mohammed Kwarah Tal** "Violence, Youth, Proliferation of Small Arms and Light Weapons, and Conflicts in 21st Century Africa" examines the nexus between the proliferation of Small Arms and Light Weapons (SALW) among the youth and conflict in Africa. The chapter lays bare the potential danger of the ever-growing youth population in Africa, which state of affairs leads, where economies and politics do not absorb the youth, to armed group violence orchestrated by the spread of SALW on the continent. The chapter suggests among other recommendations that African leaders must adopt honest aggressive policies that will engage the youth in productive ventures in order to prevent violence and crimes.

**Witness Chikoko's** chapter "Violence against children on the streets in sub–Saharan Africa: Cases of Harare, Lusaka, Nairobi, and Johannesburg" explores issues of the exposure to different forms of violence of street children in sub-Saharan African cities with special reference to Harare, Lusaka, Nairobi and Johannesburg. The chapter mainly examines three forms of violence, namely sexual, physical, and psychological. The chapter concludes by lobbying and advocating full implementation of children's rights laws, policies, and programmes so as to reduce the vulnerabilities of street children.

**Thabile Anita Samboma's** chapter "Violence against Disabled Children in Botswana" reveals how children living with disability in Botswana are vulnerable to violence in the form of sexual abuse, emotional abuse, corporal punishment, and exploitation in the form of child labour.

# 4 Part IV: Nature, Religion, and Cultural Violence in Africa

Violence may be considered to be a part of the experience of the African traditional way of life (see chapter by Obert Mlambo and Kudzanai Mlambo). For this reason, this section contains chapters that explore a variety of topics on the cultural perceptions of violence in Africa.

The section also explores how violence may be analysed and how it is shaped and functions within the particular cultural constructs of the traditional African worldviews. Cultural experimentation with certain beliefs has provided opportunities for ritual practices which reflect the currency of belief systems in juju that can be violently murderous among some African communities. Some chapters examine how such religion and culture have also imposed violent practices and rituals.

Religious beliefs may be so deeply engrained into cultures that conflicts arise at times of religious change or when different religions come into contact. Thus some chapters also explore a variety of topics relating to the cultural perceptions of violence in Africa, the role of religion in violence in Africa, and the cultural aspects and appropriation of violence in Africa. This, among other things, sheds some light on the ritualistic murder of twins, people with albinism, and the cultural motivations behind sexual violence.

Traditional beliefs, taboos and sacred places have for long been viewed as vehicles for the avoidance of environmental degradation in conservative African communities. **Obert Mlambo and Kudzanai Mlambo** in the chapter "Violence against Nature in African Traditional Thought and Practice" depart from a romanticized view of the role of African traditional beliefs and myths in shaping attitudes to nature. Their discussion decouples cultural reasoning and critical thinking (McClymont 2018). They argue that myths and traditional beliefs are part of culture and often involve cultural reason as opposed to critical reasoning, although not all myth and tradition lacks critical reason. They argue that violence against nature committed in certain cultural processes betrays cultural reasoning as opposed to critical thinking.

**Ezra Chitando** in his chapter "Yearning for Old Time Religion in the Face of Globalization? Interpreting Fundamentalisms and Violent Extremism in Africa" contributes to the debate on the impact of globalization on religious consciousness in Africa. Without reducing violence attributed to religion to religious factors, the chapter contends that there is merit in reviewing how fundamentalisms and violent extremism might be regarded as reactions to globalization in Africa.

**Jacinta Chiamaka Nwaka's** chapter "In God's Name: Drivers of Violent Extremism in Northeast Nigeria" discusses motivations and drivers in the intensification and sustenance of Boko Haram insurgency in north eastern Nigeria, an area marred by religious extremism. The chapter proffers calculated measures that focus on other drivers of violence, without completely ignoring religious motivations, as a more effective strategy in countering insurgency in the region.

**Evarist Ngabirano's** chapter "Beyond Ethnicity: Reflections on the History and Politics of Violence in Uganda" explains postcolonial ethnic violence as driven by the cultural differences that exist between ethnic groups in Uganda.

**Rabson Hove's** chapter "The Intersectionality between Violence and Poverty in Africa: Sketching the Prevalence of Various forms of Violence in South Africa" surveys the different forms of violence in South Africa, discussing their causes, nature, and effects. The chapter examines the extent to which poverty is the main cause of violence in its different manifestations in South Africa.

**Marlino Eugénio Mubai's** chapter "Violence against Nature in Africa: A Historical Assessment" discusses how violence against nature represents direct and indirect attacks on socio-ecological systems and symbolizes an act of violence towards the earth and the diverse inhabitants or species that depend on it. **Martin Mujinga's** chapter "Xenophobia, Afrophobia, or Promoting Xenophilia? Semantic Explorations of Violence and Criminality in South Africa" analyses the terms used to describe acts of violence on foreign nationals in South Africa: xenophobia and Afrophobia. The chapter argues that although these terms have dominated scholarship, they are a disguise for criminal acts by some black South Africans.**Francis Benyah's** "Enchanted Worldviews and Violence against Persons with Albinism in Sub-Saharan Africa" explores the religious and superstitious beliefs in Africa that cause violence against people living with albinism.

**Jones Hamburu Mawerenga's** "Violence against Persons with Albinism in Malawi" touches on the ritualistic aspect of violence against people with albinism in Malawi.

Susan M. Kilonzo's chapter "Globalization, Islamic Fundamentalism, and Violence through the Youth in Kenya" frames violence in terms of globalization in its manifold conceptualizations, and how it may serve as a catalyst for religious fundamentalism, radicalization, and violence in Africa.

# 5 Part V: Gender and Violence in Africa

This section marks the beginning of the second volume of this Handbook. Chapters under this section explore the issues of violence and gender in Africa. Different genders in Africa violate each other on the basis of conceptions and misconceptions of gender ideologies, and they determine power relations, attitudes and behaviours. Some chapters in this section explore how gender-based violence can also be exacerbated by poverty, climate change, culture and others.

**Veronica Fynn Bruey's** chapter "Sexual Violence against Girls and Women in African Conflict" focuses on how sexual violence disproportionately affects girls and women in African conflict. The chapter adopts a discursive approach to examine sexual violence in African conflict, essentially attending to the occurrence, meaning, concepts, impacts, and implications of sexual violence in African conflict.

**Tshenolo J. Madigele and Mutsawashe Chitando's** Chapter "The Cost of Violence against Women in Africa" discusses the cost of violence against women in Africa. It highlights the impact of violence against women on Africa's development.

**Yasmin M. Khodary's** chapter "Violence against Women in Egypt: A Closer Look at Intimate Partner Violence and Female Genital Mutilation" maps the different forms of violence against women (VAW) in Egypt, with a special focus on female genital mutilation (FGM), and intimate partner violence (IPV). The chapter answers the following question: To what extent do factors such as gender, residence, wealth, and education shape women's exposure to violence and increase the risk of their exposure to certain forms of VAW in Egypt over others? Using a quantitative survey method with a sample of 400 Egyptian men and women in the Qalyoubia Governorate (Lower Egypt) and the Minia Governorate (Upper Egypt), the chapter provides an overview of the prevalence of FGM and IPV while testing the significance of various categories of inequalities, such as gender, the urban-rural division, wealth, and education on the prevalence of FGM and IPV in Egypt.

**Lindiwe Princess Maseko's** chapter "'Wait, Let's Talk About It': A Feminist Assessment of the Response of the Church of Cross Hayfield (NELCSA) to Gender-Based Violence in Pietermaritzburg, South Africa" examines gender-based violence (GBV) as a new public health pandemic and sexual reproductive health right concern in the 21st century. The chapter assesses The Church of the Cross (Hayfields) NELCSA's response to GBV in Pietermaritzburg, South Africa. It uses feminist cultural hermeneutics as a study tool to examine and expose the imbalances of gender representation from a cultural perspective.

**Susan Monyangi Nyabena's** "Breaking The Silence: Exploring the Challenges and Support Mechanisms for Male Survivors of Gender-Based Violence in Sub-Saharan Africa" focuses on gender-based violence against male survivors, who often remain invisible in research and practice. The chapter addresses this gap by examining the challenges faced by male survivors of GBV in sub-Saharan Africa and exploring the available support mechanisms. By shedding light on the experiences of male survivors, the chapter contributes to developing inclusive interventions and policies that address the specific needs of male survivors.

In their chapter "Changing Contexts, Changing Violence Patterns? The Case of African Diaspora Women" **Nomatter Sande** and **Amos Muyambo** explore how migration has become a global phenomenon, and how diasporic contexts are upsetting tradition and the cultural roles of men and women. Using the United Kingdom as a case study, the chapter examines how some women in diasporic contexts are responding to opportunities that favour them against men. Some African diaspora women are using their privileges to perpetrate violence against men. The chapter qualitatively analyses data gathered from social media, newspaper articles, news channels, and text-based research. This chapter concludes that diasporic contexts can be spaces for violence and some African diaspora women perpetrate violence against men.

In the chapter "Gender Violence: A Portrait of Women for Change's Fight against Gender-Based Violence in Zambia" **Nelly Mwale and Joseph Chita** argue that women are critical drivers of change, especially when they initiate avenues for dealing with gender-based violence against women. Therefore, the efforts of women to curb gender-based violence and ultimately contribute to the actualization of Sustainable Development Goal Number 5 on gender equality deserves documentation for posterity.

**Mary Nyasimi and Veronica Nonhlanhla Jakarasi** in their chapter "Persisting Inequalities: An Intersectional View of Climate Change, Gender and Violence" shed light on the convergence of climate change, gender, and violence. They explore the adverse effects of climate change, particularly extreme weather events such as floods, droughts, and rising temperatures, and how these impacts are disproportionately affecting women, girls, the elderly, and disabled individuals. They show how the effects of climate change increase the rate of violence faced by these vulnerable groups. They demonstrate, for example, how coastal and inland water fish vendors, predominantly women, have experienced sexual violence due to the scarcity of fish, primarily caused by climate change and excessive harvesting. Furthermore, they show how men's traditional roles as providers are also disrupted by climate change challenges, leading some to resort to increased violence, particularly during disagreements with their partners and children.

**Sonene Nyawo's** chapter "Women's Sexuality Captured: Another Form of Gender-Based Violence (GBV) in the Swati Patriarchal Space" explores women's representation in patriarchal spaces, which simultaneously influences their identities and prescribes acceptable standards of behaviour and action, causing physical and psychosocial distress and trauma.

**Mutsawashe Chitando's** chapter "Adolescent Boys, Young Men and Mental Health in Southern Africa" draws on the opportunities, challenges, and joys relating to the mental health of adolescent boys and young men in Southern Africa. The chapter further advances the discourse on mental health in Southern Africa using adolescent boys and young men as a lens. Chitando asserts that through advocating mental health in one's different spheres of influence, one may make significant strides towards the realization of positive mental health outcomes for adolescent boys and young men in Southern Africa. She posits that the inability to do so could be interpreted as a form of structural violence against adolescent boys and young men.

**Telesia Kathini Musili's** chapter "Towards a Reconstruction of Sacralized Traditions to Avert Gender-Based Violence Prevalent in Girl-Child Marriages amongst the Akamba" argues for the deconstruction and reconstruction of repressive cultural norms that provide a fertile ground for girl-child marriages to thrive amongst the Akamba people in Kenya. The chapter proffers an understanding of violence through storytelling in the form of a case scenario of one Muthike.

## 6 Part VI: Violence, Memory, and the Law in Africa

Memory is another dimension through which violence is conceived, remembered, and imagined. Some chapters in this section explore the role of memory in discourses of violence. Without assuming any water-tight relationship between violence, memory and the law, the section contains chapters that deal with how the law is deployed to deal with violence in Africa.

**Oliver Nyambi** in his chapter "Pre-Colonial and Colonial Violence in Zimbabwe: a Literary Exegesis" analyses purposefully selected scenes of pre-colonial and colonial violence from several Zimbabwean literary texts, to explore their representations of violence. The chapter focuses on what the texts reveal concerning the immanence of violence in the historical evolution of group identities and relations. Drawing on Fanon's insights on the psychology, materiality, and race of violence, the chapter centres violence as a temporal motif and concept that is fundamentally rhizomic in the social and political ordering of societies, branching out into many different leads that unravel its "necessity," causes, forms, and nature.

In their chapter "'Living in the Shadow of Death': Understandings of Political Violence and its Aftermath in the Zimbabwean Context" **Chenai Matshaka** and **Ruth Murambadoro**, explore the challenges of unresolved and entrenched violence in colonial and postcolonial Zimbabwe, and the difficult and complex ways of breaking cycles of violence. The chapter examines meanings of violence and trauma as an important part of how individuals and society respond to violence. Such responses, they argue, are central to breaking cycles of violence and building peace, hence the importance of capturing them and reflecting upon them in processes and dialogues that are inclusive.

**Collium Banda** in his chapter "Forgetting as Psychological Weapon? Critiquing the Call to Forget in a Zimbabwe Founded and Ruled by Violence" examines President Mnangagwa's use, (at the time of writing) of the concept of forgetting as a psychological tool of oppression in Zimbabwe's political landscape. The chapter describes the importance of a critical theological-ethic of memory for the church's engagement with the political call to forgive and forget, in contrast with Mnangagwa's rhetoric. It critiques Mnangagwa's ironic plea to let bygones be bygones as psychological tool while still subscribing to violent politics.

**Parfait Akana's** chapter "Incest as Dismissal: Anthropology and Clinics of Silence" proffers a critical description of how the injunction to silence constitutes the keystone of denials about sex crimes against minors. He analyses the various motives that make it possible to configure anthropologically the "good" reasons for keeping quiet, postulating that what makes the enunciation of such reasons possible is not only the anchoring of the various anthroposocial structures that constitute our common world in a violent ecosystem, but the inscription of this violence in a daily practice where it sometimes represents a major term of the negotiation between individuals in the struggle for survival.

## 7 Part VII: Preventing Violent Conflict in Africa

This section emphasizes the hindrances and opportunities that accompany the prevention of and attempted curbing of violence in Africa. More crucially, chapters in this section propose strategies to minimize or prevent violence in Africa. This is critical for development initiatives in Africa, such as Agenda 2063, For The Africa We Want, and the 2030 United Nations Sustainable Development Goals (SDGs).

**James Tsabora** in his chapter "Confronting Military Violence in Africa's Electoral Spaces: Law, Institutions, and Remedies" problematizes the kind of violence perpetrated by the military and proposes an institutional response mechanism that could be appropriated and deployed to address the problem.

**Victor H. Mlambo, Ernest Toochi Aniche, and Mandla Mfundo Masuku** in their chapter "Managing Conflict in Africa: Challenges and Opportunities for the African Union" explore the role of the African Union in managing conflict in Africa, examining the extent to which the African Union has been successful in addressing widespread conflicts in Africa. Most importantly, they discuss what can be done to capacitate the African Union to effectively address the widespread conflicts on the continent.

In the chapter "Beyond Xenophobia or Afrophobia: Strategies and Solutions" **Nomatter Sande and Martin Mujinga** reflect on and harmonize recommendations from both inductive and deductive research to function as strategies and solutions to move from Afrophobia, criminality, and xenophobia to xenophilia. The study deploys the social identity theory as a theoretical framework.

**Kalu Kingsley Anele's** chapter "Violent Piracy off the Coast of Nigeria: A Theoretical Analysis" analyses the nexus between piracy and violence, arguing that Nigerian piracy is coterminous with violence in the Niger Delta region of Nigeria. He locates other forms of violence in Nigeria, namely, attacks on offshore oil installations, violent elections, transnational organized crime and resource control agitation in the Niger Delta, as typical causes of violent piratical attacks off the Nigerian coast. These violent piratical attacks in the waters of Nigeria require solutions by the government of Nigeria centred on political will to suppress piracy. Thus, good governance, adequate funding, prosecution of pirates and their enablers, and the funding, training, and equipping of maritime enforcement agencies and regional cooperation, among other things are masures to curb violent piracy in Nigeria.

**Victor H. Mlambo, Mandla Mfundo Masuku, and Daniel Nkosinathi Mlambo** in their chapter "Insurgency in Mozambique: Incorporating

NATO's Article 5 to the Region's Quest for Collective Defence" critically analyse the possibilities of enhancing a binding security framework to eliminate future security threats in the SADC region. The chapter explores the possibility for SADC to develop a responsive binding security framework, and the challenges of initiating such a framework for addressing the insurgency in Mozambique and future threats that might emerge in the region. The chapter suggests that security challenges affecting the SADC region could be addressed through the use of African epistemology, which supports the view that African challenges require African solutions through an Ubuntu approach.

In their chapter "Mediatized Conflict: A Case of Nigerian Media Reportage of Farmer-Herder Conflict" **Ridwan Abiola Kolawole** and **Babatunde Raphael Ojebuyi** proffer an analysis that contrasts two types of journalism—"peace journalism" and war journalism. Attending to escalatory and (de)escalatory narratives involving farmer-herder conflicts in Nigeria, they examine the roles of the Nigerian media in constructing frames of reference of the conflict, for example, ethnicity and cultural identities. Their study demonstrates that the media undermine the peace approach as they are overtly or covertly implicated in the escalation of the farmer-herder conflict by foregrounding the cultural traits of the headers to depict their aggressiveness in achieving a better environment for their animals, as well as the sustainability of the herding business. Their analysis offers an appraisal of the peace approach, finding that the approach ought to be properly articulated to actualize the attainment of Sustainable Development Goal 16 in Nigeria.

## Bibliography

Champion, M., & O' Sullivan, L. (2017). 'War Is the Father and King of All': Discourses, Experiences, and Theories of Hellenistic Violence. In: M. Champion & L. O'Sullivan (Eds.), *Cultural Perceptions of Violence in the Hellenistic World* (pp. 1–20). Routledge.

Falola, T., & Yacob-Haliso, O. (2023). *African Refugees*. Indiana University Press.

Fourie, W. (2015). Four Concepts of Africa. *HTS Teologiese Studies/ Theological Studies, 71*(3), Art. #2847, 10 pp. https://doi.org/10.4102/hts.v71i3.2847

Hovland, I. (2003). Macro/Micro Dynamics in South Africa: Why the Reconciliation Process Will Not Reduce Violence. *Journal of Peacebuilding and Development, 1*(2), 6–20. https://doi.org/10.1080/15423166.2003.194812506437

Kalyvas, S. N. (2006). *The Logic of Violence in Civil War*. Cambridge University Press.

Lee, B. X. (2019). *Violence: An Interdisciplinary Approach to Causes, Consequences, and Cures*. Wiley Blackwell.

Lunstrum, E. (2009). Terror, Territory, and Deterritorialization: Landscapes of Terror and the Unmaking of State Power in the Mozambican 'Civil' War. *Annals of the Association of American Geographers, 99*(5). 884–892.

Mamdani, M. (2002). Making Sense of Political Violence in Postcolonial Africa. In O. Enwezor, C. Basualdo, U. M. Bauer, S. Ghez, S. Maharaj, M. Nash, & O. Zaya (Eds.), *Experiments with the Truth* (pp. 21–42). Documenta11_Platform2. Hatje Cantz Verlag.

Mamdani, M. (2004). *Good Muslim and Bad Muslim: America, the Cold War, and the Roots of Terror*. Pantheon Books.

Mlambo, O. B. (2020). Robert Mugabe and the Politics of Civil Renewal. In E. Chitando (Ed.), *Personality Cult and Politics in Mugabe's Zimbabwe* (pp. 160–172). Routledge.

Mlambo, O. (2024). Introduction. In *Africa: The Definitive Visual History of a Continent*. Penguin Random House.

Mlambo, O. B., & Zimunya. C. T. (2016). Rethinking the Role of Group Thought in Religious Violence and Extremism. In J. Kuegler, L. Togarasei, & R. M. Gunda (Eds.), *The Bible and Violence in Africa* (pp. 59–73). University of Bamberg Press.

Mbembe, A. (2001). *On the Postcolony*. University of California Press.

Mbembe, A. J. (2006). Decolonizing the University: New Directions. *Arts and Humanities in Higher Education, 14*(1), 20–45.

Scarry, E. (1985). *The Body in Pain: The Making and Unmaking of the World*. Oxford University Press.

Scott, J. C. (1985). *Weapons of the Weak: Everyday Forms of Peasant Resistance*. Yale University Press.

Verweijen, J. (2015). *Understanding Violence by African Government Forces: The Need for a Micro-Dynamics Approach*. London School of Economics and Political Science Blog. https://blogs.lse.ac.uk/africaatlse/2015/01/02/understanding-violence-by-african-government-forces-the-need-for-a-micro-dynamics-approach/

# Conceptualizing Violence in Africa

# Violence in Africa: Reflecting on a Broad Concept

Ezra Chitando and Obert Bernard Mlambo

Violence has been integral to human history. Various human communities across space and time have performed and experienced violence. They continue to do so at the time of writing, and most probably, reading. To reflect on violence in Africa – as this Handbook does—is not to assign a peculiar place to Africa. Thus, this Handbook does not in any way suggest that Africa is home to violence in ways that other spaces do not experience violence. If the dominant explanation has been that "violence in Africa is senseless," in this Handbook we seek to make the violence intelligible, even as it is expressed and experienced in manifold ways. While some readers might experience "violence in Africa" as a form of violence itself, our quest is to clarify and explain the different forms of violence (Brankovic 2019), in the hope that the collective scholarly and human family can contribute towards mitigating violence in Africa.

Violence is never a simple concept and should never be presented as such. This Handbook is suitable for a broad coverage of countries across the African divisions of the North, East, Central, South, and West, and enables the

---

E. Chitando (✉)
Department of Philosophy, Religion and Ethics, University of Zimbabwe, Harare, Zimbabwe
e-mail: chitsa21@yahoo.com

O. B. Mlambo
Classical Studies Section, School of Languages and Literatures, Rhodes University, Makhanda, South Africa

coverage of diverse themes such as: the topography of violence, technologies of violence, terrorism, civil war and insurgent violence, child soldiers and violence, epistemic violence, structural violence, violence and memory, violence and the law, cultural mechanisms for creating, sustaining, resisting, and mitigating violence, political violence, violence in moments of religious, social, and geo-political transformation, gender and violence, and violence against nature, among many other themes.

Chapter contributions in this Handbook demonstrate high levels of reflexivity as they variously pose profound and illuminating questions regarding violence and its various manifestations in respective contexts. Whereas existing studies on violence in Africa relate more particularly to a specific theme of violence, a country or a region, we provide in this Handbook, a global view of violence, its definitions, its various forms of expression, its psychological and cultural dimensions, mechanics, constitutive elements, patterns, progression, characteristics and so forth. We must state at once that we do not at all claim any universal validity for our definition of violence; it is a heuristic device to enable our readers to gain an appreciation of how we have generally sought to approach this highly complex and widely variegated phenomenon. This Handbook is cross-national and cross-disciplinary.

We strive to show how violence may be understood as a force that gives meaning to goals by individuals, by governments or by groups of people. For example, state formation can be a result of violence in an armed conflict. Conquest and competition for power and resources are often achieved through military violence. Violence can be deployed in religious conflicts and can be unleashed to impose a particular order or objectives.

Our task in this Handbook is to make sense of the violence that is found in Africa. Some of the violence is done by Africans. Some of the violence is done on Africans. Yet still more violence is done by Africans in concert with others on Africa. This Handbook is inspired by the African Union's Pan-African vision of: "An integrated, prosperous and peaceful Africa, driven by its own citizens, representing a dynamic force in the international arena" (African Union 2015). Contributors to this Handbook seek to lay the foundations for this vision by reflecting, clearly and intensely, on the various forms and causes of violence in Africa, as well as proposing interventions that can contribute towards minimizing or overcoming violence. Whereas the dominant paradigm overviews of violence in Africa tend to create the impression that it is innate, unique (see for example, the question in Leys, 1965: 17), unavoidable (this is critiqued in Chabal et al., 2005) and perennial, contributors seek to clarify the multiple forms of violence, explain their occurrence and propose strategies for overcoming them. While conceptual clarity is vital, we contend that providing practical solutions is even more important. Thus, by proposing strategies for overcoming violence in Africa, this Handbook strives to be "relevant to the needs and concerns of African societies" (Kaya & Seleti, 2013: 32).

The continuing terror of violence in its various forms in Africa gives rise to the need among African scholars to split hairs over this phenomenon, and to explore its forms, mechanisms, and effects from a perspective diversity across many African countries discussed in this volume. Historians have often recorded the African past and present precisely for its violence, exploring themes and narratives of war, colonialism and its attended effects, dictatorships, terrorism, bloody diamonds, and so forth. This volume goes further to draw attention, among other things, to cultural, social, political, economic, and religious discourses generated by, sustaining, and contesting violence in the African continent. It includes attention to military violence, racial violence, violence in economic and political systems, violence in structures of civic space, and ideology, religious dynamics and dimensions of violence. The volume ventures across different locations, topographies and times in Africa. Some chapters explore cultural discourses of violence to shed a light on key elements of African culture, and to reveal cultural mechanisms for creating, sustaining, resisting, and mitigating violence in Africa.

This Handbook also attends to a conceptual challenge involving the nature and definition of violence. Owing to its elusive nature, violence tends to trap its investigators into the pursuit of long-established conceptual categories (Riess, 2016). By bringing together 57 chapters on the topic of violence in this handbook, we hope that the definitional issues and the multivariant nature of violence can be explored, dissected, and nuanced from different thematic angles, positionalities of expertise, experiences, geographical locations, and theoretical and conceptual entry points.

This Handbook is one of the very few attempts at academic research on violence in Africa in one volume, indeed one of the first in terms of the depth and breadth of coverage of issues of violence. We admit that violence is an intrinsic part of every human society, and even within different African countries is always culturally defined. As Werner Reiss (2016: 1) notes: "the highly heterogeneous forms of violence make the phenomenon elusive and hard to define." Drawing the expertise from academics and practitioners from various disciplines in the humanities and social sciences, this volume brings together consideration of a multitude of divergent aspects, forms, expressions, definitions, meanings etc. of violence. The volume therefore affords the reader some appreciation of a much broader picture of what violence signifies in a variety of specific cultural African contexts.

By consolidating reflections on violence in Africa, this Handbook extends the frontiers of knowledge in a number of related ways.

First, it expands our understanding of the complexity of violence, in Africa and beyond. Whereas there is a preoccupation with physical violence and the role of the state (see for example, Kirwin & Cho, 2009), violent extremism (see for example, Chingotuane et al., 2021), genocide (see for example, Collins et al., 2019) and gender-based violence/violence against women (see for example, Budoo-Scholtz & Lubaale, 2022; Onditi & Odera, 2021), youth and violence (see for example, Ismail & Olonisakin, 2021), this Handbook brings other forms of violence to the fore. Thus, the Handbook provides conceptual refinement of one of the most central concepts within African Studies, more broadly conceptualized (see for example, Veit et al., 2011). The concept of epistemic violence, mostly overlooked in studies on violence in Africa, informs the approaches adopted by many contributors to this Handbook. This refers to the dominance of Western ideas and the suppression of African ways of knowing (Masaka, 2021; Ndlovu-Gatsheni, 2018; Nyamnjoh, 2004), thereby stifling uniquely African experiences of diverse phenomena (Afolabi, 2020). Thus, prioritizing African experiences, rather than forcing these into a Procrustean bed, promises more effective solutions.

Second, contributors to this Handbook are drawn from diverse disciplines. We have taken seriously the call for African Studies to embrace transdisciplinarity in African Studies (for example, Zeleza, 2006; Bongmba, 2014). Methodological fanaticism is antithetical to the quest to understand multifaceted phenomena, in Africa and elsewhere. Fundamentalist attachment to only one approach prevents researchers and practitioners from achieving holistic understanding. Thus, we contend that violence is too complex to be clarified by researchers from one exclusive field. By bringing together contributors informed by different disciplinary axioms, this Handbook seeks to do justice to the intricacies of violence in Africa. Thus,

> a multiplicity of multilayered and interrelated, local and global, causal and escalation factors coalesce to generate violent conflicts in Africa. The most important and recurrent factors in causing conflict include, political governance, social structures and processes, individual personalities, ethnicity, religion, ideology, economic motives (both greed[y] and grievances), the colonial legacy, the international capitalist system, and global power politics. The importance of these factors varies in different conflicts and contexts, in different phases of a conflict, and some factors are overshadowed by others during conflict. (Chingono, 2016: 213–214)

Third, we have sought to integrate the theme of technologies of violence in this Handbook. Many of the extant works on violence, in Africa and elsewhere, tend to overlook technologies of violence when analysing the architecture of violence in Africa. For violence to occur, it is aided by various technologies. What are these technologies of violence in Africa? Technology refers to a body of knowledge about the useful arts (Misa, 2003: 7)—a systematic appropriation of useful arts, devices, systems, tools, materials, procedures and knowledge in order to commit violence. Globalization also plays a part. It opens(ed) Africa to new religions, new politics, new cultures, and new technologies which literally became "technologies of violence" in Africa. These include military hardware and software such as guns, teargas, and tankers, as well as religion, and radical and fundamental ideologies.

Fourth, it is anticipated that the Handbook will contribute to the emergence of more decidedly African traditions in the study of violence in Africa. This is closely related to the urgency of addressing epistemic violence that we broached above. Essentially, "African traditions" relate to the formation of a consistent trajectory of African scholars across different generations reflecting on a theme of existential significance for Africans using categories that are informed by African realities and experiences (see for example, Chitando et al.). In order for Africa(ns) to have a fighting chance in addressing violence, there is need to develop intellectual traditions tackling violence that are nourished by an African ethos. This Handbook, we hope, contributes to the emergence of thriving, critical and robust African traditions in the study of violence in Africa.

Fifth, and dependent on the foregoing, we anticipate the growth and consolidation of networks of African scholars (and other allies) actively working to counter violence in Africa. Whereas the section on strategies to overcome violence in Africa in this Handbook is limited owing to thematic considerations, ultimately we are persuaded that the peacebuilding and conflict transformation will be central to African scholars' engagement with Agenda 2063 and its vision of "an integrated, prosperous and peaceful Africa." Pan-African thinktanks such as the Council for the Development of Social Science Research in Africa (CODESRIA) are well placed to coordinate such initiatives (see for example, Assié-Lumumba, 2006). We envisage the Handbook as providing a possible take-off point for further engagement on overcoming violence among African scholars. Whereas scholars, peace activists, governments and non-governmental organizations in other parts of the world can contribute towards overcoming violence in Africa, it is Africans who have the primary responsibility to achieve this (Jackson, 2008: 979;

Marongwe et al., 2019). The Handbook takes seriously the need to interrogate knowledge production on Africa, including the visibility and impact of African scholarship (Okech, 2021: 2) on violence and security.

## 1 Violence: Some Notes on a Slippery Concept

Providing a comprehensive, universally binding and timeless definition of violence is, ultimately, an exercise in futility. This is because essentialist definitions that purport to cover the past, present, and future meanings of specific concepts are severely flawed. This is as true of violence as it is of other concepts in both the humanities and the sciences. For example, reflecting in relation to the problematic of defining religion, Jan Platvoet, a Dutch scholar of religion with keen interest in indigenous spirituality, writes:

> A universally valid definition would have to produce a perfect, and perfectly matching adequatio mentis et rei, 'congruence of mind and thing', in everyone in whatever time, past, present, and future, and in whatever society, culture and language. It seems highly unrealistic to expect this to be achieved in the foreseeable future for the group of cultural phenomena that we loosely refer to by the terms 'religion' and 'religions'. (Platvoet, 1999: 248)

We are convinced that Platvoet's reflections in relation to the possibility of developing a universally applicable definition of religion apply with equal force to the concept of violence, in Africa and elsewhere. We are not likely to be able to coin a definition of violence that applies to the past, present, and future, in all places, for everyone. Violence is perpetrated, experienced, and conceptualized differently by diverse actors in disparate contexts. Another scholar of religion, Afe Adogame, while battling to delineate "religious violence" from, "violence" is forced to concede that, "An appropriate definition of violence has remained a vexed enigma"(Adogame, 2009: 176). In this Handbook, contributors embraced open and flexible definitions of violence, but all within the ambit of intelligibility. Thus, instead of the editors supplying an a priori and fixed definition of violence, we encouraged the contributors to be informed by contextual factors in their approach to violence in specific African settings. To say this is not to succumb to some dangerous relativism, but to promote flexibility in the study of violence in Africa.

We readily acknowledge the numerous efforts that have been undertaken both to analyse violence in Africa, as well as to project its possible occurrence in the future (see for example, Cilliers, 2018). Reflections on the origins of violent conflict in Africa (Aremu, 2010; Nhema & Zeleza, 2008) are equally helpful in terms of assisting us to appreciate how violence comes about. Thus, for example, Aremu (2010) discusses the arbitrary boundaries drawn by the colonialists, ethnicity, inept leadership, corruption, and poverty. However, for us, without a rigorous contextualized analysis, these factors are not adequate to account for violence in Africa. This is because, for example, inept leadership and corruption are realities in many other contexts. However, these factors have not led to violence in other contexts beyond Africa. Similarly, the World Health Organization (WHO) has provided a partial, though useful informative definition of violence, articulating as follows:

> The intentional use of physical force or power, threatened or actual, against oneself, another person, or against a group or community, that either results in or has a high likelihood of resulting in injury, death, psychological harm, maldevelopment or deprivation. (WHO, 1996)

The definition above is helpful to the extent that it highlights issues of intent, physicality, as well as directionality in understanding violence, as well as the effects of the same. However, perhaps because the definition was coined in the context of understanding violence as a public health issue, it embodies a limited appreciation of the intricacies of violence, including violence against non-humans. Thus, for example, the WHO definition does not cover ecological violence. Yet, the climate emergency globally, and especially in Africa, confirms the importance of investing in understanding of ecological violence, namely, violence against the environment (see for example, Navas et al. 2018). This has led some to conceptualize "Peace Ecology" (Kyrou, 2007) where humans seek to promote and secure peace with the environment.

Rutherford et al. (2007) provide valuable insights into violence. While operating from within the public health perspective, they highlight definitions that focus on the doers of violence (self-directed, interpersonal, and collective violence), sexual violence, gender-based violence, and intimate partner violence. They cover other forms of violence within the family or domestic setting (violence against children, youth, elder abuse), workplace violence, structural violence, terrorism, and genocide. On her part, Hamby makes the following submission:

> A precise definition of violence requires four elements. Violence is behavior that is (a) intentional, (b) unwanted, (c) nonessential, and (d) harmful. All four elements are necessary to properly include all acts that belong in the category and to properly exclude similar acts that are not violence, such as self-defense

(a form of aggression but not a form of violence), accidents, and horseplay. (Hamby, 2017: 168)

The criteria spelt out in the foregoing definition is informative. However, it does have its own limitations. Whereas the idea that violence is behaviour that is intentional is useful, it overlooks the fact that, ultimately, the key feature is the use of force rather than the motivating factor. Further, it is difficult to ascertain the motivation behind certain actions and to conclude with certainty that a person or a group sought to use force to cause harm. For example, ecological violence is often understood by its perpetrators, such as multinational oil companies, as "development." However, their actions are harmful to the environment.

We also acknowledge the challenges relating to personal and ideological standpoints regarding violence (see for example, Tripplet et al., 2016). Thus, whether one classifies a particular act as an expression of violence is more often than not influenced by one's location. Writing on the law and violence in America, Sklansky (2021: 5) rightly avers that, "[T]he ideas about violence embedded in the law are deeply entangled with race, with gender, with class…" as well as the emergence of new forms of violence such as cyber-violence (see for example, Malanga, 2021). Malanga's (2021) study confirms the presence of cyber violence against women in one African setting. His study "found that women experienced cyber violent behaviours that ranged from cyber bullying, online defamation, cyber stalking, sexual exploitation to hate speech, and nonconsensual pornography. Perpetrators used digital platforms such as Facebook, WhatsApp, online personal accounts, dating sites, and smartphones to carry out their acts of cyber violent behaviours against women" (Malanga, 2021: 631). However, owing to the increase in internet penetration in Africa, it is sustainable to assume that cyber violence against women is widespread.

As we have already highlighted, defining violence is rendered difficult by the ethical and ideological standpoints of the people defining. The classical line, "one person's terrorist is another person's freedom fighter" (see for example, Kennedy, 1999), demonstrates the challenge of defining violence. Thus, for example, Nelson Mandela, widely celebrated as a freedom fighter, was on the United States terror list. Similarly, while many would regard activists who seek to protect the environment as "the good guys," there are some who regard them as eco-terrorists (see for example, Spadaro, 2020). It is also significant that some environmental and animal rights activists use the multivalent term "jihad" (Posłuszna, 2020) to characterize their activism and to rally their supporters to protect the environment and animals. Thus, classifying certain actions as violent is to a large extent shaped by one's prior ethical and ideological stance. This has the effect of complicating the discourse on violence.

A critic might accuse us of specializing in critiquing those who have been brave enough to propose some definitions of violence, without having the courage to propose one ourselves. Indeed, this would seem to be a fair observation. However, we contend that perhaps the more strategic approach is to adopt an inductive approach. Thus, in the ensuing section we seek to discuss various forms of violence found in Africa. We surmise that, being informed by the reflections of other scholars in this section and reviewing the diverse forms of violence in the next section will provide a firm foundation for us to formulate an open definition of violence.

## 2 Forms of Violence in Africa

As the chapters in this Handbook confirm, the term "violence" serves as a shorthand and placeholder for diverse phenomena. In this section, we seek to highlight the different forms of violence that occur in Africa. At the risk of repetition, we would like to underscore that by cataloguing the various expressions of violence we do not seek to project Africa as any more violent than other contexts. This exercise emerges from our conviction that only an in-depth appreciation of the scope and spaces of violence in Africa will facilitate a more effective engagement with violence in order to actualize Agenda 2063. However, our discussion of the various forms of violence in this introductory chapter is tentative and indicative, rather than definitive and absolute. Many of the themes raised here are discussed in greater detail in the different sections and chapters. Further, we should hasten to add that while we have isolated different forms of violence for brief analysis, in reality there is considerable overlap across the categories. Also, the order in which we present the forms of violence in Africa below is somewhat arbitrary and in no way suggests that we deem some forms of violence as less consequential than others. Thematic considerations, rather than any sense of some forms of violence deserving more urgent attention than others, guided our organizations of the ensuing sections.

### Epistemic Violence

Although indigenous Africans were not hapless victims of colonialism and are not uncritical consumers of postcolonial postulations by their former oppressors, it remains true that colonialism had an indelible mark on the former colonial subjects. This impact is both systemic, collective, and individual. As colonialism was a violent episode with a long aftermath (see for example, Simatei, 2005), its far-reaching impact includes epistemic violence. Although South African higher education has emerged as an arena of the call for the dismantling of the hegemony of colonial and Global-North-related ways of knowing (see for example, Heleta, 2016; Mbembe, 2016), there has been an insistent argument on the need for Africanization (see for example, Chitando, 2016) and the acceptance of indigenous knowledge systems (IKS) in Africa. All these are efforts to counter epistemic violence, which is often hidden in plain sight.

Epistemic violence emerges from the arrogance of colonialism and its vicious assault on indigenous ways of being and knowing. By definition, colonialism projects itself as unrivalled and bringing superior knowledge. It trivialized African knowledge systems and deemed them inferior. Crucially, it instituted a relentless assault on IKS by mocking, rubbishing, and curtailing them. The colonial project was ruthless in its attack on all things deemed "local and native," investing heavily in initiatives aiming at exclusion, injury, and erasure. This violence is informed by arrogance and a fundamentalist sense of conviction that Africa, by definition, is incapable of possessing any knowledge that can count for anything. According to Moira Pérez:

> The notion of epistemic violence refers to the different ways in which violence is exercised in relation to the production, circulation and recognition of knowledge: the denial of epistemic agency for certain subjects, the unacknowledged exploitation of their epistemic resources, their objectification, among many others. (2019: 81)

Epistemic violence has an impact across various spaces in Africa. It is violence expressed in dispossession—of memory, land, dignity, and confidence. Although epistemic violence has been contested, negotiated, and sometimes negated by Africans, its effects continue to linger. It remains difficult for many African intellectuals, politicians, and activists to accept the validity of African ways of knowing. Consequently, the struggle against epistemic violence in Africa is a long and drawn-out one. Achieving "epistemic freedom" and "epistemic justice" (Ndlovu-Gatsheni, 2018) continues to require courage and creativity. Acknowledging the primacy of epistemic violence in Africa is an important step towards creating cultures of peace. Since epistemic violence emerges from racist and colonial constructions, epistemic racism is a threat to more harmonious international relations (Brunner, 2021) and it must be replaced by new paradigms of relating among the different peoples of the world.

Space considerations imply that we cannot furnish numerous examples of epistemic violence in Africa, although various chapters in this Handbook provide useful examples. However, the dominant political and administrative systems in Africa continue to operate on Eurocentric assumptions, many decades after the attainment of political independence. The Global North remains the referral point for African "standards," with its stamp of approval continuing to be pursued for many processes initiated in Africa. This is confirmed within the higher education sector in Africa, where Western epistemologies ride roughshod over indigenous ways of knowing. African students continue to be subjected to the old formula where all ideas, concepts, and examples in the disciplines are drawn from the Global North. It is within this context that the calls for decoloniality, epistemic freedom, Africanization and IKS are growing in African institutions of higher learning. It is vital for African realities and ways of knowing to be the focus and point of departure in higher education in Africa. Reflecting on the teaching of business studies in (South) Africa, Schutte writes as follows:

> Future research needs also to be done on indigenous knowledge regarding concepts such as sustainability, business ethics, negotiation techniques, leadership, hierarchy, profit and loss, investments, insurance, ownership, accountability, long term planning, indigenous township and rural marketing, time management, risk management, procurement planning, street vendors, contracts and agreements, accounting principles, economic growth, budgeting, banking, infrastructure development, change management, paradigm shifts, innovation, entrepreneurship, responsibility, citizenship, tax, team work, quality management, organizational structures, decision-making processes, future studies and many more. The practice of business in South Africa has proved that a Eurocentric understanding of these concepts differs in some instances from indigenous African knowledge. Therefore, research into the indigenous understanding of concepts like these is necessary to find common ground and a workable platform for Africa and the West to understand each other when entering global business relations. (Schutte, 2019: 197–198)

## Sexual and Gender-Based Violence

It is now widely recognized that sexual and gender-based violence (SGBV) is global and endemic (Heise et al., 2002). The 16 Days of Activism against Gender-Based Violenc (GBV), a global campaign, is shedding light on this widespread form of violence. While different definitions and alternative terms have been used, including "domestic violence," "violence against women and girls," "intimate partner violence" and others, there is no denying the fact that the challenge is a huge one indeed. Each one of these terms has its own nuances, underscoring the need for closer scrutiny than can be undertaken herein. One helpful definition has been given as follows:

> Violence involving men and women, in which the female is usually the victim; and which is derived from unequal power relationships between men and women. Violence is directed specifically against a woman because she is a woman or affects women disproportionately. It includes, but is not limited to, physical, sexual and psychological harm (including intimidation, suffering, coercion, and/or deprivation of liberty within the family, or within the general community). It includes that violence which is perpetrated or condoned by the state.... This widely accepted definition of gender-based violence is now often expanded to include violence that results from unequal power relations between men and between women (e.g. homophobic violence). (WHO, 2009: 3)

There is a growing appreciation of the need to address SGBV in Africa, with the theme drawing the attention of African scholars and activists (see for example, "Section V" in Yacob-Haliso & Falola, 2021). Although sometimes the casting of some countries, for example, South Africa and the Democratic Republic of the Congo (DRC) as "the rape capital of the world" or the "epicentre of SGBV" is problematic in that it entrenches stereotypes, it remains true that men have been responsible for violence against women and girls. Power inequality has ensured that many women and girls have been at the receiving end of violence perpetrated by men (Vetten & Ratele, 2013).

Toxic notions of masculinity have authored pain for women and girls in diverse African settings. Ademiluka's (2018) recent attempt to absolve patriarchy in violence against women (and ascribing it to a psychological malady) is unconvincing, to express it mildly. It remains true that men's quest to assert themselves over women reminds us that SGBV is not sexual but is about power. Further, women's bodies have been theatres of violence in various African contexts, including the phenomenon that Denis Mukwege, a medical doctor who has treated women victims in the DRC and won the Nobel Peace Prize in 2018, has called, "rape with extreme violence" (see for example, Mukwege & Nangini, 2009; Mukwege et al., 2010). This includes the violence by groups that espouse a religious agenda, such as Boko Haram in northern Nigeria (see for example, Matfess, 2020). Significantly, intimate partner violence increases in contexts characterized by war and armed conflict (see for example, Ekhato-Mobayode et al., 2020).

The COVID-19 pandemic that wreaked havoc globally from 2020 and was underway during the time of writing, necessitated lockdowns. However, these lockdowns resulted in a sharp upsurge in SGBV throughout the world. Women with violent partners became more susceptible to attacks (AUC-WGDD, 2020). COVID-19, therefore, is being experienced within the other pandemic, namely, the SGBV pandemic. Further, the climate emergency is threatening to worsen women's vulnerability to SGBV. This dimension of climate change and SGBV is emerging as a major issue of interest. Thus:

> Climate change is rarely discussed in relation to violence against women. It has become a global common concern due to its role as a contributing factor in exacerbating SGBV. Though entire populations are affected by climate change, women and girls face double victimization as human beings as well as because of their gender. During emergencies, especially conflicts and disasters, women are at high risk of SGBV because of crisis in the family and society as well as due to sudden breakdown of family and community structures arising from forced displacement. As a result, women and girls become more vulnerable and face physical, sexual, psychological harm as well as denial of resources or necessary services. (Desai & Mandal, 2021: 138)

One form of SGBV that is gaining attention is that directed at women in politics (UN Women Leadership & Governance Section, 2021). In certain regions of the world, women who dare to enter the political space must anticipate violence in all its diverse forms. Misogyny and a patriarchal sense of entitlement combine to project women as followers, not leaders. In different African contexts, women struggle against violence directed towards them by mostly male competitors. Thus, "In many African states, politics is marred by violence, persecution, intimidation and torture. While both genders are victims of this, political violence presents particular barriers to women's engagement and political participation" (International IDEA, 2021: 23). Further,

> Violence against women in politics (VAWP) limits women's political opportunities and discourages or prevents them from exercising their political rights, including their rights as voters, candidates, party supporters or public officials. VAWP can occur during electoral campaigns, but not only: as women assume various political positions, they may, for example, be pressured to resign from their posts on the basis of gender, or verbally threatened or intimidated because they are women in politics; and VAWP may take many other forms, including in sexist stereotypes and images portrayed in the media, which, particularly in the digital age, focus on women's bodies, sexuality and traditional social roles, rather than their competence, capacity and contributions as leaders. (iKnow Politics, 2016: 2)

It is becoming clear that SGBV is one global pandemic that requires urgent action. Emerging forms, such as technology-facilitated gender-based violence (TFGBV) imply that more work is required to overcome SGBV. In Africa, socio-cultural, religious, political, economic and other factors have combined to make SGBV an intractable issue (see for example, Alesina et al., 2021; Akamike et al., 2019). Patriarchy generally normalizes violence against women and girls. Initiatives to explore violence against women in religion in Africa (see for example, Chitando & Chirongoma, 2013; Le Roux et al., 2020; Nyangweso & Olupona, 2019), in literature and film (Nkealah & Nnaemeka, 2021), in the media (Green et al., 2020; Okorie, 2011) and elsewhere confirm the widespread nature of SGBV in Africa. The impact of SGBV on women's vulnerability to HIV in Africa has also been explored in detail in the many publications by the Circle of Concerned African Women Theologians (see for example, Modie-Moroka, 2016; Siwila & Kobo, 2021). Critically, within the last decade, there has been a notable commitment by governments, non-governmental organizations, faith-based organizations and other players to prioritize responding to SGBV in Africa. In particular, there is an appreciation of the need to engage men and boys as partners in addressing SGBV in Africa (see for example, Freedman, 2012).

## Violence Against Men and Boys

To emphasize violence against women and girls is not to gloss over or even to deny violence against boys and men in society. We, however, do not subscribe to the notion that violence against men is at the same level as violence against women (Gesinde, 2019), although we agree that it does require attention. We concur that toxic masculinities also endanger the health and well-being of some men, particularly in contexts of violence. Thus, for example, Schultz (2020) has presented survivors' testimonies of men who experienced SGBV in Northern Uganda. Similarly, another study presents violence against men and boys in the Central African Republic (All Survivors Project, 2018). Violence against men and boys in conflict settings is associated with notions of power, where those who are enjoying an upper hand at specific points in time seek to "de-masculinize" those they would have overcome. Clark (2019) refers to men's susceptibility to violence in conflict and security contexts as "the vulnerability of the penis." In our opinion, the following definition is quite detailed and informative:

> Sexual violence against men includes actions directed at the victim's sexual or reproductive health or identity, for example: rape, whether oral or anal,

involving objects, the perpetrator or two victims; enforced sterilization; enforced nudity; enforced masturbation and other forms of sexual humiliation; castration; genital violence (for example beatings of genitals or the administration of electric shocks to the genital area); and enforced incest or enforced rape of female or male others. These are common forms of sexual violence committed particularly in armed conflict. Sexual violence directed against men and boys can similarly take place in many settings, including in the home, the workplace, schools, on the streets, in the military, as well as in prisons and police custody. (Solangon & Patel, 2012: 418)

There is also the "muted reality" of GBV against men (Thobejane et al., 2018) within the domestic sphere. Due to the patriarchal nature of most African societies, there is an assumption that men will always be the perpetrators of violence against women. However, a more balanced perspective confirms that GBV against men is more widespread than is often assumed. Patriarchal constructions of men as strong and commanding have led to most men failing to report cases of abuse against them. "Men fear that if they report abuse by women people will doubt their sexual orientation. Men, therefore, hide and deny any victimization just to protect their ego" (Mbandlwa, 2020: 6755). This aspect of male survivors of GBV remaining silent has also been noted in other settings outside Africa (see for example, Cook, 2009: xvi). Yet "[M]ale victims of domestic violence deserve the same recognition, sympathy, support, and services as do female victims" (Dienye & Gbeneol, 2009: 338).

Despite the conspiracy of silence, secrecy, and shame surrounding GBV against men, a number of researchers have begun drawing attention to this phenomenon. Obarisiagbon and Omage (2019: 52), writing with special reference to Southern Nigeria, identify men as facing verbal abuse, physical abuse, sexual abuse, emotional/psychological abuse and economic abuse. Commenting on the situation in Ghana, Zuure (2018) underscores men's tendency to suffer in silence. This pattern is replicated in diverse other settings. Without downplaying violence against women, we submit that more research needs to be undertaken into GBV against men in Africa.

## Violence Against Sex Workers

The adage that sex work is the world's oldest profession is a well-known one. Sex work is a global phenomenon, with virtually every society on earth having sex workers. However, the status of sex work remains contested, with religious, ethical, ideological, and other considerations often overriding public health considerations on how to make sex work safer, even if only in the interim, for those who participate in the industry. There is much stigma associated with sex work in Africa and women sex workers are particularly at the receiving end of some of the most vicious attacks, including from those who have the responsibility of protecting them, such as the police. The following observation is instructive:

> African sex workers are the victims of physical and sexual abuse and rarely receive protection from the state as victims of gender-based violence. There is a general perception that gender-based violence is part and parcel of sex work and not a crime from which they should be protected. Statistics involving gender-based violence very rarely include instances in which the woman at issue is a sex worker. Far from protecting sex workers from abuse, African states are often complicit in the abuse of sex workers through tolerance of routine police abuse and harassment of sex workers. Police often demand exorbitant bribes from sex workers, detain sex workers through arbitrary arrests, and subject sex workers to sexual abuse. African women engaged in sex work also experience sexual and physical abuse from clients. They risk contracting HIV/AIDS and other sexually transmitted infections ("STIs") from clients who refuse to wear condoms or vicious beatings and sexual assaults from clients that object to condom use. (Mgbako & Smith, 2011: 1180–1181)

The foregoing citation details the vulnerability of female sex workers in Africa to violence. However, as we argued regarding women and GBV, there is the need to acknowledge the existence of male sex workers on the continent. They are also vulnerable to violence, particularly due to the stigma and discrimination associated with men selling sex. Although there are attempts to promote dialogue between male sex workers and the police in some settings (see for example, Woensdregt & Nencel, 2021), violence remains one major characteristic of sex work by both women and men in different African contexts.

## Violence Against Children

Children are highly valued in most African settings. They are associated with blessings from God and the ancestors, bring status to the parents and can continue the lineage (see for example, Mbiti, 1969), offer social security, contribute to labour, and provide emotional satisfaction (Dyer, 2007). Despite the valorization of children in Africa, we must concede that children still face violence, especially at home and at school. A report on children and violence in Africa offers the following detailed analysis:

> Violence against children takes different forms: physical violence, including corporal punishment; sexual violence, including harassment and abuse; and mental violence, including verbal abuse, cruelty and harassment of a type that can damage a child's psychological and emotional health and wellbeing. As well as threatening children's survival and development, violence erodes family structures, jeopardizes children's education, generates social insecurity and consumes precious national resources. (ACPF, 2014: x)

Corporal punishment has emerged as a highly emotional and divisive issue, with many parents deploying postcolonial arguments. They charge that the very idea of regarding corporal punishment as "violence" is a confirmation of the imposition and dominance of Global North ideas and practices on the Global South. Many maintain that they would not have succeeded in life without having been "straightened" by corporal punishment. The impact of Christianity is clear when many African Christians declare that corporal punishment is "biblical" (see for example, Pete & du Plessis, 2000). Although some countries in Africa have made progress in banning corporal punishment for children in school, fear of losing political support, as well as the notion that corporal punishment is "cultural," means that the practice continues in many homes (and schools! See: for example, Mahlangu et al., 2021). Thus, "Only 8% of children in Africa live in countries where they are protected in law from punitive assault by adults; globally, just 10% of children enjoy this protection" (End All Corporal Punishment of Children, 2017).

The debate over corporal punishment confirms the complexity of postcolonial African identities. Due to the fact that many contemporary African parents (particularly the fathers) were subjected to corporal punishment, they now embrace the practice as "African." However, it was brought by missionaries and used liberally by the colonialists (Van Wyk & Chifamba, 2019). Tolerating corporal punishment for children often results in society's acceptance of GBV, as well as state violence against citizens. It socializes people to embrace the notion that using violence guarantees compliance, thereby entrenching the use of violence.

## Violence Against Sexual Minorities

Whereas the dominant image of a homophobic Africa is problematic, as it overlooks the general tolerance shown towards sexual minorities, including within faith communities (see for example, Van Klinken & Chitando, 2021), it remains true that there is significant violence against homosexuals in some African settings. There have been instances where those who are perceived as having a "different" sexual orientation and gender identity have experienced violence. In particular, transgender persons identifying as female tend to be more exposed to violence (Müller et al., 2021) than other sexual and gender minorities. A study on violence against sexual minorities in the Kenyan coastal region shows that politicians, religious leaders, and the media periodically whip up emotions, resulting in attacks on lesbians and gays (Human Rights Watch, 2015). In Malawi, politicians have deployed the notion of "God-fearing Malawi" to justify the suppression of the rights of homosexuals (Chanika et al., 2013).

The status of lesbian, gay, bisexual, transgender, intersex, queer or questioning+ (LGBTIQ+) in most African countries contributes to the violence that is directed at sexual minorities. While there has been some progress in decriminalizing homosexuality in Africa, most African countries continue to regard homosexuality through the frame of the politics of the Global North seeking to impose its values on the Global South. Hence, they have not invested in protecting sexual minorities against violence. The net effect is the following:

> LGBTQI persons often suffer physical violence foremost from their families and members of their communities. Sexual violence has been identified as a common threat to LGBTQI persons, as it is used to 'punish' persons who defy traditional gender norms because of their sexual orientation, gender identity or expression. Lesbian-, Queer-, Bisexual-, and transgender women have been identified as a group particularly vulnerable to violence. This violence occurs within a context where womxn are considered inherently less valuable than men. It has been revealed that Lesbian-, Queer-, Bisexual-, and transgender womxn are prone to violence as it is believed that their sexual orientation and gender expressions are a threat to dominant masculinities. (ArcusFoundation & Iranti, 2019: 9)

## Ecological Violence

The world is becoming more alert to the impact of ecological violence in the wake of the climate emergency. There is unanimity that climate change does not merely happen but is caused by human actions. The capitalist exploitation of humans and the environment has seen the environment being subjected to multiple forms of exploitation. Greed of unique proportions has seen multinational companies visiting violence on the African landscape in search of mineral resources and merciless deforestation. The "cut and run" (Glastra, 1999) strategy that characterizes the illegal logging and timber trade in Africa (and other parts of the world) has seen Africa bleeding. Although some indigenous people are involved in perpetrating ecological violence, their effect pales in comparison with the devastation wrought by multinational companies.

Iheka (2018) has provided some valuable insights into ecological violence from the perspective of African literature. He offers an ecocritical reading of works of art that highlight ecological violence in Africa. For him, whenever humans are unable to appreciate nature on its own terms and adopt an exploitative attitude, they are engaging in ecological violence. Ecological violence stems from the dangerous anthropocentrism that creates a hierarchy of beings, with humans at the very top. The so-called "progress" by humans often entails destroying forests and resisting co-existing with other creatures (Iheka, 2018: 33–34).

Ecological violence in Africa has been generally understated. This could be due to a number of factors, including the somewhat hidden nature of the violence and the cost of naming ecological violence for what it is. For example, mining is regarded as a legitimate economic activity and the industry is seen as promising Africa's economic liberation. Indeed, Africa has every right to benefit from its abundant mineral resources. The concept of a "resource curse" is inherently contradictory and we do not endorse it. Resources are meant to benefit those who own them, that is, all the citizens of a particular country, and, by extension, the continent. However, mining, as done by multinational companies, is detrimental to the environment, as well as to the health of the local population (see for example, Stewart, 2020).

It is important to make a conceptual distinction between ecological violence and violence that is related to environmental conflicts. Thus, the emerging interest in climate change, violence, and security in Africa (Schmidt & Muggah, 2021), for example, must be separated from violence directed towards the environment. Climate-change related conflict and violence is often public, spectacular, and attracts the media. However, ecological violence is what Nixon calls, "slow violence." Thus:

> By slow violence I mean a violence that occurs gradually and out of sight, a violence of delayed destruction that is dispersed across time and space, an attritional violence that is typically not viewed as violence at all. Violence is customarily conceived as an event or action that is immediate in time, explosive and spectacular in space, and as erupting into instant sensational visibility. We need, I believe, to engage a different kind of violence, a violence that is neither spectacular nor instantaneous, but rather incremental and accretive, its calamitous repercussions playing out across a range of temporal scales. (Nixon, 2011: 2)

Crucially, it is vital to acknowledge that humans' violence against nature has precipitated nature's own violence. The frequency of violent and exceedingly destructive cyclones in Southern Africa has increased, while devastating droughts have hit parts of East and West Africa. Nature is not passive, simply being there and waiting to quietly absorb the violence meted on it by humans. Nature fights back and unleashes its own ferocious violence, resulting in immense human suffering. Indeed, the climate emergency is a result of humanity's violence against nature.

## Violence by the State

The postcolonial state in Africa is mostly a product of a violent history. Particularly in Southern Africa, the state has emerged out of the brutal process of colonialism and militant struggles against colonialism.[1] Created by violence, the postcolonial African state has generally not hesitated to unleash violence for its own survival. Although it is simplistic to attribute all the violence in Africa to "weak states," (Kirwin and Cho, 2009)[2] given that some powerful states do sponsor violence against their opponents and citizens, it remains true that the state is often implicated in violence in Africa. Here, we have to contend with both the errors of commission or omission, namely, that the state is either directly behind acts of violence, or that it has failed to distribute goods and services fairly, thereby giving rise to violence (see for example, Bay & Donham, 2006). Pan-African think-tanks such as CODESRIA have expended considerable intellectual energy in trying to understand the African state and to find ways of increasing its efficiency, and critical African intellectuals have sought to provide alternative interpretations from the Eurocentric ones (see, among others, Ikpe, 2021).

On the part of countries in an area, we are more circumspect in relation to identifying violence in Africa. We are persuaded that the capacity of the state, whatever the size of the area that it superintends over, is more critical and relevant, rather than the sheer number of countries. States that care for (love) their citizens, protect them from harm and invest in their flourishing. State violence often stems from insecurity, where the state invents and multiplies "enemies, dissidents and renegades" in the name of protecting sovereignty and territorial integrity. While we do accept that there are "terrorists, rebels

---

[1] Herbst's (1990) provocative comparison of the role of war in state formation in Europe and what he regards the relative peaceful formation of the African state is vitiated by his refusal to acknowledge the violence of colonialism in the first instance.

[2] For a helpful review of the literature on "failed states," see Di John (2008). On the other hand, Gentili (2009) rightly proposes that the very concept itself is a failure.

and warlords" in Africa (Varin & Abubakar, 2017), we do not share the state's tendency to see these everywhere and in everyone!

One of the biggest threats to the security of many citizens in Africa is the concept of "protecting national security" as adumbrated by the postcolonial state. Once this concept is unleashed, literally every form of violence by the state becomes sanctioned and acceptable by the state. Across diverse African settings, "protecting national security" is code for extreme violence by the state. Although coming from an earlier period, the report, "Deadly Marionettes: State-Sponsored Violence in Africa" (Article19, 1997) highlights how state operatives in different countries use underhand tactics to harm perceived opponents. On the other hand, when faced with communal violence, the state's interventions are mostly guided by enlightened self-interest (see for example, Elfversson, 2015).

When state operatives operate with impunity and are convinced that they are above the law, they can torture opposition activists without any fear of consequences. Young people and workers protesting against corruption, for example, are routinely beaten or shot at in different African countries. During the COVID-19 lockdowns, police in Nigeria, Kenya, South Africa, Uganda, and other countries, for example, used maximum force to compel citizens who were battling to secure their livelihoods, to comply (Mugabi, 2020). It does not help for defensive African scholars to insist that the same violence was exhibited by police in other contexts beyond the continent. The issue at stake is the violence suffered by African citizens.

Overall, then, the state in Africa has generally demonstrated a huge appetite for violence. Musical shows, national activities held in stadia, soccer matches, and other activities where huge numbers of people are involved tend to quickly degenerate into violence. Perhaps the general construction of the state as the all-powerful patriarch (Togarasei, 2020) with the right to discipline errant and mischievous "children" (citizens) serves to account for this tendency by the state in Africa. On his part, Mlambo (2020) maintains that some heads of state, such as the former president of Zimbabwe, Robert Mugabe, regard themselves as the "fathers of the nation" and can, therefore, generously administer corporal (or worse) punishment on any of their subjects who do not seem ready to follow the orders that they bellow from their lairs.

## Electoral Violence

We must begin by acknowledging the notable progress that Africa has made in abandoning one-party states and engaging in multiparty politics and holding of elections regularly. While some wish to adopt a more cautious stance (see for example, Mattes, 2019), by their nature elections are often charged and divisive. Due to the high stakes, some political actors simultaneously become entrepreneurs of violence. In a recent study, Animashaun (2020) reflected on electoral violence in Kenya, Nigeria, and Zimbabwe. He concluded that the "pervasive nature of electoral violence in Sub-Saharan Africa could be linked to politicized land rights, ethnic marginalization, patrimonialism, state-sponsored violence and youth unemployment" (Animashaun, 2020: 20). While many peaceful elections continue to be held throughout the region, it is helpful to acknowledge that some elections have been marred by electoral violence.

Electoral violence in some parts of Africa has resulted in loss of life, internal displacement of citizens, destruction of property, psychological harm and other negative outcomes. Some political actors deploy electoral violence to intimidate opponents in an effort to retain or gain power. Although some may want to classify electoral violence under political violence, it does appear analytically prudent to separate these two forms of violence. Thus:

> Electoral violence can be distinguished from other forms of political violence by its timing (before an election, on election day, or after an election); objectives (winning, sabotaging, preventing, altering, or challenging election outcomes); and methodology (it may be physical, verbal, or psychological). Electoral violence functions as one of many tools used by political actors to acquire or retain power. (Bekoe & Burchard, 2020: 258)

For Omotola (2010: 52), electoral violence in Africa is, among other types of violence, related to the neo-patrimonial character of the African state, the influence of the military and what he dubs, "the weak institutionalization of democratic architectures."

## 3    Conclusion

In this chapter, we have sought to provide an overview of the multiple and complex forms of violence found in Africa. However, as we conceded in the opening paragraph, we are painfully aware that for some African intellectuals and activists, a volume such as this one constitutes the ultimate betrayal. They will most likely contend that it reinforces the stereotype of Africa as some permanently lawless space characterised by perpetual violence (Chiwanza 2021; Obijiofor 2009 and Manzo 2018). While we understand such concerns and are sensitive to them, we hold a different perspective. Our motivation comes from what we consider a good place: achieving an in-depth appreciation of the diverse expressions and experiences of violence in Africa equips us to provide more effective interventions to overcome or minimise violence. We anticipate that this Handbook will inspire further engagement around the theme of violence in Africa and contribute towards more effective strategies that will bring sustainable peace and development. This will ensure securing "The Africa We Want," as envisaged by the African Union's development blueprint, Agenda 2063.

# References

ACPF. (2014). *The African Report on Violence Against Children*. The African Child Policy Forum (ACPF).

Ademiluka, S. O. (2018). Patriarchy and Women Abuse: Perspectives from Ancient Israel and Africa. *Old Testament Essays, 31*(2), 339–362.

Adogame, A. (2009). Fighting for God or Fighting in God's Name! The Politics of Religious Violence in Contemporary Nigeria. Religions/Adyan: *Journal of the Dohan International Centre for Interfaith Dialogue, 1*, 174–192.

Afolabi, O. S. (2020). Globalisation, Decoloniality and the Question of Knowledge Production in Africa: A Critical Discourse. *JHEA/RESA, 18*(1), 93–109.

African Union. (2015). *Agenda 2063: The Africa We Want: Popular Version*. African Union Commission.

Akamike, I. C., et al. (2019). Predictors and Facilitators of Gender-Based Violence in Sub-Saharan Africa. *Journal of Global Health Reports, 3*, e2019076. https://doi.org/10.29392/joghr.3.e2019076

Alesina, A., et al. (2021). Violence Against Women: A Cross-Cultural Analysis for Africa. *Economica, 88*, 77–104.

All Survivors Project. (2018). *"I Don't Know Who Can Help": Men and Boys Facing Sexual Violence in the Central African Republic*. https://allsurvivorsproject.org/wp-content/uploads/2018/03/ASP-Central-African-Republic.pdf. Accessed 30 December 2021.

Animashaun, M. A. (2020). Democratization Trapped in African Violence: Is Sub-Saharan Africa a Dangerous Place for Democracy? *Contemporary Journal of African Studies, 7*(2), 18–30.

ArcusFoundation and Iranti. (2019). *Data Collection and Reporting on Violence Perpetrated Against LGBTQI Persons in Botswana, Kenya, Malawi, South Africa and Uganda*. Iranti.

Aremu, J. O. (2010). Conflicts in Africa: Meaning, Causes, Impact and Solution. *African Research Review, 4*(4), 549–560.

Article 19. (1997). *Deadly Marionettes: State-Sponsored Violence in Africa*. Article 19.

Assié-Lumumba, N. T. (2006). *Higher Education in Africa: Crisis, Reforms and Transformation* (Working Paper Series). CODESRIA.

AUC-WGDD (The African Union Commission—Women, Gender and Development Directorate). (2020). *Gender-Based Violence During the COVID-19 Pandemic* (Policy Paper). AUC-WGDD.

Bay, E. G., & Donham, D. L. (Eds.). (2006). *States of Violence: Politics, Youth and Memory in Contemporary Africa*. University of Virginia Press.

Bekoe, D. A., & Burchard, S. M. (2020). The Use of Electoral Violence. In G. Lynch & P. VonDoepp (Eds.), *Routledge Handbook of Democratization in Africa* (pp. 258–272). Routledge.

Bongmba, E. (2014). Interdisciplinary and Transdisciplinarity in African Studies. *Religion and Theology, 21,* 218–250.

Brankovic, J. (2019). *What Drives Violence in South Africa? Research Brief*. Centre for the Study of Violence and Reconciliation.

Brunner, C. (2021). Conceptualizing Epistemic Violence: An Interdisciplinary Assemblage for IR. *International Politics Reviews, 9,* 193–212.

Budoo-Scholtz, A., & Lubaale, E. C. (Eds.). (2022). *Violence Against Women and Criminal Justice in Africa: Volume II Sexual Violence and Vulnerability*. Palgrave Macmillan.

Chabal, P., et al. (Eds.). (2005). *Is Violence Inevitable in Africa? Theories of Conflict and Approaches to Conflict Prevention*. Brill.

Chanika, et al. (2013). Gender, Gays and Gain: The Sexualised Politics of Donor Aid in Malawi. *Africa Spectrum, 48*(1), 89–105.

Chingono, M. (2016). Violent Conflicts in Africa: Towards a Holistic Understanding. *World Journal of Social Science Research, 3*(2), 199–218.

Chingotuane, E. V. F., et al. (2021). *Strategic Options for Managing Violent Conflict in Southern Africa: The Case of Mozambique*. Situation Report. Friedrich Ebert Stiftung, Maputo. http://library.fes.de/pdf-files/bueros/mosambik/18479.pdf. Accessed 6 December 2021.

Chitando, E. (2016). The Africanization of Biblical Studies in Zimbabwe: Promises and Challenges. *Journal of Theology for Southern Africa, 156,* 54–70.

Chitando, E., & Chirongoma, S. (Eds.). (2013). *Justice Not Silence: Churches Facing Sexual and Gender-based Violence*. African Sun Media.

Chiwanza, T. H. (2021, December 26). "I Stopped Watching CNN, BBC, Sky News"-Kenyatta Rejects Western Propaganda. The African Exponent. https://www.africanexponent.com/post/17674-i-stopped-watching-cnn-bbc-sky-news-kenyatta-rejects-western-propaganda. Accessed 28 December 2021.

Cilliers, J. (2018). *Violence in Africa: Trends, Drivers and Prospects to 2023*. Africa Report 12. Institute of Security Studies, Pretoria. https://media.africaportal.org/documents/Violence_in_Africa_ISS.pdf. Accessed 9 December 2021.

Clark, J. N. (2019). The Vulnerability of the Penis: Sexual Violence against Men in Conflict and Security Frames. *Men and Masculinities, 22*(5), 778–800.

Collins, L., Lyons, T., & Adeboye, W. (2019). Guest Editorial: Rethinking Genocide, Mass Atrocities, and Political Violence in Africa. *Genocide Studies and Prevention: An International Journal, 13*(2), 2–13.

Cook, P. W. (2009). *Abused Men: The Hidden Side of Domestic Violence* (2nd ed.). Praeger.

Desai, B. H., & Mandal, M. (2021). Role of Climate Change in Exacerbating Sexual and Gender-Based Violence against Women: A New Challenge for International Law. *Environmental Policy and Law, 51*, 137–147.

Di John, J. (2008). *Conceptualising the Causes and Consequences of Failed States: A Critical Review of the Literature* (Working Paper No. 25). LSE.

Dienye, P. O., & Gbeneol, P. K. (2009). Domestic Violence Against Men in Primary Care in Nigeria. *American Journal of Men's Health, 3*(4), 333–339.

Dyer, S. J. (2007). The Value of Children in African Countries. *Journal of Psychosomatic Obstetrics and Gynecology, 28*(2), 69–77.

Elfversson, E. (2015). Providing Security or Protecting Interests? Government Interventions in Violent Communal Conflicts in Africa. *Journal of Peace Research, 52*(6), 791–805.

End All Corporal Punishment of Children. (2017). *DAC Briefing: Prohibiting All Corporal Punishment of Children in Africa: An Essential Step Towards Fulfilling the 2030 Agenda for Sustainable Development*. http://endcorporalpunishment.org/wp-content/uploads/regional/DAC-briefing-2017-EN.pdf. Accessed 1 January 2022.

Freedman, J. (2012). *Engaging Men in the Fight against Gender-Based Violence: Case Studies from Africa*. Palgrave Macmillan.

Gentili, A. M. (2009). Failed States or Failed Concept? *Studia Diplomatica, 62*(2), 9–22.

Gesinde, A. (2019). Victimisation of Men and the Veracity of Wife-to-Husband Abuse in Research Reports: Implications for Domestic Violence Counselling. *African Journal for the Psychological Study of Social Issues, 22*(3).

Glastra, R. (Ed.). (1999). *Cut and Run: Illegal Logging and Timber Trade in the Tropics*. International Research Centre.

Green, D. P., Wilke, A. M., & Cooper, J. (2020). Countering Violence Against Women by Encouraging Disclosure: A Mass Media Experiment in Rural Uganda. *Comparative Political Studies, 53*(14), 2283–2320.

Hamby, S. (2017). On Defining Violence, and Why It Matters. *Psychology of Violence, 7*(2), 167–180.

Heise, L., et al. (2002). A Global View of Gender-Based Violence. *International Journal of Gynecology and Obstetrics, 78*(Suppl. 1), S5–S14.

Heleta, S. (2016). Decolonisation of Higher Education: Dismantling Epistemic Violence and Eurocentrism in South Africa. *Transformation in Higher Education, 1*(1), a9. https://doi.org/10.4102/the.v1i1.9

Herbst, J. (1990). War and the State in Africa. *International Security, 14*(4), 117–139.
Human Rights Watch. (2015). *The Issue is Violence: Attacks on LGBT People on Kenya's Coast.* https://www.hrw.org/sites/default/files/report_pdf/kenya0915_4upr.pdf. Accessed 30 December 2021.
Iheka, C. (2018). *Naturalizing Africa Ecological Violence, Agency, and Postcolonial Resistance in African Literature.* Cambridge University Press.
iKnow Politics: International Knowledge Network of Women in Politics. (2016). *Consolidated Reply of the e-Discussion on: Violence Against Women in Politics.* https://iknowpolitics.org/sites/default/files/vawip_cr_0.pdf. Accessed 24 December 2021.
Ikpe, E. (2021). Transcending the State–Market Dichotomy, Developmentalism and Industrial Change: Learning from Critical African Scholars. *Africa Development, 46*(3), 21–43.
International IDEA. (2021). *Women's Political Participation-Africa Barometer.* International IDEA.
Ismail, F., & Olonisakin, F. (2021). Why Do Youth Participate in Violence in Africa? A Review of Evidence. *Conflict, Security and Development, 21*(3), 471–399.
Jackson, A. (2008). Review Article: War, Violence and Peace in Africa. *Journal of Southern African Studies, 34*(4), 969–979.
Kaya, H. O., & Seleti, Y. N. (2013). African Indigenous Knowledge Systems and Relevance of Higher Education in South Africa. *The International Education Journal: Comparative Perspectives, 12*(1), 30–44.
Kennedy, R. (1999). Is One Person's Terrorist Another's Freedom Fighter? Western and Islamic Approaches to 'Just War' Compared. *Terrorism and Political Violence, 11*(1), 1–21. https://doi.org/10.1080/09546559908427493
Kyrou, C. N. (2007). Peace Ecology: An Emerging Paradigm in Peace Studies. *International Journal of Peace Studies, 12*(1), 73–92.
Kirwin, M. F., & Cho, W. (2009). *Weak States and Violence in Sub-Saharan Africa* (Afrobarometer Working Paper 111). https://afrobarometer.org/sites/default/files/publications/Working%20paper/AfropaperNo111.pdf. Accessed 6 December 2021.
Le Roux, E., et al. (2020). Engaging with Faith Groups to end VAGW in Conflict-affected Communities: Results from Two Community Surveys in the DRC. *BMC International Health and Human Rights, 20*(27). https://doi.org/10.1186/s12914-020-00246-8
Leys, C. (1965). Violence in Africa. *Transition, 21*, 17–20.
Mahlangu, P., et al. (2021). Prevalence and Factors Associated with Experience of Corporal Punishment in Public Schools in South Africa. *PLoS ONE, 16*(8), e0254503. https://doi.org/10.1371/journal.pone.0254503
Malanga, D. F. (2021). Survey of Cyber Violence Against Women in Malawi. In *Proceedings of the 1st Virtual Conference on Implications of Information and Digital Technologies for Development* (pp. 623–634). https://arxiv.org/ftp/arxiv/papers/2108/2108.09806.pdf. Accessed 10 December 2021.

Manzo, K. (2018). Images of Africa in World Press Photo. In M. I. de Heredia & Z. Wai (Eds.), *Recentering Africa in International Relations Beyond Lack, Peripherality, and Failure* (pp. 97–119). Routledge.

Marongwe, N., et al. (Eds.). (2019). *Violence, Peace and Everyday Modes of Justice and Healing in Postcolonial Africa*. LANGAA RPCIG.

Masaka, D. (2021). Knowledge, Power, and the Search for Epistemic Liberation in Africa. Social Epistemology. *A Journal of Knowledge, Culture and Policy, 35*(3), 258–269.

Matfess, H. (2020). Part and Parcel? Examining Al Shabaab and Boko Haram's Violence Targeting Civilians and Violence Targeting Women. *Studies in Conflict & Terrorism*. https://doi.org/10.1080/1057610X.2020.1759262

Mattes, R. (2019). *Democracy in Africa: Demand, Supply, and the "Dissatisfied Democrat"* (Afrobarometer Policy Paper No. 54). Afrobarometer.

Mbandlwa, Z. (2020). Analysis of a One-Sided Narrative of Gender-Based Violence in South Africa. *Solid State Technology, 63*(6): 6754–6767 [8].

Mbembe, A. J. (2016). Decolonising the University: New Directions. *Arts and Humanities in Higher Education, 15*(1), 29–45.

Mbiti, J. S. (1969). *African Religions and Philosophy*. Heinemann.

Mgbako, C., & Smith, L. A. (2011). Sex Work and Human Rights in Africa. *Fordham International Law Journal, 33*(4), 1177–1220.

Michira, J. (2002). *Images of Africa in the Western Media*. http://web.mnstate.edu/robertsb/313/images_of_africa_michira.pdf. Accessed 6 December 2021.

Misa, T. J. (2003). The Compelling Tangle of Modernity and Technology. In T. J. Misa, P. Brey and A. Feenberg (Eds.), *Modernity and Technology*, 1–30. Massachusetts Institute of Technology.

Mlambo O. B. (2020). Robert Mugabe and the politics of civic renewal in Zimbabwe: A case of comparison with Emperor Augustus? In: Chitando, E. (Ed.), *Personality Cult and Politics in Mugabe's Zimbabwe*, 160–172. Routledge.

Modie-Moroka, T. (2016). Masculinities, Gender-Based Violence, HIV and AIDS in Botswana. *Pula: Botswana Journal of African Studies, 30*(2): 284–297.

Mugabi, I. (2020, April 20). *COVID-19: Security Forces in Africa Brutalising Civilians Under Lockdown*. DW. https://www.dw.com/en/covid-19-security-forces-in-africa-brutalizing-civilians-under-lockdown/a-53192163 Accessed 2 January 2022.

Mukwege, D., & Nangini, C. (2009). Rape with Extreme Violence: The New Pathology in South Kivu, Democratic Republic of Congo. *Plos Med, 6*(12), e1000204. https://doi.org/10.1371/journal.pmed.1000204

Mukwege, D., et al. (2010). Commentary. Rape as a Strategy of War in the Democratic Republic of the Congo. *International Health, 2*(10), 163–164.

Müller, A., et al. (2021). Experience of and Factors associated with Violence against Sexual and Gender Minorities in Nine African Countries: A Cross-Sectional Study. *BMC Public Health, 21*, 357. https://doi.org/10.1186/s12889-021-10314-w

Navas, G. et al. (2018). Violence in Environmental Conflicts: The Need for a Multidimensional Approach. *Sustainability Science, 13*, 649–660.

Ndlovu-Gatsheni, S. (2018). *Epistemic Freedom in Africa: Deprovincialization and Decolozation*. Routledge.

Nhema, A., & Zeleza, P. T. (Eds.). (2008). *The Roots of African Conflicts: Causes and Effects*. James Currey.

Nixon, R. (2011). *Slow Violence and the Environmentalism of the Poor*. Cambridge University Press.

Nkealah, N., & Nnaemeka, O. (Eds.). (2021). *Gendered Violence and Human Rights in Black World Literature and Film*. Routledge.

Nyamnjoh, F. B. (2004). A Relevant Education for African Development—Some Epistemological Considerations. *Africa Development, 29*(1), 161–184.

Nyangweso, M., & Olupona, J. K. (Eds.). (2019). *Religion in Gender-Based Violence, Immigration, and Human Rights*. Routledge.

Obarisiagbon, E. I., & Omage, M. I. (2019). Emerging Trend in the Culture of Domestic Violence Against Men in Southern Nigeria. *International Journal of Humanities and Social Science, 9*(3), 50–56.

Obijiofor, L. (2009). Is Bad News from Africa Good News for Western Media? *Journal of Global Mass Communication, 2*(3/4), 38–54.

Okech, O. (2021). Governing Gender: Violent Extremism in Northern Nigeria. *Africa Development, 46*(3), 1–19.

Okorie, N. (2011). Development Journalism and Africa: Tackling Violence Against Women. *Africana, 5*(2), 171–184.

Omotola, S. (2010). Explaining Electoral Violence in Africa's 'New' Democracies. *African Journal on Conflict Resolution, 10*(3), 51–73.

Onditi, F., & Odera, J. (2021). *Understanding Violence Against Women in Africa: An Interdisciplinary Approach*. Palgrave Macmillan.

Pérez, M. (2019). Epistemic Violence: Reflections Between the Invisible and the Ignorable. *El lugar sin límites, 1*(1), 81–98.

Pete, S., & du Plessis, M. (2000). A Rose by Any Other Name: 'Biblical Correction' in South African Schools. *South African Journal on Human Rights, 16*(1), 97–120. https://doi.org/10.1080/02587203.2000.11827590

Platvoet, J. G. (1999). To Define or not to Define: The Problem of the Definition of Religion. In J. G. Platvoet & A. L. Molendijk (Eds.), *The Pragmatics of Defining Religion: Contexts, Concepts and Contests* (pp. 245–266). Leiden: Brill.

Posłuszna, E. (2020). A Prognostic View on the Ideological Determinants of Violence in the Radical Ecological Movement. *Sustainability, 12*(16), 6536. https://doi.org/10.3390/su12166536

Riess, W. (2016). Introduction. In W. Riess & G. G. Fagan (Eds.), *The Topography of Violence in the Greco-Roman World*. University of Michigan Press. 1–17.

Rutherford, A., et al. (2007). Violence: A Glossary. *Journal of Epidemiology and Community Health, 61*(8), 676–680.

Schmidt, P., & Muggah, R. (2021). *Climate Change and Security in West Africa* (Strategic Paper 52). Igarapé Institute. https://igarape.org.br/wp-content/uploads/2021/02/2021-02-04-AE-52-Climate-Change-and-Security-in-West-Africa.pdf. Accessed 21 December 2021.

Schultz, P. (2020). *Male Survivors of Wartime Sexual Violence: Perspectives from Northern Uganda*. University of California Press.

Schutte, F. (2019). Epistemic Violence: A Case for the Decolonisation of South African Business School Curricula. *South African Journal of Higher Education, 33*(2), 195–211.

Simatei, T. (2005). Colonial Violence, Postcolonial Violations: Violence, Landscape, and Memory in Kenyan Fiction. *Research in African Literatures, 36*(2), 85–94.

Siwila, L. C., & Kobo, F. A. (Eds.). (2021). *Religion, Patriarchy and Empire: Festschrift in Honour of Mercy Amba Oduyoye*. Cluster Publications.

Sklansky, D. A. (2021). *A Pattern of Violence: How the Law Classifies Crimes and What It Means for Justice*. The Belknap Press of Harvard University Press.

Solangon S., & Patel, P. (2012). Sexual Violence against Men in Countries affected by Armed Conflict. *Conflict, Security & Development, 12*(4): 417–442.

Spadaro, P. A. (2020). Climate Change, Environmental Terrorism, Eco-Terrorism and Emerging Threats. *Journal of Strategic Security, 13*(4), 58–80.https://doi.org/10.5038/1944-0472.13.4.1863. https://digitalcommons.usf.edu/jss/vol13/iss4/5

Stewart, A. G. (2020). Mining Is Bad for Health: A Voyage of Discovery. *Environmental Geochemistry and Health, 42*(42), 1153–1165.

Thobejane, T. D. et al. (2018). Gender-Based Violence against Men: A Muted Reality. *Southern African Journal for Folklore Studies 28*(1), 1–15.

Togarasei, L. (2020). State as Patriarch and Biblical Discipline: Theorising State-Sponsored Violence in Zimbabwe. *African Identities*. https://doi.org/10.1080/14725843.2020.1813549

Tripplet, R., et al. (2016). Does "Violent" Mean "Bad"? Individual Definitions of Violence. *Deviant Behaviour, 37*(3), 332–351.

UN Women Leadership and Governance Section. (2021). *Preventing Violence Against Women in Politics*. Guidance Note. UN Women Leadership and Governance Section. https://www.unwomen.org/sites/default/files/Headquarters/Attachments/Sections/Library/Publications/2021/Guidance-note-Preventing-violence-against-women-in-politics-en.pdft. Accessed 24 December 2021.

Van Klinken, A., & Chitando, E. (2021). *Reimagining Christianity and Sexual Diversity in Africa*. Hurst.

Van Wyk, A., & Chifamba, J. (2019, October 12). Analysis: Hitting Children Is Not an African Tradition. *Premium Times*. https://www.premiumtimesng.com/features-and-interviews/357207-analysis-hitting-children-is-not-an-african-tradition.html. Accessed 1 January 2022.

Varin, C., & Abubakar, D. (Eds.). (2017). *Violent Non-State Actors in Africa Terrorists, Rebels and Warlords*. Palgrave Macmillan.

Veit, A., et al. (2011). Violence and Violence Research in Africa South of the Sahara. *International Journal of Conflict and Violence, 5*(1), 13–31.

Vetten, L., & Ratele, K. (2013). Men and Violence. *Agenda, 27*(1), 4–11.

WHO. (2009). *Promoting Gender Equality to Prevent Violence Against Women*. World Health Organization.

WHO Global Consultation on Violence and Health. (1996). *Violence: A Public Health Priority*. World Health Organization.

Woensdregt, L., & Nencel, L. (2021). Taking Small Steps: Sensitising the Police Through Male Sex Workers' Community-Led Advocacy in Nairobi, Kenya. *Global Public Health*. https://doi.org/10.1080/17441692.2021.1954681

Yacob-Haliso, O., & Falola, T. (Eds.). (2021). *The Palgrave Handbook of African Women's Studies*. Palgrave Macmillan.

Zeleza, P. T. (2006). The Disciplinary, Transdisciplinary and Global Dimensions of African Studies. *International Journal of African Renaissance Studies, 1*(2), 195–220.

Zuure, D. N. (2018). Domestic Violence against Men in the Nabdam District of Ghana. *International Journal of Pedagogy, Policy and ICT in Education, 6*(1), 69–80.

# The Rate of Oppression (ROp): The Apartheid Studies Approach to the Study of Harm

Nyasha Mboti

## 1 Introduction

Apartheid Studies (AS) is an emerging interdisciplinary field of study and approach that treats the hitherto neglected notion of apartheid as a theoretical framework, paradigm, and forensic methodology to understand *how* the world—in which we live, subsist, and die—is the way it is (Mboti, 2019, 2023a, 2023b, 2023c). In essence, AS examines how harm persists. How does oppression—and poverty, inequality, violence, loss, and injustice—not go away? Departing from existing approaches to the study of power, oppression, and injustice—approaches which are preoccupied with what the powerful and institutions do—AS charts its own independent analysis which focuses on the central theme of the Rate of Oppression (ROp), a construct that defines how the oppressed everywhere typically experience oppression differently, at adjusted rates, such that the costs of oppression and the costs of maintaining oppression are invoiced on the oppressed themselves. That is, oppression is conducted and maintained at the oppressed's own expense. When oppression is billable on the oppressed and maintained at the expense of the oppressed, it can persist indefinitely and undetectably. In fact, oppressors can go on holiday, or on sabbatical. Hence, I define apartheid as *oppression on holiday*

---

N. Mboti (✉)
Department of Communication Science, University of the Free State, Bloemfontein, South Africa
e-mail: mbotin@ufs.ac.za

(Mboti, 2023a). This is because oppressors no longer need to directly supervise or command-and-control those they oppress. Instead, oppression can go on in distributed fashion, undetectably. As oppression goes on, life goes on, and so oppressors go on holiday.

Apartheid Studies does not preoccupy itself with the study of the oppressor, the colonizer, or the slave master. This overstudied direction of enquiry was once important but has become sterile, infected as it is with the main virus of giving unearned—and too much—credit to useless elites. Since oppressors are in fact on holiday, their thoughts, actions, and motivations constitute a mere footnote in the frequently untelevized drama of daily life. So, AS operationalizes its own definitive shift in emphasis by focusing, almost exclusively, on the oppressed themselves—how they transact, relate, discourse, interact, and behave from day to day. The answer about what is going on in the world, and *how harm goes on instead of going away*, is to be found in the transitive direction of the oppressed, what they do, what they think they are doing, where they live, with whom they live, and how they live.

Formally, AS seeks to understand and, ultimately, to resolve the fundamental conflict of interest at the heart of daily human life—whereby life goes on without the oppressed directing themselves to end oppression. The urgency to eradicate harm is adjusted and demoted. It is not that people are under a spell or are mentally colonized or that there is a Stockholm Syndrome at work. Far from it. It is simply that life goes on, in a highly calculated, densely layered fashion. So, children must go to school and, in many cases, be picked up after school. (The school run is very important.) School fees and rents must be paid. Bus fare and transport money must be set aside. Debit orders must go off and loans be paid off. Food must be put on the table. Levies, tariffs, airtime, medical bills, and groceries must be seen to. All of these get in the way, structurally, of the immediate focus on ending oppression and ending it now. It is as if the business of liberation, freedom, and emancipation is not only postponable, but is intrinsically substitutable and exchangeable. If it is exchangeable, then it has an exchange rate. The Lonmin Massacre of August 16 2012 did not put a stop to the school run, to sweet teeth, addictions, sex, fees, bills, and rentals. Rather, life went on. One only needs to study household expenditure to see how life goes on. Check the receipts and the till slips. Upton Sinclair's assertion in *I, Candidate for Governor* (1935 [1994]) that "It is difficult to get a man to understand something, when his salary depends on his not understanding it" has renewed meaning. A person's understanding of his or her own salary and, in this case, his or her own Rate of Oppression, is far more urgent in all cases.

It is as if people have other urgent business, or more personal immediate business, to prosecute—business that has quite little to do with directly and immediately undoing the harmful status quo. Some will say that it is what it is, which is a fair point. But that it is what it is, is not the same as explaining *how it is what it is*. We still need to explain the "how" of the status quo. So, people live in harm's way and live with harm endemically. Endemicity explains, for instance, the general vocabulary used to suggest that people across the globe at the end of 2022 had learnt to live with the COVID-19 virus. The moment one learns to live with harm is the moment the problem appears to have disappeared, not because it has actually gone away or gone anywhere but merely because it has been reverse-transcribed by human circadian rhythms. How do people live with harm? How do people live in harm's way? How will people get out of it? We notice that, once people have learnt to live with harm, such that life goes on, global emergencies are called off. There is no more crisis. For AS, the fact that people live with harm so often and so frequently explains the persistence of oppression. When life goes on amid harm, such that harm persists instead of ending, and when people inhabit uninhabitable places, and drink undrinkable water, and live unliveable lives, and bear the unbearable, this is not resilience at all but, rather, a conflict of interest. Unless and until this fundamental conflict of interest at the heart of social life is resolved, harm hardens into permanence—permanence hidden in frequent sight by circadian rhythms. That is, harm is still there, as persistently, prevalently, and virulently as ever, perhaps more so, but now in progressively undetectable form.

Undetectability does not mean that harm is invisible. There is a difference between *invisibility* and *undetectability*. While invisibility suggests that I would not be able to see something with my naked eyes, for instance, I can still detect invisible things with the other senses such as hearing, taste, smell, and touch. So, an invisible thing can still make a sound. It can still smell. Undetectability, on the other hand, belongs to a wholly different order of sense data. That is, undetectability defines that which none of the five senses can detect, even if it were visible, tangible, audible, smellable, or tasteable. The tale, below, of the "stamped out" passport, for example, indicates how important an account of undetectability is to the business of unravelling the puzzle of the indefiniteness of harm, injustice, and oppression in human relations. Note how, once COVID-19 became officially endemic, it became undetectable, because people had supposedly learnt to live with it. That is, people could now move to, or get back to, other business. In AS, this is called *demotion*. Thus:

> Whereas psychologists have concluded that humans and animals faced with threatening situations react in two main ways, i.e., fight or flight, this is a fundamentally limited way of looking at the problem. The Apartheid Studies framework indicates that there is, in fact, a third reaction which is more frequent and more important than fight or flight; freeze, flop or faint. This reaction occurs mostly amongst the oppressed who make up most of the world's population. This third reaction is called demotion. That is, the threatened human being basically lives in harm's way all his or her life. They cannot get out. They cannot fight and they cannot run. They cannot hide. Indeed, the oppressed go towards harm, like minesweepers and deminers. They seek work in gold and coal mines where mine disasters have happened and continue to happen. They inhabit uninhabitable places and eat things that are not fit for human consumption. They queue for harm, like the oppressed in South Africa queuing at No. 80 Albert Street for the hated Pass Book. The Apartheid Studies framework thus shows not only that there is fight, flight, and demotion, but that demotion is the most common and most frequent reaction to harmful situations. (Mboti, 2023a: 28)

The "demotable" is the correct sense in which I am interested in undetectable events. Gil Scott-Heron stated, famously, that "The revolution would not be televised" (Ongiri, 2010: 16). But the untelevisable may still be detectable. The undetectable is televisable but will still not be seen! In large part, undetectable events happen because people move on to other things or have other things to do.

Undetectability simply means that noticing harm-that-is-there is hardly an urgent concern. Rather, it is postponed, substituted, and exchanged away. Harm thus persists side by side with livelihood-making, with the diurnal flow of the goods and items indexed on the receipts and the till slips. There was a time when my children and I used to watch *SpongeBob SquarePants*. Notice how, for instance, the Krusty Krab restaurant is, in fact, designed after a lobster or crab trap. The fact that Mr Krabs—the money-grubbing capitalist crab—makes his living from and within the very same accessory to the capture, storage, and killing of his own kind is successfully *demoted* and reverse-transcribed into the deeper background of the story, in such a way that, in the end, it is merely décor, a setting, for the daily silliness and transactions of veggie burgers. So, if you "looked" for apartheid today through direct observation, you would only find shards and fragments of it, never the whole thing. This was, of course, always the case. It is true that, for some decades, apartheid came up for air in South Africa and announced itself in pseudo-civic form through the *dompas*, a desperation-at-scale that owed much to the historical tetchiness of the Boer than anything else.[1]

Most of the time people are not directly persecuted but, rather, "merely" live with harm, with the only interface with oppression provided in the form of household expenditure. The AS approach identifies household expenditure as being, by far, the most universal indicator of the ROp. By this I mean that the goods, forms, objects, commodities, items, reflexes, wants, desires, anxieties, aspirations, and relations around which a person's daily life ebbs and flows are the true indicators and the true interface with apartheid. Each cup of tea you have, each fragment of bus ticket or supermarket till slip, the phone contacts, the debit orders, your social media, the bills, fees, itineraries, groceries, utilities, and levies: all these are the *interface* with apartheid; the shards and fragments of its golden thread illustrating how it is dispersed, diffused, and distributed. These are the elements of the fundamental conflict of interest about which I keep speaking. You cannot subsist from day to day—eating, cheating, and drinking—in these conditions and not be fundamentally conflicted. It is this many-sided interface that is the subject of our inductive and forensic analysis in AS.

## 2 Apartheid Studies: Motivations, Itineraries, and "Where Were You When X"

The AS approach is one that I pioneered in the decade between 2012 and 2022, leading to the publication of my first book, *Apartheid Studies: A Manifesto*, by Africa World Press in 2023. This first publication is the first of four volumes (the other three volumes are already in press) that map the emerging field. I set up AS to address the global absence of the systematic study of apartheid and the widespread neglect of the notion of "apartheid" as a heuristic, theoretical framework, paradigm, and method of analysis (see Mahlaela, 2022; Mboti, 2019, 2023a, 2023b, 2023c; Sirvent, 2023). In the first place, I was irritated and motivated by the absence of the formal and systematic study of the topic, question, phenomenon, and problem of apartheid in South Africa and globally. I was obviously drawn by the crying

---

[1] In the chapter titled "Lobengula's Inkatha Forensics: Goldilocks' One-Third, Eric Garner Can't Breathe" in *Apartheid Studies: A Manifesto* (Mboti 2023a: 369–404), I draw on Ndebele King Lobengula's forensic way of describing the British and the Boers, the former as chameleons and the latter as lizards, to show the differences—and similarities—in how the two sibling races utilise apartheid as a policy.

need for a public education project to fill this gap. To this day, apartheid is yet to be formally and properly interrogated and defined from the point of view of the people who carried the *dompas*.

If the conceptual elitism is shocking, the pedagogical neglect is absurd. There is not a single module or course, research chair, institute, or centre for AS, that formally teaches, researches, or educates about apartheid, at any of South Africa's 26 public universities, or at any university anywhere in the world, anyway. This neglectful *status quo* would not be allowed to persist if South Africa and the world needed to definitively say "never, never, and never again" to such pervasive, prevalent, persistent, and virulent forms of injustice, harm, and oppression as apartheid. So, then, why were there no Apartheid Studies? At any rate, how does one, conceivably, say "never again" to something that he or she does not study? To my mind, one of the most important ways South Africa and the world could properly say "never, never, and never again" to apartheid is through taking its study seriously in the same way that, for instance, Holocaust Studies is resourced and taken seriously. In any case, there seemed to be a causal link between South Africa's current significant and persistent national problems and the neglect of systematic diagnostic study of apartheid (see Mboti, 2023a). (Interesting. We study slavery and racism, go to Elmina and other slave castles, visit Robben Island, we go to the Genocide Memorial in Kigali, Holocaust Memorial in Berlin, etc. We solemnly declare, "never, never again!" Slavery still happens. Racism remains rampant. Genocide still happens. Why?).

Second, I had unsettled questions about the aetiology of apartheid. Who says apartheid began in 1948 (and ended in 1994)? Where do such definitive dates flow from and where do they flow to? So, are the events described in Peter Abrahams' *Mine Boy*, first published in 1947, not apartheid? How? Once again, the definition of apartheid is tied to the narrative of *when* it is supposed to have begun, and such a narrative exclusively reflects the haggling of white historians about such and such origins (see Beinart, 1995; Clark & Worger, 2013; Dubow, 2014, 2017; Giliomee, 2003a, 2003b, 2012; Guelke, 2005; Harvey, 2002; Legassick & Innes, 1977; Lovell, 1956; Marks & Trapido, 1987; Posel, 1987, 1991; Rich, 1980; O'Meara, 1983; Simpson, 2017;Sonneborn, 2010; Welsh, 2009; Worden, 2012).[2] That is, the people who define apartheid never actually carried a *dompas*. So against what do white historians test their knowledge of apartheid? Not only do the received

---

[2] Some South African historians like to speak of "high apartheid" or "apartheid's golden age," a mysterious time from the mid-1960s to the mid-1970s. Breckenridge (2014) maps the "golden age" as beginning in 1966, from the assassination of Verwoerd, until 1973, when international oil and domestic labour crises began (see also Breckenridge, 2014: 233; Dubow, 2017; Simpson, 2017).

accounts sit on an embarrassingly white-sided foundation, but they fail to propose even the most basic framework by which to understand how it was possible for a minority to rule and dominate over a majority for over three centuries.

Third, I was interested in the itinerary and whereabouts of apartheid after 1994 in South Africa. The standard practice is to regard apartheid as having "died" in 1994 (see Beinart, 1995; Clark & Worger, 2013; Dubow, 2014; Guelke, 2005; Harvey, 2002; Sonneborn, 2010; Sparks, 2003; Welsh, 2009; Worden, 2012). It bugged me that, even though apartheid was officially dead, no one has yet to show its corpse. How would one independently test and verify this claim of apartheid's death? If it is true that apartheid died in 1994, this assertion ought to be empirically testable and provable. One could theoretically test for so-called "change" and "transformation." A formal index and indicator could be developed. What if apartheid persisted in a shifted shape?

I was aware, for instance, of the practice of "stamping out" passports by some foreign travellers who are in South Africa illegally. Upon arrival in South Africa, every foreign arrivant mandatorily presents his or her passport to immigration services at the Beitbridge border post. The passport is stamped, indicating the number of days, up to 90, during which the owner of the passport can stay legally in South Africa. Beyond the stipulated days, the passport holder becomes, officially, an "undesirable" if he or she fails to get a valid visa to extend their stay in South Africa. As it happens, some of the cross-border travellers routinely stay in South Africa beyond the days stipulated by the immigration stamp—without a visa—and, yet, without officially becoming undesirable. The overstayed, illegal status is never officially recorded, and the owner of the passport stays in South Africa for months or years without immigration knowing this. How does this happen? The passport owner, after some weeks or months in South Africa, sends the passport back to the border via a courier (typically a cross-border bus or haulage truck driver). This is done to get the document "stamped out," for a fee, before the official expiry of the allocated days. "Stamping out" means that the passport gets a stamp from immigration indicating that the owner of the passport has exited South Africa. Essentially, the courier bribes an immigration officer or officers to stamp the passport to indicate that the passport holder has left South Africa and returned to his or her country of origin prior to the lapse of the stipulated 90-day period. The truth, however, is that the passport owner is already living and possibly working in South Africa. The courier returns to South Africa with the "stamped out" document and hands it back to the owner. In the official immigration records, the owner of the passport is designated as having legally and officially exited South Africa, and so has a clean record and not at risk of being labelled an undesirable. Yet only the passport *document* and immigration records indicate this official record of exit. In reality, the flesh-and-bone human being behind the passport has not gone anywhere. The documented, official, legal exit is not the same as an exit in substance.

Could this be the same trick that apartheid pulled in 1994, where the official record indicates that apartheid is no longer in South Africa, yet it stayed on by rigging how we keep records and keep track of harm? Could it be that, in 1994, South Africa's passport got "stamped out" and yet apartheid itself is alive and well in the country and in people's quotidian lives? What does apartheid, in post-apartheid South Africa, look like? How do we recognize—and diagnose—it? How does it operate? So, I set up AS, in part, to get to the bottom of this absurd mystery. In fact, the interest in the whereabouts of apartheid led to a secondary preoccupation. If apartheid persists in a shifted shape, outside official recognition, how exactly does it persist? What form does persisting apartheid take? What is its mode of conduct?

I got the answer to these secondary questions on August 17 2012, the day after the Lonmin Massacre in Marikana. While most people remember the events of Lonmin through the lens of August 16, when the brutal shootings took place on live television, I was even more disturbed and impressed by the events of August 17, the day after. Then residing in Durban and appointed as a postdoctoral researcher at the University of KwaZulu-Natal, I was impressed by how "normal" August 17 was—how like any other non-Massacre day it was. People did not seem to have lost their breakfast appetites, or forgotten the school run, or shopping. I had assumed that, considering the events of August 16, surely daily life in South Africa would grind to a halt on August 17, so that a serious and urgent national inquest could take place—the goal being that such an event would never be allowed to happen again. To my mind, this moment marked a national and constitutional crisis, one that necessitated a declaration of a national emergency where people had to pause and drop everything, focus on this one issue together at the same time, and fix it before any sort of normal daily life could return.

But, to my utter surprise, life went on. It was not that people did not care about the events that had occurred. It was simply that a massacre in another province of the country was fully compatible with picking up children and dropping them off at school, or with queuing at the municipal office to pay utility bills, or with buying and selling, work shifts, and so on. Essentially, these massacres and daily itineraries can happen side-by-side. I was shocked by this "good neighbourliness" of states of affairs. I remembered, hurriedly, that H. F. Verwoerd, the putative father of apartheid, had, in March 1961, defined apartheid as "a policy of good neighbourliness." The observation of life-going-on compatibly with the Lonmin Massacre was the first window I got into how oppression persists, often permanently. If the oppressed can still do other things at different times, then will there ever be a moment when everything stops for everybody to confront the same oppression? Hence, one could sum this problem by asking: "Where were you when the Lonmin Massacre took place?", "What were you doing when the Lonmin Massacre took place?", "What were you doing on August 17?"

Essentially, fundamentally, life went on. The sun rose in the east and set in the west as it has always done. What changed?

The same "Where were you when X" and "What were you doing when X" questions can be asked of many other seminal events. What were you doing as Steve Biko was murdered in the jail cells of Pretoria in September 1977? Where were you as Hurricane Katrina raged? My epistemic interest sought to bypass the historical record, and focus, say, on September 12, 2001, rather than the much-cited 9/11. For my purposes, *the-morning-after* and *the-day-after* were much more seminal: 9/12 instead of 9/11; August 17 rather than August 16. I was bound to be more impressed if I learnt that people remembered their bills and debit orders, fuelled their cars, showered, watched the weather, and had an appetite for breakfast and lunch on 9/12 and August 17. There is nothing, empirically, that said or demonstrated that life could *not* go on. Life did not grind to a halt just because 34 miners had just been gunned down in cold blood by police with R5s.[3] There was no natural, anterior, or independent constraint or restriction to life going on. The massacre was compatible with drinking coffee, sucking a cigarette, playing at PlayStation, browsing a social media feed, or remembering to bring along an umbrella because the weather forecast said it might rain.

These observations, about how life went on and about these strange compatibilities, set me on a journey of relating the quotidian flow of daily life with the persistent flow of oppression itself. How did oppression persist? It did so anomalously, through—and as a function of—the gap between the duration of harm and the human capacity for demotion. Suddenly, I had an answer to the question of how ordinary people lived with apartheid. (People lived with apartheid the same way people now live with COVID-19). It was because, under apartheid itself, life went on. People can live with harm—not because they like to be harmed or that they do not care about the sorry state of the world, but simply because they can live with harm. It is a capacity. The capacity exists. If there is a slight delay in the urgency with which *x* is

---

[3] The R5, used in 2012, at Lonmin, became the standard service rifle of the South African Defence Force (SADF) in 1980.

confronted with harm, that delay is all $x$ needs for his or her life to go on. The lives of the families of the Lonmin miners ground to a halt on August 16, as did the life of Ntsiki Biko on 12 September 1977, or Betty Shabazz on 21 February 21 1965, or Coretta Scott King on 4 April 4 1968, but for other people outside that immediate cycle, radius, and circle where the disaster was urgent, the morning after and the day after were not unlike any other non-disaster day. These putatively distant people, for whom the disasters on these select dates were not seemingly urgent, would themselves get to face their own urgent moments of crisis, loss, trauma, and bereavement. But crises take place on different days, for different durations, in different forms, and in different contexts (for different people!). The durations and contexts of crisis were always already adjusted such that crisis would never be experienced uniformly. Instead, there was an important interval of delay, a difference in duration, and an endemicity, that made sure that life went on for whoever lived long enough with harm. Anyway, it was this density of thoughts, reflections, pauses, and puzzles that led to the ground-breaking formulation of the notion of the Rate of Oppression (ROp).

The widespread endemicity of harm, and apartheid's passport that is conveniently "stamped out," mean that the topic of apartheid is, today, treated as non-urgent, even as old news. In this conventional account, only the "legacies of apartheid" still exist, not apartheid itself. Policy focus is deliberately limited to addressing these seemingly isolated and episodic "legacies." In such an epistemic fog, trolls are already raising doubts if apartheid was really as harmful as previously thought.[4] Meanwhile, the oppressed's time is continuously taken up with precise calculations and managements of how much, how long, and how far harm can be lived with, observing and tracking the quantity and duration of intervals during which individuals can leverage margins in the Rate of Oppression to put food on the table, pay rent, bills, transport, and school fees. As we will see, the sum of intervals identifies one's ROp—how much, how long, and how far one can go and manage without considering and before calculating that the direct and definitive confrontation of oppressive institutions and the system of oppression is an urgent matter.

---

[4] In April 2018 the CEO of AfriForum, a Mr Kriel, maintained that apartheid was not a crime against humanity. It had too few victims, he said.

# 3   The Rate of Oppression (ROp) and the Experience of Harm: A Discussion

The construct of the ROp defines *how the oppressed experience the same oppression at different rates, and how this differential distributed experience is behind the persistence of harm and oppression.* The ROp explains the undetectable violence of apartheid—how under apartheid, for instance, the oppressed can queue for the *dompas*, the very thing they hate. Why would the oppressed queue for the *dompas*? Well, because there is a fundamental conflict of interest at the heart of the behaviour of the oppressed. Any oppressed person who does not fight oppression (that is, any oppressed person for whom life goes on) exhibits this fundamental conflict of interest. The architecture of the violence of apartheid is threaded tightly around this conflict of interest. The discussion below indicates, in outline, how this happens.

The ROp is a surcharge—an extra cost to living under oppression. This added sum is different for each oppressed person. We refer to this surcharge, in AS terminology, as the invoice. Apartheid invoices all of us differently, and it is the (difference in the) rate at which we are invoiced that is the most significant factor in how we behave towards oppression and towards each other. We may all be living under the same oppression, but the rate—indeed the cross rate—at which we are invoiced is differently adjusted for everybody. If all the oppressed were charged the same premiums for living under apartheid, they would all definitely react to oppression in the same way. But this is far from being the case. Because the surcharge—that is, the ROp—invoiced each oppressed person who lives with harm is different, we all experience and react to the same oppression differently. This account of the ROp is a radical departure from the standard conceptions of how power, institutions, and systems function. It is no longer necessary to study the National Party to understand apartheid, or colonizers to understand colonialism. Rather, one merely proceeds to the study of how oppressed people live with harm from hour to hour and day to day. Indeed, this emerging account compels us to alter fundamentally how we study and understand oppression, harm, and injustice which, we now understand, are never uniform and are never experienced at the same rate even by people who live on the same street in the same community. Indeed, Rates of Oppression differ even for people who live in the same household (for instance, observe how differently domestic workers, "garden boys," and "maids" interact in the household). Like exchange rates, Rates of Oppression, move about from minute-to-minute, hour-to-hour, and day-to-day. Changing contexts shift and alter Rates of Oppression, too. A general principle is that the poorer one is, the more unstable one's rate.

Essentially, oppressed people live differently under the same sort of oppressions. There is no way it can happen otherwise. This essential difference in Rates of Oppression shifts oppression so much that when one family next door is starving, another neighbouring family might be at a graduation, shopping, or *lobola*. Recently, in Carletonville, outside Johannesburg, I got directions to a cemetery at a shopping mall! There is nothing in the essential make-up of oppression that excludes the side-by-sideness (that is, "good neighbourliness") of different levels of oppressed states. Instead, all forms of oppression are structurally "good neighbourly." That is, all forms of oppression adjust themselves from individual to individual, and from household to household, allowing different persons and households to "domesticate" their own problems in a manner that allows life to go on. In Shona, we say *chakafukidza dzimba matenga* (what covers houses are roofs)[5] and *nhamo yeumwe hairambirwi sadza* (one person's predicament does not cause others to refuse to eat sadza, the staple food). From household to household, the surcharge is different, meaning that urgent matters are urgent at different times, rates, intervals, and durations. Our losses are invoiced differently, at different rates, just as workers at the same company are paid varying salaries at the end of the month, incorporating all sorts of adjustments, and each worker has different budgetary calculations to make in their heads according to their own situations. We may say, quoting Karl Marx (1970 [1890]): *jedem nach seinen Bedürfnissen* (to each according to his needs). More precisely, to each according to his or her own rates.

The fundamental point that I am making here, and that must be properly absorbed and understood if one is to grasp the crucial premise of the ROp, is that *not everyone pays the price of oppression at the same rate*. The bill of living under oppression is always adjusted differently for all of us. Basically, all the oppressed are harmed at different rates and intervals. Some pay the bill today, sooner or later, while others pay up tomorrow or next week. Some pay half-down or quarter-down while others pay with interest or at different interest rates and premiums. In certain cases, the payment itself is borrowed, with interest, or stolen, or the proceeds of bribery. Some among the oppressed can muster collateral and sureties, others, of course, cannot. Some others can get away with various forms of default for given periods of time. There is such a dizzying density of differences and rates that the phenomenon is almost a black box! It is all this differentiation in the rate

---

[5] Basically, you cannot know fully what is going on next door. If only you knew!

at which our debits are ordered, and our debts called in that is the critical factor in the persistence of harm and injustice. After all, if the amount payable quoted in X's invoice is different to that in Y's, this leads to differently adjusted payment plans and therefore anomalous outcomes. As long as there are anomalous outcomes, the oppressed will not experience harm the same way and, therefore, will not muster a truly shared response. Without a truly shared response, it is impossible to see how the oppressed can muster a coherent theory of liberation. In such conditions, everyone is constrained by his or her own peculiar household expenditure, so that we constantly address each other in peculiarly differentiated, anomalous terms (that is, in terms of our Rates of Oppression). It is as if we are constantly at cross-purposes. The truth, however, is that we are constantly at cross-rates. Until we resolve the problem of anomalous cross-rates, all attempts at achieving justice and peaceable outcomes are already contaminated by the default persistence of the very problem that they are trying to solve. Indeed, all remedial attempts at justice and peace—partly because they borrow the vocabularies, source codes, and grammars of the same violence, harm, and oppression that they are trying to undo—in fact end up maintaining oppression. The ROp is thus an attempt to explain the anomalous persistence of oppression, the anomalous outcomes among the oppressed, and the anomalousness of daily contemporary life. The anomaly is that life goes on—that we somehow live with harm. That we live with harm expresses the fundamental conflict of interest of our lives. The two, anomalousness and conflict of interest, are the true subjects of AS.

So, the fact that a person could have been digging yams by the river, or fixing a broken sandal, or visiting Sweden, when, say, 9/11 happened, indicates that a signal global crisis not only can co-occur within the same ontological orbit as a mundane occurrence, such as visiting relatives or digging for yams or looking for a lost goat, but also that both have the same chance of taking place. What this means is that life goes on elsewhere too—a capacity that must not imply that one does not care about what is happening in such and such a place, but simply reflects that humans take turns to experience harm. Harm is so distributed that its experience takes place in intervals—almost as if (chances in) human lives were ordered in a physical queue. While Steve Biko was being murdered in the cells in a Pretoria jail on September 12 1977, what do you think other Africans (in South Africa) were doing? Where were they? Certainly, they did not stop whatever they were doing. Other Africans, themselves living under the same apartheid that was at that moment depriving Biko of his life, were at *lobola*, at school, in shebeens, visiting sick relatives in hospital, at church, at soccer matches, at work, selling things, stealing, making love, preaching, digging for gold, watching television, reading in a library, lounging under a shady tree, at a graduation, fetching water at the river, closing out a transaction, and so on. To reiterate: life goes on. And again, this does not mean that the oppressed who are doing other things "when x" do not care or do not see what is going on. Rather, it is simply that harm is undetectable: one does not stop eating pap, *sadza* or *garri*, wooing a lover, taking a leak behind the house, buying tomatoes for the evening cooking, scratching an itch, betting at horses, or watching a soccer final, simply because another person somewhere is being murdered or harmed at that moment. People cannot be in more than one place at once[6] and, of course, *nhamo yeumwe hairambirwi sadza*.

But the problem is far denser, and far more than that still. What the ROp does is draw our attention to a capacity for the experience of harm to be so distributed and differentiated that there can never be a true shared experience and solidarity in the world about what to do about oppression—since the experience of oppression itself is always queued. Hence, each attempt to act towards, or even just to talk about, a common problem, and to find a common denominator, is always constrained by the fact that each participant experiences the same common problem at a different and differently adjusted rate. Whereas Biko's family experienced such an unbearable loss on September 12 1977, and hence their world stopped on that day, other oppressed South Africans could afford to do other things (i.e., to live in harm's way) for some unspecified duration until it was their own turn to be stopped and harmed at a roadblock for not having a *dompas* or whatever harm and loss they experienced—by which time Biko's family would then be doing other things too.

Observe how, at any given protest, it is never the *whole* community present at such an event. Only some people ever pitch up at a protest, or at any event. In that moment, most people are elsewhere, doing something else. So, it is impossible that an observer will ever see everybody being there, even if the protest is about sanitation, water, or electricity, which might be problems affecting everyone in the community at that time. The presence-of-some and the absence-of-others is because sanitation, water, and electricity problems are experienced differently from household to household. There is an adjustment in the nature of the problem as a problem moves from household to household. Even within the same crowd at a protest, some are actually anxious about other things as well, such as unpaid rent or school fees, or a sick relative at the hospital, or an upcoming job interview, or an upcoming televised game in the English Premier League, or a shortage of

---

[6] See the "availability problem" in the Introduction of Mboti (2023a).

bus fare—so that what everyone is willing to do in that protest, and how far everyone is willing to go in their actions, is always different and differentiated. This phenomenon explains differences of opinion about tactics and strategy amongst "comrades" who might be engaged in the same struggle. It is, principally, the ROp that would explain how (not why) musical bands like the Beatles or Destiny's Child, and political parties such as ZANU and ZAPU, and MDC, in Zimbabwe, and ANC, DA, COPE, and EFF in South Africa, split. Banding together does not eliminate differences. It merely demotes and queues them. In so far as differences are queued, they are magnified. They enter a state of endemicity. That is, splits are endemic for musical bands and political parties.

Oppression persists precisely when it leverages human beings' capacity for life to go on—the capacity to have intervalled Rates of Oppression. It means that we can never actually talk about the same oppression even if we all live under it. We can never actually locate the same colonialism. The same colonialism is experienced differently by each of the colonized, which complicates the business of independence: whose colonialism ended on April 18 1980 in Zimbabwe? For whom did colonialism end on March 6, 1957, in Ghana and October 1, 1960, in Nigeria? When the Sharpeville Massacre happened, it was not every single oppressed African who was in attendance. Rather, it was a minority that came to hand over *dompases*. It is always a minority that comes. Most were off to work, to work for their families and provide food on the table. In fact, chances are some of the oppressed would see a job opening if another went ahead and turned in their *dompas* at the police station or, even, if another oppressed person was killed in the protest. After mining disasters, like the one at Coalbrook in 1960, exactly two months before Sharpeville, when 435 miners were buried alive, new workers replaced them. In fact, even as the disaster was going on, mining continued in another structurally unaffected part of the mine. True, the tragedy-as-a-whole and the loss-as-a-whole hurts. But life goes on—life must go on. A job is a job. You mourn and shake your head and grieve visibly for a few minutes or hours—and then you must get up and again think about that cow with a broken leg that needs veterinary attention early tomorrow morning, or the summons from the chief about the quarrel over the *muganhu* (boundary line) or the unpaid taxes or *vana vadzingwa kuchikoro* (children sent away from school due to unpaid tuition fees), and so on. That sort of activity never stops. Some had television in the poor township, when others did not (so what?); some had and have sugar for tea, others bread, others a four-roomed house, and so on. All these are affordances which matter significantly in queuing humans up—in structuring how much and how far we can still go if, as, and when others' lives have been harmed to a stop.

So, when I got lost on my way to a funeral and got the directions to the cemetery at a shopping mall, it was clear what was going on: it meant that, while some are dying and being mourned for, others are, in that same moment, shopping. Such activity always goes on, such that when such-and-such is happening, such-and-such is also happening. This is what is meant by the assertion about things that co-occur within the same commutative ontological orbit. A funeral is co-extensively compatible with shopping, shopping with Biko being murdered in the cells, Biko's murder with graduation, graduation with watching television soccer or television wrestling, watching television with being at a protest, a protest with a municipal election, an election with queuing for money at a bank, banking with digging yams, digging yams with visiting a relative, and so on. It is this commutative compatibility—a form of good neighbourliness—that oppressors everywhere cultivate and depend on to guarantee that no two oppressed people ever experience the same oppression at the same rate.

By this mechanism, oppression, initially temporary (i.e., oppression that must end), persists. A 2 × 3 m plastic and cardboard shack, clearly a temporary structure, becomes a home for a family of six in Epworth, Harare, for 20 years. It is this permanence of the temporary which provides training data to those policymakers who talk of "shack upgrading" schemes[7] or so-called tiny homes,[8] or permanent refugee camps[9] as solutions to the housing crisis or to displacement of communities. A refugee camp in Palestine, like all camps naturally a temporary phenomenon, has been there since 1948, for instance. Poverty and inequality can persist like this forever until even the Bible says that the poor will always be with us (cf. Matthew 26:11). So, the ROp is like stages in a video game or the children's *nhodo* game—while some players are at *mamu-*1 (level), others are at *mamu-*2 (level 2), or *mamu-*3 (level 3), and so on, of the same game. (Hahahahahahaha!) The "rate" seals a person in. One thus experiences the world in terms of one's own "rate," and in terms compatible with that rate, constraining at what rate one lives in harm's way.

---

[7] Government of South Africa. (2013, December 4). *Shack Dwellers to Become First Time Home Owners in Eastern Cape*. https://www.gov.za/shack-dwellers-become-first-time-home-owners-eastern-cape. Accessed 23 March 2018.

[8] D'Silva, B. (2022, January 4). *Why the Tiny House Is Perfect for Now*. https://www.bbc.com/culture/article/20211215-why-the-tiny-house-movement-is-big. Accessed 13 February 2022.

[9] Elmasry, F. (2018, March 22). *Re-imagining Refugee Camps as Livable Cities*. https://www.voanews.com/science-health/re-imagining-refugee-camps-livable-cities. Accessed 23 March 2018.

So, on August 17 2012, the day after the Lonmin Massacre, the world did not stop: as has been said, the school run continued as normal, and birds chirped in the trees, and minibus taxis operated their routes. This does not mean that the oppressed had and have no solidarity. It simply means that oppression enrols us in endless queues of "rates." A Zimbabwean who crosses a crocodile-infested Limpopo, knowing fully well that another Zimbabwean was killed by a crocodile just the day before, in probably that same spot, does so on the basis of the ROp.[10] A cigarette smoker who continues to smoke even when the cigarette carton clearly says "Smoking will kill you" does so because of the ROp: because there is an interval. The smoker never dies immediately. Rather he may die in the next hour, next week or next year or next decade, but meanwhile he can smoke. That is, there is always a duration. This duration expresses the ROp. The capacity to smoke—until, whenever death happens—is *durationally present*, durationally there, just as the capacity to cross the Limpopo until and unless death happens, is durationally there too. Death, meanwhile, is *durationally absent*, until whenever one dies. It is these durational presences and absences that determine the course of human actions. That is, the oppressed live in harm's way according to these intervals. Seen this way, the ROp—rather than, say, Marxist class analysis or Freudian and Jungian psychoanalysis, or the sociology of resilience—seems a far more fact-friendly and rigorous explanation for the behaviour of the oppressed under oppression. The ROp, thus applied, might explain sex work, or the opioid crisis, or why abused women stay, and so on. Certainly, it explains the permanence of temporary spatialities such as apartheid townships, hostels, and compounds.

We measure my ROp simply by measuring the duration; the interval. The interval explains how some are going to carnival or to parties at KwaMereki leisure spot in Harare while others are taking their dead to Warren Park Cemetery nearby, and others still are picking up trash at the Warren Park dumpsite—all in the same moment and almost within earshot. Those going to KwaMereki *vakatombofirwawo* (they have been to funerals before) or *vachafirwawo* (they will be at funerals sooner or later)—but *nhamo yeumwe hairambirwi doro negochi-gochi* (another's funeral is no reason not to plan to get drunk and braai). Those at the dumpsite picking up trash have, as per their own Rate of Oppression, more urgent pursuits at that moment compared to those mourning or braaiing. These differences in the rate at which humans experience loss explain how, say, poverty and inequality can

---

[10] Ngoepe, K. (2022, January 18). *Crocodile Attacks in Limpopo Over the Years*. https://www.iol.co.za/sundayindependent/news/crocodile-attacks-in-limpopo-over-the-years-646034a8-1f7b-4fb8-9644-999d3d4e53d3. Accessed 15 February 2022.

go on for far longer than they should, and even why dictators remain in power. Not every Zimbabwean experiences the same ZANU-PF in the same way. Some benefit from it, others benefit from being against it, and still others benefit from having nothing to do with it, while most just leverage intervals to survive from day to day—hence in Zimbabwe one often hears a person saying "*Zvangu zvaita*" (my things are sorted)[11] or "*Ndapinda, ndapinda!*" (I'm in!). Once you get yours, you leverage it, for marginal gain, and move on to the next problem. The gains are always marginal and fractional. Hence people can buy cooking oil only for that evening's cooking or sugar only in half a cupful, or one cigarette. These fragments are called *zvitsaona* (accidents) in Harare's townships. This extreme breaking of bulk and extreme retailing reflects the ROp—how *tese takasiyaniswa* (we are all differently adjusted or differentiated) from hour to hour, day to day, week to week, month-end to month-end, and year to year. Thus, some might be mourning at one house while others, after a brief respectful wait, may be playing music or watching football (perhaps with the volume turned conveniently low for the time being) at a house down the street. On the next street, out of earshot of the wailing, the music might even be playing full blast. Taken to their logical conclusion, durational absences and presences of harm may explain phenomena as disparate as "tribal" division and civil wars, endemic corruption, why some colonized people collaborate with their colonizers, the existence of Bantustans, and so on.

In sum, once harm goes on long enough in human society, in whatever corner of the world, it generates enough training data to shape the world in that data's image. That is, at that point, harm is empirically attestable as a going concern, and whoever lives with harm is invoiced for this habit. After all, one cannot just live in a long-lived system at no ongoing cost. Just as slave owners were compensated for their losses when slavery "ended," so oppressors everywhere live off the proceeds of oppression whereby they are compensated for the harm incurred by others. As Lord Farquaad in *Shrek* says, "Some of you may die, but it's a sacrifice I am willing to make." The point is that there is a cost to being poor, victimizable, and vulnerable. When that cost is billed on the oppressed themselves, we get apartheid. The ROp, then, is the bill and invoice of living with harm. A new understanding of harm is necessary to arrive at this new theorization of socio-economic relations. Remember, if a person keeps a *dompas*, in whatever form, then that person is funding his or her own oppression. One is paying for harm as a service. That is, you are being billed for the apartheid "privilege" of letting you live in a crowded,

---

[11] This would be after, say, finally collecting money from the bank after having been in the queue all day with other strangers.

crime-infested township, letting you navigate a life of shortages and scarcity, and letting you be employed in a low wage, dehumanizing job, and so on. Essentially, nothing is wasted. Apartheid wastes nothing. If slaveowners can be compensated for "losing" their slaves, and if the oppressed queue for the *dompas*, pay for it, and keep it securely, then this is all the evidence needed that harm has now transitioned into a mere service.

## 4  By Way of Conclusion: Harm and Circadian Rhythms

The ROp is the central construct of the emergent theoretical framework of AS. It provides a viable, testable explanation of how harm, oppression, injustice, and poverty persist in human society. The reliable index for mapping Rates of Oppression is to look, simply, at whether life goes on. Life going on is a function of whether people in households have, among other things, eaten (which is not necessarily the same as having eaten well), slept (which is not necessarily inclusive of having slept well), or washed (without it being the best wash in the best facilities), or been treated for illnesses (without it, necessarily, being the best treatment), and so on. In this account, people's lives are constrained by what I will call *lifelihood*.

Lifelihood is "life going on", expressly the actual evidence of life going on, not mere livelihood as normatively understood.[12] Lifelihood is indexed, for instance, in *kwaziso* (greetings, in Shona), of which there are three main ones: *Mamuka sei?* (supposedly "Good morning" but literally "How did you wake up?" which is always asked in the morning); *Maswera sei?* ("How did you spend the day?" which is asked later in the day) and *Makadii?* ("How are you?" which is only asked if you last met a person a day ago or more).[13] In isiZulu and isiXhosa people ask about *impilo* (life). That is, all of this is a discourse of *signs-of-life*. Thus, lifelihood is an index of signs-of-life, which is always assessed in a three-token set: *Mamuka sei?* is always asserted in the morning, upon first sighting of another human being, if one is close enough to do *kwaziso*; *Maswera sei?* is always late in the day, asked only of somebody you saw and greeted in the morning; and *Makadii?* can be asked at any time of the day on meeting someone that you last saw at least 24 hours ago. This is the *kwaziso* test of signs-of-life. People are harmed and oppressed within the

---

[12] Note that lifelihood is not life itself. It is simply what one observes.
[13] I am excluding the greetings *Mangwanani* (good morning), *Masikati* (good afternoon), and *Manheru* (good evening), which are not "asked" and are shortcuts, to which the response is generally a repetition which may include "asking" something.

bounded parameters of *kwaziso* and in terms of its three tokens: *Mamuka sei? Maswera sei?* and *Makadii?* That is, if the whole exercise of harm is premised on Rates of Oppression (the means by which life goes on), then the longest duration of Rates of Oppression begins at two days, where *Makadii?* is used to assess for lifelihood, and the minimum duration to check up on lifelihood is 12 hours (*Mamuka sei?* and *Maswera sei?*) You cannot say *Mamuka sei?* or *Maswera sei?* twice to the same person, for instance, because you have already done the test.

My preoccupation with household expenditure, as the expenditure of the signs-of-life *kwaziso* tokens, is non-standard. Rather, it is a direct translation of the Shona axiom that *chakafukidza dzimba matenga"* (literally, what covers houses are roofs). The saying that what covers houses are roofs is an axiom of knowledge which makes the observation that, from the outside, the household is a black box. Because of this ineffability and inscrutability, one cannot study Rates of Oppression by direct observation but, rather, only by signs-of-life, or whether life goes on. I retain the normative term, household expenditure, because it is already widely known. In my hands, however, it means *chakafukidza dzimba matenga*, which we can shorten to just *chakafukidza* or *dzimba-matenga*. Thus, my proposition of household expenditure as a unit by which to explain causality is far wider and richer than what is captured by, say, the price of a basket of commodities and utilities, or the flow of supply and demand. This is because household expenditure, in terms of *dzimba-matenga*, indicates, at the same time, (1) what people are going through as a result of life going on, and (2) how people are adjusting to life going on. Lifelihood is a function of *dzimba-matenga*.

Thus, what the ROp, as an expression of how people live with harm, demonstrates, is that we need a new understanding of the circadian rhythm. Essentially, all forms of harm are reticulated circadian rhythms. You cannot properly study the human without a theory of the socialization of the circadian rhythm. In the end, this is what the ROp boils down to: a model of the circadian rhythms of people living in harm's way and people living with harm. Our accumulated knowledges of *dzimba-matenga*, communicable and observable as the tokens *Mamuka sei? Maswera sei?* and *Makadii?* suggest (indeed, indicate) that the optimal unit of time in which to study what is going on in the social lives of humans must take place, precisely, between 12 hours and 2 days after you last saw a person. That is, 36 hours.[14]

*Dzimba-matenga* basically confirms that the true duration of a "day" need not be the normative 24 hours but, rather, between 12 and 36 hours. 24

---

[14] 36 hours = 48 hours minus 12 hours.

hours is just arbitrary clock time. Empirically, the 12 to 36-hour *dzimba-matenga* day, in fact, is more reflective of the true flow of life, circadian rhythms, and signs-of-life. Think, for instance, of domestic workers and market women from the townships, who must wake up at 3am to catch scarce public transport, or security guards who sleep irregularly. Every morning, at 8am, I bump into the Mme Lydia who cleans our department's offices. She tells me that she wakes up at 3am to put the bathing water to boil and to prepare for the school children who would still be asleep. By 4am, she has left the house for the bus rank, to queue for public transport to the city. She lives in the township of Botshabelo, 50 kilometres away from the Bloemfontein city centre. Botshabelo was designed by apartheid to be that way, to be so far away from the "white" city. Like other Africans, she spends most of her income on commuting to and from work. This woman and mother is paying for the apartheid design of her life. She must wake up at 3am and spend more than 50% of her income just to be cleaning our departmental offices at 8am. Meanwhile, I live just 10 kilometres from the office, in the formerly all-white city, and so only set my bedside alarm to ring at 15 minutes before 7am. To observers, Mme Lydia and I are both at the office at 8am. That is all that counts. In reality, if we apply the Rate of Oppression to it, we are not living in the same reality, even if we greet and walk side-by-side in the corridor. Thus, the livelihoods of the oppressed consist of very different flows of life than is allowed by the arbitrary divisions of a 24-hour clock. The best way to study what is going on in the *dzimba-matenga* black box of people's lives is not by checking watches, clocks, alarms, hooters, and bells, or break time, lunch time, or knock-off time, but, rather, circadian rhythms. As noted, the circadian rhythms of the oppressed flow around *Mamuka sei? Maswera sei?* and *Makadii?* Thus, the "measurement" of Rates of Oppression consists of tokens of lifelihood falling in the 12-to-36-hour interval. Any unit less than this is too short for study, and anything longer is probably superfluous. Therefore, if a *dzimba-matenga* "day" is 36 hours, the optimal duration of each ROp is between 12 to 26 hours long. This 14-hour period marks the optimal window of observation of the oscillation between rest and activity[15] and the ongoing conflict interest of the oppressed. This is the external manifestation of the circadian rhythm, its externalization. Together the three lifelihood tokens of *Mamuka sei? Maswera sei?* and *Makadii?* express the socialization of the circadian rhythm. The circadian rhythm, I believe, is the most important, most fundamental, human sign-of-life which can ever be studied. It is the human circadian rhythm which is the foremost access point of harm.

---

[15] For an in-depth account of rest and activity as they relate to apartheid, see Mboti (2023a).

# References

Beinart, W. (1995). *Segregation and Apartheid in Twentieth-Century South Africa*. Routledge.

Breckenridge, K. (2014). The Book of Life: The South African Population Register and the Invention of Racial Descent, 1950–1980. *Kronos, 40*, 225–240.

Clark, N. L., & Worger, W. H. (2013). *South Africa: The Rise and Fall of Apartheid*. Routledge.

Dubow, S. (2014). *Apartheid, 1948–1994*. Oxford University Press.

Dubow, S. (2017). New Approaches to High Apartheid and Anti-Apartheid. *South African Historical Journal, 69*(2), 304–329.

Giliomee, H. (2003a). The Making of the Apartheid Plan, 1929–1948. *Journal of Southern African Studies, 29*(2), 373–392.

Giliomee, H. (2003b). "The Weakness of Some": The Dutch Reformed Church and White Supremacy. *Scriptura, 83*, 212–244.

Giliomee, H. (2012 [2003]). *The Afrikaners: Biography of a People*. Cape Town: Tafelberg.

Guelke, A. (2005). *Rethinking the Rise and Fall of Apartheid: South Africa and World Politics*. Palgrave Macmillan.

Harvey, R. (2002). *The Fall of Apartheid: The Inside Story from Smuts to Mbeki*. Palgrave Macmillan.

Legassick, M., & Innes, D. (1977). Capital Restructuring and Apartheid: A Critique of Constructive Engagement. *African Affairs, 76*(305), 437–482.

Lovell, C. R. (1956). Afrikaner Nationalism and Apartheid. *The American Historical Review, 61*(2), 308–330.

Mahlaela, T. (2022). *Universities in SA Should Offer Compulsory Module in Apartheid Studies*. https://w2.unisa.ac.za/CW/SITES/CORPORAT/DEFAULT/COLLEGES/HUMAN_SC/NEWS_EVE/ARTICLES/UNIVERSI.HTM. Accessed 7 May 2023.

Marks, S., & Trapido, S. (1987). The Politics of Race, Class and Nationalism. In S. Marks & S. Trapido (Eds.), *The Politics of Race, Class and Nationalism in Twentieth-Century South Africa* (pp. 1–67). Routledge.

Marx, K. (1970 [1890]). Critique of the Gotha Programme. In K. Marx & F. Engels, *Selected Works* (vol. 3, 9–30). Progress Publishers.

Mboti, N. (2019). Circuits of Apartheid: A Plea for Apartheid Studies. *Glimpse, 20*, 15–70.

Mboti, N. (2023a). *Apartheid Studies: A Manifesto* (Vol. 1). Africa World Press.

Mboti, N. (2023b). Introducing Apartheid Studies: A New Forensic-Inductive Philosophy for Abolishing Harm. *Filosofie & Praktijk, 44*(1), 58–73.

Mboti, N. (2023c). What Is Apartheid Studies? https://networks.h-net.org/node/10670/discussions/12535475/what-apartheid-studies. Accessed 7 May 2023.

O'Meara, D. (1983). *Volkskapitalisme: Class, Capital and Ideology in the Development of Afrikaner Nationalism, 1934–1948* (pp. 171–177). Cambridge University Press.

Ongiri, A. A. (2010). *Spectacular Blackness: The Cultural Politics of the Black Power Movement and the Search for a Black Aesthetic*. University of Virginia Press.

Posel, D. (1987). The Meaning of Apartheid Before 1948: Conflicting Interests and Forces within the Afrikaner Nationalist Alliance. *Journal of Southern African Studies, 14*(1), 123–139.

Posel, D. (1991). *The Making of Apartheid, 1948–1961: Conflict and Compromise*. Clarendon.

Rich, P. (1980). The Origins of Apartheid Ideology: The Case of Ernest Stubbs and Transvaal Native Administration, c.1902–1932, *African Affairs, 79*(315), 171–194.

Simpson, T. (2017). Rethinking 'Apartheid's Golden Age': South Africa, c.1966–1979. *South African Historical Journal, 69*(2), 151–152.

Sinclair, U. (1935 [1994]). *I, Candidate for Governor*. University of California Press.

Sirvent, R. (2023). *Nyasha Mboti's Book. Apartheid Studies: A Manifesto*. BAR Book Forum. https://www.blackagendareport.com/bar-book-forum-nyasha-mbotis-book-apartheid-studies-manifesto. Accessed 7 May 2023.

Sonneborn, L. (2010). *The End of Apartheid in South Africa*. Chelsea House.

Sparks, A. (2003 [1990]). *The Mind of South Africa* (p. xiii). Jonathan Ball.

Welsh, D. (2009). *The Rise and Fall of Apartheid*. Jonathan Ball.

Worden, N. (2012). *The Making of Modern South Africa: Conquest, Apartheid, Democracy*. Wiley-Blackwell.

# On Systemic and Epistemic Violence in Africa

Patricia Pinky Ndlovu and Sabelo J. Ndlovu-Gatsheni

## 1 Introduction

This chapter examines the dynamics of systemic and epistemic violence in Africa. It delves into how such systems as racism, colonialism, capitalism, heteronormative patriarchal sexism underpinned by the intrusive cognitive empire generated various forms of violence ranging from physical, subjective, objective, epistemic, and many others. In the current conjuncture, epistemic violence is sustained by the global economy of knowledge, with its uneven intellectual and academic division of labour. The chapter is informed by a decolonial epistemic perspective linked to the Black radical tradition, which delves into modern history of violence in its institutional, systemic, structural and epistemic dimensions, bequeathed on the modern world by Euromodernity. Violence is constitutive of Euromodernity. The Latin American decolonial theorists have termed this constitutive violence of Euromodernity, coloniality—an underside/negative side of modernity. The decolonial epistemic perspectives uncover, unmask, and decrypt those forms of violence that tend to hide in plain sight—in institutions, systems, structures, and knowledges.

P. P. Ndlovu (✉) · S. J. Ndlovu-Gatsheni
University of Bayreuth, Bayreuth, Germany
e-mail: Patricia.P.Ndlovu@uni-bayreuth.de

S. J. Ndlovu-Gatsheni
e-mail: Sabelo.Ndlovu-Gatsheni@uni-bayreuth.de

The chapter is divided into six sections. The first section introduces the forms of violence haunting the modern world in general and Africa in particular. The second section reflects on the institutions within which systemic, structural, institutional, and epistemic violence is incubated and launched into society. The third section turns to the specific subject of epistemic violence and introduces the concept of the cognitive empire—an empire which invades the mental universe of other people to commit theft of history, epistemicides, linguicides, culturecides, and indeed ontolocides. The fourth section highlight how an expansive decolonial archive from Africa, Latin America, Asia, the Black radical tradition, and feminist scholarship has grappled with the question of epistemic injustices. The fifth section suggests decolonial ways of overcoming violence in general and epistemic injustices/epistemic violence, drawing from the resurgent and insurgent decolonization of the twenty-first century. The last part is the conclusion and draws together all the arguments raised in this chapter as it highlights how violence remains a major challenge today.

## 2  Mapping the Forms of Violence Beyond Common Conceptions

Ricardo Sanin-Restrepo (2020: 8) posited that that *potestas* (power as domination) "works through a primary violence." What is this primary violence? This is the foundational systemic and structural violence constitutive of the social classification, racial hierarchization, and gendering of human population as part of encryption of power (see Sanin-Restrepo, 2016). The violence of encryption of power resulted in the construction of a transcendental model of power that the Latin American decolonial theorists have termed "coloniality" (see Mignolo, 2012; Quijano, 2000). Carl Schmitt (2006) referred to the emergence of a transcendental model of power as the "second nomos of the earth."

Racism, enslavement, genocides, colonialism, imperialism, racial capitalism, forced religious conversions, and heteronormative sexism were all vectors of the constitutive foundational violence of Euromodernity. One has to read such early writings as those of Frederick Douglas to understand how the category of foundational violence emerged and was inflicted on the bodies and lives of those who were classified as Black and native (see Douglas, 1845). It was through efforts to make sense of this foundational violence that the Black radical tradition emerged (Robinson, 2000). The Black scholars concerned with enslavement as systemic, structural, institutional and indeed foundational violence long understood violence in its multidimensional categories and developed an extended concept of violence. For example, Saidiya V. Hartman (1997) examined "scenes of subjection" and "terror" constitutive of enslavement. This is how she put it:

> The scenes of subjection considered here—the coerced spectacles orchestrated to encourage the trade in black flesh; scenes of torture and festivity; the tragedy of virtuous women and the antics of outrageous darkies—all turn upon the simulation of agency and the excesses of black enjoyment. (Hartman, 1997: 22–23)

The extended conception of violence also appealed to those peoples who were subjected to such violence systems as racism, enslavement, colonialism, imperialism, capitalism, religious conversions, colonial education, heteronormative sexism, and Eurocentrism—all of which reverberated at the centre of Euro-American-centric modernity (Ake, 1979; Amin, 1989; Cesaire, 1955; Chinweizu, 1975; Fanon, 1963; Memmi, 1957; Nandy, 1983; Ngũgĩ wa Thiong'o, 1986; Nkrumah, 1965; Quijano, 2000). It was through the efforts of anticolonial and decolonial struggles that such systems as colonialism and apartheid were condemned internationally as constitutive of violence/crimes against humanity.

Of course, it took time for consensus to emerge among scholars and activists, especially those who were never subjected to such systems as racism and colonialism, to realize that the common and narrow understanding of violence as physical (personal violence) has to be extended. Among European scholars the work of the leading theorist of peace Johan Galtung (1969: 168) is often taken as foundational and he made a strong case for "an extended concept of violence" because even "Highly unacceptable social orders would still be compatible with peace."

Thinking from the perspective of peace, Galtung noted that a narrow conception of violence would have negative implications for peace—reducing it to mere absence of physical violence. He termed absence of visible physical violence as speaking to a restricted conception of peace, which he named "negative peace" (Galtung, 1969: 170). In seeking to deepen the conception of peace, Galtung wrote of "positive peace" which, fundamentally, means the absence of injustices and structural, systemic and institutional violence, which cannot be easily seen on the surface of society.

Galtung's case for extension of the concept of violence to embrace structural violence resonated with Marxists whose Marxist science was concerned with capitalist as an exploitative and violent system. The Marxist-oriented scholars tended to divide violence into revolutionary, non-revolutionary, and reactionary/counter-revolutionary violence. Revolutionary violence is that which targets the powerful oppressor (the bourgeoisie) who are the beneficiaries and stockholders of capitalism. Counter-revolutionary/reactionary violence is that which is launched in defence of the status quo of domination and exploitation. Non-revolutionary violence is that performed by the poor against each other borne of failure to correctly identify the enemy (see Mamdani, 2007).

The agenda of extension of the concept of violence also attracted the European philosopher Slavoj Zizek in his slim volume *Violence: Six Sideways Reflection* (2008: 1–2):

> This is the starting point, perhaps even the axiom, of the present book: subjective violence is just the most visible portion of a triumvirate that also includes two objective kinds of violence. First, there is a 'symbolic' violence embodied in language and its forms, what Heidegger called 'our house of being.' As we shall see later, this violence is not at work in the obvious—and extensively studied—cases of incitement and the relations of social domination reproduced in our habitual speech forms: there is a more fundamental form of violence still that pertains to language as such, to its imposition of a certain universe of meaning. Second, there is what I call 'systemic' violence, or the often-catastrophic consequences of the smooth functioning of our economic and political systems.

Zizek elaborated on his extension of the concept of violence:

> The catch is that subjective and objective violence cannot be perceived from the same standpoint: subjective violence is experienced as such against the background of a non-violent zero level. It is seen as a perturbation of the 'normal,' peaceful state of things. However, objective violence is precisely the violence inherent to this 'normal' state of things. Objective violence is invisible since it sustains the very zero-level standard against which we perceive something as subjectively violent. Systemic violence is thus something like the notorious 'dark matter' of physics, the counterpart to an all-too-visible subjective violence. (Zizek, 2008: 2)

The extension of the concept of violence is also discernible in the gender and feminist scholarship the intersectionality theory emerged capturing multifaceted nature of forms of oppressions and violence affecting women. To be specific, the intersectionality theory emerged from feminist movements and scholarship of "women of colour" (racialized and feminized as Black) to enable understanding of converging racism, classism, and genderism as forms of oppression (see Collins, 2000). This multiplicity of oppressions and violence is well-captured by Sara C. Motta (2018) who depicts women's position as "liminal subjects" and explains that:

> Many have spoken of the wounds inflicted upon us as feminized and racialized peoples by patriarchal capitalist coloniality; of our systematic negation as subjects which Frantz Fanon described as 'a furious determination to deny the other person all attributes of humanity' [...]. This negation is experienced as invisibility, the White gaze of suspicion, and denial of the capacity of gift in which the question is always asked 'are you like us human' [...]. This denial of the capacity of gift legitimizes the idea that there is nothing to learn from us; we are absent as (knowing) beings. In this the state, as sovereign, legitimizes an anti-ethics of war and conquest in which the exception of removal rights, denial of humanness, and logics of elimination becomes the norm which structures our reality as raced 'southern' women. (Motta, 2018: 5)

It is clear that violence as a leitmotif of subjection, oppression, exploitation, and indeed denial another people's humanity, cannot be singularized. It has to be understood in its various forms: foundational, systemic, institutional, structural, symbolic, psychological, epistemic, and other dimensions. There is also a need to identify the structures, institutions, and systems (infrastructures), which incubate and unleash violence.

## 3  The Modern Infrastructures of Systems of Violence

The modern infrastructures of violence range from the plantation, colony, factory, school, church, border, prison, police camp, refugee camp, to the street in a modern world governed according to white supremacy. Achille Mbembe (2019: 92) call these infrastructures of violence "the repressive topographies of cruelty" underpinned by "necropolitics" and driven by "necropower".

The victims of systemic, structural, institutional, epistemic and physical violence have been those people who were classified as Black and native in an anti-Black world. This was made possible by the fact that the very concepts of "the human" and "the social" were conceived within Euromodernity against Black and native peoples (Vargas & Jung, 2021; Walcott, 2014). The plantation became the site of subjection of African people to enslavement and its brutalities. Enslavement as a foundational regime for primitive mercantile accumulation formed the basis for other regimes of subjection of labour to exploitation ranging of indentured labour to the modern contractual labour practices. This is why Marcus Garvey in 1925 in New York said that enslavement did not come to an end; in fact the enslaved people became factory slaves. This means that abolition and emancipation were just transitional arrangements from one form of violence to another (see Hartman, 1997).

Besides the plantation being a site of social death, it was also in the plantation that racial capitalism drew its power as it unfolded into a globalized system of exploitation and violence. On top of this, it was within the plantation that the racial category of Black crystallized and was concretized into a badge of sub-humanity and inferiority (Manjapra, 2020). This is why Kris Manjapra (2020: 7) pointed out that:

> Colonizers attempted to commodify, extract, and appropriate land and labour surplus from differentially racialized groups. Different forms of colonial coercion and racial differentiation were employed to 'cheapen' the price of labour and to dehumanize labourers in emerging capitalist economies.

Racialization was and is "infrastructural to capitalism, with legacies that persist into our modern times" (Manjapra, 2020: 8). The plantation was succeeded by the colony. Mbembe (2019: 2021) posited that colonialism was fundamentally about who owns the earth, as he underscored the planetary character of colonialism. Mbembe's point was initially raised by the novelist Joseph Conrad (1993), who wrote that "The conquest of the earth, which mostly means the taking it away from those who have a different complexion or slightly flatter noses than ourselves, is not a pretty thing when you look into it too much." Mbembe (2019: 78) explained that the colony is a site of terror par excellence where there was denial of co-presence and where "the sovereign right to kill is not subject to any rule in the colonies." Mbembe (2019: 46) clearly understood the meaning of colonialism:

> Colonizing broadly consisted in a permanent work of separation: on one side, my living body; on the other, all those 'body-things' surrounding it; on the one side, my human flesh, through which all those other 'flesh-things' and 'flesh-meats' exist for me.

It was with specific reference to the colony that Frantz Fanon (1963) depicted violence as atmospheric. Everything was governed through violence. Explaining this violence, Fanon painted this vivid picture:

> The colonial world is a world cut into two. The dividing line, the frontiers are shown by barracks and police stations. In the colonies it is the policemen and

the soldiers who are the official, instituted go-betweens, the spokesmen of the settler and his rule of oppression. (Fanon, 1963: 29)

Violence was a mode of governance in the colonies and plantations. Mbembe (2001) categorized colonial violence into three. The first was the foundational violence known in colonial historiography as pacification. The second was the legitimation violence which sought to legitimize colonial governmentality. The third was the maintenance violence which was meant to maintain colonial domination, repression and exploitation (Mbembe 2001: 12–15). These threefold modes of violence constituted what Mbembe (2001) termed the commandment.

The systemic and structural violence rooted in the plantation and the colony is still ruining lives today as it is being reproduced at a global scale and also at national scales by states. It is this reality that led Francoise Verges (2022: vi) to posit that violence is normalized and the structural and systemic frames of it include: "neoliberal capitalism, racism, imperialism, white supremacy and patriarchy, homophobia and transphobia." In *A Feminist Theory of Violence* (2022) Verges identifies the modern state and its policing practices as the major violence machine especially against women. She argues that the violence of the state is hidden in the very initiatives that are said to be for protection noting that "Protection is understood in the colonial tradition: keep the barbarians at the gates; militarize the public space; create social, environmental, and cultural segregation; use artwashing, politics of bourgeois respectability, and white feminism to justify this segregation" (Verges, 2022: vi). This is possible because "the state condenses all forms of imperialist, patriarchal, and capitalist oppression and exploitation" (Verges, 2022: 3). This is why it is the state which foment and encourage "hatred against minorities, trans people, queer people, sex workers, racialized people, migrants, and Muslims" (Verges, 2022: 3). This takes us to the epistemic dimensions of violence and epistemic injustices.

## 4  The Cognitive Empire and Epistemic Violence

The concept of the cognitive empire invokes a different empire from the well-known physical empire, which physically (directly violently) invades, conquers, dominate, repress and exploit the colonized people. The cognitive empire uses invisible technologies to invade the mental universe of its targets and it seeks to colonize the minds (Ngũgĩ wa Thiong'o, 1986). It is a foundational empire on which the very "colonizer's model of the world" is predicated (Blaut, 1993). It is a very successful empire which managed to impose its own epistemology that framed the modern systems, structures and institutions as well as shaping the consciousnesses of the modern subjects. It operates at a planetary scale in its routinization and naturalization of what it has imposed (Ndlovu-Gatsheni, 2018a, 2018b, 2021). In short, the cognitive empire is better understood as the invisible elephant in the domain of knowledge, which commits such forms of violence as theft of history, epistemicides, culturecides, linguicides and ontolocides. Like the current troublesome Coronavirus, it survives through camouflaging itself, disguises, invisibility, and indeed mutations.

While Boaventura de Sousa Santos (2018) used the term "the end of the cognitive empire" in a title of his book, insinuating that this empire is coming to an end because of epistemologies of the South, which are "coming of age," he did not elaborate on the operations of this empire. It is vital to say that the cognitive empire is the pillar of all empires—the physical and commercial empires. Ngũgĩ wa Thiong'o (1986) called it the "metaphysical empire," Robert Gildea (2019) termed it the "empire of the mind" and Ashis Nandy (1983) depicted it as an "intimate enemy" (an enemy that resides like virus in the body and mind of the host). These related but different descriptions and names highlight its amorphous character and invisible operative logics as it commits epistemic injustices across the world.

To gain a deep understanding of the cognitive empire, there is need to make further reflections on Euromodernity. This is because Euromodernity materialized through the colonization of time and human subjectivity. Gurminder K. Bhambra (2007) captured this in terms of "rupture and difference" as the key logics of Euromodernity. Euromodernity's self-representation and indeed autobiography is that of emerging out of a "rupture" in time, leading to the monopolization of the temporality "modern" by Europe and the designation of all others as "primitive/ancient" (pre-modern)—that is, outside modern time and thus backward.

Thus at the centre of Euromodernity pulsated a paradigm of difference, which enabled the colonization of being human itself through techniques of social classification of human population and racial hierarchization in accordance with invented differential ontological densities (Maldonado-Torres, 2007; Ndlovu-Gatsheni, 2020; Wynter, 2003). Those human beings who found themselves pushed to the subhuman category had their knowledge, history, culture and language questioned, devalued and even said to be nonexistent. Here was born a biocentric and teleological European accounts of the human, with the European "Man" at the centre as the master and owner of the world (Ndlovu-Gatsheni, 2013, 2018a, 2018b; Wynter, 1995). This colonial logic was always underwritten by a "colonial turn" backed up by what Valentin Y. Mudimbe (1988) termed the "colonial library" in knowledge, which advanced Eurocentric epistemologies as the only valid, legitimate, truthful, and universal ones.

The long-standing "colonial turn" was at one level underpinned by equally long-standing discourses of Hellenocentrism (all started in Greece), Westernization (the West as the template of complete human being), Eurocentrism (Europe as the centre of the world), Secularism (de-godding/death of God and rule of European "Man" armed with scientific knowledge), Periodization (linear conceptions of time marked by ruptures), and Colonialism (conquest and occupation of a world that was deemed to be empty) (see Dussel, 2011). At a second level, it was symbolized by the historic Valladolid Debate (1550–1551), in which Bartolomé da las Casas and Juan Ginés de Sepúlveda argued the ontological question of the humanity of the "natives." Las Casas's position, which viewed them as subhumans who worshipped wrong gods, were primitive, and could be rescued through conversion to Christianity, laid the foundation for anthropology and ethnography, whereas Sepúlveda's take, which dismissed the very humanity of Indigenous people, formed the basis for scientific racism in knowledge production (Castro, 2007; Suárez-Krabbe, 2015).

The epistemic violent dimensions and consequences of all this are well-captured by Lewis R. Gordon (2022) in terms of invisibilization/erasure of the Black and the native. Gordon distilled five kinds of invisibility namely: racial, Indigenous, gendered, exoticized, and epistemic. "Racial invisibility involves not being seen as human being by virtue of hyper-visibility—a state of being perceived excessively because of not belonging" writes Gordon (2022: 129). This is the first form of violence of invisibility. The second form pertains to the Indigenous people whereby "The settler regards the Indigenous people as belonging to the past because their land will never be returned to them; the future is foreclosed" (Gordon, 2022: 133). Therefore, the survivors of genocides and their descendants exist in the modern as haunting "ghosts" as they were not expected to be part of the modern time. The third violence of invisibilization pertains gender in which women are denied "voice" as well as "speaking without being heard" (Gordon, 2022: 135).

Exoticism is the fourth kind of invisibilization whereby there is seeming "love and valorization" while "the racist exoticist plays a bad-faith game of bestowing an intrinsic sense of superiority through being supposedly able to identify the intrinsic virtues of racially deprecated people" (Gordon, 2022:

136). The consequence is: "In exoticism, the humanity of racially valorized people is lost. Their extolled visibility hides—renders invisible—their humanity" (Gordon, 2022: 137). The fifth is epistemic invisibilization: "It combines the others by what we could describe as a movement from illicit appearance to the consequence of illegitimate knowledge" (Gordon, 2022: 137). Gordon explains: "The logic of this form of invisibility is that black, brown and red people cannot produce knowledge" (Gordon, 2022: 137). Gordon (2022: 138)'s conclusion is that "Examining all five forms of invisibility together, we see how matrices of dehumanization distribute invisibility across many people in the Euromodern or white supremacist world."

Regarding the practical unfolding of the cognitive empire, Ngũgĩ wa Thiong'o (2009) is very insightful. He identified two techniques which were deployed in the invasion of the mental universe of the colonized people. For the first technique, he gave the example of a computer whereby the removal of the hard disk of a previous memory and the downloading of a new software results in total change to demonstrate how the cognitive empire works. This means that using church, school, and university, the cognitive empire is actively involved in the process of removing the hard disk of previous indigenous people's knowledge and memory and is constantly downloading into their minds the software of European knowledge and memory (Ngũgĩ wa Thiong'o, 2009). The consequences amount to what Ali A. Mazrui (1978) has termed "cultural schizophrenia," and Ngũgĩ wa Thiong'o articulates it very well:

> The colonial process dislocates the traveler's mind from the place he or she already knows to a foreign starting point even with the body still remaining in his or her homeland. It is a continuous alienation from the base, a continuous process of looking at oneself from the outside of self or with the lenses of a stranger. One may end up identifying with the foreign base as the starting point toward self, that is, from another self towards oneself, rather than the local being the starting point, from self to other selves. (Ngũgĩ wa Thiong'o, 2012: 39)

The second technique of the cognitive empire is the one that Ngũgĩ wa Thiong'o has likened to the detonation of a "cultural bomb" at the centre of the universe with far-reaching consequences. This is how he puts it: "The effect of the cultural bomb is to annihilate a people's belief in their names, in their languages, in their environment, in their heritage of struggle, in their unity, in their capacities and ultimately in themselves" (Ngũgĩ wa Thiong'o, 1986: 3). A people who has experienced this "cultural bomb" tends to develop complicated consciousness of themselves to the extent of aspiring to be like their colonizers and always falling on each other trying to emulate what the cognitive empire delivered as standards in knowledge production.

Of course, the colonized people across the world rose against the physical empire and rolled out the decolonization struggles of the twentieth century. Those struggles became mainly ranged against the physical empire—that is, they aimed at dismantling direct colonial administrations. Indeed, the direct colonial administrations were rolled back and a modicum of political sovereignty was granted, albeit within an unchanged imperial world system and global coloniality. This is why Ramón Grosfoguel (2007) posited that the decolonization of the twenty-first century was a myth, as direct colonialism metamorphosed into global coloniality to sustain the colonial matrices of power. Within this context, attainment of a modicum of political sovereignty did not change the epistemic injustices committed by the cognitive empire.

The cognitive empire enabled the current global political economy of knowledge, in which there is a belief among what one would term the "globalists" that because of globalization process, knowledges of the world have coalesced into a commonwealth with no centre and periphery, with no binaries and dichotomies. This debate came out prominently in Collyer et al. (2019: 1), where they noted that "there is a widespread idea that we live in a knowledge society, an information society, or a technological society. Yet in most fields of research, there is also an idea that the disciplines we work in, and the concepts we work with, do not come from any particular place in that society. They are just in the air, so to speak."

We just wish the resolution of epistemic violence would produce a commonwealth of knowledge and, better still, ecologies of knowledges. We are far from this reality. There are a number of reasons for this. The first is that despite frantic efforts to speak across the North–South divide or the pretences that these binaries no longer exist. The reality is that Europe and North America continue to enjoy a privileged position in knowledge production (Hountondji, 1990). There is still the resilient uneven intellectual and academic division of labour with Africa and the Global South still performing the position of where raw data is hunted for, gathered and extracted in raw form to be processed into theory in Europe and North America (Hountondji, 1997). Intellectual and academic dependence remains endemic, if not pandemic, with scholars of the Global South still compelled by power dynamics to publish in journals and leading presses located in the Global North if they are to gain any recognition as knowledge producers (Ndlovu-Gatsheni, 2018a, 2018b).

While this situation is indeed being challenged, contested, negotiated and subverted to the extent that there is increasing talk of partnerships, Paulin

J. Hountondji (1997: 1) has insisted that "The fact bears repeating: in the field of science and technology, Third World countries, especially those in Black Africa, are tied hand and foot to the apron strings of the West." It was also Hountondji (2002) who adapted Samir Amin's concept of economic extraversion and applied it to the domain of knowledge to reveal that there is a structural condition that sustains the dominance of Europe and North America to the extent that the rest of the majority world (the Global South) finds itself saddled with standards, protocols, methodologies, theories, and indeed epistemologies developed in the Global North. This reality takes us to the discussion of the complex issues of epistemic injustices.

## 5 Existential, Justice and Epistemic Dimensions of Violence

At the root of epistemic violence is the existential question of denied humanity of Black and native people, which is directly connected to the epistemic problems of non-recognition of diverse ways through which diverse people make sense of the world and their lives (Ndlovu-Gatsheni, 2013; Santos, 2014, 2018). It is a foundational injustice that is linked to "coloniality of being"—that is, denial of the very humanity of other people and their reduction to a subhuman status (Maldonado-Torres, 2007). In epistemic justice, one finds the convergence of the "color line" and the "epistemic line" (Du Bois, 1903; Ndlovu-Gatsheni, 2018a, 2018b). Boaventura de Sousa Santos introduced the concept of "abyssal thinking," which is predicated on refusal of the "copresence" of worlds and peoples, in the process generating epistemicides (the killing of other people's knowledges) (Santos, 2007).

Epistemicides are underwritten by genocides (the physical killing of people whose humanity is questioned). This open floodgates to linguicides (killing the languages of those who are targeted for enslavement and colonization and the imposition of colonial languages), and cultural imperialism (attacking the cultures of the enslaved and colonized peoples) (Ndlovu-Gatsheni, 2018b). The theft of history (denying non-European peoples' possession of history) is connected with ontolocides (exiling people from their languages, cultures, histories and from themselves through alienation, resulting in dehumanization and dismemberment) (Ndlovu-Gatsheni, 2018b).

Since epistemic injustices are committed through epistemological colonization, which targets the minds of the victims, it is one of the most resilient crimes of Euromodernity and its technologies of racism and colonialism. Therefore, the dismantling of the physical empire does not solve the problem of epistemic injustices because they remain deeply etched in the minds of the colonized peoples (psyche), in curriculum, institutions, modern systems and iconography.

But another dimension of epistemic injustice is that of ignoring other archives and privileging others as pioneering. For example, with regard to the very question of epistemic injustice, there is a tendency to credit Miranda Fricker (2007) as the pioneering work on the subject of epistemic injustice. One wonders why such a recently published work can be considered pioneering on a subject that had preoccupied other scholars for a long time before Fricker? There are indeed such seminal works as Claude Ake (1979), Ngũgĩ wa Thiong'o (1986), Linda T. Smith (1999), Jack Goody (2006), and many others which had dealt with the question of epistemic injustices long before Fricker's interventions. This argument is not meant to minimize Fricker's contributions to the question of epistemic injustices but to highlight how scholars from Africa in particular experience epistemic injustice in the form of their work not being taken seriously and treated as though it does not exist at all, while works produced by Europeans and North Americans are privileged.

There is a rich archive produced by Latin American scholars such as Enrique Dussel (1993, 1995), Walter D. Mignolo (1995, 2000), Aníbal Quijano (2000), and many others on the question of epistemic injustices, tracing it back to the very moment of the unfolding of the European Renaissance and Euromodernity and highlighting the often-ignored reality of coloniality of power, knowledge, and being. They have meticulously linked the questions of genocides, enslavement, racism, patriarchy, sexism, and heteronormativity as key coordinates of epistemic injustices (Grosfoguel, 2013, 2019; Lugones, 2007).

In Southeast Asia, the whole project of Subaltern Studies which emerged in the 1980s sought to address the epistemic injustices inflicted on the poor people whom they termed "the subaltern," drawing on the work of Antonio Gramsci (Guha, 1983, 1997). It was from Subaltern Studies that the famous question of whether the subaltern can speak emerged (Spivak, 1988). Feminist scholarship in its various iterations and schools has been pioneering in raising issues of epistemic injustices linked with race, gender, and class (Collins, 2000). It was feminist scholarship that introduced the concepts of "intersectionality" in understanding multiple forms of oppression and their differential multiple impacts on women depending on their race, class, and ethnicity (Crenshaw, 1995; Lorde, 1984; Lugones, 2003). The seminal work *Engendering African Social Sciences* (1997) edited by Imam, Mama, and Sow, highlighted the core issues of androcentrism and sexism, patriarchy in knowledge production and social science, concluding that any social science which ignored the question of gender was an impoverished one. What emerges poignantly from feminist scholarship is the fact that at the centre of epistemic injustices, there are deep-rooted entanglements of race, sex, and gender, which are well expressed as "epistemic racism/sexism and four genocides/epistemicides of the long 16th century" (Grosfoguel, 2013).

The Black radical tradition, with W. E. B. Du Bois (1903) as its leading light, highlighted the question of epistemic injustices long ago, including raising the question of how Black people feel about anti-Black racism and its epistemic implications, which depicted those deemed to be Black as a problem. It was from the staple of Black radical tradition that Cedric J. Robinson offered the seminal work *Black Marxism: The Making of the Black Radical Tradition* (1983 [2000]), critiquing European Marxism for complicity in epistemic injustices. Therefore, it does not make sense to argue that the recent work of Miranda Fricker is pioneering on the subject of epistemic injustices (Dunne, 2020).

Even the Eurocentric idea of Greece as the cradle of knowledge has been vigorously challenged by African scholars such as Cheikh Anta Diop (1954, 1974a, 1974b) who highlighted how Egypt instead of Greece was a seat of knowledge, which was then taken to Greece by those who studied in Egypt. This is a debate that is well-captured in Martin Bernal's *Black Athena: The Afroasiatic Roots of Classical Civilization* (1987), where the very question of civilization is brought into the centre of contestations about epistemic injustices aligned to Eurocentrism. The Afrocentricity school pioneered by scholars such as Diop and today led by Molefi Kete Asante (2007) has been grappling with the question of epistemic injustice for a very long time, in the process recovering African endogenous knowledge that has been pushed to the margins by Eurocentrism. Perhaps what can be said is that these works did not use the term "epistemic injustice" specifically and perhaps Fricker coined it. This analysis takes us to the most difficult part of how to resolve the problem of epistemic injustices.

## 6  Towards the Resolution of Epistemic Violence

What can be said with certainty is that there are resurgent and insurgent planetary decolonization struggles, which target epistemic injustices as well as iconographies of peoples who committed genocides and epistemicides across the world. This planetary decolonization is embodied by the Rhodes Must Fall and Black Lives Matter movements today. These movements are confronting a planetary cognitive empire which has successfully invaded the global mental universe of the people while privileging epistemologies from Europe and North America as well as the theories, concepts, and scholarship of white men from Germany, Britain, Italy, France, and the United States of America, mainly.

The reality on the ground is that there is no easy way out when it comes to decolonizing thought and dealing with hidden epistemic injustices and violence. This difficulty arises from the fact that the cognitive empire has successfully delivered a world governed by what Mudimbe (2013) has termed "the line," on which he thus elaborates:

> As a metaphor, the line operates in everyday life with such efficiency that we forget that this simple word not only organizes our spatial perception but determines our conceptualization of basic rapports between front and back, deep and shallow, in and out, near and far, on and off, up and down, past and present, and today and tomorrow.

In short, we live in a world that is epistemically colonized, with lines being its signatures. These are not innocent lines. They are, in the words of Boaventura de Sousa Santos (2007), "abyssal lines." This reality means that epistemic injustices cannot be fully resolved without changing the foundational colonial crime of pushing non-European people out of the human family and without the de-imperialization of the modern world system. This is why one finds such scholars as Sylvia Wynter (2001) proposing a new "counter-cartography of a history of human life" pivoted on "a relational conception of human existence" and drawing from Frantz Fanon's concept of sociogeny (see also Erasmus, 2020).

In this counter-cartography of the history of human life, the key aspect is the definitive entry of the descendants of racialized, feminized, enslaved and indeed dehumanized people into the academies across the world, vehemently rejecting the subhuman category they have been consigned to (Maldonado-Torres, 2008; Ndlovu-Gatsheni, 2018a). These descendants of dehumanized people are openly challenging all aspects of Eurocentrism, and they are declaring for the whole world to know that as human beings, they were born into valid and legitimate knowledge systems (Mudimbe, 1994). The recovery of subjugated knowledge is made possible by the fact that, except where absolute genocide was involved, elements of pre-colonization knowledges have survived.

With specific reference to India, Aditya Nigam (2020) has empirically demonstrated how pre-colonization knowledges have survived and continue to influence the present in the process, even undercutting the Eurocentric impositions of secularism. According to Nigam, the pre-colonization knowledges and spiritualties which he termed "non-synchronous synchronicities" have never obediently succumbed to Euromodernity, Eurocentrism, and colonization.

The first important move in dealing with epistemic injustices for the victims is to undertake the painstaking process of self-introspection with a view to confronting, at individual and collective levels, the problematic consciousness imposed by the cognitive empire. It was this consciousness that Du Bois (1903) depicted as cascading from two souls, two thoughts, two unreconciled strivings, and two warring ideas in one black body. This process is necessary but very difficult because the intellectuals and academics from the Global South are produced by the modern world university system, which itself is a culprit in the commission of epistemic injustices and sustenance of global colonial matrices of power.

The issue here is the agenda of dealing with miseducation while working towards re-education as an essential prerequisite for the decolonization of the mind (Ngũgĩ wa Thiong'o, 1986). This is what has been rendered by feminist movements and Indigenous people's movements as learning to unlearn in order to relearn (Ndlovu-Gatsheni, 2018a). While there are numerous pedagogies of learning new knowledge, there is a scarcity of those that help in unlearning what was imposed by the cognitive empire. Unlearning entails self-exorcism of coloniality. Therefore, the pedagogies of unlearning have to be developed in struggle as the victims of the cognitive empire grapple with how to abandon what was meant for colonization.

Within the academies and universities that claim to be advancing the agenda of resolution of epistemic injustices, there are many steps that have to be taken. The first is that of re-provincializing Europe while de-provincializing those areas like Africa, Asia, the Caribbean, and Latin America that were marginalized and peripherized (Ndlovu-Gatsheni, 2018b). This agenda has to build on the concepts of "moving the centre" and shifting the biography and geography of knowledge so as to make sure that the definitive entry of the descendants of the enslaved, racialized, feminized, and dehumanized substantially stir the toxic pond of knowledge to the point of reaching an epistemic rupture which enables an opening for ecologies of knowledges (Ndlovu-Gatsheni, 2018a; Ngũgĩ wa Thiong'o, 1993; Santos, 2007). A number of moves have to be practically taken within the academy to de-parochialize social theory; diversify and pluralize the syllabus and the curriculum; shift and deliberately digress from what has been given as the canon; decentring of exhausted and irrelevant knowledge; and de-hierarchization of hierarchies in epistemology so as to open spaces for previously marginalized and excluded voices (Ndlovu-Gatsheni, 2018b).

## 7 Conclusion

It is the inextricable entwinement of structural, systemic, institutional, psychological, and epistemic violence which a decolonial epistemic perspective, which embraces the Black radical tradition that enables their unmasking and decryption. There is a clear case for taking forward the unfinished business of epistemological decolonization as it directly confronts all the crimes of the cognitive empire while also rising against the physical manifestations of racism which continue to enable the making Black lives of not to matter. Epistemological decolonization has successfully led to the reopening of basic epistemological questions and is making the reorganization of the world of knowledge a priority in the current conjuncture. Of course, this epistemic revolution has provoked conservative political elements working together with conservative intellectuals mainly in Europe and the United States of America to dig in and try to push for the outlawing of critical race theory, intersectionality theory, postcolonial theory and decolonial theory—accusing them of being nothing but identity politics.

What gives hope is that the current conjuncture is dominated by profound dissatisfaction with the dominant and hegemonic knowledge. This fundamentally means that epistemic violence and injustices have to be confronted as the world looks forward to epistemic reconstitution involving the embracement of ecologies of knowledges, thinking across traditions, and indeed the adoption of mosaic epistemologies that make convivial scholarship and epistemic freedom possible.

**Funding:** Federal Ministry of Education and research through the Postcolonial Hierarchies in Peace and conflict.

## Bibliography

Ake, C. (1979). *Social Science as Imperialism: The Theory of Political Development*. University of Ibadan Press.

Amin, S. (1988 [2009]). *Eurocentrism: Modernity, Religion and Democracy: A Critique of Eurocentrism and Culturalism.* Monthly Review Press.

Amin, S. (1989). *Eurocentrism, Modernity, Religion, and Democracy: A Critique of Eurocentrism and Culturalism.* New York Monthly Review Press.

Asante, M. K. (2007). *An Afrocentric Manifesto: Toward an African Renaissance.* Polity Press.

Bernal, M. (1987). *Black Athena: The Afroasiatic Roots of Classical Civilization.* Rutgers University Press.

Bhambra, G. K. (2007). *Rethinking Modernity: Postcolonialism and the Sociological Imagination.* Palgrave Macmillan.

Blaut, J. M. (1993). *The Colonizer's Model of The World: Geographical Diffusionism and Eurocentric History.* The Gilford Press.

Castro, D. (2007). *Another Face of Empire: Bartolomé de Las Casas, Indigenous Rights, and Ecclesiastical Imperialism.* Duke University Press.

Cesaire, A. (1955 [2000]). *Discourse on Colonialism.* Monthly Review Press.

Chinweizu, I. (1975). *The West and the Rest of Us: White Predators, Black Slavers and the African Elite.* Random House.

Collins, P. H. (2000). *Black Feminist Thought: Knowledge, Consciousness, and the Politics of Empowerment.* Routledge.

Collyer, F., Connell, R., Maia, J., & Morrell, R. (Eds.). (2019). *Knowledge and Global Power: Making New Sciences in the South.* Wits University Press.

Conrad, J. (1993). The conquest in Joseph Conrads's Heart of Darkness.available: https://www.123helpme.com/essay/the-conquest-in-joseph-conrads-heart-of-darkness. Accessed on 6 November 2023.

Crenshaw, Kimberlé. (1995). Mapping the Margins: Intersectionality, Identity Politics and Violence Against Women of Color. In K. Crenshaw, N. Gotanda, G. Peller, & K. Thomas (Eds.), *Critical Theory: The Key Writings that Formed the Movement* (pp. 283–313). The New Press.

Diop, C. A. (1954) *Nations nègres et culture* (Negro Nations and Culture). Présence Africaine.

Diop, C. A. (1974). *The African Origins of Civilization: Myth and Reality* (M. Cook, Ed. & Trans.). Lawrence Hill Books.

Diop, C. A. (1974). *Precolonial Black Africa* (H. J. Salemson, Trans.). Lawrence Hill Books.

Douglas, F. (1854 [1968]). *Narrative of the Life of Frederick Douglas, an American Slave, Written by Himself.* New American Library.

Du Bois, W. E. B. (1903). *The Souls of Black Folk.* Dover Publications.

Dunne, G. (2020). Epistemic Injustice. In M. A. Peters (Ed.), *Encyclopedia of Educational Philosophy and Theory* (pp. 3–8). Springer.

Dussel, E. (1993). Eurocentrism and modernity (Introduction to the Frankfurt Lectures). *Boundary 2, 20*(3), 65–76.

Dussel, E. (2011). *Politics of liberation: A critical world history* (T. Cooper, Trans.). SCM Press.

Dussel, E. (1995). *The Invention of the Americas: Eclipse of "the Other" and the Myth of Modernity*. Continuum Press.
Erasmus, Z. (2020). Sylvia Wynter's Theory of the Human: Counter-, Not Post-Humanist. *Theory, Culture & Society, 37*(6), 47–65.
Fanon, F. (1963). *The Wretched of the Earth*. Grove Press.
Fricker, M. (2007). *Epistemic Injustice: Power and the Ethics of Knowing*. Oxford University Press.
Galtung, J. (1969). Violence, Peace and Peace Research. *Journal of Peace Research, 6*(3), 167–191.
Gildea, R. (2019). *Empires of the Mind: The Colonial Past and the Politics of the Present*. Cambridge University Press.
Goody, J. (2006). *The Theft of History*. Cambridge University Press.
Gordon, L. R. (2022). *Fear of Black Consciousness*. Farrar, Staus and Giroux.
Grosfoguel, R. (2007). The Epistemic Decolonial Turn: Beyond Political-Economy Paradigms. *Cultural Studies, 21*(2–3), 211–223.
Grosfoguel, R. (2013). The Structure of Knowledge in Westernized Universities: Epistemic Racism/Sexism and the Four Genocides/Epistemicides of the Long 16th Century. *Human Architecture: Journal of the Sociology of Self-Knowledge, 11*(1), 73–90.
Grosfoguel, R. (2019). What Is Racism? Zone of Being and Zone of Non-Being in the Work of Frantz Fanon and Boaventura de Sousa Santos. In J. Cupples & R. Grosfoguel (Eds.), *Unsettling Eurocentrism in the Westernized University* (pp. 264–273). Routledge.
Guha, R. (1983). *Elementary Aspects of Peasant Insurgency in Colonial India*. Duke University Press.
Guha, R. (1997). *Dominance Without Hegemony: History and Power in Colonial India*. Harvard University Press.
Hartman, S. V. (1997). *Scenes of Subjection: Terror, Slavery and Self-Making in Nineteenth-Century America*. Oxford University Press.
Hountondji, P. J. (2002) *The Struggle for Meaning: Reflections on Philosophy, Culture, and Democracy in Africa* (J. Conteh-Morgan, Trans.). Ohio University Research in International Studies Africa Series No. 78.
Hountondji, P. J. (1990). Scientific Dependence in Africa Today. *Research in African Literatures, 21*(3), 5–15.
Hountondji, P. J. (Ed.). (1997). *Endogenous Knowledge: Research Trails*. CODESRIA Books.
Imam, A., Mama, A., & Sow F. (Eds.). (1997). *Engendering African Social Sciences*. CODESRIA Book Series.
Lorde, A. (1984). *Sister Outsider: Essays and Speeches*. Crossing Press.
Lugones, M. (2003). *Pilgrimages/Peregrinajes: Theorizing Coalitions Against Multiple Oppressions*. Rowman & Littlefield.
Lugones, M. (2007). Heterosexualism and the Colonial/Modern Gender System. *Hypatia, 22*(1), 186–209.

Maldonado-Torres, N. (2007). On the Coloniality of Being: Contributions to the Development of a Concept. *Cultural Studies, 21*(2–3), 240–270.

Maldonado-Torres, N. (2008). *Against War: Views from the Underside of Modernity*. Duke University Press.

Mamdani, M. (2007, October 1–33). *Political Violence and State Formation in Post-Colonial Africa* (International Development Centre Working Paper Series No. 1).

Manjapra, K. (2020). *Colonialism in Global Perspective*. Oxford University Press.

Mazrui, A. A. (1978). *Political Values and the Educated Class in Africa*. University of California Press.

Mbembe, A. (2001). *On the Postcolony*. University of California Press.

Mbembe, A. (2010). *On Private Indirect Government*. CODESRIA Books.

Mbembe, A. (2019). *Necropolitics*. Duke University Press.

Mbembe, A. (2021). *Out of the Dark Night: Essays on Decolonization*. Columbia University.

Memmi, A. (1957). *The Colonizer and the Colonized*. Beacon Press.

Mignolo, W. D. (1995). *The Dark Side of the Renaissance: Literacy, Territoriality, and Colonization*. The University of Michigan Press.

Mignolo, W. D. (2012). *Local histories/global designs: Coloniality, subaltern knowledges and borderthinking*. Princeton University press.

Motta, S. C. (2018 [1965]). *Liminal Subjects: Weaving (Our) Liberations*. Rowman & Littlefield.

Mudimbe, V. Y. (1988). *The Invention of Africa: Gnosis, Philosophy and the Order of Knowledge*. Indiana University Press.

Mudimbe, V. Y. (1994). *The Idea of Africa*. Indiana University Press.

Mudimbe, V. Y. (2013). *On African Fault Lines: Meditations on Alterity Politics*. University of KwaZulu-Natal Press.

Nandy, A. (1983). *The Intimate Enemy: Loss and Recovery of Self under Colonialism*. Oxford University Press.

Ndlovu-Gatsheni, S. J. (2013). *Empire, Global Coloniality and African Subjectivity*. Berghahn Books.

Ndlovu-Gatsheni, S. J. (2018a). *Epistemic Freedom in Africa: Deprovincialization and Decolonization*. Routledge.

Ndlovu-Gatsheni, S. J. (2018b). Metaphysical Empire, Linguicides and Cultural Imperialism. *The English Academy Review: A Journal of English Studies, 35*(2), 96–115.

Ndlovu-Gatsheni, S. J. (2020). *Decolonization, Development and Knowledge in Africa: Turning Over a New Leaf*. Routledge.

Ndlovu-Gatsheni, S. J. (2021). The Cognitive Empire, Politics of Knowledge and Africa Intellectual Productions: Reflections on Struggles for Epistemic Freedom and Resurgence of Decolonization in the Twenty-First Century. *Third World Quarterly, 42*(5), 882–901.

Ngũgĩ wa Thiong'o. (1986). *Decolonising the Mind: The Politics of Language in African Literature*. James Currey.

Ngũgĩ wa Thiong'o. (1993). *Moving the Centre: Struggles for Cultural Freedom*. James Currey.

Ngũgĩ wa Thiong'o. (2009). *Something Torn and New: An African Renaissance*. Basic Civitas Books.

Ngũgĩ wa Thiong'o. (2012). *Globalectics: Theory and The Politics of Knowing*. Columbia University Press.

Nigam, A. (2020). *Decolonizing Theory: Thinking Across Traditions*. Bloomsbury India.

Nkrumah, K. (1965). *Neocolonialism: The Last Stage of Imperialism*. Monthly Review Press.

Quijano, A. (2000). Coloniality of Power, Eurocentrism, and Latin America. *Nepantla: Views from the South, 1*(3), 533–579.

Robinson, C. J. (1983). *Black Marxism: The Making of the Black Radical Tradition*. Zed Press.

Robinson, C. (2000). *Black Marxism: The Making of the Black Radical Tradition*. University of North Carolina Press.

Said, E. W. (1993). *Culture and Imperialism*. Vintage Books.

Sanin-Restrepo, R. (2016) *Decolonizing Democracy: Power in a Solid State*. Rowman & Littlefield.

Sanin-Restrepo, R. (2020). Decrypting the City: The Global Process of Urbanization as the Core of Capitalism, Coloniality and the Destruction of Democratic Politics of Our Times. In A. Osman (Ed.), *Cities, Space and Power: The Built Environment in Emerging Economies (BEinEE): Cities, Space and Transformation* (Vol. 1, pp. 1–27). AOSIS Press.

Santos, B. D. S. (2007). Beyond Abyssal Thinking: From Global Lines to Ecologies of Knowledges. *Binghamton University Review, 30*(1), 45–89.

Santos, B. D. S. (2014). *Epistemologies of the South: Justice against Epistemicide*. Paradigm Publishers.

Santos, B. D. S. (2018). *The End of the Cognitive Empire: The Coming of Age of Epistemologies of the South*. Duke University Press.

Schmitt, C. (2006). *The Nomos of the Earth in the International Law of the Jus Publican Europaeum*. Telos Press.

Smith, L. T. (1999). *Decolonizing Methodologies: Research and Indigenous Peoples*. Zed Books and Otago University Press.

Spivak, G. C. (1988). Can the Subaltern Speak? In C. Nelson & L. Grossberg (Eds.), *Marxism and Interpretations of Culture* (pp. 271–313). University of Illinois Press.

Suárez-Krabbe, J. (2015). *Race, Rights and Rebels: Alternatives to Human Rights and Development from the Global South*. Rowman & Littlefield.

Vergas, J. H. C., & Jung, M.-K. (2021). Antiblackness of the Social and the Human. In M.-K. Jung & J. H. C. Vargas (Eds.), *Antiblackness* (pp. 1–14). Duke University Press.

Verges, F. (2022). *A Feminist Theory of Violence*. Pluto Press.

Walcott, R. (2014). The Problem of the Human: Black Ontologies and "the Coloniality of Our Being. In S. Broeck & C. Junker (Eds.), *Postcoloniality-Decoloniality-Black Critique: Joints and Fissures* (pp. 93–108). Campus Verlag.

Wynter, S. (1995). 1492: A New World View. In V. L. Hyatt & R. Nettleford (Eds.), *Race, Discourse, and the Origin of the Americas: A New World View* (pp. 5–57). Smithsonian Institution Press.

Wynter, S. (2003). Unsettling the Coloniality of Being/Power/Truth/Freedom: Towards the Human, After Man, Its Overrepresentation—An Argument. *CR: The New Centennial Review, 3*(3), 257–337.

Wynter, S. (2001). Towards the Sociogenic Principle: Fanon, Identity, the Puzzle of Conscious Experience, and What It is Like to Be 'Black.' In M. Durán-Cogan & A. Gómez-Moriana (Eds.), *National Identities and Sociopolitical Changes in Latin America* (pp. 30–66). Routledge.

Zizek, S. (2008). *Violence: Six Sideways Reflection*. Picardo.

# Technologies of Violence in Africa

Wesley Mwatwara and Obert Bernard Mlambo

## 1 Introduction

In 2023, that Africa stands out as one of the continents with the largest ongoing violent armed conflicts is beyond doubt, and often the world's attention is caught by some of most horrible images of the vagaries of violent conflict on society especially non-combatants. Indeed, Tiyambe Zeleza (2008: 7) has observed that violence against unarmed civilians has been on the rise in African conflicts as militants thrive "on perpetrating systematic violence against civilians to demonstrate the incapacity of the state to protect them." While significant effort has been made by both state and non-state actors to reduce the incidence of violent conflict, the continent continues to feature a number of countries that are expected to continue having high levels of armed violence including Somalia, the Democratic Republic of the Congo, Central African Republic, South Sudan, Sudan, Burundi, Libya, Cameroon, Angola, and Chad (Cillier, 2018). Prior to 2000, and in the early 2000s, countries such as Liberia, Sierra Leone, Zaire, Burundi, Rwanda, Somalia,

W. Mwatwara (✉)
Department of Art & Culture, History, and Antiquity, Vrije Universiteit Amsterdam and Research Associate, Walter Sisulu University, Amsterdam, Netherlands
e-mail: w.mwatwara@vu.nl

O. B. Mlambo
Classical Studies Section, School of Languages and Literatures, Rhodes University, Makhanda, South Africa

Côte d'Ivoire, and Guinea-Bissau experienced crippling conflicts and civil strife in which violence and incessant killings were prevalent (Annan, 2014).

Although by 2023, it was broadly accepted that there had been a general decrease in the prevalence of violent conflict, new modes of violent conflict had also emerged. Violent insurgencies have increased in Mali, Niger and Mauritania as well as low intensity conflicts within relatively stable countries like Ghana, Nigeria, and Senegal (Annan, 2014). In the Democratic Republic of Congo (DRC) war, an estimated three to four million lives were lost between 2002 and 2004. The vast majority of these victims died not from bullets, but as a result of malnutrition and disease (Wordofa, 2010). Furthermore, as the Darfur conflict also shows, violent conflict claims lives not just through bullet wounds, but also through the broader erosion of human security and by breeding more poverty (ibid.). Given the prevalence of violent conflict, it is, therefore, not surprising that historiographically, much is known about armed violence in Africa from the cusp of independence in the early 1960s to the present. In particular, ethnicity, poverty, greed, and oppression have been listed among the major drivers of violent conflicts and civil strife within and among communities and states in the subregion. The costs and consequences of violent conflicts are immense, affecting society, the economy, and the environment through deaths and injuries, sexual crimes and intimidation, population dislocations within and across national borders, the devastation of the ecosystem, agricultural lands and wildlife, the destruction of society's material and mechanical infrastructures, and outflow of resources including "capital flight" and "brain drain" (Zeleza, 2008: 23).

Yet since 2000, there has also been both change and continuity in how armed violence has been meted on African societies. Between 2001 and 2023, recurrent violent uprisings, skirmishes between various armed groups, and spates of lynchings in countries such as Mozambique and Sudan have been apparent and have added another dimension to the effect of warfare on society (de Brito, 2017). For instance, in March 2021, the world got to know about the armed violence that had been going on in northern Mozambique for almost three years when armed militants killed and injured thousands in Mocimboa da Praia (Bonate, 2019; Fabricius, 2017; Hanlon, 2018). Elsewhere, in October 2022, in the eastern DRC, civilians were forced to flee to neighbouring countries such as Rwanda and Uganda for safety. Indeed, over 120 armed groups operate in eastern DRC, a region which hosts around 4.5 million internally displaced people—the highest number in Africa (CROrg, n.d.). Furthermore, between 11 April and 10 May 2023, armed clashes between the military and the paramilitary group Rapid Support Forces (RSF) in the Sudanese capital Khartoum resulted in hundreds of deaths (de Waal,

2023). By 10 May, the conflict had claimed the lives of 604 people and injured 5,100, while over 700,000 had been displaced internally (DW, 2023). These figures were in addition to 3.7 million people who had already been internally displaced before the conflict (ibid.). These conflicts offer vignettes of the challenges that military conflict has brought to both civilians and state operators since the turn of the century. Thus, it remains important to study how combatants (youths, rebels, government security forces, and religious sects) have systematically appropriated various arts, devices, systems, tools, materials, procedures, and knowledge in order to commit their violence usually on non-combatants. As this chapter will demonstrate, the complexity of actors in African conflicts and their roles in controlling technology, diplomacy, information, territory, and economies also complicate the technologies of violence.

Given the opacity of war-time violence in Africa, modes of dealing with these vagaries have also developed over time as society attempts to heal from scars left by war. Thus, the proliferation of cleansing ceremonies for both victims and perpetrators in war and post-war societies speak to issues connected to curing technologies of violence's residual effects. Indeed, as Alcinda Honwana (1996) has argued, these ceremonies are aimed at "re-humanizing those de-humanized by an intensity of violence that was widely seen by Mozambicans [read Africans] as irreducible to individual human actors." So grievous are the technologies of violence that one survivor has described the war situation as turning people into animals. Helder, a survivor of the Mozambican Civil War, explained:

> I know the man who killed my uncle. I greet him. I talk to him. I can drink with him. *It was the war that killed. Not people. Because during the war people were animals. Now we are not. And we should forget about when we were animals* [italics for emphasis]. It was no good. (Bertelsen, 2021)

The above anecdote attests to a soldier's body deployed by the state or bodies of armed bands, and their deployment by rogue individuals wielding state power. Such bodies can conceptually be understood as a technology of violence. Following Bourdieu's (1977) concept and characterization of social space as dependent on the rank of the human beings who move within the space, their sex and gender, their age, their hierarchical relationships, and the kind of social practice in which they engage, it is possible to conceptualize activities by armed soldiers deployed to man political space as a technology of violence. What is more, Michel Foucault conceptualized how the constitution of activity centrally consists in the fashioning of human bodies' aptitudes within disciplinary practices and performativity (Foucault,

1979: 138; see also Butler, 2004). Foucault's theoretical perspective on the human body allows visualization of how armed soldiers or groups function through their bodies and their guns, as a technology of violence. Humans operating as soldiers are in this sense a technology of armed violence operating like machines. The movement of well-trained soldiers in the streets of Harare, for example, figure the soldier's body as a part of the weapons system powered by his physical abilities and training (see Phang). Mlambo (2022: 174) describes the deployment and appearances of Zimbabwe's liberation war veterans in the streets of Harare by the late president Robert Mugabe's government in palpable ways that suggest the spectacle of a military, violent, and threatening group. Their ritualistic assembling, marching and dancing, Mlambo argued, clearly fused the masculine, the beefy, the aggressive, the husky and the athletic as they showed the grand leap, the stamping of the feet, and the vigorous movements of their bodies which all acquired martial and muscular connotations. In August 2018 and February 2019, soldiers were deployed by the Zimbabwean state to quell protests during which they strutted and postured their physical toughness and their habits of combat in military fatigues in Harare, which resulted in the deaths of civilians from gunshot wounds.

A significant variable in the manufacture and dispensation of violence in Africa since the turn of the century has been the emergence of warlords and "terrorists" with no capability for taking over or restructuring state power, which in turn breeds their banditry as well as their "lack of interest in exercising state power" (Zeleza, 2008: 7). Post-Siad Barre Somalia stands out as a typical example of social banditry in postcolonial Africa which has led to "great loss of life" and prolonged warfare between ethnic and regional militias which "threaten the viability of the nation-state" (ibid.). Overall, incessant conflict has led to the spread of infectious disease, chronic hunger and malnutrition, lack of water, the destruction of private and public property, and the disruption of basic social services such as education and health (Wordofa, 2010). In the following section we frame the terms "technology" and "violence" in the context of the African continent.

## 2  Concepts: "Technology" and "Violence"

This chapter's focus is on technologies of violence in Africa, consequently, we would like to furnish some reflections on the word "technology." Misa (2003: 7) has described technology as a body of knowledge about the useful arts and their systematic deployment. Misa also mentions a range of examples of useful arts in the practice of violence: systems, materials, devices, tools, procedures, and knowledge for practical tasks. Thus, technologies of violence may be understood as systems or methods of doing violence. These are a complex of industries and devices— materials, machines and processes through which violence is produced. Technologies of violence comprise those forms of technology which are designed and most useful for violence and violent conflict. These include, among other things, weapons of various kinds, as well as "technologies of repression," such as methods of torture and incarceration. It is important to indicate that the technology of weapons can only exist in the presence of other support systems. Thus, we make particular mention of transport, communication, geography, infrastructure, and water sources, that play a role in facilitating technologies of violence in Africa.

Violence may involve injury or enforcing of the will. We apply the term "violence" to include actions involving application of force in its crude and subtle processes. These two modes of violence; the subtle and the crude range from violence's visible and tangible forms like warfare to its abstruse expressions, for example, the imposition by a powerful individual or group of ways of thinking that favour submission (Mlambo, forthcoming). In this respect, ideology becomes a subtle expression of violence in manufacturing consent and loyalty, which operates beyond the torture chamber and the prison (see McDonough, 2016: 78 cited in Mlambo, forthcoming). To preserve power, African governments also use spies. There is also widespread use of hit squads to eliminate political enemies and use of lawfare to stifle freedoms of speech, social and political activities deemed dangerous to the ruling elites, and to capture institutions of learning as potential breeding grounds for independence and self-confidence. We, therefore, examine the various forms of violence and processes through which violence in Africa is unleashed as a systematic appropriation of useful arts, devices, systems, tools, materials, procedures, and knowledge to effect practical tasks (Misa, 2003), and how such actions and processes are developed and appropriated into versions and sub-versions of technologies of violence in Africa.

## 3  The New Millennium

The close of the twentieth century and the beginning of the twenty-first offered renewed, albeit misplaced, hope for a more peaceable global society in general and in Africa in particular. Generally, even though there has been a decline in large-scale violent conflict and civil strife, pockets of simmering tensions, insurgency, and the re-emergence of coups in countries like Zimbabwe, Guinea-Bissau, Chad, Niger, Madagascar, Burkina Faso, Sudan, and Mali; as well as insurgency in Mali, Niger, and Mauritania are serious sources of the uncertainty of lasting peace (Annan, 2014). Between 2000 and 2003, there were high numbers of cases of rape and torture, and high death rates, hence, for example, the 2009 report of the Liberian Truth and Reconciliation Commission (TRC) indicated that 250,000 people were killed in the almost 14-year conflict and one million displaced. The improvement of communicative power in Africa during this period brought new dimensions to how violence was dispensed. For instance, radio broadcasts by Hutu extremists were found to have accelerated the production of violence against the Tutsi during the Rwandan Genocide (Warren, 2015). In countries like Zimbabwe, Uganda, and Kenya, digital technologies have been deployed by political elites to foment hatred among rival political parties leading to violence. Yet paradoxically, the same communication technologies were also used to foster peace in the postconflict phase. For example, in the Economic Community of West African States (ECOWAS) region, the most commonly used technology for peacebuilding in 2021was social media, which was used to conduct trainings, run online campaigns for sensitization and awareness raising on various social issues, as well as for storytelling and countering harmful narratives online (Buildup, 2022). Peacebuilders have tapped into the youth's disposition towards digital platforms to connect with them.

In this period, the region also faced a serious problem of the proliferation of small arms. In 2011, West Africa alone hosted about seven to ten million of the world's illegal SALW as well as eight million out of the 100 million circulating in Africa. Critically as technologies of violence, 77,000 of these small arms were within the control of West African insurgent groups (Ebo & Mazel, 2003). Arguably, there is an indelible link between the proliferation of these weapons and the fact that small arms and light weapons account for most of the African continent's conflict-related deaths. At regional level, the precarity of the situation is better placed into context when considering that out of an estimated 100 million light weapons that circulate in Africa, about eight million are in the hands of non-state actors in West Africa (Banini, 2023). Furthermore, the vibrant nature of the illegal weapons market complicates the situation. Between 2000 and 2011, Côte d'Ivoire under Laurent Gbagbo was one of the top violators of the small arms conventions as it brazenly purchased weapons using illegal documents (ibid.). In the 2010 election, won by Alassane Ouattara, Gbagbo procured weapons illegally to hold on to political power while, in response, Ouattara's fighters solicited illicit small arms from foreign and from neighbouring sources (ibid.). Similar acts of arms proliferation were happening in Burkina Faso, which obtained authorization for the shipment of 68 tonnes of defence equipment and ammunition, which, however, ended up in Liberia in March 1999. Similarly, Guinea obtained military equipment for Liberia in a series of shipments from Kyrgyzstan, Moldova, and Slovakia in 2000 and 2001 as did Côte d'Ivoire, which bought five million cartridges from the Ukraine for Liberia in July 2000 (ibid.). In 2003, there were serious allegations that Guinean troops in the United Nations Mission in Sierra Leone (UNAMSIL) regularly supplied weapons to the Liberian rebels (Vines, 2005).

## 4 End of Old-Type Wars

The period after 2000 saw Africa's geopolitical importance to European powers and the USA skyrocket due to the "war on terror" they were mounting against "militant" Islam. In particular, Africa's "fragile" states were perceived as potential sanctuaries of global terrorist networks, and the need for "safe" energy resources outside the volatile Middle East (Zeleza, 2008: 13). Yet this geopolitical consideration by western countries had a severe impact on African denizens as the

> ...war on terror provided alibis for governments, [...] as well as international agencies, to violate or vitiate their human rights commitments and to tighten asylum laws and policies. In the meantime, military transfers to countries with poor human rights records have increased which portends ill for human rights. (ibid.: 14)

This window allowed many African governments to

> pass broadly, badly or cynically worded anti-terrorism laws and other draconian procedural measures, and to set up special courts or allow special rules of evidence that violate fair trial rights, which they use to limit civil rights and freedoms, and to harass, intimidate, and imprison and crackdown on political opponents [...] helping to strengthen or restore a culture of impunity among the security services in many countries. (ibid.)

Countries such as Morocco and Zimbabwe witnessed "a sharp escalation of state-sponsored intimidation, torture, arbitrary arrests and political killings, and orchestrated attacks on the independence of the media and the judiciary" (ibid.).

Although the global war on terror had these consequences, Chinese investment and geostrategic involvement in Africa during the same period also had a significant impact. While Chinese trade, investment, and infrastructure aid have fundamentally reshaped Africa's developmental trajectory, its rise has also posed a "security dilemma" not only in the global balance of power but also in the technologies of violence as the US seeks to stifle its rise (Ayabei, 2017). Whereas, as already noted, Africa has a serious challenge with small weapons proliferation to both state and non-state actors, China further complicated this quandary through alleged "irresponsible" arms transfers to African governments in exchange of minerals (Ayabei, 2017: 32). For instance, Chinese military arms exacerbated the Darfur Crisis (2003–2020) where they were utilized to commit serious human rights abuses (ibid.). From Darfur to Zimbabwe, Democratic Republic of Congo (DRC) to Guinea, China has been criticized for its role in causing conflicts in Africa. Yet, it is important to underscore the fact that it is not only the Western Europeans and the USA that have exacerbated existing conflict trends within Africa. Similarly, some Russians and Ukrainians allegedly registered front companies in Ghana and tried to use false letterheads from the Ghanaian defence and foreign ministries to sell weapons in 2003 (ibid.).

In Southern Africa, the infamous purchase of arms, tankers, and water cannons by the Robert Mugabe government just after the March 2008 electoral loss stands out as an example of how African governments gear up to brutalize citizens during elections. At the centre of the conflict was a Chinese ship loaded with armaments for Zimbabwe which put pressure on both China and South Africa after dockworkers refused to unload the cargo pointing out that it was destined to be used in Mugabe's crackdown on his rivals after a disputed election (Dugger, 2008). Backed by South Africa's powerful trade unions, who vowed protests and threatened violence if the government tried to transport the weapons without them. Indeed, as Dugger observed:

> The Chinese ship, packed with ammunition, rockets and mortar bombs, quickly became a symbol of clashing approaches to the Zimbabwean dilemma: Should South Africa confront Zimbabwe's autocratic president, Robert Mugabe, in power for 28 years, or continue to pursue the policy of quiet diplomacy. (Dugger, 2008)

Paradoxically, Chinese involvement has not only escalated tensions but it has also played both a critical role in conflict resolution and postconflict reconstruction in supporting a political transition to a new independent republic of South Sudan (ibid.). China's involvement is largely influenced by its desire to protect oil interests in South Sudan yet it was one of several states including France, Iran, and Saudi Arabia that exported large amounts of small arms and light weapons and ammunition to Sudan. The scale of the human rights disaster and the killing of people and destruction of major parts of Darfur were massive: an estimated 1.6 million people were displaced within Darfur and 200,000 Sudanese refugees fled to Chad and thousands were killed (ibid.). Overall, by 2013, Chinese military involvement in African conflicts had earned China top position as the largest supplier of major conventional weapons in the world. Ironically, China believes that its arms exports enable African countries to guard their sovereignty from external threats and, therefore, do not have a negative effect on peace, security, and stability of the recipient region and the world as a whole (ibid.). The Chinese boast that their activities are not an interference into domestic politics in recipient countries yet these have been shown to entrench dictatorships and to tip the odds against democratic actors in the regions concerned.

The exploitation of natural resources by major powers is not a new phenomenon in Africa but it has also spawned the emergence of militant gangs/violent vigilante groups purporting to represent the interests of affected communities. Not surprisingly, therefore, the exploitation of natural resources amidst abject poverty has fuelled violence is countries like Mozambique (Appel, 2019). In Mozambique, the participation of several mercenary groups including the Wagner Group (Russian) and the South African Dyck Advisory Group demonstrates new dimensions in African conflicts, that is, mercenary groups that possess military hardware that state security forces actually do not possess. By their participation, these groups have also been accused of "obfuscating simple visions of a war comprising merely civilians, state forces and insurgents" (Bertelsen, 2021). In the Niger Delta, there have also emerged micro-level conflicts which have now become part of a complex conflict system that is issue-based, ethnic, and geographic in nature. Hundreds of criminal and politically motivated gangs have emerged including the Blood Suckers, the Gentlemen's Club, and the Royal House of Peace, the Niger Delta People's Volunteer Force, and the Niger Delta Vigilante Group which by 2004 were making threats to disrupt the oil industry with potential to impact on world oil prices for a short period (Vines, 2005: 354). Their criminal networks were supported by local politicians and were linked into regional networks, from Sao Tome, Liberia, Senegal, Côte d'Ivoire, and the Gambia, and international (involving Moroccans, Venezuelans, Lebanese, and French (Vines, 2005: 355). These groups have fuelled the crisis in the delta by employing large numbers of unemployed young people, empowering them with money and guns resulting in high levels of violence (ibid.). For instance, in October 2004 in Abuja two main armed groups, the Niger De People's Volunteer Force and the Niger Delta Vigilante Group agreed to a disarmament process under which 1,000 guns (mostly AK-47s) were surrendered while there were suspicions that the best weapons were retained (ibid.). This conflict led to several kidnappings of expatriates, casualties, and the increased use of sophisticated weaponry by militant groups such as the Movement for the Emancipation of the Niger Delta (MEND) (Annan, 2014: 3).

Besides these local level armed groups, there are also groups such as Boko Haram and the Lord's Resistance Army that operate regionally (Cillier, 2018: 3). In the post-2000 period, the link between transnational organized crime and terrorism grew as Africa's violent groupings coalesced with their Middle Eastern counterparts, firstly, with al Qaeda and, later, the Islamic State (ISIL) (ibid.). Although the absolute number of fatalities in African conflicts involving these warmongers has been declining since the turn of the century, the level of barbarity is yet to be properly interrogated. However, from 2001 to 2017 the seven countries that experienced the highest number of fatalities were Sudan, Nigeria, the DRC, Somalia, South Sudan, the Central African Republic (CAR), and Libya (ibid.: 5).

## 5   Technology of Xenophobic and Genocidal Violence in Africa

René Girard (1989) has conceptualized the practice of myth-making to justify extermination of ethnic groups as a technology of violence (Mlambo, forthcoming). This technology has been appropriated in Africa in the context of collective violence against minority groups. The logic of myth-making involves identifying an ethnic group to target as a scapegoat for whatever accusations. Girard's well-specified scapegoat theory explains internal violence within a society as reflecting a need to distinguish self from other (Mlambo, forthcoming). This genocidal violence occurs when a kind of purgation is done against an ethnic group, which in Girardian terms, is accomplished as an expulsion of a scapegoat. We can see a reflection of his pattern in contemporary hostility to immigration in countries like South Africa and Botswana where outsiders are excluded and even killed. We must hasten to indicate that we do not here refer to actual myths, like that of Oedipus, but to historical events in which the practice of making them conform to a mythical pattern may be described as a technology, whereby myths rationalize episodes of violence.

There is discrimination and sometimes violence meted against minority groups for not having belonged to the formal societal structure in a given country. Zimbabweans, for example, are treated as *Makwerekwere* (a derogatory term used by South Africans to refer to foreign Africans) in Botswana and in South Africa. Their real crime in most cases is that of doing exceptionally better than South Africans at work places. The fight by Zimbabweans on special permits which the South African had scrapped unconstitutionally has largely been viewed by ordinary South Africans as intransigency and, in turn, has fomented the hatred of Zimbabweans within the country (Venter, 2023). Similarly, belief in the sinister but undefinable advantages in commerce enjoyed by Jews in English society justifies discrimination against them—whereas their real offence is always to have been outside the formal structure of Christendom.

Mogekwu (2005) argues that xenophobes usually act out of ignorance about the people they hate, and narrowly perceive them as threats (Solomon & Kosaka, 2013, 2). Moreover, Misago et al. (2015: 13) assert that xenophobic expressions vary from discriminatory attitudes and remarks to institutional and social exclusion of particular groups, to harassment and overt forms of interpersonal and collective violence. Minority groups in some cases in Africa are stereotypical. A Zimbabwean living in South Africa reported to us an incident where he was verbally abused by a South African taxi driver for causing electricity shortages in South Africa. In his rant, the taxi driver was bitter that the South African government was supplying Zimbabwe with electricity, thus causing shortages in South Africa. Xenophobic violence is usually inflicted on people accused of various trumped-up charges: theft, drugs, sexual crimes, including rape, and so on. Thus, when foreign nationals were persecuted in Botswana or South Africa, their persecutors convinced themselves that a threat was posed to society as a whole by a small number of people, despite their relative weakness. The mechanism sought a significant cause of a crisis targeting a foreigner or a group of foreigners as a scapegoat. Such stereotypical accusations demonstrate the insignificance of small groups or the individual. A technology of violence, thus, as a mechanism of violence in the accusations and in the acts of brutality. A violent mob, for example, searches for an accessible cause that would appease its appetite for violence (see Girard, 1989: 16). In Girard's formulation, a mob, in which there is an act of "mobilization" works like a military operation against a wanted enemy, to purge the community of elements that corrupt and undermine it. The mobs that lynch and burn people with tyres and inflammable materials in

South Africa are cases in point. This scourge of xenophobic violence spiralled in most South African cities in recent years.

## 6   Technologies of Infrastructure and Geography in Africa

In this section, we discuss how violence is determined by technologies of infrastructure and the geography of the African continent. Rebel groups have taken advantage of the forests in central Africa. Joseph Kony has for many decades terrorized civilians in Uganda, CAR, and the Democratic Republic of Congo, taking advantage of the dense forests in the region. The same can be said about Alfonso Dhlakama's RENAMO (Resistência Nacional Mocambicana) in Mozambique. The forests are still enabling rebel activities, and it has not been possible for the Mozambican government to hunt down the RENAMO insurgent movement, as the forests provide affordances to banditry. The word "affordance" was originally used by James Gibson (1986), to refer to what an environment furnishes or provides to the living creatures depending on it. We deploy it to refer to the untamed forests in Africa as affording conditions that furnish or equip rebel or insurgent movements in Africa. Sun Tzu Wu (Giles, trans. 1910) observed that the art of war is governed by five factors: (1) the Moral Law, (2) Heaven, (3) Earth, (4) the Commander, and (5) method and discipline (Sun Tzu Wu, Giles, trans. 1910: 3). For our purposes, we will single out just one to illustrate the role of geographical terrain in violent conflict in Africa, namely: Earth which we conceptualize as the geographical terrain. Sun Tzu's insights in his *The Art of War* demonstrate how ancient technologies of violence cannot be fully appreciated without attention to the spaces within which warfare occurred (Mlambo, forthcoming). Violence is located in particular physical locations, and, as Clifford Ando (2019: 16) observed, focalizes war through the movements in space or terrains of armies. African geographical terrains involving the sea, mountains, rivers, deserts, flat plains, and forests are relevant to the operation of the systems of technologies of violence. For instance, piracy around the Horn of Africa by young Somalis has risen to a level serious enough for the international community to take concerted action to secure an international sea lane. As J. H. Ho (2009: 3) has shown, pirates usually target the Gulf of Aden, which is a transit point for 20,000 ships a year, and had seen the number of attacks on ships rising to, for instance, 111 in 2008 from 44 in 2007. Furthermore, forests have also played their part. Agrippah Mutambara's (2014) vivid account of the Rhodesian bush war is revealing of the role played by the dense rain forests and terrain in Eastern Zimbabwe and in Mozambique where he operated as a guerrilla fighter. The forests were conducive to guerrilla tactics. Guerrilla military strategies and tactics depended on the geographical terrain and its natural resources as providing a background to violence. In Nigeria, the Sambisa forest, is utilized as shelter by the Boko Haram terrorist organization and is believed to be where hostages from the Chibok schoolgirls kidnapping in April 2014 are kept (Okoli, 2019). Forests in the DRC and Liberia have also served as sources of resources for funding conflict (Van Solinge, 2008).

## 7   Religious Wars/Terrorism

Religion in Africa has increasingly functioned in important ways as a technology of violence. Brutal and indiscriminate attacks on Christian communities have been carried out by extremist Islamic groups, and justified as Allah's wars. Extremist Islamic movements have been used in recent years to extend and buttress martial power and to impose Sharia law and doctrine, and the Islamic way of life. The Boko Haram's and the ISIL's missions to create a caliphate in Nigeria and Mozambique respectively are recent examples of how religion has been weaponized by Islamic fundamentalists. Yet it is equally important to state that Christian religious movements have also been operating with similar visions. Joseph Kony's rebel group in north-east Uganda poses as a religious military force: the Lord's Resistance Army (Mlambo, 2017).

In the previous section, we have already noted that the "war on terror" resulted in the proliferation of militant non-state actors that cost civilians their lives and property. From 2013 to 2015, the increase in fatality levels was mostly driven by events in Nigeria associated with Boko Haram and the Nigerian military response to combat violent Islamist extremism (Cillier, 2018: 5). Whereas in 2010, only five countries experienced sustained activity from violent Islamist extremism (Algeria, Mali, Niger, Nigeria, and Somalia), that number grew to 12 countries (Algeria, Burkina Faso, Cameroon, Chad, Egypt, Kenya, Libya, Mali, Niger, Nigeria, Somalia, and Tunisia) by 2018 (ibid.). Long destabilized by several coups and ethnic tensions in the pre-2000 years, violent conflict resurfaced in Mali by the National Movement for the Liberation of Azawad (MNLA) Tuareg rebels and al Qaeda in the Islamic Magreb (AQIM) in 2007 and the coup d'état in 2012 resulted in killings, and mass forced displacement of civilians (Annan, 2014: 3). In Nigeria, the Boko Haram insurgency in northern Nigeria took many lives, displaced several thousand and destroyed state property (ibid.: 4). By 2015 and 2016, the number of conflicts in Africa was at an all-time high, the increase in the number of conflicts can in large part be explained by the rise of the Islamic State (IS) (Bakken & Rustad, 2018). In northern Mozambique, violence manifested itself through looting, murder, and seizure of political and military power (Morier-Genoud, 2020). Perpetrators of violence were allegedly linked to Somali Jihadists and IS/Daesh, but there was insufficient evidence to buttress the claim. Instead the influence of a local breakaway Islamic sect comprising young Mozambican men was emphasized (Bertelsen, 2021; Morier-Genoud, 2020).

In these conflicts with religious pretensions, young women and girls aged between 12 and 24 years have been the most vulnerable, with many being kidnapped by the insurgents and used as (sex) slaves or informants. In Nigeria, for instance, the whereabouts of many women kidnapped by Boko Haram remains unclear, while those rescued have not received professional therapy, hence, trauma continues to haunt them (Gichohi & Kishara, 2021). However, the creation of international links with either al Qaeda or ISIL escalated intra-group violence due to differing ideologies within these movements. Boko Haram connected to al Qaeda in the Islamic Maghreb in 2010 causing dissidence within the Nigerian movement resulting in a split in 2017, one faction retaining its connections to ISIL while the other returned to its original identity and autonomy (Morier-Genoud, 2020: 406). Thus, in a way, ISIL has become the main driver of conflicts that already existed before its dominance. Indeed, in 2017, five of the state-based conflicts in Africa in Chad, Libya, Mali, Nigeria, and Niger were related to ISIL (Bakken & Rustad, 2018). Furthermore, the number of non-state conflicts also increased dramatically during the same time peaking in 2017 with 50 non-state conflicts, compared to 24 in 2011 (ibid.).

In Nigeria, the asymmetric nature of the war against Boko Haram resulted in untold suffering among civilians and suspected enemy combatants. In fact, by 2015, Nigeria's military forces had extrajudicially killed 1200 persons, illegally arrested 20,000 young males, while 7,000 persons died due to conditions in military custody (Oriola, 2020: 13). Soldiers killed in battle also regularly received undignified treatment: Boko Haram routinely pours acid on the corpses of soldiers (ibid.). Boko Haram used a hybridized weaponization strategy: sophisticated technological equipment and tools made from indigenous knowledge ensconced in cultural beliefs and practices, particularly voodoo (ibid.: 14).

Another important part of the conflict picture is one-sided violence. One-sided violence is defined as violence against civilians by a formally organized group, which can be either the state or a non-state actor. From 2011, there was a substantial increase in the number of actors carrying out one-sided violence, the prominent one being Boko Haram in north-eastern Nigeria (Bakken & Rustad, 2018). There was a peak in such deaths in 2014 with 8,760 deaths, while in 2017, the number was 5,694 (ibid.). Indeed, by 2017, Boko Haram stood out as the worst perpetrator, followed by various groups in the CAR (ibid.). Yet it is important to underscore that the general consensus is that Boko Haram is "excessively and unnecessarily violent and deploys spectacular and atrocious means to kill" (ibid.). One observer reported, "[T]errorists or whatever are not supposed to carry something like RPG to kill one person. You are not to carry something like AA (antiaircraft missile) to fire somebody [...] But them, they will use it on one person" (Oriola, 2022: 16). Yet this violence has also been reported to be perpetrated by state security forces as children who were detained by the military claimed that were sexually assaulted while "Boko Haram treated us better" (Paquette, 2019). Suspected thousands of Boko Haram were tried secretly in military facilities in a dehumanizing manner (Burke, 2017).

As the venues, actors and mechanisms of war have become complex with the proliferation of intrastate wars, informal fighting forces, small arms, and terror tactics, the costs of war for women have risen (Zeleza, 2008: 21). Many more women have died from the indirect consequences of war including injuries, hunger, exhaustion, diseases, and the disruptions of flight, relocation, and economic devastation. Widowhood and the growth of female-headed households impose severe strains on women. Rape, sexual slavery, and forced marriages as well as increased rates of sexually transmitted infections including HIV/AIDS have emerged as some of the major war crimes. Women have fallen victim to different combatants and sometimes to peacekeeping forces, and wartime conditions generate increased demand for sexual services, thus promoting prostitution and the trafficking of women (ibid.). Yet women also participate in wars as combatants, active supporters, and provocateurs (ibid.). Such has been the level of systematic rape that the United Nations Population Fund (UNFPA) helped with the deliveries of 16,000 babies within one year (i.e., 2014–2015) in Boko Haram–ravaged north-eastern Nigeria. Boko Haram's strategy of systematic rape and deliberate attempt to produce progeny from such rapes meant that women's bodies became an integral part of armed conflict and terrorism (Oriola, 2017: 108). Other human costs that are less immediately visible are psychological stress and trauma, for example the impact of the disintegration of families and communities, life as a child soldier and the rape of women and girls. In the long term, violent conflict has wiped out the useful and essential "social fabrics" and "social cohesion" which is more costly to a society than destabilized governments, undermined economies, and damaged major infrastructure (Wordofa, 2010: 92).

## 8 Conclusion

This chapter has demonstrated that there are several technologies of violence that currently dominate Africa. A significant variable in the manufacture and dispensation of violence in Africa since the turn of the century has been the emergence of warlords and "terrorists" in countries such as post-1991 Somalia where social banditry now dominates. Incessant conflict has led to the weaponization of infectious disease, chronic hunger, and malnutrition. Violence and its attendant challenges such as death, lack of water, the destruction of private and public property, and the disruption of basic social services have had a serious impact on non-combatants. Violence has partly been determined by technologies of infrastructure and the geography of the African continent. Rebel groups have taken advantage of the dense forests in Uganda, Nigeria, CAR, and the DRC. Historically, military movements such as RENAMO had utilized forests in a similar fashion in Mozambique. Thus, forests provide affordances to banditry. Genocidal violence on ethnic minorities has also been on the rise across the continent, especially in terms of contemporary hostility to immigration in countries like South Africa and Botswana where outsiders are excluded and even killed. However, the improvement of communicative power in Africa during this period has brought new dimensions to how violence has been dispensed. For instance, in countries like Zimbabwe, Uganda, and Kenya, digital technologies have been deployed by political elites to foment hatred among rival political parties leading to violence. Yet paradoxically, the same communication technologies have also been used to foster peace in the postconflict phase. Indeed, social media has increasingly been used to conduct training, run online campaigns for sensitization and awareness raising on various social issues, as well as for storytelling and countering harmful narratives online. Peacebuilders have tapped into the youth's disposition towards digital platforms to connect with them.

# Bibliography

Annan, N. (2014). Violent Conflicts and Civil Strife in West Africa: Causes, Challenges and Prospects. *Stability: International Journal of Security & Development, 3*(1): 3, 1–16.

Ando, C. (2019). The Space and Time of Politics in Civil War. In C. Rosillo-Lopez (Ed.), *Communicating Public Opinion in the Roman Republic.* Historia Einzelschriften (pp. 175–188). Franz Steiner.

Appel, F. (2019). *Nietzsche Contra Democracy.* Cornell University Press.

Ayabei, C. (2017, February). The Rise of China and Conflicts in Africa: The Case of Sudan. *African Journal of Political Science and International Relations, 11*(2), 29–35.

Bakken I. V. & Rustad, S. A. (2018). *Conflict Trends in Africa, 1989–2017,* 4–27. Peace Research Institute Oslo.

Banini, D. (2023, May 12). West Africa Has a Small Weapons Crisis—Why Some Countries Are Better at Dealing With It Than Others. *The Conversation.* https://phys.org/news/2023-05-west-africa-small-weapons-crisiswhy.html. Accessed 13 May 2023.

Bertelsen, B. E. (2021). Civil War and the Non-Linearity of Time: Approaching a Mozambican Politics of Irreconciliation. *Journal of the Royal Anthropological Institute, 28*(S1), 50–64.

Bonate, L. (2019, June 14). *Why the Mozambican Government's Alliance with the Islamic Council of Mozambique Might Not End the Insurgency in Cabo Delgado.* Zitamar. https://zitamar.com/mozambican-governments-alliance-islamic-council-mozambique-might-not-endinsurgency-cabo-delgado. Accessed 27 January 2022.

Bourdieu, P. (1977). Outline of a Theory of Practice (R. Nice, Trans.). Cambridge University Press.

Buildup. (2022). *Digital Tech and Peacebuilding in West Africa.* https://howtobuildup.medium.com/digital-tech-and-peacebuilding-in-west-africa-23b42ae03158. Accessed 10 July 2023.

Burke, J. (2017). Secret Trial of Thousands of Boko Haram Suspects to Start in Nigeria. *The Guardian.* https://www.theguardian.com/world/2017/oct/09/nigeria-begin-secret-trials-thousands-boko-haram-suspects

Butler, J. (2004). *Precarious Life: The Powers of Mourning and Violence.* verso.

Camber W. T. (2015). Explosive Connections? Mass Media, Social Media, and the Geography of Collective Violence in African States. *Journal of Peace Research, 52*(3).

Cillier J. (2018). *Violence in Africa Trends, Drivers and Prospects to 2023.* Institute for Security Studies, Africa Report 12.

CR.Org. n.d. https://www.c-r.org/programme/east-and-central-africa/democratic-republic-congo-conflict-focus?gclid=Cj0KCQjwk5ibBhDqARIsACzmgLSOOubEH-Yw2lFbwiPEY9-DVhglg8Fkf0gt7NJIyoM2Ps2WbXV94jMaAvcCEALw_wcB. Accessed 5 November 2022.

de Brito, L., et al. (2017). Authoritarian Responsiveness and the Greve in Mozambique. *Food Riots, Food Rights and the Politics of Provisions*, 158–176.

De Waal, A. (2023). *Sudan Conflict: Hemedti—The Warlord Who Built a Paramilitary Force More Powerful Than the State*. https://theconversation.com/sudan-conflict-hemedti-the-warlord-who-built-a-paramilitary-force-more-powerful-than-the-state-203949. Accessed 9 May 2023.

Dugger, C. W. (2008, April 19). Zimbabwe Arms Shipped by China Spark an Uproar. *The New York Times*.

Ebo, A., & Mazel, L. (2003). Small Arms Control in West Africa: Monitoring the Implementation of Small Arms Controls (MISAC). *International Alert*.

Fabricius, P. (2017, October 27). *Mozambique: First Islamist Attacks Shock the Region*. Institute for Security Studies (Tshwane/Pretoria). http://allafrica.com/stories/201710280066.html

Foucault, M. (1979). *Discipline and Punish: The Birth of the Prison* (A. M. Sheridan Smith, Trans.). Vintage.

Gibson, J. J. (1986). *The Ecological Approach to Visual Perception*. Taylor & Francis.

Gichohi, W., & Kishara, W. (2021). *Wilton Park Report Conflict and Peacebuilding in Mozambique*, Tuesday 21–Wednesday 22 September, WP1761V2.

Girard, R. (1989). *The Scapegoat* (Y. Freccero, Trans.). The John Hopkins University Press.

Hanlon, J. (2018, June 19). Mozambique's Insurgency: A New Boko Haram or Youth Demanding an End to Marginalisation? *Blog LSE*. https://blogs.lse.ac.uk/africaatlse/2018/06/19/mozambiques-insurgency-a-new-boko-haram-or-youth-demanding-an-end-tomarginalisation. Accessed 27 January 2022.

Ho, J. H., 2009. Piracy around the Horn of Africa. *The Korean Journal of Defense Analysis*, 21(4).

Honwana, A. M. R. M. (1996). *Spiritual Agency and Self-Renewal in Southern Mozambique* (Doctoral Dissertation, School of Oriental and African Studies, University of London).

McDonough, S. J. (2016). A Question of Faith? Persecution and Political Centralization in the Sasanian Empire of Yazdgard II (438–457 CE). In H. A. Drake (Ed.), *Violence in Late Antiquity: Perceptions and Practices* (pp. 69–84). Routledge.

Misa, T. J. (2003). The Compelling Tangle of Modernity and Technology. In T. J. Misa, P. Brey, & A. Feenberg (Eds.), *Modernity and Technology* (pp. 1–30). Massachusetts Institute of Technology.

Misago, J. P., Freemantle, I., & Landau, L. B. (2015). *"Protection from Xenophobia: An Evaluation of UNHCR's Regional Office for Southern Africa's Xenophobia-Related programmes*. UNHCR.

Mlambo Obert B. (2017). I Am Evelyn Amony: Reclaiming My Life from the Lord's Resistance Army. *Afrikanistik Aegyptologie Online, 14*. https://www.afrikanistik-aegyptologie-online.de/archiv/2017/4546. Accessed 22 May 2023.

Mlambo, O. B. (forthcoming) Technologies of Violence in Antiquity. In F. McHardy (Ed.), *A Cultural History of Violence in Antiquity*. Bloomsbury Academic Publishers.

Mlambo, O. B. (2022). *Land Expropriation in Ancient Rome and Contemporary Zimbabwe: Veterans, Masculinity and War.* Bloomsbury Academic Publishers.

Mogekwu, M. (2005). African Union: Xenophobia as Poor Intercultural Communication. *Ecquid Novi, 26*(1), 5–20.

Morier-Genoud, E. (2020). The Jihadi Insurgency in Mozambique: Origins, Nature and Beginning. *Journal of Eastern African Studies, 14*, 3.

Mutambara, A. (2014). *The Rebel in Me: A ZANLA Guerrilla Commander in the Rhodesian Bush War, 1975–1980.* West Midlands: Co-published by Hellion and Co Ltd and 30° South Publishers Pvt Ltd.

Okoli, A. C. (2019). Boko Haram Insurgency and the Necessity for Trans-Territorial Forestland Governance in the Lower Lake Chad Basin. *African Journal on Conflict Resolution, 19*(1).

Oriola, T. (2020). Nigerian Troops in the War Against Boko Haram: The Civilian–Military Leadership Interest Convergence Thesis. *Armed Forces & Society 2022, 0*(0).

Oriola, T. (2022). Nigerian Troops in the War Against Boko Haram: The Civilian–Military Leadership Interest Convergence Thesis. *Armed Forces and Society*, 13.

Oriola, T. B. (2017). 'Unwilling Cocoons': Boko Haram's War Against Women. *Studies in Conflict and Terrorism* 40(2).

Paquette, D. (2019). *Nigerian Children Who Escaped Boko Haram Say They Faced Another 'Prison': Military Detention.* Washingtonpost.com.

Perlo-Freeman, S., Solmirano, C., & Wilandh, H. (2013). Global Developments in Military Expenditure. *SIPRI Yearbook, 2013*, 127–134.

Phang, S. E. (2008). *Roman Military Service: Ideologies of Discipline in the Late Republic and Early Principate.* Cambridge University Press.

Solomon, H., & Kosaka, H. (2013). Xenophobia in South Africa: Reflections, Narratives and Recommendations. *Southern African Peace and Security Studies, 2*(2), 5–30.

Sudan Death Toll Climbs, With 700,000 Internally Displaced. https://www.dw.com/en/sudan-death-toll-climbs-with-700000-internally-displaced/a-65561649?maca=en-GK_RSS_SmartNews_Volltext_ENG-20051-xml-media. Accessed 10 May 2023.

Van Solinge, T. B. (2008). Eco-Crime: The Tropical Timber Trade. In *Organized Crime: Culture, Markets and Policies* (pp. 97–111). New York, NY: Springer New York.

Venter, C. (2023). *Court Gives One-Year Lifeline to 178,000 Zimbabwean Exemption Permit Holders.* https://www.iol.co.za/pretoria-news/news/court-gives-one-year-lifeline-to-178000-zimbabwean-exemption-permit-holders-928eef16-8304-42aa-b4d2-46b10465fdee. Accessed 10 July 2023.

Vines, A. (2005). Combating Light Weapons Proliferation in West Africa. *International Affairs, 81*(2).

Wordofa, D. (2010). Violent Conflicts Key Obstacles for Sub-Saharan Africa to Achieving the Millennium Development Goals—Where is the Evidence?" In R. Bowd & A. B. Chikwanha (Eds.), *Understanding Africa's Contemporary Conflicts: Origins, Challenges and Peacebuilding*. Institute for Security Studies Monographs, No. 173.

Zeleza, P.T. (2008). Introduction: The Causes and Costs of War In Africa: From Liberation Struggle to the "War on Terror." In A. Nhema & P. T. Zeleza (Eds.), *The Roots of African Conflicts: The Causes and Costs*. Ohio University Press.

# Border Violence in Africa

## Rachel Ibreck and Souhayel Weslety

Africa's borders are notorious for their "arbitrary" origins in colonial designs (Herbst, 1989). But borders are always more than static boundary lines on a map. They are also relations and "processes" with legal, institutional, and sociocultural dimensions (Kearney, 2004: 131) that vary over time and space. They work to classify and filter people, producing "differentiated forms of access and rights" (Casas-Cortes et al., 2015: 57), and intervening in the making of social identities, economic status, and political order (Kearney, 2004). From a critical standpoint, borders constitute expansive, versatile sites, or "borderscapes" through which sovereign power operates, and where "resistances and struggles" might also emerge (Brambilla & Jones, 2020). This provokes us to question how and in what ways borders are experienced and "embodied" (ibid.: 289) and to examine their relations to violence in Africa "from below," from the perspectives of people on the move.

For states, as for colonial authorities, borders explicitly function to produce sovereign power; they are "a tool of founding violence" (Brambilla & Jones, 2020: 290). Political authorities, therefore, strive to maintain physical boundaries and to dictate the political outcomes of border-crossings and cross-border exchanges. They employ borders as governance instruments to define

R. Ibreck (✉)
Goldsmiths, University of London, London, UK
e-mail: r.ibreck@gold.ac.uk

S. Weslety
Université Tunis Carthage, Tunis, Tunisia

and entrench political hierarchies, and to allocate economic opportunities. People seek, and sometimes attain, opportunities and freedoms by crossing borders. Yet the very existence of borders, and the discontinuities in access to rights between places on either side of them, produces the impetus for crossing and the grounds for contestation and violence (Jones, 2019: 37). This violence is not confined to incidents at crossing points, and instead permeates society and manifests in diverse locations and forms.

At first sight, border violence might be read as the criminal actions of armed groups or human traffickers operating in "lawless" environments at the peripheries of "weak states" that dominate media and policy discourses (e.g. UN, 2022). In practice, its scope is far more extensive, encompassing the actions of legal and security actors and mirroring a broader continuum of violence that stretches from physical to symbolic forms in warzones and unequal societies (see Scheper-Hughes & Bourgois, 2004). At the sharp end are mass deaths, murder, rape, and torture by both criminal and security actors at crossing points, or in the name of border control. Less overt are more routine repressive security practices such as the indefinite incarceration of migrants. Beyond this, processes of bordering are implicated in structural violence on global and individual scales—as Achiume (2019: 1519) argues: "national borders have played and continue to play in maintaining Third World subordination." Border logics are embedded in everyday norms and practices, fostering racism, discrimination, and gender-based violence (Tyszler, 2021). The commonality between these various modes of violence is that they are suffered by people on the move, whether fleeing conflicts and economic deprivation, or seeking opportunities, rights or protection with "horizons of hope" (Brambilla & Jones, 2020: 290). In this discussion, humanitarian categories that differentiate between refugees and migrants are immaterial—all are vulnerable to this violence (de Genova, 2016: 37).

The meaning of borders and their relations to violence has shifted over time in Africa, as elsewhere. With the rise of neoliberal globalization by the 1990s, economies opened but free markets were reified to the point that politically "the value of things" began "surpassing the value of people" (Mbembe, 2000: 260). Mobility increased for the rich but diminished for the poor, in the interests of capital: "laborers today are constrained by borders and therefore wages are artificially suppressed" (Jones, 2017: 166). The fundamental contradictions of market-led development were implicated in proliferating conflicts, widening economic inequalities, and deepening environmental crisis. But networked governance arrangements conspired to trap populations, promoting "containment" (Duffield, 1997) and bare survival at margins while the borders "multiplied" (Casas Cortes et al., 2015: 57). As

Mlambo and Chitando point out, borderlands are now among the spaces where violence is rampant; they are "combat zone[s] where people vie for power and its retention" (this volume). In particular, the continent's most strategic borders, located on routes and shorelines to Europe, have become intense sites of "necropolitical" violence (Tyszler, 2021; Van Houtum, 2010), determining "who matters and who does not, who is *disposable* and who is not" (Mbembe, 2003: 27).

This chapter focuses on the heterogenous forms of border violence occurring on refugee and migrant journeys along routes towards and across the Mediterranean from Africa to Europe. First, we situate this violence in context, exploring the history and meaning of borders on the African continent—their origins in colonial interventions, and their contemporary harnessing by European states. Second, we conceptualize the violence of Eurocentric border "externalization" in Africa, drawing upon previous studies. Finally, we present a case study of memories and experiences of border violence, based upon our ethnographic research, cataloguing blinding abuses on journeys to Tunisia, inside the country, and in Mediterranean waters. But we also reveal a Tunisian "borderscape" where intensifying racism and violence against "foreign" migrants is woven into domestic political struggles. Tunisians "burn the border" (*harraga*) (see M'Charek, 2020) with subversive migration practices; they also counteract it with social solidarities, and justifications for freedom of movement. With attention to these experiences, we illuminate how border violence relates to state violence and affects migrants, refugees and citizens alike.

## 1 Africa's Border Politics

The need for mobility is not sufficiently considered in debates about Africa's borders that have historically been dominated by concerns about boundary dilemmas inherited from colonial rule. We know that anticolonial nationalists adopted a flawed map with socially incongruent, geographically questionable (and oddly linear) borders as a matter of political expediency—despite the knowledge that these were products of colonial conquests and epistemic violence. Postcolonial leaders sought to establish people's right to self-determination on the continent by removing alien rule rather than problematizing either colonial boundaries or their notions of territoriality. Their understandable priority was to deal with prevailing racial hierarchies (in the South) and persistent neo-colonial interventions in independent states (Herbst, 1989: 686). This shaped the framework for the Organization of

African Unity (OAU) and the regional norm to uphold non-interference in the internal affairs of member state. But less obviously, postcolonial states inherited not only the literal boundaries marked on the map, but also exclusionary Eurocentric concepts of security, political community, sedentarism, and the related military or legal frameworks and practices.

The rationale for the inviolability of borders was to prevent inter-state conflicts but it reproduced other forms of conflict and suppression. Cartographic decisions made by colonial mappers have fuelled border disputes and wars of succession (Amadife & Warhola, 1993). Eurocentric ideas about borders, nation-state governance and belonging have been harnessed in violent ethnonationalist projects, and the targeting of minorities (for instance in Eastern Democratic Republic of Congo, Mathys, 2023). The problem is not only that Africa's postcolonial boundaries are plagued by "uncertainty" and needed to be "Africanized" (Zartman, 2001: 61), it is also that a conception of hard national borders was entrenched, leaving the door open for contemporary neo-colonial processes of "rebordering" (Yuval-Davis et al., 2019: 2).

African states are now "partners" in European agendas aimed at "securing" African borders, that aim to keep people on the continent and away from European shores (e.g. European Commission, 2023). This Eurocentric bordering is made possible partly because diverse African histories of borders are being forgotten. Precolonial orders varied in their political and spatial imaginaries yet tended to conceptualize sovereignty in terms of its relations to people rather than spaces, depending on popular allegiance not territorial control. Many left blurry zones, "frontier marches" defined by overlapping laws rather than border controls (Zartman, 1965: 160–161). Tunisia's post-independence president, Habib Bourguiba, echoed something of this flexibility in tactical responses to Tunisia's border disputes in the Sahara—his "theory of dépassement" (Zartman, 1965: 169) envisaged joint sovereignties. Historically, African borders were "interlaced spaces" that might expand or contract, not only through conflict, but also in response to the mobilities of people and trade relations (Mbembe, 2000: 263). They were not concretized in linear maps and "the concept of territorial delimitation of political control was … culturally alien" (Englebert et al. cited in Laine, 2020: 109).

This reminds us that borders are historically contingent and therefore open to change. Africans continue to imagine borders differently—not necessarily by carving out new sovereign states, like Eritrea, South Sudan, or continually striving to, like Somaliland and Western Sahara—but by profoundly questioning the terms of sovereignty and territoriality. On the cusp of independence, several African leaders pushed against the colonial approach, engaging in alternative "worldmaking" (Getachew, 2019) aimed at regional federation and building international institutions that might, had they come to fruition, have placed stronger constraints on state violence and enhanced rights to mobility. Many decades later, the continental body was the focus for a reconsideration: the Constitutive Act of the African Union (2002) established limits on a previous principle of non-interference in the political affairs of its member states, adding a commitment to responsible sovereignty—although it only licenses intervention in exceptional circumstances and focuses on violations against citizens within state borders, rather than those against the people who strive to cross them.

Regional institutions steer the continent positively towards integration, cross-border trade, and free movement. Historical and informal patterns of movement also persist on the ground and many Africans freely cross land borders (Adepoju et al. (eds.), 2020: 1–5). Meanwhile, scholars are developing new ideas, including with compelling arguments for a decolonial ethics of international law that would reflect global interconnections by imposing obligations upon former colonizers to host economic migrants (Achiume, 2019). Existing and emerging progressive narratives, policies, and practices of mobility are, however, up against entrenched national policies and the ongoing imposition of the EU's border regimes in Africa.

## 2   Conceptualizing Eurocentric Border Violence

Border violence against migrants within Africa and on routes to Europe has spiralled upwards. Humanitarian sources generally indicate that the Central Mediterranean route, a direction of travel through Libya or Tunisia towards Italy is the "most deadly route" in the world (Missing Migrants Project 2023) and that a parallel Western Mediterranean route through Morocco to Spain is not far behind. IOM (2022) recorded more than 29,000 deaths on these routes, since 2014. The data indicates that deaths and disappearances in the Central Mediterranean are continual. The identities of the victims are often unknown, although most have likely travelled from countries in East and West Africa, and sometimes the immediate cause of death is listed, but the underlying reasons, or who is responsible are not stated.

There are blind spots in our knowledge of this violence. Existing evidence on irregular migration is, at best, partial and "better data is needed not just on irregular migration flows, but also the profiles and experiences of those on irregular journeys" (Africa Migration Report, 2020: 35). The scale and potential of movements from North Africa to Europe may be depicted in "exaggerated and sensational terms" (ibid.: 27), but the multiple harms experienced by migrants within African countries, or in border crossings to Europe are hardly calculated. Human rights reports provide evidence of "excessive force" by border security actors in especially egregious cases, such as when 23 African migrants died at the Melilla-Morocco border in June 2022 (HRW, 2022). Activist groups and media publish stark accounts of deaths, abductions, torture, and racism against migrants (e.g. InfoMigrants, 2023). Yet none of these reports provide a comprehensive picture. The scale and nature of border violence is uncertain, not least because clandestine journeys are marked by silences and disappearances.

What is undeniable is that the surge in violence and death on border crossings has increased over the past two decades. It is axiomatic that this related to measures taken by European states and the European Union to fortify their borders and to shift the burden of migration management onto the African countries from which migrants originate, and those through which they transit. Scholarly research has done much to illuminate the violent impacts of this border externalization, and to expose the circularity of border (in)security measures—as Jones puts it: "The hardening of the border through new security practices is the source of the violence, not a response to it" (2019: 37).

## Eurocentric Bordering Practices

European states continue to tighten asylum criteria, reduce their commitments to refugees (Zetter, 2015), and increase restrictions on visas in a systematic effort to control migration. Migration governance that is being pursued in the name of security is designed to keep "the world's poorest out"—it is "global apartheid geopolitics" (Van Houtum, 2010: 957). As legal routes close, many migrants have instead taken irregular paths. European policymakers have viewed these journeys as either a problem to be tightly managed, or a threat to be directly countered, leading to a series of intertwined measures that are generally summed up as border "externalization" (e.g. Tyszler, 2019).

Currently, European border management largely rests on bilateral partnerships with key states, and multilateral agreements such as the Khartoum process—which explicitly aims to combat human trafficking, while effectively offering development money for migration control. It also entails the subcontracting of African security forces to serve as EU border guards, and support to Frontex (the European Border and Coastguard Agency) and African coastguards to intercept and "push back" migrant vessels. As M'charek puts it: "Everyone, including the airlines, has been enrolled in this process of stopping people from moving illegally" (2020: 425). Security actors are in the foreground, but humanitarian regimes are also implicated in "biopolitical warfare" to govern and contain migrants, using diverse instruments: "humanitarian discourses and practices, legal regimens, and military strategies of control" (Garelli & Tazzioli, 2018: 182). These interventions are militarizing and modifying African borders, at the behest of European states—and at the expense of African people.

Through a genealogy of Libya's borders, Brambilla captures some of the preliminary agreements and interventions that redefined African borderscapes. She finds that the Murzuq oasis, situated near a formerly open frontier with Chad, was transformed in the early 2000s into a "closed border gate" with government-run migrant detention centres to limit Sub-Saharan African mobility. Behind this shift, lay a rapprochement between Italy and the Gaddafi regime and a series of Italian/Libyan bilateral agreements aimed at dealing with terrorism, drug trafficking and illegal immigration. Since then, in Libya and beyond we see "new forms of Euro/African borderland in Africa originated by Europe" (Brambilla, 2014: 222). The "ripple effects" (Chemlali, 2023: 1) enter politics and society. For example, migration controls that were introduced in cooperation between the Moroccan government, Spain and the EU explicitly targeted Central and West African nationals, fuelling racial discrimination (Tyszler, 2021: 955). Over time, European interventions in border control have deepened, and so have their violent consequences.

There is rich literature theorizing the nexus between the "fierce" EU border regime, irregular migration, and violence (e.g. Jones, 2019; Van Houtum, 2010; Van Houtum & Boedeltje, 2009). Scholars have also paid attention to the ways in which the process of securitizing the border continues to be contested by migrants in "daily strategies, refusals, and resistances" (Casas Cortes et al., 2015: 80). To build on this, we turn to ethnography and foreground the experiences and perspectives of people on the move. Our aim is not to "stare at suffering" (Donham, 2007) or to gratuitously repeat descriptions of "dire and intolerable conditions, the torture, enslavement, and violence" (Mezzadra, 2020: 428) that already feature in numerous human rights reports (e.g. Amnesty International, 2022; Human Rights Watch, 2022). Instead, we are interested in analysing the violence that migrants— a term used here to include refugees and all who cross borders—themselves make visible, in specific places and times.

## Researching Border Violence

Our findings are empirically grounded in intermittent research at sites of protests by and for the rights of migrants in Tunisia. Interviews and observations were gathered outside the offices of international humanitarian organizations in Tunis in March 2022, November–December 2022, and April 2023. We also visited Zarzis, a town located near the Tunisia-Libya border, at the height of a protest at the end of November 2022.

The experiences of violence at the centre of our analysis here, vividly emerged from our ethnography, rather than explicitly being the focus of inquiry (we gathered unstructured accounts of the histories and concerns of protesters—who graciously shared their stories despite their difficult circumstances). The research was ethically sensitive, given the political and economic vulnerabilities and trauma of all migrants. We sought to mitigate this both through respect for standard ethical procedures required by institutional ethics approval—for instance we mainly use pseudonyms, except when asked to attribute quotations—and by remaining attentive to unequal power relations between ourselves and many of our respondents, and to our own individual positionalities. We are both "outsiders,"—albeit differently positioned since Wesley identifies as a Tunisian man while Ibreck identifies as a Ugandan-born British woman. But we are also "engaged" researchers, driven by scholarly and activist concerns. We study and write in solidarity with our research participants' struggles. Indeed, we agree with Halilovich (2022) that to claim objectivity while recording egregious human rights violations and injustices would "be almost impossible, as well as ethically problematic."

## The Tunisian Case

Our focus on border violence in Tunisia was feasible and relevant from a case selection perspective. The country is a strategic priority for border management from the perspective of European policymakers (Cuttitta, 2020: 2; European Commission, 2023). Since 2015, European states have funded programmes to support Integrated Border Management, including working with border agencies to "strengthen capacity," training officials in border management, and equipping border agencies with cutting edge surveillance technologies (see ICMPD, n.d.). It has long been a country of origin, a transit country for Sub-Saharan African migrants, and it is becoming a destination in the context of EU border fortification. Yet domestic political actors engage with EU externalization policies selectively and strategically

(Cassarino, 2018) and some civil society actors actively challenge them (Cuttitta, 2020: 9).

In comparison to its neighbours, Tunisia is notable for its sustained democratic and human rights movements, earning it a reputation as the only success story of the 2011 Arab spring revolutions. Tunisians have driven important legislative changes, notably the "historic" Law 50 of 2018 that was the first legislation to criminalize racial discrimination in the region (Parikh, 2021). Moreover, Tunisia's history has been defined by mobilities and entanglements across the Mediterranean, including established circular migration with Europe (Natter, 2015). Indeed, after the revolution, thousands of young people exercised their demands for freedom and the right to work by taking boats for Italy (Garelli et al., 2013).

Tunisia is now sliding backwards in terms of economic and political opportunities, with rising authoritarianism and populism (Souilmi, 2023). But it is also a site of resistance—both Tunisians and migrants are challenging violence and exclusion through acts of solidarity, networking for justice (Rees et al., 2023), or persistently crossing and critiquing the border. In this politically unsettled context, we encountered plural forms and perpetrators of border violence.

## 3  Memories and Experiences of Border Violence in Tunisia

Our ethnography enables us to sketch a trajectory of border violence along refugee and migrant routes. We include the legacies of violence that people bring with them, as well as the violence they experience within Tunisia or during attempts to cross to Europe. We identify flashpoints of violence on routes through Algeria, Morocco, and Libya to Tunisia, and trace violence that has taken root in memories and trauma. We then explore the violence experienced in two Tunisian hotspots, Zarzis and Tunis.

We do not suggest that all migrants follow a similar path. Some travel circular routes, making it across the Sahara or into the Mediterranean but then being forced back, sometimes crossing the borders of several transit countries before they reach Tunisia (interviews, March 2022; April 2023). Their journeys can take from months to several years. In addition, there are thousands of migrants (and increasingly also refugees) leaving Tunisia, who might depart either from Zarzis or from any other well-known Mediterranean crossing point, such as the shores near Sfax. What we present is merely a snapshot, based exclusively upon our fieldwork. It is by no means representative of the scale or locations of the violence. Yet disturbingly, it is more than sufficient to illuminate the depth of the violence, the multiple forms it takes, and the diverse actors who either participate or are affected.

## Algeria: A Racist Jungle

Crossing the Algerian desert is a prerequisite to enter Tunisia from the south. The journey leaves both physical scars and traumatic memories. It may take at least a week and potentially more than a month of walking, often without food or water. Along the way, migrants are attacked by armed insurgents, but cannot even bury the victims: Bob from Sierra Leone labelled it the "journey of no return," having witnessed his best friend getting shot by rebels "when he refused to give them money." Abdul recalled being abandoned by smugglers and seeing fellow travellers perish: "I feel so bitter. Five people died on the journey including some of my colleagues from Guinea." The desert path puts migrants' resilience and resistance to the test in the jungle in the most excruciating ways. "It's a journey of survival," Stephen attests. It is recalled as a nightmarish "forest" where violence, robbery, and deprivation are to be expected—"The rebels… take anything of value"—and dehydrated and starving migrants are forced to drink their own urine (interviews in Tunis, March 2022; November 2022; April 2023).

Not only young men, but also families are exposed to these dangers. As two Yemeni parents recounted their journey, their children added their own troubling recollections: a seven-year-old boy described it as: "too hot death!"; his older brother recalled seeing two men getting eaten by dogs released by Algerian security forces; "I run and I run," he said. His trauma lingered in sleepwalking when they arrived in Tunisia—his mother detailed how he would wake up in the middle of the night and leave the tent running (group discussion, April 2023).

Women also travel these routes. They confirm how border violence is gendered, with high rates of sexual abuse and rapes, especially of female migrants (Tyszler, 2019). Elizabeth described how the driver of the car she was travelling in pulled up in middle of the desert and raped her. She was (visibly) on her period and had told him that she was married, contributing to her trauma at this physical and *moral* violation. Her expression of relief that "I did not get pregnant" further illustrates the determination of women migrants to keep moving (interviews, April 2023) and the risks and the burdens they carry as vulnerablized "daily fighters" (Tyszler, 2019: 13). Such crimes also harm the survivor's community, including the transient groups of migrants that witness them. Mohammed was forced to watch as armed men raped women in the group: "they rape women in front of you... There is not security... there are no rights in the desert... you can do nothing" (interview, November 2022).

Walking through the desert is life-threatening, but travelling by car or by boat may turn out to be equally risky. Ibrahim from Sierra Leone and two others were stuffed in "the trunk of a car like sardines" for several hours and then had to walk for two more hours before they could find the next "agent" (interview, April 2023). Ahmed from Sudan watched smugglers remove the seats of vehicles to fit as many people as possible. He and his brother were among fifteen people crushed into one taxi. Smugglers placed "an Arab man" in the front seat of the vehicle to "deceive the police" (interviews, IOM protests, April 2023), highlighting not only the "professionalization" (Mlambo, 2020) but also the racialization implicit in smuggling methods.

The desert is physically gruelling and dangerous, but towns are also filled with threats. To say the least, Algeria "is not good for blacks" in the words of a migrant from (Sierra Leonean protester at IOM, Tunis, April 2023). Migrants are humiliated, called names, chased down streets and even stoned (interviews, March 2022; April 2023). They may find menial jobs, but these are confined to compounds and they cannot venture out. Construction sites are "a place to hide" said Bachir from Sudan, because they "can't walk freely" in the streets, as Bob from Sierra Leone explained (interviews, April 2023). Militarized Algerian forces, who our interlocutors referred to as *Zandam*, hunt migrants inside and outside the city. Abdul described witnessing them shoot at a group of migrants at the top of a 12-storey building. One of them died on the spot as he fell, and another who initially survived later committed suicide in the hospital when the police threatened him with either going to prison or being thrown back into the desert (interview, December 2023).

## Morocco: An Externalized Police State

Only a handful of our participants travelled through Morocco. Those who did, testified to similar episodic state violence as in Algeria. The Moroccan police posed an overarching threat. A Sudanese refugee recounted how the agent hid him and his group from the police at the Spanish-Moroccan border. It was eight days of agony trapped in a small container. Forty-five migrants had to live off nothing but two dozen loaves of bread every day for over a week. They were given buckets in which to release themselves (interview, April 2023). In another shocking incident, a Sudanese migrant witnessed how two people in his group were battered to death by the Moroccan police then dumped by them at the Algerian border post. He and his remaining friends were forced to keep going: "we just had to leave their dead bodies there… Algerians allowed us to come in, but they said they can't take dead bodies… We got in touch with the families to tell them" (interview, November 2022).

Such ordeals illustrate migrants' suffering at the other end of EU border securitization. As Mlambo (2020: 94) argues, these policies "prolong the misery of migrants who are at the mercy of smugglers who prey on their desperation." The scattered bodies of the migrants who do not make it to the finish line now make the hitherto "invisible" borderlines (Brambilla, 2014: 226) into painful markers on the landscape.

## Libya: Detention and Torture in a Mafia Zone

In blatant proof of their determination to keep irregular migrants out (Mlambo, 2020), the EU and Italy established partnerships with fractured and opaque political authorities in Libya, a country "torn by civil war." The violence against migrants there is so deadly, a UN investigation identified potential "crimes against humanity" (UN, 2023); the "dire and intolerable conditions" and torture are notorious (Mezzadra, 2020: 428). Our interlocutors were subject to all manner of physical and emotional assault in Libyan waters and soil, whether in the oasis of Quatrum or in Libya's infamous prisons such as Osama prison in Zawiyah (interviews, Tunisia, March 2022; April 2023).

Libyan border violence is experienced by people of all ages. A Sudanese boy, aged 14, when incarcerated in 2019, vividly recalled the brutality and humiliation he endured at the hands of Libyan prison authorities. He was thrown paltry amounts of food and stripped off his clothing in front of everyone for random searches. Similarly, a Sudanese man in his twenties told us of his imprisonment and torture in Libya. "I was stripped naked, deprived of food, beaten and videoed… You should think the unthinkable in Libya prisons. There were cases of people getting raped because the guards were high on drugs." The only possibility of escape relied upon bribing the guards, who ran a labour racket loaning money to some prisoners, who would then be released and put to work to repay it (interviews in March and November 2022).

The ways that migrants are exploited, detained and abused, stands in stark contrast to Libya's "historical socio-cultural values" and longstanding relationships with other African countries (Brambilla, 2014: 228). Libyan waters have become yet another "gated border site" ruled by militia whose sole job, under the support of the EU, is to intercept migrant boats and hand them over to criminal gangs (Mlambo, 2020). Ultimately, this only strengthens migrants' resolve to travel: they will genuinely "take all risks" to cross to the other side of the Mediterranean (group discussion, April 2023).

## Zarzis: Fishing and Mourning Migrants

Zarzis lies at the nexus of Europe's "warfare" on migrants (Garelli & Tazzioli, 2018) along the Mediterranean coast from Libya to Tunisia. The effects of externalization policies are literally "felt" in the everyday, and witnessed when bodies of dead migrants wash up on the shores (Chemlali, 2023: 13). These shipwrecks and deaths are the lethal consequences of militarized borders; either directly or indirectly (Cuttitta, 2020: 12).

Border deaths have shaken the lives and livelihoods of Zarzis' fishermen. Facing an unrelenting tide of migrant deaths and decomposing bodies, they have made it a moral mission to search for migrant boats in distress, to save lives, and to recover dead bodies from the sea: "In summer on a normal day we would come across 10–15 bodies in the sea" (fisherman, November 2022). These are the corpses of migrants who "have been mercilessly sacrificed" (de Genova, 2016: 34). Many of them are Sub-Saharan Africans: "they are in the more fragile boats… they get a worse deal," as Imed Soltani of *Terre pour tous* explained (December 2023). Migrants take "small and uncomfortable boats" that were designed to fit half of the passengers they carry (interviews, March 2022). Some of these "precarious vessels" Mezzadra (2020: 433) now lie in Zarzis's dry harbour, remnants of unfinished journeys. Together with the corpses and cemeteries, the wrecked boats are material traces of a mounting death toll.

Many fishermen have individually saved hundreds of lives over the years, yet they are also haunted by memories of those who perished, and are worried about how to care for their physical remains. Kamel recalled how several migrants died of dehydration during a 16-hour rescue operation, among them a pregnant woman and a toddler: "I couldn't sleep for two days until I heard that they were able to bury the baby." Chamseddine Marzouk was so determined to "give dignity for these bodies" (interviews, November 2023) that he created a "makeshift cemetery" for unknown migrants with his own hands (Zagaria, 2020: 541). An Algerian artist later contributed to a formal cemetery and memorial, *Le Jardin d'Afrique*. But both cemeteries are now at "saturation point" (Chemlali, 2023: 17).

Alongside the tragic deaths of strangers, the deaths and disappearances of many locals who try to cross the border are "omnipresent" in Zarzis. They cast a shadow and a "collectively felt trauma" over the local community (Chemlali, 2023). The anguish and emotional burdens that flow from border violence "reverberate" in this small town (Zagaria, 2020: 541), as they surely must in other communities in "migrant-sending" African countries. People spoke of the ways in which border violence tears the social fabric, stealing young lives and producing grieving families all over Tunisia. As one activist put it: "it used to be that the mothers of the popular quartiers used to say they want young people to get jobs now these same mothers say we want the bodies of our young people" (Soltani, December 2023).

In the past, Zarzisians could migrate (and return) legally because visas were available. Now only a privileged educated elite, the "brains" that Europe wants, can do so (M'Charek, 2020: 419). Every other young person's mobility is blocked: "every time they apply for a visa they get rejected; they study for years and years and then they are unemployed," as a grieving father explained. If family members want to visit relatives in Europe, or if they seek new educational or work opportunities, they can only do so by clandestine means. Many of those who take these dangerous crossings vanish from the town—either forever, if they do not survive the voyage, or for many years, because of their illegal status.

When migrant lives are lost, there is generally little or no prospect of justice. People in Zarzis increasingly refuse to accept this iniquity. Families, fishermen, and townspeople protested consistently for more than three months after a boatload of their children disappeared (17 young people lost in September 2022). This struggle continues. This grieving community attributes these disappearances to a "state crime." This is more than speculation—there is now a file of evidence. Survivors share videos that show Libyan or Tunisian coastguards attacking migrant boats to force their return. Fishermen record the failure of the coastguard to mount a search for survivors and the findings of their massive voluntary initiative to comb the seas. Family members describe locating bodies of their loved ones that were apparently scarred from beatings; or were covertly buried without DNA testing or informing the parents, until the protesters found and dug them up.

This peaceful resistance to Eurocentric border violence in Zarzis has been met with new forms of brutality. When demonstrators and mourners marched with thousands of townspeople, the police responded with tear gas and beatings of some of the protesters. They even assaulted and handcuffed the father of one of the victims. People who support migrants in Europe have been criminalized in "political rhetoric and in legislation" (Mezzadra, 2020: 428), in Zarzis they have become direct targets for political repression: "police stopped and threatened to shoot them and fired bullets to scare them off.... Even old ladies were struggling. They were throwing tear gas. Police were also raiding homes" (interview with father of disappeared boy, November 2023).

Zarzis is simmering with grief and anger in the wake of European "containment" strategies. Both young Tunisians and migrants from elsewhere in Africa feel trapped there. The only option for these marginalized and economically disenfranchised groups is to try to keep moving on, either out of the country, or to elsewhere in Tunisia.

## Tunis: Humanitarian Neglect and Wavering Hospitality

Deliberately thrown from pillar to post, many migrants converge in Tunis. But increasingly they find no safety or support there either. The violence of the city is less overt than in other flashpoints, but it is insidious, and it is also intensifying.

On the structural level, there are few means of basic survival for displaced people. By the time they reach there, many are destitute. They have spent the equivalent of thousands of dollars to smugglers, in bribes to Libyan prison guards, or in inflated rents, food, and other necessities, as an economic crisis hits. Their lives turn into a routine search for work, that sometimes only ends in exploitation in a context where they lack rights or protection, as Abdul from Sierra Leone explained: "I started working in the restaurant. They didn't pay me all day. I asked 'when are you going to pay?'… Another guy didn't get paid… Some of the Arabs don't pay. I work for nothing here" (interview, November 2023).

In addition, there is scant support from international humanitarian organizations. Some migrants have taken up residence on the streets outside UNHCR and IOM, demanding help and protection. National borders determine whether you will be labelled a deserving refugee or an irregular migrant in the international humanitarian lexicon. But the outcomes are not that different. After months, one Sudanese refugee said he received recognition and a card from UNHCR only to find that still the "conditions are unliveable, and the card is completely useless. They don't provide food or rations for us." Another said "the organisation told us to figure things out on our own. We tried to find menial jobs in the area but not possible. We are just living off donations." Ibrahim had given up and just wanted to be repatriated. But even this process of return took months, and in the meantime: "No place to sleep; no food. You just beg in the streets. No help from them—they say you need to wait for your documents" (interviews November 2022). When migrants' protests escalate, as they did in March 2022 and April 2023, the UNHCR tends to compound the problem by calling upon the police. As a local human rights activist observed: "the UN have competence to intervene when there are disputes and harassment, but instead they immediately called the police" (interview FTDES activist, December 2022), at the risk of complicity with border violence.

Beyond economic deprivation, humiliation, and risks of incarceration, migrants in Tunis also have racism to contend with. This is border violence that rebounds onto Black Tunisians—"the construction of a racialised category of undesirables at the border associating black skin colour with a status of illegality" (Tyszler, 2021: 955) seeps into everyday life. As one migrant put it, "if you're dark people, the police can catch you and put you in prison" (November 2022). Quotidian racism in Tunisia—where inequalities borne of historical slavery persist—is being reinforced (interview FTDES activist, December 2022).

People on the move used to say that there is less racism in Tunisia than in other North African transit states (interviews, March 2022, November 2022). Troublingly, this changed in early 2023, when migrants became the target of systematic violent beatings, racist abuse, and discrimination following a hate-speech by President Kais Saied that depicted them as criminals and threats. This was state-sanctioned violence by a leader who had gained power through a slow-moving coup. His scapegoating of migrants was a means to whip up domestic support, but also to threaten chaos at the border to silence European states growing critical of his rising authoritarianism. He wielded Tunisia's border-management partnership for political leverage. The violence was so extreme that it led to a humanitarian exodus with mass repatriations of some migrants. At the same time, the president pursued arrests of domestic political opponents and civil society, and threats to other vulnerable people, including LGBTQI+ groups, intensified (Rees et al., 2023). For migrants who remained, the situation is ever more precarious, though the search for a "better future" continues (interviews, April 2023).

## 4  Conclusion

Border violence is concentrated not only in deserts but also at sea and in towns, proliferating in diverse forms and degrees. It consists of unspeakable violations by security actors including police, prison officials and border guards who brutalize, torture, detain, rape and either directly or indirectly kill people on the move, as well as by criminal smugglers. It includes "invisible wounds" (Crepet et al., 2017) left by experiencing and witnessing these horrors. It also encompasses racist brutality and dehumanization; inequality, discrimination, and exploitation; and the indignity and humiliation of economic deprivation. Lives are cut short; families are torn apart;

time, money and labour are stolen in the wake of border regimes that explicitly devalue African lives. We find this array of violations even in Tunisia—formerly the most hospitable North African state, with strong civic movements that are struggling against authoritarianism and racism and for mobility rights. Moreover, in this comparatively open setting, we can also see how harsh border policing designed to target people on the move returns home, in attacks on citizens and rising authoritarianism.

Border violence is a direct extension of colonial violence. Not just because the boundaries were a product of colonization but because Europe is *rebordering* the continent, enabling various extractions, while severing historical connections and strengthening the forces of authoritarian and military rule. The borders are filters in the sense that materials and useful migrants can cross, but most Africans are classified as threatening or surplus life; "after salt and brains have been mined and shipped out" from towns like Zarzis, the remaining young people generally "consider *harraga* (burning the borders)" (M'charek, 2020: 419).

Unquestionably, the European quest to constrain and divert African mobilities is morally in tension with the obligations generated by colonialism (Achiume, 2019) and with global inequalities that represent "the postcolonial harvest of centuries of European exploitation and subjugation" (de Genova, 2016: 43). African lives are disrupted and lost as "colonial ghosts" (Mezzadra, 2020) selectively promote international human rights abroad while closing borders at home. What is more, it is deeply counterproductive. Despite the increased border securitization, as Mlambo (2020, citing UNDP) explains, the number of people crossing the sea has not, and likely will not decrease.

Many African governments, like Tunisia, are swallowing European border directives in return for aid. They may well have a mutual interest in militarizing "security." But regional leaders and democrats on the continent must urgently take lessons from people who know the effects of externalization and securitization on the ground. In Tunisia, refugees, migrants, and citizens alike are making violence visible, and demanding and forging new transnational relations. They know that, in the words of Zarzisian activist Ali Kniss: "this system of borders and visas is a capitalist, racist system marginalizing people in the south and globally." It reflects the rise of authoritarian, nationalist groups in Europe, (Mezzadra, 2020: 428) and emboldens similar forces in Africa. As new episodes of catastrophic military violence erupt and climate emergency takes hold on the continent, mobility is an essential and intrinsically African survival strategy. Eurocentric border concepts and policies are fuelling violence and must be re-imagined and reformed.

# Bibliography

Achiume, E. T. (2019). Migration as Decolonization. *Stanford Law Review, 71*(6), 1509–1574. https://blogs.law.columbia.edu/abolition1313/files/2020/08/Migration-as-Decolonization.pdf

Adepoju, A., Fumagalli, C., & Nyabola, N. (eds.). (2020). *Africa Migration Report: Challenging the Narrative*. African Union and IOM.

Amadife, E. N., & Warhola, J. W. (1993). Africa's political boundaries: Colonial cartography, the OAU, and the advisability of ethno-national adjustment. *International Journal of Politics, Culture, and Society, 6*(4), 533–554. https://doi.org/10.1007/BF01418258

Amnesty International. (2022). *Morocco: They Beat Him in the Head, to Check If He Was Dead: Evidence of Crimes Under International Law by Morocco and Spain at the Melilla Border*. https://www.amnesty.org/en/documents/mde29/6249/2022/en/. Accessed 9 May 2023.

Brambilla, C. (2014). Shifting Italy/Libya Borderscapes at the Interface of EU/Africa Borderland: A "Genealogical" Outlook from the Colonial Era to Postcolonial Scenarios. *ACME: An International Journal for Critical Geographies, 13*(2), 220–245.

Brambilla, C., & Jones, R. (2020). Rethinking Borders, Violence, and Conflict: From Sovereign Power to Borderscapes as Sites of Struggles. *Environment and Planning D: Society and Space, 38*(2), 287–305. https://doi.org/10.1177/0263775819856352

Casas-Cortes, M., Cobarrubias, S., De Genova, N., Garelli, G., Grappi, G., Heller, C., & Tazzioli, M. (2015). New Keywords: Migration and Borders. *Cultural Studies, 29*(1), 55–87. https://doi.org/10.1080/09502386.2014.891630

Cassarino, J.-P. (2018). Beyond the Criminalisation of Migration: A Non-western Perspective. *International Journal of Migration and Border Studies, 4*(4), 397–411. https://doi.org/10.1504/IJMBS.2018.096756. Accessed 9 May 2023.

Chemlali, A. (2023). Rings in the Water: Felt Externalisation in the Extended EU Borderlands. *Geopolitics*, 1–24. https://doi.org/10.1080/14650045.2023.2198125

Crepet, A., et al. (2017). Mental Health and Trauma in Asylum Seekers Landing in Sicily in 2015: A Descriptive Study of Neglected Invisible Wounds. *Conflict and Health, 11*(1), 1. https://doi.org/10.1186/s13031-017-0103-3

Cuttitta, P. (2020). Non-Governmental/Civil Society Organisations and the European Union-Externalisation of Migration Management in Tunisia and Egypt. *Population, Space and Place, 26*(7), e2329. https://doi.org/10.1002/psp.2329

Donham, D. L. (2007). Staring at Suffering: Violence as Subject. In E. G. Bay & D. L. Donham (Eds.), *States of Violence: Politics, Youth, and Memory in Contemporary Africa* (pp. 16–36). University of Virginia Press.

Duffield, M. (1997). Humanitarian Intervention, the New Aid Paradigm and Separate Development. *New Political Economy, 2*(2), 336–340. https://doi.org/10.1080/13563469708406309

European Commission. (2023, July 16). *The European Union and Tunisia: Political Agreement on a Comprehensive Partnership Package.* https://neighbourhood-enlargement.ec.europa.eu/news/european-union-and-tunisia-political-agreement-comprehensive-partnership-package-2023-07-16_en

Garelli, G., Sossi, F., & Tazzioli, M. (Eds.). (2013). *Spaces in Migration. Postcards of a Revolution.* Pavement Books.

Garelli, G., & Tazzioli, M. (2018). The Biopolitical Warfare on Migrants: EU Naval Force and NATO Operations of Migration Government in the Mediterranean. *Critical Military Studies, 4*(2), 181–200. https://doi.org/10.1080/23337486.2017.1375624

Genova, N. D. (2016). The "Crisis" of the European Border Regime: Towards a Marxist Theory of Borders. *International Socialism* (150), 31–54. http://isj.org.uk/the-crisis-of-the-european-border-regime-towards-a-marxist-theory-of-borders/

Getachew, A. (2019). *Worldmaking After Empire: The Rise and Fall of Self-determination.* Princeton University Press.

Halilovich, H. (2022). The Ethnographer Unbared: Academic Kinship, Elective Affinities and (Re)Negotiating Researcher Positionality. *Forum Qualitative Sozialforschung/Forum Qualitative Social Research, 23*(1). https://doi.org/10.17169/FQS-23.1.3831

Herbst, J. (1989). The Creation and Maintenance of National Boundaries in Africa. *International Organization, 43*(4), 673–692.

Human Rights Watch. (2022, June 29). *Morocco/Spain: Horrific Migrant Deaths at Melilla Border.* https://www.hrw.org/news/2022/06/29/morocco/spain-horrific-migrant-deaths-melilla-border. Accessed 4 May 2023.

ICMPD. (n.d). *Support Programme to Integrated Border Management in Tunisia 2015–2019.* IBM Tunisia\. https://www.icmpd.org/our-work/projects/support-programme-to-integrated-border-management-in-tunisia-ibm-tunisia. Accessed 9 May 2023.

InfoMigrants. (2023). https://www.infomigrants.net/en/. Accessed 4 May 2023.

IOM. (2022). *Data.* Missing Migrants Project. https://missingmigrants.iom.int/data. Accessed 4 May 2023.

Jones, R. (2017). *Violent Borders: Refugees and the Right to Move.* Verso Books.

Jones, R. (2019). From Violent Borders: Refugees and the Right to Move. *NACLA Report on the Americas, 51*(1), 36–40. https://doi.org/10.1080/10714839.2019.1593688

Kearney, M. (2004). The Classifying and Value-Filtering Missions of Borders. *Anthropological Theory, 4*(2), 131–156.

Laine, J. P. (2020). Reframing African Migration to Europe: An Alternative Narrative. In I. Moyo, C. C. Nshimbi, & J. P. Laine (Eds.), *Migration Conundrums, Regional Integration and Development: Africa-Europe Relations in a Changing*

*Global Order* (pp. 93–116). Springer (Africa's Global Engagement: Perspectives from Emerging Countries).

Mathys, G. (2023, May 2). *Lines Through the Lake: Why the Congo-Rwanda Border Can't Be Redrawn*. African Arguments. https://africanarguments.org/2023/05/lines-through-the-lake-why-the-congo-rwanda-border-cant-be-redrawn/. Accessed 5 May 2023.

Mbembe, A. (2000). At the Edge of the World: Boundaries, Territoriality, and Sovereignty in Africa. *Public Culture, 12*(1), 259–284. https://muse.jhu.edu/related_content?type=article&id=26186

Mbembe, A. (2003). Necropolitics. *Public Culture, 15*(1), 11–40. https://muse.jhu.edu/related_content?type=article&id=39984

M'charek, A. (2020). *Harraga*: Burning Borders, Navigating Colonialism. *The Sociological Review, 68*(2), 418–434. https://doi.org/10.1177/0038026120905491

Mezzadra, S. (2020). Abolitionist Vistas of the Human. Border Struggles, Migration and Freedom of Movement. *Citizenship Studies, 24*(4), 424–440. https://doi.org/10.1080/13621025.2020.1755156

Mlambo, V. H. (2020). Externalization and Securitization as Policy Responses to African Migration to the European Union. *African Human Mobility Review, 6*(3). https://doi.org/10.14426/ahmr.v6i3.916

Natter, K. (2015). *Revolution and Political Transition in Tunisia: A Migration Game Changer?* Migrationpolicy.org. https://www.migrationpolicy.org/article/revolution-and-political-transition-tunisia-migration-game-changer. Accessed 9 May 2023.

Parikh, S. (2021, Summer). *The Limits of Confronting Racial Discrimination in Tunisia with Law 50* (Middle East Report, 299). https://hal.science/hal-03384138

Rees, P. Raach, F., Weslety, S., & Ibreck, R. (2023). *For Migrants in Tunisia, Life Is Just Getting Worse*. OpenDemocracy. https://www.opendemocracy.net/en/beyond-trafficking-and-slavery/migrant-solidarity-in-tunisia-offers-hope-after-racist-attacks/. Accessed 9 May 2023.

Scheper-Hughes, N., & Bourgois, P. (2004). Introduction: Making Sense of Violence. In N. Scheper-Hughes & P. Bourgois (Eds.), *Violence in War and Peace: An Anthology* (pp. 1–27). Blackwell.

Souilmi, H. (2023). A Tale of Two Exceptions: Everyday Politics of Democratic Backsliding in Tunisia. *The Journal of North African Studies, 28*(2), 1–19. https://doi.org/10.1080/13629387.2023.2207226

Tyszler, E. (2019). From Controlling Mobilities to Control over Women's Bodies: Gendered Effects of EU Border Externalization in Morocco. *Comparative Migration Studies, 7*, 25. https://doi.org/10.1186/s40878-019-0128-4

Tyszler, E. (2021). Humanitarianism and Black Female Bodies: Violence and Intimacy at the Moroccan–Spanish border. *The Journal of North African Studies, 26*(5), 954–972. https://doi.org/10.1080/13629387.2020.1800211

UN. (2022). *Organized Crime Perpetuating Instability, Violence, Poverty Across West Africa, Sahel, Executive Director Tells Security Council*. https://press.un.org/en/2022/sc14761.doc.htm. Accessed 3 May 2023.

UN. (2023). *Human Rights Council Hears That There Are Reasonable Grounds to Believe That Crimes Against Humanity Have Been Committed Against Libyans and Migrants Throughout Libya Since 2016 and That New Mechanisms Are Needed* (no date). OHCHR. https://www.ohchr.org/en/news/2023/04/human-rights-council-hears-there-are-reasonable-grounds-believe-crimes-against. Accessed 11 May 2023.

Van Houtum, H. (2010). Human Blacklisting: The Global Apartheid of the EU's External Border Regime. *Environment and Planning D: Society and Space, Vol 28*, 957–976. https://doi.org/10.1068/d1909

Van Houtum, H., & Boedeltje, F. (2009). Europe's Shame: Death at the Borders of the EU. *Antipode, 41*(2), 226–230. https://doi.org/10.1111/j.1467-8330.2009.00670.x

Yuval-Davis, N., Wemyss, G., & Cassidy, K. (2019). *Bordering*. Wiley.

Zagaria, V. (2020). "A Small Story With Great Symbolic Potential": Attempts at Fixing a Cemetery of Unknown Migrants in Tunisia. *American Behavioral Scientist, 64*(4), 540–563. https://doi.org/10.1177/0002764219882994

Zartman, I. W. (1965). The Politics of Boundaries in North and West Africa. *The Journal of Modern African Studies, 3*(2), 155–173. https://doi.org/10.1017/S0022278X00023600

Zartman, I. W. (2001). *Bordering on War*. Foreign Policy, Washington. https://www.proquest.com/openview/1bbe8109393698373f5dd3cfd542e548/1?pq-origsite=gscholar&cbl=47510. Accessed 5 May 2023.

Zetter, R. (2015). *A Fragmented Landscape of Protection*. Forced Migration Review. https://www.fmreview.org/dayton20/zetter. Accessed 5 May 2023.

# Diaspora and the Afterlife of Violence: Eritrean National Narratives and What Goes Without Saying

## Victoria Bernal

Violence has a long afterlife; it lives on after the events are over, leaving its mark on individuals and on institutions. Thus, we should understand terms such as "post conflict" as drawing attention to the significance of conflict as the context of ongoing lives rather than as demarcating a break between a past crisis and the present. Violence is destructive, but violence is also formative and is part of what constitutes community. Where nations are founded through conflict, "the story of lives enmeshed in violence is part of the story of the nation" (Das, 2008: 2). Media are significant in these processes, as Zizi Papacharissi, writing about brutal state violence against protesters in 1973 Greece, explains: "Collective memory of the event, imprinted in our psyches and recycled via the media, rendered it a permanent part of our history and identity" (2015: 2).

Collective experiences of violence are inextricably entwined with what it means to be Eritrean. War conducted on Eritrean soil for three decades (1961–1991) created the nation of Eritrea while also establishing its diaspora. The struggle for independence from Ethiopia has been mythologized by the national leadership, and its "martyrs" (as those killed during the war are called) are officially memorialized. The suffering of the nation and sacrificing for the nation are dominant themes of the Isaias regime that has governed the country since independence. In contrast, there is a distinct silence among

V. Bernal (✉)
Department of Anthropology, Gender and Sexuality Studies, University of California, Irvine, Irvine, CA, USA
e-mail: vbernal@uci.edu

© The Author(s), under exclusive license to Springer Nature Switzerland AG 2024
O. B. Mlambo and E. Chitando (eds.), *The Palgrave Handbook of Violence in Africa*,
https://doi.org/10.1007/978-3-031-40754-3_6

Eritreans about the horrors and personal losses they have actually experienced. Silence, acquiescence, and complicity with the authoritarian state on the part of Eritreans inside the country can be explained by the harsh treatment facing those who deviate. But the silence in the dynamic online public sphere created and maintained by Eritreans in diaspora is puzzling.

In this chapter I interrogate the silence on Eritrean diaspora websites regarding personal suffering related to the war that produced Eritrea as an independent nation, elevated its current president and ruling party to government leadership, and established the Eritrean diaspora (Connell, 2011; Iyob, 1995). What is and is not stated on diaspora websites yields insights into the legacies of political violence, the workings of state power in mobilizing identities around collective suffering, and the dynamics of the Internet. Posts on these websites reveal the struggles of Eritreans to come to terms with the upheavals that have shaped their lives and the ways the social effects of war extend beyond the temporalities and spatialities of the violence itself. My primary concern is to understand what it means for people and for society when the process of making sense of past violence is entangled with political struggle in a context where powerful official narratives frame how people live with what they have lived through. I argue that national narratives of the Eritrean state that celebrate sacrifice for the nation operate on Eritreans as a secondary form of violence that renders their personal losses unspeakable.

My research concentrates on three important websites established by Eritreans based in the United States. The first website, Dehai, was established in 1992 (originally as an email list), and two significant rivals, Asmarino and Awate, were established in 2000 and 2001, respectively. While Dehai attracts posters who support the regime, and the ruling party now features a link to it on its own website, the diaspora websites all stand out as independent initiatives undertaken by ordinary Eritreans in a context where political engagement has been controlled from the top down by authorities. Initially all content was in English, which is not only a language of diaspora but is also one of Eritrea's three semi-official languages. Now content appears in Tigrinya and Arabic, and the websites stream video as well. Eritreans in diaspora have greater access to the Internet, and they contribute most of the content.

The founders of these three websites and many of the long-time posters are members of the generation most impacted by Eritrea's independence struggle and are part of the first wave of migrants and refugees from Eritrea who established the diaspora. While the identities and locations of posters are not always knowable from their posts, many Eritreans use their real names online and often make their locations known as well. The second wave of Eritrean mass exodus is more recent, taking shape in diaspora over the past decade. Members of the first generation established these websites, set down the formal guidelines, and through their practices created informal norms and expectations about posting (see Bernal [2014] for a more detailed social history of Eritrean cyberspace). Those posters who have been participating online from earlier days are distinguishable as members of the first wave, and, as in some of the posts I quote here, references to years spent in diaspora or to particular events provide clues as to whether someone is a first- or second-wave migrant. In the course of my research I have met the founders of all three websites.

In the twenty-first century many diasporas sustain themselves and their homeland connections in part through digital media, a process sometimes described as "digital diasporas" (Brinkerhoff, 2009; Gajjala, 2008; Oiarzabal & Alonso, 2010). What is distinctive about the long-standing Eritrean websites is that they are devoted to national politics and serve as a comparatively open public sphere that has no counterpart inside Eritrea, where information and political expression are forcefully dominated by the state. Even online critics risk harassment by purported government trolls, but critics inside Eritrea risk imprisonment or even death. Online Eritreans are able to produce and circulate knowledge, express themselves, and participate in politics in ways not possible in Eritrea.

Research inside Eritrea is limited by the government's restrictions on the access of researchers (including the denial of entry visas) and being associated with researchers could put informants there in danger. But what drew me deeply into online research was the range of creative ways Eritreans use the Internet to engage in politics. Internet activities, I argue, are not a surrogate for "real" politics; rather, they are powerful in creating and mobilizing publics. This chapter draws on my many years of research on Eritrean politics online and is informed by my observations of conditions in Eritrea, from my first visit in 1980 to my most recent in 2016, and my familiarity with Eritrean life in diaspora, particularly in North America and Europe. Eritrea's transnational political field and the affordances of the Internet challenge the notion of a homeland/diaspora binary, suggesting instead complex, shifting, and elastic networks of connection and cleavage that are neither entirely independent of nor defined by territorial sovereignties and locations, and that likewise complicate the online/offline dichotomy since these are all integral components of a world that Eritreans inhabit and seek to affect.

Communication and expression are widely seen by scholars as part of a post-violence healing process (Henry, 2006; Sanford, 2003). The proliferation of optimistically named truth and reconciliation commissions is premised on this (Das, 2008). Moodie, writing about violence in El Salvador, observes that "suffering, like any experience, must be represented in comprehensible signs to have meaning" (2006: 67; see also Dickson-Gomez, 2004). Yet what is "comprehensible" rests on social understandings and existing narratives about how the world works. Kapteijns and Richters note that scholars and those who have lived through violence struggle with how to "define and represent [a subject matter] so hard to contain in standard vocabularies, and so disruptive and yet so deeply intertwined with enduring social conditions" (2010: 6–7). There is, moreover, a complex dynamic between historical processes and collective histories, on the one hand, and individual lives formed by particular knowledge and circumstances, on the other hand. Cvetkovitch observes that "politics and history manifest at the level of lived affective experience" (2007: 461). Cvetkovitch's notion of "public feelings" (2007) and Dana Seitler's question about whether "affect is located in the body, the psyche, or cultural discourse at large" (2016) point to the complexity of the interface where individual loss and hurt are produced by and subsumed within societal histories.

The project of making sense of political violence is fraught with social struggles over facts and interpretations and possibilities of exclusions and betrayals (Feuchtwang, 2003). Speech in such contexts cannot be conceived "as merely referential" but rather as "constituting powerful action in the world" (Theidon, 2013: 115). But how, then, should we conceive of silence? Yong suggests "anthropologists have to listen and talk to these silences without banishing them" (2006: 463). Shaw argues that "neither silence nor forgetting are necessarily pathological 'symptoms.' Rather, there are different modes of silence and forgetting" (2010: 255). Part of what I seek to uncover here is an Eritrean mode of silence production, revealing silence not as a thing or an action but as a relationship.

In the case of the Eritrean independence struggle, violence and suffering are connected to a set of ideologies and beliefs through which the Eritrean Peoples' Liberation Front (EPLF) successfully mobilized the Eritrean population, including those in diaspora (Woldemikael, 1991). Belonging to a political community under siege, rather than simply sharing cultural affinities or native origins, defined the diaspora experience of those who fled during the 1961–1991 war for independence. Diaspora communities were organized by leaders in Eritrea to serve the nationalist cause. The experience of diaspora was also shaped by the fact that during those decades Eritrea was effectively closed off so that no visits home were possible (with the exception of illegal, dangerous crossings into EPLF territory through the Sudan). Thus, while Eritreans are part of global migration patterns from the south to the economic centres of Western Europe and North America, the political conditions that formed their diaspora give it distinctive characteristics. As Africans, Eritreans are among the "new African diasporas" confronting and transforming racialized notions of what it means to be European, African American, or black (to name a few contested identity categories), and perhaps unsettling the notion of diaspora itself (Iyob & Knight, 2014; Okpewho & Ngegwu, 2009; Rahier, 2010; Shelemay & Kaplan, 2015). For African migrants, racist social exclusion in the West contributes to the process of diaspora identification (Abusharaf, 2002; Besteman, 2016). Eritreans' experiences under the totalitarian Marxist regime of Mengistu Hailemariam, their political education by the EPLF, and their engagements with Isaias Afewerki's authoritarian state apparatus mean that Eritreans share experiences not only with other post-colonial and racialized populations but also with other post-socialist populations that were caught up similarly in radical, dogmatic attempts to remake society through centralized politics from which no dissent and no legal means of escape were permitted (Kligman, 1998; Yurchak, 2005). The powerful political culture established by the EPLF and institutionalized by the Isaias regime has sought to define what it means to be Eritrean for those inside and outside the country. One aim of this chapter is to uncover the power and violence of a political culture that resides in people even after they have left the space of violence and the territory governed by the guerrillas who became the state.

Liberation wars and revolutions aim to make a better world, but their effects, even on their intended beneficiaries, may be devastating. The warfare that won Eritrea's independence and the ongoing militarization of society that are celebrated and enshrined as national values have inflicted vast losses upon Eritrean people. The story of Eritrea has been told by the EPLF and by the state it formed as a triumphal story of heroic sacrifice. This narrative, I argue, leaves ordinary people with little scope to express the personal losses they have suffered or to construct independent alternative narratives as they seek to make sense of personal and national histories and futures. Indeed because Eritrea's violent history has had such a powerful impact across its society, personal histories are simultaneously national histories. The accounts of scholars and journalists contributed to mythic narratives about the EPLF and the achievements of Eritrean nationalism in the early years of the Isaias regime (Dorman, 2005; Reid, 2006). For well over a decade, however, critical reports and analyses of the post-independence regime have accumulated (Bozzini, 2011; Kibreab, 2009; Riggan, 2009). The tide of political sentiment has also shifted on Eritrean diaspora websites where dissenting views and calls for regime change are now dominant themes. Eritreans' political engagement online is often driven by passionate emotions as evidenced by the expressive posts they write addressing national conditions. However, personal experience and individual accounts of suffering remain largely left out.

In the pages that follow I seek to uncover the processes that produce this gap and find meaning in the silence. The section below details the kinds of violence experienced and witnessed by the generation of Eritreans who lived through the independence struggle. This is followed by an examination of how the state constitutes Eritreans through narrating this history. Then I analyse the ways that personal experiences of violence and loss are revealed and concealed in the online public sphere.

## 1    Living with Losses: Eritrean Experiences of Violence

For Eritreans who lived through the struggle for independence from Ethiopia, experiences of political violence generally began with Ethiopian rule. Initially an Italian colony and briefly a British protectorate, Eritrea was federated to Ethiopia in 1950 (Finaldi, 2016; Trevaskis, 1960; Wrong, 2005). Under Emperor Haile Selassie, Eritreans endured escalating repression and violence. According to a UNICEF report,

> the Ethiopian government made every effort to suppress Eritrean identity, culture and tradition … all books written in Eritrean languages were destroyed. Influential Eritrean nationalists were either imprisoned or deported to Ethiopia Eritreans joined the liberation movement. This in turn led to more oppressive responses from Ethiopia, including mass arrests and the burning of entire villages. (1994: 17)

An armed struggle began in 1961 (Cliffe & Davidson, 1988). Ethiopia annexed Eritrea in 1962. Cultural and religious affinities between Ethiopians and Eritreans gave the conflict aspects of civil war. Resistance was first organized by the Eritrean Liberation Front (ELF), which was formed by Eritreans in exile, primarily in Egypt. The EPLF splintered from ELF in 1972, led by Isaias Afewerki and Ramadan Nur. While fighting Ethiopian forces, the ELF and the EPLF battled each other, killing more Eritreans between 1972 and 1974 than had died at the hands of Ethiopians up to that point (HRW, 1991: 42). Purges conducted within the two fronts led to additional killings. Following the overthrow of Haile Selassie in 1974, a brutal Marxist dictatorship known as the Dergue and led by Mengistu Hailemariam took power in Ethiopia and escalated the war in Eritrea. Intermittent conflict continued among the liberation movements into the 1980s when the EPLF pushed most of the ELF fighters into Sudan as part of Eritrea's refugee diaspora. In 1991 the EPLF's victory over the Dergue's troops won Eritrea's independence. Isaias Afewerki became the president of Eritrea and the EPLF became the ruling party, the People's Front for Democracy and Justice (PFDJ) (Pool, 2001; Welde Giorgis, 2014).

Eritreans who were adolescents or young adults in the 1970s and 1980s were especially affected by the war as they were drawn into the fronts, harassed by Ethiopian forces, and sometimes forcibly conscripted. In his book on refugees, Eritrean scholar Gaim Kibreab mentions the extreme conditions he and his friends faced in Eritrea in 1975: "To be a youth and an Eritrean in Asmara was at that time very dangerous. Most of us were aware of the danger that awaited us if we fell into the hands of the [Ethiopian] security forces" (1987: 26). Some young men joined the EPLF rather than risk conscription into the Ethiopian army. While EPLF fighters were mainly volunteers, the conditions under which Eritreans lived often left them little alternative to joining the guerrillas. Many Eritreans lived, worked, or studied in Ethiopia proper, and experienced the state violence there known as the "Red Terror" that marked the beginning of the Dergue. At least 10,000 people were killed in Addis Ababa alone in 1977.

In Eritrea the war was "not fought between the government army and the fronts; it was fought between the army and large sections of the people," including "reprisal killings of civilians" (HRW, 1991: 7, 14). The counterinsurgency strategies used by Ethiopia have been used by other governments. However, "the Ethiopian case stands out as particularly destructive because of the extraordinarily prolonged level of sustained violence" (HRW, 1991: 4). From 1980 EPLF-controlled areas and contested areas were subject to frequent air raids that kept the population in a constant state of fear and made normal life impossible, forcing people to carry out activities at night and in underground caves. In contrast to Ethiopia's disregard for the distinction between civilians and combatants, the EPLF's policy was to respect civilians and to treat prisoners of war humanely. However, the ELF and the EPLF regularly assassinated accused collaborators (HRW, 1991: 47, 251). Ethiopian forces routinely pillaged the Eritrean countryside, in part for their own survival as troops were commonly deployed with few or no supplies (HRW, 1991: 43, 284). Ethiopian soldiers subjected women to kidnapping and rape, forcing some to accompany troops as servants and concubines (HRW, 1991).

Summary executions and massacres were carried out in Eritrea, including the murder of civilians taking refuge in mosques and churches. While there is comparatively little detailed documentation of these events, historian Habtu

Ghebre-Ab gathered first-hand accounts in 2002 about mass killings in 1975. His book, *Massacre at Wekidiba*, was published by Red Sea Press, another important initiative founded and run by a diaspora Eritrean. Explaining the motivation for his project, Ghebre-Ab writes,

> the fact that I did not have first hand experience of the tragedies does not in any way mean I was unaffected by massacres that took place in Eritrea. In fact, one would be hard pressed to find any person of Eritrean origin who is not personally and profoundly touched by the horrors of mass killings that took place in Eritrea during the three-decade long armed struggle for independence. (2013: 10)

Like many Eritreans, he also lost two brothers who joined the EPLF and were killed in battle. His project is one of historical documentation that records names and dates, what people saw, and what people did, but it is not able to convey the emotional effects and after-effects on survivors.

UNICEF, reporting that the war destroyed Eritrea's infrastructure, adds that "the damage to individual lives has also been extensive," leaving roughly 95,000 orphans and other children with "traumatic memories of armed conflict" that along with life-threatening drought "add to children's suffering" (1994: 19, 109). Researchers from the War-Torn Societies Project of the United Nation report,

> the war sent about 1,000,000—a third of the entire Eritrean population—in exile. ... Many others became internally displaced. There is no record on casualties, but some estimate that as many as 70,000 combatants and 250,000 civilians lost their lives during the war. (Woldemichael & Sorensen, 1995: 4–5)

Lives and ways of life in what is now the nation of Eritrea have been destroyed in such a way that the losses are literally incalculable. One reason we lack detailed information is Eritrea's restrictions on journalists and scholars. A growing body of scholarship on Eritreans in diaspora has emerged partly as a response to such restrictions but has not taken up the question of how far and with what consequences actual wartime and liberation movement experiences might diverge from the established national narratives. These narratives are often readily repeated by informants themselves instead of their personal histories. Conrad, among others, found a formulaic uniformity in many Eritreans' accounts, although she describes how once dissent began to be voiced, ELF supporters and members of minority ethnic groups in diaspora put forth alternative narratives of Eritrea's history, even including an alternate Martyrs' Day (Conrad, 2006a). Such narratives are politically significant, but to the extent that they are similar in theme to the dominant narrative with other (stigmatized) groups playing heroic and sacrificial roles instead of the EPLF, they do not reveal how Eritreans experienced Ethiopian violence and life on the fronts as human beings (rather than as nationalists). Furthermore, there is almost a total absence of information about abuses within the EPLF or the kinds of suffering fighters (many of whom were young people cut off from their families for the duration) experienced. The published "reminiscences" of EPLF member and nationally acclaimed writer, Alemseged Tesfai, give a picture of the hardships of life on the front lines and the culture of martyrdom for the cause, but through the lens of admiration for selfless sacrifice. One exception is when a group of young fighters are killed, and he writes a sentiment rarely aired in public: "Our revolution is too costly" (2007: 71). On the following page he seems to correct himself for this response, however, observing that a soldier "has no time for sorrow, sentimentality, and sympathy" (2007: 71–72). In all wars there is a discrepancy between heroic ideals and lived experience (Das, 2008), but with the EPLF's former leaders in power, the veneration of the front and the ideal of sacrifice for the nation have been institutionalized.

## 2    Suffering for the Nation

Control over information, political education, and the dissemination of propaganda, which were keys to EPLF's wartime strategies, are central to the way the Eritrean state has governed since independence. Within Eritrea there is no free press, civil society, or independent public sphere. As an Awate poster put it, "one of the last remaining pillars that continue to hold the roof over [the regime's] dilapidated power structure is its almost total control of information by its monopoly over mass media" (Awate post, 27 June 2013).[1] Censorship, secrecy, and propaganda are obvious tactics. But the ways that people are rendered silent by national narratives that purport to represent them are complex and subtle.

The national narratives produced by the Eritrean state locate Eritrea's existence as an independent nation and the future security and development of the nation in the enormous sacrifices made by Eritreans. As Conrad puts it, "the key themes of 'Eritrean official history' revolve around issues of unity, solidarity, self-reliance, and readiness to die for the nation" (2006a: 254). Those killed in the war are known as martyrs, and their sacrifice of life for

---

[1] Except for occasional ellipses or brackets for clarifications, I have not altered the spelling or grammar in any of the web posts quoted in this article.

the nation is, I have argued, held up as an ideal of citizenship I have called "sacrificial citizenship" (Bernal, 2014). The Eritrean National Charter states:

> We fought against enemies who had superior capacity, with meagre outside support, relying on our people and own capacity, with heavy sacrifices, tremendous effort, vigilance, political maturity and ingenuity. Our struggle was not limited to combating the enemy; we laid the proper foundation for an independent country. Finally, in a referendum in which the entire population consciously and enthusiastically participated, 99.8% voted for national independence. It would be no exaggeration to claim that such an achievement has few equals in the history of liberation movements. (EPLF/PFDJ, 1994: 1)

The Eritrean Constitution that was ratified in 1997 but never fully implemented begins with this preamble:

> We the people of Eritrea, united in a common struggle for our rights and common destiny: With Eternal Gratitude to the scores of thousands of our martyrs who sacrificed their lives for the causes of our rights and independence, during the long and heroic revolutionary struggle for liberation, and to the courage and steadfastness of our Eritrean patriots; and standing on the solid ground of unity and justice bequeathed by our martyrs and combatants; Aware that it is the sacred duty of all Eritreans to build a strong and advanced Eritrea on the bases of freedom, unity, peace, stability and security achieved through the long struggle of all Eritreans, which tradition we must cherish, preserve and develop.[2]

The Isaias regime established 20 June as Martyrs' Day, when the nation officially recognizes its losses. Independence Day celebrations on 24 May also begin with a minute of silence "in memory of fallen heroes."

The national narratives promoted by the Eritrean state that construct Eritreans as heroic sacrificers and elevate the martyr as an iconic figure inflict a secondary form of violence on Eritreans. Through such narratives the state makes personal experiences of suffering unspeakable because Eritrean identity and belonging are constructed through collective sacrifice and the victimization of the nation, not through the losses that many Eritreans actually experienced. Where collective suffering serves as a foundation of group identity, to exit from that script is to risk setting oneself outside the community. This national community remains important for Eritreans in diaspora. They were an organized element of the nationalist struggle, and they continue to see themselves (and are recognized by the state) as a component of the nation.

---

[2] See http://www.eritrean-embassy.se/government-agencies/eritrea-constitution/.

There are significant parallels with the ways the Tamil separatist organization, the Liberation Tigers of Tamil Elam, dominated the cultural life of Tamils in diaspora such that the Tamil Tigers came to define Tamilness itself (Thiranagama, 2014). Thiranagama observes, "with few alternative views of Tamilness available, to go against LTTE ideologies about Sri Lanka and Tamil Eelam had become tantamount to rejecting one's own community" (2014: 272). Unlike the Tamil Tigers, the EPLF succeeded in forming a state, gaining even greater power to define Eritrean culture and identity.

Eritrea is not unique in connecting death to nationalism. As Ledgerwood writes of Cambodia, "the master narrative of the state … provides an explanation for the inexplicable and creates from death a re-established sense of national identity" (2001: 104). Benedict Anderson observed, "the deaths that structure the nation's biography are of a special kind … exemplary suicides, poignant martyrdoms, assassinations, executions, wars, and holocausts [that] must be remembered/forgotten as 'our own'" (1991: 205–206). But the degree to which national identity and the legitimacy of the regime in power in Eritrea are bound up with a narrative about martyrs who sacrificed their lives for the nation to exist is distinctive. Furthermore, as Jackie Feldman points out, "the ways in which such practices of necromancy are constructed are culturally specific and teach us much about the cosmology of particular nations" (2010: 122). For the Eritrean state, martyrs serve a political purpose similar to what Feldman describes for Israel: "Were it not for the State, what happened in Auschwitz could happen to Jews today. Jewish existence thus becomes contingent on the State, and this contingency charges the taken-for-granted life-world of Israel with emotion and ultimately, reinforces commitment to the state" (2010: 104). Violence is foundational to the state, which then produces a taken-for-granted association among identity, survival, and the state. In the Eritrean case, this association holds that the nation would not exist without the EPLF and the Isaias regime and that Eritrean existence thus rests on the sovereignty of the regime and the sacrifice of the Eritreans who died to create it. As Feldman indicates, this is much more than a political logic; it is an emotional orientation where the powerful feelings evoked by violence are harnessed to political loyalties.

In their discussion of commemorations, Jelin and Kaufman write of the societal "labors of memory" through which "facts are reorganized, existing perspectives and schemes of interpretation are shaken, voices of new and old generations ask questions, tell stories, create spaces for interaction, share clues about what they experienced, what they heard, and what they silenced before" (2001: 39). In Eritrea, repression makes it very difficult for such participatory processes to take place. According to Reid, while the politics of silence are characterized by a remarkable degree of patience on the part of the population upon which the government can continue to depend, the latter has rooted its legitimacy in a flame-keeper role, positing itself as the sole interpreter of national destiny, which is obviously unsustainable in the longer term. (2009: 211)

The Eritrean leadership maintains a siege mentality that demands ongoing collective sacrifice such that "individual interests are by definition considered as treason" (Treiber, 2007: 243). The state strives to control citizens' lives to an extreme degree and to orchestrate their expression of emotions through public events such as Martyrs' Day. Everyone's experience is supposed to be writ large in the collective history and any independent expression is seen as a threat to unity. Silence is not an absence, but something produced through relations of power. Even in the relative freedom of diaspora websites, silence and self-censorship reflect and produce particular forms of belonging.

## 3   Diaspora and the Afterlife of Violence

The three decades of mass mobilization by nationalist movements and war with Ethiopia were formative experiences for more than a generation of Eritreans. Those who escaped Eritrea to other lands lost an entire life-world as they sought safety. The war is not just an event or even a series of events that members of the diaspora have survived but a rupture of their individual life course and of their social world that can never be put back to what it was or continued toward what it might have become. All Eritreans who lived through the era of the independence struggle (whether in Eritrea or abroad) must be understood as survivors of a national trauma that changed their life courses irrevocably even as it tore Eritrean society apart and put it back together in a new form. New waves of migrants from Eritrea have different experiences of their homeland and reasons for escape (Conrad, 2006b; Hepner & Tecle, 2013; Poole, 2013). Here I focus on the first generation of diaspora that was formed by the liberation struggle and whose members experienced first hand aspects of this now mythologized national history. This first wave of Eritreans in diaspora are the peers of Eritrea's president and ruling-party members. The ruling party calls this generation *yekealo* ("the capable ones" in Tigrinya) and calls the next generation *warsay* ("my heirs"), meaning those who inherited Eritrean independence.

Members of the diaspora have lived through war, death of loved ones, displacement, and loss of home and property, serial migration, alienation, racism, and isolation in places of resettlement. Even after reaching safety,

Eritreans in diaspora faced the dangers and frustrations of negotiating legalities and illegalities in exile: not having freedom of movement to leave refugee camps or travel from one country of refuge to another; lacking important documents; being stateless; seeking visas; seeking political asylum; pursuing numerous attempts to migrate over the course of years; attempting to reunite with family members; trying to financially support, rescue, or help relocate other family members in dire situations; and struggling to adjust to multiple, serial "host" societies and settings (Arnone, 2011; Conrad, 2006b).

The 1998–2000 border war, the continuing instability of relations with Ethiopia, and the conscription of all Eritrean youth into open-ended military and national service mean that war, flight, and refuge are not simply events in the past but loom in the present and the future for Eritreans, including the family members back "home" to whom those in diaspora remain attached despite their separation. The diaspora suffer differently than survivors within Eritrea not least because they are surrounded in daily life by people who did not share those experiences and know little or nothing about them. There is a great deal of diversity across and within diasporas, yet as Sonia Ryang writes, "what all of these examples hold in common is their tie to the homeland is cut off with more or less pain, more or less violence" (2009: 3).

Across the ruptures of war, forced migration, and diaspora, Eritreans established websites that have drawn posters and attracted readers since the 1990s. The kinds of connections formed online by members of the diaspora arise from their alienation from the social locations where they find themselves as well as from their shared experiences in Eritrea and in flight. Part of what draws readers and posters to diaspora websites is the sense of communicating with others who know the shared losses and the absent presences, the "ghosts and shadows" that haunt them (Matsuoka & Sorenson, 2001). Eritreans read into each other's posts many unstated understandings about Eritrean history, politics, and culture that contextualize posts. This common framework, however, has been largely constructed by the dominant voice of the state, whose narratives could be considered "canonical and institutional memory" (Feldman, 1999: 8). Whether posters write against the backdrop of official narratives or whether they stand in a self-consciously critical relationship to them, neither they nor their readers are independent of the dominant framework.

# 4 What Goes Without Saying

Violent disruptions of people's lives, families, and communities are part of what tie Eritreans together and bind members of the diaspora to one another and to the nation, even when they have made new lives as citizens of other countries. Yet rarely are the traumas and losses actually experienced by individuals ever mentioned. It is as if the most important understandings are those that cannot be articulated. This is not only because the experiences are painful to recall, but also, more significantly, because expressions of pain (and in some cases the actual experiences themselves) run counter to the heroic national narrative that constitutes cultural and political membership. Allen Feldman writes,

> the victim is an irreconcilable absence. The political victim, deceased or alive, is always partially the disappeared. Something has been subtracted even from those who survive and return, something that can only accommodate symbolic mediation, emotions, and memory, new social networks, micro-communities of pain, are formed around the particularity of the removed, the subtracted, and the returned. (1991: 238)

By following the complex links connecting the power of the state to Eritreans' unstated feelings, I trace the ways the unexpressed takes shape and perhaps even draws power through its omission. An unusual example of someone expressing personal pain was posted on Dehai in December 22, 1996:

> Like thousands of fellow Eritreans, I had the opportunity to participate in the Eritrean struggle as "Teghadalai" [guerrilla fighter]. I do not take lightly what the word "teghedalai" meant. Like many others, the Eritrean inside conflict has caused us to migrate to the west without plans and desire. I happen to be here in the Washington DC Metropolitan area physically, but part of my soul is back home in my native homeland. You could visualize from the tone of my writing that I am not a person who smiles much; my life is over shadowed by the affection that I have for those unable to see the torch of glory, unable to tell their story & those veterans who are physically & mentally disabled. After the last paragraph, I was unable to continue & stopped for two days. Is it emotion or compassion for reasons that I could not understand; I was not able to control my tears. (Dehai post, December 31, 1996)

This post suggests some of the hidden dimensions of experience and emotion that many other Eritreans who lived through similar events may share but refrain from articulating publicly.

By reading between the lines and by bringing into focus the negative space—the gaps left by what is not stated—the various means by which people obliquely refer to loss and suffering become visible. Sometimes posters conjure up known or shared experiences with a single word or two. Words such as "martyrs," *meda* ("the field"—i.e., as a fighter), and *ghedli* ("the front") are powerfully evocative, calling up entire histories and strong emotions. In an exchange of views on Asmarino about the government's dismantling of Asmara University in 2006, one poster in replying to another underlines his point that President Isaias is threatened by the educated with this statement: "You know this very well. You were in meda" (Asmarino post, August 6, 2006). Thus, not only do these two posters know something about each other, but they also share knowledge of the war that can be evoked by a single word.

The issue of silence about personal experience was addressed in a post a few days after the emotional post from the former guerrilla fighter. Titled "How we paid for Freedom," it begins:

> We all talk about the Eritrean struggling years for freedom, but we seldom put a face and a name to specific events to know and calculate how it had impacted us. For sure each and every one of us have been touched by it. (Dehai post, December 31, 1996)

The timing of these disturbing posts around Western Christmas and New Year could be coincidental but might suggest that being surrounded by celebrations reminds some Eritreans in diaspora of the sadness they carry inside and evokes feelings of alienation that prompt them to turn to the websites. The author then writes, "I would like to present you stories, different versions of our experiences." Significantly, the author chooses to express herself through the fictional representation of collective experience, rather than memoir or another genre that would make truth claims based on individual experience. The first instalment describes a young woman's return visit to Eritrea after 16 years in diaspora:

> Guilt ate away at MbraQ [transliterated Tigrinya name] … for surviving her younger siblings and for not having served to the cause of Eritrea's struggle along with them … The festive mood in the house changed into chaos of wailings and agonized crys that gave fresh life to the hidden sorrows of her parents. (Ellipses added)

The reunion becomes an occasion of mourning as the return of the living child simultaneously represents the loss of the children who will never return.

Notice, too, that the sorrows over the deaths have been "hidden." The focus on parents' suffering follows a pattern in Eritreans' posts where emotional pain is often expressed obliquely as empathy for others, particularly parents. Thus, for example, one post starts by criticizing the regime as "those who are gambling with the country and our brothers' blood," and goes on to say, "our parents are crying day and night ... their bones are broken, their knees are shaking, their backs are shivering and their hope is shattered forever" (Asmarino post, July 3, 2007; ellipsis in original).

The most common references to the war in posts deal with martyrs. Frequently martyrs are invoked through slogans like "remember our martyrs." For the state, the figure of the martyr represents the nation's sacrifices to achieve independence, but for many Eritreans, the loss is personal. The dead include loved ones, relatives, friends, comrades in arms, schoolmates, and neighbours. One poster writes, "the blood of the martyrs runs through our veins, arteries, and our hearts" (Asmarino post, November 27, 2006). He represents the dead as inseparable from the living. As such they cannot be relegated to the past or left behind. Those who survived lived and in some cases fought under similar conditions as those who died. Martyrs thus stand for the suffering associated with the war and for everything the survivors escaped. The "martyr" figure constructs the identities of the living as survivors. As the story about MbraQ suggests, this is sometimes a source of guilt for those who fled to diaspora. At other times, reminders of the martyrs may suggest that whatever present grief is felt and however hard one's current condition may be the alternative literally was death. In all of these ways, posters' invocations of the dead indirectly allude to the living and to what I call "the afterlife of violence."

The issue of personal experiences of loss as opposed to national loss was raised by someone posting from Asmara who asserted that those in power did not experience the same losses as other Eritreans. He turns what I have called sacrificial citizenship against the state to find it wanting:

> Almost every one of us has paid the dear life of a big brother, an uncle, an aunt, a father and a mother. A son, a daughter, a little brother. Some have paid four to five per family. We can't have them back, we will only see them in heaven. ... Sadly for us, GOD's test for us is that those in power and those who have made Eritrea their playground have paid nothing. ... They do not cry for anybody on Martyr's Day ... The Man the world call our President lost no brother nor sister nor uncle nor friend in the revolution. (Awate post, July 4, 2007; ellipses added; originally posted with a note that it was translated from Trigrinya by Awate)

As in the example above, posters often use "we" and write in the plural, emphasizing shared concerns and experiences. The priority of individuals' feelings, rights to security, happiness, or other aspects of well-being are not taken for granted in the communicative context in which Eritreans connect online or offline. Stoicism, moreover, has served Eritreans as a survival tactic under the Ethiopians, who forbid mourning of those they killed as traitors, and under Isaias Afewerki, who urged mothers to celebrate rather than mourn their children killed in war. Another poster apologized for writing about a family he knows that lost all but one of their sons: "Everyone for sure do have his/her story to tell about what they passed during the difficult time. I raised the example only to be provoke your memories" (Dehai post, October 16, 1997). While Eritreans' orientation towards collective experience rather than personal suffering may have long historical and cultural roots, it is actively fostered by the regime. A 2007 post on Asmarino reflects critically on the way Eritrean belonging is constructed through sacrifice:

> I lost six immediate brothers in the war ... but this doesn't make me or my families more Eritreans than the rest citizens of Eritrea. But don't tell me whether I am a pure Eritrean or not (according your judgements) ... I did not ask you to give me a citizenship or to approve me for Eritrean citizenship. (Asmarino post, June 9, 2007; ellipses and parentheses in original)

One of the things readers and posters on Eritrean websites are doing is participating in a community of suffering. Even people who do not voice their own stories or feelings can see that their pain is shared, and their losses are part of a collective history. However, the extent to which that history has been edited and mythologized by the state in effect appropriates people's experiences and emotions from them for political purposes. A poster discussing Independence Day celebrations writes,

> since PDFJ controls the communities, they will exploit the occasion. I am watching ERI-TV [on livestream] and everything is on high drive. ... As you can see, they are exploiting our legacy that is your legacy, mine, and everyone else's. In such an occasion, do you let them own your history or you use that occasion as a moment of reflection. (Awate post, May 24, 2015; brackets and ellipsis added)

Personal accounts and reflections are important for revising history and also for reclaiming experience for private, social life, where the state treats suffering and sacrifice only as nationalist and instrumental in their significance.

In 1998 a Dehai poster argued against the border war, which the diaspora generally ardently supported at that time, by drawing on personal knowledge of the disputed area. His post begins with an understated account of how as a youth he was forced into the ELF and later escaped to the Ethiopian border:

> In 1978 I (with 14 youngsters from the same village) was recruited without mine or my parents will, to join ELF. Opposing not to join the fighters, as we know, was detrimental. Thus the only thing I could do was to escape [to the border region]. (Dehai post, June 23, 1998; parentheses in original; brackets added)

Clearly much pain and fear are concealed in these spare sentences. Another poster recalled events of August 30, 1965, when he was engaged in clandestine activities of the ELF, helping to establish rebel cells in Keren and Asmara. He says he is driven to set this down because national narratives (constructed by the EPLF) underplay the contributions of Muslim Eritreans. While focused on comrades who were caught by the Ethiopians and sent to prison, his account shows he nearly missed being captured himself. The individuals he mentions were killed which he indicates by writing "martyr" after their names.

> In the morning hours of that fateful 30th August, this writer and **Michael Ghaber** (martyr) met and discussed with their former middle school teacher, Memhir **Seyoum Negassi** (martyr), who immediately volunteered to meet with the ELF envoys from Kassala. We took him to the hideout ... When we returned to take out Memhir Seyoum from the place at about mid-day, no one was there! ... In my youth, I witnessed the Jeberti and Bedjuk [Muslim Eritrean ethnic groups] contributing more than their share in the nationalist awakening ... It is sad to see that all those who made Eritrean nationalism happen at the end of the long journey to be treated with disrespect ... by the first head of the new Eritrean state. (Awate post, October 16, 2002; bold and parentheses in original; brackets and ellipses added)

As difficult as Eritreans find it to tell such stories, as long as the villains are Ethiopians or even the ELF, the mythic status of the EPLF is not directly challenged. Another poster, however, reports things he saw in the EPLF that cast not only the present leadership but also the very nature of the liberation movement in a critical light:

> When I read Ali Said's [a government official] interview and his response to the rights and situations of the prisoners of conscience, [jailed Eritrean critics of the government] I was astonished that nothing have changed since the time

> I had acquaintance with him and as a matter of fact also with Isaias. The year was 1994 [editor: 1974] and I was young and innocent. But from the first day I joined the then EPLF, I was terrorized by what I started to observe and especially when I was advised by a high school friend (now a high official in the government) not to inquire about the prisoners of conscience … I perfectly knew where they were kept (in foxholes in Bleqat) and I sometimes saw some of them from a distance when they were fetching water and still that photographic image lingers in me. (Awate post, December 23, 2003; parentheses in original; brackets and ellipsis added except for the date, which was edited by the webmasters)

The author's mention of being "terrorized" at the time and of how what he saw "lingers in me" after three decades provides a glimpse of the feelings that often go unspoken. This post is significant, moreover, for thinking about the "speech impediment" that has prevented many more Eritreans from reporting their experiences, because the oppression he witnessed was being carried out by the liberation movement of which he was a part. During the war, the EPLF enjoyed mass support among Eritreans and was sustained in part by Eritreans in diaspora. Thus, unlike harm done to a community by external forces, the EPLF was not something that simply acted on Eritreans. Many passionately believed in it and supported it emotionally and materially for decades. EPLF fighters were people's relatives and friends. To openly reveal its flaws casts personal histories, sacrifices made, and losses exacted in a new light.

The post above prompted someone else to post his own even more troubling memories of the EPLF a few days later:

> I also witnessed this horror 30 years back, but mostly as a foot soldier. Unlike [the previous poster], I was not privy to the meetings of the polit bureau, but I too have a story to tell … The year was 1972, I had just joined the then Selfi Nasnet armed faction led by Isaias … The fate of many combatants in this armed group—the politically active, the war weary, and disillusioned—was mostly incarceration, followed by execution … of all the military gears of a Tegadelay [guerrilla fighter], the plastic rope sends shivers to me, to this day … Disarmed victims were tied behind their backs with this rope before being led to execution grounds. It was also used to garotte the victims. The *mesera nesela* [plastic rope] was a gruesome "self-reliance" weapon, one which spared the use of scarce bullets … I hope a museum will accord it a space for people to see during the expected Reconciliation Era. (Awate post, December 26, 2003; brackets and ellipses added)

His mention of "this horror" makes clear how powerfully he was affected. Not only does he still remember and physically recoil after 30 years, but also he suggests that this piece of history is so important that a museum should display it. His prediction of a "Reconciliation Era" suggests he believes a truth and reconciliation process will be necessary to expose such hidden histories.

These last two posts appeared after 2001, a political turning point when Eritrean dissent arose following the disastrous border war. The posters recount events that took place in the early 1970s, after 30 years of silence (at least in the public forum of diaspora websites). While the reasons for posting or remaining silent about personal experiences are multiple and complex, in this case it seems that posters are emboldened by other posters and by the burgeoning criticism of President Isaias and the ruling party. In his text the first poster draws a direct connection between what he observed in the EPLF, and the jailing of critics being carried out in Eritrea in the early 2000s. Yet despite the steady rise of dissenting voices in diaspora since then and posters who criticize the harsh political culture developed by the EPLF and expanded throughout society by the Isaias regime, few personal testimonials have been unleashed. The accounts that are posted hint at all that remains unsaid.

A recent post by a woman former EPLF fighter broached the taboo topic of sexual assault within the ranks. "How I hated those nights, those sleepless nights," she writes, "he was groping and harassing me the whole night is what you could tell or keep it to yourself the next day and retain it your—and only your—memory" (Awate post, February 10, 2016). Her post interestingly appeared alongside an illustration that presented the map of Eritrea in the form of a person being choked at the neck by a rope. She mentions she wrote the post in response to government claims that rape is rare or non-existent in Eritrea, and she argues that "if we are honestly seeking for 'hard evidence,' well, then let us create a conducive climate that enables the concerned, the victims to speak out and share their experience."

The posts quoted in this article suggest that there are many stories yet to be told about what happened to Eritreans and how it affects them now. Members of the generation that experienced the struggle for independence are aging and are scattered among Eritrea and diverse diaspora locations. Their secret knowledge may never be shared, and their untold stories may never be heard. The Isaias regime bases its claims to legitimacy in the EPLF's successful war of liberation. As the regime has increasingly alienated Eritreans through its internal repression and bellicose foreign policies, people's efforts to make sense of the present and to envision possible national futures are entangled with history. Propaganda, censorship, and national narratives centred on collective struggle and sacrifice have produced not just strategic self-censorship among Eritreans but a more subtle political aphasia that renders some things unsayable.

## 5 Conclusion

Even as thousands of Eritreans flee their country every month and contribute to what Europe sees as a migrant crisis, we lack insights into the perspectives and personal histories of migrants themselves. Migrants' stories do not begin in refugee camps or on overcrowded boats and their stories do not end when they find a safe haven in another land. What migrants leave behind remains with them, and there are sentiments and publics that are hidden from view. The Internet may help to reveal some dimensions of these emotions and communities (Turner, 2008).

Anthropology was at the forefront of research into transnationalism, migration, refugees, and diasporas (Basch et al., 1994; Hannerz, 1996; Malkki, 1995; Vertovec & Cohen, 1999), and our discipline has long contributed to the understanding of contemporary political violence (Feldman, 1991; Nordstrom & Robben, 1996; Sluka, 1999). The discipline has been comparatively slow, however, to grasp the significance of digital media for cultural research and to demonstrate what anthropological perspectives have to contribute to Internet research (see Coleman [2010] for an overview of early research). My analysis of the politics of silence brings into focus aspects of Internet communications that have been overshadowed by interest in the role of the Internet in providing access to information and freedom from censorship.

Eritreans are engaged in a profound ongoing struggle over the meaning of life and death and the politics of nationhood. Understanding this struggle is important not least because Africa often is regarded as "a space in which universal reason somehow does not operate and therefore in which 'senseless' violence erupts" (Donham, 2006: 17; see Thomas [2009] for a similar discussion in relation to Jamaica). As Eritreans seek to make sense of their lives and their history, they do so against the backdrop of the world's indifference and in confrontation not only with an authoritarian regime but also with a regime of truth that has served to anchor them in an identity defined by the leadership to serve its purposes. Franz Kafka famously observed: "A book should work like an axe to break up the frozen sea inside us." The violence of that image makes us consider how writing can be an act of violence, an act of destruction that makes something new possible. Eritreans may not yet have found a way to explode the logjam of state mythologies that inhibit the recounting of their own experiences. The websites established by Eritreans in diaspora are vital for such processes and have proven to be sites of knowledge production where critical perspectives are developed.

Eritrean websites reveal complex communicative terrains where power is constructed and contested in ways that cannot be captured by the opposition between the diaspora and the homeland, between online and offline, or between silence and speech. Eritreans may leave Eritrea behind, but they cannot fully escape Eritrea's violent history or its transnational political culture. What emerges is a picture of the dynamic processes of visibilization and concealment in which Eritreans are engaged as they construct relations of citizenship, reconstruct communities in the aftermath of war, weigh the costs of war, and interpret the significance of their suffering. The relative safety of Eritrean websites must be seen in contrast to the ongoing violent repression within Eritrea and the threat posed by a government preoccupied with its own defence from enemies both internal and external. Eritrean narratives reveal how the effects of violence endure. The ways dominant narratives shape what is expressed online offer a cautionary counterpoint to the idea that the Internet is inherently liberating or that physical exit from a dangerous homeland yields political freedom.

**Acknowledgements** I am grateful to *AA* editor Deborah Thomas and three anonymous reviewers for their stimulating feedback. Much of the article was written during my 2015–2016 fellowship at the Centre for Advanced Studies in the Behavioral Sciences at Stanford University, and I thank CASBS and its director, Margaret Levi, for the great gift of time for thinking, researching, and writing.

# References

Abusharaf, R. (2002). *Wanderings: Sudanese Migrants and Exiles in North America*. Cornell University Press.
Anderson, B. (1991). *Imagined Communities: Reflections on the Origin and Spread of Nationalism*. Verso.
Arnone, A. (2011). Talking About Identity: Milanese Eritreans Describe Themselves. *Journal of Modern Italian Studies, 16*(4), 516–527.
Basch, L., Schiller, N. G., & Blanc, C. S. (Eds.). (1994). *Nations Unbound: Transnational Projects, Post-colonial Predicaments, and De-territorialized Nation-States*. Gordon and Breach Science Publishers.
Bernal, V. (2014). *Nation as Network: Diaspora, Cyberspace, and Citizenship*. University of Chicago Press.

Besteman, C. (2016). *Making Refuge: Somali Bantu Refugees and Lewiston, Maine*. Duke University Press.

Bozzini, D. (2011). Low-Tech Surveillance and the Despotic State in Eritrea. *Surveillance and Society, 9*(1/2), 1–22.

Brinkerhoff, J. (2009). *Digital Diasporas: Identity and Transnational Engagement*. Cambridge University Press.

Cliffe, L., & Davidson, B. (Eds.). (1988). *The Long Struggle of Eritrea for Independence and Constructive Peace*. Spokesman Books.

Coleman, G. E. (2010). Ethnographic Approaches to Digital Media. *Annual Review of Anthropology, 39*, 487–505.

Connell, D. (2011). From Resistance to Governance: Eritrea's Trouble with Transition. *Review of African Political Economy, 38*(129), 419–433.

Conrad, B. (2006a). Out of the 'Memory Hole': Alternative Narratives of the Eritrean Revolution in Diaspora. *Africa Spectrum, 41*(2), 249–271.

Conrad, B. (2006b). A Culture of War and a Culture of Exile: Young Eritreans in Germany and Their Relations to Eritrea. *Revue Europeene Des Migrations Internationales, 22*(1), 59–85.

Cvetkovitch, A. (2007). Public Feelings. *South Atlantic Quarterly, 106*(3), 459–468.

Das, V. (2008). Violence, Gender, and Subjectivity. *Annual Review of Anthropology, 37*, 283–299.

Dickson-Gomez, J. (2004). One Who Doesn't Know War, Doesn't Know Anything: The Problem of Comprehending Suffering in Postwar El Salvador. *Anthropology and Humanism, 29*(2), 145–158.

Donham, D. (2006). Staring at Suffering: Violence as Subject. In E. Bay & D. Donham (Eds.), *States of Violence: Politics, Youth, and Memory in Contemporary Africa* (pp. 16–33). University of Virginia Press.

Dorman, S. (2005). Narratives of Nationalism in Eritrea: Research and Revisionism. *Nations and Nationalism, 11*(2), 203–222.

EPLF/PFDJ. (1994). *National Charter Adopted by the 3rd Congress of the EPLF/PFDJ*. http://alenalki.com

Feldman, A. (1991). *Formations of Violence: The Narrative of the Body and Political Terror in Northern Ireland*. University of Chicago Press.

Feldman, A. (1999). The Event and Its Shadow: Figure and Ground in Violence. *Transforming Anthropology, 8*(1/2), 3–11.

Feldman, J. (2010). Nationalising Personal Trauma, Personalizing National Redemption: Performing Testimony at AuschwitzBirkenau. In N. Argenti & K. Schramm (Eds.), *Remembering Violence: Anthropological Perspectives on Intergenerational Transmission* (pp. 103–134). Berghahn Books.

Feuchtwang, S. (2003). Loss: Transmissions, Recognitions, Authorisations. In S. Radstone & K. Hodgkin (Eds.), *Regimes of Memory* (pp. 76–89). Routledge.

Finaldi, G. (2016). *A History of Italian Colonialism, 1860–1907: Europe's Last Empire*. Routledge.

Gajjala, R. (2008). South Asian Technospaces and 'Indian' Digital Diasporas. In R. Gajjala & V. Gajjala (Eds.), *South Asian Technospaces* (pp. 37–48). Peter Lang.

Ghebre-Ab, H. (2013). *Massacre at Wekidiba: The Tragic Story of a Village in Eritrea*. Red Sea Press.

Hannerz, U. (1996). *Transnational Connections: Culture, People, Places*. Routledge.

Henry, D. (2006). Violence and the Body: Somatic Expressions of Trauma and Vulnerability During War. *Medical Anthropology Quarterly, 20*(3), 379–398.

Hepner, T. R., & Tecle, S. (2013). New Refugees, Development-Forced Displacement, and Transnational Governance in Eritrea and Exile. *Urban Anthropology, 42*(3/4), 377–410.

HRW (Human Rights Watch). (1991). *Evil Days: Thirty Years of War and Famine in Ethiopia*. Human Rights Watch.

Iyob, R. (1995). *The Eritrean Struggle for Independence: Domination, Resistance, Nationalism, 1941–1993*. Cambridge University Press.

Iyob, R., & Knight, F. (Eds.). (2014). *Dimensions of African and Other Diasporas*. University of the West Indies Press.

Jelin, E., & Kaufman, S. (2001). Layers of Memories: Twenty Years After in Argentina. In D. Lorey & W. Beezely (Eds.), *Genocide, Collective Violence, and Popular Memory* (pp. 31–52). Rowman & Littlefield.

Kapteijns, L., & Richters, A. (Eds.). (2010). *Mediations of Violence in Africa: Fashioning New Futures from Contested Paths*. Brill.

Kibreab, G. (1987). *Refugees and Development in Africa: The Case of Eritrea*. Red Sea Press.

Kibreab, G. (2009). *Eritrea: A Dream Deferred*. James Currey.

Kligman, G. (1998). *The Politics of Duplicity: Controlling Reproduction in Ceausescu's Romania*. University of California Press.

Ledgerwood, J. (2001). The Cambodian Tuol Sleng Museum of Genocidal Crimes: National Narratives. In D. Lorey & W. Beezely (Eds.), *Genocide, Collective Violence, and Popular Memory* (pp. 103–122). Rowman & Littlefield.

Malkki, L. (1995). *Purity and Exile: Violence, Memory, and National Cosmology Among Hutu Refugees in Tanzania*. University of Chicago Press.

Matsuoka, A., & Sorenson, J. (2001). *Ghosts and Shadows: Construction of Identity and Community in an African Diaspora*. University of Toronto Press.

Moodie, E. (2006). Microbus Crashes and Coca-Cola Cash: The Value of Death in 'Free Market' El Salvador. *American Ethnologist, 33*(1), 63–80.

Nordstrom, C., & Robben, A. (Eds.). (1996). *Fieldwork Under Fire: Contemporary Studies of Violence and Culture*. University of California Press.

Oiarzabal, P., & Alonso, A. (Eds.). (2010). *Diasporas in the New Media Age: Identity, Politics, and Community*. University of Nevada Press.

Okpewho, I., & Ngegwu, N. (Eds.). (2009). *The New African Diaspora*. Indiana University Press.

Papacharissi, Z. (2015). *Affective Publics: Sentiment, Technology, and Politics*. Oxford University Press.

Pool, D. (2001). *From Guerrillas to Government: The Eritrean People's Liberation Front*. James Currey.

Poole, A. (2013). Ransoms, Remittances, and Refugees: The Gatekeeper State in Eritrea. *Africa Today, 60*(2), 67–82.

Rahier, J. M. (2010). The Diversity of Diasporic Subjectivities: Different and Separate Ontologies? A Response to Kamari Clarke's 'New Spheres of Transnational Formations.' *Transforming Anthropology, 18*(1), 66–69.

Reid, R. (2006). War and Remembrance: Orality, Literacy and Conflict in the Horn. *Journal of African Cultural Studies, 18*(1), 89–103.

Reid, R. (2009). The Politics of Silence: Interpreting Apparent Stasis in Contemporary Eritrea. *Review of African Political Economy, 36*(120), 209–221.

Riggan, J. (2009). Avoiding Wastage by Making Soldiers: Technologies of the State and the Imagination of the Educated Nation. In D. O'Kane & T. R. Hepner (Eds.), *Biopolitics, Militarism, and Development: Eritrea in the Twenty-First Century* (pp. 72–91). Berghahn Books.

Ryang, S. (2009). Introduction: Between the Nations: Diaspora and Koreans in Japan. In S. Ryang & J. Lie (Eds.), *Diaspora Without Homeland: Being Korean in Japan* (pp. 1–20). University of California Press.

Sanford, V. (2003). *Buried Secrets: Truth and Human Rights in Guatemala*. Palgrave.

Seitler, D. (2016). *The Affect Project*. http://www.humanities.utoronto.ca/wg_16-17_affect

Shaw, R. (2010). Afterword: Violence and the Generation of Memory. In N. Argenti & K. Schramm (Eds.), *Remembering Violence: Anthropological Perspectives on Intergenerational Transmission* (pp. 251–260). Berghahn Books.

Shelemay, K., & Kaplan, S. (Eds.). (2015). *Creating the Ethiopian Diaspora*. Tsehai Publishers.

Sluka, J. (1999). *Death Squad: The Anthropology of State Terror*. University of Pennsylvania Press.

Tesfai, A. (2007). *Two Weeks in the Trenches: Reminiscences of Childhood and War in Eritrea*. Hdri Publishers.

Theidon, K. (2013). *Intimate Enemies: Violence and Reconciliation in Peru*. University of Pennsylvania Press.

Thiranagama, S. (2014). Making Tigers from Tamils: LongDistance Nationalism and Sri Lankan Tamils in Toronto. *American Anthropologist, 116*(2), 265–278.

Thomas, D. (2009). The Violence of Diaspora: Governmentality, Class Cultures, and Circulations. *Radical History Review, 2009*(103), 83–104.

Treiber, M. (2007). Dreaming of a Good Life: Young Urban Refugees from Eritrea Between Refusal of Politics and Political Asylum. In H. P. Hahn & G. Klute (Eds.), *Cultures of Migration: African Perspectives* (pp. 239–60). Lit Verlag.

Trevaskis, G. (1960). *Eritrea: A Colony in Transition, 1941–52*. Oxford University Press.

Turner, S. (2008). Cyberwars of Words: Expressing the Unspeakable in Burundi's Diaspora. *Journal of Ethnic and Migration Studies, 34*(7), 1161–1180.

UNICEF. (1994). *Children and Women in Eritrea*. United Nations.

Vertovec, S., & Cohen, R. (Eds.). (1999). *Migration, Diasporas, and Transnationalism*. Edward Elgar.

Welde Giorgis, A. (2014). *Eritrea at a Crossroads: A Narrative of Triumph, Betrayal, and Hope*. Strategic Book Publishing.

Woldemichael, B., & Sorenson, B. (1995). *Management of Social and Institutional Rehabilitation: Eritrea Case Study*. War-Torn Societies Project. United Nations.

Woldemikael, T. (1991). Political Mobilization and Nationalist Movements: The Case of the Eritrean People's Liberation Front. *Africa Today, 38*(2), 31–42.

Wrong, M. (2005). *I Didn't Do It for You: How the World Betrayed a Small African Nation*. HarperCollins Publishers.

Yong, K. H. (2006). Silences in History and Nation-State: Reluctant Accounts of the Cold War in Sarawak. *American Anthropologist, 33*(3), 462–473.

Yurchak, A. (2005). *Everything Was Forever Until It Was No More: The Last Soviet Generation*. Princeton University Press.

# The Chemical Violence of Colonial Encounters in Africa: Historiographical Reflections and Theoretical Perspectives

Elijah Doro

## 1 Introduction

In October 2020, residents of Kabwe, a small mining town in Zambia brought a class action lawsuit before the South African High Court against global mining giant Anglo-American Corporation. The plaintiffs filing on behalf of 140,000 women and children argued in their case that their clients had suffered multiple injuries and medical defects from lead poisoning (Amnesty International, 2023). Chemical exposure to lead from soils in children's playgrounds, homes, and township prompted adverse health effects such as miscarriages, anaemia, stillbirths, brain damage, physical disabilities, and sometimes death. The plaintiffs alleged that the Anglo-American mining company was culpable through its direct involvement in "irresponsible" mining practices between 1924 and 1974. The lawsuit further argued that Anglo-American Corporation knew of the dangers of lead poisoning for over a century but deliberately chose to turn a blind eye. The Kabwe lead mine at Broken Hill was closed in 1994 leaving behind vast stockpiles of toxic waste. In 2022, the United Nations Special Rapporteur on Toxics described Kabwe as "one of the most polluted places on earth" and threatened by a severe environmental crisis (Corporate Justice Coalition, 2022). The verdict in this historic lawsuit is still pending but, whatever its outcome, this case will

E. Doro (✉)
Rachel Carson Centre, Ludwig Maximillian University, Munich, Germany
e-mail: elijahdoro0@gmail.com

have substantial significance in illuminating the potential of colonial encounters to disrupt present landscapes and communities in Africa. If successful this lawsuit will not only serve as judicial precedence in the prosecution and conviction of colonial chemical violence, but it will also amplify the imperative for extensive investigation of similar historical incidences of chemical violence in Africa that are currently obscured from scrutiny.

The Kabwe lead poisoning lawsuit illustrates that violence is not always there, readily available for analysis and examination. It is not always visible and tangible. Rather, its scars and scratches are sometimes lodged in the invisible molecular structures and genetic materials of life. In such circumstances, victimhood becomes contested and culpability and accountability fraught with many complexities. It raises a myriad questions. How do we confront the violence whose trail is ephemeral and transient, disparate, and undefined in temporal spaces? How do we contend with broken narratives of chemical violence when the victims are disempowered by knowledge hegemonies that reinforce their precarities, and the perpetrators have bulwarks of knowledge that reinforce plausible deniability? These existential questions evoke the imperative for a critical rethink and epistemological reflections on the constitutionality of violence within the colonial and postcolonial state building projects in Africa. Palpably, violence is ubiquitous to projects of power and authority. It is a function of modernity and the modern state, and as Mamdani puts it, violence is the "midwife of history" (Mamdani, 2005). Violence is a construct of power relations and is reproduced through authority, control, coercion, and dominance. The colonial state-making project and settler colonialism in Africa was predicated on the logic of violence to subjugate indigenous people and their lands and keep them in the condition of subjects (Fanon, 2005: 35–94). Violence was a mundane and quotidian aspect of colonial life (Muschalek, 2019). It was usual, routinized, and embedded into normative aspects of colonial culture. Decolonial scholarship has depicted the coloniality of violence in postcolonial Africa and its afterlives as chronic strife (Comaroff & Comaroff, 2006; Ndlovu-Gatsheni, 2013), thus, denoting the temporal durability and institutionalized nature of violence that transcends historical epochs. Violence does not die; it just assumes new forms and metamorphosizes. Therefore, forensic examination of the many new forms in which colonial violence manifests in the politics of the present is a useful endeavour. Chemical violence is much subtle, persistent, transgenerational, and latent. It is "slow violence" displaced across time and space (Nixon, 2011). Its diagnosis and the quantification of its cause and effect and severity is elusive and contested. Justice, redress, compensation, and accountability become problematic in this terrain.

Chemical violence is structural. It is perpetrated and accessorized through infrastructures and processes. Murphy (2013a, 2013b) designates the processes that accessorize the perpetration of chemical violence as "chemical infrastructures." Chemical infrastructures constitute the spatial and temporal distribution of industrial chemicals in the air, waterways as they are absorbed and accumulate in cells of life and bodies over time and persist. The infrastructures are not physical or tangible things but consist of a multidimensional set of relational properties that becomes what Susan Star (1999) terms an "ecology of infrastructure". Chemical infrastructures pervaded the settler colonial capitalist project and entangled human bodies in toxic chemical relations during its molecular production churning out chemically altered lives or "alterlives" (Murphy, 2017). Armiero (2021) identifies the epoch of industrial capitalism as the "wasteocene" and distinct from the Anthropocene to denote the embodied stratigraphy of power and toxicity. The "wasteocene" is not just about toxic waste as a thing but waste as a set of wasted relationships centred on structural violence perpetrated against subaltern colonial subjects to produce wasted people. Humans become part of the toxic waste from these violent settler capitalist entanglements. The violent encounters of the wasted people are invisibilized, erased, and domesticated in toxic narratives. The narrative architecture of official memory in toxic narratives marginalizes the injustices of chemical violence suffered by victims such as the Kabwe women and children through deniability, scapegoating, and hegemonic knowledge regimes that scuttle retrieval of the historical truth. Strategic ignorance is reinforced to absolve and abscond. The infrastructures of chemical violence are spatially and temporally extensive, translocal, and transversive. They are etched in power structures and global power relations. Their spatial and temporal dispersion is uneven and so are the concomitant diverse effects on life. Victimhood, susceptibility, and proximity of exposure to chemical violence is defined by the matrix of power and the hierarchies in social relations manifesting in race, class and gender. As a distinct form of violence, colonial chemical violence refers to the discriminately disproportionate exposure of indigenous people and ecologies to industrial and environmental toxins during settler colonial production processes and the impact of these toxic substances on their bodies, the future generations, and natural ecosystems. While most epistemic approaches to violence in Africa have conceptualized and empiricized on the physical, tangible, and concrete forms of brutalization whose scars are more discernible, visible, and traceable (such as the manifest social and political cultures of strife), the insidious and molecular forms of colonial assault and genetic disruptions of chemical encounters have remained outside the gaze of scholarship. This chapter seeks to recentre chemical violence as a conceptual tool through which we can grasp the persistent and durable nature of colonial cultures of violence and the pathways through which we must approach, understand, and address violence in modern Africa. It argues for a historiographical and theoretical engagement with chemical violence in narratives of African scholarship in ways that further identification and articulation of how the spectre haunts and inhabits contemporary physical and biological spaces.

## 2   Toxic Colonial Histories: Chemicalized Landscapes and Disposable Bodies

The object of colonial conquest in Africa was expropriation, exploitation, extraction, and exportation. The white settler society was built on violent dispossession and coercive administration. The colonial economy required the mobilization of subject bodies in extractive spaces as disposable labour and the simultaneous conscription of indigenous landscapes and ecosystems into the orbit of capitalist exploitation and enterprise. Human bodies and landscapes were disposable entities, transient materialities within the infrastructure of colonial capitalist production. From King Leopold II's atrocious rubber regime in the Congo, to the infectious gold mines in South Africa, and the Herrero genocide in German East Africa millions of African bodies were dispensed in orgies of colonial violence. But these are the more visible encounters of colonial violence whose scars and lacerations are conspicuously etched in history. Other forms of imperial assault were subtle, and the perpetration of the violence and its manifestation have been latent and unquantifiable across time. The slow violence of colonial encounters is directly linked to disproportionate levels of chemical exposure in industrial, mining, and agricultural processes and the concomitant contamination and pollution of landscapes, ecosystems, and human bodies that predisposed them to vulnerabilities, sickness, ecological disruptions, and death in the long term. This slow violence has dormancy and latency that crossed temporal boundaries of colonial and postcolonial to be reactivated in contemporary communities. It is transgenerational and endures within the cells of life and biological ecosystems with potency. The latency of colonial chemical violence is the wait for the effects and sediments of the past to arrive in the present and alter the future (Murphy, 2013b). Thus, the past defers its violence into the present. Ann Stoler (2013) calls the afterlives of colonial violence the "debris" of empire. The debris of empire are the "toxic corrosions" and violent accruals of colonial aftermaths and the many persistent forms in which they impinge on the material environment and human bodies. In the words of Stoler, while the violent crimes of the colonial past have been named, the corrosion of the less visible elements of soil and soul have not.

Colonial labour regimes in mining, agriculture, and industry were systematically hierarchized and racialized such that Africans performed the most dangerous tasks that gave them proximity to exposure from toxic chemical waste, pesticides, insecticides, herbicides, and poisons. Colonial pest control programs to eradicate tsetse-flies, mosquitoes, and locusts, and to contain tropical diseases, utilized chemical technologies and extensive spraying campaigns that not only poisoned landscapes, water, and natural ecosystems but also conscripted thousands of Africans as disposable manual labourers handling the toxic sprays in usually unsafe and hazardous conditions (Ford, 1971; Giblin, 1990; Hoppe, 2003; Scoones, 2014). Thousands of tonnes of dangerous poisons were deployed in African areas and distributed for uncontrolled use for the extermination of insect and wildlife vermin. Colonial officials irresponsibly handed out poisons for use to Africans during pest destruction campaigns and these dangerous chemicals were difficult to control (*Natal Agricultural Journal*, 1908). In southern Africa, dangerous poisons such as lead arsenite were used in wholesale quantities to poison wild animals that were classified as vermin and threatened the white settler farming economy (Gargallo, 2009; Mavhunga, 2011; Mutwira, 1989). The wildlife poisoning campaigns were extensive and well-coordinated. Drums of poisons were left in various African villages under the supervision of chiefs for indiscriminate use to eradicate wildlife (NAZ S138/34). The long-term impact of these chemical pogroms on nature and wildlife in Africa was the near extinction and endangerment of various species of animals such as wild dogs which today are protected (Richards et al., 2018). Cultures of wildlife poisoning have also been appropriated in contemporary illegal hunting practices and poisons such as potassium cyanide that has been used to kill elephants and other game.

Poisons such as strychnine, arsenic, and cyanide were also used as political tools in bio-warfare and counterinsurgency in southern Africa to fight nationalist guerrillas in South Africa, Zimbabwe, Namibia and Mozambique (Gould, 2005; Purkitt & Burgess, 2002). Water sources such as rivers and watering wells were indiscriminately poisoned, threatening large African populations and aquatic life and chemicalizing landscapes with toxic sediments that embedded into soils. Chemical residues of this bio-warfare and chemical violence have been activated at certain points in human bodies as sicknesses, and in landscapes as outbreaks of bacteriological diseases such as anthrax (*Mail and Guardian*, 2000). Bergman (2013) designated biochemical weapons as a public health threat to civilian populations whose consequences are difficult to manage. The use of Agent Orange in Vietnam and Laos during the 1960s and its accompanying devastating toll across many generations illustrates the deadliness and durable perils of chemical weapons used during colonial wars (Biggs, 2023). Long-term consequences of chemical and biological weapons include chronic mental and physical illnesses and new infectious diseases and these can be mediated by ecological changes (Committee on Toxicology, 1985). Some delayed transgenerational effects of exposure to chemical and biological weapons are carcinogenesis, teratogenesis, and mutagenesis (Bergman, 2013; Reutter, 1999). Biological agents such as anthrax are persistent and resistant to environmental degradation and can last in soils for many years. The combined impact of all these factors can affect food supplies, agriculture, trade, tourism, and economic development. Psychic spaces and memories are also other sites of residual chemical violence from bio-warfare as trauma and panic still inhabit communities and terrains. Chemical weapons result in intense social and psychological distress and physical exposure can induce mental disorders such as organic psychosis, delirium, and dementia (WHO, 2005). The burden of all this to national healthcare facilities and medical infrastructure requires no further emphasis.

## 3 Toxic Timescapes of Colonialism: Temporalities of Chemical Violence in Africa

Temporalities of violence are pervasive, intrusive, endemic, and transgressive. They are not bound or confined to the neat chronological categories of historical time and demarcations. Like thermal entities, violence cannot be erased, destroyed or expunged; it can only be transformed into many alternative manifestations. To grapple with the epistemic identity of chemical violence in Africa is to posit fundamental questions about the past and its role in the construction of contemporary vulnerabilities and insecurities. However, to juxtapose the past and the present should not be a ritual that seeks to find alibis and acquit current political processes and leadership in Africa for the atrocities and violence in the continent. It is not a project in nationalist and pan-Africanist historiographies and romanticized narratives of postcolonial Africa. While making the decolonial point on violence as a legacy of empire we must guide against descending into the conceptual whirlpool of "colonial determinism" and "anti-colonial fixation" wherein our quest for colonial effects will dilute our critical edge and we ultimately sound like apologist scholars registering political demands and constructing convenient scapegoats for failed regimes in Africa. Thus, decoloniality if not critically structured can become a bulwark for alibi and scapegoat political narratives that entrench the precarity of the continent. This is not a criticism of decoloniality, but we need to contest colonial and hegemonic ideologies while simultaneously strengthening accountability and good governance in Africa. As Ann Laura Stoler (2013) puts it, to posit that colonial situations bear on the present is not to suggest that the contemporary reality can be accounted for by colonial histories alone. Rather, it is to understand how the colonial histories yield new damages and renew disparities. Thus, the "coloniality of violence" must not be deployed as an absolute and "open sesame" concept to analyse the recurrent logic of violence in Africa. Some modes of postcolonial governance can be explained by colonial experiences, but postcolonial governance cannot be reduced to colonial encounters.

Investigating chemical violence requires excavating timescapes, landscapes, and bioscapes. Timescapes denote timing and time windows within which exposure, latency, and effect occurs. It is the intersectionality of time, space, and bodies (Davies, 2023). Landscapes are the various physical sites of exposure and contamination such as the abandoned lead mines in Kabwe, Zambia. Bioscapes are the human and animal body surfaces on which the evidence of chemical violence is inscribed. Bodies, or bioscapes are powerful tools that absorb and make visible the "toxic soup" and chemical violence embodied in flesh and blood (Armiero, 2021). The manifestation of chemical violence in epidemics of disease, sickness and health crises is a complex historical process that is spread across many generations and localities (Müller & Nielsen, 2023). The United Nations Economic Program (2012) and World Health Organization have conceded that there is indeed a global "toxic epidemic" conspicuous in frequent occurrences of noncommunicable diseases that are linked to ubiquitous exposure to endocrine disrupting chemicals that will affect future generations. However, while the WHO/UNEP report acknowledges the chemical violence, it presents it as a ubiquitous global problem and does not nuance it to situate and contextualize the disproportionate scales and hierarchized infrastructure of victimhood that accompanies it. This projects a "we are all victims" perspective or, as Tom Davies (2023) puts it, a "we are all in this together" narrative which appears progressive and inclusive but is inherently discriminative and hegemonic. The "we are all victims" narratives disempower the real victims of systemic and systematic violence by equitably apportioning the suffering while ignoring the inequitable and structural processes that deployed the violence. It is perhaps the equivalence of the "all lives matter" counter-narratives to "Black lives matter." Eventually, it is fallacious and ahistorical to argue that the toxic epidemic is a homogenous global threat. It is not, and the health problems emanating from the hormone-disrupting chemicals are historical and vary according to power, race, and class, all of which mediated levels of exposure, chronicity, and latency. The toxic epidemic, therefore, has a power and social dynamic and investigating the predisposition factors and tracking the vulnerabilities across history to see how these have been most virulent in some communities is a much useful project than generic conceptualizations. We should never assume, for instance, that the African lead mine worker in colonial Zambia and his progeny living on the environs of abandoned toxic lead mines in postcolonial Zambia share a similar burden of the toxic epidemic as a white lead mine worker in colonial Zambia and his progeny in postcolonial Zambia. Most sites of chemical violence in the colonies were not just sites of extraction, but they were also spaces of livelihood, homes, and domestic zones that continued to be integral to people's lives as everyday landscapes. In southern California's "cancer alley" descendants of slaves lived alongside chemical factories and suffered disproportionate exposure, while white landowners moved elsewhere from the mid-twentieth century (Davies, 2023). The toxic legacies of the plantation slave economy bequeathed a legacy of uneven vulnerability to death and chemical violence. The cycle of exposure became perpetual even after the physical infrastructures of chemical violence had been disassembled. Studies in Canada's chemical valley, which is a historic landscape for petrochemical processing, revealed how the indigenous Aamjiwnaang communities have been exposed to carbon disulphide and the violent effects have been tracked in the last decade through health surveys and body mapping (Murphy, 2013b). These included manifestations of an "ongoing colonial violence" in the form of changed sex ratios, unborn lives, and Minamata disease from eating mercury-contaminated fish. Understanding the timescapes of chemical violence involves examining continuities between past contamination, past exposure, present contamination, present exposure, and the immediate or acute effects, and the chronic and transgenerational effects.

Violent colonial power relations entangled themselves into the fabric of biological life systems, ecosystems, microscopic organisms, soils, landscapes, waterscapes, and the atmosphere. Toxic sediments were integrated into everyday life. Soils were poisoned with chemicals such as arsenic, lead, and mercury. Water sources were also contaminated threatening human health and well-being. Children's playgrounds became toxic spaces and infants have been slowly poisoned from ingesting contaminated soils (Dooyema et al.,

2012; Kanda et al., 2019, 2020). Agricultural lands have been rendered unproductive, posing threats to food security and livelihoods. Harmful trace elements and metals have accumulated in many African ecosystems over the years, reaching unprecedented levels (Nriagu, 1992). This has been compounded by growing industrialization with estimates in the 1990s suggesting that 15–30% of infants in African urban areas may be suffering from lead poisoning. Global focus on environmental degradation in Africa has concentrated on soil erosion, bad agricultural practices, deforestation, the anthropogenic challenges of climate change, climate adaptation, and mitigation. This has marginalized and invisibilized the deleterious impact of harmful and toxic chemicals and impeded on the progress to streamline their effects in national development, environmental and public health policy formulation and implementation. Nriagu (1992) laments the "benign neglect" that accompanies the management of hazardous toxic contaminants in Africa which concomitantly scuttles the efforts to combat and prevent the high rates of infant mortality and endemic non-communicable and chronic diseases in Africa. The precarious vulnerabilities of African populations to these toxic contaminants are not only rooted in material residues from the past, but also in how colonial relations have embedded institutions that have reactivated and perpetuated these vulnerabilities in modes of production in the postcolonial present. Chemical infrastructures from the colonial period, built on the logic of "permissibility of pollution" of indigenous landscapes that are not efficiently regulated or accountable to responsible environmental governance, pervade every aspect of the African industrial, mining, and agricultural complex. These are in petrochemicals, fossil fuel production, agro-industry, bio-technology, and metallurgy and they have colluded with powerful political elites to get favourable government contracts and operate unrestrained and with impunity dumping toxic waste in waterways, polluting streams, and disrupting the livelihoods of rural farmers and fishermen and youth incomes, running down wetlands, displacing communities, and raising a spectre of disease and death for millions across the continent. The air, water, soils, and vegetation in communities living close to these chemical infrastructures is heavily contaminated with toxic metals and this violence is rarely acknowledged let alone remedied. Thus, the "chemical violence of colonial encounters" morphs into the "chemical violence of neo-colonial encounters" crossing temporal frontiers of the past into the present and actuating itself indelibly into the processes of life.

The Zambian case which was highlighted in the introduction illuminates more candidly the many temporal layers of colonial chemical violence, the complexities of historically diagnosing it, tracking it and linking its continuities in present spaces and landscapes. It shows how the threat of chemical violence does not go away even when the physical infrastructure and political institutions that sustained it have been disbanded. In Derek Walcott's poetic words, it is the figurative and metaphorical "rot" that remains clinging tenaciously to the ruins of a great house when the evil man that presided over it is long gone. The Zambian lead mining industry dates back to 1906 at Kabwe Broken Hill, contributing significantly to the country's colonial economy and export revenue. Mining was conducted around African communities in the Kabwe area that had around a population of around 17,000 in the 1970s (Clark, 1975: 1–2). These people were directly exposed by the direction of the prevailing winds from the smokestacks and smelting plants that produced toxic fumes. The dangers of mining pollution and toxic mining waste were well known by colonial officials, but these were concealed during much of the colonial period until the 1990s (Pesa, 2022). Thus, for over two generations the Zambian colonial lead mines deliberately dispensed lead poison to tens of thousands of African mine-workers and their families. The scale of the concealed systematic and systemic chemical violence was obviously so huge that it constitutes a genocide and pogrom of almost Auschwitz proportions. Between 1973 and 1975 the lead concentration of air in one of the townships in Kabwe, with a population of 10,000 people, was as high as 145 milligrams per cubic meter measured against a threshold safety guideline of 1.5 milligrams per cubic meter (Clark, 1975). Studies done in the early 1970s revealed dozens of cases of lead poisoning of infants around the Kabwe townships, and contamination of vegetables and maize used for human consumption. The investigations showed the transmission of lead poison from pregnant mothers to their unborn babies and established a transgenerational spiral of chemical violence. There are many more such sites of chemical exposure in Africa that have not received the scientific focus and historical glare to bring the victims into visibility and to understand how their lives and their future have been altered by the chemical violence and the ways in which their landscapes and contaminated biological bodies can be rehabilitated.

## 4 Towards a New Analytical Frontier of Studying Violence in Africa

Scholarship of violence in Africa needs to transcend the normative epistemic culture of examining the visible and conspicuous categories of political and social violence that is endemic to the colonial and postcolonial state-making projects. It must strive to illuminate other less visible, subtle, and latent forms of victimization and brutalization whose scars are much more difficult to discern and empirically quantify across time. The violence that cannot be immediately seen and evoked with gory images and graphic depictions of affliction and turmoil oft escapes the glare of spectacle, diminishes in memory, and slides away from the public arenas. The victims of such violence are forgotten and remain trapped in the miseries of powerlessness and invisibility. Their future generations also become enmeshed within a toxic cocktail of perpetual vulnerability and institutionalized historical amnesia. Chemical violence is subtle, yet potent and persistent. It endures in the genetic materiality of life, slowly poisoning generations, mutating and deforming the unborn destinies of communities, hampering and disrupting the full potential of life. The magnitude and scale of destruction may not be fully appreciated due to the staggered instalments in which the violence is administered, the chronicity and latency, but the cumulative impact is severe and tremendous.

A critical analytical focus on chemical violence in African scholarship requires integrating environmental justice approaches, subaltern studies, racial and class theories, as well as decoloniality and environmental science methods to strengthen our understanding of problems of power, authority, and coercion in colonial and postcolonial Africa. Environmental justice and subaltern studies approaches are useful for identifying the structural inequalities that predispose people to exposure and vulnerabilities in landscapes of toxic contamination. Decoloniality will illuminate the organic linkages between colonial chemical violence and its many postcolonial manifestations as legacy of empire, while environmental science methods will provide empirical vindication and forensic evidence. The thrust of this new outlook in studying violence in Africa must be not only to expand the conceptual frontiers of the subject, but also to engage with the many landscapes and humans entrapped within violent spaces of chemical exposure and slow death.

# 5 Conclusion

The Kabwe lead-poisoning litigation saga provides a critical conceptual and empirical case study of the chemical violence of colonial encounters in Africa and the afterlives of such violence in postcolonial landscapes and future generations of unborn babies. It provokes critical questions about the infrastructures of violence that are not so visible but have devastating effects on the livelihoods and well-being of millions of people in Africa. The extensive nature of the colonial extractive economy and its many sites of chemical production within a racialized system that treated Africans as animals and less than humans and concealed the extent of chemical exposure and toxic risk evokes grim scenes of mass poisoning and slow death. The violence festered insidiously outside the gaze of official narratives and multiplied in blood, DNA, tissues, geological materialities, plants, water, and living organisms, and was transmitted and teleported into the future. How do we document such violence in scholarship so that it is appropriately and adequately framed as urgent and imperative? How do we mobilize outrage against hegemonic systems that entrench toxic vulnerabilities within systems of production that are still premised on the logic of structural chemical violence? These questions obviously demand a proactive epistemic engagement with violence as a concept whose identity and manifestations shift in time and space. Understanding violence in Africa assumes the ability not only to define its nature and occurrence but to explain its many subtle forms and complex processes that are not always readily available.

# References

Amnesty International. (2023). *South Africa Hears Historic Class Action for Lead Poisoning Launched by Zambian Children and Women.* https://www.amnesty.org/en/latest/news/2023/01/south-africa-hears-historic-class-action-for-lead-poisoning/. Accessed 24 June 2023.

Armiero, M. (2021). *Wasteocene: Stories from the Global Dump.* Cambridge University Press.

Bergman. Å., et al. (Eds.). (2013). *State of Endocrine Disrupting Chemicals.* World Health Organization and United Nations Environment Program.

Biggs, D. (2023). The Chemical Platoon, the Abandoned Base and the Village: Human Experiences of Multiple Toxic Timescapes in Vietnam. In S. Muller & M. O. Nielsen (Eds.), *Toxic Timescapes: Examining Toxicity Across Time and Space.* Ohio University Press.

Clark, A. R. L. (1975). *The Sources of Lead Pollution and Its Effects on Children Living in the Mining Community of Kabwe, Zambia*. London School of Hygiene and Tropical Medicine.

Comaroff, J., & Comaroff, J. L. (Eds.). (2006). *Law and Disorder in the Postcolony*. University of Chicago Press.

Committee on Toxicology. (1985). Possible Long-Term Health Effects of Short-Term Exposure to Chemical Agents. Vol. 3. *Final Report: Current Health Status of Test Subjects*.

Corporate Justice Coalition. (2022). *Kabwe: Anglo-American Lead Poisoning Legacy*. https://corporatejusticecoalition.org/wp-content/uploads/2023/05/CJC_CaseStudy_Kabwe.pdf. Accessed 13 June 2023.

Davies, T. (2023). Slow Observation: Witnessing Long Term Pollution and Environmental Racism in Cancer Alley. In S. Muller & M. O. Nielsen (Eds.), *Toxic Timescapes: Examining Toxicity Across Time and Space*. Ohio University Press.

Dooyema, A., et al. (2012). Outbreak of Fatal Childhood Lead Poisoning Related to Artisanal Gold Mining in Northwestern Nigeria, 2010. *Environmental Health Perspectives, 120*(4), 601–607.

Fanon, F. (Ed.). (2005). *The Wretched of the Earth*. Groove Press.

Ford, J. (1971). *The Role of Trypanosomiasis in African Ecology: A Study of the Tsetse Fly Problem*. Clarendon Press.

Gargallo, E. (2009). A Question of Game or Cattle? The Fight Against Trypanosomiasis in Southern Rhodesia (1898–1914). *Journal of Southern African Studies, 35*(3), 737–753.

Giblin, J. (1990). Trypanosomiasis Control in African History: An Evaded Issue? *Journal of African History, 31*(1), 59–80.

Gould, C. (2005). *South Africa's Chemical and Biological Warfare Program* (PhD thesis). University of Rhodes.

Hoppe, K. A. (2003). *Lords of the Fly: Sleeping Sickness Control in British East Africa, 1900–1960*. Praeger.

Kanda, E., et al. (2019). Contamination and Health Risk Assessment of Trace Elements in Soil at Play Centres of Urban Low-Income Settings. *Human and Ecological Risk Assessment: An International Journal, 20*(6), 1663–1675.

Kanda, E., et al. (2020). Contamination of Soil Around an Abandoned Mine Tailings Dam with Trace Elements in a Small Town in North-Eastern Zimbabwe. *International Journal of Global Environment, 18*(4), 283–302.

*Mail and Guardian*. (2000). Zimbabwe on Brink of Anthrax Epidemic. https://mg.co.za/article/2000-12-18-zimbabwe-on-brink-of-anthrax-epidemic/. Accessed 11 March 2023.

Mamdani, M. (2005). *Good Muslim, Bad Muslim: America, the Cold War and Roots of Terror*. Pantheon Books.

Mavhunga, C. (2011). Vermin Beings: On Pestiferous Animals and Human Game. *Social Text, 29*(1), 151–176.

Müller, S., & Nielsen, M. O. (2023). Living with Poison: Exploring Generations as Toxic Timescapes. In S. Müller & M. Nielsen (Eds.), *Toxic Timescapes: Exploring Toxicity Across Time and Space*. Ohio University Press.

Murphy, M. (2013a). Distributed Reproduction, Chemical Violence, and Latency. In *Life Un(Ltd): Feminism, Bioscience, Race* (11:3). https://sfonline.barnard.edu/distributed-reproduction-chemical-violence-and-latency/. Accessed 20 June 2023.

Murphy, M. (2013b). Infrastructures of St Claire River. In S. Boudia & N. Jas (Eds.), *Toxicants, Health and Regulation Since 1945*. Pickering and Chatto.

Murphy, M. (2017). Alterlife and Decolonial Chemical Relations. *Cultural Anthropology, 32*(4), 494–503.

Muschalek, M. (2019). *Policing and the Colonial State in German East Africa*. Cornell University Press.

Mutwira, R. (1989). Southern Rhodesian Wildlife Policy (1890–1953): A Question of Condoning Game Slaughter? *Journal of Southern African Studies, 15*(2), 250–262.

*Natal Journal of Agriculture*. (1908). Locust Destruction: Report on 1907–1908 Campaign, 865–874.

National Archives of Zimbabwe, S138/34, Game Control 1924–1934.

Ndlovu-Gatsheni, S. (2013). *Coloniality of Power in Postcolonial Africa: Myths of Decolonization*. CODESRIA.

Nixon, R. (2011). *Slow Violence and the Environmentalism of the Poor*. Harvard University Press.

Nriagu, J. O. (1992). Review: Toxic Metal Pollution in Africa. *The Science of the Total Environment, 121*, 1–37.

Pesa, I. (2022). Mining Waste and Environmental Thought on the Central African Copperbelt, 1950–2000. *Environment and History, 28*(2), 259–284.

Purkitt, H. E., & Burgess, S. (2002). South Africa's Chemical and Biological Warfare Programme: A Historical and International Perspective. *Journal of Southern African Studies, 28*(2), 229–253.

Reutter, S. (1999). Hazards of Chemical Weapons Release During War: New Perspectives. *Environmental Health Perspectives, 107*(12), 985–990.

Richards, N. L., et al. (2018). The Killing Fields: The Use of Pesticides and Other Contaminants to Poison Wildlife in Africa. *Encyclopedia of the Anthropocene, 5*, 161–167.

Scoones, I. (2014). *The Politics of Trypanosomiasis Control in Africa* (STEPS Working Paper).

Star, S. L. (1999). The Ethnography of Infrastructure. *American Behavioral Scientist, 43*(3), 377–391.

Stoler, A. L. (2013). The Rot Remains: From Ruins to Ruination. In A. L. Stoler (Ed.), *Imperial Debris: From Ruins to Ruination*. Duke University Press.
UNEP. (2012). *State of the Science of Endocrine Disrupting Chemicals*.
Walcott, D. (1953). *The Ruins of a Great House*.
WHO. (2005). *Mental Health of Populations Exposed to Biological and Chemical Weapons*.

# Epistemic Violence in the Postcolony: Interrogating the Colonial Legacy and War in Francophone African Literature

Gibson Ncube

## 1 Introduction

In his foundational text, *The Wretched of the Earth*, Martiniquais writer and political philosopher Frantz Fanon (1963: 311) points out that "Europe undertook the leadership of the world with ardour, cynicism, and violence." He argues quite convincingly in this book that the grammar of violence came to be ingrained in the very organization of the colonial world. The violence of the process of colonization, as well as the violence that was needed to maintain it, could only be challenged by and through violence itself: "Colonialism is not a thinking machine, nor a body endowed with reasoning faculties. It is violence in its natural state, and it will only yield when confronted with greater violence" (Fanon, 1963: 61). Ultimately, the very quest for liberation from colonial domination was itself imagined as an effort that needed to be violent: "Between oppressors and oppressed everything can be solved by force" (Fanon, 1963: 72). In considering Fanon's conceptualization of the intersection of colonialism and violence, Rebecca Romdhani and Daria Tunca (2022: 1) attest that "a deeper understanding of colonial violence must necessarily start with an awareness of its multiple forms before examining its continuing presence in the contemporary world." These reflections highlight the way in which colonial violence has afterlives that stretch into the contemporary world.

G. Ncube (✉)
Stellenbosch University, Stellenbosch, South Africa
e-mail: gncube@sun.ac.za

I evoke these ideas on Fanon's thinking about colonialism and its multifaceted forms of violence because in this chapter I set out to examine how literary texts from Francophone Africa have grappled with the trope of violence. I ponder if the different forms of violence that play out in postcolonial Francophone literature can be traced back to the violence of colonialism or whether it is necessary to think beyond colonialism. Can colonialism continue to be the sole source of violence that we see today, more than half a century since many countries became independent of European rule? Moreover, I examine the meanings and the uses of violence. In this way, I seek to demonstrate that violence should not be seen merely as a negative and destructive force. I contend that it can be a productive and generative force which makes it possible to rethink the postcolonial moment in Africa.

This chapter focuses specifically on Francophone literary texts. African literary and scholarly production has often been framed around rigid linguistic boundaries. These linguistic boundaries themselves, I think, are one of the palpable afterlives of the colonial project (2022: 20). Anglophone literary texts have dominated literary production on the continent owing to the way English has grown to be a "global lingua franca" (Crystal, 2003: x). A focus on African literature in French is thus important for two main reasons. First, this chapter makes available literary narratives and discourses that would ordinarily not be easily available to non-speakers of French. Second, I concur with Thérèse Migraine-George (2013: x) who acknowledges that literature is "a borderless or worldly practice" but equally calls for a decentring of France and French from African literary and knowledge production. Migraine-George (2013: x) points out in this regard that it is important not to "reinstate a literary homogeneity that would subsume all differences and argue for a decentred approach to literature." Migraine-George (2013: x) further rejects "an exclusively metropolitan conception of French and the levelling of a history that uniformly collapses writers from former colonizing and colonized nations within an allegedly colour-blind French 'Republic of Letters.'" My attempt to read African Francophone literary texts and the critical discourses that they embed makes them available to English speakers. Such an analytical endeavour can be read as a decolonial praxis which sets out to overcome the linguistic boundaries imposed on Africa and African scholarship by colonialism. For ease of referencing, I make use of English translations of different novels, in instances where such translations exist. Where no translations exist, I offer translations of the direct citations that I make from the selected novels.

## 2    Violence and Its Literary Representation

In the book *Violence: Six Sideways Reflections*, Slavoj Žižek (2008: 1) identifies three main forms of violence. The first is termed "subjective violence" and it refers to "violence performed by a clearly identifiable agent." The second is called a "symbolic violence" and it is "embedded in language and its forms." The third is "systemic violence" which Žižek describes as "the often catastrophic consequences of the smooth functioning of our economic and political systems." In conceptualizing these different forms of violence, Žižek underscores that violence has to be seen as "a perturbation of the 'normal', peaceful state of things" (2008: 2). Also important in Žižek's theorization is the way violence infiltrates and is also expressed through language. This idea is particularly important for the analysis that I propose in this chapter, in that it examines how language embedded in literary narratives represents and negotiates different forms of violence in Africa.

The point made by Žižek on the perturbation of a normal and peaceful state of things is particularly relevant when we think of colonization and its afterlives in Africa. As Dierk Walter (2017: 4) highlights, the "process of Western penetration of the world was, as has often been remarked, extraordinarily violent." Walter (2017: 5) further explains that "violence was omnipresent in the extension of European power; it might even be said to have become a permanent state." In this way of reasoning, colonialism can be seen as having been instituted, maintained, and ultimately dislodged through different forms of violence.

Yambo Ouologuem's (1968) epic novel entitled *Le Devoir de Violence* (Bound to Violence) is important for the way it offers a counter-narrative to the idea that colonialism and contact with the West through the slave trade inaugurated the cultures of violence that are now prevalent in Africa. *Le Devoir de Violence* challenges the idea of a pristine precolonial Africa. Keguro Macharia (2020), in a tweet, also questions this idea and states:

> The fantasy of precolonial Africa amazes me. […] In that Africa, there were no wars, no ethnocidal intentions, no people who were forced to migrate because of wars, no deep, multigenerational hatreds. […] Can we not lie to ourselves? Or at least, let us tell more interesting lies.

Ouologuem's *Le Devoir de Violence* refuses to reproduce the fantasy of a flawless and utopian precolonial Africa. In this novel, Ouologuem presents the history of a fictitious kingdom named the Nakem Empire. The novel presents a long and bloody history of violence in this imaginary kingdom well before any encounter with Arabs and Europeans. In her analysis of *Le*

*Devoir de Violence*, Susan Gorman (2008: 3) attests that this novel "draws on the past but does so very differently from other authors. Instead of accepting the stories of the past unqualifiedly, Ouologuem constantly raises questions concerning their authenticity." One important question that Ouologuem raises is on the need to do away with the linear temporal fixations with/on the origins of violence in Africa. What becomes significant, then, is to consider the postcolonial manifestations of violence in Africa within the long genealogies and continuum of violence on the continent. We, thus, need to make sense of what Achille Mbembe (1992: 12) terms the vulgarity of power in the postcolony within its multifaceted geohistorical framings and contexts. In his analysis of the political history of Cameroon, Mbembe (2001: 105) refers to how rule in the postcolony is characterized by "excess and the creativity of abuse." Mbembe (2001: 108) further explains that confrontation arises when the *commandement* of those who wield power is unable to instil obedience:

> Confrontation occurs the moment the *commandement*, with vacuous indifference to any sense of truth, seeks to compel submission and force people into dissimulation. The problem is not that they do not obey or pretend to obey. Conflict arises from the fact that the postcolony is chaotically pluralistic, and that it is in practice impossible to create a single, permanently stable system out of all the signs, images, and markers current in the postcolony.

The exercise of power becomes vulgar when there is "a series of corporate institutions and a political machinery that, once in place, constitute a distinctive regime of violence" (Mbembe, 2001: 102). I make use of these ideas on the intersection of the exercise of power and violence to understand the specificities of the expression of violence in postcolonial Africa.

Against this background, literary production, fiction in particular, is a pivotal site of representing and trying to understand violence. Fiction offers an alternative vision of violence that history and archives provide. Fiction offers new ways of knowing violence and creating new knowledge on violence. Although Allan Pasco (2004: 373) cautions that literature should not be considered as a historical fact because "art is not fact, and one should not confuse history with fantasy," I contend in this chapter that literary narratives have the potential to help us understand and appreciate better the "general historical backgrounds, person histories, preconceptions, assumptions, states of mind and other personal nuanced attitudes that might not be easily captured by official historical documents" (Ncube, 2016: 7). In this way, the writer is a social thinker who is concerned with capturing all that they observe in the societies in which they live.

In thinking through the narration and representation of violence in fictional texts, I am aware of the deep ethical issues that this entails. Bruce Lawrence and Aisha Karim (2007: 10) observe the same issues in the introduction to the book *On Violence: A Reader* and ask the following pertinent set of questions:

> In our view, superseding all other questions and also informing them is the central question without which the focus on violence becomes a mere reflex of dominant stereotypes with no analytical advance: what is the relationship between knowledge about violence and action? That is, how does one speak about violence without replicating and perpetuating it? And how can one apply knowledge about violence to advocate strategies that either reduce its incidence or deflect its force?

In reading of violence in Francophone African literary texts, I contend that literature offers an innovative way of recognizing violence and appreciating its dynamics and thereby facilitating our understanding of it. As a reader and interpreter of texts depicting violence, I concur with Laura Tanner (1994: 3) who attests that "the reader in the scene of violence must negotiate a position relative not only to victim and violator but to the attitudes about violation encoded in representation and experienced through reading." In this line of thinking, it is imperative to develop an ethic of reading and interpretation that recognizes the intricacies and effects of violence at different levels and is also mindful of the potency of reading and interpreting violence.

Having considered the definitions of violence and explored the different types of violence, as well as the theoretical issues inherent in reading and interpreting violence, in the following sections I will analyse different forms of violence and the diverse literary texts that represent them. For the purposes of this chapter, I will focus on two distinct forms of violence: epistemic violence and the violence of wars in Africa. Exploring these two forms of violence will make it possible to examine the place of violence in texts from different time periods that cover different geopolitical zones of the Francophone world on the continent, and in the process offer a diversely textured analysis of the causes and effects of these types of violence.

## 3   Epistemic Violence

As previously pointed out, colonialism was in its very nature a violent process and system. Cheikh Hamidou Kane's novel *L'Aventure Ambiguë* (Ambiguous Adventure) (1972) tells the story of the arrival of the Europeans in the African country of the Diallobé. The narrator of the story explains how the arrival was violent: "The morning of the Occident in Black Africa was spangled over with smiles, with cannon shots, with shining glass beads" (Kane, 1972: 48). This violent arrival, signalled by cannon shots, leaves the Diallobé completely disoriented after attempts to fight off the Europeans fail dismally:

> Some among of the Africans, such as the Diallobé, brandished their shields, pointed their lances, and aimed their guns. They were allowed to come close, then the cannons were fired. The vanquished did not understand. (Kane, 1972: 48)

Beyond this initial physical violence faced by the Diallobé, I am interested in a more disquieting form of violence which had far more reaching effects and consequences. I term this form of violence "epistemic violence." Epistemic violence primarily involves the progressive erasure of indigenous knowledge systems and ways of life by Western modes of thinking and being. This marginalization and erasure of indigenous African epistemologies treats Western knowledge systems as the correct and rightful ways of thinking and being. Epistemic violence in the novel *L'Aventure Ambiguë* did not merely seek to change how the Diallobé (a metonymy of Africans) were progressively robbed of their ways of living, thinking, and being, but this process was an epistemicide. Epistemicide, according to Boaventura de Sousa Santos (2014: viii), refers to the "intellectual instruments" that were used to sustain and legitimate colonialism and colonial violence by subjugating indigenous ways of knowing and creating knowledge. De Sousa Santos (2014: 243) further explains that: "the destruction of knowledge is not an epistemological artefact without consequences. It involves the destruction of the social practices and the disqualification of the social agents that operate according to such knowledges." In the same line of thought, Siseko Kumalo (2020: 19) refers to "epistemic erasure" and defines it in terms of attempts at impositions that displace indigenous knowledge systems and practices.

In the novel *L'Aventure Ambiguë*, one of the first steps in the process of epistemicide is the imposition of European education. Master Thierno, the teacher at the traditional school, expresses his rejection of the European school, stating: "We reject the foreign school in order to remain ourselves, and to preserve for God the place He holds in our hearts" (Kane, 1972: 10). Master Thierno seems to understand two important things about the new education. First, this education will change the way of living and being of the Diallobé people. Second, the foreign education has the potential to displace and distort their religious and belief systems.

In the face of the dilemma of whether to send the Diallobé children to the European school or not, the Most Royal Lady, the sister of the Chief, finds that it would be more profitable to send the children to the new school: "I believe that the time has come to teach our sons to live. I foresee that they will have to do with a world of the living, in which the values of death will be scoffed at and bankrupt" (Kane, 1972: 27). The Most Royal Lady suggests that the traditional way of life and learning relies heavily on espousing death, and that such a view would not lead to any advancement of their society. To encourage the adoption of European education, the Most Royal Lady suggests that her nephew, Samba Diallo, be sent to this new school. Her hope is that Samba will "learn better to join wood to wood" (Kane, 1972: 32). This means that the children will learn technical methods which, through joining wood to wood, will help them construct better homes for their people. For the Most Royal Lady, European education represents "knowledge of the arts and the use of arms, the possession of riches and the health of the body" (Kane, 1972: 32). Master Thierno, however, asks an important question on the meaning of this new form of learning:

> They would learn all the ways of joining wood to wood which we do not know. But, learning, they would also forget. Would what they would learn be worth as much as what they would forget? I should like to ask you: can one learn this without forgetting that, and is what one learns worth what one forgets? (Kane, 1972: 30)

Master Thierno touches on one of the most important issues of the subtle violence that is epistemic violence: forgetting. Would the learning of Western knowledge not lead to the forgetting of African ways of being? Indeed, this process of forgetting has worked hand in hand with the erasure of indigenous epistemologies and the displacement of indigenous belief systems. *L'Aventure Ambiguë* shows that the colonial strategy of "civilizing" Africans was engineered in such a way that Africans were decultured. Deculturation involved an ingenious form of violence which, according to the Chief, leaves them vulnerable: "I am a poor thing, that trembles and does not know" (Kane, 1972: 33).

The next level in epistemic violence can be seen in the way in which Samba Diallo navigates the treacherous line of maintaining the traditional education that he had received as a child and assimilating Western ways of thinking and being. This is particularly visible when Samba moves to France to pursue his university studies. His initial impression is one of bedazzlement at Western knowledge: "With these new skills I was suddenly entering, all on one floor, a universe which was, at the very first, one of marvelous comprehension and total communion" (Kane, 1972: 144). However, this initial bedazzlement turns to disillusionment as he is faced with the difficult problem of integration and assimilation. He fails to assimilate into French society because of the fundamental differences in epistemologies. He finds that in Africa he had been able to guard preciously certain beliefs and practices, especially intimate closeness to nature and to God. In the West, though, he finds a secular world in which belief in God has almost altogether ceased, a world that is completely cut off from nature:

> You have not only raised yourself above Nature. You have even turned the sword of your thought against her: You are fighting for her subjection—that is your combat isn't it? I have not yet cut the umbilical cord which makes me one with her. The supreme dignity to which, still today, I aspire is to be the most sensitive and the most filial part of her. Being Nature herself, I do not dare fight against her. I never open up the bosom of the earth, in search of my food, without demanding pardon, trembling, beforehand. I never strike a tree, coveting its body, without fraternal supplication to it. I am only that end of being where thought comes to flower. (Kane, 1972: 125)

What is important about Samba Diallo's experience in France is the fact that it prefigures what would happen in Africa once Western education had entirely transformed African society. Samba finds himself disoriented. He is unable to integrate into Western society and upon his return to the country of the Diallobé, he finds himself a stranger amongst his own people: "Here, now, the world is silent, and there is no longer any resonance from myself. I am like a broken balafon, like a musical instrument that has gone dead. I have the impression that nothing touches me anymore" (Kane, 1972: 166). Samba feels that he has all sense of direction in his life, and this ultimately culminates in him losing completely all the beliefs that he had been taught as he was growing up.

The coup de grâce in this long process of epistemic violence is described in Samba Diallo's death at the hands of a Fool who had himself spent some time in France. Samba's death is symbolic of the complete annihilation of African epistemologies in the face of a seemingly omnipotent Western civilization. *L'Aventure Ambiguë* is important for the way in which it articulates issues that continue to resonate in the contemporary age. These are issues that have to do with which kinds of knowledge systems are valued and given value, and also which bodies of knowledge continue to be looked down upon. Decolonial discourses have in the past decade or so become more and more salient in articulating the importance of the violently imposed imbalances in knowledge production. As stated by Sabelo Ndlovu-Gatsheni

(2015: 485), this decolonial turn represents a "liberatory language of the future [which] seeks to ask new and correct questions about the human condition, going beyond Euro-American-centric epistemology that deliberately posed some human problems wrongly to continue deception." The epistemic violence that was instituted by colonialism through the "imposition of foreign worldviews often involved a demonization of African traditions and knowledge systems" (Ncube, 2021: 131) and *L'Aventure Ambiguë* compels us to ask different questions about what is important for the development of the African continent.

## 4 War as Violence/The Violence of War

In the previous section, I pointed out in the analysis of the novel *L'Aventure Ambiguë* that the arrival of the Europeans in the country of the Diallobé came in the form of a war, of guns and cannons. I also pointed out in the case of *Le Devoir de Violence* (Bound to Violence) that war in Africa did not begin with the advent of the Europeans. War was a form of violence that preceded colonialism. The argument that I make in this section is that war is a metaphor of conflict. This conflict can take the form of a literal war where there is armed confrontation in which people are either killed, maimed or both. Beyond this literal war, I consider the figurative of the portrayal of other diverse violent conflicts in which people are killed or maimed, physically, emotionally, and psychologically. Such a consideration of war and metaphors of war will allow me to examine the complexity of violent conflicts in postcolonial Africa. Wars and figurative wars in different parts of the continent have had unfathomable effects on different people. This section examines four novels which broach different kinds of war and how these wars affect different people. The first is the novel by Ivorian writer Ahmadou Kourouma, *Allah Is Not Obliged* (2007), and the second is *Harvest of Skulls* (2017) by Abdourahman A. Waberi from Djibouti. *Allah Is Not Obliged* is a story recounted by a young boy named Birahima who lives in a village on the border of Guinea and Côte d'Ivoire. When his mother dies, he sets off to Liberia to search for his aunt. Liberia is at that time in the throes of a bloody civil war. Birahima describes his experiences as a child soldier after he has been conscripted into a rebel force. Within this rebel group, Birahima traverses Liberia as well as Sierra Leone. Despite the grotesque atrocities that he faces, Birahima's narrative tone remains largely light-hearted and at times comical. As for *Harvest of Skulls*, it is a collection of short stories recounting different facets of the 1994

Rwandan genocide. The stories are largely based on ethnographic interviews that Waberi had with survivors of the genocide.

Ahmadou Kourouma's novel, told through the eyes of a young protagonist narrator, shows how wars have a profound effect on the most vulnerable: women, children, and the disabled. From the very opening words of the novel, it is evident that Birahima is an emotionally and psychologically wounded child who has possibly experienced suffering and violence in his ten years of life:

> The full, final and completely complete title of my bullshit story is: Allah is not obliged to be fair about all the things he does here on earth. Okay. Right. I better start explaining some stuff.
>
> First off, Number one ... My name is Birahima and I'm a little nigger. Not 'cos I'm black and I'm a kid. I'm a little nigger because I can't talk French for shit. That's how things are. You might be a grown-up, or old, you might be Arab, or Chinese, or white, or Russian—or even American—if you talk bad French, it's called *parler petit nègre*—little nigger talking—so that makes you a little nigger too. That's the rules of French for you. (Kourouma, 2007: 1)

What is important in this novel is the way in which language becomes the scene of violence, as the text is itself inscribed in linguistic violence. The use of language that would be called vulgar and uncouth, as well as the bastardization of the French language in the original text, become important sites through which to understand how this juvenile protagonist-narrator comes of age in a place in which violence is ubiquitous. Birahima himself traces how he has had to negotiate different violent circumstances in his life:

> Before I got to Liberia, I was a fearless, blameless kid. I slept anywhere I wanted and stole all kinds of stuff to eat. My grandmother used to spend days and days looking for me: that's because I was what they call a street child. Before I was a street kid, I went at school. Before that, I was a *bilakoro* back in the village of Togobala (according to the *Glossary*, a *bilakoro* is an uncircumcized boy). I ran through the streams and down to the fields and I hunted mice and birds in the scrubland. I was a proper Black Nigger African Native Savage. Before that, I was a baby in maman's hut. I used to scamper between maman's hut and grandmother's hut. Before that, I crawled around in maman's hut. Before I was crawling around on all fours, I was in maman's belly. And before that, I could have been the wind, or maybe a snake, or maybe water. You're always something like a snake or a tree, or maybe water. You're always something like a snake or a tree or an animal or person before you get born. It's called life before life. I lived life before life. (Kourouma, 2007: 11)

Birahima seems to be fully aware that his past plays a part in how his future turns out be. The constant repetition of "before that" in this quotation highlights how the past has an impact on what happens in his life. He traces this vicious cycle to a time that precedes even his birth. Thinking through this affirmation by Birahima using Jacques Derrida's (1994) concepts of "traces" and "hauntology," it can be argued that the past continues to be "this non-object, this non-present present" (Derrida, 1994: 5). According to Derrida, a "trace" refers to a mark that is visible in the present moment and represents something that was, but is no longer, there. This conjuring of the past into the present represents a way in which the past haunts the present.

One of the ways in which Birahima processes the violent and traumatic past experiences is in the way in which he uses language. John Walsh (2008: 196) offers an interesting reading of the way in which Birahima uses language:

> Birahima seems to be aware of his own arrested development and shields himself from the violence around him with the self-protective quality of language. The child uses language as a critical transitional object to preserve the self during its transformative confrontation with the world outside. Birahima's language, however, is not one that builds toward a future harmony between self and other; it is a language of vituperation that, in its derisiveness, seems to leave a curse on the very environment that created him.

Two important issues can be identified in Walsh's intervention. To begin with, it is clear that Birahima uses language in a way that reflects the kinds of violence he has faced in his life. His violent use of language mirrors his tumultuous up-bringing in equally volatile West Africa. Secondly, Walsh highlights that Birahima's use of violent and graphic language is itself not generative, as it does not bring him closer to others. In fact, it alienates him as he becomes more and more trapped in an almost endless cycle of violence.

In addition to the violence that he expresses through words, Birahima also talks of how he perpetrates physical violence when he is part of the rebel group:

> And me, I've killed lots of innocent people in Liberia and Sierra Leone, where I was in a tribal war, where I was a child-soldier, where I did some really hard drugs. I'm followed by evil spirits, so everything is rotten in me and with me. Bastard! (Kourouma, 2007: 12)

Birahima states, in a very matter-of-fact way, that he killed people. However, beyond this unembellished statement, regret and remorse can be felt. He refers to how he is haunted by the spirits of those he killed, and states that everything inside of him is putrescent and repulsive. Birahima's experiences and deeds, as heinous and sadistic as they might be, nonetheless, still need to be considered as those of a child. Birahima, like many child-soldiers, is forced to grow up and experience the violence of war as if he was an adult.

Given that Birahima acts like an adult, he can be read as what Smith (2002: 131) calls a "representative of the unfinished (grotesque) body of the post-colonialism." In this way, Birahima embodies all that has gone wrong with postcolonial African states. From their very inception, African countries had to contend with numerous haunting spirits which appear to be unappeasable. Through the candid protagonist-narrator, Kourouma not only shows the failures of African postcolonial nations but also the continued interference of the West in African affairs. One symbol of the West in Africa and how it emboldens the culture of violence is the Kalashnikov, the rifle that was used by the child-soldiers: "Small-soldiers had every-fucking-thing. They had AK-47s. AK-47s are Kalashnikov guns invented by the Russians so you can shoot and keep shooting and never stop. With the AK-47s the small-soldiers got every-fucking-thing" (Kourouma, 2007: 47). The violence of the Kalashnikov, as previously pointed out, is amplified by the linguistic violence of the narrator. In my view Birahima's butchering of the French language "displays the struggle to escape the colonizing tendencies of the French language in Africa" (Walsh, 2008: 196). Kourouma deftly uses this protagonist-narrator to capture how war and its violence stunts growth in Africa, the same way in which it inhibits Birahima from having a somewhat normal life.

War and its violence and the way this affects Africa's development is the central concern in Waberi's *Harvest of Skulls*. This book deals with the Rwandan genocide, its violence and its aftermath. Waberi (2017: xi) in the preface of the novel explains what his writing sets out to do:

> ...erect a pantheon of ink and paper dedicated to all the victims; call on those consciences willing to listen. Revisit the history of this country set on a path of self-destruction or, more accurately, ushered along in its demise by a long-standing criminal regime. [...] The nature of our humanity calls on us to give, if only momentarily, a face, a name, a voice, and, leaving, a living memory to the hundreds of thousands of victims so that they don't end up as mere numbers.

For Waberi, the short stories that he composes attempt to tell the stories of those who did not live to be able to tell them. The stories also tell the tales of those who survived but are unable to verbalize or put their experiences into words.

In more recent literary texts, the representation of war and its violence has involved grappling with the idea of the state being at war with its own citizens. The recurrent depiction of this violence of the state against its own citizens has involved the use of the trope of dirt. Ashleigh Harris (2008: 44) argues that this trope of dirt needs to be "read as a palimpsest, superimposed onto colonial and Afrocentric discourses of cleanliness and dirt, and as such, neither unexpected nor new, but rather, eerily predictable in their entanglement with the violent and exclusionary discourses of nationalist politics." What Harris suggests here is that the evocation of dirt speaks to inherited colonial forms of violence in which blackness was considered as dirty. In her analysis of the same trope of dirt in post-independent Zimbabwe, Tendai Mangena (2022) explains that the state has always bestowed upon itself a cleansing role against dissenting voices. According to Mangena (2022: 124), "the purported cleaning […] is contestable. It is a misnaming of state violence aimed at concealing and obscuring its criminality." As for Gibson Ncube (2018: 51), he contends that the "medicalisation and pathologising of dirt and filth thus frames state violence against [dissenting voices and] bodies as necessary in order to remove the vile, foul and revolting constituent. Like a surgical operation, the clean-up intervention set out to bring about order and cleanliness."

Florent Couao-Zotti's collection of short stories entitled *L'Homme Dit Fou et la Mauvaise Foi des Hommes* (2000) (The So-Called Madman and the Bad Faith of Men) offers an apt presentation of this trope of dirt in an unnamed African country. In the short story that carries the same name as the collection, Couao-Zotti tells the story of a man called Prosper Natchaba who is homeless with his young daughter, Viscencia. As the story progresses, we learn that Prosper is not in fact a madman but a former civil servant who lost his job and was forced to be homeless. Ironically, he lives in an alley that is behind the country's central bank. Prosper decides that he will approach the CEO of the central bank to inform him of the diverse challenges that are faced by many citizens in this country. He is, however, not allowed to enter the bank as he is dirty and smelly and, therefore, not dignified enough to meet the CEO. He is violently kicked out of the bank by Zéphyrin, the chief brigadier of the police. The violence of Zéphyrin symbolizes how the state crushes all dissenting voices. The state in this short story, as is certainly the case in many post-independent African countries, is ruthless in meting out violence to quell any sort of dissent or voice that opposes its power.

Having failed to see the CEO of the central bank, Prosper decides to seek audience with the mayor of the town so he can deliver to him the same message of the suffering of the ordinary citizens. The mayor accepts and Prosper demands that their meeting be televised live. Prosper is naked during this televised meeting. He calls his nakedness "*la tenue de combat et de vérité*" (the attire of combat and truth) (Couao-Zotti, 2000: 45). Wearing his outfit of combat and truth, he addresses the mayor and those in power and articulates the diverse challenges that he and others face:

> Monsieur le maire, c'est simple: il y a vingt mille fonctionnaires de l'État qui ont perdu leurs protège-faim mensuels et qui tirent à la maison le diable par le cul. Les jeunes diplômés sont pris à la gorge par le chômage. Je ne parle pas du SIDA et de qui a déjà étendu ses cantons dans les collèges et les universités. (*L'Homme Dit Fou et la Mauvaise Foi des Hommes* 2000: 46)

> [Mr Mayor, it's simple: there are twenty thousand civil servants who have lost their monthly sources of income and who are at home, struggling to make ends meet. Young graduates are being choked by unemployment. I will not speak about AIDS which has already ravaged the colleges and universities.]

The mayor is unable to offer any plausible answer to Prosper's question. Instead, he accuses Prosper of orchestrating a coup against him. It is at this point that Prosper stands up, exposing his genitals to the television screen. This white screen represents a form of violence that is prevalent in many post-independent countries, and this is the quasi-silent and bloodless violence of censure. The screen goes blank, but the sound is not muted. The commander of the military is heard instructing soldiers to shoot at will. Hundreds of rounds of ammunition are shot at Prosper. This killing of Prosper marks the ultimate form of violence in which dissenting and other voices are completely eliminated. It characterizes the definitive removal of the dirt and filth that threatens the "proper" functioning of the state. Mbembe (2001: 103) explains that such use of brutal force and violence speaks to how the exercise of power in the postcolony is often "grotesque and obscene". Mbembe (2001: 105) further contends that in the postcolony "the state considered itself simultaneously as indistinguishable from society and the upholder of law and the keeper of the truth. The state was embodied in a single person, the president. He alone controlled the law, and he could, on his own, grant or abolish liberties—since these are, after all, malleable." Mbembe's argument resonates with what happens in this particular short story and, indeed, with what happens in contemporary Africa where state power is used to violently quell any form of voice or action that challenges it.

This idea of violence being used to quell forms of challenge and defiance also relates to another form of violence which is often depicted as a gruesome war, namely the intimate or gender-based violence which is faced by women. This form of war or violence is displaced from the public and spectacular. It is an intimate kind of war and violence which is expressed and experienced in the private spaces of home, spaces in which individuals are normally supposed to be at their safest. To illustrate this form of violence, I will briefly analyse Calixthe Beyala's novel *Tu T'Appelleras Tanga* (1988) (You will be called Tanga), which I take to be representative of the portrayal of gender-based violence in Africa. This novel tells the story of Tanga, a young woman who is on her deathbed and tells her life story to a fellow prisoner, a white French woman called Anne-Claude. Tanga was abused by her father and later became a sex worker in order to make ends meet. She talks of the violence that she had to face in her profession at the hands of the different men with whom she had intercourse. She decided to leave sex-work when she found a man, Hassan, whom she found loving. She was ready to start a new life, be a wife, look after her husband and home, and eventually be a mother. However, this man that she thought was different raped her:

> Hassan me prend dans ses bras. Pas à pas, sans me lâcher, il me pousse vers le lit. Il s'effondre sur mon ventre. 'Embrasse-moi', demande-t-il. Ses lèvres me subjuguent. Il saisit une de mes jambes, puis l'autre, les met sur ses épaules. Il me pénètre. Ses pas me transpercent. (Tu T'Appelleras Tanga 1988: 19)

> [Hassan takes me in his arms. Step by step, without letting go of me, he pushes me onto the bed. He collapses onto my tummy. 'Put your arms around me,' he asks. His lips overcome me. He takes hold of one of my legs, and then the other, puts them on his shoulders. He penetrates me. His strokes pierce me.]

Tanga soon realized that Hassan was no different from any other man. Hassan felt entitled to her body and did not require any consent from her should he want sex. Tanga was reduced to a mere sexual object which is at the disposal of the man. In Beyala's novel, such objectification of women is normalized and violence on and against women's bodies is ubiquitous. Several scenes describe how they are raped. In one particular scene, a young women named Kadjaba Dongo is gang-raped:

> Un jour... Kadjaba s'est couché sur une natte sous un manguier ... Ils sont venus seuls ou en groupe. Ils ont parlé, elle n'a pas répondu ... Ils sont partis. Puis il y a eu un silence. Elle respirait profondément, prête à s'abandonner au sommeil quand le dernier est arrive ... Il s'est approché d'elle, a renforcé son pagne et l'a pénétrée brutalement. (Tu T'Appelleras Tanga 1988: 24)

> [One day ... Kadjaba was sleeping on a mat under a mango tree ... They came alone or in groups. They spoke, she did not respond ... They left. Then

there was silence. She breathed heavily, ready to abandon herself to sleep when the last one arrived. ... He approached her, tore her loincloth and brutally penetrated her.]

This violence against women can be explained by the very manner in which patriarchy works and the way in which women are subservient to men and their bodies and lives are not their own. Langa et al., (2020: 9) offer a different explanation for the violence that men direct at women. According to them, colonialism infantilized black men, and in order for them to regain their masculinity, they aimed their frustrations at the easiest and closest targets: women and children. "Black men were positioned as 'boys' and black masculinity as inferior to white masculinity" (Langa et al., 2020: 9). Pumla Gqola (2015: 157) also explains in this regard that:

> This claim to recover from emasculation very often requires the performance of hypermasculinity that women are expected to support as part of enabling men to attain manhood. In some of its brutal manifestations, it directly trivialises sexual violence by these men.

The violence that women have to contend with is in this way seen as a way in which black men set out to regain their lost masculinity. It is with this in mind that Steve Biko (1978: 130–131) concludes:

> The black man we have today has lost his manhood. Reduced to an obliging shell, he looks with awe at the white power structure, and accepts what he regards as the inevitable position. Deep inside him, his anger mounts at the accumulating insult, but he averts it in the wrong direction—on his fellow black men in the township, on the property of black people... All in all, the black man has become a shell, a shadow of man, completely defeated and drowning in his own misery, a slave, an ox bearing the yoke of oppression with sheepish timidity.

In the case of Tanga, she refused to be used as an abusable and rapeable object or body. She used violence to free herself from the violence that she had to face. She did this by killing Hassan. In this instance, violence can be seen to be generative in that it allowed Tanga to free herself from the objectification and abuse with which she had to constantly deal.

In this section, I have argued that war is in its nature violence. I have demonstrated that war takes different forms which include militarized assaults and state violence against citizens as well as intimate gender-based violence. The depictions of these different forms of violence highlight, on the one hand, how wars, be they militarized or domestic, point to inherited past forms of violence. On the other hand, these wars and the violence that they enact highlight that the past cannot continue to be used as an excuse for present violence. The war and violence against women, for example, needs to be dealt with as a problem stemming from the contemporary moment and requiring contemporary solutions and interventions.

## 5   Conclusion

Cultures of violence can be inherited. They can be passed from one generation to another, from one dispensation to another. Yet violence is, in some instances, not inherited at all. It emerges organically from the contemporary moment and takes on a life of its own. Different forms of violence overlap and are interrelated. Violence at a national scale finds resonance with the intimate violence which takes place within the private space of the home.

I have demonstrated in this chapter that contemporary Africa not only has had to contend with different forms of violence but has also had to negotiate violence inherited from as far back as the precolonial period. Yambo Ouologuem's novel *Le Devoir de Violence* suggests that we are bound to violence and that it is almost impossible to escape the vortex of past violent experiences. The present and the future are, in this way, tainted by past experiences of violence. I contend, as I bring my argument to a close, that literary texts are important in creating and enabling spaces in which it is possible to image different futures, futures that are liberated from yoke of past experienced violence.

I conclude this chapter by arguing that literature presents a space of (re)negotiating and (re)thinking violence, its meaning, its expression and its effects in contemporary Africa. While one of the primary objectives of literature is to entertain, not all subjects treated in literary texts are entertaining. This is certainly the case when we consider the theme of violence in Africa. Literary narratives are important in depicting diverse forms of violence in post-independent Africa. Such depictions allow readers to imagine new futures in which violence has been stripped of its destructive force. Adebanwi (2014: 407) explains this function of literature when he attests that:

> In observing the social process, both past and present, they reflect, and reflect on, extant perspectives in understanding reality by creating new maps of existence through ideas that not only generate, but also transcend existing possibilities and ways of apprehending those possibilities. In contributing to the common store of social, political and moral ideas in society, they also become wellsprings of new ideas and new ways of thinking.

The depiction of violence in literary texts, therefore, transforms this fictionalized violence into something that is productive and generative. Readers of the texts examined in this chapter can potentially be moved, emotionally and intellectually, when they face different forms of violence in the novels. Ato Quayson (2003: xv) advances a theory involving what he terms "calibration" which he describes as "a procedure of attempting to wrest something from the aesthetic domain for the analysis and better understanding of the social." According to Quayson (2003: xvi), literary texts have the potential to influence the everyday world we live in: "the crucial index for evaluating any particular configuration of ideas is whether it illuminates new ways of experiencing existence, whether this involves literary criticism, social analysis, and activism or the quotidian round of human relationships." Accepting that the impact of literature remains minimal compared to other forms of cultural production, I contend that it does enable us to see much that is ill in the worlds that we inhabit and, in so doing, it compels us to think of better futures. As argued by Ncube (2018: 52):

> For as long as human societies continue to exist, literature will continue to capture its complex and diverse functioning. Violently marginalised, side-lined and muffled histories and discourses are afforded a space in which they cannot only be revisited but can be rethought in a bid to better understand them and to accord them the rightful recognition they deserve.

It is possible, through literature and reading literature, to understand the world we live in and also imagine new worlds in which we would want to live.

## References

Adebanwi, W. (2014). The Writer as Social Thinker. *Journal of Contemporary African Studies, 32*(4), 405–420.

Beyala, C. (1988). *Tu T'Appelleras Tanga*. Editions Stock.

Biko, S. (1978). *I Write What I Like. Steve Biko: A Selection of His Writings*. Picador.

Couao-Zotti, F. (2000). *L'Homme Dit Fou et la Mauvaise Foi des Hommes*. Le Serpent à Plumes.

Crystal, D. (2003). *English as a Global Language*. Cambridge University Press.

Derrida, J. (1994). *Spectres of Marx: The State of the Debt, the Work of Mourning and the New International*. Routledge.

De Sousa Santos, B. (2014). *Epistemologies of the South: Justice Against Epistemicide*. Routledge.

Fanon, F. (1963). *The Wretched of the Earth*. Grove Press.

Gorman, S. (2008). Don't Let Yourself Be Made Game Of: Yambo Ouologuem's Le Devoir de Violence and the Game of Genre. *Postcolonial Text, 4*(2), 1–14.

Gqola, P. D. (2015). *Rape: A South African Nightmare*. MF Books.

Harris, A. (2008). Discourses of Dirt and Diseases in Operation Murambatsvina. In M. Vambe (Ed.), *The Hidden Dimensions of Operation Murambatsvina* (pp. 40–52). Weaver Press.

Kane, C. H. (1972). *Ambiguous Adventure*. Heinemann African Writers Series.

Kourouma, A. (2007). *Allah Is Not Obliged*. Anchor Books.

Kumalo, S. H. (2020). Resurrecting the Black Archive Through the Decolonisation of Philosophy in South Africa. *Third World Thematics: A TWQ Journal, 5*(1–2), 19–36.

Langa, M., Kirsten, A., Bowman, B., Eagle, G., & Kiguwa, P. (2020). Black Masculinities on Trial in Absentia: The Case of Oscar Pistorius in South Africa. *Men and Masculinities, 23*(3–4), 499–515.

Lawrence, B. B., & Karim, A. (2007). Theorising Violence in the Twenty-First Century. In B. B. Lawrence & A. Karim (Eds.), *On Violence: A Reader* (pp. 1–17). Duke University Press.

Macharia, K. (2020). [@keguro_]. The fantasy of precolonial Africa amazes me. […] In that Africa, there were no wars, no ethnocidal intentions, no people who were forced to migrate because of wars, no deep, multigenerational hatreds. […] Can we not lie to ourselves? Or at least, let us tell more interesting lies [Tweet]. Twitter. https://twitter.com/keguro_/status/1299332057525415936

Mangena, T. (2022). "We Must Aspire to Be a Clean Nation": Ambivalences of Transition in "New Dispensation" Metaphors of Dirt. In O. Nyambi, T. Mangena, & G. Ncube (Eds.), *Cultures of Change in Contemporary Zimbabwe: Socio-Political Transition from Mugabe to Mnangagwa* (pp. 121–139). Routledge.

Mbembe, A. (1992). The Banality of Power and the Aesthetics of Vulgarity in the Postcolony. *Public Culture, 4*(2), 1–30.

Mbembe, A. (2001). *On the Postcolony*. University of California Press.

Migraine-George, T. (2013). *From Francophonie to World Literature in French: Ethics, Poetics, and Politics*. University of Nebraska Press.

Ncube, G. (2016). Knowledge, Power and Being: Literature and the Creation of an Archive of "Marginal" Sexualities in the Maghreb. *Journal of Literary Studies, 32*(4), 1–16.

Ncube, G. (2018). Of Dirt, Disinfection and Purgation: Discursive Construction of State Violence in Selected Contemporary Zimbabwean Literature. *Tydskrif vir Letterkunde, 55*(1), 41–53.

Ncube, G. (2021). The Role Ubuntu Could Have Played in Restorative Justice in Zimbabwe. In: J. Mukuni & J. Tlou (Eds.), *Understanding Ubuntu for Enhancing Intercultural Communications* (pp. 130–140). IGI Global.

Ncube, G. (2022). *Queer Bodies in African Films*. NISC.

Ndlovu-Gatsheni, S. J. (2015). Decoloniality as the Future of Africa. *History Compass, 13*(10), 485–496.

Ouologuem, Y. (1968). *Le Devoir de Violence*. Éditions du Seuil.

Pasco, A. H. (2004). Literature as Historical Archive. *New Literary History, 35*(3), 373–394.

Quayson, A. (2003). *Calibrations: Reading for the Social*. University of Minnesota Press.

Romdhani, R., & Tunca, D. (2022). *Narrating Violence in the Postcolonial World*. Routledge.

Smith, E. (2002). I have been a Perfect Pig": A Semiosis of Swine in" Circe. *Joyce Studies Annual,* (13), 129–146.

Tanner, L. E. (1994). *Intimate Violence: Reading Rape and Torture in Twentieth-Century Fiction*. Indiana University Press.

Waberi, A. A. (2017). *Harvest of Skulls*. Indiana University Press.

Walsh, J. (2008). Coming of Age with an AK-47: Ahmadou Kourouma's *Allah n'est pas Obligé*. *Research in African Literatures, 39*(1), 185–197.

Walter, D. (2017). *Colonial Violence: European Empires and the Use of Force*. Oxford University Press.

Žižek, S. (2008). *Violence: Six Sideways Reflections*. Picador.

# Geographies of Violence and Informalization: The Case of Mathare Slums in Nairobi, Kenya

Maurice Omollo and Solomon Waliaula

## 1 Introduction

Many informal settlements in urban environments are visibly represented by dilapidated structures, congestion and lack of essential services for large numbers of dwellers. These circumstances are informed by the very little public recognition they elicit from the city authorities, as may be observed in Nairobi, Kenya where 60% of the residents are informal settlement dwellers (Pamoja Trust, 2009). This staggering number of residents, therefore, have to struggle through a myriad activities for survival. Indeed, slums, as informal settlements are often referred to in the city county of Nairobi, have been linked to insecurities espoused through violent behaviour (UN-Habitat, 2007) and this has been observed as a normal but necessary survival technique in informal settlements. However, violence as understood has the characteristic of forceful imposition of one's will on another, thereby causing harm, which may be physical or psychological, but this does not capture the wider violence that unfolds in slums such as Mathare. Moser (2005) has provided a typology distinguishing between social, economic, institutional, and political violence. Social violence is linked to gender power relations and also to gangs;

---

M. Omollo · S. Waliaula (✉)
Maasai Mara University, Narok, Kenya
e-mail: solomonwaliaula@gmail.com

M. Omollo
e-mail: omollo@mmarau.ac.ke

© The Author(s), under exclusive license to Springer Nature Switzerland AG 2024
O. B. Mlambo and E. Chitando (eds.), *The Palgrave Handbook of Violence in Africa*, https://doi.org/10.1007/978-3-031-40754-3_9

economic violence is motivated by material gain, institutional violence is associated with state institutions as well as social cleansing vigilante groups, and political violence to paramilitary conflicts and political assassinations. This chapter highlights occasions where these forms of violence are observable in the context of Mathare Valley area of Nairobi County and summarizes them into hidden violence, circuit violence and existentialism violence. It is based on the perspective that violence in the slum area is a feature that permeates society so that the residents are able to survive in the otherwise difficult circumstances of the informal settlement, which is characterized by lack of government services. The objectives here include an investigation of the violence, as espoused in the typology already mentioned, and providing a geographical context.

## 2 The Study Area and Methodology

Mathare Valley slum area is found within Nairobi County, which also doubles as the capital city of Kenya. The city's functions dominate the political, social, cultural, and economic life of the people of Kenya, as well as the rest of the East African region comprising Uganda, the whole of the former Sudan, Somaliland, Tanzania, Rwanda, and Burundi (Mitullah, 2003). Mathare Valley slum area is located at about 6 km from the city centre of Nairobi and is estimated to cover an area of about 73.2 hectares of land (Corbum et al., 2012; Kamau & Ngari, 2002; Pamoja Trust, 2009). It is predominantly found within Mathare Constituency which is considered to be notorious for its high rate of crime and low-income families. Poverty and deprivation is concentrated in this area as well as human activity, energy, and creativity (Duara Foundation, 2010). The slum area as described in this chapter includes all the 11 villages of Kosovo, Mabatini, Mashimoni, Number 10, Area 4B, Gitathuru, Area 3A, Area 3C, Village 2, Bondeni, and the upgraded Mathare 4A. These were identified by the researcher from a pilot study and augmented by literature on Mathare Valley. The location of the study area together with the villages accessed is shown in Fig. 1.

All the 11 villages of Mathare Valley: Mathare Village 2, Mathare Area 3A, Mathare Area 3C, Mathare Gitathuru, Mathare 4B, Mathare Number 10, Mabatini, Kosovo, Mashimoni, Bondeni, and Mathare 4A (see Fig. 1) were extracted from a reconnaissance undertaken before the actual study (Kenya, 2011; UN-Habitat, 2008; Wasikeh, 2002). From each of these villages an equal choice of five household heads were selected through the snowball sampling method and information was also augmented by known village

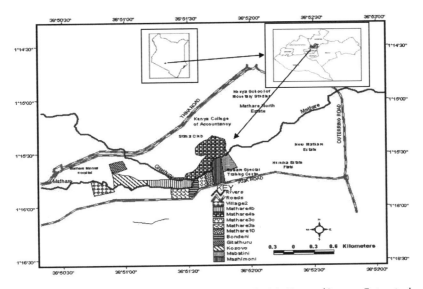

**Fig. 1** The Slum Villages of Mathare Valley in Nairobi, Kenya (*Source* Extracted and modified from Data Exchange Platform for Horn of Africa [DEPHA, 2008])

elders from each of the village, as informed by a research assistant who is a resident in the slum area. A total of 55 sample household heads were interviewed about forms of violence that are common in Mathare Valley slum area. The 11 village elders were brought together for a focus group discussion on violence in Mathare.

## 3 Slums and Structured Violence

Contemporary society has been characterized by an increasing influence of the structures of the global economy in every part of the world (Pilisuk, 1998) and the inevitable impact on low-income societies such as Kenya is the increasing disparity between the rich and the poor. This has led to a progressive detachment of the government from the poor. These places are then left to operate as vulnerable societies. They become the context of the hidden violence based on happenings that take place away from obvious visible instances of force meted on the residents of the slum people. Among these includes what a respondent described in the discussion as follows: "my wife handles the selling of groceries, and she knows I expect some income from the undertaking" (respondent during a Focus Group Discussion [FGD] on 23 September 2021).

What this implies is that there must be some income from the groceries, which the wife must work very hard to access. In the event that nothing is received, the woman may be beaten up and, hence, a physical form of violence results.

The reality of living in an informal settlement causes jitters to the residents, especially because their eviction could take place any time, even though the political class assures them of protection, which is mainly for the purposes of gaining votes, for these areas have large numbers of people living in small quarters that are not up to the standards of the local authority. Politicians, therefore, use the residents as a voting block for their election, violating their rights to be in decent houses: "the MCA (member of county assembly) said he will make sure we don't get evicted from the area, and we believe him! And so we live here, earn our livelihoods from here" (respondent to a question about assistance by the political class. 23 September 2021).

Politicians in the slum view the residents as a voting machine because their numbers are higher than in other urban areas. Violence is indirectly meted on them by this class by virtue of their status as poor and vulnerable. Indeed, being a densely populated area, Mathare Valley has provided a market for a variety of businesses to thrive. Here, many items might be found, and all are sold at low prices, including what has become known as the '*kidogo economy*' (instances where items that ideally are sold whole can be halved or reduced further to be accessible to the residents in small bits): "bread that is normally sold at KES 50 can be divided into three and each sold at KES 20, which is affordable" (Extract from FGD, 23 September 2021).

In terms of affordability this works. However, in the totality of the costs, the resident of the slum area pays more for items sold in small bits. Indeed, "a bar soap that ordinarily costs around KES 100 can produce 10 pieces with each being sold at KES 20" (FGD, 23 September 2021).

The bar soap example above translates to buying the item at KES 200, a 100% increase in costs that is unparalleled elsewhere! Though the economic basis of this arrangement works, the violation of the poor, forced to buy at higher costs, deprives them of their savings and, therefore, the ability to improve their welfare.

## 4   Circuit and Existentialist Violence

The fact that the residents of Mathare Valley slum area have lived and adapted to their circumstances does not negate the very nature of their challenges. Circuit and existential violence are forced by having to get on with residing in an informal settlement. The everyday struggles residents go through to access an income that should satisfy a household's basic needs is not a conducive environment for improvement of welfare. The following extract from the focus group discussion brought out a very interesting perspective of violence:

> It is interesting that we are here together but during elections we are divided into our ethnic groups and when you are in Kosovo village you will never set foot in Mathare Area 4A, simply because historically the two areas have had strong inclination to particular opposing ethnic groups who have always been against each other politically. (FGD 23 September 2021)

Insecurity and violence coming about due to political rivalry has been a regular feature whenever national elections are held. This regular occurrence is cyclic in that it happens every election time and takes its toll on the residents, ranging from damage to property, to loss of life. The predictability of this type of violence means it could be mitigated if anticipated early enough, but not much is done to achieve this.

There is a sense of insecurity when the presence of gangs has been observed in slums, especially in the context of the gangs achieving their aims forcefully. According to Okombo and Sana (2010), Nairobi slum dwellers have to pay a certain amount as a protection fee, or some form of violence may be meted on them. Among the more known of such groups are the Mungiki and the Taliban which have fought wars within the slums of Mathare for different reasons. These two have strongly been associated with their ethnic backgrounds, with the Mungiki being linked to Kikuyu youth, and the Taliban to the Luo youth and more so due to the common conglomeration of ethnic groups in particular sections of the slums. (Interestingly, though these gangs have been banned, they still exist in a hidden form.) In fact, to a large extent ethnicity determines where one resides within the slums of Nairobi. Such arrangements have resulted in balkanization of ethnic groupings within the slums and people from a different ethnic background would feel resentment at residing in a section associated with a particular ethnic group. However, Mutisya and Yarime (2011) dispel this balkanization proposition as seen through an ethnic lens, since it should actually be viewed through a socio-economic lens because most of the inequalities in the slums are more class-oriented than ethnic-based.

The presence of gangs suggest an institutionalized criminality that may be obvious to the law enforcers who may either ignore it, or are too weak to handle it, which could then mean a dysfunctional state security apparatus. In this context, the hidden nature of the violence meted on the residents by the groups may not be known to an outsider who passes by. In the words of a member in the focus group discussion:

> You put up a '*kibanda*' (a small shop), they come to demand for some payment for taking up space that would otherwise, be useful to another resident for a similar undertaking… it is worse for one who has a motorcycle and uses it as a livelihood activity to carry passengers… the owner would have to be part of a group which is then forced to pay some protection fee… you cannot have your motorcycle for business and do it alone. (FGD 23 September 2021)

The perspective of the motorcyclist may be useful in generating income for many people, but it is done in a way that leaves no alternative. The gangs' influence in the activities carried out in the slum area is quite obvious:

> I have actually seen a victim of the gang's crudeness when a *matatu* (bus) driver refused to part with some money that they required from him… he was manhandled, and the vehicle was not allowed to move from the stage till some cash was given… he was also lucky because they knew him. (A respondent during a face-to-face interview with a household head.)

A similar view was also observed from a question posed to another female household head who was sampled for an interview about an encounter with the known gang in her village:

> If you need some form of peace, just pay the required amounts (they may be small but picked at a regular interval). This will make work easier in trying to engage in income-earning activity in the slum area. (A female household head during a face-to-face interview.)

In the elaborated cases above it can be observed that the residents of Mathare have more-or-less been subdued to the extent that the routine of extorting money has become accepted. This acceptance has made this approach of accessing cash by the local youth routine. Indeed, there was general justification that the groups have provided some semblance of order and security to the residents of Mathare Valley:

> The young people have made sure there is order and any disagreements between those undertaking activities in the slum area can be solved by the groups' directives… in fact, that cash given out is used to help those without source and still reside in the area. (An interviewee.)

There was a feeling that, despite the subtle force used by the gangs in getting cash from the residents, they are able to repulse any moves that could be detrimental to their sources of income. Their activities were supported by some interviewees in the context that: "At times they organize themselves into groups and just decide to clean up the area… of course, we would be expected to give out something."

Such positive engagements would give the groups a good reputation, but this extends up to where "the giving out of something" begins.

## 5   State Violence on Mathare Residents

Despite the fact that the government of Kenya has made attempts to improve the status of the slum dwellers through Kenya Slum Upgrading Program (KENSUP) which was conceived and entrenched in the 2004 National Housing Policy, the insecurities visited on the people by violent evictions and demolitions by sections of its agents are not directed at solving the myriad problems of slums. The Kenya National Police Service is the agency charged with the responsibility of providing security in the country. The City of Nairobi is responsible for service provision in all parts of the County including the informal settlements such as Mathare. Historically, the slum areas have never been provided with municipal services due to their informal status and therefore not being recognized in City bye-laws. It is only recently that some municipal services have begun to penetrate in the informal structures especially water supply. The following is extracted from the discussion with the residents:

> We do get water and power although for water it is not frequent. Both these are available but there is a payment for them… water is not in the houses, this can be accessed from standpipes in designated areas within the villages… for power, the structure owners have made arrangements that we receive it using one meter box for a number of households… and there are conditions like only for lighting!

Another discussant interjected and added: "We do not pay for power because I think ours is tapped… we just pay a flat rate for rent since I came in here."

The existential violence here has to do with having to access some basics by either using less, or applying some illegal means to acquire them. In an interview with a head of household the following was reported: "I prepare *chang'aa* (local alcohol) for my livelihood… it has helped me provide for fees for my children… whenever they come (the police) I give them something to keep me going on with my business."

A similar case happens for those who own businesses within the slum area: "I have opened up a place where people come to watch movies and football, but I don't have a license… I part with some shillings to the security people and my business runs on… in fact, most of us here do not have business licenses."

It should be noted that the majority of these activities undertaken in the slum are not legalized. In this case, the law enforcers could take advantage of the situation to extort money from the small entrepreneurs. As observed in the interviews and discussions, this is always the case, and a routine is maintained when they come and collect their cash and leave the residents to undertake their activities.

## 6  State Action on Managing Slum Issues

Slum and informal settlement dwellers of Nairobi City comprise over 60% of all the residents of Nairobi (Amnesty International, 2009; Mitullah, 2003) and, therefore, the lack of service to them represents a significant disregard of a population that makes the City what it is. To wish away over 128 slum settlements in the city of Nairobi (Pamoja Trust, 2009) in terms of services, is an outrageous option since they make up the most populous sections of the city, which the local authority is mandated to serve. Many who work in the industrial areas of the City come from these settlements, and their contribution cannot be overemphasized on the economic front. One direction that seems to have been attractive to the government has been to consider a variety of slum-upgrading options and to limit the development of these informal and unregulated residential structures. The government has therefore provided for an upgrading of the slum structures through its KENSUP programme. This has had some initial repercussions, for instance, where the upgraded structures meant for the slum dwellers have ended up being occupied by the middle-income earners who were never residents of the slums. It is in the spirit of upgrading that the slums were to be demolished and the occupants relocated. However, the would-be beneficiaries of the new buildings end up in other similarly dilapidated structures and the whole effort of upgrading housing becomes futile and does not meet the objectives for which it was initiated (Dafe, 2009). The spread of slums has its impetus from such efforts, if not well addressed, because how these residents get to manage elsewhere is a matter of concern not only to themselves, but also to wider society, especially with recent issues about land ownership and the place of squatters and internally displaced persons.

It is imperative to consider if the dwellers are forewarned about the impending destruction to their structures (majority are actually tenants). It is also questionable if these city residents are relocated elsewhere before the demolitions begin. This is important because the slum dwellers may not be able to pay the levels of rent demanded in the other residential areas. In fact, most of the slum dwellers reside in their present locations because they are near to their livelihood sources of income—these being the industrial areas of Nairobi. Often after the slum residents have been relocated and the locations recovered by the city authorities, such land has been sold to other occupants who are the rich and powerful, and at times in a very well-orchestrated and executed exercise linking the City authority and the local elected people together with the local chiefs. Indeed, the Nairobi City Council has always been ranked very highly as being one of the most corrupt institutions in the country (Transparency International, 2008).

The most common thing that happens in the event that the local residents resist eviction is that a confrontation pitting the slum residents against the agents of the local authority ensues. Consequences have been catastrophic, with injury or even loss of life, affecting mainly the residents. Often the responsible government arm has managed to subdue the residents to either push them away from what they may consider their homes, or to make their life difficult in the slum by not providing basic public services. It is the city authority and the police who have inflicted most pain on the residents of the slums by forcefully evicting them from where they have lived for a long time. Some of the children from these slums know no other homes than the slums.

Residents have always been apprehensive about their status in these settlements and fearful of a possibility of violent evictions carried out with no warning. It is also possible that even when the slum dwellers are to be relocated to pave way for upgrading many have been afraid of missing out in the new structures, and much more significantly and which may increase their fear, of being unable to sustain the cost of occupying the upgraded structures. The rent paid in the upgraded section is often higher than would be paid for the same in the former slum areas. Not only does the cost implication affect rent, but it also affects other sectors of life including the establishment of a livelihood strategy such as a kiosk—which would require a license and monthly, weekly, or even yearly taxation. This is not the case in the slums, because most businesses are informally handled with the great goodwill of the residents.

The National Police are also accomplices to the inhumane treatment of the residents when they provide protection while the structures of the slum dwellers get demolished. This armed section of the government often reacts violently whenever the residents protest about their eviction. It must be appreciated that this organ of the state is supposed to provide security to all and has the responsibility of making sure that peace is maintained. However, it is the brutality with which they engage with residents of the slum and many other low-income residents that leaves a lot to be desired. The perception is that the police would consider whoever resides in the slum a criminal. This may be attributed to the general view that slums are settlements whose residents are mainly violent or are used to violent and criminal experiences (Moser, 2005; UN-Habitat, 2003a, 2003b) and, therefore, must be treated violently.

There is no justification to the application of force on the slum dwellers who are not violent. In fact, rough encounters often result in more protests which trigger even more violence and, hence, injury or loss of life. The brutality visited on the slum dwellers must be restrained as better methods of engaging with these residents of the city are sought. In the end, dialogue is the best way to solve issues affecting slum residents and their perceived fears. Force only increases the resentment of the residents towards the police.

There is the aspect of police activity, where the law enforcers allow illegal activities to take place within the slum, but the rogue ones get some payment in return. This captures the hidden violation of the rights of the residents of the slum who have to succumb to this extortionist tendency to earn a living, even though outside the law.

## 7 The Origin and Activities of Vigilantes in Nairobi's Slums

Vigilantes have sometimes been referred variously as militias, gangs, or "*jeshi*." The origin of these groups in the slums is attributed to the KANU Youth Wingers who got official support during the government regime in the 1990s (Okombo & Sana, 2010). The opposition party to the government then also recruited its own militia and there were violent conflicts between the two in the early days of multiparty politics. These groups were mainly used to frustrate the efforts of opposing political groups in recruitments and public rallies by engaging in political violence. Although, in 2002, through a gazette notice, the government banned such organizations which included Mungiki,

Taliban, Jeshi la Mzee, Jeshi la Embakasi, and Kamjesh, they still thrived in Nairobi.

Vigilantes have had their presence in the informal settlements and their activities were felt most in the large slums such as Mathare and Kibera. According to Okombo and Sana (2010) it was only after the 1992 election that these groups realized their potential to get money from undertaking illegal activities on behalf of politicians that they re-organized themselves with well-defined structures. These groups knew how to use the threat of violence to subdue individuals to their demands. This is what has continued to happen in the slums of Nairobi where security has often been considered lacking and people succumb to the authority of the gangs.

During the 2007 post-election violence in Kenya, among the most affected were persons living in slums and other informal settlements. Nairobi's situation was the worst hit because here live a cosmopolitan range of communities from different ethnic backgrounds in a situation where politics has been tribalized to such an extent that when a candidate from one tribe has won, the opposing candidate of a different tribe disputes the results and members of their communities physically fight each, with dire consequences.

Slums, therefore, offer themselves as the bedrock of rivalry due to the distinctive segmentation of different sections of such residences and overwhelmingly being occupied by members of particular communities in isolation of the others. It must be mentioned here that the vigilante and militia organizations in the slums cannot be isolated from the socio-economic and political development of the country, because it is this that established them. In this respect, the militias have run and controlled affairs in the slums, be it in livelihood endeavours or lifestyle—there have been cases where women have been forced not to dress in a particular way such as wearing "indecent clothing" as dictated by members of the organizations—(Masika et al., 1997).

Militia groups in the slums of Nairobi have therefore positioned themselves as powerful forces which dictate the happenings in the informal settlements. This may be viewed in both positive and negative terms. For instance, they have offered an alternative order in a situation lacking one. They have also provided some semblance of security where the concerned arm of government has been inadequate. This, however, represents a parallel "government" different from the formal engagement with the government, and, therefore, in direct competition with it. This can be seen in the context when they have engaged in activities that have forced adherence to certain conditions and payment of some fees, all of which is illegal (an example being protection fees). This is, in all considerations, extortion of money from the residents where they have no say over the running of their lives in as far as their residential area is concerned. Indeed, the negative aspects of these groups undermine their overall good.

There are some circumstances that may have lured young people into joining the vigilante groups in the slums and these have their basis in poverty. An idle and unemployed youth is fertile ground for criminal engagement. It is also observed that a majority of the slum dwellers in Kenya are poor (Amnesty International, 2009) and therefore susceptible to criminality and other illegalities to access some income. The very nature of their residential area, such as poor infrastructure, presence of many dark alleys, and other similarly deplorable conditions, make the residents sometimes vulnerable to mugging and even actual injuries inflicted on them by such groups of young people who want to survive. These circumstances also make the informal settlements insecure places since some form of violence may then be meted on any individual. This, perhaps, could be a perception the police have had, so that whenever they patrol these segments they deal ruthlessly with these youths, too. It could also be a way of discouraging any resistance from the residents when they enter these sections of the city in order to avoid any large-scale confrontation; a survival strategy for both the residents and the police.

## 8 Engaging in Violence Perpetrated By Formal Institutions and Vigilantes

The threat of violence degrades the slum residents, preventing them from fully exploiting their abilities. Indeed, no one may invest one's resources in an atmosphere of fear. It is in such a state that individuals would undertake their activities in total submission to the "authority" that controls the area, in the case of the militias. The same applies when residents are in constant fear of demolition and destruction of their properties as sometimes perpetrated by the local authority—an arm of government. In fact, any attempt at improving a livelihood activity would, for instance, be limited to petty endeavours which may not suffer great loss once violence engulfs the area. It is, however, possible to see individuals engaged in a variety of activities to satisfy basic household needs. There are many cases where residents of the slum would put a lot of energy into enhancing their circumstances but due to their poor status would only get into those activities which have the potential of immediately bringing in some income. These are activities that often attract serious competition since many of the slum dwellers engage in them.

These include small businesses relating to groceries, selling of second-hand goods like shoes and clothing among others (Mitullah, 2003; Pamoja Trust, 2009). It is in the undertaking of such activities that the local militias intercept to finance their members. Okombo and Sana (2010) describe this as well structured, such that the activities and shops considered as large are made to pay more to the vigilante as compared to the much smaller undertakings, and no one is spared the "taxation."

The state, after evicting people from their structures in the slums, often do not provide alternative shelter. In fact, these people move to other areas of similar status because the conditions in such residences offer them opportunities to move on with life and earn some income. The example of the slum-upgrading effort in the Kibera upgraded settlement has yielded to the would-be beneficiaries giving up their houses to the middle-income earners and going back to a slum life. This means something has not worked and, therefore, the slum condition is spreading in Nairobi in an unprecedented manner. Whereas the intention of the upgrading was to uplift the standard of living of the slum people, circumstances have militated against them and the only way to manage is to get into another slum where the requirements of trying to make a living are not as demanding as is the case in the upgraded settlement.

There is also a need to recognize that when people are relocated from where they have spent all their lives it takes time for them to establish a semblance of their previous state in another location. Any effort directed towards slum upgrading should be alive to the fact that a pattern that was established in the old residence is always replaced with a totally new one, and some people may not be able to sustain themselves there. When this happens some would look for a way of moving back to the old slum (if it still exists) or moving into another slum altogether. This is indeed a challenge that the government of Kenya must address. It is also possible some who are evicted are left totally unattended to, mainly because they have been illegal occupants of the areas they lived in. This group may have nowhere else to go, especially after living in the area they are being evicted from for a long time, to the extent that their children know no other place they could call home.

Any effort directed at relocating people must take into consideration that they have a livelihood to depend on and that establishing a livelihood source takes time and money. The kind of undertakings engaged in may also not be easy to start in another location. For example, one depending on the large market in the slum may not be comfortable in a structured residential area where there are restrictions on establishing a business and a far smaller market. In fact, the rent charged in an upgraded settlement is also upgraded to fit with the new facilities available.

Residents living in the slums would, therefore, undoubtedly have to contend with either the illegality of their structures and their associated controlled status by the vigilantes that undertake their activities within the settlements, or, wait for the state organ to evict them from these structures and relocate them (which does not happen very frequently) to other locations considered upgraded. In this regard, the illegality of the slums is an aspect to be dealt with by the state, and this is well done through its agents (the city authority and the police). The subjugation of the rights of the residents by the vigilantes or militias is also well articulated when they determine what to do or not do in the slum. Slum dwellers in Nairobi are therefore completely subdued to respect these two groups of authority, which makes them insecure and utterly vulnerable.

## 9  The Way Forward

The violence meted on the residents of the slums must not continue. It is completely inhumane, and people should be able to trust the security system of the state. It is in this regard that the state organs must work to change the negative attitude the residents of the slums have towards them. The local authority must be seen to provide basic services to all, regardless of the status of the urban dwellers. This means the provision of infrastructure such as piped water, properly lit streets, and formal education must reach the slum dwellers where they are. The challenge may be to cooperate with the people in making this work. It is upon the local authority to determine where to come in because it has the capacity and expertise to follow up such endeavours. Such efforts have the potential of positively improving the attitude of the residents towards the local government.

Although it may be a challenge for the government to easily provide security of tenure for the land in the slums, it is important to show efforts towards this end because some of these areas are public land and displacing such a large population would not stop the spread of slums. Security of tenure reduces chances of violence caused by forceful evictions. It is incumbent that proper consultation is enhanced between the residents of the informal settlements and the local authority in the realization of this endeavour.

If the government provides efficient and effective security the activities of the vigilantes will cease. It is only where order is lacking that one would seek an alternative. The militias are a consequence of a security system that is not working. This informal arrangement has mainly been utilized to extort residents of the slums in Nairobi for provision of "security." The young people who join these groupings are often unemployed youth. It is therefore necessary that efforts are directed towards the provision of opportunities to make a living for this group of young people. Once a majority are engaged in decent income-earning activities there would be no need of vigilantes, especially when the government provides effective security.

These factors when considered together should be seen as potentially enhancing trust in the government organs and consultation on ways to improve the status of the residents in the informal settlements. It may be noted that slums are not the best form of settlements a government should aspire to have (Mitullah, 2003). However, in order to deal with the challenge of the slums, violence must be avoided in all its forms. The slum people need not be subdued violently to conform to the local formal institutions. It needs a government that is ready to listen to the fears of the residents and work towards creating an atmosphere of trust and consultation. Indeed, it is the government that has indirectly allowed the proliferation of slums and it has to take precautions to deal well with their impact. Once government is effective, the fears developed from the activities of the vigilantes would dissipate.

## 10 Conclusion

Moser has aptly explained that violence does not only "affect people's health and well-being, but it also has a devastating impact on the social fabric and economic prospects of entire cities" (Moser, 2005: 10).

This means the very presence of this vice makes people unable to perform and live a fulfilling life. It connotes an impact that goes beyond the slums of Mathare or Nairobi but the entire country. Violence breeds violence and there is no way a subdued people are able to undertake their duties effectively. It has been noted that the most probable sources of violence meted on the slum dwellers of Nairobi originate from both "hidden" activities which are found within households or "cyclic and/or existential violence" that are external as exhibited by actions of the Nairobi city authority and the police as well as of vigilante groups. Whereas the latter relate to informalized exploitative activities, the former imply a form of "formal" violence that makes the residents live in fear of demolitions and confrontations. These have worked to cause slum dwellers to live under pressure–they have succumbed to the fear of these organizations which portend loss of a livelihood, injury, or even death. In this case, they have engaged little effort to contribute to their well-being and that of their households. It has been shown that the government holds the key to improving the welfare of the slum people and letting them engage their full potential and skills towards the realization of better circumstances of living. This is only possible through a government that can be trusted and ready to listen to its residents and can provide effective and efficient security to all. It is through this engagement that even the vigilantes will not survive because there would be no vacuum for them to fill.

## Bibliography

Amnesty International. (2009). *KENYA—The Unseen Majority: Two Million Slum-Dwellers*. Amnesty International.

Corbum, J., Ngau, P., Karanja, I., & Makau, J. (2012). *Mathare Zonal Plan—Nairobi, Kenya: A Collaborative Plan for Informal Settlement Upgrading*. Report of the collaboration between University of California—Berkeley, University of Nairobi, Muungano Support Trust and Slum Dweller International.

Dafe, F. (2009, February). *No Business Like Slum Business? The Political Economy of the Continued Existence of Slums: A Case Study of Nairobi* (Working Chapter Series No. 09-98). Development Studies Institute, London School of Economics and Political Science, London.

DEPHA (Data Exchange Platform for the Horn of Africa). (2008). *Map of Mathare Slums, Nairobi–Kenya*. Available at http://www.depha.org also at http://reliefweb.int/sites/reliefweb.int/files/resources/CC0FA8800D90FE0E852573C9005A673F-unep_REF_ken080105_a.pdf

Duara Foundation. (2010). *Mathare Valley*. Retrieved July 12, 2010, from http://www.duara.org/Mathare.html

Kamau, H. W., & Ngari, J. (2002). *Assessment of the Mathare 4A Development Programme Against the Sustainable Livelihoods Approach*. A project funded by DfID. Working Paper No. 4.

Kenya. (2011). Kenya Slum Upgrading Programme (KENSUP), Ministry of Housing. Retrieved June 7, 2012, from http://www.housing.go.ke/?p=124

Masika, R., de Haan, A., & Baden, S. (1997). *Urbanisation and Urban Poverty: A Gender Analysis' Report prepared for the Gender Equality Unit* (Bridge Development—Gender Report No. 54).

Mitullah, W. (2003). Urban Slum Reports: The Case of Nairobi, Kenya. In UN-Habitat (2003) *Understanding Slums: Case Studies for the Global Report on Human Settlements*. Nairobi.

Moser, C. O. N. (2005). City Violence and the Poor. In *In Focus* (pp. 10–12). UNDP-International Poverty Centre.

Mutisya, E., & Yarime, M. (2011). Understanding the Grassroots Dynamics of Slums in Nairobi: The Dilemma of Kibera Informal Settlements. *International Transaction Journal of Engineering, Management and Applied Sciences and Technologies, 2*(2), 197–213. http://TuEngr.com/V02/197-213.pdf

Okombo, O., & Sana, O. (2010) *Balaa Mitaani: The Challenge of Mending Ethnic Relations in the Nairobi Slums.* Friedrich Ebert Stiftung (FES) and Citizens against Violence (CAVI).

Osha, S. (2007). The Informalization of Urbanity. *African Identities, 5*(3), 331–353.

Pamoja Trust. (2009). *An Inventory of the Slums in Nairobi.* Nairobi.

Pilisuk, M. (1998). The Hidden Structure of Contemporary Violence, Peace and Conflict. *Journal of Peace Psychology, 4*(3), 197–216.

Transparency International. (2008, April 17). *Kenya Bribery Index 2008—Employment Related Bribes Highest as Service Delivery Is Hampered.*

UN-Habitat. (2007). *Sustainable Urbanisation: Local Action for Urban Poverty Reduction, Emphasis on Finance and Planning.* The Twenty-First Session of the Governing Council.

UN-Habitat. (2003a, May). *Guide to Monitoring Target 11: Improving the Lives of 100 Million Slum Dwellers—Progress Towards the Millennium Development Goals.* Global Urban Observatory.

UN-Habitat. (2003b). *Facing the Slum Challenge.* Advanced Draft on global report on Human Settle.

UN-Habitat. (2008). *UN-Habitat and Kenya Slum Upgrading Programme: Strategy Document.* Nairobi: UN-Habitat.

Wasikeh, P. (2002). *The Redevelopment of Large Informal Settlements in Nairobi: The Case of the Mathare 4a Development Project.* Retrieved March 24, 2005, from http://www.hdm.lth.se/TRAINING/postgrad/HD/papers/2002/HD2002-1.pdf

# Through the Afrocentricity Lens: Terror, Insurgency and Implications for Regional Integration in Southern Africa from Cabo Delgado Province, Mozambique

Daniel Nkosinathi Mlambo, Victor H. Mlambo, and Mandla Mfundo Masuku

## 1 Introduction

Colonialism has always been blamed for Africa's slow pace of development and integration blueprints. However, the internal problems in most African states have gradually changed the status quo. After gaining independence, the majority of African countries continuously experienced political and economic challenges instigated by ethnic and tribal competition for political power to control the distribution of state resources. This has been evidenced by weak political institutions, constitutional challenges, and political instability, leading to military coups and terrorism-driven conflicts (Jiboku, 2016).

Mwanawina (2011) further highlights the fact that the twenty-first century has brought with it immense challenges in the global arena, such as terrorism, poverty, economic decline, and respect for human rights, which have, in turn, prompted a change in governance trends. What has become more evident is that no state can exist in isolation, and there is a need to enter regional

D. N. Mlambo
Tshwane University of Technology, Pretoria, South Africa

V. H. Mlambo
University of Johannesburg, Johannesburg, South Africa

M. M. Masuku (✉)
University of KwaZulu-Natal, Durban, South Africa
e-mail: masukum@ukzn.ac.za

integration arrangements to survive in an increasingly independent world. Studies on regional integration and terrorism are scattered among various disciplines. Previously, political scientists had a long-standing interest in the two. Still, historians, lawyers, international relations (IR) scholars, development specialists, and public policy analysts have recently shown interest in this field. Hence, the literature on this subject continues to grow as scholars from diverse disciplines delve into the various discourses and debates on regional integration and terrorism strategies. From an African standpoint, the need for regional integration has been demonstrated by policies and programmes constantly formulated by African heads of state and continental and regional organizations. Although Africa is blessed with numerous natural resources, it has continued to remain underdeveloped, chiefly because it has been plagued by immense challenges, such as poor health facilities, cultural and religious crises, intrastate and interstate conflicts, economic underdevelopment, and resource depletion, to name but a few. The continuous acts of extensive civil wars, rebellions, coups, child soldiers, and terrorism have attracted much Afrocentrism scholarly attention, predominantly in West and East African states such as Sudan, Nigeria, Chad, Ethiopia, and the Central African Republic (CAR).

In Southern Africa, while political instability has been persistent in states such as Lesotho and Zimbabwe, and the many rebel insurgencies in the Democratic Republic of Congo (DRC), the region has been a relatively peaceful one in the continent and has kept its regional integration blueprints intact in comparison with other regions. However, the recent resurgence of terrorism in Mozambique's northern Cabo Delgado province (since 2017) has brought back the need to revisit African insurgency and its effect on regional integration from a Southern African perspective (Mlambo, 2021). The issues of weak governance, weak security structures, and porous borders have been prone to steer the continent's regional integration frameworks. Likewise, political instability and conflict have dire effects on economic growth. In the view of the ambivalent positions, a further investigation is warranted, predominantly from an Afrocentric perspective, since in Africa, most states have various forms of instability, albeit in varying degrees. This chapter delves into the repercussions of the rise of insurgency in Cabo Delgado and what ramifications this will have for Southern Africa's regional integration outlook.

## 2   Africa, Regional Integration, and the Economic Growth Agenda: A Concise Analysis of Literature

Regional integration has manifested itself historically in Europe, America, and Africa as an essential doctrine to stimulate the expansion of capitalism and political unification; hence, it has a long historical tradition. Regional integration in Africa has a long-standing history dating back to 1910 with the formation of the Southern African Customs Union (SACU). The twenty-first century has brought mammoth socio-economic challenges globally. Because of such challenges, it has become more evident that no country can exist in isolation, and there is a need to enter into regional integration arrangements (Mwanawina, 2011; Palloti, 2004). Chitsa (2016), putting it in its simplest form, noted that regional integration refers to a process whereby a group of states joins forces and vows to be administered by similar rules, protocols, and policies about political, economic, and social issues, intending to accomplish common goals for their citizens. From van Niekerk's (2005) assessment, regional integration can thus be robustly understood from three points of view:

1. *Geographical scope*—has to do with the number of countries in regional integration arrangements, whether from an economic, political, or social consideration.
2. *The substantive coverage*—has to do with available sectors or activity (labour, trade, macro policies, and so forth).
3. *The depth of integration*—has to do with the extent of sovereignty a particular state aims to surrender.

Aworaro (2015) points out that neighbouring states drive regional integration in a specific geographic region that needs to stimulate and enhance regional integration facilitation and cooperation by establishing institutions that steer and shape mutual action with the vision of realizing socio-economic and political benefits. Similarly, these states must be prepared to share their sovereignty and undertake some sacrifice and political commitment. Jiboku and Okeke-Uzodike (2016) further maintain that such obligations should be driven by the fact that states pool their human, financial, and material resources towards national and continental development blueprints. These, in turn, should drive the movement of goods, enhance development, and economic growth, lessen poverty, harmonize socio-economic policies, and promote the fight for peace and security. Other envisioned benefits may include making markets more competitive, stimulating investment opportunities, and strengthening political and economic reforms and cooperation through security mechanisms.

Gibbs (2012) joins several scholars in arguing that regional integration became even more pivotal when most African states gained or were about to achieve their respective freedom from European colonizers from the 1950s onward. While it is important to note that regional integration offers myriad benefits, these are not always guaranteed, as they depend on the degree and extent of commitment from involved member states. Likewise, the lack of engagement and robust participation toward regional integration blueprints is a massive challenge for Africa's regional integration endeavours, mainly because of the continent's political landscape. Other obstacles include poverty, low-income levels, civil conflicts, human rights abuse, dependence on foreign aid, and terrorism-driven activities (Mwasha, 2011).

Since then, African leaders have promoted several development plans, frameworks, and programmes. Even though these are diverse in nature and scope, they are uniting, prioritizing, and privileging regional integration as a prerequisite for political independence and economic development. In Gibb's (2009) assessment, colonialism had created an extremely fragmented state system, which, combined with economic and political marginality, needed Africa to develop innovative ways to stimulate economic growth blueprints. Hence, the quest for forging technical links among African states was driven by Pan-African desires for collective self-reliance, solidarity, development, peace, and security. From this came the Organization of African Unity (OAU) and the formation of other continental, regional groupings and regional development initiatives. Among these was the OAU's Lagos Plan of Action, the Abuja Treaty establishing the African Economic Community (AEC), and the New Partnership for Africa's Development (NEPAD). These were driven by the notion that African states would struggle to survive by themselves without some form of unity. This was also driven by the quest for the region to fight against political instability, colonial rule, apartheid in South Africa, poor economic prospects, and extreme geographical fragmentation. From a Southern African perspective, regional integration was envisioned to steer regional progression forward as in the rest of Africa.

During apartheid, regional integration was mainly characterized by an exceptional degree of economic integration, driven by much hostility and political divisions motivated by South Africa's destabilization policies (Mlambo, 2020). Given the political balkanization of Africa into arbitrary nation-states with a sparse population, minor markets, porous borders, continuous conflict, and terrorism, it is not surprising that regional integration has been seen as a means of overcoming some of these challenges while intending to forge a practical African unity both from a political and an economic perspective (Asante, 1995). Again, unique geographical characteristics make regional integration imperative. This is because the continent is home to many landlocked nations, making addressing issues such as trade a daunting task.

Hence, most African states participate in regional integration; by this, we mean that all agree to operate common institutions and cooperate governmentally to stimulate benefits such as peace and security and additional non-economic benefits. Nevertheless, regional integration in Africa has continued to be a challenge. Notwithstanding some achievements, the continent has suffered constant setbacks in its regional integration agenda. In addition, apart from emerging powers such as South Africa and Nigeria, most African states are weak and vary in their levels of development, societal norms, and resource endowment. Continuous political instability, ethnic fractionalization, ethnic centrism, corruption, weak governance, law and order, coups, famine, poverty, unemployment, and dictatorial rule have played a significant part in this. Apart from these problems, there is also a lack of private sector investments in regional integration. Despite the quest for regional peace, the region has, over the years, been fraught with armed revolts.

Events in Zimbabwe, the DRC, and Lesotho provide evidence that the region still has peace and security challenges. Thus, Qobo (2007) opines that in most African states, it would be challenging to stimulate regional integration frameworks without robust governance structures driven by the rule of law.

## 3 Historically Africanizing Terrorism and Insurgency

Since the dawn of independence, some African states have not only struggled against domestic terrorism but have also been challenged over the last few decades by the resurgence of transnational terrorist groups that have used Africa to carry out attacks. Many socio-economic and political conditions in Africa have produced grievances that militant groups have utilized to rationalize their recourse to violent actions. Some of these can be made so that physical terrain is often used for these violent actions. In the case of the physical landscape, this includes securing a location (typically a region and mainly a dense forest) that serves as an operational base to plan attacks, receive support, offer training, and act as a recruitment source. Bahgat and Medina (2013) further narrate that studies on terrorism are not recent, originated many decades ago, and were based on the belief that there is an urgent need to understand this form of political violence formally.

Approaching a socio-political problem such as terrorism from a social science perspective leads to a more nuanced understanding of terrorists, and their activities, social networks, connections, systematic social operations, and political and other systems. Although studies on terrorism have been common in the global arena, the term "terrorism" has been difficult to conceptualize. Indeed, as Asuelime and David (2015) observed, there are more than 100 diplomatic and academic definitions of terrorism. In recent scholarly debates, terrorism has been conceptualized through the lenses of (1) crime, (2) politics, (3) warfare, (4) propaganda, and (5) religion. Most of the points mentioned above, if not all, are commonly perpetrated by terrorists and are typically considered illegal by the international community. However, this study embraces Matsena's (2011) conceptualization of terrorism as violence that targets unarmed and vulnerable civilians to achieve specific political objectives.

This sentiment is also shared by Martha Crenshaw's 1994-edited volume titled *Terrorism in Africa*. It clarifies that terrorism is a tactic that utilizes violence or threat as a coercive strategy to cause fear and political intimidation. Terrorism is made up of features encompassing, among other things, resistance movements, military coups, political assignations, and numerous intra- and interstate conflicts that have affected African states at some point during the continent's transition to independence and the subsequent postcolonial period. Drawing on the above, Onapajo and Ozden (2020), using Lee's push-and-pull theory, believe that push factors explain the structural detect in a society that makes individuals into violent extremism, including bad governance, poverty, and unemployment. On the other hand, pull factors (which describe an extremist group's attractive attributes that motivate individuals to join) include group ideology, fame, and glory, reputation, and group protection. According to Schmid (2005), critical characteristic elements of terrorism include:

1. The demonstrative use of violence against human beings
2. The threat of further violence
3. The deliberate production of terror/fear/dread, and anxiety in a target group
4. The frequent targeting of civilians
5. The purpose of intimidation, coercion, and propaganda

6. The fact that it is a method, tactic, or strategy of conflict waging
7. The illegal, criminal, and immortal nature of the acts of violence
8. The predominantly political character of the act
9. Its use as a tool of psychological warfare
10. The importance of communicating the acts of violence to a larger audience

During the twenty-first century, the repercussion of the terrorist attacks on the Twin Towers of the World Trade Center in the United States of America (USA) on the 11 September 2011 has given renewed incentive to the continuous causes of terrorism (Ajide & Raheem, 2020). There has been a steady rise in violent extremist attacks throughout Africa. This violence is not only setting motion a dramatic reversal of the developmental and economic gains already accrued. Still, it is also threatening again, threatening to halt political and economic development prospects for years to come. Makinda (2007) aptly illustrates that, from an African perspective, the continent's history has manifested itself in four forms. First, it was mainly limited to African issues, particularly the liberation struggles. Such a form of political violence, directed at forces of foreign occupation, was justified in terms of self-determination. Second, terrorist activities in the continent have manifested in civil wars in many African countries, such as Angola, Congo, Rwanda, and Sudan. In this form of terrorism, the struggle took the form of violence by Africans against African and ethnic groups. Third, some African governments have embraced the Palestinian cause and transplanted the Israeli–Palestinian problem to the continent. Fourth, Al-Qaeda into a much-feared network on the continent.

While terrorism may be based on political, religious, social, cultural, economic, and environmental factors, not all have contributed to African terrorism. Over the last few decades, acts of terrorism on the continent have steadily increased as many terrorist groups have multiplied and gained further confidence in the lack of repercussions for their actions. Various acts of killing, rape, abductions, bombing, and mass murder in multiple countries on the continent have gone unpunished to a large extent (Abioye, 2019). Terrorism activities are operationally distinct from guerrilla warfare in the sense that their perpetrators must operate within a territory that is effectively controlled by their enemies and in which they must, therefore, avoid detection on an individual basis. There are some points at which the ultimate aims of terrorist groups affect the activities they engage in. One of these is when they accept death as the price of their actions (Clapham, 2003).

Terrorism constitutes an imminent threat to Africa's peace, security, stability, and development. The factors mentioned above, and the continent's constant postcolonial development failures, have made Africa susceptible to being a breeding ground for terrorist activities. While the scale of terrorist activities in the continent varies from region to region, some regions like West Africa have, over the years, become a terrorism hotspot. This situation (predominantly after the colonial era) has been driven by economic resources ranging from crude oil and minerals to gas, weak economies and democracies, ethnic rivalry, religious beliefs, and corruption. Without a doubt, the failure of Africa's security mechanisms and the role played by terrorism is especially pertinent, given the combination of the unfolding revolutions and political transformation on the continent and the ever-growing Islamic terrorist threats in many African countries.

## 4 The Resurrection of Terror and Insurgency in Capo Delgado: Unpacking the Driving Motives

Since its independence from Portugal in 1975, Mozambique has witnessed two long periods of war and peace. The first was a 15-year-long civil war between the ruling party, the *Frente de Libertação Moçambique* (FRELIMO), and the rebel forces of the *Resistência Nacional Moçambicana* (RENAMO), that caused millions of deaths and displacements. However, after signing the Rome "General Peace Accords" in 1992, Mozambique witnessed relative peace and a steady gross domestic product (GDP) growth between 2003 and 2013. Nevertheless, the resurgence of low-intensity armed conflict between FRELIMO and RENAMO from 2013 to 2016 further provided a reality check, indicating that all was not well. Mozambique's danger is no longer limited to the politico-military confrontation between FRELIMO and RENAMO. The country has witnessed a paradigm shift of violence encompassing terrorism and gaining speedy momentum continuously (Faleg, 2019).

As indicated, African states have not been spared from terrorism generally. Nevertheless, Southern Africa has, over the years, been relatively spared from this. Yet, the Cabo Delgado province in Mozambique has, over the last five years, seen a relative resurrection of terror-related incidents. Besides Mozambique, no other Southern African country has witnessed terrorism. Indeed, given the recent activities, this could have spillover effects for other countries in the region. History has shown that (as with Boko Haram) these movements can start small and become a severe regional security threat. While accurate data varies, it has been shown that thousands of people have been killed and displaced in the northern parts of Mozambique since 2017. These attacks have been carried out by Ansar Al Sunna (also known as Ahlu Sunnah Wal-Jamo). This Mozambican-based Islamic extremist insurgent group rose to prominence in October 2017 after attacking civilians and government property in Cabo Delgado.

This was first a religious movement in Cabo Delgado, and the group often claims that the Islam that is practised in Mozambique has been corrupted and no longer follows the teaching of Muhammad. The region of Cabo Delgado has a Muslim population of about 58%. The Islamic group is driven by anti-Christian and anti-Western values. One of their goals, like other African terrorist groups, is to enforce strict Sharia and Islamic law in their localities. Driven by the marginalization and high unemployment rates in northern Mozambique, the group has attracted young and vulnerable men to join their ranks and has hidden militant camps in the Cabo Delgado districts of Macomia, Mocimboa da Praia, and Montepuez (Mutasa & Muchmwa, 2021).

Makonye (2020) asserts that Cabo Delgado is situated in the northern parts of Mozambique and bordered by the Republic of Tanzania to the north, Niassa province to the west, and Nampula province to the south. The province has an estimated population of 2.3 million people and is made up mainly of three ethnic groups: (1) the Makonde, (2) the Macau, and (3) the Mwani. The province has witnessed a boom in the oil and gas industry; however, it remains the poorest province in Mozambique. Again, its relatively large Muslim population, unemployment, and marginal economic development have provided a suitable environment for the Islamic group to grow its membership. Hence, the province is caught up in an insurgency lockdown that has attracted continental and global interest.

The insurgency in Mozambique has had far-reaching implications within the social, economic, humanitarian, and political spheres. Cilliers et al. (2021) have lucidly noted that this insurgency would threaten Foreign Direct Investments (FDI), infrastructure investments, mining, other significant short- and long-term projects, and Southern African regional integration. Further contributing to this have been governance challenges, including large-scale corruption in the ruling FRELIMO. It is noticeable that Mozambique has not yet been able to contain and subdue as they need more capacity in training, military intelligence, and equipment. Against this background, continental assistance is essential in preventing the situation.

## Implications for Southern African Regional Integration

Regional integration is a strategy that sees states, through their governments, agreeing to commit to working collectively with interest in specific focal areas such as development, governance, and peace and security. Despite a positive outlook since the transformation from the Southern African Development Coordination Conference (SADCC) to the Southern African Development Community (SADC) in 1992, the regional integration agenda in Southern Africa faces several new challenges, including terrorism. The region has always experienced relative peace, but recent incidents in Mozambique require us to delve into the conflict. In postcolonial Africa, persistent insecurity in some parts of the continent and the ineffectiveness of peace-building mediations in preventing this necessitate revisit approaches to continental conflict.

Ibeanu (2015) concedes that the end of the Cold War and the much-needed transition from military and authoritarian rule to civil democratic governance in some continental states in the 1980s and 1990s gave impetus to the view that continuous fighting would be outdated. In many African states, robust transition procedures were brought to the fore, elections were held, and new governments came into office. However, since this period, instability seems to have occurred. From a global perspective, any state, intrastate, and interstate instability brings dire developmental and economic challenges. Suppose we narrow this down to a regional point of view. In that case, conflict can halt regional processes such as trade, the flow of resources, and human capital development, bringing spillover effects to other member states. From a Mozambican point of view, these spillover effects may affect South Africa and Tanzania, Malawi, Zimbabwe, and Zambia. They may also bring significant displacements, refugees, the flow of weapons, crime, illegal arms trading, more terrorist activities, and money laundering, among other things (Mlambo, 2021; Mutanga, 2017).

To further enhance peace, maintain shared security, and advance progress in Southern Africa, what ought to be done is to bring forward robust and well-maintained and evaluated mechanisms for further formulating and applying reforms, with the notion of making political governance socially relevant. At the same time, to counter such measures, resources meant for the general populace are diverted to assist in fighting conflict. They may, among other things, include:

1. The consolidation of peace and physical and social security for people
2. The implementation of social, political, and legal institutions which ought to sustain peace, development, and economic growth

3. The promotion and protection of gender equality, civil, and human rights
4. The formation and implementation of integrated and coherent regional programmes and priorities

For regional integration to be justifiable, these must be effectively established. However, without proper institutional frameworks and capacity, they cannot accomplish their role effectively and constantly. In Cabo Delgado, the beginnings of terrorism are relatively early, hence, swift steps in identifying such threats should be taken. Despite what is happening in Cabo Delgado, the problem in Africa is that short-term methodologies have driven us. Terrorism requires short-term and long-term solutions, encompassing robust transformation policies, peace-building mechanisms, governance structures, and collective bargaining power.

Another vital factor that might create conditions that could make terrorism likely is the phenomenon of state failure or collapse. Makinda (2007) emphasized that there is no clinical definition of failed or failing states. However, policymakers have often used these terms interchangeably to refer to African and other developing countries that have experienced or may be experiencing governance problems. This is particularly acute for Mozambique, where the continuous governance challenges continue to hamper needed economic reforms and development and have caused many people to live below the poverty line.

We believe that as long as governance issues at the national level, which are sometimes incarnated through interstate disputes, are not properly managed, regional integration aspirations will not be realized in the region. In general, conflict brings repercussions that take years to fix and many resources to reverse. Peace and security are vital for economic growth, and it is a solid challenge to steer economic growth when displaced individuals are in camps and infrastructure is demolished; this is true of Cabo Delgado (Mulindwa, 2020).

## Possible Recommendations

Since the birth of the SADC in 1992, the Southern African region has not experienced terrorism of this scale before. These attacks have shown and continue to offer the violent extremists' determination to carve out part of the country to establish a caliphate or haven to plan and execute terror-related activities. This is not a crisis Mozambique can solve on its own, and there is a need for intervention by regional bodies and states deemed relatively advanced. From a Southern African perspective, this is the SADC and South Africa as emerging powers. However, any interventions must also draw on examples from other parts of the continent, such as West, North, and East Africa and the Sahel region; where terrorist activities have over the years caused havoc. Peace and security are prerequisites for growth and development anywhere in the world. This is important in Africa because of the continent's underdevelopment driven by years of conflicts.

As long as some parts of the continent remain unstable, needed development and economic growth plans will take forever. Any intergovernmental organization involved in the fight against terrorism in the continent must have to confront at the practical level the big debate which emerged after 9/11 as to whether terrorism, in its current state and manifestations, constitutes a threat to the continent on the same scale as poverty, health risks, and internal conflicts. The role of the SADC is essential for preventing and combating any regional conflict, including terrorism, to fill the gaps where its member states or regional mechanisms are lacking (Ewi & Aning, 2006). As a regional body, any plan brought to the fore by the SADC should amply deal with the humanitarian, security-related, political, and economic challenges and *terrorist hotspots (hiding places) that must be liberated.

The use of military action by the Mozambican government has not brought the envisioned results; in fact, it has created warfare in Cabo Delgado. This is even though, from an African perspective, this is never an easy thing to do (1) because of the types of locations these terrorists use as hiding spots, (2) because the way they manoeuvre from one location to another makes them hard to track, and (3) because they always split and form smaller groups in different locations. The ISS (2020) identified some of the following protocols that perhaps the SADC should take:

1. Develop a comprehensive operational strategy that allows for a range of military, economic, political, and humanitarian measures
2. Send a fact-finding mission to northern Mozambique to determine the extent of the crisis and the humanitarian needs of the population
3. Consider appointing a special convoy to coordinate efforts to assist Mozambique
4. Assist the Mozambican government in developing long-term strategies to address the root causes of terrorism, including confiscating land for mining, unemployment, underdevelopment, and the lack of resources

While the points mentioned earlier are crucial, the SADC has, over the years, not applied them in other regional states that, unlike Mozambique, have witnessed an array of political instability. In Okunade and Ogunnubi's

(2019) view, the continent's massive size in land mass and population, natural resources, open seas, and oceans have had consequences for its security, peace, and stability.

On the one hand, these factors offer prospects for economic development. Abundant land, mineral, and raw materials enhance productive and profitable economic activities. The seas and oceans provide less costly means of transportation for personal and commercial interaction with the rest of the world.

On the other hand, such geographic circumstances have rendered part of the continent vulnerable to internal and external threats since the fifteenth century. The continent's rich resource reservoirs have attracted criminals, terrorist organizations, and traffickers to exploit the undefended coastal waters and porous borders to engage in criminal activities that have continued to threaten regional and continental stability, peace, and security. This has imposed a heavy responsibility on both continental and regional actors. At its disposal, the SADC possesses a plethora of instruments to facilitate an intervention; the SADC Treaty of 1992, the SADC Protocol on Politics, Defence, and Security of 2001, and the SADC Common Agenda (amended in 2009), the Strategic Indicative Plan for the Organ on Defence, Politics, and Security (SIPO), and the SADC Mutual Defence Pact of 2003.

Mozambique satisfies the conditions under which the SADC must intervene in member states, as provided under the SADC Protocol on Politics, Defence, and Security. These structures and institutions can be used to include the Summit of Heads of States or Government, Council of Ministers, Organ on Politics, Defence and Security Cooperation (OPDSC), and the Troika. Article 11(2) (b) of the protocol provides that the SADC OPDSC shall seek to resolve large-scale violence between sections of the population or between the state and sections of the population (Vhumbunu, 2021). By working together with Mozambique's police and military, SADC forces must act impartially and within the law if they are to stabilize Cabo Delgado and gain the community's trust. This is necessary not only for the province's safety but also to avoid giving locals a reason to support the insurgents further.

The regional body firmly understands that insurgency in Mozambique risks exploding into a full-blown regional challenge. However, some have criticized the regional body for not taking an early initiative in the Mozambican conflict that started as early as 2017. This is also driven by the fact that over the years, the SADC has failed to intervene in other cases of regional instability in states such as Lesotho, the DRC, and Zimbabwe. As this has severe ramifications for Mozambique and the region, the lack of action will fuel more attacks on innocent civilians.

The unequal balance of African states has led more powerful actors to take an interest and intervene in the affairs of their neighbours. States such as Nigeria, South Africa, and Egypt are expected to advocate for regional cooperation and offer support to their neighbours. From a global perceptive, and especially since the Cold War era, there has been a need for emerging regional powers to be involved and be the drivers of conflict resolution within their regions. Depending on the magnitude of such conflict, this entails the utilization of mediation, preventive diplomacy efforts, peacekeeping, peace support, operations, peacebuilding and postconflict reconstruction (Mlambo & Adetiba, 2019). Sidiropoulos (2007) observes that since 1994, when the late Nelson Mandela's government assumed office, Africa has become the most crucial element in South Africa's foreign policy documents, and this is driven by the following factors:

1. South Africa's responsibility to the continent was born of the support many African countries provided for the national liberation struggle, and because of which, countries were subjected to cross-border raids by the apartheid government
2. The particular South African experience of internal negotiation and agreement could serve as an example to other countries
3. The recognition that its political and economic success depends largely on the continent's fortunes and that its well-developed economy could lead in Africa's development

South Africa, as an emerging power, has, since the democratic dispensation, played a central and pivotal role in formulating both the regional and the continental security architecture. South Africa's ongoing interest in the continuous Islamic attacks in Mozambique is not without careful consideration for its security and that of the region. The current lack of South African involvement in Mozambique is alarming given its proximity and emerging power status in Southern Africa, as it remains a leading actor in Southern Africa regarding soft and hard power credentials.

This is further attested in the (2021) Global Firepower rankings, in which among 140 modern military powers, South Africa was ranked 32 (with a score of 0. 5665) in terms of its hard power credentials. For the West, South Africa's democratic transition, liberal 1996 constitution, and large and diverse economy further cement its status as a regional powerhouse. In addition, in the twenty-first century, there have been other ways of conducting diplomacy. While power is still seen as the central prism concerning how countries interact, philosophies of power have altered remarkably. While a country's power is often measured along with its hard power currencies (military and economic), recent developments in the global arena are allowing other diplomatic approaches apart from hard power. This is what Nye Jr (2002) refers to as soft power. For him, a state must utilize soft rather than hard power. Most African states do not yield soft-power currencies, mainly, because of autocratic regimes, conflicts, underdevelopment, and marginalization from the global economy; however, South Africa possesses both soft- and hard-power attributes. Soft power pertains to the capability of an agent (a state) to effectively project its objectives to an audience (the foreign public) in a manner that positively alters the audience's attitudes, thus, also facilitating a sort of moral belief (Chiroro, 2012; Mlambo & Adetiba, 2020; Sidiropoulos, 2014).

When a state's power is superior to that of other regional or continental states, that country is considered a hegemonic state or an emerging power because its superiority gives it considerable influence over other regional or continental states. Similarly, economic dominance is closely linked with social, cultural, and political hegemony (Modesto & Sajeev, 2016). However, van der Westhuizen (2016) reminds us that it should be noted that just because a country possesses soft-power currencies, this does not automatically confirm it will yield soft-power actions. Instead, how leaders can conceive and utilize soft-power attributes should influence policy outcomes in the short and long run.

Over the years, South Africa has tried to be an influential emerging power in the region, with both successes and failures. In the literature, it is somehow accepted that the behaviour and role of emerging powers are linked to the failure or success of regional integration. As the only African state in the Brazil, Russia, India, and China (BRIC) grouping, South Africa becomes the voice of Africa in international fora. There is significant evidence that successful regional integration will depend on the extent to which there exist regional institutions with sufficient competence and capacity to stimulate and manage, effectively and efficiently, the complex process of regional integration.

## 5 Conclusion

The insurgency in Cabo Delgado is escalating. Its political, security-related, humanitarian, and cross-border implications are far-reaching, not presenting a good picture for Southern African regional integration. It is in the interest of the SADC, South Africa, and other organizations to urgently address what is happening in Cabo Delgado before it spirals out of control. Continuous conflict and terrorism in Africa indicate that the continent is facing a problem in dealing with this surge. It is, therefore, vital that we strongly analyse the dynamics in Cabo Delgado, as by doing this, policymakers and heads of state will come up with better initiatives that may be effective in not only diminishing instability but also dealing with issues that drove it. For the region to accrue the benefits of regional integration, limiting regional and continental conflicts will be of utmost importance both in the short and the long run. In the same vein, addressing the continuous national, political, and socio-economic challenges is essential. This will require full responsibility, accountability, good governance, and competent state-society relations. Irrespective of other external factors, the Mozambican government itself needs more security resources (police and military) present at the terrorist hotspots, such as Cabo Delgado, and able to navigate easily by road, air, and sea. Again, the government must be at the forefront in fighting the insurgency to gain the local population's trust, as no foreign support can entirely replace political leadership.

## Bibliography

Abioye, F. (2019) *Terrorist Groups in Africa: Quo Vadis?* https://www.jstor.org/stable/26873434?seq=1#metadata_info_tab_contents. Accessed 30 June 2021.

Ajide, K. B., & Raheem, I. B. (2020). Does Democracy Really Fuel Terrorism in Africa? *International Economic Journal, 34*(2), 297–316.

Asante, K. B. (1995). The Need for Regional Integration: A Challenge for Africa. *Review of African Political Economy, 22*(66), 573–577.

Asuelime, L. E., & David, O. J. (2015). Interrogating the Concept and Practice of Terrorism within a Changing Global and Historical Context. *African Renaissance, 12*(1), 7–26.

Aworaro, F. (2015). Regional Integration and Development in Africa: Between the Present Realities and Overcoming the Future. *African Journal of Governance and Development, 4*(2), 5–16.

Bahgat, K., & Medina, M. (2013). An Overview of Geographical Perspectives and Approaches in Terrorism Research. *Perspectives on Terrorism, 7*(1), 38–72.

Chiroro, B. (2012). *South Africa: Optimising the Currency of Soft Power in the International Arena.* https://media.africaportal.org/documents/No-79.-Optimising-the-currency-of-soft-power-in-the-international-Arena.pdf. Accessed 30 July 2021.

Chitsa, T. A. (2016). *Challenges of Regionalism in Africa. A Case of the Southern African Development Community (SADC)* (Honours Dissertation). Midlands State University, Zimbabwe.

Cilliers, J., Louw-Vaudrain, L., Walker, T., Els, W., & Ewi, M. (2021). *What Would It Take to Stabilize Cabo Delgado?* https://issafrica.org/iss-today/what-would-it-take-to-stabilise-cabo-delgado. Accessed 1 August 2021.

Clapham, C. (2003). Terrorism in Africa: Problems of Definition, History, and Development. *South African Journal of International Affairs, 10*(2), 13–28.

Ewi, M., & Aning, K. (2006). Assessing the Role of the African Union in Preventing and Combating Terrorism in Africa. *African Security Studies, 15*(3), 32–46.

Faleg, G. (2019). *Conflict Prevention in Mozambique. Can There Be Peace After the Storm?* https://www.iss.europa.eu/content/conflict-prevention-mozambique. Accessed 4 August 2021.

Gibb, R. (2009). Regional Integration and Africa's Development Trajectory: Metatheories, Expectations, and Reality. *Third World Quarterly, 30*(4), 701–720.

Gibb, R. (2012). The Southern African Customs Union: Promoting Stability Through Dependence. In C. Saunders, G. A. Dzinea, & D. Nagar (Eds.), *Region building in Southern Africa: Progress, problems, and prospects*. Zed Books.

Global Firepower. (2021). *Global Firepower 2021.* https://www.globalfirepower.com/. Accessed 1 June 2021.

Ibeanu, O. (2015). *Political Instability and the Challenges of Democratization in Africa: A Conceptual Analysis.* https://media.africaportal.org/documents/Political-Instability-and-the-Concept-of-Democraticization-In-Africa.pdf. Accessed 27 July 2021.

ISS. (2020). *Mozambique Insurgency Requires Urgent Response from SADC and the AU.* https://issafrica.org/about-us/press-releases/mozambique-insurgency-requires-urgent-response-from-sadc-and-the-au. Accessed 15 July 2021.

Jiboku, P. A. (2016). *The Quest for African Economic Integration: An Assessment of NEPAD's African Peer Review Mechanism* (PhD Thesis). University of KwaZulu-Natal, South Africa.

Jiboku, P. A., & Okeke-Uzodike, U. (2016). Regional Economic Integration and the Governance Challenge in Africa: Missing Link in the African Peer Review Mechanism. *Africa Development, 41*(2), 47–70.

Makinda, S. M. (2007). History and Root Causes of Terrorism in Africa. In W. Okumu & A. Botha (Eds.), *Understanding Terrorism in Africa: In Search for an African 'Voice'*. Institute for Security Studies.

Makonye, F. (2020). The Cabo Delgado Insurgency in Mozambique. Origin, Ideology, Recruitment Strategies, and Social, Political, and Economic Implications for Natural Gas and Oil Exploration. *African Journal of Terrorism and Insurgency Research, 1*(3), 59–72.

Matsena, K. K. (2011). *Revisiting the African Union's Responsibility in Addressing the Terrorism Conundrum in East Africa* (Honours Mini Dissertation). University of Venda, South Africa.

Mlambo, D. N. (2020). The Quest for Post-Colonial Regional Integration: Examining the SADC in Southern Africa Post-1992. *Journal of African Foreign Affairs, 7*(1), 23–24.

Mlambo, D. N. (2021). Africanizing Rebel Insurgency in a Postcolonial State and Ramifications for African Regional Integration: Insight(s) from the Democratic Republic of Congo (DRC). *Journal of Social Political Sciences, 2*(3), 205–224.

Mlambo, D. N., & Adetiba, T. (2020). South Africa and Regional Integration in Southern Africa Post-1994: Realities, Challenges, and Prospects. *Journal of Nation-Building and Policy Studies, 4*(1), 5–33.

Mlambo, D. N., & Adetiba, T. C. (2019). Post-1994 South Africa's Peacekeeping and Military Intervention in Southern Africa, Reference from the Democratic Republic of Congo (DRC) and Lesotho. *Journal of Public Affairs, 20*(1). https://doi.org/10.1002/pa.1984

Modesto, S. T., & Sajeev, M. (2016). As Assessment of South African Economic Dominance and its Influence on Regional Integration. *European Journal of Business and Accountancy, 4*(4), 55–86.

Mulindwa, P. (2020). Interstate Border Conflict and Their Effects in Region Building and Integration of the East African Community. *African Journal of Governance and Development, 9*(2), 599–618.

Mutanga, J. M. (2017). Economic Integration: The Impact of Conflict on Economic Development in Africa. *African Journal of Public Administration and Management, 25*(1), 1–24.

Mutasa, M. N., & Muchmwa, C. (2021). Ansar Al Sunna Mozambique: Is It the Boko Haram of Southern Africa? *Journal of Applied Security Research, 17*(3), 332–351.

Mwanawina, I. (2011). Regional Integration versus National Sovereignty: A Southern African Perspective. *Law and Politics in Africa, Asia, and Latin America, 44*(4), 456–481.

Mwasha, O. N. (2011). The Benefits of Regional Economic Integration for Developing Countries in Africa. A Case Study of East African Community (EAC). *Korea Review of International Studies, 1*(8), 69–92.

Niekerk, M. V. (2005). Surinam Country Study. ESRC, Centre on Migration. *Policy and Society (COMPAS),* 15.

Nye, J. S. (2002). *The Paradox of American Power: Why the World's Only Superpower Can't Go It Alone.* Oxford University Press.

Okunade, S. K., & Ogunnubi, O. (2019). The African Union Protocol on Free Movement: A Panacea to End Border Porosity? *Journal of African Union Studies, 8*(1), 73–91.

Onapajo, H., & Ozden, K. (2020). Non-Military Approach Against Terrorism in Mozambique: Deradicalization Strategies and Challenges in Countering Boko Haram. *Security Journal, 33*(1), 1–17.

Palloti, A. (2004). SADC: A Development Community Without a Development Policy. *Review of African Political Economy, 31*(101), 513–531.

Qobo, M. (2007). *The Challenge of Regional Integration in Africa: In the Context of Globalisation and the Prospects of a United States of Africa.* https://issafrica.org/research/papers/the-challenges-of-regional-integration-in-africa-in-the-context-of-globalisation-and-the-prospects-for-a-united-states-of-africa. Accessed 30 June 2021.

Schmid, A. P. (2005). Terrorism is a Psychological Warfare. *Democracy and Security, 1*(2), 137–146.

Sidiropoulos, E. (2007). *South Africa's Regional Engagement for Peace and Security.* https://www.saiia.org.za/wp-content/uploads/2008/04/south.africa.comment1.pdf. Accessed 1 July 2021.

Sidiropoulos, E. (2014). South Africa's Soft Power. *Current History, 113*(763), 197–202.

Van der Westhuizen, J. (2016). South Africa's Soft Power Conundrum: How to Win Friends and Influence People in Africa. *Journal of Political Power, 9*(3), 449–456.

Vhumbunu, C. H. (2021). Insurgency in Mozambique: The Role of the Southern African Development Community. *Conflict Trends, 1,* 3–13.

# The State and Violence in Africa

# Discourses on Political Violence and the Mechanics of Legitimation in Official Commissions of Inquiry in Africa

Claire-Anne Lester

## 1 Introduction

Weber's assertion that the state is the "human community which (successfully) lays claim to the *monopoly of legitimate physical violence*" has become a foundational premise of modern theorizations on the state (Weber, 1919). Yet, to what extent can we say that this assertion holds in postcolonial Africa? While many have studied the causes and nature of violence in Africa (Kalyvas, 2003; Lemarchand, 2021; Straus, 2012) there is less analytical focus given to the modalities and techniques by which the state legitimates its claims to violence. I contend that one such model, which is used extensively in the contemporary African context, is the commissions of inquiry. These investigatory bodies are frequently used as official instruments to investigate incidents or periods of political or state violence.

Since 1990 there have been more than seventy commissions of inquiry in Africa that have investigated incidents, periods, or patterns of violence, from the various truth commissions seen in South Africa (1995), Rwanda (1999), Sierra Leone (2000) and Kenya (2009) to commissions investigating (post-)election violence in Kenya (2007) and Liberia (2011) and Zimbabwe (2018). Official commissions that investigate state violence, such as those listed above, centre on a subject that strikes at the very heart of state power on the one

C.-A. Lester (✉)
Department of Sociology and Social Anthropology, Stellenbosch University, Stellenbosch, South Africa
e-mail: clairel@sun.ac.za

hand, and the limits of democratic participation on the other hand; events that call into question the legitimacy of the state's use of violence. When there is an official investigation into the state's violent excesses, which have resulted in the killing of citizens, the question of the state's legitimacy hangs suspended in the air.

Commissions of inquiry have become the go-to institution in Africa through which to officially demarcate legitimate from illegitimate violence. Moreover, distinguishing between the two relies on whether violence is identified as political violence. This means that disentangling discourses on violence in official commissions becomes pivotal in constituting the state itself as legitimate. In this chapter I reflect on commissions of inquiry as repertoires of colonial practices with their origins in British state formation and imperialism processes. However, in the way they are frequently used today, and particularly their role in investigating past violence, or patterns of violence, official commissions produce official discourses on violence that contribute to processes of state legitimation in postcolonial Africa. Moreover, their efficacy as tools of legitimation varies. In some cases, they are whitewashing devices that blatantly justify the state's use of force to restore law and order. However, in other cases, such as that of powerful truth commissions with support from civil society, they can operate to delegitimize state violence and triumph accountability for security forces that have acted illegally. In this chapter, I provide some clarity in conceptualizing forms of violence and, drawing on various commissions held to investigate violence in colonial and postcolonial Africa, shed light on how discourses on violence are connected to techniques of legitimation.

## 2  Conceptualizing Political Violence

As will be shown in the sections that follow, commissions of inquiry are used ubiquitously to investigate instances or patterns of violence. Yet, there is a need to qualify their relation to *political* violence as distinct from more general forms of violence. A focus on political violence is necessary for a more lucid understanding of official commission of inquiries' relation to legitimation, the legitimation of violence and indeed the legitimation or delegitimation of the state as well as the violence inflicted by the state. We tend to distinguish political violence from other forms of violence by two mechanisms: (1) by claiming a special moral or public *legitimation* for the harm inflicted, and (2) by the *representative* character of the agents or the targets of those acts of violence (Du Toit, 1990). The violence displayed by activists throwing stones at police, or security forces shooting rubber bullets (or live ammunition) to quell an uprising is considered qualitatively different to violence enacted between a group of people brawling in a pub because the activists and security forces believe their actions to be sanctioned by some higher morality or greater public cause, whether that be the struggle for justice against oppression, or to maintain law and order. It is, in accordance with certain social codes, violence that is considered more legitimate. Hence, when Weber asserts that the state is the "human community which (successfully) lays claim to the *monopoly of legitimate physical violence,*" one should add that this violence is construed as political: violence wielded in the defence of public law and order.

The concept of political violence is complex and contested, particularly when one introduces the notion of structural violence. Structural violence invokes a more metaphorical use of the word violence and is, thus, delinked from the ordinary meaning of violence. Structural violence is widely invoked to argue that even in contexts where there may be no evidence of violence in the literal sense, we can still discern serious cases of political violence. An example is apartheid South Africa, whose segregationist and racist laws were themselves generative of economic and social inequality and persecution. For Galtung, who coined the term structural violence, structural violence is "present when human beings are influenced so that their actual somatic and mental realizations are below their potential realizations" and where such violence is built into structures, like legal frameworks, that prohibit people from having "equal power and equal life chances" (Galtung, 1969). Hence, policies of paternalism (as was colonialism) and selective or unequal development are construed as examples of structural violence (Kotze, 1978).

The Black Lives Matter movement, which arose in the context of the United States from 2013, and which critiques anti-Black racism and police violence draws attention to both violence in the regular sense as well as structural violence. The movement has spread around the globe, inciting renewed outrage against police brutality and forms of quotidian structural violence like poverty and inequality where Black people are construed as the main victims of oppression. From a perspective like this, it is the so-called "normal order" of society that becomes the subject of critique. Here, structural oppression is equated with *political* violence, under the term *structural violence*. As stated by Garver, "Any institution which systematically robs certain people of rightful options generally available to others does violence to those people"

(Garver, 1970). Hence, structural violence forms part of a normative argument that raises questions about the legitimacy of a social order in which structural violence is present and, indeed, perpetuated by state law and policy.

These different notions of violence are relevant to understanding the work of commissions of inquiry and their legitimating role. In the sections that follow I show how part of commissions' legitimating schemes involves discursively differentiating political violence from gratuitous or non-political violence. Violence that is not construed as political is less likely proven to be legitimate. Particularly where the commission is investigating the state's violent suppression of the civil uprising, the ability of the commission to show that violent protest was illegal and disordered acts as a justification of the police retaliation.

## 3 Commissions and (Colonial) State Formation

### Commissions on the Continent

Commissions of inquiry originated as a key part of the British state apparatus as Royal Commissions, tasked to investigate problems arising for the crown (Burton & Carlen, 1979; Corrigan & Sayer, 1985). As such, they predate modern forms of governance and parliamentary legislative procedure. With the governmentalization and modernization of the state, around the 1840s, the British state became more concerned with establishing a functional bureaucracy to perform its administrative role, a role which relied on gathering accurate information about citizens' health and welfare (Clokie & Robinson, 1937; Sitze, 2013).

These investigative institutions became entrenched as instruments of official fact-finding during this period. They combined the proto-scientific zeitgeist of 19th-century Britain with a public investigatory and reporting regime, which, according to their proponents, provided an objective and inclusive policy-making process (Keller, 2009). In their more recent form, they derive their authority either from Parliament, the Executive, or in some cases, like the South African Truth and Reconciliation Commission (TRC), from particular legislation.[1]

---

[1] The South African TRC was established by its own legislation: the Promotion of National Unity and Reconciliation Act, which laid out the TRC's mandate and powers.

Official commissions have various roles, the foremost one being instruments of objective fact-finding (Hanser 1965). However, it is well documented that commissions' work can also be influenced by a political agenda, which has led critics to accuse them of being tools for political obfuscation and delaying substantial political reforms (Herbert, 1961). Following this line of argumentation, the public and inquisitorial stage of the commission, which invites input from civil society, is merely a "phase of discourse"—one which presents the state authorizing the commission as caring and responsive to the public (Ashforth, 1990a). A staunch critique, however, is that commissions are merely devices used, to tell a "truth" that the state wishes to tell or that they serve to hide the truth rather than reveal it (Ashforth, 1990b; Hamilton, 2015; Sitze, 2013). It is for this reason that commissions like the Marikana Commission of Inquiry, which investigated the state killing of 34 protesting mine workers in South Africa in 2012, have been referred to as commissions of *omission* (Mahlakoana, 2019; McKinley, 2015; Shapiro, 2015). Here, the contention is that official commissions exclude glaring facts concerning the violence they investigate, effectively serving to justify police violence.

However, a review of various commissions of inquiry over time reveals that not all commissions, all the time, serve only the interests of the state. As I have argued elsewhere, whether an official commission will advance progressive change or not or contribute to holding state agents accountable for acts of illegitimate violence, depends on the balance of political forces in a particular historical formation (Lester, 2020). For example, they were increasingly used as investigatory bodies to advance political reforms in Britain in the 1830s, fuelled by pressure from Reform Ministries and groups of organized factory workers. Although the term would not have existed at the time, the Factories Commissions in Britain, cited at length by Engels in *The Conditions of the Working Class in England*, can be read as investigations into structural violence. The reports detailed the gruesome effects of protracted working hours, low pay, and few or no health and safety regulations on factory workers, including child labourers. In this context, the commissions were able to reveal the violence and inhumanity upon which the Industrial Revolution and Britain's economic prowess, had been built. This outcome was buttressed by the fact that there was a strong labour movement advancing the struggle to reduce the hours of the working day, which was supported by members of parliament and other prominent figures in society. Hence, there was a historical and social process, whereby forms of violence and violation previously considered acceptable (like children working in factories) becomes constituted in both discourse and practice as unacceptable, undesirable, immoral, and finally, illegal.

This attests to the ambivalent nature of commissions of inquiry. Fused with the requisite social forces, resources and political will, their outcomes will have a foregone conclusion that is less secure. Instead, when various sectors are invited to make submissions, the official space may be cracked open to hear contestatory contributions which, in some cases, can sway findings towards progressive social change (Lester, 2020). In these instances, commissions of inquiry can oppose or delegitimize forms of political violence.

## Colonial Commissions, Law, and Indirect Rule

As common features of British political life, commissions became essential tools in advancing Britain's colonial and imperial projects. However, in colonial Africa, commissions of inquiry operated far differently from how they were in nineteenth-century Britain. Imperialism involved extending the British state to its colonial outposts and navigating how to effectively rule 'subject' populations through indirect rule, as so eloquently explained by Mahmood Mamdani in *Citizen and Subject* (Mamdani, 1996). As legal instruments, these commissions employed the techniques and language of the law—or "Lawfare"—to dominate colonized people (Comaroff & Comaroff, 2006). For example, in one commission established in the Colony of Natal, after it was annexed by Great Britain in 1843, it was stated:

> The natives' own laws are superseded; the restraints which they furnish are removed. The government of their own chiefs is at an end; and although it is a fact that British rule and law have been submitted in their stead, it is not less true that they are almost as inoperate as if they had not been proclaimed, from a want of the necessary representatives and agents to carry them out. (Welsh, 1973)

The next step for colonial authorities was to entrench colonial rule through the formation of functional bureaucracies that relied on detailed knowledge of "native" ways of life and social organization (Evans, 1998). As argued by Ashforth (1990a, 1990b) in managing society, commissions of inquiry became essential 'schemes of legitimation' used to design ways to meet the objectives of state planning, particularly for economic and extraction purposes. Commissions effectively became tools of liberal governance; an institutional form used by the government to "relate, develop, civilize, and improve the lives of populations," like indigenous people, who were presumed to be incapable of representing themselves through political institutions (Sitze, 2013).

While stabilizing colonial rule through bureaucracy was a central concern of the British colonial state, colonialism was in most cases a violent endeavour. Resistance to colonial violence and dispossession is evident in the manifold examples of indigenous people rising up against colonial regimes. Early examples of this resistance include the several battles that constituted the Anglo-Zulu War of 1879 (Greaves, 2012; Lieven, 1999), but of course, there are many others.

In many cases, the British colonial state used commissions of inquiry in an attempt to legitimate its use of force in quelling a riot or uprising. Sitze argues that similar to the "grand tradition" of commissions of inquiry into the "Native Question," which investigated relations between indigenous and colonial subjects (Ashforth, 1990a); there is another thematic sub-type of commission set up in the wake of imperial violence: tumult commissions. Sitze (2013: 160) identifies the Jamaica Royal Commission established following the Morant Bay rebellion in 1865 as the archetypal tumult commission, and cites some 24 of these in South Africa, including the Bulhoek (1921), Bondelswart (1923), Witieshoek (1951), Sharpeville (1960) and Soweto (1976). For Sitze, these official investigations into the state's violent excesses in suppressing rebellion gave a semblance of genuine remorse. However, when their establishment ran parallel to indemnity laws (like a State of Emergency or marshall law) like they often were; tumult commissions rather operated to legitimate impunity for extrajudicial state killing. Writing about the tumult commission model as it was deployed in South Africa, Sitze states:

> Even though commissions could, in principle, give rise to prosecutions, they were more often substitutes for prosecutions… Under apartheid South Africa, the more that Commissions of Inquiry would be created to investigate state massacres, the less they would produce public debate and discussion…Here, the Commission of Inquiry was not a fact-finding device; it was a whitewashing machine. (Sitze, 2013)

The "whitewashing machine" metaphor suggests a device able to disguise the fact that something has been soiled. It suggests that what is being presented as the final product has in some way obscured a less pristine reality and that there is a misrepresentation. In the case of tumult commissions, that which is being misrepresented then, or repackaged is the violence enacted by the state. The packaging, then, is the discourse in the official report, the use of language which comes to constitute the official account, or narrative, of the event in question.

## 4 Discourses on Violence in Official Commissions

Amidst the various roles of commissions of inquiry, one of the most convincing arguments is their role in producing official discourse on a social problem (Ashforth, 1990a, 1990b; Burton & Carlen, 1979; Moon, 2008). Official discourse, in this context, is discourse produced in and by the state. This is to be distinguished from the discourse produced in an unofficial commission of inquiry. There are indeed many examples of unofficial truth projects, like commissions of inquiry or truth commissions established by bodies other than the state (Bickford, 2007).[2] These may in all respects carry out their work in the same way that an official commission would and produce credible and sophisticated reports. However, official truth-seeking projects mean that findings are afforded the label of being an *official* truth, which becomes part of the *official* archive of national and social memory. When established to investigate instances or a period of violence, state commissions produce official discourses on the violence.

Studying discourse involves the way language is used, the way beliefs and ideas are communicated, and how people interact (van Dijk, 1997). One can also refer to discourse as one might commonly refer to a "legal discourse," "medical discourse," or a "feminist discourse." In this way, discourse refers to:

> A fairly comprehensive and systematically articulated ensemble of specific ways and modes of talking about particular areas of social life associated with general institutions, professions and disciplines or with certain general ideological and political positions. (Du Toit, 1990)

Using this conceptualization, it is true that there can be multiple discourses that emerge as a commission undertakes its work, as it conducts its hearings and those which are evident in the final commission report. Many truth commissions, for example, in their efforts to support peaceful transitions from periods of conflict and national building, tend to exhibit a reconciliation discourse (Verdoolaege, 2008a). Much of the work of official commissions involves seeking solutions to problems of governance and this requires finding the appropriate language with which to speak of the problem and articulate a solution to that problem. However, when it comes to investigating instances or patterns of violence, the commission of inquiry has a pivotal

---

[2] UTP examples.

role in producing official discourses on that violence which frame how the public comes to view that violence.

Pertaining to political violence, elaborated on above, discourses on violence are bound up with processes of legitimation and delegitimation. As will be explicated in the sections below in which I draw from examples of various commissions of inquiry, as official investigations into violence, the public definition of what constitutes violence is primarily a political act. It is inherently political as it involves the naming of certain actions as "violence" or as "violations." The remainder of this piece draws on various commissions of inquiry as they have emerged in Africa to focus on how the official discourses on violence function in legitimating certain forms of violence.

## 5 Not a Strikers' Demonstration But a Looting Mob

One of the key ways in which forms of political violence become naturalized, legitimized or sanctioned is through the discourse, that is, through the language used to describe the violence in official statements and texts. This is often evident in the way those wielding the violence are described. One may think of the adage that one person's terrorist is another's liberation fighter. But descriptions are often more subtle. A reoccurring pattern is the tendency in official commissions to refer to those who had been on strike not as "strikers," but as looters, or a mob. The following section draws examples from South Africa.

An early example is the 1913 Witwatersrand Disturbances Commission, established shortly after the Union of South Africa in 1910. The strikes arose in relation to low wages, rising living costs and job reservations for white mine workers (Visser, 2016). The unrest was suppressed brutally by the military and 25 strikers were killed (Visser, 2003). A legitimist discourse on violence is already evident in the commission's terms of reference in which it sought to establish "were the circumstances such as to render it *necessary* for the government to take special precautions to preserve and restore order and to protect life and property" and "whether the acts of violence were such as *to justify* the police defence, or military forces in using forcible measures…" (Gladstone, 1913) [emphasis added].

These words imply that the state, and only the state, is authorized to wield violence to preserve social order. There was no commensurate investigation by the commission into whether the violence used by the strikers was necessary for them to acquire higher pay and thus be in a position to meet their basic needs of subsistence to preserve a level of human dignity in relation to the type of labour performed, or in defence of their health or safety. Instead, the report emphasized that the strike had occurred unlawfully and recounted evidence that the strikers had "terrorized" the population to join and support the strike. In its concluding statements, it defended and praised the "unpleasant" work of the police, stating, "A mob has no right by our law or by the law of any civilized country to attack the police by hurling stones at them" (Gladstone, 1913). This language and explicit reference to the law presents the protesting subjects as having acted illegally and in an uncivilized manner, which is in distinction to the state law enforcement who are right in their mission to restore law and order. It is through the state's legitimate operationalization of violence that civilization is restored.

The Witwatersrand Disturbances Commission concluded that the police and other military forces had every right to employ "rigorous measures to quell a riot" and went on to assert that had the military not performed in the way it had, the violence would have been more severe and continued for longer. The state's violence was framed not only as necessary, but as the *duty* of those in authority, and the failure of the military to intervene in the way it did would have been "an offence" (Gladstone, 1913). Here the commission cannot be said to be merely a tool of the state. It is through the commission that the issues related to the legitimate use of violence by the state vis-à-vis other institutions—the police and the military—were deliberated.

Another example is in 1973 when 12 African mine workers were killed at Anglo American's Western Deep Levels Mine at Carletonville, South Africa after police opened fire to quell an uprising. The men were on strike for a wage increase. Official reporting denied that the mobilization was political violence at all and like in other instances of mine violence, conflict was attributed merely to inter-tribal differences or irrational agitation. When addressing the National Party in a meeting the Prime Minister denied that the violence was political at all, stating that it was, "not a strikers' demonstration but *a looting mob* out to destroy life and property with dangerous and murderous weapons" (Horrell and Horner, 1974)[emphasis added]. An inquest was held which exonerated the police from blame but was never made public. In a copy of the correspondence sent from the American embassy in Pretoria to the secretary of state in Washington, it stated the following about the official inquiry:

> Badenhorst concluded that company officials and police had to deal with a rampaging mob which refused appeals for restraint and was threatening to overwhelm whites in mine compound. He said mine officials were justified in

calling police and, although noting that arrival of police acted "like a spark which caused a fire," that they came in fulfilment of their duty.

The report continues to cite Badenhorst—the judge who presided over the judicial inquest—as having made an "honourable and correct assessment of the situation, that police officers' concern for their men was *reasonable* and well-founded and that shooting of ringleaders was *justified*" (Press Release: *Committee Informed Police Exonerated in Carletonville Mine Shootings in South Africa*, Special Committee on Apartheid. 27 November 1973) [emphasis added]. In this case, the official discourse on violence presented the violence by the strikers as illegitimate in that the violence they caused was not acknowledged to be politically motivated. Acknowledging this would have meant accepting that there was something about the "normal" social order that required change, that there was something illegitimate about the state and the apartheid social order.

From these two examples, legitimist discourses on violence can be read as ideological formulations that operated to legitimize colonial or minority rule over Africans. The narrative that violence was necessary to restore law and order, as was often a narrative in colonial tumult commissions, can be read in line with Peter Ekeh's notion of colonial ideologies; ideologies "invented by the colonizing Europeans to persuade Africans that colonization was in the interest of the Africans" (Ekeh, 1975). By extension, the colonial tumult commissions functioned to effectively persuade Africans that colonial violence was also justified as serving their interests to restore law and order.

While one might have expected this in a colonial context, one would not expect this legitimation of state violence to occur in the context of an independent and democratic polity. However, we see a comparable kind of discursive delegitimation occurred in the case of the Marikana Commission of Inquiry which began its work in 2012. This is evident in the terms of reference, which set out what and how the commission should investigate the various actors involved: the mine workers, the mining company (Lonmin Plc) and the police (Farlam, 2015: 2–5).

Concerning Lonmin Plc, the mining company, the terms of reference state that the commission should investigate whether the response to the "threat and outbreak of violence which occurred on its premises" was appropriate. This phrasing suggests an underlying assumption that Lonmin was not directly responsible for the "violence," but that the "violence" was carried out by other parties on the company's premises. We see that euphemistic language is employed to describe the violence associated with Lonmin's actions, compared to that associated with the strikers. It states that the

Commission ought to investigate whether Lonmin contributed to an "environment...conducive to the creation of tension, labour unrest," or "disunity among its employees," and ascertain whether Lonmin directly or indirectly caused "loss of life" or "damage to persons or property" (Terms of Reference of the Commission of Inquiry into the Tragic Incidents at or Near the Area Commonly Known as the Marikana Mine in Rustenburg, North West Province, South Africa 2012, in Farlam, 2015: 2–5).

In comparison, the discourse on violence in the terms of reference related to the conduct of the labour unions is far more suggestive of the illegitimacy of their actions (Lester, 2023). For example, it mandates that the Commission should investigate the extent to which the unions had "exercised effective control over its membership and those allied to it in ensuring that their conduct was lawful and did not endanger the lives and property of other persons." The phrasing suggests that the striking mineworkers were operating without the authorization of the union and were out of control. The criterion for the assessment of the union's actions is also suggestive of a more severe causal relationship to the violence expressed in the words "lawful" and "endanger...lives and property." It also potentially steers the inquiry towards findings that are more incriminating for the unions. If the actions of union members are found to be unlawful (for example, engaging in an *unprotected* strike) then the unions are shown to be unable to "control" their members, and the members' actions are presented as unlawful and having endangered the lives and property of other persons. The locution used concerning the actions of the unions is vastly different to that used in relation to Lonmin. The linguistic formulation of the terms of reference assumes that Lonmin acted lawfully. The men on strike can *endanger*, while Lonmin can only potentially contribute to disunity (Lester, 2021: 160–171).

The legitimist discourse on violence is evident in relation to the police who shot live ammunition at the group of strikers, killing 34. First, the terms of reference contain that the Commission should inquire into, "the nature, extent and application of any standing orders, policy considerations, legislation or other instructions in dealing with the situation." This indicates that the Commission had to evaluate whether the police were acting in line with the law and regulations related to the legitimate use of force. The terms of reference stated that the Commission should determine the "precise facts" related to the "use of all and any force and whether this was reasonable and justifiable." There seems to be a systematic bias built into the framing of the inquiry into the police's use of force because the police, as a state institution is expected to wield legitimate force. Here, we see echoes of the Weberian idea that the state holds a monopoly on the legitimate use of violence.

This is further evident in the final report and the way the striking mine workers were not referred to as "strikers" but as a "crowd," or a mob (Farlam, 2015: 57–59). Using this terminology, as opposed to a more active description like "strikers" depoliticizes the action, deflating the group of agency—political and rational motivation for risking their livelihoods (the workers were threatened with dismissal if they continued the strike) and subsequently lives by engaging in the strike. As noted previously, political violence is distinct from other kinds of violence, such as being hit by a car for example, in the way it makes claims to moral or public legitimation for the injury sustained, and the representative character and target of the violence. Using the term "strikers" would mean taking seriously that which was being struck for (or against) and would necessitate engaging with the substance of the strike, the demands, and assessing the conditions that led to the strike. The imagery one gets when reading the report is one of a criminal crowd moving about the Lonmin mine campus and violently intimidating other mine workers into joining the strike action.

The discourse of the "crowd" evokes a foreboding potential for harm. It is a threat to the disruption of law and order. As Freud asserts, people are capable of a certain madness or excess when in a crowd; they become hypnotized and lose themselves (Freud, 2018). Where crowds are concerned, violence will always be senseless, irrational, and illegitimate. It is through discursive constructions such as these that official commissions construct legitimist discourses on violence that in turn, serve to legitimate the state's monopoly on legitimate violence.

## 6    Truth-Seeking to Critique State Violence in Africa

The previous section showed how commissions of inquiry have been used to legitimate state violence and undermine civil protest. However, as I stated previously in this paper, whether a commission of inquiry will lead to progressive outcomes or not depends on the balance of political and social forces in a particular social formation. Hence, in this section, I draw from other examples in colonial and postcolonial Africa where commissions of inquiry have become avenues from which to critique undesirable forms of state violence and seek accountability (moral, political, or legal) for such violence. Instead of being "whitewashing machines," in the right context, led by a particular presiding officer, or with sufficient social (national or international) support, certain commissions have defied the trajectory of the "tumult commission," and have been authoritative instruments to critique oppressive dispensations and illegitimate violence.

There are examples from both the colonial and postcolonial eras. In Belgian Congo, news of King Leopold II's policy of "maximum exploitation" and atrocities inflicted on local people had spread, particularly the "hand cutting affair" in which indigenous people were mutilated by having their hands cut off when they were considered to not be productive enough, or refusing forced labour. As a response to increased pressure in Europe, the British consul Robert Casement released a report which publicized these atrocities and in response, the Belgian parliament, headed by socialist leader Emile Vandervelde and others who opposed Leopold II's regime pressured the king to undertake another commission of inquiry. The commission was mandated to investigate "whether, in certain parts of the territory, acts of ill-treatment were committed against the natives, either by private individuals or by agents of the state…" (Janssens et al., 1905). It was an international commission comprised of foreign judges, which meant the commission operated independently from the Belgian crown and the commissioners used this independence to collect hundreds of testimonies from local populations (Jain, 2020). The testimonies detailed the gruelling policies and abuses by the state and the report's contents had a profound effect when publicized among European countries. It eventually led to a change in Congo's status when on 15 November 1908 the parliament voted to annex the Congo Free State and assume control of its administration, as had been recommended in the commission report (Janssens et al., 1906). In this case, far from whitewashing the atrocities, the commissioners used the independent inquiry to denounce the violence inflicted on local people, and the outcome was a lasting transfer of political power.

There are additional examples from British colonial Africa, such as the 1929 Aba Commission of Inquiry in Nigeria which investigated the violent suppression of a women's peasant revolt (*Ogu Umunwaanyi*) in which thousands of women protested the introduction of taxes, the oppressive warrant chief system, and the effects of the low prices of agricultural produce due to the global financial crisis in the late 1920s (Isichei, 1976). The women destroyed property like European factories, native courts, and the houses of warrant chiefs, calling for the eradication of the warrant chief system. They wanted a system of rule by democratically elected indigenous clan leaders. Approximately 50 women were killed and another 50 wounded by British troops in an attempt to quell the uprising. Two commissions were established in late December 1929 and in January 1930.

Whilst the first commission operated similarly to the colonial tumult commission model mentioned in the previous section, which exonerated the soldiers' use of force to distinguish the "savage passions" of the "mob" of women; the second commission acknowledged the directness and resolve shown by the women. The Commission stated, "No one listening to the evidence given before us, could have failed to be impressed by the intelligence, the power of exposition, the directness and the mother-wit, which some of these leaders exhibited in setting forth their grievances" (Kies, 2013). This presents the women protestors not as an unruly, senseless mob, but the contrary: a reasoned group whose wielding of political violence was to raise grievances. This quote can be understood as acknowledging that the use of political violence was legitimate, and used to pursue and advance legitimate, even noble ends.

The revolt and subsequent responses catalysed lasting changes in the British administration of the territory. The warrant chief system was abolished, and several administrators called for reforms of the system of rule by incorporating indigenous social practices (Kies, 2013). Hence, in this case, the commission of inquiry's narration of political violence was such that the protestors' use of violence was presented as legitimate. This became an official discourse on the violence which countered the narrative of the women as a "mob" that required quelling. There are other such examples of commissions during the colonial era, as noted by Jain (2020) such as the 1959 Nyasaland Commission of Inquiry. This commission went beyond the critique of violence and was, according to Jain (2020: 62) instrumental in excelling the process of decolonization.

Truth commissions are another type of commission that has become ubiquitous, as instruments of transitional justice. These are established to inquire into patterns of human rights violations and as part of a transition to democracy following a period of authoritarian rule (Hayner, 2011). A truth commission is an "ad-hoc, autonomous, and victim-centred commission of inquiry" which investigates the causes and consequences of patterns of violence occurring in a state and makes "recommendations for the redress and future prevention" (Freeman, 2006: xiii) of such violence. These institutions have been designed for the specific purpose of official truth-seeking into human rights abuses and to rebuke those violations. As they also tend to be victim-centred, these commissions have an additional role concerning past political violence, which is often to form the grounds for victim healing, reconciliation, and empathic repair through truth-telling (Boraine et al., 1995; Gobodo-Madikizela, 2008; Verdoolaege, 2008b). As such, truth commissions often have the task of addressing the psychological trauma of protracted societal violence. One of the most well-known truth commissions from the African continent is the South African Truth and Reconciliation Commission (TRC), established following the overthrow of the apartheid regime and the first democratic election in 1994. Since then, truth commissions have been ubiquitous on the African continent, particularly in former British colonies where commissions of inquiry were the norm following state violence. These institutions are now used in the attempt, not to legitimate state violence, but to critique it in the hope that cycles of violence will not continue and effect some form of accountability for such violations of human rights.

An example is the Commission of Inquiry into Post-Election Violence (CIPEV), set up to investigate the facts relating to the 2007 post-election violence in Kenya. The elections precipitated a political crisis, leading to the eruption of violence throughout the country. President Mwai Kibaki, running for re-election, was challenged by a former member of his cabinet, Raila Odinga and election officials reported that during the campaigning period violence had already erupted between different ethnic groups. When Kikabi was announced president, thousands of opposition supporters took to the streets in protest around the country, attacking those suspected of voting for Kibaki. This largely took place in the Kikuyu regions of the Rift Valley and Nairobi's slums, which gave the violence an ethnic character (HRW, 2008). In the two months following the election, a humanitarian crisis ensued with approximately 500,000 people losing their homes and more than 1,000 people killed.

There were widespread, violent attacks on persons and property, with sexual violence being another distinctive feature. The CIPEV was established on 23 May 2008, two months after the violence had come to an end. The commission, also referred to as the "Truth, Justice and Reconciliation Commission of Kenya" was an international commission funded by the government of Kenya and a multi-donor trust fund for National Dialogue and Reconciliation managed by the United Nations Development Programme (UNDP). Its main task was to investigate who was responsible for planning, organizing, and perpetrating egregious human rights violations, which included investigating the role of state security agencies. However, the commission seemed to go a step further. Its report sets out factors to explain "how and why violence has become a way of life in Kenya, a country once known for peace, prosperity, and its potential for development" (Truth, Justice and Reconciliation Commission, Commissions of Inquiry, CIPEV Report [Waki Report], 2008). This indicates that it sought to explain a broader culture of violence in Kenya and how this developed historically, and in its analysis of the nature of this violence, the report goes into great detail locating the instance of violence in a broader historical and social context.

For Ashforth (1990a) one of the main reasons a commission of inquiry is appointed is when the state needs to transcend politics as there are important issues that need to be addressed in a "non-political" way. This commission was significant in its engagement with political violence because rather than depoliticizing the violent events, the Waki Commission made it explicit that the violence was distinctly political in most cases and located this in a pattern of "growing politicization and proliferation of violence in Kenya…following the legalization of multi-party democracy in 1991" (Waki Report, 2008: 22). Although the term "structural violence" is not used, it is hinted at when the report roots the burgeoning culture of violence in structural deprivation: "the increasing problem of a growing population of poor, unemployed and youth…who agree to join militias and organized gangs" (Waki Report, 2008: 23). The experience of relative deprivation among certain ethnic groups who perceive inequality in terms of land and other resources is also cited as a sentiment harnessed by politicians to spur political unrest (Waki Report, 2008: 23). Hence, as a truth commission, this commission did not merely seek to legitimate the state's use of violence but instead, used a public fact-finding and truth-seeking process to articulate the various forms of violence and how they were rooted in historical processes.

To do this, the Waki Commission classified the violence into three types: spontaneous, planned, and police or state-directed violence (Waki Report, 2008: 118). The distinction was significant when compared to past commissions in Kenya, which tended to paint election violence as spontaneous reactions to an unfavourable outcome, which meant that the determined and political character of the violence was undermined and precluded the possibility for prosecutions as no clear perpetrator was evident. The Waki Report states that whilst there were some spontaneous acts of violence, others were planned as targeted ethnic attacks, and, hence, accountability for that violence was necessary. Another key point here is that ethnic violence was conceptualized as political violence. The commission found that since the 1990s politicians had been instigating the use of violence and that a failure to prosecute and punish those responsible for past violations had caused a "culture of impunity and a constant escalation of violence" (Waki Report, 2008: 22).

The Waki Commission avoided this trend by compelling high-level politicians to participate and to answer for their role in the violence (Oyieke, 2020). There was a recommendation to set up a special tribunal in Kenya to try the alleged perpetrators, but this did not come into effect. Instead, the

"Ocampo 6" were brought before the International Criminal Court (ICC). Among the six were Uhuru Kenyatta and William Ruto, later elected president and deputy president in the 2013 elections. Hence, the commission's findings signalled to international bodies like the ICC that perpetrators instigating violence of this nature would be held accountable for their actions. In its efforts to enforce some measure of accountability, the commission striving for a role that went beyond being merely a whitewashing device. Since the report was publicized, there have been several significant reforms of the justice system, judiciary, and police institution. Recommendations included the establishment of a special National Task Force on Police Reforms, which issued additional police reform recommendations, later incorporated into the 2010 final constitution (Oyieke, 2020).

## 7 Conclusion

Drawing on various examples of official commissions investigating violence in Africa, I have shown how they are instruments through which the legitimacy of forms of political violence are deliberated. As postcolonial African states reckon with enduring forms of violence, commissions remain fascinating institutions to analyse discursive modalities and narrative techniques through which the state legitimates its claims to violence. The multiple instances where they have had an instrumental function for colonial states or democratic administrations attempting to paper over instances of violence and human rights violations, have led them to rightfully being viewed with suspicion as "whitewashing" tools.

I offered examples from South Africa to provide detail on how the official discourse of commission reports present different instances and actors of violence in distinct ways, which served to legitimate the use of violence by state functionaries. This is evident in the language used to frame the violence and those accused of wielding it as a "mob" rather than as political actors protesting. However, other examples show how the outcomes of official commissions are not always a foregone conclusion. Just as in the case of the British Factory Commissions, which led to reduced working hours for factory workers, and improvements in worker rights, commissions of inquiry in Africa have also been leveraged to critique objectionable forms of state violence and even undesirable forms of political rule, in some cases contributing to processes of decolonization and judicial reform. These commissions' official discourse on the violent period instead argued that the state's violence was illegitimate and that opened space to critique an oppressive order rather than bolster it. Hence, commissions' enhanced accountability role is seen in the wake of the third wave (Huntington, 1993) of democratization, with the rise of truth commissions. Truth commissions continue to be used as an institutional tool to uncover facts about past violence, to seek accountability for such violations, and to assist victims in healing from traumatic experiences. That is not to say that all truth commissions operate in this way, and there are indeed instances where state-led commissions lack public legitimacy. With their focus on narrowly defined forms of violence, truth commissions can still be used to paper over past violence, without the requisite commitments to social justice and accountability (Mamdani, 2000). When truth-seeking is not coupled with institutional reform and reparations, even the most effective investigations into violence can obscure or naturalize enduring forms of structural violence, like poverty and inequality.

The significant point, however, is that these institutions are uniquely poised as those through which issues of legitimacy and political violence are debated, contested, entrenched, and disrupted. Depending on the context and balance of social forces, these commissions of inquiry become public lenses into political violence which influence the way the public comes to view the violence. As such there is more work to be done on the way these institutions operate in an African context, and how contemporary iterations reproduce or depart from colonial uses.

# Bibliography

Ashforth, A. (1990a). *The Politics of Official Discourse in Twentieth-Century South Africa*. Clarendon Press.

Ashforth, A. (1990b). Reckoning Schemes of Legitimation: On Commissions of Inquiry as Power/Knowledge Forms. *Journal of Historical Sociology, 3*(1), 1–22.

Bickford, L. (2007). Unofficial Truth Projects. *Human Rights Quarterly, 29*(4), 994–1035 [Online]. http://sun.worldcat.org/title/unofficial-truth-projects/oclc/5183516756&referer=brief_results. Accessed on 11 April 2018.

Boraine, A., Levy, J., & Asmal, K. (Eds.). (1995). *The Healing of a Nation? Justice in Transition*.

Burton, F., & Carlen, P. (1979). *Official Discourse: On Discourse Analysis, Government Publications, Ideology and the State*. Routledge & Kegan Paul.

Clokie, H. M., & Robinson, J. W. (1937). *Royal Commissions of Inquiry: The Significance of Investigations in British Politics*. Oxford University Press.

Comaroff, J., & Comaroff, J. L. (2006). *Law and Disorder in the Postcolony*. University of Chicago Press.

Corrigan, P. R. D., & Sayer, D. (1985). *The Great Arch: English State Formation as Cultural Revolution*. Blackwell.

du Toit, A. (1990). Discourses on Political Violence. In N. C. Manganyi & A. du Toit (Eds.), *Political Violence and the Struggle in South Africa*. Macmillan.

Ekeh, P. (1975). Colonialism and the Two Publics in Africa: A Theoretical Statement. *Comparative Studies in Society and History, 17*(1), 91–112.

Evans, I. (1998). *Bureaucracy and Race*. University of California Press.

Farlam, I. (2015). The Marikana Commission of Inquiry: Report on Matters of Public, National and International Concern Arising out of the Tragic Incidents at the Lonmin Mine in Marikana in the Northwest Province.

Freeman, M. (2006). *Truth Commissions and Procedural Fairness*. Cambridge University Press.

Freud, S. (2018). *Group Psychology and the Analysis of the Ego* (J. Strachey, Ed.). Logos Books.

Galtung, J. (1969). Violence, Peace and Peace Research. *Journal of Peace Research, 6*(3), 167–191.

Garver, N. (1970). What Violence Is. In A. K. Bierman & J. A. Gould (Eds.), *Philosophy for a New Generation*. Macmillan.

Gladstone, H. J. V. (1913). Witwatersrand Disturbances Commission Report.

Gobodo-Madikizela, P. (2008). *Empathetic Repair After Mass Trauma When Vengeance Is Arrested* [Online]. www.sagepublications.com

Greaves, A. (2012). *Crossing the Buffalo: The Zulu War of 1879*. Hachette UK.

Hamilton, W. (2015). *South Africa: The Marikana Report—A Whitewash* [Online]. https://www.socialistalternative.org/2015/07/05/south-africa-the-marikana-report-whitewash/. Accessed on 11 April 2019.

Hanser, C. (1965). *Guide to Decision: The Royal Commission*. Bedminster Press.

Hayner, P. B. (2011). *Unspeakable Truths: Transitional Justice and the Challenge of Truth Commissions*. Routledge.

Herbert, A. (1961). *Anything but Action? A Study of the Uses and Abuses of Committees of Inquiry*. Published for the Institute of Economic Affairs by Barrie and Rockliff.

Horrell, M., & Horner, D. (1974). *A Survey of Race Relations in South Africa*. South African Institute of Race Relations.

HRW. (2008). Ballots to Bullets: Organised Political Violence and Kenya's Crisis of Governance.

Huntington, S. P. (1993). *The Third Wave: Democratization in the Late Twentieth Century*, Vol. 4. University of Oklahoma press.

Isichei, E. (1976). *A History of the Igbo People*. Macmillan.

Jain, M. (2020). "Lawfare", Instruments of Governmentality and Accountability, or Both? An Overview of National Commissions of Inquiry in Africa. In T. Probert & C. Heyns (Eds.), Pretoria *National Commissions of Inquiry in Africa: Vehicles to Pursue Accountability for Violations of the Right to Life?* (pp. 45–69). Pretoria University Law Press.

Janssens, E., Nisco, G., & de Schumacher, E. (1905). Rapport de La Commision d'enquete. In *Bulletin Officiel de l'État Indépendent Du Congo, No 9 & 10*.

Janssens, E., Nisco, G., & de Schumacher, E. (1906). *The Congo: A Report of the Commission of Enquiry*. Appointed by the Congo Free State Government, a Translation.

Kalyvas, S. (2003). The Ontology of Political Violence: Action and Identity in Civil Wars. *Perspectives on Politics, 3*, 475–494.

Keller, M. (2009). Commissioning Legitimacy: The Global Logics of National Violence Commissions in the Twentieth Century. *Politics and Society, 37*(3), 352–396.

Kies, S. M. (2013). *Matriarchy, the Colonial Situation, and the Women's War of 1929 in Southeastern Nigeria*. Eastern Michigan University.

Kotze, D. A. (1978). Development and Structural Violence. *Politikon, 5*(1), 30–41.

Lemarchand, R. (2021). *The Dynamics of Violence in Central Africa*. University of Pennsylvania Press.

Lester, C.-A. L. (2020). Commissions of Inquiry and the Role of Law: Towards a Materialist Approach. *Social Dynamics, 46*(1), 86–103.

Lester, C.-A. L. (2021). *Legal Truth and Discourses of Violence in Post-apartheid Commissions of Inquiry: The TRC and Marikana Commission*. Ph.D. diss., Stellenbosch University.

Lester, C.-A. L. (2023). Legalism in the Marikana Commission of Inquiry Report: Veiling "Sociological Causes" of the Massacre. *South African Review of Sociology*, 1–23.

Lieven, M. (1999). "Butchering the Brutes All Over the Place": Total War and Massacre in Zululand, 1879. *The Journal of the Historical Association, 84*(276), 614–632.

Mahlakoana, T. (2019, August 15). Mathunjwa: Farlam Commission One of Omission. *Eyewitness News* [Online]. https://ewn.co.za/2019/08/15/mathunjwa-farlam-commission-one-of-omission

Mamdani, M. (2000). The Truth According to the TRC. In I. Amadiume & A. An-Na'Im (Eds.), *The Politics of Memory: Truth, Healing and Social Justice*. Zed Books.

Mamdani, M. (1996). *Citizen and Subject: Contemporary Africa and the Legacy of Late Colonialism*. Princeton University Press.

McKinley, D. T. (2015). *Commissions of Inquiry or Omission?* [Online]. https://sacsis.org.za/site/article/2347. Accessed on 7 April 2018.

Moon, C. (2008). *Narrating Political Reconciliation: South Africa's Truth and Reconciliation Commission*. Lexington Books.

Oyieke, A. Y. (2020). Public Hearings and Secret Envelopes: The Waki Commission as a Case Study of Accountability in Kenya. In *National Commissions of Inquiry in Africa: Vehicles to Pursue Accountability for Violations of the Right to Life?* (pp. 181–216). Pretoria University Law Press.

Press Release: Committee Informed Police Exonerated in Carletonville Mine Shootings in South Africa, Special Committee on Apartheid. 27 November (1973) United Nations Office of Public Information.

Shapiro, J. (2015, July 1). Omission of Inquiry. *The Times* [Online]. https://www.zapiro.com/component/zoo/advanced-search/55654?Itemid=464&page=5

Sitze, A. (2013). *The Impossible Machine: A Genealogy of South Africa's Truth and Reconciliation Commission*. The University of Michigan Press.

Straus, S. (2012). Wars Do End! Changing Patterns of Political Violence in Sub-Saharan Africa. *African Affairs, 111*(443), 179–201.

Terms of Reference of the Commission of Inquiry into the Tragic Incidents at or Near the Area Commonly Known as the Marikana Mine in Rustenberg, Northwest Province, South Africa (2012). http://www.politicsweb.co.za/party/marikana-terms-of-reference-for-the-farlam-inquiry. Accessed on 7 May 2018.

Truth, Justice and Reconciliation Commission. (2008). *Commissions of Inquiry—CIPEV Report* (Waki Report). IX. Government Documents and Regulations. 5. https://digitalcommons.law.seattleu.edu/tjrc-gov/5

van Dijk, T. (1997). The Study of Discourse. In T. van Dijk (Ed.), *Discourse as Structure and Process* (pp. 1–34). Sage.

Verdoolaege, A. (2008a). *Reconciliation Discourse: The Case of the Truth and Reconciliation Commission*. John Benjamins.

Verdoolaege, A. (2008b). *Reconciliation Discourse* [Online]. Discourse Approaches to Politics, Society and Culture, Vol. 27. John Benjamins. http://www.jbe-platform.com/content/books/9789027291615. Accessed on 26 June 2018.

Visser, W. P. (2016). *Governments, Parliaments and Parties, Labour, Labour Movements and Strikes (Union of South Africa)* [Online]. https://encyclopedia.1914-1918.online.net/article/governments_parliaments_and_parties_labour_labour_movements_and_strikes_union_of_south_africa. Accessed on 18 November 2020.

Visser, W. P. (2003). The South African Labour Movement's Response to Declarations of Martial Law, 1913–1922. *Scientia Militaria, 31*(2), 144–145.

Weber, M. (1919). The Profession and Vocation of Politics. In P. Lassman & R. Spiers (Eds.), *Weber: Political Writings*. Cambridge University Press.

Welsh, D. (1973). *The Roots of Segregation: Native Policy in Colonial Natal, 1845–1910*. Oxford University Press.

# Party Politics, Violence, Impunity, and Social Injustices in Zimbabwe (1980–2022)

### Vellim Nyama and Pedzisai Ruhanya

## 1 Introduction

There has been a tendency in African national politics for political parties to confront each other in violent encounters to subdue each other. The main culprits in trying to secure dominance are the revolutionary parties that led liberation struggles, who propel themselves on a false premise of entitlement to doing as they please because they feel they are the government itself, and not the governing party. The ruling ZANU PF party in Zimbabwe has persistently perpetrated what this research observes as social injustice on members of the opposition parties in spirited efforts to eliminate any form of counter opinions on how the country must be governed in order that the general populace can enjoy their freedoms (Matasva, 2022). Zimbabwe gained independence from British colonial rule on 18 April 1980. From that year to date, ZANU PF has dominated the political scene in Zimbabwe (Mlambo, 2014).

This chapter looks at the period from 1980 to 2022 and highlights critical and unjust historic political and social events which expose injustices and impunity inflicted against the opposition by the party/state conflation machinations. These events and activities have allegedly been perpetrated by

V. Nyama (✉)
University of the Free State, Bloemfontein, South Africa
e-mail: vellimnyama@gmail.com

P. Ruhanya
Department of Creative Media and Communication, University of Zimbabwe, Harare, Zimbabwe

the ruling party, including through several spheres of government institutions and also through party organs and activists. Social injustice is regarded as that situation where a dominant population or section of the population is privileged in the political and social power structures, leading to their influence extending to the suppression of the rights of the less privileged members of that society (Farooq, 2015; Maus, 2015). Zimbabwe has experienced incidences of political suppression and violence from the colonial era to the post-independence era (Macheka, 2022). Ndlovu-Gatsheni and Ruhanya (2020) call this circle of state politics "a repetition without change" following the military coup against founding president, Robert Mugabe, in November 2017, arguing that impunity, violence, and injustices remain in post-Mugabe Zimbabwe because of the ubiquitous role of the securocracy in the political and public affairs of the state.

## 2 Background to the Study

Zimbabwe attained independence that was recognized by the free world on 18 April 1980 with Canaan Banana as its first president and Robert Mugabe as prime minister. The government structure changed in 1987 when the country became an executive presidency as it transitioned from the government led by Banana to the one led only by the president, with Robert Mugabe becoming the first executive president having absolute control of the military set up of Zimbabwe (IPSS, 2018). Post-independent Zimbabwe's political climate has had outbreaks of political violence and even though some countries have experienced similar challenges, in Southern Africa the country has been regarded as the most violent nation, after civil wars that occurred in the former Portuguese colonies of Mozambique and Angola (Macheka, 2022; Research and Advocacy Unit, 2018). Before attaining its independence, the exiled population of Zimbabwe living in Mozambique, Botswana, Tanzania, and Zambia were raided and massacred by the Rhodesian forces at Freedom Camp, Chimoio, and Nyadzonya in the liberation struggle years of the 1970s. This means peace has been very fragile for the politically weaker sections of the Zimbabwean population even before independence was attained. Violence, therefore, has a colonial, liberation, and post-independence trajectory.

Since 1980, ZANU PF activists, sometimes aided by the security forces, the police and traditional leaders like chiefs and headmen, have treated the opposition party members and supporters as enemies of the state. In 2008 the government refused to allow international agencies to distribute food aid to rural dwellers in Masvingo Province, as announced by the then Minister of Social Welfare, Nicholas Goche on 29 May 2008 (Human Rights Watch news release, 4 June 2008). The reason for the ban was that the rural dwellers had voted for the opposition during the 29 March 2008 elections. In the face of poor harvests, the donations from international humanitarian organizations were taken over by government and distributed as handouts from the ruling party in sinister political manipulations in which opposition supporters were skipped in the food parcel distribution. Post-election violence has become the norm rather than the exception each time elections are held, and the Zimbabwean opposition is always on the receiving end (Motlanthe, 2018; Mungwari, 2019; UN Press Statement, 21 April 2008; 13 May 2008). The Motlanthe Commission of Inquiry, which investigated the violence experienced on 1 August, heard a witness in its sitting session in Bulawayo who referred to the Gukurahundi killings of his parents amongst a total of approximately 20,000 people in the provinces of Midlands and Matabeleland in the mid-1980s. The Gukurahundi genocide needs to be resolved for people to experience social justice. Austin (2013) avers that actions that can be regarded as social injustice are targeted at groups of people, the grouping materializing from tribe, race, economic class, or such, with the purpose of eradicating their privileges and rights. The study focused on unfair treatment of opposition parties by the ruling party, which infringes on their rights and often results in marginalization. Ruhanya and Gumbo (2022) posit that the problem in Zimbabwe emanates from the party/state/military conflation associated with the liberation struggle. The ruling party has a history of organized violence, even during the liberation struggle.

## 3 Literature Review

This section reviews debates and discourses on the deployment of violence against political opponents as a mode of construction of hegemony in both colonial and postcolonial Zimbabwe. Sachikonye (2011) avers that the current political rivalry has its roots in the colonial era which did not entertain opposition parties. In the colonial era the opposition would be fighting for independence and the colonial government would not give in. Some of the struggles were armed and protracted. Sachikonye posits that when any strategy to usher in peace is crafted it must take into consideration existence of generational violence. This means the violence is shared from generation to generation and efforts to end the scourge must include changing the mindset. Protests in Zimbabwe surfaced against Mugabe's government for the first time at the close of the 1990s decade (Ncube, 2013). Protests or street demonstrations were met with stern police measures with the help of soldiers and on some occasions injuries or deaths were inflicted on the demonstrators.

Farooq (2015) gives examples of social injustice as including discrimination and homophobia. Zimbabwe's opposition activists are the victims of Farooq's (2015) proposition as people from the lower echeleons of power suffer the most. This study focuses on the marginalization suffered by opposition parties in Zimbabwe as social injustice to the ordinary citizen who chooses to have a different opinion from that of the ruling party. Denying citizens their right to have a different opinion undermines all other types of freedoms such as freedom of assembly and association, political rights, equality, and non-discrimination among other rights as articulated in the Zimbabwe Constitution 2013.

According to Al Gharaibeh (2011), cultivating human rights culture in any country must be a government responsibility. Human rights belong to human beings for them to practise and cannot be bought or inherited. Humans co-own human rights without reference to race or political opinion. Mtetwa and Muchacha (2013) posit that, despite the indivisibility of human rights, the political quagmire Zimbabwe finds itself in post-2000 has impacted negatively on the realization of other rights like social, cultural, and economic rights. The arena in which both political and civic rights are supposed to be practised in Zimbabwe has been uneven, unstable, and toxic as it has denied political opponents of the ruling party space to exercise these rights (Masunungure & Shumba, 2012; Murisa, 2010; Zimbabwe NGO Human Rights Forum, 2005). Human rights are interconnected and cannot be enjoyed in isolation. If the population or a section of the population is denied civic and political rights then the social and economic rights cannot be fully enjoyed, neither can a stable political environment be achieved (Crisis in Zimbabwe Coalition, 2011; Ploch, 2010; United Nations, 1992).

Ife (2001) posits that both civic and political rights are referred to as the first generation of human rights. These bestow upon human beings a variety of rights: voting rights with free choice, freedoms of speech, expression, assembly and the inalienable right that one cannot to be imprisoned in the absence of fair trial. Citizens must have access to the law and be protected from torture. They have the right to choose to be a member of a labour union and be exposed to minimum labour standards in the workplace (Bratton, 2014; Chikwanha, 2010; Ife, 2001). According to Austin (2013), social justice equal rights, opportunities, and treatment for all people must be respected as people are equal as posited in Article 1 of the universal declaration of human rights.

Another set of rights is the so-called third generation rights. Al Gharaibeh (2011) refers to these as collective rights. These include the right to economic development, political stability, and the right to clean air or clean environment. As Ife (2001: 3) puts it, "there is not much point in having good education or health services, and adequate legal protection for the right of free speech, if people are dying because they cannot drink clean water, or breathe polluted air, and if people are unable to participate in the benefits of economic development."

Ruhanya and Gumbo (2022) argue that the military has been used by the ruling party to protect them and the judiciary will rubberstamp decisions that are made by the ZANU PF politburo as there is party/state conflation. The military has been perceived as a tool that is used by the ruling party elites to target members of the opposition.

This chapter is underpinned by retributive justice theory that focuses on punishing offenders for imagined wrongdoing. The state views dissenting voices as people who need retributive justice as they are easily targeted, so as to send a strong signal to whoever would be an offender, not to become one. Members of the opposition parties have been on the receiving end of the justice system as they are getting "unfair" treatment rather than receiving restorative justice. Through the state-party conflation, ZANU PF has been using statutory instruments to stifle dissenting voices from the opposition as a way of sanctioning them and keeping them in check.

## 4 Methodology

This study was located in the constructivism and interpretivism paradigms which afforded the researchers talking and interacting with participants in order to understand the complex circumstances in which they live (Schwandt, 1994). The respondents told their own stories, and the researcher was keen to listen to how they relate(d) to their world. Participants thereby constructed the knowledge about their worldview (Schwandt, 2000). The study utilized the qualitative approach in a case study design. A case study research design facilitates a deep investigation of a real-life contemporary phenomenon in its natural context (Woodside, 2010). Twenty people were interviewed, amongst them party cadres from the ruling and opposition parties, victims of political violence, academics, and social analysts. The testimonies are presented as the views of the respondents from their own lived experiences which could be disputed by other testimonies. Their testimonies reflect how the participants interpreted their lived realities. That is how the chapter sought to understand them without verifying their testimonies. The participants are entitled to articulate their experiences, but it should be noted that there could be variations to their views.

## 5  Findings and Discussion

Conflict has mostly been recorded during political campaigns for elections, national or local, as well as when rallies are planned by the ruling or opposition parties. In times of drought events surrounding food distribution in rural communal areas have been characterized by discriminatory practices which side-line non-members of the ruling party and members of the opposition parties as narrated by interviewees. The following section of the chapter will give narratives/testimonies from the people reached during the data collection.

### Post-Election Evictions 1985

The second elections after attaining independence in 1980 were held in 1985. The political atmosphere then was charged with tensions between ZANU PF as the ruling party and Zimbabwe African People's Union (PF ZAPU) as a co-ruling party that had a strong backing from the Matabeleland and Midlands provinces. The minority United African National Council (UANC) party which ruled in the short-lived Zimbabwe-Rhodesia government was a spent force and had lost most of its following to the ruling ZANU PF.

> The political understanding in the ordinary population was that PF ZAPU was an opposition party that had been co-opted into government but was still regarded as an enemy opposition on tribal basis. After the election results were announced the townships in Harare experienced a hitherto unknown type of violence as ordinary citizens who did not subscribe to ZANU PF were forcibly evicted from their houses. R3

The narration by R3 reveals an underlying current of tribalism which is often expressed in ruling party politics through allocation of posts. This appears to be stereotyping the two political parties as Ndebele and Shona. Historical facts show that ZAPU was a national political party and so was ZANU. More, so ZANU broke away from ZAPU. Most critically both the leadership of ZAPU and ZANU were under Joshua Nkomo in ZAPU and the National Democratic Party (NDP) before it was banned in 1961. Nkomo was, therefore, a national and not an ethnic leader. This explains why he was nicknamed "Father Zimbabwe" denoting a nationalist leader in the struggle for Zimbabwe's independence.

> Few days after ZANU PF won the 1985 elections, their party youths came to our house in Mufakose just before midnight on that fateful night. They shouted slogans demeaning of opposition parties and the Ndebele people. They said we were not attending their political rallies and so this meant we were opposition supporters. Now that the election result shows ZANU PF having won, they said we must go to Bulawayo where ZAPU PF is located. They emptied our 5-roomed house of all the property and dumped it by the side of the road. They placed a chain on our gate and locked us outside with their own keys. R2

Freedom of citizens must guarantee their right to associate with any organization of their choice, whether religious, social, or political. The year 1985 saw people being forced to attend rallies by the ruling party in the more densely populated areas of the city, mostly.

> In Zengeza 4, Chitungwiza we were evicted and our property vandalized. The group of ZANU supporters that came to our house numbered around one hundred people. They sang the so-called revolutionary songs, terrifying us in the process. They came into the yard and threw us out of our house in a short space of time. They also broke our windows by throwing stones. R5

The other respondents revealed similar victimization in Kadoma, Marondera, and Mutare amongst other towns. A ZANU PF ex-political commissar (R10) for Highfield township branch disclosed:

> The early 1980s were years in which the party was gearing towards establishing a one-party state in Zimbabwe. This was a common political structure in communist countries and others that had fought for independence in Africa. We had UNIP in Zambia and FRELIMO in Mozambique and it was common understanding these parties ruled without official oppositions. As members of the ruling party and as young and excited youths then we believed one-party state, whether voluntarily or by force, was the best recipe for good governance and peace. R10

The Zimbabwe Republic Police (ZRP) did not get involved in trying to protect victims of ruling party violence or non-members, as one senior officer recalled:

> We were under strict instruction from our high command that we would not attend to cases of evictions, not even attempt to stop these as the party regarded them political matters beyond the jurisdiction of the ZRP police. Thus the people suffered in silence without recourse. Even when the opposition members came seeking assistance at the police charge office we confessed we were not attending to political matters. Of course this was unprofessional on our part. R15

Evicting opposition members and people not even interested in party politics from their houses are criminal acts that the police ignored as they were instructed not to interfere in politics by the ruling party. This meant the ordinary citizen was being forced to abandon their own choices for political affiliation and become ZANU PF-card-carrying members.

## Gukurahundi, 1982–1987

The era of dissidents is characterized by sustained combat against the opposition PF ZAPU by the ruling party. Indeed, there was government road and dam construction equipment destroyed by dissidents in District Development Fund depots. These acts were prevalent in the Matabeleland and Midlands provinces. One participant from the Midlands province where the dissidents operated in the mid-1980s revealed some of his encounters with the soldiers who came to their village in the summer of 1986. He (R7) narrated their ordeal:

> The soldiers came to our village and rounded up men and boys, made them to sit down and addressed everyone, including women and girls. The soldiers had no time to waste as they alleged that they were weeding out dissidents who were destroying government equipment from DDF sites by burning caterpillars, bulldozers and vehicles which the government used in making infrastructure in that area. According to the soldiers we were all dissidents but some were more active than others. They made the males to line up at gun point and force-marched them towards a waiting military truck. They used a language that was not Ndebele or Shona. Later we came to know they were using a Korean language coupled with many gestures and broken Ndebele. I was only 12 years of age and one soldier just looked at me and asked me to get out of the line and go to my mother. Three days later we heard these men and boys had been shot dead and buried after being asked about dissidents and tortured: more than a dozen males. R7

Other narratives revealed that some soldiers who hailed from these areas somehow sent messages warning their male relatives to migrate to towns and leave only the women in the villages because all males were presumed to be dissidents as long as they were Ndebele. That way some survived the onslaught by the soldiers who were determined to rid the southwestern provinces of the dissident menace. Another input from a ZAPU PF member was that the so-called dissident era was targeted at eliminating the Ndebele tribe from Zimbabwe under the pretext of fighting dissidents.

## Land Invasions, 2000

The land invasions of the year 2000 changed the tenor of attack by ZANU PF activists from the black opposition parties to white-owned farms.

> Two years prior to the farm invasions, the former freedom fighters had been vocal against the government asking to be compensated for participating in the war of liberation. They fought the war, they missed chances of advancing their own lives in Rhodesia, they risked their lives and therefore they demanded to be compensated in recognition of their sacrifice. The advent of farm invasions side tracked their attention as comrades to vent their anger on whites. There was a temporary relief on the opposition in form of ZAPU and Zimbabwe United Movement (ZUM) of Edgar Tekere. The anger was directed to the new kid on the block Movement for Democratic Change (MDC) which had just been launched as a political party by the labour union under the leadership of Morgan Tsvangirai but ZANU PF was quick to brand it as being sponsored by whites. Therefore, it justified taking over their farms so as to destroy the income base which they thought would be used to sustain the MDC. R4

The farm invasions in most areas were spearheaded by ZANU PF activists, both men and women, who violently confronted the white farmers with accusations of sponsoring the opposition Movement for Democratic Change, MDC. Thus, hatred for the opposition party drove these activists to evict white farmers from their farms. True, good agricultural land was in deficit for the black majority, but the chaotic invasions were rooted in crippling the sponsorship of the MDC, according to ZANU PF propaganda.

## Operation Murambatsvina, 2005

In the year 2005, the process that became labelled as *Murambatsvina* ("clear the filth") made worldwide waves when the ZANU PF government executed it under the then President Mugabe. The war veterans were the ones whose houses in the suburb of Kambuzuma in Harare first came under the force of bulldozers and other road construction equipment like caterpillars and front-end loaders, levelling well-constructed houses to the ground in broad daylight. The official line proffered by the central government was that they were removing suburbs that had structures built without its authorization. However, the narrative by some ex-combatants gave a different motivation for why these houses were destroyed:

> I am an ex-combatant myself and as comrades resident in Harare we came under the venomous attack of President Mugabe for failing to win the parliamentary seats in Harare for the ruling ZANU. The MDC was strong in elections in the capital since it was the biggest base of labour, and its roots are in the organized labour unions. To get back to us in retribution the president and first secretary of ZANU PF demonstrated how subordinate we were to him by destroying our houses. He made us homeless, and the world cried out. As a way of damage control Mugabe went on to destroy ordinary citizens' houses in Zimbabwe so as to cover up the political thrust he was putting on us comrades by force. The cause was the loss of seats in Harare to the opposition MDC. He breathed bitterness to us. R9

This means anger against the opposition MDC was the cause for the wanton destruction of houses belonging to innocent citizens which made the UN secretary general send an envoy to investigate this action that had been condemned worldwide. The houses destroyed had been built decades before, except for the areas where the ex-combatants had settled a few years before the Murambatsvina operation.

## 2008 Election Violence—The Presidential Run-Off

The most violent elections in post-2000 Zimbabwe were the June 2008 presidential elections run-off following the defeat of ZANU PF and President Mugabe in a relatively peaceful general election in March 2008. The period before the re-run elections was marked by beatings, evictions, and torture in rural areas which the ruling ZANU PF had declared as no-go areas for the opposition MDC.

> The March 2008 elections were held, and results were not announced for more than a month. The nation was waiting in suspense. Leaked information was that Tsvangirai had won the presidential election. Mugabe wanted to concede defeat, but his henchmen refused and asked him to stay. They forced a re-run through manipulating votes in favour of Mugabe that justified and permitted the re-run to occur. Hell broke loose on the opposition before the re-run. R25

The veracity of Mugabe's outright defeat in March 2008 remains unconfirmed. What is on public record is that the Zimbabwe Electoral Commission (ZEC) took more than five weeks to announce a re-run because Morgan Tsvangirai had not won with 50% plus one vote as provided by the constitution. This move by the army, whose allegiance was with ZANU PF, denied the opposition their right to assume power under the constitution of Zimbabwe.

> In our rural area we were forced to attend meetings which the ZANU PF activists called sessions for re-education. These were meant to force MDC supporters to vote for Mugabe in the re-run. In one such meeting in our Chiweshe area as many as six men were beaten to death by ruling party officials. In just one week a total of seventy men and women had been subjected to unbearable torture. A grandmother of 76 years was publicly flogged Islamic style in front of all the villagers. The death of six men and the public beating of the grandmother took place on the 5th of May in 2008. R17

The cruelty unleashed on the opposition party after the announcement of a re-run in 2008 was one of the bloodiest that independent Zimbabwe ever witnessed associated with elections. R17 gives that harrowing narrative which was duplicated in other rural areas. The ruling party towed a path to annihilate the opposition.

> What you need to know about 2008 elections is that the ruling party got the biggest shock of its life. Our president R G Mugabe was beaten in the presidential race and MDC got the largest number of MPs in the parliamentary vote as well as all the urban and some peri-urban councils. This had never been fathomed in ZANU PF. The Joint Operations Command, the Central Intelligence Organization, ZRP, ZDF, the Prison Services and all ZANU activists were called into action to cause and maintain mayhem in the opposition ranks so that the rerun of the presidential vote would be in favour of Mugabe. Even soldiers addressed villagers campaigning for ZANU PF. This was done with its success realized in the withdrawal of Morgan Tsvangirai from the second vote as a way of protecting citizens who were being maimed and murdered without recourse to the justice system as all law-and-order institutions were captured to favour only the ruling party. R16

The use of soldiers to address rallies in villages is the ultimate unconstitutional behaviour. There is no rule of law in such a scenario. Institutions meant to protect citizens like the police and army were under the complete control of the ruling ZANU PF. Even during current events, as the nation prepares for the 2023 elections, there is evidence of party-state conflation and collusion against the opposition:

Some rural people fled persecution to take refuge in the South African Embassy for weeks until the police flushed them out as the Thabo Mbeki government refused to openly condemn the ZANU PF extremist actions to annihilate the opposition MDC. Other villagers fled to neighbouring countries to hide from persecution by the ZANU PF activists. The official numbers came to more than three thousand refugees in Botswana, Mozambique and Zambia. R11

The narrative by R11 reveals the failure by the former South African government under Thabo Mbeki to protect the tortured and harassed opposition members who had taken refuge in its embassy. There has been no official condemnation of the heinous acts of the ZANU PF by most of the neighbouring governments in the SADC, except by the former president of Botswana, Ian Khama. He was the only president bold enough to condemn the ZANU PF atrocities against the Zimbabwean population.

Human rights lawyers have been on the receiving end in the election violence as they have suffered arrests and detentions. The police were under directives from their hierarchy to ignore matters relating to the ruling party and the opposition. The violence perpetrators acted with impunity as they could not be arrested under instructions from the ruling party. R13

The lawyers who took up the cases of opposition members faced arrest by the police and secret service members. The perpetrators of violence were not arrested because they were protected by a partisan police and army.

## Post-Mugabe Election Violence in 2018

As the country was going for 2018 elections, there was a semblance of peace as the opposition was allowed to campaign. However, there was a delay in announcing election results. Fearing that the 2008 scenario would repeat itself, some citizens embarked on a march to demand the release of election results on the 1 August 2018 in Harare. Soldiers were deployed into Harare's central business district where they indiscriminately fired live bullets at protesters, killing six people and injuring scores of others. President E. D. Mnangagwa appointed the Motlanthe Commission of Inquiry to carry out an independent investigation, vowing that those responsible would be brought to book. The recommendations of the Motlanthe Commission have not been implemented by the government. Members of the security forces who carried out the atrocities have not been brought to court. The victims of the violence or their survivors have not been compensated for loss of life or loss of property. The second republic led by Mnangagwa, who had pledged to behave differently than politicians during the Mugabe era, has not succeeded in taking concrete measures that improve ordinary people's lives, especially regarding corruption and the rule of law. The rule of law has played second fiddle to ZANU PF priorities.

> It is common knowledge that security forces in Zimbabwe have committed post-2018 elections deplorable atrocities. These include abductions or disappearances of opposition members, vitriolic attacks and torture in detention after unlawful arrests of opposition activists. Up to now security personnel who killed and maimed opposition members have not been brought to book. No single summons has ever been issued. R6

The failure to prosecute perpetrators of violence against the opposition parties is a strong indication that the ruling party ZANU PF has captured the state institutions into their political ranks. They are no longer independent to act according to the Zimbabwe constitution but they have become partisan.

The latest report on compensation for the 1 August 2018 shootings was reported by the *Newsday Weekender* of 1 October 2022. The relatives of the victims have been compensated a total of Z$2,000. The equivalent of the Zimbabwean dollar on Reserve Bank of Zimbabwe (RBZ) rate is 1US$: Z$621.5 which means the compensation stands at US$3.20. On the parallel market, where most exchanges are done by the general population and businesses, US$1: Z$800 as on 3 October 2022 (Ignite Media Zimbabwe 544). This means at parallel or black-market rates the compensation is US$2.50. This is a mockery of justice: less than $3 compensation for opposition victims killed by during protests in August 2018. The compensation amount can only buy two or three loaves of bread at most.

## Pre-2023 Election Conditions

In January 2022 Nelson Chamisa, an opposition leader, formed the Citizens Coalition for Change (CCC) as a splinter group from the Movement for Democratic Change Alliance. Matasva (2022) says that CCC officials accused the youth wing of ZANU PF of attacking its offices in Mutare as a way of intimidating the opposition as a forerunner to the 2023 election violence.

## Banning of Opposition Rallies

The opposition CCC has been failing to hold rallies in preparation for 2023 elections as the Zimbabwe Republic Police always comes up with reasons not to grant permission citing security concerns.

> The ZRP police are always denying us to hold rallies, citing baseless concerns. One such concern is that they do not have enough policemen to monitor our rally or that the venue has been pre-booked by ZANU PF. That way the opposition is muscled out of their anticipated rally through the use of the police by the ruling party. R1

By law the police do not sanction a rally but are supposed to be informed about such gatherings. However, abuse of authority by the ZRP makes them an accessory to machinations of the ruling party.

## Delayed Court Cases Involving Opposition Members

Cases brought to court are perpetually delayed if they involve the opposition to allow frustration and fatigue to set in the opposition camp. One notorious case of detention without trial is that of Job Sikhala, legislator for Zengeza West and member of the opposition CCC. He is detained together with a fellow legislator Godfrey Sithole at Chikurubi Maximum Prison. The legislators were arrested on 14 June 2021 while attending a funeral service and have spent more than 242 days in prison without trial. The funeral was for a CCC female member who was murdered by a ruling ZANU PF activist. The allegation by the state is that Sikhala wanted to avenge the death of CCC member, Moreblessing Ali. Sikhala sent a communique to from prison to sympathizers when the two legislators clocked 100 days in remand prison:

> Beloved Zimbabweans, we dearly love our country and everyone living in it to the core. Zimbabwe belongs to all of us, and we will strive forever for a society of equality and happiness. Your overwhelming support is echoing here through the walls of Chikurubi Maximum Security Prison. We are not criminals. We are political prisoners of a regime that is scared of its people. R24

The speech by Sikhala shows the bitter struggle of the opposition in exercising their political rights. Reiterating that Zimbabwe belongs to all citizens presupposes there are political powers who deem the opposition to be an enemy of the state. He laments the uneven nature of current political dispensation which treats citizens unequally. The speech acknowledges they are detained as political prisoners and they are not criminals. Arrested law breakers are brought to court within 48 hours and these CCC MPs have not been to court for trial in over 100 days.

## 6 Making Every Civil Servant a ZANU PF Card-Carrying Member

The ruling ZANU PF has a policy of forcing every civil service member to become a member of the governing party. Testimonies from civil servants bear witness to the fact that if you are not a ZANU PF card-carrying member then you will not be promoted:

> I am a college principal. I received a call to attend a seminar from someone who called me by my full name. All expenses for accommodation, bed and breakfast, meals were paid for. From 20 to 27 April 2022 we gathered at the hotel, as civil servants occupying positions of leadership and influence. Attendance had been emphasized to be compulsory. From day one of the seminar each session started with ZANU PF slogans and the singing of chimurenga songs. These are the songs that were used in the war of liberation. If you stood up to contribute and you had excuses not to sloganeer, the facilitator would shout the slogans and start singing before you contributed. When I returned from the seminar, I divulged the new regulations to my non-teaching and lecturing staff of just under 200. R12

The narration by R12 shows the push by the ZANU PF to brainwash civil servants by making them repeat slogans and sing liberation war songs which were sung during the war which ended in 1979 after negotiations called the Lancaster House talks. Everyone has a right to choose a political affiliation of their choice, and not to be assigned one. You may choose not to belong to any political party because it is not mandatory. However, the ruling party has usurped these rights from individuals with the obvious threat that if you are not a ZANU PF member then you cannot be given that opportunity to occupy senior position in government.

> The explanation for becoming a card-carrying member whether you like it or not for any government institution was explained. You are implementing policies of ZANU PF wherever you are leading: primary or secondary school, college, vocational, parastatals like ZIMRA, ZIMDEF, National Railways and others. Whoever is elevated to leadership position must be a card-carrying member of ZANU PF regardless of your wish, inclination, or opinion. You

are entered into the party data base. Your salary is docked for any amounts the party wishes to raise through its membership. R8

Government must be separated from the ruling party. These are two distinct entities which ZANU PF has endeavoured to merge by misinformation. The gullible public have been told at rallies that the party is the government and that the police and the army belong to ZANU PF. Failure to practise democratic principles by the ruling party has led to a situation where concerted disinformation and persistent lies at rallies and through mass media, which is controlled by government, have made the ordinary citizens think that ZANU PF is government and vice versa.

> All business people who get tenders in government institutions are ZANU PF card holders otherwise they would not get any business with a government institution. R19

The condition to award government tenders to party card holders is a system that holds the whole population of Zimbabwe to ransom. Tenders are awarded to card-carrying members who have no knowledge or expertise in delivery of technical services. There are party business people who are awarded road construction tenders when they do not even have a single piece of earth-moving equipment. After the tender is awarded to such an individual, or partnership, they then start to hire both equipment and expertise from other people or businesses which are not affiliated to ZANU PF. Such projects fail dismally, the winner of the tender is politically connected, and no action is taken against him.

> In every institution there are workers who are government agencies recruited by the dreaded Central Intelligence Office (CIO) and who are commonly referred to as CIO (cten). R3

The network of government spies spans all facets of businesses the entire state. Even in churches some of them are known to be CIOs. Some are pastors running their own churches but are connected to the central intelligence.

> Some opposition members are abducted after giving a speech to a seemingly innocent audience and they disappear for months on end or suffer extrajudicial death. There are abductees who have not been found for years on end. As we approach the next crucial elections, like the 2023 ones, we can be sure to expect such abductions to increase in tempo. R23

Freedom to speak one's mind is not accorded those who oppose the ruling party. Those who do, do so at their own peril. The atmosphere is toxic as you never sure about the presence of spy agents, some respondents testified. This is in line with the operation of competitive authoritarian regimes that emerged after the fall of the Soviet Union in 1989. They abused and captured state institutions in order to create unfair competition against the opposition (Levitsky & Way, 2002).

# 7 Conclusion

The failure by the ruling party to afford space for the political activities of the opposition parties is a gross violation of human rights. The events discussed in this chapter show a focused effort to annihilate opposition politics in Zimbabwe since the country gained independence in 1980. Forcing civil servants to support ZANU PF or risk not being promoted violates basic tenets of freedom for individuals. The Zimbabwe Constitution prohibits civil servants to take part in political activities before they resign under section 165(4). Election violence that involves abductions, maimings, and killings of opposition members has been the pattern in Zimbabwe ever since it gained independence in 1980. Opposition politics could be the riskiest occupation in the country. Indeed, the Zimbabwe opposition has suffered social injustice over the years. The chapter recommends the total independence of the National Peace and Reconciliation Commission in its operations, so that it becomes more effective. Political and government leaders should take peace building seriously rather than a fallacy at international stage, they should practise peace. Civil society organizations that are involved in peacebuilding initiatives should be allowed to perform their mandate without any threats and they should employ their strategies for the betterment of the country. There is a need to implement section 210 of the constitution which says that an Act of Parliament must provide an effective and independent mechanism for receiving and investigating complaints from members of the public about misconduct on the part of security services, and for remedying any harm caused by such misconduct. This will assist in curtailing the partisan role of security forces in the electoral and public affairs of Zimbabwe.

# Bibliography

Al Gharaibeh, F. (2011). Human Security, Terrorism and Human Rights in Middle East: Implications for Social Work Practice. *European Journal of Social Sciences, 20*(2), 228–239.

Austin, M. J. (Ed.). (2013, March 26). *Introduction to Social Justice in Social Work: Rediscovering a Core Value of the Profession* (1st ed.). Sage. ISBN-10: 1452274207.

Bratton, M. (2014). *Power Politics in Zimbabwe*. Lynne Rienner Publishers.

Chikwanha, B. A. (2010). *Human Rights and Governance in Zimbabwe—Formulae for Engaging the Diaspora Residents*. A discussion paper for the DFZ Conference on Engaging Zimbabweans in the Diaspora, Elephant Hills. www.dfzim.com

Crisis in Zimbabwe Coalition. (2011, October 12–18). Zimbabwe Briefing a Crisis in Zimbabwe. *Regional Office Weekly Report* (47).

Farooq, U. (2015). Social Injustice Definition, Issues and Example. *Study Lecture Notes*. 7 May 2015 and 19 November 2015. https://www.honorsociety.org/articles/social-injustice-discrimination

Government of Zimbabwe. (2001). *Social Workers Act* (Act 9/2001) of 2001. Zimbabwean Government Gazette: Government Printer.

Ife, J. (2001). *Human Rights and Social Work: Towards Rights-Based Practice*. University Press.

Institute for Peace and Security Studies. (IPSS). (2018). Zimbabwe Conflict Insight. IPSS.

Lange, K. (2019, August 12). *The Current Conflict Situation in Zimbabwe: Young Initiative on Foreign Affairs and International Relations*.

Levitsky, S., & Way, L. A. (2002). Elections Without Democracy: The Rise of Competitive Authoritarianism. *Journal of Democracy, 13*(2), 51–65.

Macheka, M. T. (2022). Political Violence and Faceless Perpetrators in Zimbabwe: Reconceptualising a Peace Building Strategy. *Cogent Social Sciences, 8*(1), 2046315. https://doi.org/10.1080/23311886.2022.2046315

Masunungure, E. V., & Shumba, J. M. (Eds.). (2012). *Zimbabwe: Mired in Transition*. Weaver Press. https://doi.org/10.2307/j.ctvk3gm41

Mlambo, A. (2014). *A History of Zimbabwe*. Cambridge University Press.

Mtetwa, E., & Muchacha, M. (2013, August). The Price of Professional Silence: Social Work and Human Rights in Zimbabwe. *African Journal of Social Work, 3*(1), 19–43.

McBride, A. (2018, August 1). *Still No Justice for Zimbabwe's 2018 Post Election Violence*.

Maus, M. (2015). What Is the Definition of Social Injustice? *Quora*. 17 September. Web. 19 November.

Matasva, F. (2022). War of Words After Alleged Zanu PF Youths Attack, Deface CCC Offices. *Manicaland Correspondent*. https://www.newzimbabwe.com/war-of-words-after-alleged-zanu-pf-youths-attack-deface-ccc-offices/

Mavhinga, D. (2021). Still No Justice for Zimbabwe's 2018 Post-Election Violence: Implement Motlanthe Commission's Recommendations; Investigate Security Forces. August 2, 2021 2:37PM EDT. Human Rights Watch.

Motlanthe, K. (2018). *Report of the Commission of Inquiry into the 1st of August 2018 Post-Election Violence in Zimbabwe*. Government of Zimbabwe.

Mungwari, T. (2019). Zimbabwe Post Election Violence: Motlanthe Commission of Inquiry 2018. *International Journal of Contemporary Research and Review, 10*(2), 20392–20406. https://doi.org/10.15520/ijcrr.v10i02.675

Murisa, T. (2010). *Social Development in Zimbabwe*. Discussion Paper prepared for the Development Foundation for Zimbabwe. www.dfzim.com

Ncube, C. (2013). The 2013 Elections in Zimbabwe: End of an Era for Human Rights Discourse? *Africa Spectrum, 48*(3), 99–110.

Ndlela, N. (2005). The African Paradigm: The Coverage of the Zimbabwean 'Crises' in the Norwegian Media. Westminster Papers in *Communication and Culture* (Special issue: 71–90).

Ndlovu-Gatsheni, S. J., & Ruhanya, P. (2020). (Eds.), *The History and Political Transition of Zimbabwe*. Springer International.

Ploch, L. (2010). *Zimbabwe: Background, Congressional Research Service Report for Congress, Congressional Research Service*. www.fas.org/sgd/crs/row/RL32723.pdf

Report of the Commission of Inquiry into the 1 August 2018 Post-Election Violence, 2018. http://kubatana.net/wp

Research and Advocacy Unit. (2018). Zimbabwe-political violence and elections. *Report produced by the Research and Advocacy Unit*.

Ruhanya, P., & Gumbo, B. (2022). The Securocratic State: Conceptualising the Transition Problem in Zimbabwe. *Third World Thematics: A TWQ Journal*. https://doi.org/10.1080/23802014.2022.2099575

Sachikonye, L. M. (2011). *When a state turns on its Citizens: 60 years of institutionalised violence in Zimbabwe*. Weaver Press, Project MUSE. https://muse.jhu.edu/book/18144

Schwandt, T. A. (1994). Constructionist, Interpretivist Approaches to Human Inquiry. In N. K. Denzin & Y. S. Lincoln (Eds.), *Handbook of Qualitative Research* (pp. 118–137). Sage.

Schwandt, T. A. (2000). Three epistemological stances for qualitative inquiry: Interpretivism, hermeneutics, and social constructionism. In N. K. Denzin, & Y. S. Lincoln (Eds.), *Handbook of Qualitative Research* (2 ed., pp. 189–213). SAGE Publishing.

United Nations. (1992). *Vienna Declaration and Programme of Action*. A/CONF. 157/24 (Part 1), Chap. III. June 1993. Geneva.

UN Press Statement. (2008, April 21). Secretary General Meets with Zimbabwean Opposition Leader Over Election Crisis. *UN Press Statement*. http://www.un.org/apps/news/story.asp?NewsID=26401&Cr=zimbabwe&Cr1. Accessed May 27, 2022.

UN Press Statement. (2008, May 13). Zimbabwe: UN Voices Concern Over Politically-Motivated Violence. *UN Press Statement*. http://www.un.org/apps/news/story.asp?NewsID=26658&Cr=zimbabwe&Cr1=. Accessed May 27, 2022.

Woodside, A. G. (2010). Bridging the Chasm Between Survey and Case Study Research: Research Methods for Achieving Generalization, Accuracy, and Complexity. *Industrial Marketing Management, 39*(1), 64–75.

Zimbabwe Human Rights NGO Forum. (2005). *The Aftermath of a Disastrous Venture*. A follow up report on Operation Murambatsvina. Document.

Zimbabwe: Reverse Ban on Food Aid to Rural Areas. (2008, June 4). Human Rights Watch News Release. http://hrw.org/english/docs/2008/06/04/zimbab19022.htm

# Preventing Electoral Violence in Africa: Towards Sustainable Peace

### Khabele Matlosa

## 1 Introduction

An election is fundamentally a conflict situation to the extent that it denotes a contestation over access to, control over, retention, and use of state power by the political elite. This chapter aims to build upon existing literature to advance our understanding of electoral violence in Africa. Anchored in political economy theory and analysis, the chapter investigates various domains and manifestations of electoral violence and how it intersects with other forms of political violence. The chapter also charts a way forward in terms of how best to institutionalize sustainable peace and have violence-free elections in Africa.

One of the major development challenges facing Africa today is election-related violence. Elections are a double-edged sword as they can either promote democracy and peace, or shield autocracy and trigger violent conflicts. Whereas democracy is unthinkable without elections, autocracy is also possible even under conditions of regular elections. This irony suggests that elections can achieve two diametrically opposed purposes depending on the prevailing circumstances in each given country. On the one hand,

K. Matlosa (✉)
Cantre for African Diplomacy and Leadership, University of Johannesburg, Johannesburg, South Africa, Gauteng, South Africa
e-mail: matlosak@gmail.com

they can serve as a fundamental anchor for simultaneous democracy-building and peace-building. On the other, they can provide a veil of legitimacy to authoritarian rule punctuated by spasms of violent conflicts and political instability.

This truism is not difficult to fathom. Elections are a political contestation for state power. Contestation over state power involves conflict among political contestants (parties and candidates). Thus, conflict around elections is natural and cannot be wished away. Some conflicts can have positive dynamics leading to democratic transformation. What should concern us, therefore, is not that elections are conflict-ridden, but rather that most of these conflicts take a violent form. Violent conflict during elections adversely affects democracy, peace, and development.

Elections are a high-stakes contestation for state power. State power in Africa is highly prized. The state is seen as the only viable avenue for elite accumulation of wealth by both fair and foul means, especially in those countries with a miniscule private sector. Under these circumstances, the political elite tends to perceive elections as a vehicle to the largesse of the state. In such countries, electoral contests become so fierce that they become war by other means. Electoral contestation is, thus, turned into a zero-sum rather than positive-sum game. This, in part, explains why most elections in Africa have been marred by political violence. According to Burchard "more than half of all elections held in Africa experience some form of violence or intimidation either before or after election day" (Burchard, 2015).

Electoral violence constitutes one of the most daunting challenges inhibiting the deepening of democratic governance in Africa today. It is one of the intractable features that mark the continent's pervasive culture of violence. Of the top ten most violent countries globally, two are in Africa (i.e. Lesotho and South Africa). Most African countries rank very low on the Global Peace Index suggesting that the continent is home to the most violent conflicts globally. This explains in part why Africa occupies a second spot to the Americas in terms of very high homicide rates. Perpetrators of political violence are many and varied and include both national and external actors. Understanding the scope and magnitude of electoral violence requires a deep-dive into the political economy analysis that reveals that this violence is traceable to both deep-seated (invisible) structural conditions and more proximate superstructural (visible) triggers/catalysts. Addressing electoral violence through the electoral cycle alone is an exercise in futility. While electoral and governance reforms are useful strategies for redressing electoral violence, a much more comprehensive approach ought to encompass democracy-building, peace-building, and deliberate pursuit of equitable and inclusive socio-economic development. This is simply because, in the final analysis, democracy, peace, and development are mutually intertwined and inextricably interwoven. They should be pursued simultaneously and concurrently and not sequentially. This is the principal thrust of this chapter. The next section provides a political economy analysis of electoral violence in Africa.

## 2  Political Economy Analysis: A Theoretical Lens

This chapter adopts a political economy analysis in understanding the roots, nature, manifestations, and repercussions of electoral violence in Africa. The political economy approach entails discovering the interconnectedness of various deep-seated drivers and proximate factors in understanding a particular phenomenon. This approach unearths how social, economic (including environmental), and political dynamics have either direct or indirect bearing on phenomena, including electoral violence in Africa, as well as how best this violence can be resolved sustainably. Political economy is one of the most useful approaches to examining and explaining conflict situations around the world in general, and in Africa in particular.

It is for this reason that political economy analysis was chosen for examination and explanation of the dynamics that propel electoral violence as well as imperatives for sustainable prevention, management, and resolution of electoral violence in Africa. At the very core of the political economy analysis, is the investigation of the structural drivers and super-structural causes that undergird political (electoral) violence. Structural factors relate to a country's socio-economic make up. The super-structural factors relate to political culture and the state of peace and security in each country. These two variables are explored in the two sub-sections below.

### Structural Roots

Structural conditions that lay a foundation for political (electoral) violence are traceable to the economic structures, social relations, and the cultural milieu of each country. Postcolonial Africa is generally marked by deep-seated underdevelopment, pervasive poverty and hunger, prevalent unemployment, and wide-spread inequality, which generate a political culture of violence. The continent's underdevelopment is a direct result of its enslavement and colonization by Europe since the nineteenth century (Rodney, 1982). In turn,

Africa's underdevelopment has translated into the development of Europe (Mhango, 2018; Nkrumah, 1965). Since Africa's self-rule in the late 1950s to date, neo-colonialism has continued Africa's underdevelopment and, in the process, has sustained the development of Europe and North America in contemporary times. Poverty, hunger, unemployment, and inequality are a direct result of Africa's underdevelopment as well as unequal distribution of its abundant natural resources, poor governance, lack of visionary and transformative leadership, corruption, nepotism, patronage, politics of identity, and patrimonialism generally (Bayart, 1989).

Therefore, when elections take place under conditions of weak economies and mismanagement of sociocultural diversity, and where the state is the main employer, they often become conflictual and oft-times violent. The stakes of winning and losing are far too high and almost all contestants would not contemplate defeat. Such contestation also involves mobilization of votes along identity lines, such as ethnicity, religion, and region among others. Hence, the pervasive trend of ethnicization of politics and politicization of ethnicity in Africa especially during elections. These structural socio-economic conditions provide a perfect recipe for electoral violence as witnessed in Kenya in 2007–2008, Zimbabwe in 2008, Cote d'Ivoire in 2010–2011, and Nigeria in 2011, for instance.

Structural root causes of electoral violence can be classified broadly into three categories, namely: (a) contestation over state power (largely by the elite); (b) struggle over resources (e.g. land), and (c) identity-based cleavages (e.g. ethnicity). These are discussed in the following three paragraphs.

First, at the heart of electoral contest is access to, control and use of state power by the elites. While the political elites are the most obvious contestants during elections, various other elites do take part in this contest, including the commercial elites who often provide resources, such as money, in support of their preferred political parties. In this contestation, the party (or a coalition of parties) wielding the state power aims to retain this power. On the other hand, opposition parties (or coalitions of opposition parties) outside the state, aim to dislodge those in power in order to access and control the levers of state power. Given that these contests are often "do-or-die" affairs, in cases where the institutional architecture and electoral governance are enfeebled, the contestations turn into political violence, particularly in situations where contestants mismanage normal electoral conflicts. In this sense, electoral violence, is caused by conflict over state power by elites, with the ordinary people (especially the workers, peasants, and unemployed etc.) used as cannon fodder in these struggles.

Second, acquisition of state power comes with several privileges including power to access and distribute national resources. Africa is awash with abundant natural resources. These resources are unevenly distributed, skewed in favour of a small coterie of the *nouveau-riche* at the expense of most of the people (especially workers, peasants, unemployed etc.) who are subjected to the vagaries of socio-economic ills such as poverty, hunger, unemployment and inequality. Based on the unequal access to, control and use of resources, social classes of haves and have-nots have formed. In more ways than one, therefore, electoral contests also turn on class struggles between and among the haves and have-nots. This manifests, among others, through ideological platforms that political parties occupy which align with social class divides. Conservative parties often tend to represent class interests of the haves, social democratic parties tend to represent the interests of the have-nots, while liberal parties vacillate between these class interests and divides. In this sense, electoral violence is caused by resource conflicts in which local and foreign elites own the lion's share of national resources, while most of the citizens are immiserated and impoverished.

The third cause of electoral violence relates to mismanagement of diversity. Simply defined, diversity is a state of being different. It defines individual and group identity in society. Its subjective and objective markers include language, religion, history, region, custom/culture, race, class, ethnicity, gender and age. Diversity cannot be wished away. That is why the 2004 Human Development Report aptly observes that "cultural diversity is here to stay—and to grow. States need to find ways of forging national unity amid this diversity. The world, ever more interdependent economically, cannot function unless people respect diversity and build unity through common bonds of humanity" (UNDP, 2004: 2–3). Being different from others ought not be a bad thing. In fact, in its article 8 (3), the African Charter on Democracy, Elections and Governance, adopted by the African Union in 2007 and which came into force on 15 February 2012 after the required 15 ratifications by AU member states, stipulates clearly that "state parties shall respect ethnic, cultural, and religious diversity which contributes to strengthening democracy and citizen participation" (AU, 2007: 14).

Diversity, in and of itself, need not lead to adversity and become destructive. In fact, it is supposed to enrich democracy given that two of the many principles of democracy are pluralism and tolerance. People ought to be free to be who they are and to choose and celebrate their various identities, being respected and also respecting others with different identities from their own. They should be "able to make cultural choices without penalty, without being excluded from other choices—for jobs, schooling, housing, healthcare, political voice and many other opportunities critical to human well-being" (UNDP, 2004: 28). This is what the 2004 Human Development Report cogently terms cultural liberty—the freedom to express one's identity without fear for any reprisal. Under conditions of cultural liberty, diversity can be a resource for national unity and advancement of nation-state building project in contemporary Africa. Unity is perfectly possible in diversity. The notion of unity in diversity is premised "on the assumption that a successful nation is one that can pool together its diverse social intermixtures in a manner that builds on their richness and does not alienate any group" (Deng, 2008: 43).

## Super-Structural Triggers

The structural conditioning for political (including electoral) violence works in consonance with superstructural triggers/catalysts. While structural conditions are often felt and less visible, superstructural factors are often both felt and visible. How the key organs of the state such as the executive, the legislature, and the judiciary play their roles in managing national affairs (governance) goes a long way in either facilitating or preventing political violence, including electoral violence. It is not just the role of these three key organs of the state that determine if elections are violent or peaceful. The roles of the security establishment, the bureaucracies, the traditional media, social media, civil society, private sector, trade unions, faith-based organizations, traditional governance institutions, students, farmers associations, women's movements, youth organizations, and communities directly and indirectly contribute in one way of the other in facilitating or preventing political/electoral violence. External actors also play an important role in either facilitating or preventing electoral violence in Africa. For instance, the current superpower rivalry between and among the United States of America, European Union, China, and Russia has also created a toxic environment for elections in Africa today.

If a country has a political culture imbued in violence, elections are also bound to turn violent. If a country has an embedded history of violence, elections are bound to be violent. In such situations, the security establishment is highly politicized. The net effect of the politicization of the military is the militarization of politics including elections. In Central Africa, this is the case in the Central African Republic, Cameroon and Gabon, while in Southern Africa, this is the case in Eswatini, Lesotho and Zimbabwe. This toxic situation is even more glaring in countries emerging from protracted violent conflict where peace agreements are difficult to implement effectively, such as South Sudan and Burundi in East Africa, the Democratic Republic of Congo in Central Africa, and Guinea Bissau and Mali in West Africa.

Sustainable electoral governance predicated upon political stability and peace is fundamentally dependent on strong, effective, and resilient institutions. These include, inter alia, the Electoral Management Bodies (EMBs) and the electoral system. Once the EMBs fail the test of 'procedural certainty and substantive uncertainty', a stage is set for violence-ridden election (Mozaafar & Schedler, 2002). This is often the case in North Africa countries such as Egypt and Mauritania and in West African countries such as Togo and Burkina Faso.

The electoral system plays an important role in determining the peacefulness or violent nature of elections. There is a plethora of electoral systems worldwide and in Africa. But all these typologies of electoral systems can be grouped into four families, namely: Plurality-Majority Systems; Proportional Representation Systems; Mixed Systems, and Others which do not fit neatly into the above three families (Reynolds et al., 2005). An electoral system denotes institutional, legal, regulatory, and procedural elements through which elections are conducted and votes are translated into seats won by parties and candidates. In assessing whether an electoral system is conflict-prone, its four key elements are crucial: the electoral formula, the district magnitude, the vote-to-seat ratio, and the boundary delimitation (Matlosa, 2004).

In sum, therefore, the political economy analysis of electoral violence in Africa suggests two main explanatory variables that are both intertwined and mutually reinforcing namely structural conditions (mainly society, culture, and economy) and super-structural factors, including politics and institutions, EMBs, electoral system, leaders, people, external actors etc. If electoral violence is to be prevented, there is a need to address it at both structural and superstructural levels. The predicament of Africa today is that much effort and resources are invested in trying to deal with only superstructural triggers of electoral violence with little, if any, attempt to root out structural conditions of violence.

## 3 Elections-Violence Nexus

In order to establish the nexus between elections and violence, three concepts are worth exploring and operationalizing. These are: elections, conflict and electoral violence. An election is a process whereby a people belonging to a particular territorial state (the electorate), under the authority of a single institutional state, choose their leaders (at various levels of government) periodically to manage their national affairs as an expression of popular sovereignty (Matlosa, 2021). An election constitutes the heartbeat of representative democracy. Lindberg reminds us that "while there are many views on what democracy is—or ought to be—a common denominator among modern democracies is elections" (Lindberg, 2006: 1).

On their own, however, elections do not guarantee democracy, nor are they synonymous with it. A perception that equates elections with democracy amounts to what Karl terms "the fallacy of electoralism" (Karl, 1986)—the perception that the mere holding of regular elections, irrespective of their quality, qualifies a country as a democracy. It is this notion that exposes elections as a double-edged sword. Electoralism is capable of advancing democratization under favourable conditions, yet it is capable of shielding autocratization in an inclement political climate. The concerns about the adverse effects of elections, and electoral authoritarianism, are articulated by Schedler (2002, 2006) when he addresses elections in the context of the "menu of manipulation." Elections are agents of democratization, but they are also the tools of manipulation aimed at anchoring authoritarianism, he contends.

Conflict refers to incompatibility of interests between/among two or more parties whereby pursuit of one's interest means a loss of the other(s). Conflict is an essential aspect of social change. Conflict is part and parcel of social change in all societies and, as such, it is not necessarily a negative phenomenon, but conflicts become destructive and counter-productive once they escalate into violence and belligerents resort to violent means of resolving them. Conflict can be defined as real or perceived divergence of interests, beliefs, and values among two or more people (parties to the conflict). This incompatibility among conflicting parties leads to the realization that the interests of party A can only be achieved at the expense of parties B and C. Conflict can manifest itself in many forms, some of which may be violent and inflict pain and suffering to both parties in conflict and to other people who may not be directly involved, due to its spill-over effect.

In elections the political elites, vying for political hegemony through the state, find themselves caught up in this incompatibility conundrum. Conflict, per se, is not a problem, much the same way as contestation over state power through electoral competition, provided conflict and electoral disputes are managed constructively and peacefully through positive-sum (win-win) strategies. But there is a lot wrong with conflict and elections when they turn violent and contestants/belligerents aim to resolve their incompatibilities by violent means, through zero-sum (winner-take-all) strategies. One of the primary reasons why elections in Africa are managed by Election Management Bodies (EMBs) is precisely to make sure that electoral competition is conducted democratically and peacefully throughout all the three stages of the electoral process (pre-voting, voting, and post-voting stages). However, often elections on the continent tend to be violent resulting in loss of lives, destruction of property, depression of the economy, and forced displacement of people internally and externally.

It could be argued, therefore, that the major problem facing Africa is not so much that there are conflicts (overt and covert, violent and non-violent) everywhere, but rather that no effective mechanisms have been built for constructive management of the conflicts. Conflict can be either constructive or destructive. Constructive conflict involves persuasion, compromises, and win-win solutions (positive-sum game). Destructive conflict involves coercion, fixed positions, and winner-take-all solutions (zero-sum game).

Electoral violence refers generally to violent election-related conflicts. Thus, electoral violence is a subset of political violence, broadly speaking. It encompasses "coercive acts carried out for the purpose of affecting the process of results of an election... either by manipulating the electoral procedures and participation or by contesting the legitimacy of the results" (Kovacs & Bjarnesen, 2018: 5). Laakso (2019) posits that electoral violence is the result of manipulation of electoral process or a reaction to that manipulation. As indicated earlier, it is a subset of political violence. According to the Armed Conflict Location and Event Data (ACLED) project, political violence denotes the use of force by an individual or a group of people "with a political purpose or motivation.... A politically violent event is a single altercation where often force is used by one or more groups to a political end" (ACLED, http://www.acleddata.com>uploads>2015).

ACLED identifies eight key actors that perpetrate political (including electoral) violence in Africa:

(1) First, state actors are associated with the government in power who unleash violence against real or perceived anti-government forces through either established security agencies and/or paramilitary forces.
(2) Second, rebel actors are groups "whose goal is to counter, replace or separate from an established national governing regime through violence. Rebel groups have a stated political agenda for national power" (ACLED, http://www.acleddata.com>uploads>2015).
(3) Third, political militias are a specific set of perpetrators of violence. They are "often created for a specific purpose or during a specific time period (i.e. Janjaweed) and for the furtherance of a political purpose by violence.

They are distinct from state actors in that they do not seek "the removal of a national power, but are typically supported, armed by, or allied with a political elite and/or act towards a goal defined by these elites or larger political movement" (ACLED, http://www.acleddata.com>uploads>2015). A widely known political militia are the Sudanese Janjaweed, often used by the state as an informal paramilitary force both during and in between elections. But in some African countries, political parties have a tendency to form their own armed militias especially around elections as a bulwark for unleashing violence against their opponents. Recently, in 2019, Ghana passed legislation aimed at banning party militias or vigilante groups. But despite this legislation, political parties in Ghana continue to operate party militias and have not yet effectively disbanded them.

(4) Fourth, communal (identity) militias are "armed and violent groups organized around a collective feature including community, ethnicity, region, religion or, in exceptional cases, livelihood.... Identity militias may have a noted role in the community, such as the long-term policing units common among Somali clans. Events involving 'identity militias' are referred to as 'communal violence' as these violent groups often act locally, in the pursuance of local goals, resources, power and retribution" (ACLED, http://www.acleddata.com>uploads>2015). Terrorism and violent extremism fall under the label communal (identity) militias.

(5) Fifth, demonstrators are groups of people that engage in "spontaneous demonstrations that may, or may not, continue beyond a discrete event" (ACLED, http://www.acleddata.com>uploads>2015). They can be "against government institutions, businesses or other private institutions" (ACLED, http://www.acleddata.com>uploads>2015).

(6) Sixth, fairly distinct from demonstrators are rioters who are "individuals who participate in either violent demonstrations or spontaneous acts of disorganized violence.... Rioters are by definition violent, and may engage in a wide variety of violence, including the form of property destruction, engagement with armed groups (security forces, private security firms etc.) or in violence against unarmed civilians" (ACLED, http://www.acleddata.com>uploads>2015).

(7) Seventh, protestors are "individuals who participate in non-violent demonstrations.... Although protestors are by definition non-violent themselves, they may be targets of violence by other groups (security institutions; private security firms; or other armed actors)" (ACLED, http://www.acleddata.com>uploads>2015).

(8) Eighth and finally, another group that engages in political (electoral) violence is referred to as external forces which are military forces operating outside of their home countries (ACLED, http://www.acleddata.com>uploads>2015). These include, inter alia, mercenaries (e.g. USA, Russia, France), private security firms, United Nations forces, and various others linked to big powers with embedded interests in Africa such as North Atlantic Treaty Organization (NATO)'s war in Libya (2011), the United States of America, and France among others. Mostly these external forces are used either for regime change purposes or in support of a sitting regime as long as external interests of the external powers are protected and secured.

In sum, elections, conflict, and electoral violence are conceptually intertwined and operationally interwoven. Elections are a normal democratic process of citizens periodically choosing leaders to manage national affairs, as an exercise in popular sovereignty. Conflict is a natural process that often accompanies elections irrespective of their democratic quality. However, if such election-related conflicts are mismanaged, they quicky turn into political (electoral) violence. While election-related conflicts may not be counter-productive, they may lead to electoral violence which, by definition, is, in and of itself, counter-productive. The next section zeroes in on the electoral cycle dimensions of electoral violence as part and parcel of the super-structural manifestations of this problem.

## 4 Electoral Cycle Dynamics

Electoral violence manifests across all the three stages of the electoral cycle: pre-voting, voting, and post-voting, as illustrated in Fig. 1.

As Table 1 illustrates, the bulk of electoral operations are concentrated in the pre-voting stage of the electoral cycle. It is no revelation, therefore, that the majority and intensity of election-related conflicts that often lead to political (electoral) violence are, almost invariably, traceable to this electoral stage.

With respect to the legal framework, the majority of electoral violence is triggered by winner-take-all electoral systems and biased electoral management bodies. With regard to planning and implementation, sources of electoral violence may emanate from budgeting and election financing as these issues have both direct and indirect impact on the extent to which the political playing field is level to guarantee the integrity and democratic quality

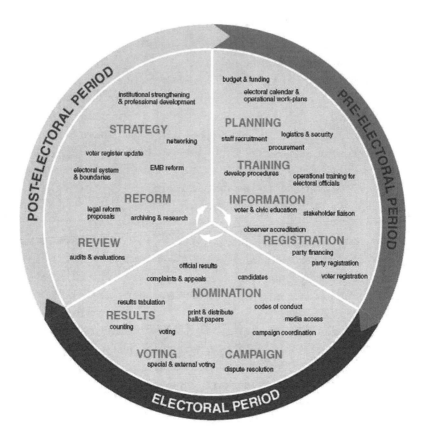

Fig. 1 Electoral cycle

of elections. Other sources of electoral violence may manifest during training and education if both civic education and voter information is biased against those constituencies or party agents that support opponents. Registration and nomination of candidates for elections do generate conflicts that also degenerate into violence. Flawed voters' rolls are a source of conflicts and violence as happened in the Democratic Republic of the Congo in 2011. Nomination of candidates often leads to intra-party tensions, violent conflicts, and party splits as Lesotho's political history amply demonstrates (Matlosa, 2021). During election campaigns, a major trigger for electoral violence is surely party funding and media access that often tends to be skewed in favour of incumbent parties and candidates, thereby tilting the political playing field against opposition parties/candidates.

In comparison to the pre-voting stage, there are fewer incidences of electoral violence during the voting phase, as illustrated in Table 2. This situation

Table 1  Pre-voting phase

| Components | Main activities |
| --- | --- |
| Legal framework | • Constitution<br>• Electoral system and boundaries<br>• Electoral bodies<br>• Codes of conduct |
| Planning and implementation | • Budgeting, funding and financing<br>• Election calendar<br>• Recruitment and procurement<br>• Logistics and security |
| Training and education | • Operational training for elections officials<br>• Civic education<br>• Voter information |
| Registration and nominations | • Voter registration<br>• Observer accreditation<br>• Parties and candidates |
| Electoral campaigns | • Party financing<br>• Media access<br>• Codes of conduct<br>• Breaches and penalties<br>• Campaign coordination |

may be explained by the mere fact that voters, parties, candidates, and electoral management bodies are all focused on the election day operations.

There may be incidences of violence especially during vote tabulation and announcement of results often perpetrated by losing parties and candidates as evidence from the Kenyan elections of 2007/2008, the Zimbabwean elections of 2008 and the Nigerian elections of 2011 vividly demonstrates.

Often times, the post-election violence in Africa is either a continuation of grievances during the pre-voting and voting stages or new grievances following announcement of election results (Table 3).

Electoral violence has devastating consequences on governance, peace, and development in countries concerned. These consequences take various forms, including: (a) loss of human life (e.g. 1,300 people in Kenya, 2007–2008); (b) forced displacement of people internally and externally, (e.g. 300,000 in

Table 2  Voting phase

| Components | Main activities |
| --- | --- |
| Voting operations and election day<br>Verification of results | • Special and external voting<br>• Vote counting<br>• Tabulation of results<br>• Complaints and appeals<br>• Official results |

Table 3 Post-voting phase

| Component | Main activities |
|---|---|
| Post-election | • Voter lists and updates<br>• Audits and evaluation<br>• Archiving and Research<br>• Legal reform<br>• Institutional strengthening and professional development |

Kenya 2007–2008); (c) decline in socio-economic and human development (e.g. Zimbabwe today, Cote d'Ivoire 2010–2011); (d) loss of faith in elections (e.g. Lesotho's plummeting voter turnout between 1993 and 2022); and (e) dwindling public trust in democratic institutions (especially political parties, parliaments and Electoral Management Bodies in Africa). Afrobarometer data suggests a worrying trend of declining public trust in key governance institutions in Africa as shown in Table 4.

From Table 4, it is evident that key institutions that are supposed to anchor democratic governance are not trusted by the majority of citizens. This is clear in the case of parliament which is not trusted by about 50% citizens, or local authorities (53%), ruling parties (54%), opposition parties (63%), and revenue authorities (50%). Institutions that enjoy the trust of the majority of citizens are the head of state/government (52%), the army (64%), traditional leaders (59%), religious leaders (69%), and the courts of law (51%). It is noteworthy that African citizens seem to have more trust in unelected institutions such as the army, traditional leaders, and religious leaders in comparison to ones that are central to democracy building and promotion such as the electoral commission, parliament, and political parties.

## 5 Towards Sustainable Peace

According to the 2022 Global Peace Index (that measures the state of peace in 163 countries), the top five most peaceful African countries are Mauritius (No. 29), Ghana (No. 40), The Gambia (No. 45), Botswana (No. 48), and Sierra Leone (No. 50). Generally, elections conducted in these countries are often violence-free. The five least peaceful African countries are South Sudan (No. 159), Democratic Republic of the Congo (No. 158), Somalia (No. 156), Central African Republic (No. 155), and Sudan (No. 154) (Institute for Economics & Peace, 2022). Elections in these countries are often marked by protracted violence. A vivid illustration of the entrenched culture of violence is revealed in homicide rates. Figure 2 shows this worrying trend on the continent.

Table 4 Public trust in institutions in Africa

| | President (%) | Parliament (%) | National election commission (%) | Local council (%) | Ruling party (%) | Opposition party (%) | Tax/revenue authority (%) | Police (%) | Army (%) | Traditional leaders (%) | Religious leaders (%) | Courts of law (%) |
|---|---|---|---|---|---|---|---|---|---|---|---|---|
| Not at all/just a little | 45.4 | 54.9 | 50.2 | 53.1 | 53.7 | 62.8 | 51.3 | 49.8 | 33.4 | 33.5 | 29.2 | 45.2 |
| Somewhat/a lot | 51.7 | 41.5 | 44.5 | 43.4 | 43.6 | 33.2 | 41.4 | 48.6 | 64.1 | 58.9 | 69.0 | 50.9 |
| Refused | 0.5 | 0.3 | 0.3 | 0.1 | 0.5 | 0.5 | 0.3 | 0.3 | 0.3 | 0.3 | 0.2 | 0.3 |
| Do not know/haven't heard enough | 1.9 | 3.2 | 5.0 | 4.4 | 2.2 | 3.9 | 7.0 | 1.2 | 2.1 | 7.2 | 1.5 | 3.7 |
| Total | 100 | 100 | 100 | 100 | 100 | 100 | 100 | 100 | 100 | 100 | 100 | 100 |

*Source* Afrobarometer (2019–2021)

**Total number of homicide victims, by region, 2017**

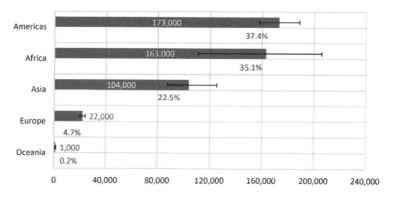

**Fig. 2** Homicide rate by continent, 2017 (*Source* UNIDOC [2019: 11])

The global comparative data on homicide rate reveals that the overall number of people killed by homicide skyrocketed exponentially from 362,000 in 1990 to 464,000 in 2017 (UNIDOC, 2019: 11). As illustrated in Fig. 2, the Americas have the highest homicide rate at 173,000 (37.4%). The second continent with the highest homicide rate is Africa at 163,000 (35.1%). The third spot is occupied by Asia at 104, 000 (22.5%). Europe sits on the second rung from the bottom of the global homicide rate at 22, 000 (4.7%). The continent that boasts the least homicide rate is Oceania at a meagre 1000 (0.2%) (UNIDOC, 2019: 11). It is clear from this data that Africa has an embedded culture of political (including electoral) violence. Of the top ten countries with the highest murder rate, two are in Africa (i.e. Lesotho with 43.6 murders per 100,000 people in 2017 and South Africa with 35.7 murders per 100,000 people in 2017 (World Population Review, 2019).

Dealing with electoral violence has to entail a holistic and comprehensive strategy that encompasses peace-building and peace-making as well as achieving equitable and inclusive socio-economic development during and between elections. The process of achieving violence-free elections, therefore, must transcend the electoral cycle. The rationale is that the structural root causes of electoral violence go deeper than just elections, including underdevelopment, poverty, hunger, unemployment, and inequality.

Dealing effectively with conflicts in order to address electoral violence, African countries must pursue four strategies, namely:

(1) *Conflict Prevention*: monitoring the electoral cycle in its entirety with a view to avoid escalation of conflict into violence (deterrence, early

warning, early response, early recovery, pre-election assessment missions, human rights monitoring, preventive diplomacy, Infrastructures for Peace [I4Ps], election observation missions etc.).
(2) *Conflict Management*: Long-term management of intractable conflicts (containing an existing conflict from escalating into violence (mediation, election observation missions, negotiations, arbitration, litigation, human rights monitoring, I4Ps etc.).
(3) *Conflict Resolution*: An effort aimed at eradicating or containing the causes of structural, super-structural, institutional conflicts (dispute resolution, peace agreements, alternative dispute resolution, reconciliation, I4Ps etc.).
(4) *Conflict Transformation*: Encompasses conflict prevention, management and resolution and weaves them together with peace-making and peace-building, socio-economic development and social justice (election observation, human rights monitoring, transitional justice systems, post-conflict reconstruction and development, reconciliation, I4Ps etc.).

During the Thirteenth Ordinary Session of the Assembly of Heads of State and Government held in Sirte, Libya, in July 2009, the AU adopted the Panel of the Wise on "Election-Related Disputes and Political Violence: Strengthening the Role of the African Union in Preventing, Managing and Resolving Conflict". This report provides a comprehensive menu of strategies and approaches for the Union to adequately tackle election-related disputes and political violence. The report emphasized that the AU, through its Panel of the Wise, and other relevant organs, such as the African Union Commission (AUC) should address root causes of electoral violence both within the electoral cycle (election-related causes) and structural factors (systemic cuases). It further highlighted the need for the Union to invest more resources in preventive measures and early warning and early response. The report details far-reaching policy recommendations which are clustered in six as follows:

(1) Risk mapping, preventive and early warning mechanisms
(2) Electoral governance and administration
(3) Coordination of electoral assistance
(4) Post-election conflict transformation mechanisms
(5) International cooperation and partnerships
(6) Strategic interventions by the Panel of the Wise (IPI, 2010).

As part of deepening democracy and inculcating a culture of peace, the African Union's long-term development blueprint, Agenda 2063—The Africa

We Want, should decisively deal with vexing problems around electoral violence. It is important that the Panel of the Wise is sufficiently capacitated to deal with the problem in all the six areas mentioned above. Furthermore, in order to adequately tackle the problem of electoral violence through fusing election observation and mediation, it is imperative that the African Governance Architecture (AGA) and the African Peace and Security Architecture (APSA) are synergized.

One of the most innovative ways in which some countries have addressed the problem of electoral violence is the establishment of solid and functional infrastructures for peace (I4Ps). Broadly, I4Ps refer to:

> the building of institutional capacities for peace-building, prevention of violent conflict and recovery from post-war violence... It is a dynamic network of interdependent structures, mechanisms, resources, values and skills which, through dialogue and consultation, contribute to conflict prevention and peace-building in a society. (Van Tongeren et al., 2012: 2)

These institutions, platforms and networks conventionally take the form of National Peace Committees (NPCs) operating at local, district, or provincial and national levels involving parties in conflict, governments, and civil society organizations (CSOs). The NPCs mediate local conflicts and facilitate constructive dialogue among disputants often using insider mediators and largely relying on customary/traditional alternative dispute resolution mechanisms. These mechanisms have worked well in most post-conflict situations, most notably in South Africa following its political transition of 1994 and Kenya following its post-election crisis of 2007–2008. Besides South Africa and Kenya, another country where I4P mechanisms have worked well is in Ghana (see Odendaal, 2012). Ghana has a strong National Peace Council established in 2011. It coordinates the work of peace councils established at local and district levels. All these mechanisms help mediate local conflicts before they spiral out of control into violent conflicts. Ghana's I4P mechanism has worked well in containing possible electoral violence following a tight election outcome of 2008 where the winning presidential candidates led the loser by less than 1% of the total votes cast. In order to ensure a peaceful contest during the election held in December 2012, seven political parties and independent presidential candidates signed the Kumasi Declaration on 27 November 2012 under the aegis of the National Peace Council. Indeed, the general election was conducted peacefully with disputes channelled through the judiciary system which finally upheld the election outcome in the latter part of 2013. Odendaal cautions that in designing NPCs, due regard has to be given to four main elements namely: (1) the nature of their mandate; (2) clarity of their roles and functions; (3) composition of their membership; and (4) their competence and technical expertise (Odendaal, 2012: 40).

# 6 Conclusion

In addressing electoral violence, a more holistic approach is required in order to deal with the deep-seated roots rather than mere symptoms of the problem. First and foremost, the structural roots of the problem have to be addressed head on through ensuring equitable distribution of national resources. Inequality, poverty, and unemployment remain the some of the major threats to democracy and peaceful elections in Africa today (witness the popular uprisings in North Africa). African countries should address electoral violence by adopting the electoral cycle approach, including addressing issues at the pre-voting stage (e.g. voter registration and demarcation of boundaries etc.), the voting stage (e.g. campaigning close to or inside voting stations, intimidation of voters etc.), and the post-voting stage (e.g. unnecessary delay in announcing results).

Credible, peaceful and transparent elections require strong, effective and independent Electoral Management Bodies (EMBs). The manner of appointment of commissioners must guarantee the independence of the EMB, and EMBs must function without any political influence from any of the contesting parties or any other authority. In addition, EMBs must enjoy financial autonomy, reporting to parliament and not to the Ministry of Finance or Justice. The electoral system design is also important in managing election-related conflicts. Evidence abounds suggesting that winner-take-all systems are highly conflict-prone. African countries, especially those emerging from protracted conflict, are encouraged to adopt systems that foster inclusive outcomes, simplicity, proportionality, and avoid winner-take-all outcomes.

African countries need to invest more in preventing electoral violence. This requires more resources aimed at early warning and preventive diplomacy. The current approach which is focused on conflict management is not sustainable as it is more of a fire brigade approach. Waiting for a fire to happen and then unleashing fire-fighters to contain the inferno is a counter-productive strategy in redressing electoral violence. Furthermore, maybe African states, in fact, need to transcend mere prevention. They need to embrace a more comprehensive approach in the form of conflict transformation (prevention, management, resolution, peace-making, peace-building, and sustainable human development).

# Bibliography

Afrobarometer Round 8 (2019–2021).

AU. (2007). *African Charter on Democracy, Elections and Governance*, Addis Ababa, Ethiopia.

Bayart, J. (1989). *The State in Africa: The Politics of the Belly*. Institut d'Etudes Politique.

Burchard, S. (2015). *Electoral Violence in Sub-Saharan Africa: Causes and Consequences*. Lynne Rienner Publishers.

Deng, F. (2008). *Identity, Diversity and Constitutionalism in Africa*. United States Institute of Peace Press.

Institute for Economics and Peace. (2022). *Measuring Peace in a Complex World, Global Peace Index*. Sydney: Australia.

International Peace Institute (IPI). (2010). Election-Related Disputes and Political Violence: Strengthening the Role of the African Union in Preventing, Managing and Resolving Conflict. *African Union Series* (pp. 63–74), July 2010.

Karl, T. (1986). Imposing Consent? Electoralism Versus Democratisation in El Salvador. In P. Drake & E. Silva (Eds.), *Elections and Democratisation in Latin America, 1980–1985*. Centre for Iberian and Latin American Studies.

Kovacs, M., & Bjarnesen, J. (Eds.). (2018). *Violence in African Elections: Between Democracy and Big Man Politics*. Zed Books.

Laakso, L. (2019). Electoral Violence and Political Competition in Africa. *Oxford Research Encyclopedias*. https://doi.org/10.1093/acrefore/9780190228637.013.1344

Lindberg, S. (2006). *Democracy and Elections in Africa*. Johns Hopkins University Press.

Matlosa, K. (2004). Electoral Systems, Constitutionalism and Conflict Management in Southern Africa. *African Journal on Conflict Resolution, 4*(2), 11–53.

Matlosa, K. (2021). Interplay Between Party Coalitions and Electoral Systems in Lesotho: Imperatives for Party Reforms. In H. Nyane & M. Kapa (Eds.), *Coalition Politics in Lesotho: A Multi-Disciplinary Study of Coalitions and Their Implications for Governance* (pp. 139–159). Sun Press.

Mhango, N. (2018). *How Africa Developed Europe: Deconstructing the History of Africa*. Langaa Research and Publishing.

Mozaafar, S., & Schedler, A. (2002). The Comparative Study of Electoral Governance—Introduction. *International Political Science Review, 23*(1), 5–27.

Nkrumah, K. (1965). *Neo-Colonialism: The Last Stage of Imperialism*. Panaf Books LTD.

Odendaal, A. (2012). The Political Legitimacy of National Peace Committees. *Journal of Peacebuilding and Development, 7*(3), 40–53.

Reynolds, A., Reilly, B., & Ellis, A. (Eds.). (2005). *Electoral System Design: The New International IDEA Handbook*. IDEA.

Rodney, W. (1982). *How Europe Underdeveloped Africa*. Howard University Press.

Schedler, A. (2002). Elections without Democracy: The Menu of Manipulation. *Journal of Democracy, 13*(2), 36–50.

Schedler, A. (2006). The Logic of Electoral Authoritarianism. In A. Schedler (Ed.), *Electoral Authoritarianism: The Dynamics of Unfree Competition* (pp. 1–26). Lynne Rienner Publishers.

UNDP. (2004). *Cultural Liberty in Today's Diverse World*. Oxford University Press.

United Nations Office on Drugs and Crime (UNIDOC). (2019). *Global Study on Homicide*, Vienna, Austria.

Van Tongeren, P., Ojielo, M., Brand-Jacobsen, McCandless, & Tschirgi, N. (2012). The Evolving Landscape of Infrastructures for Peace. *Journal of Peacebuilding and Development, 7*(3), 1–7.

World Population Review. (2019). https://worldpopulationreview.com. Accessed 8 March 2023.

# "Dirge to Slit Bodies": EndSARS, Police Brutality, and Nigerian Dystopia in Jumoke Verissimo and James Yéku's *Soro Soke: When Poetry Speaks Up*

### Ayokunmi Ojebode

> *"The man dies in all who keep silent in the face of tyranny" (The Man Died Soyinka, 1972).*

## 1 Introduction

Post-independent Nigeria is bedevilled by complex and multifarious socio-political and economic crises like corruption, political instability, inflation, infrastructural deficit, ethnic, religious and ritual killings, and abductions and ransom collection which threaten national amity and development. On the one hand, there is the Islamic terrorist group Boko-Haram in Northeast Nigeria that has been responsible for countless killings and abductions, notably, the kidnapping of over 276 female students in Chibok in Borno State on 14 April 2014 and 110 female students in the Dapchi in Yobe State on 19 February 2018 respectively, under the guise of revolting against Western education. Also, inter-ethnic/religious killing and land disputes, especially among the predominantly Christian farmers and Muslim herders in Middle-Belt (North Central) since 1999, and the biased distribution of public resources and marginalization of minority groups, particularly from

---

A. Ojebode (✉)
SOAS University of London, London, UK
e-mail: ao38@soas.ac.uk

the oil-producing Niger Delta states, that have led to social unrest and continuous kidnappings and ransom-collection in the region.

On the other hand, police brutality in Nigeria, which has skyrocketed into a national crisis and menace, vividly expresses the theme of violence in the urban space underscored in protest literature or literary activism in Nigeria. Notably, Human Rights Watch estimated that police have shot and murdered over 10,000 individuals in Nigeria since January 2000 to date, which equals more than 1,700 victims annually (Ewang, 2019). Subsequently, Nigerian police officers are dreaded as "invincible" and as "bullies" who abuse, maim, rape, torture, and kill citizens with impunity. As a result, many Nigerians cringe in fear and succumb to bribery at police checkpoints to escape sheer dehumanization and incivilities from the police officers who act as being above the law and dangerously wielding the instrument of death—guns. However, police brutality in Nigeria has not gone unchallenged, with different public indictments and protests against the agency since 2010. Perhaps, the most prominent of such is the nationwide #EndSARS demonstration of the public outrage and pent-up frustration of Nigerians with despicable police killings, but which was eclipsed by the Lekki Massacre on 10 October 2020.

Following George Floyd's death and the aftermath of public protest in the United States on 25 May 2020, Nigerian youth exploited social media in different Nigerian states, especially Lagos and the diaspora, to demonstrate public outrage against the Nigerian Police Force's Special Anti-Robbery Squad (SARS)'s horrendous brutalities. The protest gained online recognition in 2017 when recordings of violent torture and killings by SARS police operatives were widely circulated on Twitter handles. However, the later digitally motivated #EndSARS protest was relaunched and sparked public outrage on 3 October, 2020, when a recorded clip of SARS officials' violation of a young Nigerian was circulated and became trending news on Twitter (Akinwotu, 2020). Within a week, #EndSARS generated over 2.4 million tweets and was the topmost hashtag on the microblogging app in different countries (Get Africa, 2020).

The #EndSARS was hosted alongside other hashtags, especially the more popular #Sòròsókè (Yoruba for "speak up"), a creative outlet for social commentaries on the Nigerian police, government, and ominous massacre of protesters at Lekki, Lagos State, later in October 2020. Previous victims of police brutality (predominantly upset and irritated Nigerian youth) triggered the protest. Initially, the Nigerian government undercut several public calls to dissolve SARS, which had started in 2017. Thus, the youth successfully harnessed digital media to voice their complaints, with the special aim of influencing the public narrative that the Nigerian police were "unfriendly" (Yeku, 2020). The two factors identified as fostering the prolonged #EndSARS in Nigeria were first, the coincidental COVID-19 pandemic, which saw many Nigerians struggle for survival against the depressive socio-economic experiences of the era like mass unemployment and languor. Second, the highly organized and strategic protest was widely circulated by youth who were in lockdown during the pandemic and who had ample time to generate mass movement through social media (Akinyetun, 2021).

In the meantime, underlying the #EndSARS protest was the recurrent theme of violence adapted into different forms, genres, and plots in Nigerian literature. Most importantly, poetry is a weapon of resistance against oppression. It is worthy of note that in the post-independent era, Nigerian political and literary activists from Fela Anikupo Kuti to Ken Saro-Wiwa and Wole Soyinka have fronted as avant-gardes of change, deploying literary tropes to contest post/neo-colonial structures and issues like the banditry, election rigging, erratic power supply, environmental degradation, ethnic rivalry, marginalization of ethnic minorities, military dictatorship, terrorism, resource exploitation, and violence. Popular Nigerian activists deploy different forms of art, especially poetry, to raise political consciousness and provoke social consciousness to foster national amity and co-existence through resolution (Aito, 2014).

In consonance with its classic functions, Aristotle's *Poetics* conceptualizes poetry as an imitation of life and human experience in mimetic and pragmatic contexts. Furthermore, Plato in *The Republic* advances the pragmatics of poetry as a mode and fashion of appeal to the imagination (Abrams, 1984). Although in Nigerian literature poetry's mimetic and expressive function is not as concretized as its pragmatic significance within the society, the genre is a tested product of conflict, political manipulations and realities that afford the poet self-expression, self-fulfilment, and maximum self-realization under poetic licence (Aito, 2014). Thus, modern Nigerian poets perceive their art as a means of upholding society and its tenets and this is achieved by drawing occasionally from oral reservoirs for social commentary and didactics. As it will be discovered in this chapter, beyond literary expressiveness, poetry is a creative asset for social therapy and documentary to protest and expose political oppression and social vices.

Prophetically, Christopher Okigbo's "Elegy for Slit-Drum" envisions a chaotic future for Nigeria due to murky corruption and political instability. The poet portrays political elites as "robbers," flaunting ill-gotten wealth and power. He draws a parallel between postcolonial Nigeria and the internecine conflict in the animal kingdom within the context of power, chaos, and betrayal. The poem, inspired by the Nigerian/Biafra civil war (from 6 July 1967 to 15 January 1970), adopts a predominant imagery of a traditional percussion instrument—a slit drum beaten to a lament. The portrait of the "slit/torn" drum is an ominous reality foreshadowing tragedy, though substituted in this study as the covert massacre/shot bodies of Nigerian youth by the Nigerian military during the #EndSARS protest in Lekki, Lagos State in October 2020. Against this backdrop, this chapter, therefore, explores Jumoke Verissimo and James Yéku's (2020) *Soro Soke: When Poetry Speaks Up*, a poetry volume by budding Nigerian poets, for imageries of violence and the underlined public encounters of police brutalities, underpinned by youth's revolutionary creative impulses.

In this chapter, the study adopts a historical approach, exploiting the selected experimental poetry as protest literature for empirical evidence of police brutalities in Nigeria plotted as prologue, climax, and epilogue to convey complex, contextual and mnemonic dimensions to the Lekki Massacre on 20 October 2020. Consequently, the study provides a chronological account of the SARS debacle in Nigeria before the #EndSARS protest synthesized creative works and eyewitness accounts to underscore the theme of violence.

## 2 #EndSARS: Police Brutality, Reforms, and Disbandment of SARS

The Special Anti-Robbery Squad (SARS), disbanded in October 2020, was an investigative arm of the Nigerian Police Force instituted by former police commissioner Simeon Danladi Midenda in 1992 to contain the upsurge of robbery, motor vehicle theft, kidnapping, cattle rustling, and firearms cases in South Nigeria. Initially, the special police unit was part of the Force Criminal Investigation and Intelligence Department (FCIID), under the auspices of the then deputy inspector general of police, Anthony Ogbizi. However, Colonel Ezra Dindam Rimdan (Nigerian Army)'s murder by some unknown policemen at a checkpoint in Lagos on September 1992, motivated the creation of SARS. The Nigerian military, who felt insulted and infuriated by a senior officer's death, led a swift strike against the police force which inadvertently resulted in massive crime rates because there was no one to man inter-state security posts (United States Department of State, 1994).

Thus, SARS substituted for the police force as a rescue operation and due to their grand achievement, the Nigerian government extended their scope to suburbs of the country to arrest and prosecute armed robbers, murderers, kidnappers, and violent criminals. However, after a dialogue lasting for two weeks, the Nigerian Army and the Nigerian Police Force reached an agreement and official police roles were reinstated in Lagos (Olagunju, 2020). Based on its mode of operation, SARS operated covertly, and officers were authorized by law to wear mufti and did not necessarily have to carry guns or walkie-talkies in public. Also, they frequently used unlicensed vehicles with or without personal/plate numbers during missions (Nnadozie, 2017).

In the meantime, from 2016 to 2020, SARS was indicted for extrajudicial execution, organ harvesting, torture, rape, physical assault, harassment, extortion, excessive use of force, abduction, unlawful arrest, illegal detention, illegal disposal of corpses into water bodies, and different human rights abuses. Nevertheless, allegations and requests for reform and disbandment from the public were to no avail. For instance, in mid-1996, the SARS Lagos branch detained at their workplace two security guards who were alleged to have committed a robbery. In January 1997, the corpses of the guards were later discovered at a morgue without any trace of their killers (Bureau of Democracy, 1997).

Furthermore, in October 2005, a SARS agent murdered a commercial bus driver in Obiaruku, Delta State, for refusing to offer a bribe. The officer was later sacked, detained, and charged with murder (Bureau of Democracy, 2005). Subsequently, by 2009, the special police unit had grown rapidly with outfits across interstates, and they were effective in curtailing and infiltrating the widespread cases of internet scams and occult fraternal activities in many Nigerian public universities. However, in the process, they also detained vulnerable suspects and citizens, especially Nigerian youths with extravagant cars, phones, dreadlocks, piercings, and seductive attire (Alake, 2019).

In May 2010, Amnesty International publicly announced their decision to sue the Nigerian Police over human rights violations, especially those perpetrated by some SARS officers in Borokiri, Port Harcourt, who apprehended and jailed three cyclists for more than a week while subjecting them to corporal punishment and torture with a metallic belt and gun butt (PM News, 2010). On 20 May 2010, a Federal High Court in Enugu State decreed that a former inspector general of police, Ogbonna Okechukwu Onovo should disclose the unidentified SARS agent who murdered a 15-year-old secondary school student, erroneously taken for an abductor, in the state (Nzomiwu, 2010). On 27 July 2010, Sahara Reporters released an editorial condemning SARS and other police outfits for making a lumpsum of ₦9.35 billion ($60 million) from daily roadblocks and extortion in 18 months (Sahara Reporters, 2010).

On 10 August 2019, SARS officers accidentally killed an expectant mother with a stray bullet in a counter-raid against kidnappers in Ijegun, Lagos State. Consequently, the incident provoked the residents who lynched two officers as an expression of "jungle justice" (Sahara Reporters, 2020). On 21 August 2019, four SARS officers were apprehended and charged with murder after they were secretly filmed manhandling and murdering two suspected phone shoplifters, already apprehended, in daylight (Folarin, 2019). On 5 September 2019, SARS officers in Lekki, Lagos, supposedly abducted, tortured, and stole money from Nigerian rapper Ikechukwu Onunaku by compelling him to make different ATM withdrawals (Odeyinde, 2019).

Previous scholarship on police brutality and violence in Nigeria which characterized the #EndSARS protest identified some underlyng factors that are worth considering but did not proffer a lasting solution to curtailing the menace. Scholars like George (2020) noted that first, meagre salaries and resources for law enforcement agencies in Nigeria have been contributory factors for its poor quality and low standards in police training. Thus, SARS/police operatives exploit their uniforms and firearms to extort what society "owes them." Ironically, the Nigerian Police Force cannot transact the supposed "credits" without bringing into question issues of corruption, bribery, rape, and extrajudicial killings. Second, scholars note the intra-class nature of police brutality as recruits are drafted from the lower class to intimidate fellow class types like motorists, students, artisans, and hawkers who lack the economic or political clout to demand redress (Buyse, 2018). Many Nigerian politicians or ruling elites often outsource their security to various paramilitary units and the state, hence, the increase in the personal entourage and bodyguards of the upper middle class.

Alternatively, it has been discovered that Nigerian police employ corporal punishment and barbaric torture as legal techniques to force "confessions" out of detainees. Historically, SARS has thrived on the violation of human rights while curbing crimes and criminalities in Nigeria for successful outcomes (Richard & Abolaji, 2018). Most importantly, since most public institutions and agencies in Nigeria, including the police, survive on successive regimes, regime security or survival is often mistaken for national security. Therefore, in an attempt to protect the regime and its interests, the police and military forces often deploy excessive and ruthless force to suppress citizens, especially during protests (Afeno, 2014). While the coercive modality includes the military, police, and prisons, the ideological apparatus includes the courts and the legislature. The coercive and ideological apparatuses of the state largely employ, respectively, violent and non-violent social orders to protect the ruling elites and promote their subjugation of the masses (Iwuoha, 2020).

The neo-colonial infrastructural dimension of violence in Nigeria was evident in the post-EndSARS event as Nigeria's media, legislative, and judicial systems, military and prison authorities, and Central Bank (CBN) connived to engage inhumane and punitive financial measures against demonstrators, freezing their bank accounts without prior notice or legal injunction. However, Reuben Abati (2020) argues that the incidence of police brutality in Africa is a consequence of political instability and failed leadership instead of a supposed colonial legacy. The next section provides a historical background of public protests against police brutality in Nigeria and its climax in the #EndSARS negotiating empirical and documentary evidence from creative and media sources, especially Jumoke Verissimo and James Yéku's (2020) *Soro Soke: When Poetry Speaks Up*.

## 3 The 2017 EndSARS Campaign—Prologue

In December 2017, Segun Awosanya fronted a social media campaign to mount pressure on the federal government of Nigeria to dissolve SARS due to incessant cases of brutality in Nigeria. He kickstarted the hashtag campaign #EndSARS using the Twitter handle @Letter_to_jack which triggered other Nigerian members of the public to start sharing personal experiences of SARS brutality (Salaudeen, 2017). By mid-December, the campaign had become intense but with a pocket street demonstration by protesters in Abuja which was short lived due to accusatory and trifling remarks from the government and police authorities (Bella, 2017). However, on 14 August 2018, the acting president of Nigeria, Yemi Osinbajo, declared a complete "overhaul" of SARS after being informed of horrific cases of human rights violations. In carrying out the acting president's directive, the inspector general of police (IGP) Ibrahim Kpotun Idris rechristened the unit "Federal Special Anti-Robbery Squad" (Sahara Reporters, 2018). On 21 January 2019, acting IGP Mohammed Adamu who succeeded Ibrahim Kpotun Idris attempted a drastic reform to decentralize SARS in Nigeria. The Nigerian police headquarters was originally situated in Abuja. The acting IGP confirmed thereafter that respective deputy inspector-generals (DIGs) of the Force Criminal Investigations Department (FCIID) and commissioners of police (CP) across the 36 Nigerian states would be held responsible for SARS' unruliness and indiscriminate killings in their states (PusleNG, 2019).

## 4 The 2020 EndSARS Campaign and the Lekki Massacre—Climax

In October 2020, the Nigerian public mounted more pressure on the government to dissolve SARS, especially after the case of the police murder of a Nigerian youth at the Wetland Hotel in Ughelli, Delta State. The recorded clip which went viral online elicited public outrage after just a few days (Omilana, 2020). The protests grew rapidly from social media advocacy to prevalent street demonstrations supported by prominent Nigerian Twitter figures Rinu Oduala, Femi Fani-Kayode, Kelvin Odanz, and Dr Dipo Awojide who rallied to broadcast the advocacy for the dissolution of SARS to a wider audience. In the meantime, non-violent #EndSARS demonstrators in the capital city of Abuja were maimed, assaulted, and intimidated by the federal police force, but they defied the violence by marching to the Police Force Headquarters. Several news agencies, including BBC Africa and Al-Jazeera, televised federal police using tear gas, live ammunition and water cannons on the protesters.

On 9 October 2020, in Ogbomoso, Oyo State, a protester, Jimoh Isiaq, was murdered by SARS officers while participating in the #EndSARS demonstrations. His "martyrdom" aggravated national outrage taken as an archetype for protesters who utilized Twitter hashtags like #EndPoliceBrutality and #RememberJimoh. On 10 October 2020, an outraged mob attacked a police station in Ijebu-Ode, Ogun State, over Isiaq's death and the deaths of other victims. Likewise, in Lagos, some demonstrators trooped to the Lagos State House of Assembly to petition for SARS' dissolution. The next day, Lagos legislators permitted protesters to join in an emergency session to monitor their proceedings as they voted to dissolve SARS, which passed to Nigeria's House of Assembly (Akinyetun, 2021).

On 11 October 2020, Inspector-General of Police Mohammed Adamu broadcast the dissolution of SARS with the promise of a rebranded police squad soonest. The IGP recommended Special Weapons and Tactics (SWAT) as a substitute for the defunct Special Anti-Robbery Squad (SARS) (The Guardian, 2020). The public protested the hurried decision on Twitter with different hashtags #EndSWAT and #SARSMUSTEND with suspicions that the police reform would maintain the status quo despite the promise of high-level training for SWAT officers. In southern Nigeria, the Rivers State government illegally barred demonstrations in the oil-rich state, decreeing that police should apprehend defiant citizens. However, on 13 October 2020, EndSARS demonstrators defied the decree as they trooped to the governor's state house (Ekoh & George, 2021).

From Abeokuta, Ogun State to Benin City, Edo State and Kaduna, Kaduna State and other states in Nigeria and the diaspora, especially in the United States and the United Kingdom, demonstrators, predominantly youths, trudged in solidarity against the prevalent police brutality and advocated the dissolution of SARS. The renowned Twitter activist Aisha Yesufu accused the police of maltreating and ramming her vehicle while hunting demonstrators in Abuja. On 16 October 2020, the then Twitter CEO, Jack Dorsey rebranded the #ENDSARS emoji on Twitter with the national colours of the Nigerian flag as a show of solidarity for the Nigerian masses. Subsequently, Vice President Yemi Osinbajo responded swiftly in a series of Twitter posts to reassure Nigerians of the setting up of judicial panels comprising governors and ministers to mete out justice to perpetrators of police brutality (Durosomo, 2018). On 18 October 2020, the Nigerian Army launched a supposed yearly training event, "Operation Crocodile Smile VI", to contain cyberattacks by identifying, tracking, and countering "false news" on social media platforms in Nigeria. The programme was aimed at repossessing firearms employed for violence during the nationwide protests allegedly infiltrated by street urchins and hoodlums (Akinkugbe, 2020).

The focal point of the EndSARS protests was the Lekki Massacre on 20 October 2020 around 6:50 pm, as the Nigerian Armed Forces covertly and horrendously murdered demonstrators at the Lekki Toll Gate in Lagos. The fact of the event is disputed, with the dead numbered as 15, 25, or more, based on eyewitnesses' and Amnesty International's evidence, while the Nigerian government continues to refute the number (Jones et al., 2020). The advocacy group claimed that a message was broadcast on social media platforms that demonstrators would not be assaulted as long as they kept calm on the ground, singing the Nigerian anthem and waving flags intermittently. Though the protests were mainly decentralized, demonstrators had large WhatsApp groups, funds, food, and medical supplies, and medical and legal backing. Amnesty International claimed that before the shootout, CCTV cameras were allegedly disconnected from the toll gate. However, the Lagos State Government countered that they were laser cameras, against popular narratives (Nnadozie, 2017). Also, there was a power outage, denying the protesters radiance from advert billboards managed by Loatsad Media (Olukoya & Oyekanmi, 2020). Evidence from the footage indicated that about 20 armed military officers stormed into the singing crowd (Jones et al., 2020).

On 24 November, CNN aired a six-minute documentary, including CCTV footage from government surveillance cameras to expose the military's covert shooting at the crowd from opposite sides of the toll gate. As a complement to CNN, the footage evidence presented by the Lekki Concession Company to the Lagos judiciary panel suggested that the CCTV was stopped at around 8 pm in an attempt to protect the military and other perpetrators who were involved in the carnage (Egbe, 2020). The Nigerian government has refused to take responsibility for the Lekki killings as they argue through different counter-evidence that the news was "false" (Olokor, 2020). Nonetheless, the popular Nigerian DJ Switch live-streamed the Lekki shooting from the start to the end from her Instagram account. The recording revealed a wounded male protester with a bullet in his leg which was wrapped with a Nigerian flag to reduce bleeding (Elusoji, 2020).

On 23 October 2020, she confirmed the presence of the Nigerian military, police force, and the disbanded SARS operatives who shot singing #EndSARS protesters at the Lekki toll gate on the night of 20 October 2020, with the death toll rising from seven to fifteen and several injured. DJ Switch confirmed that during the sporadic shooting, she and other survivors took the dead to the soldiers who carted them away. Incidentally, the *People's Gazette*, a Nigerian newspaper, confirmed that the military liaised with the police force to help them bury nine dead bodies, which the latter rejected (People's Gazette, 2020). Nonetheless, the DJ regretted that she could not complete the livestream due to a flat phone battery. At the time of writing, she had relocated to Canada due to continued threats to her life (Elusoji, 2020).

On 18 November, CNN in partnership with the Balkan Investigative Reporting Network, clarified that they had discovered several bullet casings from the Lekki Toll Gate which have been traced to Serbia from where the Nigerian military had imported bullets from 2005 to 2016. Initially, the Nigerian Army had blatantly denied any involvement in the Lekki killings, maintaining that its officers were "professional in their conduct" and did not breach rules of engagement (Sahara Reporters, 2020). Nigeria's Minister of Information at the time, Lai Mohammed, accused CNN of "irresponsible journalism" and tagged their documentary as a product of false news and misinformation (Nwosu, 2020). Meanwhile, the *Wall Street Journal*, an investigative US-based news outlet, publicized their analysis of different clips from social media which revealed a massacre at Lekki (Parkinson, 2020).

## 5 The 2020 EndSARS Campaign and the Lekki Massacre—Epilogue

On 22 October 2020, Nigerian President Muhammadu Buhari announced the disbandment of SARS and also indicted some former officers for perpetrating "acts of excessive force" like hanging, mock execution, beating, punching and kicking, burning with cigarettes, waterboarding, near-asphyxiation with plastic bags, and forced sexual violence on detainees during the unit's active operations (Ewodage, 2020). Thus, he informed the Nigerian public about the prosecution of the operatives (Olubajo, 2021). Likewise, on 26 October 2020, the Lagos State government set up a Judicial Panel of Inquiry to probe the events of the EndSARS protests and to identify the armed perpetrators who shot protesters while arranging commensurate compensation for the victims (Mbah, 2020). The eight-member panel comprised the chair, Doris Okuwobi, a retired justice, retired Deputy Inspector General of Police Fredrick Taiwo Lakanu, a lawyer, Mr Ebun-Olu Adegboruwa SAN and Ms Patience Patrick Udoh, both popular Lagos-based lawyers who represented civil society. Segun Awosanya (Segalink), a foremost EndSARS advocate, was drafted to the panel as a human rights activists' representative while Mr. Lucas Koyejo represented the National Human Rights Commission, and Mrs. Toyin Odunsanya, later a Judge of the High Court of Lagos, was appointed by the Lagos State Government from the Directorate of Citizens Right, the Lagos State Ministry of Justice Rinu Oduala, and Majekodunmi Temitope for the Nigerian youths (Akinsanmi, 2021).

The forensic analysis conducted by the panel through Sentinel Forensics based on evidence from military interrogations, bullet shells, and CCTV footage at the Lekki Toll Gate revealed that cold-blooded disbanded SARS operatives, police, and military officers engaged nonstop firing at harmless protesters even when they were scampering for refuge. The report submitted by the panel revealed nine dead protesters at the scene (Olubajo, 2021). During the panel's investigation, they were delayed for more than 30 minutes at a nearby military hospital, supposedly the dump site for dead victims but when access was eventually granted, it was discovered the building was unoccupied and under renovation (Sahara Reporters, 2020).

On 30 November 2020, the Nigerian Army eventually caved in to prevalent allegations of killings at Lekki, explaining that its officers had live ammunition and opened fire on demonstrators. Brigadier Ahmed Taiwo, Chief of Army Staff and the General Commander of the (GOC) 81 Division, while giving testimony to the Judicial Panel, shifted the blame and claimed that the military was invited by the governor of Lagos State, Babajide Sanwo-Olu, on a false call of being "overrun" by protesters (Ewodage, 2020). Just a few hours after the massacre, the Lagos State Governor visited the injured victims in hospitals in Lagos and released a statement on Twitter linking the horrific event to "forces beyond our direct control" (Sanwo-Olu, 2020). Paradoxically, on 21 October 2020, the governor who originally rebuffed allegations of deaths during the shooting eventually admitted to a CNN journalist that "only two persons were killed" (Adediran, 2020). The event of the EndSARS is complicated and seemed a systemic violence act as the Nigerian authorities through the minister of information and culture, Lai Mohammed, feloniously snubbed media evidence at Lekki as "the triumph of fake news and the intimidation of a silent majority by a vociferous lynch mob" (Nimi, 2021).

Given the above, the turbulent political climate in Nigeria has always been a source of poetic inspiration and imagination as Nigerian poets craft different forms and idioms to designate the genre's uniqueness and their redefined identity, role, and social status (Okunnoye, 2009). Three political events that influenced Nigerian poetry are the post-independent era in the 1960s, the Nigerian civil war (1967–1970), and military rule (1966–1979 and 1983–1999), out of which the military era has been the most insidious and devastating to national development. Nevertheless, Helon Habila (2007: 55) attests that:

> [I]n a way, the dictatorship was good for literature because it supplied some of us with our subject matter, and also while it lasted, gave us an education in politics that we couldn't have acquired in school or anywhere else. We saw pro-democracy activists being killed or arrested or exiled—unfortunate for the victims but great stuff for writing.

Likewise, Jumoke Verissimo and James Yéku's *Soro Soke: When Poetry Speaks Up* is a vantage point from which to explore police brutality as a macro aspect of complex socio-political schisms between the state and society, social and civil actors, and legal sectors. This study will reveal that violence is a dominant phenomenon and psyche in Nigeria, especially to underpin the police and military's involvement in the Lekki massacre on 20 October 2020. Although at the face level, #EndSARS was about terminating the reign of terror in Nigeria typified by the heavily-armed elite police squad and law enforcement agents, however, on a deeper level, it was a proximate and collective release of pent-up anger at an ailing system which required a quick recharge. Thus, the study's adoption of Christopher Okigbo's poetic sensibility in "Elegy for Slit-Drum" to foreground the ominous covert massacre/

"slit" bodies of Nigerian youth shot by the Nigerian military which re-echoes the prevailing themes of violence, resistance, and the irremediable state of police brutality in Nigeria.

## 6 #EndSARS: Police Brutality and Protest Voices in Jumoke Verissimo and James Yéku's *Soro Soke: When Poetry Speaks Up*

Stephen Kekeghe's documentary account in "They Hauled Him Away" reveals the poet's eye-witness account of one of the several cases of the brutality of the SARS. The poet's use of the first-person pronoun "I" validates his account of an unidentified persona, who was forcefully ejected from his car to withdraw from his bank account via a point of sale (POS) before being shot. The poet's satirical/paradoxical description of the Nigerian SARS as "those in Khaki of blood" attests to the Nigerian masses' flawed perception of the military/police force tagged by the poet as exploiters and harbingers of death instead of being protectors. The poet reveals that the innocent citizen was victimized for merely "his elegance and the sanguine stare that stood in his eyes." The manic nature of the "above-the-law" assailants who kill with impunity undermining the value of human lives validates Kekeghe's previous description of SARS agents as cold-blooded murderers who dragged a victim to an undisclosed site at the "end of the road" in the "blistering" sun and shot him "as his blood glistened on the tars" in broad daylight.

Like Kekeghe's eye-witness style, Obehi Aigiomawu also deploys a first-person pronoun "I" in "Violence" as a general appraisal of recurrent violence in Nigerian society. There is a solid emphasis on the nouns "Men," "Time" and "Violence," with the latter two repeated twice. Of course, "Men" based on its usage refers to both the ruling elites and police force, but much more the latter, who consistently perpetuate and allow themselves to be possessed by the spirit of "Violence" personalized by the poet as having the ability to choose or take hold of them (SARS police) as its medium. The underlined notion of the act of mediumship and spirit-possession or "obsession" in the case of police brutality is popular in most African cultures. On the other hand, Jumoke Verissimo's "Nigeria Will Not End Me" adopted "We," the first-person plural pronoun, to highlight the collective Nigerian masses' serious concern about the ominous killings of young Nigerians, especially Okechukwu Obi-Enadhuze, a fresh computer science graduate from the Federal University of Agriculture, Abeokuta (FUNAAB), Ogun State.

The poet's adapted title was from Okechukwu Obi-Enadhuze's final tweet before his gruesome death after a stabbing by a group of hoodlums who attacked his home in Mafoluku, Oshodi area of Lagos State on 21 October 2020. The poem's first line reveals the poet's bewilderment about Nigerians' inattention to the land's (society) mystical craving for "only young blood." The poet's deployment of personification intensifies the gustatory imagery of death and the utter disregard for human lives in Nigeria. Furthermore, in the second line, the poet balances the underlined African theme of ritual sacrifice with a biblical allusion to sacrificial giving in Luke 11:13 altered to foreground the indiscriminate injustice and murders of Nigerian youth in their Fatherland. Paradoxically, the poet contrasts the heavenly Father's benevolence and Mother Nigeria's inhumane disposition to her vibrant citizens.

In the second line, the poet begins to employ the paradoxical statements; "We ask for bread; it gives us stone; we ask to live; it takes our breath/We stand up tall; it cuts our legs; we sit wearily; it shoots us down." The latter statement is subtle kinaesthetic imagery; "stand up tall" and "sit wearily" complementing "cut" and "shoot" subtly alludes to the historic yet traumatic Lekki killings during the EndSARS protest in Lagos, Nigeria on 20 October 2020. Subsequently, the Nigerian military hounded and murdered innocent young protesters who had assembled at the Lekki Toll Gate to vocalize their outrage at the incessant cases of police brutality across the country. The #EndSARS movement led by Nigerian youth received huge support nationwide and in the diaspora, physically and virtually, as a national protest against the horrendous abuse, killing and repression of the Nigerian masses by their Mobile Police Force motivated by George Floyd's death in the United States on 25 May 2020. The online protest, which started with the hashtag #EndSARS, motivated other hashtags, especially the #Sòròsókè which fostered a creative outlet for social commentaries and literary activism on the Nigerian police, government, and the subsequent barbaric massacre and aftermath covert operation on dead protesters at Lekki, Lagos State.

Like other poets in the collection, Jumoke Verrisimo's dominant "gun" symbol has an equivalence in Ibiene Bidiaque's "Bullets" and Ndubuisi Martins' "Wreck & Wreath for Lekki" which give horrific yet satirical portrayals of the episodic event. Bidiaque's deployment of enjambment reflects the poet's intense passion and anger as he lumps the cascades of events from the moment when the Nigerian military men arrived at the Lekki Toll Gate where "unarmed" protesters were seated and "singing flag-waving" until the "blood-thirsty soldiers" arrived in the dead of the night to dislodge by shooting into the "wearily sitting" crowd. The poet expresses his sheer disgust for the incumbent Nigerian President Muhammadu Buhari (a retired Nigerian Army major-general and military head of state from 31 December 1983 to 27 August 1985, following the coup d'état in 1983 to topple Alhaji Shehu Shagari's Second Republic) and suggests that he probably authorized the shootout.

The poet deploys alliterative adjectives, "callousness," "disdain," and "dictatorship," to lampoon the Nigerian commander-in-chief who perhaps endorsed his soldiers to use "guns cocked" ironically to "battle" the "singing" civilians. Ndubuisi Martins extends Bidiaque's purview by adding specific details about the Lekki shootout; he emphasizes that the fateful event occurred at the Lekkigate, the 'placid gate, scene of horror' on 20 October 2020 at around 7.45 pm with graphic stained flags resulting from the bloody spray bullets from the Nigerian military "zombies" in a covert operation in thick darkness and ensuing silence. The poet deployed visual colour imagery "stained green, white and then red" to depict the gory scene of stained Nigerian flags, typically green, white, green, indicating the pitiful dystopia in the country.

Interestingly, both Verissimo and Martin corroborated that the protesters were in "sitting" and "kneeling" postures before the abrupt shooting spray. Nevertheless, Bidiaque and Martins emphasized the following day's treacherous and double-faced tactics of the federal and state authorities with the combined efforts of the judiciary, legislative, and media arms to falsify and wipe evidence of the genocidal slaughter at the Lekki Toll Gate with "CCTV off," "trail of blood, mopped for the morning," and recurrent hypocritical "tribunals" to crush the "threatening" EndSARS movement and edit the public narratives into a mere "fiction." Indeed, Bidiaque in "Bullets" adds that the Nigerian government tried to tactfully deceive the public into believing that there were no "dead bodies and that aliens" not the Nigerian military were responsible for the shooting.

Uchechukwu Peter Umezurike's "Who is Counting?" contended the fake Nigerian in his stylishly confidential and sealed-like poem as he exposed that at least 65 individuals were killed in the shootout. The poet's apprehension was for Muhammadu Buhari, the supposed Nigerian president or "dictator" who "ordered the kill," yet, he could not have been "sipping tea or watching *The Dictator*?" Yet, Yusuf Balogun Gemini's "This Country Still Cracks Us" is an artistic compilation of unrewarded named heroes—Nigerian activists and martyrs who had vocalized and others who were sacrificed by the pitiless SARS police. The list memorializes Jimoh Isiaka, Ayomide Taiwo, Peter Ofurum, Ifeoma Abugu, Victor Maduamagu and Daniel Adewuyi, mainly vibrant Nigerian youths killed without befitting "royal coffins" and "a month-long holiday."

Likewise, in Kola Tubosun's "Blood-Spangled Banner," the poet draws a historical correlation between the covert killing during the EndSARS Lekki Toll Gate and the Ezu River to emphasize the state of anomy and dystopia of Nigeria. In the first two lines of the poem, "In the Ezu River of bones and blood/The bodies sing with the reddened mud," the poet deploys a metaphor and simile to uncover the shocking trajectory of inhumane and vicious cases of homicide perpetrated by the Special Anti-Robbery Squad of the Anambra State Police Command in the dumping of about 35 corpses into the Ezu River, Amansea in the state since 19 January 2013. In the report "The Untold Story Of Ezu River Police SARS Killings," the International Society for Civil Liberties and the Rule of Law in Awka, Anambra State, indicted the police force for the floating dead bodies discovered on Ezu River, on the boundary between Anambra and Enugu States.

The INTERSOCIETY uncovered the alarming homicide cases and revealed the continual torture and killings at Anambra Police SARS headquarters at Awkuzu and its annexes or unit locations in the State (Okafor, 2017). Thus, Tubosun reiterates a dirge similar to Ndubuisi Martins' "Wreck & Wreath for Lekki." The former poet laments the hopelessness of a failed Nigerian state and the unpardonable blood of killed youths that taint its national sanctity "the white of a flag, the bleeding soul."

The poet duplicates the shocking death by stabbing of the 21-year-old Nigerian graduate as hinted in Jumoke Verissimo's "Nigeria Will Not End Me," to underscore the horrid "Ghosts of the nation's past haunting," premised on the recent Lekki killing during the EndSARS protest. Thus, the Yoruba proverb summarizes the horrific event: "The dead that was concealed has their legs exposed." Tubosun is heartbroken and feels repulsed at the despicable covert killing of protesters by the Nigerian military ("marauders") who hurriedly "mask the proof" of "casings of their killing rounds" as they add yet more to the sickening death toll and violent bloodsheds in Nigeria qualified by the poet as a "butcher's slab." The premature termination of the EndSARS revolution and its aftermath political schemes and Nigerian president Muhammadu Buhari's unresponsiveness contributed to the spates of violence in Nigeria.

Thus, James Yeku indicts the former Nigerian military head of state as a culprit in the violent killings given his subtle dictatorial and nepotistic tendencies reminiscent of the Russian monarchs "'tsars' or 'czars'". The poet is vexed that despite the "tales of griefs" which pour from "screens and smartphones," Buhari or "Bubu," a satirical pseudonym/nickname for the former

Nigerian president who remained docile and insensitive to the violence in the country. The poet suggests that the president's muteness is beyond contributory, yet conspiratorial. Perhaps, the tribalistic leader was unnerved by the death toll at Lekki because the victims were not "the cattle of Daura." Daura is the Nigerian president's hometown and is located in Katsina State, North Nigeria, predominantly inhabited by the native Fulanis, mainly herders and nomads who highly prioritize their grazing cattle and pastures. The public trust in the Nigerian president declined drastically after his assumption into office on 29 May 2015, given the perceived failed administration, ineptitude, and docility during critical moments like the EndSARS protests. Muhammadu Buhari campaigned under the auspices of the All People's Congress (APC) with false propaganda of "change" and "restructuring" but failed to tackle Nigeria's myriad challenges. On the one hand, Buhari is unapologetic about his religious-tribalistic ideals and incompetence motivating national concerns that Northern Fulanis were prioritized over other Nigerian ethnic groups. On the other hand, the #EndSARS is an allegory of Nigerian politicians' or ruling elites' ambitious and materialistic traits "typical" African maladies like the corruptible power lust and a facile resort to force during public protests. Thus, the above premises consolidate Abati's (2020) postulation that police brutality in Nigeria/Africa is a consequence of political instability and failed leadership instead of a supposed colonial legacy.

## 7 Conclusion

The study reveals that socio-political issues in post-independent Nigeria have been a primary preoccupation of writers, particularly poets who act as "towncriers" and as the conscience of society like the late Ken Saro-Wiwa, who was hung by a former head of state General Sani Abacha for advocating and writing against the oppressive structures in the oily Niger-Delta region in 1996. Furthermore, drawing from Christopher Okigbo's poetic sensibility in "Elegy for Slit-Drum," the poet seems to underscore a salient history of an ominous crisis and national dystopia which blends with the irremediable police brutality in Nigeria. Thus, poetry is not only for archiving but a prophetic foresight into an impending conflict. Therefore, Jumoke Verissimo and James Yéku's poetic volume served as a creative asset for social therapy and documentary to protest and expose political oppression and schemes and social vices. The selected poems blend emotive and cognitive, creative, and realistic portraits of Nigerian youths' visionary and unyielding quest for social reformation and justice in Nigeria. The antecedents of the October 2020

#EndSARS protest suggest first, that there is a mistrust between the government and protesters, and second, that the protest is far-reaching than police brutality. The clampdown on the #EndSARS protesters implicated both the Nigerian state and its police force in the sheer brutality as security forces became an instrument of private and sectional interests undermining civil rights protection.

## Bibliography

Abati, R. (2020, November 4). #EndSARS: Almost a Nigerian Revolution. Proshare.
Abrams, M. (1984). Orientation of Critical Theories. In D. Lodge (Ed.), *Literary Criticism* (pp. 1–25). Longman Group Ltd.
Adediran, I. (2020, October 22). #EndSARS: Sanwo-Olu Confirms Two Deaths from Lekki Shooting. *Premium Times*. Archived from the original on 24 October 2020. Retrieved 25 October 2020.
Afeno, S. (2014). *Killings by the Security Forces in Nigeria: Mapping and Trend Analysis, 2006–2014*. IFRA-Nigeria.
After Osinbajo's Order, Police Rename SARS 'Federal Special Anti-Robbery Squad' (FSARS). *Sahara Reporters*. 14 August 2018. Retrieved 26 February 2020.
Aito, O. (2014). The Poet as Town-Crier* in a Nation in Conflict: Okigbo's and Ojaide's Poetry. *Borno Studies in English, 40*(2), 5–26.
Akinkugbe, P. (2020). #EndSARS: Nigerian Army to Unleash Operation Crocodile Smile as Anonymous Targets Its Website. *Techuncode News* (formerly *AskIfa*). Archived from the original on 15 December 2020.
Akinsanmi, G. (2021). Lekki Shooting: Judicial Panel Begins Sitting Tuesday. *THISDAYLIVE*. 25 October 2020. Archived from the original on 10 February 2021. Retrieved 6 November 2020.
Akinwotu, E. (2020, October 6). Outcry in Nigeria over Footage of Shooting by the Notorious Police Unit. *The Guardian*. https://www.theguardian.com/world/2020/oct/06/video-of-Nigerian-police-shooting-man-in-street-sparks-outcry
Akinyetun, T. S. (2021). Reign of Terror: A Review of Police Brutality on Nigerian Youth by the Special Anti-Robbery Squad. *African Security Review*. https://doi.org/10.1080/10246029.2021.1947863
Alake, M. (2019, January 23). EndSARS: What Exactly Is the Status of SARS? *Pulse Nigeria*. Retrieved 26 October 2020.
Amnesty Slams Nigeria for Rights Abuse. *P.M. News*. 27 May 2010. Retrieved 26 February 2020.
Bella, N. (2017, December 11). #EndSARS: Nigerians Take to the Streets in Protest. *Bellanaija*. Retrieved 14 October 2020.
Buyse, A. (2018). Squeezing Civic Space: Restrictions on Civil Society Organizations and the Linkages with Human Rights. *The International Journal of Human Rights, 22*(8), 966–988.

Country Reports on Human Rights Practices—2005—Nigeria (Page 2) Bureau of Democracy, Human Rights and Labor. Accessed 18 October 2020.

Durosomo, D. (2018). Nigerians React to VP Osinbanjo's 'Overhaul' of SARS After Public Outcry of Rampant Abuse. Retrieved on August 15, 2018 from https://www.okayafrica.com/nigeria-end-sars-public-outcry-overhaul-reform-vice-president-buhari-yemi-osinbanjo/

Egbe, R. (2020). Why Lekki Tollgate Surveillance Camera Stopped Working. Latest Nigeria News, *Nigerian Newspapers*, Politics. 4 November 2020. Archived from the original on 10 February 2021. Retrieved 24 November 2020.

Ekoh, P., & George, E. (2021). The Role of Digital Technology in the EndSars Protest in Nigeria During the Covid-19 Pandemic. *Journal of Human Rights and Social Work, 6*, 161–162.

Elusoji, S. (2020). #EndSARS: DJ Switch Will Be Exposed in Due Course, Says Lai Mohammed. Channels Television. Archived from the original on 10 February 2021. Retrieved 19 November 2020.

#ENDSARS: Buratai Reacts to CNN Report on Lekki Massacre, Insists Nigerian Army Observed Rules of Engagement. *Sahara Reporters*. 18 November 2020. Archived from the original on 10 February 2021.

#ENDSARS: Lagos Panel Pays 'Unscheduled Visit' to Military Hospital Over Lekki Shootings. *Sahara Reporters*. Archived from the original on 10 February 2021. Retrieved 6 November 2020.

#EndSARS Protests Expose Nigeria's Fault Lines. Bonn, Germany: DW Akademie. 20 October 2020. Archived from the original on 21 October 2020.

Ewang, A. (2019, November 26). Nigerians Should Say No to Social Media Bills. *Human Rights Watch*. https://www.hrw.org/news/2019/11/26/nigerians-should-say-no-social-me

Ewodage, R. (2020). Nigerian Army Not Happy That Gov Sanwo-Olu Denied Inviting Us—Brigadier Taiwo. www.channelstv.com. Retrieved 7 March 2023.

Fatal Police Shooting Video of Nigerian Man Reignites Call to #EndSARS. guardian.ng. Retrieved 17 October 2020.

Folarin, S. (2019, August 21). "Police Arrest Officers Who Killed Suspected Lagos Phone Thieves" punchng.com. Accessed 18 October 2020.

George, A. (2020, October 25). The Roots of the #EndSARS Protests in Nigeria. *The Washington Post*.

Get Africa. (2020, October 12). #EndSARS: The Latent Power of Hashtag Activism. *Get Africa Weekly* (40). https://www.getrevue.co/profile/getafrica/issues/endsars-the-latent-power-of-hashtag-activism-282947

Habila, H. (2007). Writing Helps Me to Keep in Touch. *The Guardian* [Lagos] 30 September, 55.

How Police Personnel Raked in 9.35 Billion Naira from Roadblocks in The Southeast-Nigeria in 18 Months. *Sahara Reporters*. 27 July 2010. Retrieved 26 February 2020.

Iwuoha, V. C. (2020). Cattle Droppings Litter Our City Roads: Herders' Encroachments, Risk Factors and Roadmap for Achieving Sustainable Development Goals. *African and Asian Studies, 19*(4), 1–27.

Jones, M., et al. (2020, October 21). End SARS Protests: People 'Shot Dead' in Lagos, Nigeria. *BBC News*. Retrieved 21 October 2023.

Laser Cameras, Not CCTV, Removed at Lekki Tollgate—Sanwo-Olu. *Vanguard*. 22 October 2020. Archived from the original on 25 October 2020. Retrieved 22 October 2020.

Lekki Massacre: Police Reject Nine Bodies from Nigerian Army: Sources. *People's Gazette*. 20 October 2020. Archived from the original on 10 February 2021. Retrieved 23 October 2020.

Mbah, F. (2020). Inquiry Probes Shooting of Lagos Protesters, Police Abuses. www.aljazeera.com. Retrieved 6 November 2020.

Nigeria Country Report on Human Rights Practices for 1997 Bureau of Democracy. *Human Rights, and Labor*. Accessed 18 October 2020.

Nigeria Sars Protests: Horror Over Shootings in Lagos. *BBC News*. 21 October 2020. Archived from the original on 10 February 2021. Retrieved 22 October 2020.

Nimi, P. (2021). Nigerian Government Rejects Report on Lekki Toll Gate Shooting as 'Fake News'. *CNN*. Archived from the original on 24 November 2021. Retrieved 24 November 2021.

Nnadozie, E. (2017, December 23). How I Found SARS in the Police—RTD CP Midenda. *Vanguard News*. Retrieved 26 February 2020.

Nwosu, A. (2020). End SARS: Nigerian Govt Threatens to Sanction CNN Over Report on Lekki Shootings. *Daily Post Nigeria*. Archived from the original on 10 February 2021. Retrieved 19 November 2020.

Nzomiwu, E. (2010). Nigeria: Ovoko Killing—Court Orders IG to Produce Police Officer. allAfrica.com. Lagos, Nigeria. Daily Independent

Odeyinde, O. (2019, September 5). How SARS Kidnapped, Assaulted, Robbed Me—Rapper, Ikechukwu. *Punch Newspapers*. Retrieved 26 February 2020.

Okafor, T. (2017). *Ezu River Dead Bodies: Report Indicts Police Four Years After*. https://punchng.com/ezu-river-dead-bodies-report-indicts-police-four-years-after/

Okigbo, C. (1971). *Labyrinths: Poems*. African Writers Series.

Okunnoye, O. (2009). Writing Resistance: Dissidence and Visions of Healing in Nigerian Poetry of the Military Era. *Tydskrif vir Letterkunde, 48*(1), 64–85.

Olagunju, D. (2020). SARS Was Created When the Police Ran Away. *Zikoko*. Archived from the original on 1 November 2020.

Olokor, F. (2020, November 24). FG protests CNN's Lekki Shootings Documentary, Calls it Irresponsible. *Punch*. Retrieved 12 October 2023.

Olubajo, O. (2021, September 11). Nigerian Soldiers Continued Shooting Even as #Endsars Protesters Were Running Away: Forensic Report. *People's Gazette*. Retrieved 12 September 2021.

Olukoya, S., & Oyekanmi, L. (2020, October 21). Nigerian Forces Killed None of the Peaceful Protesters, Amnesty Says. *AP*. Archived from the original on 10 February 2021. Retrieved 23 October 2020.

Omilana, T. (2020, October 4). Fatal police shooting video of Nigerian man reignites call to #EndSARS. *The Guardian*. Retrieved 12 October 2023.

Parkinson, J. (2020, October 22). Young Nigerians Came to Protest Police Brutality. Then the Shooting Started. *Wall Street Journal*. Archived on 23 October 2020. Retrieved 12 October 2023.

Plato. "Book X" *Republic* (354–430). Translated by John L. Davies and David J. Vaughan. Hertfordshire: Wordsworth Classics, 1997.

Police Commiserates with Family of Woman Killed by Operative. *Sahara Reporters*. 10 August 2019. Retrieved 26 February 2020.

PusleNG. (2019, January 21). IGP Adamu orders immediate disbandment of SARS. *PulseNG*. Retrieved 12 October 2023.

Richard, A., & Abolaji, A. O. (2018). Systematic Brutality, Torture and Abuse of Human Rights by the Nigerian Police: Account of Inmates of Ogun State Prisons. *Nigerian Journal of Sociology and Anthropology, 15*(1), 1–16.

Salaudeen, A. (2017, December 15). Nigerians Want Police's SARS Force Scrapped. *Al-jazeera*. Retrieved 14 October 2020.

Sanwo-Olu, B. (2020). The Toughest Night of Our Lives. Archived from the original on 10 February 2021. Retrieved 25 October 2020.

Soyinka, W. (1972). *The Man Died: Prison Notes of Wole Soyinka*. Rex Collings Limited.

The Guardian. (2020, October 13). IGP Announces New Squad 'SWAT' to Replace SARS. *The Guardian*. Accessed 18 October 2020.

United States Department of State. (1994). U.S. Department of State Country Report on Human Rights Practices 1993—Nigeria, 30 January 1994 Refworld—UNHCR. Accessed 18 October 2020.

Yeku, J. (2020, November 12). #EndsSARS Shows Why the Police Are Not 'Your Friend'. *Africa at LSE*. Blog Entry. https://blogs.lse.ac.uk/africaatlse/2020/11/12/endsars-shows-why-the-police-is-not-your-friend/

# The Resource Curse and Structural Violence in Angola: A Path for Perpetual Conflicts

Jeremiah Bvirindi

## 1 Introduction

Among the many natural resources that Angola is known to have in abundance are oil, diamonds, iron, phosphates, copper, gold, bauxite, uranium, and wood. Large petroleum and natural gas reserves are concentrated in the Cabinda enclave's maritime zones, which are north of the Congo river estuary (Barros & Managi, 2011). It is asserted that Angola is currently the second-largest producer of oil in sub-Saharan Africa, behind Nigeria, and the fourth-largest producer of diamonds worldwide.

The nation has enormous untapped potential for the growth of industries related to agriculture, fisheries, and minerals. The majority of food consumed is imported. There are 18 provinces and a total of about 30 million people living there (World Bank, 2020). Despite the wealth the nation possesses, the IDREA 2018–2019 Report on Poverty and Inequality in Angola found that there is severe poverty and hunger against a backdrop of high illiteracy, subpar road networks, a high rate of youth unemployment, subpar healthcare services, poor maternal health and nutrition, a high vulnerability to poverty, and early pregnancies among adolescent girls.

---

J. Bvirindi (✉)
Africa University, Mutare, Zimbabwe
e-mail: bvirindi@yahoo.com

## 2  Background

In 2002, following the death of Jonas Savimbi, the head of the National Union for the Total Independence of Angola (UNITA), Angola experienced peace for the first time after 27 years of post-independence civil war. According to Ferreira (2006), a war between rival liberation movements quickly developed out of the armed struggle for independence that started in 1961 against the Portuguese. Angola gained independence in 1975 after a shaky year-long transition process, but the People's Movement for the Liberation of Angola [MPLA]-led government and two rebel movements—the National Front for the Liberation of Angola (FNLA) and the more tenacious and persistent National Union for the Total Independence of Angola (UNITA)—quickly erupted into a devastating civil war.

In Angola, the game of power became a brutal war. According to Barros and Managi (2011), Angola's colonial history under the Portuguese is a significant contributor to the post-independence instability that has plagued the country. The two authors contend that two key factors contributed to this situation: first, Portugal's failure to adequately prepare its colonies for independence; and second, the ethnic and regional divisions within nationalist movements that initially opposed their colonial overlords before turning against one another. As a result, the MPLA, UNITA, and the FNLA engaged in a bloody power struggle when the country gained independence in 1975. The MPLA was supported by the Soviet Union and Cuba, while the West, South Africa during apartheid, and even China (up until the middle of the 1980s) provided financial assistance to the government.

After the Mujahedeen in Afghanistan, UNITA rebels received the second-highest level of covert American assistance by the middle of the 1980s (Vines & Weimer, 2011). The civil war was so destructive and expensive that it destroyed the nation's institutions and infrastructure. According to the UNDP (2015), there were approximately one million fatalities and an untold number of injuries and disfigurements. An estimated 3.7 million people were internally displaced or became refugees, frequently relocating to urban areas. According to the United Nations Development Programme [UNDP], there were significant social costs as a whole generation of Angolans were left without access to quality healthcare and education. Regional disparities were further exacerbated by the depopulation of rural areas because of the colonial period's emphasis on coastal regions.

The Luena Memorandum of Understanding, which was signed in April 2002 and largely restated commitments made in 1994 in Lusaka, Zambia, followed the murder of UNITA's founding leader and the subsequent death of his successor, Antonio Dembo, as a result of the two sides resuming peace talks (Barros & Managi, 2011). Later, UNITA declared itself disarmed and registered as a democratic political party. Both the ability and the desire to wage war are currently lacking in UNITA. The MPLA was now free to rule and advance Angola without being inhibited by political or military constraints.

## 3   Overview of Angola: Hidden Violence

The people of Angola suffered a protracted and devastating conflict for over 40 years, but now there is new hope from the new president Joao Lourenco who came into power in 2017 after the 35-year rule of Jose Eduardo Dos Santos.

The country has a population of about 30.1 million people (World Bank, 2018), with over 27% living in the Luanda Province, where the capital city of Angola is situated. About 37% of the population live in rural areas. According to the International Monetary Fund [IMF] (2018), the period from 2006 to 2014 registered extreme economic growth and expansionary fiscal policy. The IMF attributed this growth as driven by high oil prices and increased oil production that had a dramatic impact on a country recovering from decades of war. The IMF (2018) posits that GDP per capita soared from US$711 in 2002 to US$4804 in 2013, with government revenue skyrocketing in the same period. This also meant a rapid ascent for Angola within the World Bank's country classification system, from the level of low-income country to that of upper-middle-income country (World Bank, 2018). According to the World Bank, official figures for government revenue show that, between 2006 and 2015, the country collected a staggering US$267.2 billion in oil-related receipts, including taxes from oil companies and proceeds from the state-owned oil company, Sonangol. On average, the Angolan government receipted around US$27 million per year during the decade, which, by comparison, exceeded the development aid given to Africa in 2013, which was US$55.7 billion. In the same year 2013, Angola's oil revenue was US$37.1 billion.

In addition to receiving oil revenue, the Angolan government negotiated a series of credit lines with Chinese financial institutions. Angola's main resources are oil and diamonds (OECD, 2015). The Organisation for Economic Corporation and Development [OECD] outlined that there were large reserves of petroleum and natural gas in Angola, concentrated in the maritime zones of the Cabinda enclave to the north of the Congo river estuary. EXX Africa (2020) has argued that Angola is currently the world's fourth-largest producer of diamonds and the second-largest producer of oil in sub-Saharan Africa, after Nigeria. It also has natural gas, iron, uranium, copper, gold, and bauxite as mineral resources. EXX Africa (2020) argued that other resources such as agricultural land and water resources must also be taken into account in assessing the country's natural resource endowment. A study by Barros and Managi (2011) revealed that oil began to be exploited in Angola in the onshore Kwanza basin. According to these researchers, exploration and production extension started in the 1960s when the oil company Chevron-Texaco discovered oil in the Angolan enclave of Cabinda.

In 1973, oil became the most important export of Angola, exceeding agricultural commodities exports. After independence in 1975, the government became involved in oil exploration by creating Sonangol, the national oil company, in 1976. Diamond exploration in Angola started in 1912 in the Luanda Province, where alluvial diamonds are most abundant (Barros & Managi, 2011). From 1971, Angola was producing 2.4 million carats a year, which was disrupted by the war of liberation and the post-independence civil war (Barros & Managi, 2011), assert that the sector was nationalized by the government in the 1980s and production declined to less than 100,000 carats a year in 1990. It is reported that the situation got worse in the early 1990s when UNITA took control of some of the most diamond-rich regions and used diamond production to finance its war activities.

According to the World Bank (2018) findings, diamonds represented about 10% of non-oil GDP, but the sector is still considered as underexploited, as many diamond-rich areas have not yet been explored. On other hand, the country has potential for agriculture and fish: Angola has vast lands and an abundance of water as well as good climatic and soil conditions, conducive to producing a large variety of foods.

Barros and Managi (2011) assert that of Angola's 57.4 million hectares of agricultural land, only about 8–14% is currently being used, and argue that agricultural productivity is very low owing to a lack of mechanization, undeveloped input markets, and poor road infrastructure. Productivity growth is being held back by limited access to agricultural finance, the insufficient use of fertilizer, a lack of market information, and an absence of food processing facilities. Failing infrastructure limits access to both domestic and international markets, pointing to the resource curse and structural violence.

## 4 The Resource Curse

Development economics researchers like Auty (1993) and Hammond (2011) observed that Third World, resource-rich countries were not developing as well and as fast as they were expected to, given that their natural resource endowment was considered a great opportunity for development. At the same time, resource-poor countries were experiencing exceptional economic growth. Auty and Gelb (2001) argued that the incomes of resource-poor countries grew faster than those of resource-abundant countries, and the gap in growth widens significantly. This phenomenon has been called the "Resource Curse," also known as the "Paradox of Plenty," by Karl (1997). This implies that resource-rich countries, like Angola, which have many more resources to boost economic development, are in fact having difficulties meeting economic growth targets.

It is often assumed that an important endowment of natural resources cannot be anything other than an advantage for developing countries. The rents generated through the process would provide the basis for generating savings, investment, and consequently growth and development. Auty and Gelb (2001) state that resource-rich developing countries performed two to three times worse than their resource-poor counterparts.

Auty and Gelb (2001) argued that the first explanations of resource-rich countries' underperformance were attributed to Dutch Disease effects on the economy. The term "Dutch Disease," according to Auty, was coined in 1977 by economists and formalized in 1982 by Corden (1982) to describe the decline of the manufacturing sector in the Netherlands after the discovery of natural gas in the 1960s. According to these authors, the fundamental principle of Dutch Disease is that a country that exports natural resources allows a major inflow of foreign currencies into its national economy. This implies an appreciation of national currencies that become relatively scarce, so that national tradable production in non-mineral sectors becomes uncompetitive in international markets.

At the same time, the inflow of foreign currencies makes the natural resource exporting sector increase its demand for production inputs such as workforce, transport, and other non-tradables. This makes the local economy allocate most of its non-exportable goods to the resource-extracting activity, shrinking the manufacturing activity. Manufactured goods cease to be exported and become imported by the local economy.

According to the theory of the "resource curse," poor countries with a large endowment of natural resources, especially oil, like Angola, often do not achieve sustainable economic growth because the size and volatility of the oil revenues encourage corruption, mismanagement, and authoritarian governments that fail to invest for the future or provide for the well-being of the majority of their populations (Hammond, 2011). According to Hammond, Angola is a classic case of the resource curse, having experienced a corrupt and authoritarian government since independence in 1975.

## 5 Governance of Resources

At the centre of inequalities in income and wealth, is governance. It has been the expectation of the Angolan people that oil revenue would translate into improved living conditions. According to the United Nations Children Fund [UNICEF] (2017), infant and maternal mortality rates in Angola remain among the highest in the world as Angola continues to reflect the characteristics of very poor countries despite its category being revised by the World Bank in 2018. The United Nations (2017) still categorizes Angola as a least developed country: one of 47 worldwide. The domestic economic crisis that began in 2014 saw Angola's per capita income drop sharply, and its World Bank classification fall back to that of a lower-middle-income country in 2017 (World Bank, 2020).

A fall in international oil prices, from over US$110 a barrel to below US$50 a barrel, exposed Angola's governance deficiencies and enduring developmental challenges. The IMF (2018) described the exposure as a reflection of the country's vulnerability to fluctuations in oil prices that sent shock waves through the economy. This led to a significant depreciation in the kwanza, (Angolan unit currency) soaring inflation, and a sharp rise in public debt, among other problems. Jensen (2018) views the government's plans for infrastructure development since the end of the civil war in 2002 as overambitious and self-defeating, citing incapacitation. Jensen argues that the advantages gained by Angola through rapid GDP growth and abundant capital have been offset by insufficient capacity, a lack of transparency, human capital deficits, corruption, and unbalanced planning.

The World Bank (2018) noted that the use of public funds in Angola lacked proper oversight, resulting in unrealistic budget assumptions, overbudgeting on transportation in preference to infrastructure development, and pro-cyclical financing, with debt accumulating rapidly both before and after the onset of the economic crisis in 2014. Lack of proper financial management is a recipe for corruption that can frustrate the efforts of development partners, resulting in the premature withdrawal of aid, leading to the suffering of the most vulnerable.

## 6     Public Sector Performance

The former president Jose Eduardo dos Santos's tenure of office ended in 2017, with him handing over power after 38 years of presidency to Joao Lourenco, who was expected to address multiple development challenges facing the country. In September 2017, Joao Lourenco was inaugurated as president after parliamentary elections, marking the first peaceful political transition in Angola since independence in 1975 (Jensen, 2018). Among Angolans, expectations were high that President Joao Lourenco would deal with corruption head-on and bring the country back to its prime, as promised during his inauguration. Critical areas he was expected to deliver on, according to Jensen (2018), were tackling corruption and repatriating illicit financial flows, as well as delivering long-promised economic, political, and social reforms, coupled with strengthening competition and furthering decentralization.

## 7     Investment Status

The World Bank (2020) observed that, contrary to the promised initiatives, Angola has the worst disinvestment rate of any sub-Saharan African country, and has continued to rely largely on the exploitation of natural resources for growth. Although Angola registered very strong growth during the oil boom, this has not translated into sustainable investments to help the poor (EXX Africa, 2020).

The World Bank (2020) attributed this lack of diversified investments to the inability of the government to convert the country's huge natural resource wealth into other forms of capital. The World Bank noted that, in Angola, resources have been used to increase consumption without reinvesting in long-term investments.

## 8     Sustainability of Oil Production

As evidenced by the Angolan database in 2017, oil production reached 1.64 million barrels a day, almost on a par with Nigeria's 1.66 million barrels per day (IMF, 2018). The IMF asserts that Angola's oil production is not sustainable as its reserves are expected to be exhausted by 2032. The Instituto Nacional de Estatistica [INE] (2016) argued that the country's dependence on oil prevents it from enjoying the benefits of economic diversification, including trade openness and export diversification leading to higher growth, noting that oil dependence has been a lasting feature of the economy and petroleum products have comprised between 87 and 98% of total annual exports since 1990. It also has to be noted that oil price volatility has caused cycles of boom and bust (Tvedten & Gilson, 2016).

## 9  Debt Sustainability

Unlike its counterparts in sub-Saharan Africa, the UNDP (2015) posits that Angola still overspends on subsidies and underspends on agriculture, education, healthcare, and social protection. In addition, the UNDP highlighted that debt sustainability has become a challenge. It reported that the debt-to-GDP ratio reached 65.3% in 2017, almost double its 2013 level, and data for the ensuing years is not readily available. This reflects wide financing gaps since 2014, but also the effect of Angola's currency devaluation on the large share of the debt denominated in foreign currency. Reports show that the debt has not only reached high levels by emerging market standards, but the speed of accumulation, the large gross financing needs in the coming years, and the deteriorating composition have become challenges. It is noted that these risks are compounded by weak debt management practices, poor communication, and lack of transparency with the market (Jensen, 2018).

## 10  The Energy Sector

In Angola, the energy sector is underdeveloped, with only 30% of the population having access to electricity in 2015 (UNDP, 2015). There is huge potential for hydropower, solar power, and natural gas-based generation, and expanding production has been one of the biggest priorities of the government over the past decades. Generation capacity and production have both been massively increased through investment valued at tens of billions of dollars, but capacity and production have still fallen short of the targets (UNDP, 2015).

## 11 Human Capital Status

According to the UNDP (2015), ANGOLA HUMAN DEVELOPMENT INDEX REPORT weak human capital outcomes constrain economic expansion and equity. It highlighted that one of the strongest engines of long-run growth will be an investment in human capital. Reporting on Angola's Human Development Index, the UNDP (2015) asserts that Angola ranks 149th out of 182 countries in the Human Development Index (HDI) of 2018, and it also stands among the lowest countries in the whole world in terms of the human capital index.

The UNDP's (2015) Human Capital Index provides a simple composite measure of the expected human capital of the next generation in a given country, combining indicators of survival, schooling, and health. On a scale of 0 to 1, Angola's Human Capital Index was 0.36 in 2018, pointing to weak education and health outcomes that limit the opportunities of the poor. It should be pointed out that, while the dimensions and factors behind, such a low level of human capital are wide-ranging, adequate investments and delivery mechanisms in health, education, sanitation, and social protection are key ingredients.

The World Bank's, 2020 annual report reveals that Angola suffers from a scarcity of trained healthcare professionals, low public health expenditure, and weak investment in water and sanitation. According to the report, Angola has only 1 physician, fewer than 23 healthcare workers, and 63 nurses per 10,000 people. Rural areas are the worst hit by this scarcity, as 85% of healthcare workers are concentrated in the capital. Poor training and education contribute to low-quality healthcare services in the country. The World Bank (2020) report went further and highlighted that public health expenditure has been declining, dropping from 2.6% of GDP in 2013 to just 1.5% of GDP in 2015 and remaining far behind the sub-Saharan average of 5.4% until the year 2020. Limited access to improved water, sanitation, and hygiene services has detrimental public health consequences such as waterborne diseases and stunted growth in children. Nationally, only 41% of the population has access to basic or improved drinking water services (63% in urban areas and 24% in rural areas) and 39% to improved sanitation (62% in urban areas and 21% in rural areas) (World Bank, 2020).

The World Bank (2020) argued that the government commits insufficient resources to education and that low education levels limit economic opportunities, especially for the rural population and women. Despite some improvements over the last few years, many children remain outside the school system, with net primary enrolment rates of only 66.4% for girls and 88.8% for boys. School attendance and school enrolment demonstrate inequality of opportunity for the rural population, as well as for women.

## 12 Private Sector Performance

A lack of growth in the private sector is another binding constraint for economic development, limiting the potential of sectors like agriculture and manufacturing (IMF, 2018). Angola's private sector is defined by weaknesses concerning available inputs, factors of production, and the role of institutions. According to the IMF (2018), these continue to be major impediments to large-scale foreign investment, and reforms will need to be enacted to improve competitiveness and facilitate the financing of new business initiatives. The World Bank's, 2020 country report outlined that the country possesses significant non-oil endowments that were previously exploited but saw productivity plummet owing to conflict. According to the report, such areas of economic potential include agriculture, mining, fisheries, manufacturing, and information and communication technology (ICT). These represent important opportunities for Angola, and a fair and freely competitive private sector can help feed their growth.

Government influence in the productive economy is still pervasive, crowding out the growth of the private sector. Large segments of the economy in Angola are not only controlled by state-owned interests but also by actors that are associated with political parties and security forces. The government of Angola holds billions of dollars (OECD, 2015) in real estate and productive assets, distributed across line ministries or in the hands of state-owned enterprises (SOEs). The SOE sector in Angola is inefficient and has only been profitable owing to oil revenues (Tvedten & Gilson, 2016).

## 13 Business Opportunities

The weak business climate is an impediment to private investment. The formal private sector in Angola is small and concentrated in commerce and services in Luanda. Foreign investment is weak outside of oil and gas: 82% of total international investment flows between 2003 and 2017 were concentrated in oil and natural gas, while agribusiness received a mere 6% (World Bank, 2020). Observation by the World Bank revealed that foreign investors were deterred by a restrictive visa regime and investment policy, as well as forex restrictions that impeded profit repatriation. However, after paying heed to the IMF's (2018) advice, the government has relaxed many of these restrictions, as it steps up its efforts to attract foreign investors. It should be noted that an unfavourable regulatory environment and high barriers to entry hinder competitiveness.

## 14 Governance Challenges Relating to Private Sector Growth

Oligopolies, barriers to entry, high operating costs, poor investor protection, and the need to pay commissions and kickbacks, mean that the private sector's growth in Angola has been constrained (Jensen, 2018). Jensen acknowledges that the new administration has, nonetheless, taken some visible steps to promote competition and reclaim public funds lost due to corruption. Local governance theories argue that institutional centralization undermines effective service delivery. According to the CMI (2020), the Angolan administration remains highly centralized, and the process of devolution was started in 2001 but never completed despite the recognized necessity for a more independent administration at the local level. The Chr. Michelsen Institute [CMI] (2020) noted that limited capacity at the local level, as well as ineffective coordination mechanisms, constrain the decentralization process and its impact.

## 15 Overall Economic Challenges

According to the UNDP (2015), Angola ranked 137 out of 140 countries on the Global Competitiveness Index, 2018. The economy continues to suffer from a difficult regulatory environment, a challenging macroeconomic framework, weak infrastructure, and inadequate human capital (IMF, 2018). A heavy bureaucracy creates opportunities for corruption and the discretionary application of regulations, although the newly elected president has taken concrete steps to improve the business climate. Market contestability is very low, and barriers to entry are high (IMF, 2018).

The World Bank (2020) report revealed that firms in Angola operate with very high input costs, including that of self-generated electricity. Market distortions through subsidies and tariffs are also common. Difficult import and export procedures undermine Angola's ability to join regional and global value chains. Failing and inadequate infrastructure is an impediment to economic growth. According to the World Bank report, only 17% of classified and urban roads are paved, and more than 70% of the country's road network was in an advanced state of deterioration at the end of the civil war.

The rural accessibility gap is a serious impediment to growth, as road density remains very low, feeder roads are few, and bridges are lacking. The transportation gap also makes it difficult for the country to develop regional trade and discourages its neighbours from making greater use of the country's ports. However, the government has committed to major public expenditures in power production to keep up with growing demand (World Bank, 2020).

## 16    Poverty and the Urban-Rural Experience

The exclusion of the poor from the benefits of growth is a binding constraint for the development of Angola.

The country has significant unrealized potential to develop industries in agriculture, fisheries, and minerals. More than 50% of the food consumed is imported. It has a total population of about 30.81 million and is divided into 18 provinces (World Bank, 2020). Despite the riches the country possesses, the IDREA 2018–2019 Report on Poverty and Inequality in Angola revealed acute poverty and hunger against a background of high illiteracy, poor road networks, a high unemployment rate among the youth, poor healthcare services, poor maternal health and nutrition, high vulnerability to poverty, and early pregnancy among adolescent girls.

The roots of poverty in Angola can be traced to the economic structures established during the colonial era and the conditions created by the 27-year civil war (Ferreira, 2006). Whereas colonialism created an export economy in Angola, the Angolans themselves were exploited and left in poverty. Foreigners without any transfer of skills did the most skilled work for Angolans (World Bank, 2020). The command economy policies enacted at independence and the long civil war pushed most foreign companies and workers holding managerial, technical, and administrative positions to leave (Krueger, 1980). By 1976, the economy and administration of the country were left with the expertise of fewer than 100 university graduates. Ferreira (2006) gives an estimation of the number of people who died over the course of the civil conflict (1976–2002) as half a million to a million, with millions of Angolans wounded and an estimated 3.7 million becoming refugees or internally displaced, often migrating to cities.

The war destroyed important infrastructure such as schools, hospitals, railways, and bridges, and this context resulted in a generation of newly independent Angolans without proper schooling or healthcare (Ferreira, 2006). The UNDP (2015) gap analysis report revealed that the poor have seen little benefit from recent economic growth, and nearly a third of Angolans still live in poverty. In the decade after the end of the civil war, GDP per capita nearly doubled, from US$2,293 (PPP) in 2000 to US$4,164 in 2014 (UNDP, 2015). This impressive expansion of the economy nonetheless did very little to reduce poverty. The proportion of people living below the US$1.90 poverty line showed only a small decline, from 32.3% in 2000 to 28.0% in 2014. Rapid population growth and increasing urban poverty meant that the absolute number of poor people in Angola increased from 4.9 to 6.7 million over this period.

The rural and slum populations have been particularly excluded from economic growth. About two-thirds of the poor live in rural areas, where poverty is widespread owing to weak connectivity, a lack of basic services (electricity, water, sanitation, and so on), and an absence of markets. While migration to urban areas can help improve livelihoods, the continuing increase of urban inequality shows the limitations of this solution (Tvedten & Lazaro, 2016). While slums are economically vibrant, many activities are informal and of limited productivity. Social protection spending in Angola has been significantly reduced and is well below levels in comparator countries. Social protection spending decreased on average by 20% per year, from 7.8% of GDP in 2010 to 2.2% of GDP in 2016. The bulk of this decrease came from the reduction of energy subsidies, which have historically represented a large share of the national budget. Spending on social assistance (war-related pensions and transfers targeting the poor) remains weak, roughly a quarter of the level of other lower-middle-income countries.

The rural poor continue to suffer from disproportionately bad health outcomes. Angola's recent growth has helped improve the health of its population, but indicators still lag far behind those of other middle-income countries. The rural poor, in particular, still contend with very low access to healthcare compared to those who can afford private care. Access to services is also a problem, with pregnancy health checks and delivery services available in only 25% of rural facilities. The incidence of poverty is almost three times higher in rural areas (54.7%) than in urban areas (17.8%). The gap between urban and rural poverty is even larger when one focuses on the depth and severity of poverty, according to the IDR 2018/2019 bridge survey carried out by the INE (2016). These disparities are major sources of structural violence (Galtung, 1969: 18).

## 17   Structural Violence

Galtung (1969) defines structural violence as harm inflicted on people through large-scale social, political, and economic institutions or systems, many of them international in scope. These entities distribute resources unevenly and are based on the unequal distribution of power. Such violence, according to Galtung (1969), works indirectly and is rarely discernible in terms of actions that can be rectified through legal, diplomatic, or other means. The salient forms of violence in Angola described above can be regarded as structural violence.

Structural violence refers to the avoidable limitations that society places on groups of people that constrain them from meeting their basic needs and achieving the quality of life that would otherwise be possible. These limitations, according to Galtung (1969), which can be political, economic, religious, cultural, or legal in nature, usually originate in institutions that exercise power over particular subjects. For example, many people desperately need education, healthcare, political power, or legal assistance but are unable to access them easily owing to restrictions in the existing social order. Unlike more visible and obvious forms of violence, where a person or group of persons physically harms someone, structural violence occurs through economically, politically, or culturally driven processes that work together in such a way as to limit victims from achieving a full quality of life. Angola, therefore, can be described as experiencing structural violence and there is a need to redistribute wealth in order to take the first steps towards curing this challenge.

Sharp inequalities are not only evident as material differences but also as social exclusion, to the point of humiliation on a social and spiritual level that is equal to an assault on human dignity (Jensen, 2018). The systematic exclusion of a group of people from the resources needed to develop their full human potential has been called structural violence (Galtung, 1969). Structural violence, defined as the physical and psychological harm that results from exploitative and unjust social, political, and economic systems, is the shadow in which the HI virus also lurks (WHO, 2004). The International Labour Organisation [ILO] (2004) observed that in poor countries, many people are trapped in wage slavery. This type of economic victimization is one of the major factors in the spread of HIV. Girls are often sent to cities to be domestic servants and are often forced to have sex with their masters. Women are unable to support themselves, and their children often become reliant on men who are neither economically reliable nor faithful. Women are less likely to be educated and less likely to find paying work. When working, women earn two-thirds of what men earn (ILO, 2004).

## 18 Conclusion

Angola has more resources than it can efficiently use to develop the country. Despite increased funding and resource abundance, it faces serious economic challenges due to corruption, disinvestment, and skill deficiencies, among other ills. The Angolan economy's overdependence on extractive resources, particularly oil and diamonds, is a potential source of instability for years to come.

The government is wary of the potential for social unrest in urban areas following the upheavals in north Africa and elsewhere since the start of 2011, but a mixture of repression and the memories of Angola's civil war have so far prevented the outbreak of protests (Vines & Weimer, 2011).

Weak governance is the final, cross-cutting binding constraint for Angola, hindering institutional capacity and jeopardizing what Jensen (2018) referred to as the existing fragile social contract. The political system has historically been characterized by discretionary decisions, rampant corruption, and crony capitalism, constraining private sector growth, and contributing to the exclusion of the poor. Following their victory in the civil war, the MPLA governed the country with weak checks and balances in a dominant discretionary presidential system. Oil revenue windfalls allowed substantial discretionary spending, ensuring loyalty at the cost of institutional efficiency and the rule of law.

In spite of Angola's status as a middle-income country due to its vast influx of oil revenues, income distribution is highly asymmetrical, and poverty levels are high. The Gini coefficient is 0.54 (UNICEF, 2017), while rural and urban poverty represent 57 and 19%, respectively (INE, 2016). The UNDP's Human Development Index lists Angola as number 149 amongst 188 countries, while the World Bank's World Development Report lists it as number 112 out of 188 countries.

The country is highly urbanized, with 62% of Angola's 25 million inhabitants living in urban areas and 41.8% in Luanda alone. Out of these, 52.3% are women, who are quite often victims of domestic violence owing to poverty (Redvers, 2011). According to Redvers (2011), the majority of Luanda's inhabitants live in informal urban and peri-urban settlements.

Redvers highlighted that these neighbourhoods are predominantly characterized by entrenched poverty, limited access to public services and employment, poor infrastructure, and highly unhealthy living conditions.

## 19 Recommendations

In the context of Angola's current structural violence, fiscal constraints and rising public debt, it is critical that Angolan authorities undertake a serious evaluation of their capacity gaps and take bold steps to reform their institutional systems and restructure state enterprises to make public investment more efficient. Angola's commodity-based economy is tied to global oil and diamond prices and is thus highly susceptible to exogenous shocks. The ability of the government to diversify the economy and open up the business environment to attract investment in other sectors, such as agriculture, will be vital to ensuring long-term stability. Urban poverty is a source of social strife, and, therefore, the Angolan government should improve service delivery and speed up social reform to avert potential unrest.

We may take the World Bank's (2020) recommendations as a way forward. Limited oil reserves in Angola are expected to be exhausted in the next decade. Angola cannot continue to consume its natural wealth in this way. Economic diversification and capital accumulation will be crucial for lessening resource dependence and fostering growth. Angola has the potential to develop other non-oil industries, including agribusiness, fisheries, mining, and manufacturing. To capitalize on these areas of potential economic expansion, government policies will need to create incentives for industry growth, such as a better business climate, improved competitiveness, access to finance, and a reasonable tax burden with low compliance costs.

Capital accumulation will be fundamental to establishing a sustainable growth path. Greater investment in produced capital, including power, transport, and water infrastructure, will serve to increase productivity and foster both domestic and international trade in the end. Greater investments in human capital, notably more effective public education, healthcare, sanitation, and social protection services will also be essential for increasing labour-force participation and boosting productivity.

The goal for Angola should be to convert its natural wealth in an environmentally conscious way into assets for the poor, in more sustainable forms of wealth, to create an inclusive society on a sustainable development path. Better governance is the key to a more sustainable economy. Weak governance holds Angola at a low level of equilibrium and is at the core of

Angola's challenge in reaching the twin goals of ending extreme poverty and boosting shared prosperity. This will help in overcoming structural violence and promote sustainable development in Angola.

## Bibliography

Auty, R. M. (1993). *Sustaining Development in Mineral Economies* (The Resource Curse Thesis). London: Routledge.

Auty, R. M., & Gelb, A. (2001). The Political Economy of Resource-Abundant States. In R. Auty (Ed.), *Resource Abundance and Economic Development*. Oxford University Press.

Barros, C. P., & Managi, S. (2011). Productivity Assessment of Angola Oil Block. *Energy, 34*(11), 2009–2015.

Collier, P., & Bannon, I. (2003). Natural Resources and Violent Conflict: Options and Actions: Washington DC, Edited by the World Bank: Angola. *Journal of Modern African Studies, 43*(1), 409.

Corden, W. M. (1982). Exchange Rate Policy and Resource Boom. *Economic Record, 58*(160), 18–31.

EXX Africa (2020). *Angola: Political Violence and State Corruption Imperil IMF and Creditor Relations, PANGEA*. https://www.pangea-risk.com/angola-political-violence-and-state-corruption-imperil-imf-and-creditor-relations/. Accessed 8 July 2023.

Ferreira, M. (2006). Angola: Conflict and Development 1961–2002. *The Economics of Peace and Security Journal, 1*(1), 25.

Galtung, J. (1969). Violence, Peace, and Research. *Journal of Peace Research, 6*(3), 167–191.

Guru, R. S. M. (2021). *Working Paper No.6: Negotiating Access to Healthcare for Populations Affected by Conflicts*. Angolan Press.

Hammond, J. L. (2011). The Resource Curse and Oil Revenues in Angola and Venezuela. *Science and Society, 75*(3), 348–508.

IDREA. (2019). Poverty Report for Angola.

ILO. (2004). *Facts on Women at Work*. International Labour Organization.

International Monitoring Fund. (2012). *Angola, 2012 Article 1v Consultation and Post-Program Monitoring*. IMF.

International Monetary Fund. (2018). *World Economic Outlook Database*. www.imf.org/external/pubs/ft/weo/2017/weodata

INE. (2016). *Resultados definitos do recenseamento geral da Populacao e da habitacao de Angola 2014*. Instituto Nacional de Estatistica.

Jensen, S. K. (2018). *Ambitions Through Booms and Bursts: Policy, Governance and Reform* (Research Paper). Africa Programme.

Karl, T. L. (1997). *The Paradox of Plenty: Oil Boom and Petro-States*. University of California Press.

Krueger, A. (1980). Trade Policy as an Input to Development. *American Economic Review, 12*(3), 162–282.

Organisation for Economic Commission and Development. (2015). *Development Aid at a Glance: Statistics by Region: 2 Africa* (2nd ed.). OECD.

Redvers, L. (2011). *Angola: Law on Domestic Violence a Step Forward for Women's Rights.* IPSNEWS.

Tvedten, I., & Gilson L. (2016). Urban Poverty and Inequality in Luanda, Angola. CMI Brief 17.

United Nations. (2017). *World Population Prospects: The 2015 Revision.* Department of Economics and Social Affairs: Population Division.

United Nations Children's Fund. (2017). *The State of the World's Children.* https://www.unicef.org/sowc.

United Nations Development Programme. (2015). *Rapid Assessment and Gap Analysis Angola.* www.undp.org.

Vines, A., & Weimer, M. (2011). A Report of Centre for Strategic and International Studies Africa Programme: Angola Assessing Risks to Stability. Vines, A, and Weimer, M. RSA.

World Bank. (2018). *GDP per capita in US$ world and database.* https//dataworldbank.org/country/Angola.

World Bank. (2020). Angolan Poverty Assessment: Poverty and Equity, Global Practice—Africa Region.

World Economic Forum. (2015). *The Global Gender Gap Report.* World Economic Forum.

World Health Organization. (2004). *Joint United Nations Programme on HIV/AIDs, Report on Global AIDs Epidemic.* WHO.

# Electoral Violence in Ghana's Fourth Republic: The Case of Party Vigilantism

Emmanuel Debrah, Isaac Owusu-Mensah, Sampson Danso, and Gilbert Arhinful Aidoo

## 1 Introduction

The 1990s began with great optimism for African democratization. The dethronement of authoritarian rulers and the creation of constitutional regimes were widely hailed as an opportunity to entrench the rule of law and multiparty politics in the continent. The holding of relatively successful founding elections in many African countries intensified the euphoria of a possible democratic consolidation in the continent. In several African countries such as Benin, Nigeria, Kenya, Malawi, Senegal, and Ghana, the holding of multiparty elections and the resultant peaceful transitions led to the conclusion that authoritarian rule and all its vestiges had atrophied (Bratton & Van de Walle, 1997; Gyimah-Boadi, 2004). After all, the new democratic system had reinstated the legislature, judiciary, rule of law, and

E. Debrah (✉) · I. Owusu-Mensah · S. Danso
University of Ghana, Accra, Ghana
e-mail: edebrah@ug.edu.gh

I. Owusu-Mensah
e-mail: iomensah@ug.edu.gh

S. Danso
e-mail: sdanso@ug.edu.gh

G. A. Aidoo
University of Education, Winneba, Winneba, Ghana
e-mail: gaaidoo@uew.edu.gh

people had begun to enjoy their liberties (Gyimah-Boadi, 2004). Also, the return of multiparty politics had enabled the critical mass of the citizens to participate in the decision-making process, where periodically they have decided on those who would govern their affairs.

However, recent commentaries have raised alarm about democratic backsliding or retrogressing due to growing carnages in the body politic. Many scholars reviewing democratic quality in Africa have questioned the preponderance of the executive powers in the governance process, the lack of judicial and media independence, transparency, accountability, and politicization of the security institutions, among others (Bratton, et al., 2005; Clapham, 1996; Prempeh, 2003). A salient attack against African democratization is the institutionalization or entrenchment of neo-patrimonialism within the body politic (Debrah, 2005; Lindberg, 2005; Van de Walle, 2007; Young, 2009). According to these scholars, the African political terrain is infested with patron-client relationships where those in superior positions would demand services from subordinates in return for benefits or both. Thus, it is a form of personalized legitimation based on reciprocal exchanges between a big man and small boy (Nugent, 1995; von Soest, 2021) and survives largely on loyalties particularly of the subordinate to the superior. Its survival further depends on the continual control and supply of resources and benefits by the patrons—usually persons who are in charge of state machinery—to their web of clienteles (von Soest, 2021; Young, 2009). While the clients' role is loyal support and delivery of several activities for their patrons, the reward of the former is in the form of financial and employment benefits even though it may go beyond these incentives (Lindberg, 2005; Nugent, 1995; Young, 2009). These clients may be the parties' activists who are oftentimes found to constitute themselves into a kind of militia cartel to promote the interests of their patrons. According to some scholars, neo-patrimonialism has been responsible for the breakdown of law and order and increasing corruption in society (Debrah, 2005; Lindberg, 2005).

Although Ghana's democratization has received much praise from the international community and domestic democratic actors, recent review of the governance literature indicates that the country has plummeted in its score on democratic quality (Debrah, 2016; Gyimah-Boadi, 2018). The governance deficits such as rising incidents of corruption, political intolerance, and interferences in the work of the judiciary have been noted in many scholarly works (Gyimah-Boadi, 2018; Prempeh, 2003). Also, much ink has been spilled on the electoral process, analysis of election outcomes, political parties' role in the political process, and intra- and inter-ethnic conflicts that have been largely framed around chieftaincy and its impact on the democratic process (Ayee, 2010; Debrah, 2005, 2016). What has been a neglected variable in the scholarly discourse of the burgeoning literature of Ghana's democratization is the extent to which violence-in-election has influenced the democratic process. Although several works have been done in the area of election violence, their link to the activities of party-sponsored militias-vigilantes have not been encapsulating. In other words, the prevailing literature that has examined election violence and party vigilante linkage applied the issues separately (Asante & Gyampo, 2021; Kyei & Berckmoes, 2021).

This chapter contributes to the prevailing literature by examining how party vigilantes' electoral violent activities permeate all facets of the electoral process. Besides, the consequences of party-vigilantes' electoral activities and democratic consolidation has been inadequately established thereby blurring our understanding of how these forces have contributed to the gradual erosion of the gains made in democratic progress in the country. Indeed, a critical examination of media and scholarly accounts as well as personal observations of the nature of electoral mobilization reveal that violence-in-elections has occurred within and among the political parties that have participated in the elections. Furthermore, to a large extent, scholarly analysis of electoral violence as the result of the activities of party vigilantes has remained at the level of anecdotal. This chapter undertakes a comprehensive discussion of how party vigilantes have carried out their election violence activities in the electoral process and their effects on sustainable democracy in the country. It is based on empirical data in order to illuminate our understanding of the imperatives of electoral violence and party vigilantism in the ongoing debate about measuring the intervening variables that have shaped the current state of African democratization.

Consequently, the chapter is organized as follows. The first part outlines the background and is followed by a short note on the methodology that guided the data used for the analysis. Next, it unveils a discussion of the conceptual issues to provide a context for analysing the imperatives. What follows is an examination of the evolution of the phenomenon in order to indicate how entrenched it is in the political and electoral processes. The next part then delineates and discusses the nature and forces that have supported its growth in the current democratic dispensation, and further examines the debilitating effect it has imposed on the democratic process. Last, the chapter proffers remedial actions needed to diffuse its negative influence on democratic consolidation and draw lessons for other African countries.

## A Note on the Methodology

Data for this paper was drawn from fieldwork undertaken from October to December 2022 to determine the extent to which party vigilantes have carried out violence in the electoral process to undermine democratic development. The qualitative method was deemed appropriate because it allows for the analysis of different interactions among the variables, and flexibility to probe for clarifications. Given the resources and operational constraints, only 90 respondents from three of Ghana's 16 regions, namely Ashanti, Volta, and Greater Accra were chosen purposively. These regions reflect the geopolitics of the country: while Ashanti and Volta regions are the ruling New Patriotic Party (NPP) and leading opposition National Democratic Congress' (NDC) strongholds respectively, the Greater Accra region swings between the two. Also, while Ashanti and Volta regions are predominantly Akan and Ewes that have developed strong political attachments to the NPP and NDC respectively, the Greater Accra region is ethnically diverse and encapsulates the overwhelming ethnic groups in the country.

Thirty (30) respondents were selected from each region. Then, two constituencies from each region were identified based on their records of electoral violence—15 each for a constituency. Thus, Ayawaso West Wuogon and Ododiodiodoo were selected from Greater Accra, Asawase and Suame (from Ashanti) and Anlo and North Tongu (from Volta). In each constituency, two polling stations where electoral violence has been perpetrated by party vigilantes were identified and each assigned seven or eight respondents depending on the specific situation. The respondents were randomly selected from the lists of polling stations and voters' register available at the EC (Electoral Commission) respectively and interviewed face-to-face and where it was not possible, the telephone option was used.

The primary data was supplemented with personal observation and archival materials retrieved from journal articles, published and unpublished books and government official reports and internet sources. Thus, the secondary data covered reviews of the theoretical and empirical literature on democratization, political parties, party vigilantes, and election violence. It must be emphasized that the overall information that was obtained through in-depth interviews and personal observations, was carefully transcribed and the critical issues were organized around salient themes based on the structure of the questions and then analysed. Also, worthy of note is that the information-gathering processes have conformed to ethical standards in research, namely they have guaranteed the anonymity and confidentiality of all respondents as well as the information they volunteered.

## 2   Conceptualizing Electoral Violence

While defying a clear-cut meaning, there is consensus among scholars that electoral violence is the act of aggression and thuggery inflicted on people during elections (Kalu & Gberevbie, 2018). It is a random or organized act to influence the electoral process through threats, verbal intimidation, hate speech, disinformation, physical assault, blackmail, destruction of property, and assassination, among others (Ijon, 2020; Kumah-Abiwu, 2017). Others refer to it as the snatching of ballot boxes with the aim to manipulate the outcome of election results while causing mayhem at polling stations, such as preventing opponents from carrying out their rightful duties by threatening and beating up election officers (Gyampo et al., 2017; Ladan-Baki, 2016).

Electoral violence manifests in diverse forms including the pursuit of exclusionary politics such as deliberate discrimination against sections of the voting population for electoral advantage, intimidation tactics and promotion of ethnocentrism to demobilize opponents' supporters (Bob-Milliar, 2014a). It also involves reckless use of inflammatory utterances by political actors (politicians) to provoke their opponents (Danso & Edu-Aful, 2012; Kumah-Abiwu, 2017). It may also take the form of rivals seeking to disrupt an opponent's campaign rallies or deployment of intimidatory tactics to influence the election process and harming other people (Birikorang & Aning, 2012; Gyampo et al., 2017).

Some political theorists have charged that democratic representation is intrinsically conflict (zero-sum game politics) because losers in elections are often left out in the political decision-making process, therefore, violence becomes an inevitable part of the game (Asamoah, 2020). From the perspective of identity-based theorists because multiparty politics reduces elections into a zero-sum game where the loser of the contest is virtually decapitated from central decision-making and a portion of the spoils of the state, the system invariably raises the stakes high for electoral violence (Asamoah, 2020; Bekoe & Burchard, 2021; Bob-Milliar, 2014a, 2014b).

In the view of the pluralists, in democratic elections where struggles/competition is a central part of the electoral process, conflict and to a large extent, violence, is an essential ingredient of the contestations for political power (Bekoe & Burchard, 2021). Similarly, the cultural pluralism theory assumes that because minority-majority dichotomy is ingrained in representative democracy, the challenge to access to power tends to engender tension. Where these tendencies are not effectively managed, electoral violence becomes the undeniable reality. According to the relative deprivation/frustration-aggression theorists, individuals who are frustrated, have the tendency to pursue violence in proportion to the severity of frustrations they suffer (Gurr, 1980). The advocates of this view contend that violence is often triggered by a blend of aggression and frustration (discontent in individuals or groups) about perceived injustice. Therefore, for the rational theorist's electoral violence is a tool for ensuring the balance of power in the electoral process. For instance, proponents of the identity-based theory maintain that ethnic polarization for purposes of electoral support—the mechanism by which the elite structure their electoral base and take the opportunity to mobilize supporters, and provide veritable grounds for violence and conflict (Bekoe & Burchard, 2021).

Despite the attempt to justify its presence in the electoral process, electoral violence is widely regarded as a condemnable act. It undermines the value of fairness on which democratic election competition is pivoted (Alidu, 2020; Debrah, 2005). Its perpetration in electoral mobilization undermines the principle of a level playing field, which is a principal barometer for measuring credibility of the election process and its outcome. Arguably, its occurrence in the electoral process could jeopardize the chances of the victims—those who suffer the violent acts—of winning. In the view of a key respondent, "as a political strategy, it has the capacity to alter voters' choices" (Interview, Teacher, Medina, June 2020).

Electoral violence undermines active popular participation in the political decision-making. This is because, it has been regarded as having the potential to suppress voter turnout and over time, to whittle away their interest in attending party campaigns and rallies, and eventually discourage them from going to the polling station to vote. Yet, persistent withdrawal from the polls due to voters' fear of being harmed by other opponents could lead to democratic recession (Interview, Lecturer in Political Science, Accra, November 2022). Moreover, it could spell doom for nascent democracies, particularly in Africa (Davenport, 2007; Hafner-Burton et al., 2013; Klaus & Mitchell, 2015; Wilkinson, 2006). The insecurity it brings to the state and the electoral process, may not only create fear and panic in society but also endanger the efforts to sustain the political peace for development to thrive (Asamoah, 2020; Bekoe, 2010).

## 3 Evolution of Party Vigilante Activities in Ghana

The literature establishes a direct link between electoral violence and party vigilantes' electoral manoeuvrings. That is, the perpetrators of electoral violence are the party vigilantes (Alidu, 2020; Asamoah, 2020; Bekoe, 2010). Party vigilantism may be defined as the planned use of threat or application of force against a party and its supporters by a rival party in response to perceived injustices or committal of electoral frauds, aiming to disadvantage them in an electoral contest (Alidu, 2020). But a careful perusal of the empirical literature reveals that the activities of party vigilantes date back to pre-independence electoral politics (Bob-Milliar, 2014a). Although group rivalries have been recorded in many communities' apolitical associations such as "Asafo Companies" and Ashanti Youth Association, among others, the phenomenon of party vigilante activities occurred between the Convention People's Party (CPP) and the United Gold Coast Convention (UGCC) and its successor, the National Liberation Movement (NLM). The period between 1951 and 1956 was remarkable for its intense intra- and inter-party political and electoral struggles. The leading political parties and their influential candidates that battled for supremacy over the governance of the country once the British colonial rule came to an end, sowed the seed of party vigilantism in the country (Birikorang & Aning, 2012; Bob-Milliar, 2014b). The sudden departure of Kwame Nkrumah from the UGCC and the formation of the CPP created the grounds for party rivalries in the body politic. In order to protect Nkrumah-CPP's independence from the UGCC, the former created a radical youth wing called "Veranda Boys." This CPP vigilante youth became the implementers of Nkrumah's "positive action" campaign against both the colonial government and the UGCC. On polling day of the 1951 election, the CPP radical youth wing (Veranda Boys) created Voters' Advice Centres which were located 50 yards from the polling stations to educate the illiterate voters on how to cast a valid ballot, however, the primary object was to "protect the ballot box from being tampered with by opposition forces" (Interview, Former MP, Accra, November 2022).

Similarly, party vigilantes' electoral support activities greeted the 1954 elections. The intense inter-party rivalries encouraged the CPP to form "Asafo Companies" to promote their particular agenda. The group hoisted "freedom flags" at the ward level of the party's structure as a strategy to deter and counter their opponents' perceived electoral machinations (Bob-Milliar, 2014b). The disappointment in the 1951 election result forced the UGCC to reorganize under a new name, National Liberation Movement

(NLM). It was the result of the combined strength of several opposition parties against the CPP. The ethnic complexion of the NLM heightened party vigilantes' activities in the electoral processes. Thus, while the Nkrumah-CPP mobilized its Veranda Boys into what became known as "Action Groupers", the NLM sought to neutralize their potency by deploying its own "Action Troupers"—drawn from its youth wing. The activities of these youth party activists (vigilantes) turned the election process into a violent field. The widespread intimidations perpetrated by the Action Groupers and Action Troupers against each other turned the otherwise peaceful election campaigns "into militancy out-manoeuvring thereby legitimizing violence as an ingredient in democratic elections" (Interview, Former MP, Accra, November 2022). Even in the aftermath of the election, the CPP continued to deploy the Action Groupers as its militant wing that unleashed terror on opponents throughout Nkrumah's reign (Austin, 1964; Chazan, 1983). The perennial violent attacks on suspected opposition forces served as a salient factor causing the immediate demise of the CPP government (Birikorang & Aning, 2012; Bob-Milliar, 2014a, 2014b; Dumenu & Adzraku, 2020). For instance:

> the Kurungugu assassination attempt on Nkrumah's life signalled the depth of violence in politics during the epoch. Finding it difficult to survive under the 'terror of the CPP veranda boys' intimidation, aggression, and harm, the opposition under its new name, United Party (UP) sponsored anti-CPP attacks via its Action Troupers. (Interview Politician, Accra, November 2022)

Again, towards the goal of dismembering the opposition parties after it turned Ghana into a one-party state, Nkrumah formed a powerful radical youth group called The Young Pioneers under the instruction of Tawiah Adamafio. Deployed as party spies, the group's activities led to the detention, execution, and self-exile of many leading opposition figures such as Dr. J. B. Danquah, and Dr. K. A. Busia among others (Interview, Politician, Accra, November 2022).

It must be emphasized that while political parties' activities were outlawed during the military interregnums, evidence of vigilante activities featured in the non-democratic regimes. For instance, the formation of the Provisional National Defense Council (PNDC) saw a resurgence of acts of vigilante violence attacks against "the enemies of the revolution" (Interview, Retired Judge, Accra, November 2022). In other to curb the growing insecurity during the period, the regime inaugurated several radical populist groups such as, Workers' Defense Committees (WDCs), People's Defense Committees (PDCs), Citizens' Vetting Committees (CVCs), Regional Defense Committees (RDCs), and National Defense Committees (NDCs) with the agenda to unleash violence on the "elite" (Ayee, 1994; Berry, 1995). For example, some cadres of the PNDC invaded the Supreme Court in Accra in June 1983 and declared their intention to replace the regular court system with the People's Tribunals, dissolve the Judicial Council, abolish the office of the Chief Justice, and close down the Ghana School of Law (Gocking, 2005).

## Nature of Party Vigilantism in the Current Dispensation

In 1992, the PNDC agreed to a transition to a multiparty system after persistent pressure from Western governments, their donors, and domestic democratic forces. In contrast to the expectation that post-Cold War electoral competition would be devoid of antagonism, it is the case that the party activists' electoral activities have continued to reflect "the revolutionary cadres" support for the regimes of yesteryears (Interview, Teacher, Accra, December 2022). Thus, despite eight uninterrupted general elections that have been held during the current constitutional dispensation with smooth power alternations, there is evidence that each of the elections has witnessed party foot-soldiers' violent activities. Although there are as many as 30 registered political parties in the country, the respondents think that "since returning to multiparty rule, electoral violence has been promoted by the two dominant political parties, namely the National Democratic Congress (NDC) and New Patriotic Party (NPP)" (Interview, Voters, Accra, December 2022). The two parties have demonstrated capacity to govern the country—the party alternations that have occurred at three different junctures have involved them. Hence, they have been the most active in the electoral process. The NDC's paramilitary organization has revolved around the erstwhile PNDC revolutionary cadres who stood firm to defend the regime. Although the return to constitutional rule theoretically ended the dreaded revolutionary CDRs, they continue to form the core of the NDC grassroots' support base and volunteered to protect the party's interests (Interview, Cadres of NDC, Accra, December 2022). With the demise of the PNDC, the CDRs metamorphosed to the popularly called "Asoka Boys"—a name derived from its dreaded revolutionary cadre. Similarly, the NPP has created its own paramilitary force called the "Invisible Forces" with the aim to counter the aggressive activities of the Asoka Boys. According to some respondents, "the formation of Invisible Forces aims to neutralize the terror activities of the Asoka Boys on the NPP and its supporters during elections" (Interview, National Executive Member of the NPP, Accra, November 2022). These unstructured and ill-organized party foot-soldiers are a mixture of partly literate and illiterate men, rather than women, who are mostly drawn from the less deprived social groups in the peri-urban communities to carry out the biddings of their parties. They are mostly "well-built young men—whose bodies show masculine features and look fearsome are often mobilized and 'indoctrinated' to be 'diabolical' to their party opponents" (Interview, Voters, Accra, December 2022).

The parties' vigilantes have embodied the most active youths within the parties. Radical in orientation and activities, "they form a constituent of the parties' youth wings some of whom are students in some of the tertiary institutions in the country" (Interview, Party Activist, Accra, December 2022). The Tertiary Educational Institutions Network (TEIN) and Tertiary Students Confederacy (TESCON) are the NDC and NPP's youth wings in the tertiary institutions respectively. These youth groups are structured and formalized. They have their own constitution to guide their internal activities. They choose their leaders at regular intervals. Many of their internal operations are informed by their respective party's orientation. In recent times, they have managed to secure a place in the membership of their respective party's national electoral colleges to participate in the election of the national leaders and presidential candidates. A second component of the group is the Fan Clubs—the most ardent followers of a particular party leader who aspires to be a flagbearer. Normally, such groups seek to propagate the ideas of their preferred candidate during intra-party candidate selection. Among others, the Youth for Mahama (YFM), John Mahama (JM) Fan Club, Bawumia Fun Club (BFM) and NPP Loyal Ladies have been prominent on the political and electoral processes. As the names imply, the groups comprise party members who have strong affinity to a particular member who have demonstrated leadership ambition. These Fun Clubs, therefore, represent the admirers of prospective candidates with the capacity to win elections who have devoted considerable time to canvass support for them during the primaries. Although some commentators believe that the latter (Fund Clubs) are less radical than the former (tertiary youth wings of the parties), there is little difference in their party and electoral activities. Indeed, the latter groups also extend to the former such that they promote antagonistic election campaigns which defy civility (Interview, Lecturer in Political Science, Accra, November 2022).

Together with others, the youth activists form the hard-core militants (radicals) of the parties' memberships. These energetic young men have operated somewhat as "private security guards" (militias) of the parties and their leading figures. In their efforts to defend the course of their parties, they have promoted violent electoral activities before, during, and post-election. First, their activities have been recorded in the pre-election process, particularly during the internal leadership contests and implementation of the activities to commence the election process. In all intra-party leadership selections, the factionalist groups within the parties have mobilized some of their youths to promote their individual leader's agenda. The intense competition by the candidates has pitted the Fun Club members against each other. In 1996 and 2000, the Kufuor and Akufo-Addo Fun Clubs clashed at several campaign outreaches with each intimidating the other to promote their candidate's interest. Similarly, in the 2000, 2008, and 2012 primaries, the NDC congress grounds witnessed dirty competition/challenges between the pro-Atta Mills, Pro-Goosie Tandoh and pro-Kwesi Botway's Fun Clubs—ardent supporters inflicted harm on each other. The heated exchanges by their ardent supporters were of a magnitude that cleaved the party. The groups that felt "brutalized" by their rivals succeeded in forming the National Reform Party in 2000 with their intimidated Goosie Tandoh as their presidential candidate. In the 2008 Koforidua leadership context, the factions that were overpowered withdrew their support from the NDC—some crossing the carpet to join the NPP while others rendered themselves neutral (Interview, Party Activists, Accra, December 2022).

The second nature of party vigilante activities have been the orchestrations of intimidations against their opponents in inter-party competitions—during the pre-election activities. The manifestations of the inter-party vigilante activities are the disruptions of opponents' campaigns. This has often taken the form of blatant obliterations of opponents' advertising materials—banners, posters and other paraphernalia aimed to weaken their opponents' competitiveness in the election. Others have involved launching physical assaults against their political opponents, (Interview, Businesswoman, Accra, December 2022). In all the election campaigns, the parties have encouraged their thugs to intimidate their opponents. Each of the parties have executed these intimidatory tactics very well in their strongholds. Thus, it is evident from the respondents' views that "a party's ability to make an electoral impact in its stronghold depends on how it is able to 'mastermind' the suppression of its opponent's supporters in its strongholds" (Interview, Party Activists, Accra, December 2022). It is the case, that "each party has used its 'machomen' to silence the opponent's supporters in areas where they command the majority support of the electorate" (Interview, Voters, Accra, December 2022). Therefore, it has become commonplace for parties to declare their enclaves as "no-go areas for their opponents" (Interview, Lecturer in Political Science, Accra, December 2022). During registration of voters, the dreaded machomen have often posed as barriers to discourage their opponents from coming out to register in their strongholds. The application of objections against their opponents who are residents in the slum areas of the communities on grounds that they are aliens have been one tactical intimidatory approach to limit their competition (Interview, Electoral Commission Official, Accra, November 2022).

The party vigilantes have also carried out their activities during elections—on polling day. Indeed, according to some respondents, "the practice where ardent party supporters constituting themselves into kind of militia groups providing security at the polling stations with the goal of securing the interests of their candidates has been a recurrent feature of post-democratization elections in the country" (Interview, Former Member of Parliament and Polling Agents, Accra, November 2022). In almost all the elections, the parties have mobilized their youth cadres to guard the ballot boxes in order to prevent their opponents from engaging in fraud to undermine their prospects of winning at the polling stations. An aspect of the threats against their opponents had been the issuance and spread of falsehoods. In their desire to win national elections, the parties have leaned on their militant foot-soldiers to promote disinformation to cause anxiety among their opponents' supporters. These militants have been found issuing counter-information to officially issued directives—such as dates for the commencements of an important electoral activity, procedures to guide voters and how to vote for one's vote to be counted (Interview, Electoral Commission Officials, Accra, December 2022). The parties' militias have not relented in their quests to manipulate the election outcome for their candidates and party by "not only intimidating voters in the queues but also beating electoral officials and general disruptions of the voting process" (Interview, Electoral Commission Officials, Accra, December 2022). Both the media and reports by observers have documented evidence of ballot-box snatching, or replacement of official ballot boxes with pre-stuffed ones at many polling stations by some party militias (Modernghana.org 2019). Thus, according to some respondents, "election contests in Ghana have turned into a boot-for-boot and all-die-be-die choices in which the parties' untrammelled desire to win elections have blinded them to the democratic rules of the game" (Interview, Voters, Accra December 2022).

The outstanding manifestation of party vigilantes' assault on the electoral process was during the conduct of the 31 January 2019 Ayawaso West Wuogon Parliamentary by-election. The violent clashes between the militias of the NDC and NPP on the afternoon of the by-election—while voting was ongoing—remains the single most intimidatory acts ever recorded since 1992 (Interview, EC Official, Accra, November 2022). The death of the NPP MP for the constituency, which offered the two parties the opportunity to fill the void in the EC's organized by-elections resurrected the NDC-NPP vigilantes' rivalries. The aggressive mobilization of the parties' militias produced a catastrophic effect on the election. The suspicion that the NDC had mobilized its vigilantes—the "Hawks"—to engineer election fraud by snatching of ballot boxes and intimidating NPP supporters to deny them access to the polls, sparked the NPP's Invisible Forces' ferocious response. The Presidential Commission Report is consistent with our findings:

The NDC dispatched its vigilante group, the Hawks, to act as its "election observers" and "do anything at all" as soon as they received instructions from their party leaders. The NDC Hawks fired gunshots close to a polling station in the constituency: The Commission established that there were arms in a warehouse around the La Bawaleshie Presbyterian Primary School—the place where gunshots were heard (Republic of Ghana, 2019a: 12).

The serious side of the NDC-NPP confrontations was the fact that the NPP had created a unit in the National Security referred to as the SWAT, membership of which were largely the party's vigilantes that had been "legitimized" under the state's cover. Thus, while voters were casting their ballots, the NPP deployed its SWAT "ostensibly, to thwart 'the NDC Hawks' fraudulent schemes thereby disrupting the voting process" (Interview, Voters, Accra, November 2022). The SWAT action led to the "retrieval of light ammunitions that had been stored in a warehouse within the constituency ostensibly to be used by the NDC Hawks to cause mayhem" (Interview, Party Activists, Accra, November 2022).

The post-election process has not escaped the party militias' destructive activities. Once they have executed the pre-and election manipulations, their next line of action has been to influence the post-election political process. Given that the vigilantes reflect the low-class memberships of the parties, they have positioned themselves to ensure that they received their rewards for their actions—electoral successes for their parties. Even in the sharing of the spoils from the elections, the vigilantes have used force and threats in the bargaining processes (Interview, Politicians, Accra, November 2022). In many instances, they have fomented troubles through threats, intimidations even against their patrons where their interests had not been met. As some respondents intimated, "the party vigilantes have become power brokers in the post-election political arrangements" (Interview, NPP Party Executive Member, Accra, November 2022). According to others, "any time their interests were sidestepped in the distributions of the largesse, they resorted to violence to achieve their aims" (Interview, MPs, Accra, November 2022). In several instances, following changes of regimes, they have applied force to remove their rival militias from the management of some state facilities such as public toilets and toll booths in order to take control over their management. Also, the party vigilantes have forcefully removed or ejected government appointees who were not their favourites. Where necessary too, they have deployed force to cause the reinstatement of their preferred candidates who had been removed from their positions (Interview, Former DCE, Accra, December 2022).

## Effects of Party Vigilante Activities on the Democratic Process

It has been argued that democracy thrives on mass participation. Therefore, getting the voters to the polls is a key responsibility of the political parties. This is where the party vigilantes' voter mobilization might have produced a positive outcome. Indeed, party cadres are noted for their abrasive campaigns to mobilize voters to the polls to ensure victory for their parties and candidates. Their door-to-door membership mobilization activities have been recognized by Debrah (2014) and Bob-Milliar (2014b). Also, their active educating of their parties' supporters on the electoral processes has been partly responsible for the relatively successful conduct of the elections (Interview, MPs, Accra, November 2022). They are the volunteers who have distributed party campaign materials and created enthusiasm in the parties' supporters thereby stimulating their interest in the electoral processes. Some respondents acknowledged that, "the innovations they have brought to the electoral process have been instrumental in the mass turnouts at the polls" (Interview, Party Activists, Accra, December 2022). In an environment of high mistrust of the managers of the electoral process and state institutions, the parties have relied on their vigilante foot-soldiers to protect their parties from those who could undermine their collective interest.

This notwithstanding, activities of party vigilantes have caused more damage to the electoral process than the claim of "acting as a mobilizing force for their parties" (Interview, Voters, Accra, December 2022). Their acts of intimidation, on the contrary, have potentially caused low participation at the polls. The sudden attacks on opponents and disruptions of electoral activities have scared more people to stay away from the polls rather than drawing them to register their names or cast their ballots (Interview, EC Officials, Accra, December 2022). In the view of some respondents, "their ill-trained unarmed machomen who are often deployed to "police" the ballots at the polling stations have demonstrated their capacity to undermine the legitimacy of state institutions" (interview, Voters, Accra, December 2022). By usurping the authority of the state institutions that are responsible for providing electoral security, the party vigilantes may be described as non-conformists whose activities obstruct the maintenance of law and order before, during and after elections (interview, Voters, Accra, December 2022). Also, their intimidatory and manipulative schemes remain palpably assaults on democracy. Their attacks on opponents and disruption of aspects of the election activities amount to a subversion on the democratic order. The boldness with which they have been deployed, and the use of threats as means to achieve their demands qualify them as "anti-democratic forces whose continuing existence within the parties poses grave hazards for the process towards democratic institutionalization" (interview, Lecturer in Political Science, Accra, December 2022). Other independent reports on the activities of party vigilantes have condemned their parallel policing at the polls as "acts in complete disregard of the standard election security practice" (Republic of Ghana, 2019b: 13).

The more debit side of their activities is the destruction of lives and properties. Thus, instead of mobilizing voters to participate in the electoral process, they have "inflicted wounds—injuries and killed innocent voters" (Interview, Voters, Accra, December 2022). For instance, a report noted, "live bullets fired by the SWAT team culminated in various degrees of injuries suffered by a section of the public residing in the vicinity … and various degrees of assault were committed by the SWAT on a section of the public including a member of parliament" (Republic of Ghana, 2019a: 43). The existence of party militia groups is a stark reality whose operations have either been sponsored, supported, or funded by some prominent persons within politics. The continuous existence of party militia groups poses a damning threat to the country's enviable constitutional democracy as their actions are an affront to the authority of the state and its democratic institutions including the EC.

## Tackling the Party Vigilantism Menace

For the sake of safeguarding democracy in the country, the activities of party vigilantes should be brought to an end. First, its demise should be promoted through direct legislation. Major legislation targeted specifically at party vigilantes should be enacted by the legislature. Once the law criminalizes the establishment of vigilante activities in the country, it will weaken the political parties' ability to promote their operations within their organizations. This way, political parties would be denied their existence when they flout the provisions of the law. In other words, it will allow the Electoral Commission (EC) to deregister a political party that entertains militia activities within its organization. The next step is to enforce the law. To this end, the security agencies should be empowered to subject the parties' internal activities to periodic reviews in order to punish acts that have promoted vigilantism. Success of the legislation will require the political will to end the canker within the parties. Therefore, the national political leadership should demonstrate their commitment to the delegitimization of vigilantes within the parties. Both the legislators that would pass the law, and the executive to enforce it should appreciate the urgency to act per their constitutional mandate to make the law active to discourage potential perpetrators. A high commitment by the members of the bench to apply the maximum sanctions on the perpetrators could serve as deterrent to the recalcitrant thereby making it an unattractive business for the youth.

Apart from formal legislation, the source of financing the activities of the party vigilantes should be axed. The party financiers that have provided funds to oil the wheels of party vigilantism in the country should be tackled by the state with a view to demobilize their activities. It is believed that once the financial supply routes are blocked, there will be little or no incentive to run the violence-cells within the parties. Although the youth have been the implementers of party vigilantes' activities, the big men and women who are embedded in the parties' apparatus have been the financiers. Therefore, a system that tracks the sources of the political parties' campaigns could be the journey towards cutting the supplies of oxygen of funds to the party vigilantes.

Public education has been identified as an important means to achieve the objective of ending party vigilantes' activities in the country. It is believed that a comprehensive public education programme should be undertaken with a view to discourage the youths from yielding to their parties' bidding to use them to perpetuate violence against other people which only serve the interests of the big men and women in their parties. Orienting the youth on democratic values and getting them to appreciate the essence of intra- and inter-party competition would have the potential to deradicalize them from their parties' indoctrinated programmes that have promoted militancy in their fabric. Two levels of public education have been presented. First, state institutions such as the National Media Commission (NMC) could capture the media space to promote persistent campaigns against party vigilantism. In addition, the National Commission on Civic Education (NCCE) may be deployed to some target communities such as the "Zongos"—slum and low-income areas in the suburbs—to promote aggressive campaigns against the menace and mobilize the youth to comprehend the incompatibility of their actions with civil political engagements. Second, since the basic unit of society in Ghana continues to remain in the domain of traditional rulers more than local governments (Debrah, 2022), it makes it trite to suggest the inclusion of the former in the public and particularly the youth education exercise. Given the respect society accords chiefs, mainstreaming them onto the campaign arena would inject a sense of action into the exercise. Also, their participation in the reorientation of the youths from party vigilantism would obtain a broad appeal among all the socio-politico-religious forces in the country.

## 4 Conclusion and Lessons

Ghana has made democratic strides in terms of having sustained and uninterrupted multiparty politics over a period of three decades, a rare feat in sub-Saharan Africa. During this period, there have been three power alternations and by Huntington's (1993) thesis, it qualifies as a democratic consolidated society, albeit electoralism being attacked as the only measuring variable for democracy. More significant of Ghana's democratic development is the role that the nascent political parties have played. In all the elections, the parties have actively mobilized the voters to the polls. They have also selected their candidates to compete in all departments of the electoral process. It is also evident that while many parties have secured a place on the electoral front, only the NDC and NPP have been progressive. Yet, Ghana's electoral politics has witnessed great upheavals due to the nurturing of vigilantes' activities within the leading political parties—the NDC and NPP. Far from being the mobilizing force for the parties' electorates and developed deep attachments to their parties which may be partly responsible for the relatively "flourishing" of democracy in the country, their activities have been obstructive to the institutionalization of democratic values in the body politic. The growing violence in the electoral process that is reprehensive, owes much to the activities of the party vigilantes. Apart from inflicting damages on the electorates and political opponents that have scared voters from the polls, they have destroyed properties, caused injuries and deaths to people. Also, the attacks on the electoral process—disruptions of voting processes, capturing of ballot boxes and other forms of orchestrations, have caused much damage to peaceful democratic exchanges. Given that elections offer the most enduring peaceful means of effecting political changes, any acts to undermine this objective is an affront to democracy. Therefore, the growing violence in elections through the party vigilantes' activities create conditions that promote democratic retrogression rather than institutionalizing it. Thus, the "militialization" of political competition only leads to violent electoral competition. It is important to emphasize that party vigilantism nurtures political radicalisms within the electorates and their growth will eventually suffocate democratic values. Furthermore, its pursuit in the electoral process undermines the electoral institution's ability to implement fair playing rules that are a *conditio sine qua non* for attaining credible elections. Therefore, only a process towards criminalizing and delegitimizing intra- and inter-party electoral competitions through the instrumentality of party vigilante activities will enable the electoral process to achieve peaceful regime change—violence-free election in Africa—a necessary condition for consolidating the nascent democratization that began with great optimism about achieving sustainable peaceful democratic transitions.

# Bibliography

Alidu, S. M. (2020). Political Vigilante Groups and Rationalism in Ghana's Electoral Democracy. *Journal of African Political Economy and Development, 5*, 3–20.

Asamoah, K. (2020). Addressing the Problem of Political Vigilantism in Ghana Through the Conceptual Lens of Wicked Problems. *Journal of Asian and African Studies, 55*(1), 457–471.

Asante, R., & Gyampo, R. E. (2021). Explaining Political Party Vigilantism and Violence in Parliamentary Bye-Elections in Ghana. *Journal of African Politics, 1*, 89–105.

Austin, D. (1964). *Politics in Ghana, 1946–1960*. Oxford University Press.

Ayee, J. R. (1994). *An Anatomy of Public Policy Implementation: The Case of Decentralization Policies in Ghana*. Avebury.

Ayee, J. R. (2010). The 2000 General Elections and Presidential Run-off in Ghana: An Overview. *Democratization, 9*(2), 148–174.

Bekoe, D. (2010). *Trends in Electoral Violence in Sub-Saharan Africa*. Washington, DC: Peace Brief 13, United States Institute of Peace.

Bekoe, D. A., & Burchard, S. M. (2021). Robust Electoral Violence Prevention: An Example from Ghana. *African Affairs, 21*(1), 543–567.

Berry, L. (1995). *Ghana: A Country Study* (3rd ed.). Library of Congress.

Birikorang, E. & Aning, K. (2012). Negotiating Populism and Populist Politics in Ghana, 1949–2012. In K. Aning & K. Danso (Eds.), *Managing Election-related Violence for Democratic Stability in Ghana* (pp. 61–96). Frederich Ebert Stiftung (FES).

Bob-Milliar, G. M. (2014a). Party Youth Activists and Low-intensity Electoral Violence in Ghana: A Qualitative Study of Party Foot Soldiers' Activism. *African Studies Quarterly, 15*(1), 125–153.

Bob-Milliar, G. M. (2014b). Verandah Boys Versus Reactionary Lawyers: Nationalist Activism in Ghana, 1946–1956. *International Journal of African Historical Studies, 47*(2), 287–318.

Bratton, M., Mattes, R., & Gyimah-Boadi, E. (2005). *Public Opinion, Democracy, and Market Reform in Africa*. Cambridge University Press.

Bratton, M., & Van de Walle, N. (1997). *Democratic Experiments in Africa: Regime Transition in Comparative Perspective.* Cambridge University Press.

Chazan, N. (1983). *An Anatomy of Ghanaian Politics. Managing Political Recession, 1969–1982.* Routledge.

Clapham, C. (1996). Governmentality and Economic Policy in Sub-Saharan Africa. *Third World Quarterly, 17*(4), 809–824.

Danso, K., & Edu-Aful, F. (2012). 'Fruitcake', 'Madmen', 'All-Die-Be-Die': Deconstructing Political Discourse and Rhetoric in Ghana. In K. Aning & K. Danso (Eds.), *Managing Election-Related Violence for Democratic Stability in Ghana* (pp. 97–132). Frederich Ebert Stiftung (FES).

Davenport, C. (2007). *State Repression and the Domestic Democratic Peace.* Cambridge University Press.

Debrah, E. (2005). *The Electoral Process and the 2000 General Elections in Ghana. Liberal Democracy and Its Critics in Africa: Political Dysfunction and the Struggle for Social Progress.* Zed Books.

Debrah, E. (2014). Civil Society Organizations and Political Party Electoral Engagements: Lessons from the 2008 and 2012 General Elections in Ghana. *Journal of Pan African Studies, 7*(3), 195–209.

Debrah, E. (2016). The Ghanaian Voter and the 2008 General Election. *Politikon, 43*(3), 371–387.

Debrah, E. (2022). Participation of Chiefs in Decentralised Local Governance in Ghana. *Commonwealth Journal of Local Governance, 26*, 53–73.

Dumenu, M. Y., & Adzraku, M. E. (2020). *Electoral Violence and Political Vigilantism in Ghana: Evidence from Selected Hotspots.* Ghana Center for Democractic Development (CDD-Ghana).

Gocking, R. S. (2005). *The History of Ghana.* Greenwood Press.

Gurr, T. R. (Ed.). (1980). *Handbook of Political Conflict: Theory and Research.* Free Press.

Gyampo, R., Graham, E., & Asare, E. (2017). Political Vigilantism and Democratic Governance in Ghana's Fourth Republic. *African Review, 44*(2), 112–235.

Gyimah-Boadi, E. (Ed.). (2004). *Democratic Reform in Africa: The Quality of Progress.* Lynne Rienner Publishers.

Gyimah-Boadi, E. (2018). *Making Democracy Work for the People: Reflections on Ghana's 25 Year Journey Towards Democratic Development.* Ghana Centre for Democratic Development (CDD-Ghana).

Hafner-Burton, E. M., Hyde, S. D., & Jablonski, R. S. (2013). When Do Governments Resort to Election Violence? *British Journal of Political Science, 42*(1), 1–31.

Huntington, S. H. (1993). *The Third Wave: Democratization in the Late Twentieth Century.* University of Oklahoma Press.

Ijon, F. B. (2020). Election Security and Violence in Ghana: The Case of Ayawaso West Wuogon and Talensi By-elections. *Asian Research Journal of Arts & Social Sciences, 10*(1), 32–46.

Kalu, T. O., & Gberevbie, D. E. (2018). Election Violence and Democracy in Nigeria: A Study of the 2011 and 2015 General Elections in Lagos State. *Kaduna Journal of Humanities, 2*(1), 60–70.

Klaus, K., & Mitchell, M. I. (2015). Land Grievances and the Mobilization of Electoral Violence: Evidence from Côte d'Ivoire and Kenya. *Journal of Peace Research, 52*(5), 622–635.

Kumah-Abiwu, F. (2017). Issue Framing and Electoral Violence in Ghana: A Conceptual Analysis. *Commonwealth & Comparative Politics, 55*(2), 1–22.

Kyei, J., & Berckmoes, L. H. (2021). Political Vigilante Groups in Ghana: Violence or Democracy? *Africa Spectrum, 53*(3), 321–338.

Ladan-Baki, I. S. (2016). Electoral Violence and 2015 General Elections in Nigeria. *Global Journal of Human-Social Science, 16*(F1), 23–29.

Lindberg, S. I. (2005). Consequences of Electoral Systems in Africa: A Preliminary Inquiry. *Electoral Studies, 24*(1), 41–64.

Nugent, P. (1995). *Big Men, Small Boys and Politics in Ghana: Power, Ideology and the Burden of History, 1982–1994*. Burns & Oates.

Prempeh, K. (2003). *The Executive-Legislature Relationship Under the 1992 Constitution: A Critical Review*. Ghana Center for Democratic Development.

Republic of Ghana. (2019a). *The Ayawaso West Wuogon Events Commission of Inquiry Final Report*. Republic of Ghana.

Republic of Ghana. (2019b). *White Paper on the Report of the Commission of Inquiry into the Ayawaso West Wuogon Events*. Republic of Ghana.

Van de Walle, N. (2007). *Meet the New Boss, Same as the Old Boss? The Evolution of Political Clientelism in Africa. Patrons, Clients and Policies: Patterns of Democratic Accountability and Political Competition* (Vol. 1, pp. 50–67). Cambridge University Press.

von Soest, C. (2021). Neopatrimonialism: A Critical Assessment. In W. Hout & J. Hutchinson (Eds.), *Elgar Handbook on Governance and Developemnt Cheltenham* (pp. 1–20). Edward Elgar.

Wilkinson, S. (2006). *Votes and Violence: Electoral Competition and Ethnic Riots in India*. Cambridge University Press.

Young, D. J. (2009). *Is Clientelism at Work in African Elections? A Study of Voting Behavior in Kenya and Zambia* (Afro Barometer Working Paper No. 106, 1–23). Accra: Centre for Democratic Development.

# Investigating the Causes and Impact of Electoral Violence in Nigeria

Usman Sambo, Babayo Sule, and Mohammed Kwarah Tal

## 1 Introduction

Electoral violence is one of the major forms of violence that affect global peace and security and, most importantly, the democratization process and good governance. It is a phenomenon that is reported worldwide; but emerging democracies are exhibiting more characteristics of violence during the electoral process (Birch et al., 2020). Across geopolitical zones in the world from Africa to Asia, Latin America and the Caribbean, several incidents of violence are recorded in every electoral cycle of most of the countries. The nature, pattern, dimension, and manifestations of electoral violence vary from one state to another; this does not make the intent any different in outlook. Most of the perpetrators of electoral violence have aimed at intimidation and subversion of the electoral process to give them an undue advantage over their opponents in the electoral contest (United State Institute for

---

U. Sambo
Department of Public Administration, Yobe State University, Damaturu, Nigeria

B. Sule (✉)
Department of International Relations, Federal University of Kashere, Gombe, Nigeria
e-mail: babayosule@gmail.com

M. K. Tal
Department of Political Science, Federal University of Kashere, Gombe, Nigeria

Peace, 2020). Electoral violence is enabled by dominant drivers that characterize the categorization of such countries in their political culture and voting behaviour. Failure to institutionalize functional political institutions, weak political parties, ethnic, religious and regional incoherence, the selfish motives of politicians, an uninformed electorate and other related factors generate the occurrence of electoral violence in the affected countries (Birch, 2020). Electoral violence has several repercussions and implications for all actors, including the politicians, parties, and voters, and affects democracy and national security. It impedes good governance, and the will and constitutional right to vote and have the votes counted for preferred candidates; insecurity is engineered, and policymaking and implementation becomes the prerogative and personal wish of the leaders instead of the collective will of the populace; and above all, electoral violence leads to the collapse of the democratic process in many instances, as witnessed in African, Asian, South American, and Caribbean countries (Wilkinson, 2004).

Africa is the region that faces the threat of electoral violence more than any other part of the world. In essence, more than 60% of elections in Africa are heralded by violence, and the outcomes are also marked with violence (Burchard & Simati, 2019). Electoral violence in Africa takes place in the context of the pre-electoral process, during the voting process, and in the aftermath of the declaration of results. The despising of the opposition, the zero-sum game, and the sit-tight nature of African rulers who in self-opinionated fashion have arrogated eternal power to themselves, has led such rulers to believe that power should be Machiavellian in nature, even when they proclaim to have fully adopted the Western liberal democratic system (Shenga & Pereira, 2019). Opposition in Africa is seen as a staunch irredeemable enemy that must be crushed at all costs. In the process, political gangsters and militias are quickly assembled by the ruling class to terrorize opposition leaders and their supporters, to the extent that even if they scaled all the hurdles of electoral bodies' technicalities and made it to the final battlefield, they would be ostracized with violence (Fjelde & Hoglund, 2014).

Nigeria has become one of the most notable states for electoral violence in the world. Incidents, reported cases, and recorded instances of electoral violence have kept on resurfacing and escalating since 2003. In essence, the 2003, 2007, 2011, 2015, and 2019 general elections have been heavily characterized and affected by electoral violence. In some cases, the violence took place before the election, during the course of the election, and after the election. Several observers, analysts, media, and academic researchers that investigated and monitored the previous elections in Nigeria from 2003 to 2019 have concluded that the elections were marred by violence on a large scale, and intimidation, as well as assault and killing in some situations (United States Agency for International Development, 2020). The manner in which the figures and incidences of electoral violence continue to escalate has necessitated an interest in investigation in the area. Nigeria is a West African state with an estimated population of over 200 million, the sixth highest in the world. It is an oil-producing country, being the tenth largest producer in the world. It is the most populous black nation in the world, has *biggest GDP in Africa, and was colonized by Britain from 1856 to 1960. Nigeria secured independence with a Westminster parliamentary model of democratic rule which only lasted for six years. The vicissitudes of military coups and counter-coups later altered the Nigerian political destiny from that of a parliamentary state to one with an American presidential style of political structure. Nigeria emerged as a federal state with three tiers of government, having the federal government at the centre with headquarters in Abuja, 36 states, and 774 local governments. Nigeria is a multi-ethnic, multi-religious and multi-geographical setting with six geopolitical zones. The Nigerian political system is volatile and highly competitive, leading the elites to make use of the fragile nature of inhabitants through the exploitation of religion, ethnic, and regional differences to secure power (Siollun, 2021).

This chapter investigates the causes and impact of electoral violence in Nigeria. The purpose is to trace the genesis of one of the crises that is threatening to pull down the hard-earned democracy in the Fourth Republic (1999–2022) which emerges as the longest surviving Republic in Nigeria's history. In doing so, the study adopts and integrates interviews conducted with specialized experts identified from the relevant field of study. The study was part of a PhD research investigation and the primary data were extracted from the interviews administered during the field survey for the PhD journey. The present chapter has been upgraded and updated to incorporate recently unfolding events. The other source of data is documentary resources. The data were interpreted using content analysis whereby the interview sources were inspected and analysed within the main body of the work, together with the existing works that supported the interview findings. The chapter is arranged in the following sections: the introduction; the nature of electoral violence; an overview of electoral violence in Nigeria; the causes of electoral violence in Nigeria; the impacts of electoral violence in Nigeria and the conclusion section. The study presents an alternative framework for practical policy implementation that will mitigate electoral violence so as to enable peaceful electoral conduct and sustained democratic governance.

## 2 The Nature of Electoral Violence

Electoral violence is observed to have been an orchestrated deliberate effort for the disenfranchisement of eligible voters, preventing them from exercising their rights, particularly in a circumstance where the perceived favoured winner is not the one desired by those who wish to subvert the process (Bratton, 2008). Inarguably, the purpose of electoral violence is to influence the outcome of electoral results by political actors after violence. The process is perpetuated by coercion, aggression, irregularities, and a targeted destruction of lives, properties, and social amenities (Birch et al., 2020). Birch et al. (2020) argue that electoral violence manifests in all electoral processes, voter registration, party primaries, the campaign process, the declaration of final results, and the aftermath of the announcement of results. Electoral violence can take various forms, dimensions, and characteristics, not necessarily the same in all societies, but the method and purpose remain the same: the use of violence and an attempt at influencing electoral outcome (Birch, 2020).

In some societies, like African states, harassment and intimidation are recorded rather than inimical violence. Electoral violence is identified as a strategy for securing electoral victory. There are various strategies available for electoral competitors to win, such as the use of campaign propaganda, money, and vote-buying; the exploitation of religious, ethnic, regional, and other social divisions; and manipulation and violence. Political actors often find the use of electoral violence as helpful for outwitting their competitors. Electoral violence differs from other forms of violence because it has the institutional frameworks associated with it that enable violence to occur in the process. Other forms of violence may erupt abruptly without recourse to any institutional basis. For example, electoral violence can be perpetrated through political parties, electoral management bodies, and political vanguards which, without any election at hand, lack any justification or opportunity to initiate violence (Birch, 2020). Birch (2020) further argues that corruption and the political order determine the nature of electoral violence, which affects opposition voters and leaders more than the ruling parties, even though the ruling parties and their supporters also face the same threat in many instances.

Electoral violence is designed by politicians to ensure an electoral victory. While there is the argument that political competition may lead to peace, it may also lead to violence if the intensity of the competition results in the politics of a zero-sum game, particularly in multi-ethnic societies. Politicians blend ethnic politics with electoral violence to disguise their purpose of achieving power. This has been exemplified in Eastern Europe in the 1990s when Milosevic's distraction led to a pogrom. In essence, election violence is used as an incentive for ethnic violence, to secure power in an ethnically dominated political environment (Wilkinson, 2004). Wilkinson's, 2004 study, using India as his frame of analysis, concludes that electoral violence is bundled into ethnic politics, and ethnic violence is unbundled through electoral violence. Patronage and clientelism motivate electoral violence in societies where formal political institutions are overshadowed by personal relationships based on resource exchange and political loyalty. Political supporters and loyalists in such political environments are more than willing to perpetrate violence in the electoral process for their preferred candidates (Taylor, 2018).

In a similar fashion to, but distinct from, that of Birch (2020) who sees electoral violence as a strategy, Mochtak (2018) views electoral violence as a form of political struggle, and it does not matter whether the environment is Thailand, Bangladesh, Pakistan, India, Kenya, Egypt, Russia, Ukraine, or the Western Balkans. Once the struggle for power becomes antagonistic, with unconventional behaviours by politicians and their supporters, the outcome will be unpleasant. Elections by themselves do not cause violence unless the intense struggles set up some causal or moderating factors to intervene and lead to violence. Electoral violence is a way of manifesting political instability during a process of transformation, as a technique used by authoritarian/hybrid rule to advance its own goal. Different political environments are influenced by different political actors in the electoral arena (Mochtak, 2018). The context of electoral violence has been affected by global political development. For instance, the era of the Cold War ideological battle and the process of democratization in the third wave (Huntington, 2004) made some cases of electoral conduct turbulent and violent. A critical example of this category is democratization in the post-communist Balkan states where violence in the transformation process was recorded due to instability (Mochtak, 2018).

Africa is a hotspot of electoral violence in the twenty-first century. The newly independent states in Africa, not used to opposition politics in their indigenous culture, but used to competitive struggles for power due to the monarchical nature of pre-colonial Africa, were forcefully initiated into competitive democracy by colonial exploiters. In post-independence African states, the assumed leaders found it difficult and intolerable to accommodate the opposition. Affected by deep ethnic division that emanated from arbitrary territorialization and deterritorialization by the colonisers, elections in Africa became volatile and totally zero-sum (Fjelde & Hoglund, 2014). Political violence in Africa takes the form of assault, murder, beating, killing battering, assassination, attempted murder, malicious damage, arson, wanton damage to property, looting, bombing, disruption of political rallies and campaigns, fighting, hooliganism, torture, thuggery, hijacking, and personal humiliation (Friedrich Ebert Stiftung, 2001). Sub-Saharan Africa had the highest incidence of electoral violence from the 1990s to 2000s, as reported in an empirical study by Fjelde and Hoglund (2014), although it has also been observed that the countries in the region have made significant progress in democratization recently (Le Van, 2015). The Social Conflict in Africa Database (SCAD) reports that sub-Saharan Africa countries conducted 390 elections from 1990 to 2012, with an estimated 57% of the elections experiencing some forms of violence, while 91 elections also witnessed post-election violence. In another report by the African Electoral Violence Database (AEVD), 60% of African elections experienced election violence from 1990 to 2008 (Burchard & Simati, 2019). Burchard and Simati (2019) conclude that about 55% of African elections had faced electoral violence as of 2015. Indeed, ethnic exploitation, vote-buying and electoral violence are the three major keys to securing victory in African elections. Political parties and politicians are found at the centre of sponsoring electoral violence. Most of the reported incidents of electoral violence in Africa are directly related to political parties and ethno-religious leanings (Fafchamps & Vicente, 2013).

## 3  An Overview of Electoral Violence in Nigeria

Electoral violence is a phenomenon that has been bedevilling Nigerian democracy and the democratization process for several decades. Central to the discourse of electoral violence in Nigeria is the question of power and power-control. Rent-seeking and patrimonialism are instrumental in determining the face of electoral violence in Nigeria, where the leaders strive to hold on to power with the purpose of allocating national resources to cohorts and cronies (Igwe & Amadi, 2021). Electoral violence in Nigeria may be categorized in terms of violence during the pre-election, mid-election, and post-election periods. Pre-election violence is normally manifested in the manipulation and subversion of the voters' registration exercise, disruption of campaigns and rallies, a campaign of terror to ostracize opposition, political assassinations, kidnappings and other related phenomena (Onapajo, 2014). This view has been empirically supported by a study (Strauss & Taylor, 2009) showing that pre-election violence is most common in Africa, where it is reported that from 1999–2007, 117 cases of pre-election violence were recorded in 124 countries. Election-day violence in Nigeria usually manifests in the form of unleashing menacing weapons across the various states in the federation, such as knives, machetes, clubs, sticks, and in some instances, guns and exploding bombs. There is also ballot snatching, the stealing of ballot boxes, the driving away of voters by force from polling stations, attacks on electoral officials and opponents and their supporters, the destruction of election materials, the alteration of results and the destruction of property (Onapajo, 2014). Post-election violence is a large-scale process that may involve killing, destruction, and the burning of public buildings in the expression of grievances against perceived manipulation (Onapajo, 2014). The question of who uses or employs electoral violence is a technical one. There is usually a rush to point out the incumbent as the perpetrator, but the Nigerian case has revealed another side, as reported by many studies (Campbell, 2010; Igwe & Amadi, 2021; Onapajo, 2014). In the Nigerian context, both ruling and opposition parties, and both politicians and supporters have engaged in the act of electoral violence.

Nigeria is an epicentre of electoral violence in Africa and in the world. In the Fourth Republic (1999–2022), out of six consecutive uninterrupted elections conducted, five in 2003, 2007, 2011, 2015, and 2019 were marred and characterized by electoral violence on a large scale. Politicians established electoral militia gangs on purpose to execute violence during elections on their behalf, in order to win at all costs. In the case of "Area Boys" in Lagos, the "Bakassi Boys" in Niger Delta, "OPC" in Southwest, "Egbesu" in Southwest, "Yan Daba" or "Jagaliya" in Kano State, "Sara Suka" in Bauchi State, "Kalare" in Gombe State, the "Banu Israeli" in Taraba State, and "ECOMOG" in Borno State, the politicians continue to form their own errand boys, supply them with intoxicants and weapons, and sponsor them to violently unleash terror against voters and opposition, which disrupts the peaceful process of electoral conduct in Nigeria (Ikelegbe & Garuba, 2011). Bratton (2008), discloses that one out of ten voters in Nigeria experienced a form of electoral violence from 2003 to 2007.

Statistically, the National Democratic Institute (NDI) reported for Nigeria's 2007 general election there were about 280 election-related deaths prior to the conduct of the election. The NDI further revealed that the Nigerian electoral body, the Independent National Electoral Commission (INEC), reported 50 deaths, and 1,093 electoral offenders after the first round of the election, but the Transition Monitoring Group (TMG) reported the number of deaths as 80 (Onapajo, 2014). Electoral violence continues to cost Nigeria many lives unnecessarily, in an atmosphere that should not only be peaceful but also full of liberty and freedom of choice. Violence and political conflicts related to elections claimed 2,000 lives in Jos, Plateau State. The post-election violence that erupted in Gombe State cost a handful of lives, with properties worth millions of naira destroyed in the aftermath of the declaration of the 2011 presidential election result; but the Kaduna State case became a gruesome one which led to the death of over 700 people. Similar violence was recorded in Kano and several other northern states with churches, mosques, police stations, shops and business set ablaze, and reported deaths totalling 1,000 (Igwe & Amadi, 2021). The 2011 electoral violence was predicted by Campbell (2010) in the build-up to the presidential election, considering the volatile nature of the environment, the deep-seated division fostered by politicians among the voters, a zero-sum game, and other factors. The warning signs and the proposed strategies by Campbell (2010) were, however, ignored by politicians, whose selfish motives of securing power at all costs superseded all logic and reasons and all considerations of national security or the supremacy of the constitution.

The US International Centre for Electoral Support (USICES) reported that over 1,000 lives were lost in Nigeria to electoral violence during the 2011 post-election violence (USICES, 2018). In 2015, about 100 were killed in electoral violence across the country (Kwarkye, 2019). A study (Demarest & Langer, 2019) reveals that media reporting on electoral violence in Nigeria does not present a true picture of the damage incurred from the phenomenon, because the Nigerian media takes sides in the process. The United States Institute for Peace reported that 100 people were killed in election-related violence in 2003, 300 were killed in 2007, while 700 were killed in Kaduna alone in the post-2011 election violence (and another 300 in other parts of Northern Nigeria), 106 were killed in the 2015 general election and hundreds of people were killed in the build-up to and during the process of the 2019 general election (Campbell, 2019). In another report, Human Rights Watch (HRW, 2019) observed that 11 deaths were documented in Kano State between the presidential and gubernatorial elections in 2019. Furthermore, according to SBM Intelligence, as reported by Human Rights Watch which monitors political and socioeconomic development in the country, 626 people were killed during the election cycle in Nigeria in 2019, after violent campaigns in 2018 (Delay, 2019). The incidence of electoral violence in the country was portrayed in a post-election survey by the United States Agency for International Development (USAID) in Nigeria which disclosed that 13% of the sampled interviewees saw the 2019 general election as weak because of electoral violence (USAID, 2020).

The 2019 general election, which was expected to consolidate a peaceful transition from the incumbent party to an opposition party, unprecedented in the history of Nigeria, turned out to be worse than the 2015 general election in terms of electoral violence. The Human Rights Watch (2019) reported

11 cases of deaths from electoral violence during the February 23 presidential election. Also, nearly 50 cases of deaths in Kano and the Rivers States were respectively reported in the gubernatorial elections in 2019 (Human Rights Watch, 2019). The security personnel either stood idly by while the violence was being perpetrated, or ran away for their safety, while in some cases, the INEC spokesman, Festus Okoye, observed that cases of complicity were witnessed on the part of security agencies (Human Rights Watch, 2019). The number of cases, however, dropped in 2019 in comparison with that of 2015. For instance, in the build-up to the 2015 general election, 80% of states recorded violence, while in 2019 only 50% recorded the same (Campbell, 2019). Irrespective of the cases of electoral violence, its nature, and the form that it takes in Nigeria, there are several reasons why it continues to resurface, and there are many implications or payoffs. The next sections examine these aspects.

## 4 The Causes of Electoral Violence in Nigeria

Theoretically, electoral violence can be traced or established in the Nigerian context using Game Theory and the consideration of political culture. From the perspective of Game Theory, Nigerian politicians engage in a type of zero-sum game where the winner takes all, and the loser loses all. Neumann and Morgenstern (1944) assume that decision-making in a competitive environment entails the employment of variant strategies by the competitors who are struggling to exert influence over each other in pursuit of the same target, with a clear and total knowledge of the environment and the critical perception of the nature of payoffs and the benefits. In the political context, and specifically, in the Nigerian environment, the political game is subject to intensive competition by political actors to win at all costs. This is because the political terrain in Nigeria is made a lucrative venture. Patronage, clientelism, nepotism, and resource allocation are all conducted on the basis of patronization of political actors instead of on their merit. In this regard, the holding of a political office in Nigeria is equated with the opportunity for wealth accumulation and well-being. Thus, politicians could not spare any technique of competition in order to cruise to victory. The patrons and clients adopted violence in the electoral process to scare away any perceived threat to victory.

The political culture of Nigeria is characterized by electoral violence and the politics of division. A study (Sule et al., 2017a), reported an interesting finding that political culture directly influenced electoral or voting behaviour in Nigeria, and the pattern of Nigerian political culture was inherent in the attitude of political players who strove to win by hook or by crook. In the quest to win at all costs, politicians adopt any opportunity available, and where none exists, they create one to push for their victory. Nigerians have become acclimatized to the politics of bitterness, violence, and manipulation. Ethnic division, religious affiliation and regional belonging are readily accentuated by politicians to secure access to national politics (Sule et al., 2017a). Campbell (2019) argued that the electoral process in Nigeria degenerated into a sharp religious division between Christians and Muslims, and whenever candidates for the presidential seat emerged from the North and South, as in 2015, the tendency towards electoral violence was inevitable in the pre-election, during the election and in the aftermath. This has been corroborated factually: when the two leading candidates in the 2019 presidential election emerged from the North and were both Muslims, the electoral violence shifted ground from the presidential to the respective gubernatorial elections across the country.

Intra-party conflicts and inter-party rivalry are identified as roots of persistent electoral violence in Nigeria. Personal rivalry between politicians has transitioned into party rivalry; because the parties are weak and devoid of ideology, individuals that formed the party are seen as the party itself. Once the intense competition affects the political stalwarts, their supporters explode into a fire of violence, which leads to their defeat. This was recorded since 2003 in the case of the former ruling PDP where intra-party disputes eventually affected their chances in 2015 and, thereby, led to their defeat in the general election (Adeniyi, 2017). The inter-party rivalry between the ruling PDP and the opposition APC in the preparation for the 2015 general election caused violence of a large magnitude, because, for the first time, a strong opposition with the wherewithal to match the strength of the ruling party emerged (Onubogu & Hassan, 2018; Sule et al., 2018). The scenario of intra-party and inter-party conflicts within the APC and the PDP and between the APC and the PDP sharply affected the 2019 general election and led to electoral violence nationwide.

The attitude of politicians and the campaign rhetoric adopted by politicians have sometimes fuelled electoral violence. In many circumstances, politicians during their rallies and public addresses in the media have urged their supporters to use all means possible to win at all costs. The four-time presidential contestant and two-time winner, Muhammadu Buhari, was reported in the build-up to the 2011 presidential election to have uttered that "if the election is rigged this time, dogs and baboons will soak in bloodbath." Expressed in more direct terms, this means: "if the election is rigged this time, there will be collateral damage" (Campbell, 2010). The post-election violence that followed later in 2011 was directly related to such an incendiary statement, believed to have been a motivator for the eruption of violence. Although Muhammadu Buhari had dissociated himself from the violence, and constantly continued to appeal to his supporters in the aftermath of the declaration of the result to stay away from any form of violence, the damage had occurred, and he had to take the larger share of the blame for the utterance. A similar incident was witnessed in the inconclusive 2019 Kano State gubernatorial election, where the APC chairman in the state, Abdullahi Abbas, in a public gathering, pronounced that the conclusion of the inconclusive election was a war that would never be compromised, and that they were ever ready to win, no matter what it would take. On the election day in Kano State, voters, journalists, observers, and INEC officials were welcomed with large scale violence by "Yan Daba" who brandished lethal weapons. Some scores of lives were lost in the process. Similar cases were recorded in Rivers, Plateau, Benue and Bauchi (Sule & Sambo, 2020). Related to the above, financial sponsors of politicians' "godfatherism" is a strong factor that propels electoral violence. Some groups of cabals with money sponsor their anointed "sons" to win power at all costs for the purpose of lording it over them when they assume power. In the process of sponsorship, they employ thugs, militias, and violence to ensure victory (Sule et al., 2018).

Weak institutions and executive arrogance are instrumental in causing electoral violence. Parties that are expected to institutionalize recruitment, training and political socialization are reduced to the personal property of powerful politicians (Onapajo, 2014). The electoral body, the INEC, which is saddled with the task of monitoring and sanctioning of electoral offences in terms of violence, violation of spending limits, and other breaches of regulations is unable to discharge its responsibilities as expected because the excessive abuse of power by the ruling class render it incapacitated in this regard (Sule et al., 2017a). The incumbent diverts national security resources, other national resources and other terms of favour and influence to their political advantage and victory. However, from a different perspective, Igwe and Amadi (2021), have identified abject poverty, excessive deprivation, unemployment, inequality, a low level of literacy and political socialization, money politics and weak institutions as the drivers of electoral violence in Nigeria. Nigeria is now the world poverty headquarters, with around 70% living in poverty, spending less than $2 per day. During the electioneering process, the majority of the populace saw the election period as an opportunity for cheap money and survival. Politicians besieged voters with money-bags and the teeming unemployed youth become a ready prey for recruitment into violence. But the United States Institute for Peace

(2020) stresses that failure to prevent perceived threats of violence before their occurrence, is the cause of electoral violence in environments like Nigeria. Numerous reports and projections have presented areas calling for a red alert, but the policymakers, who were often beneficiaries of the violence, neglected the reports (USIP, 2020).

The presence of pre-existing social conflicts in a society very often triggers electoral violence. Once a hostile section senses an opposition victory, an old rivalry outside the electoral process is reactivated and violence erupts. In Nigeria, politicians are found to have opened old wounds in campaigns to set voters against their opponents. For instance, the Nigerian Civil War polemic is easily rekindled when a Northern candidate is being campaigned against, and the same is true in the North when an Igbo candidate is projected. The outcome is that electoral violence is likely to manifest right from the outset of the campaign (Taylor, 2018). A typical example is the way in which the PDP presidential candidate, Dr Goodluck Ebele Jonathan, was pelted with pebbles, together with his convoy, in many Northern states having pronounced that he had an Igbo lineage in his blood. A false alarm or electoral fraud has sometimes orchestrated electoral violence in Nigeria (Taylor, 2018). The 2011 post-election violence in Northern States was projected when the popular favourable Northern candidate, Muhammadu Buhari, uttered that if this election was rigged, there would be collateral damage, as noted above. Some political reasons in the Nigerian context have contributed to electoral violence since 1999. These factors consist of failure to secure justice in courts by the oppressed, political repression, intolerance towards the opposition, political greed, and incitement (Friedrich Ebert Stiftung, 2001). All these factors have several repercussions on Nigerian democracy, national security, and peaceful co-existence of the country as one. These threats are presented below to expose the implications with the purpose of awakening all stakeholders concerned to understand the magnitude of the threats, and to put all hands on deck to mitigate or eradicate the phenomenon.

## 5 The Impact of Electoral Violence in Nigeria

Electoral violence has several forms of impact in Nigeria. The country which battled with prolonged exacerbated military rule has now turned over a new leaf by practising democratic governance, which is gradually proving to be successful in comparison with past experiences. Unfortunately, the hard-earned democratization is threatened by the reckless handiwork of political actors. In the forefront of all the implications, insecurity is the prime factor. Studies by Burchard and Simati (2019), USAID (2020), USIP (2020) and Igwe and Amadi (2021) have linked electoral violence in Nigeria with the current trend of insecurity. The devastating insecurity in the country has reached an alarming rate recently, threatening to collapse the country. It is believed that the deliberate sponsorship of political militias, failure to sanction them and the act of arming them with weapons has led to the manifestation later of a complex situation of insecurity in the country. Before the emergence of democratic rule in the Fourth Republic, several security threats existed in the country, but they had not been as bad as when democratic rule commenced. By 2010, all of the geopolitical zones in the country were deeply involved in one form of armed violence or another, reminiscent of electoral violence. The Niger Delta militias in the South, Boko Haram in the Northeast, farmers-herder conflict in Northcentral, the IPOB secessionist agitation movement in the Southeast, rural banditry and kidnapping in the Northwest and separatist agitation in the Southwest are all perceived as spillover effects of electoral violence, purposely engineered by the ruling class to secure victory at all costs. The consequence is that Nigeria is now one of the most terrorized and insecure states in the world. In essence, Collier (2007), submitted that the cases of electoral violence in Nigeria and other related places had put democracy in danger of extinction globally. Besides, domestically, ethnic and religious clashes were compounded by electoral violence across the nation, which has been one of the main security challenges that the country is facing today.

Electoral violence in Nigeria has the potential of causing democratic governance to collapse as it did historically in the past. Most of the reasons that the military advanced for their intervention in politics in Nigeria in the 1960s, the 1970s and even the 1980s are anchored in such issues. And the factors of violence that were witnessed in those periods were not in any way more palpable than the ones that are manifesting today, except perhaps, the Civil War, which was believed to have been the ill-advised action of the military itself. Africa has not been spared military coups even in the twenty-first century (Kwarkye, 2019). The developments in Egypt in 2013, in Zimbabwe in 2017, in Mali in 2020, in Sudan in 2020 and 2021 and in Chad in 2021 imply that Nigeria may not be immune if political actors continue to interfere with the democratic process. The collapse of democratic rule in present-day Nigeria will not bode well for all stakeholders. The loss of liberty, freedom of speech, and participation in the decision-making process, international collaboration and several other benefits that authoritarian regimes may not entertain will stall Nigeria's quest for twenty-first century progress and development. The politicians, as the first constituents that benefit from the proceeds of democratic rule, should know that posterity will never forgive their disservice if they allow their selfish motive of securing power at all costs to terminate civilian rule in the country.

Electoral violence impedes the institutionalization of strong democratic institutions in the Nigerian context. Democracy is expected to flourish when institutions such as parties, electoral bodies, civil societies, parliament, the judiciary, executive and other critical institutions are able to discharge their responsibilities diligently without any undue advantage to any section or disadvantage against any section. Unfortunately, parties in Nigeria's Fourth Republic are personalized, the electoral body is compromised, the judiciary is hampered, security agencies are manipulated, and parliament is emasculated by the executive arm. This indicates how electoral violence opens up space for allowing criminals to break laws with impunity, leading to political brigandage and a regime of personal benefit (USAID, 2020). From this perspective, the building of a strong democracy is continuously eluding the country despite the long experiment of over 20 years. Parties can sponsor violence, the compromise of electoral process by the electoral body can trigger violence, security personnel are sometimes reported as active collaborators of electoral violence in many instances, the judiciary is allegedly bribed and justice is subverted while members of parliament employ violence to secure victory (Human Rights Watch, 2019). Hence, sanction or prevention is difficult but the consequences are that the democratic practice is trapped in a vicious circle of stagnation.

There is an argument by some scholars that electoral violence is responsible for affecting the integrity, credibility, and legitimacy of elections in Nigeria. But, most importantly, credible candidates are sacrificed for mediocrity and selfish greedy leaders (Fjelde & Hoglund, 2014; Human Rights Watch, 2019; Igwe & Amadi, 2021; Shenga & Pereira, 2019; Taylor, 2018; USIP, 2020). However, such a view has been countered by such a group of studies on electoral violence (Birch, 2020; Birch et al., 2020; Campbell, 2010; Mochtak, 2018; Onapajo, 2014; Wilkinson, 2004) indicating that electoral violence in places like Nigeria cannot be scientifically linked with the credibility of candidates even if this will undoubtedly affect the integrity of the process and the legitimacy of the leaders after the election. This is because, in Nigeria, the opposition and popular candidates also adopt violence and other subversive means when they have the opportunity. This is because of the pattern of Nigeria's political culture, where it is believed that violence is a strategy of dodging the competition and where voters accepted that electoral violence is not sanctioned, thereby allowing people to perpetrate it and get away with it (Sule et al., 2017a). Most of the elections and their results are questioned by the opposition, the electorate observers and civil society because from the beginning, many voters have been disenfranchised during the voters' registration exercise; they are deterred from participating in the electoral process by the danger of assault and harm from hired thugs and political militias, and in many cases the results of the final elections do not reflect the wishes of the voters.

Misgovernance is a result of electoral violence in Nigeria. The politicians, who are quite aware that they have misused and abused the electoral process to secure power, would not be given pause by any thought or fear of public opinion and performance appraisal. They have indulged in various forms of dubious and corrupt practices. Corruption, mismanagement, embezzlement, and misplacement of priorities have occurred while detrimental neoliberal Western super-economic policies have been superimposed. Infrastructural deficiency has not been met by a remedial policy. Instead, successive governments have continued to announce non-realistic projects and programmes to divert the attention of the governed away from their failed campaign promises and mischief in political office (Campbell, 2010). Political apathy has resulted in the process which has given the ruling class further opportunity to apply more violence in future elections. Nigeria's precious resources are squandered while its inherited functional infrastructures from the colonial and early post-colonial nation-building period has been frittered away. A racket of corrupt oligarchs has formed a gang who are busy raping the national treasury in subversive ways such as the fuel subsidy regime, the intended collapse of national refineries for awarding contract for the extraction of crude oil and the importation of refined oil of, creating overnight billionaires among friends and cronies. These are all the proceeds of misgovernance, originating from the use of electoral violence to secure power since the rulers do not feel obliged to respect the rule of law and enhance accountability and transparency.

One area in which electoral violence is creating problems for Nigeria is the invitation of international cynicism, hostilities, and mild sanctions on the pretext of human rights abuses and other violations of democratic tenets. Observers in most cases have been left disenchanted and disappointed with the manner in which the electoral process has been violently conducted. For instance, in the 2019 gubernatorial election in Kano, Rivers, and Benue, international observers and reporters of international media agencies suffered attacks that endangered their lives. They narrowly escaped and later released a joint statement condemning the election and the attacks (Human Rights Watch, 2019). The supposed international partnership relating to good governance, grants and other interventions have been lost owing to the dastardly act of politicians and their errand-boys. However, the major concern is that in many cases the international community is perceived as a supporter of electoral violence in Nigeria, in cases where they seem to feel that the perpetrators can continue to serve their permanent interest in the country. A good example of this is the position of the US government on the 2007 general election where they disclosed that the election in 2007 in Nigeria had been marred with rigging, violence, irregularities, malpractices, violence, the influence of financial sponsors of politicians godfathers, subversion of the electoral process and state assault on opposition but they accepted the results in the US national interest (Sule et al., 2017b).

## 6 Conclusion

Electoral violence is one of the security threats and democratic challenges that Nigeria is presently facing. The phenomenon has been gradually institutionalized by politicians with their selfish motives of acquiring power by all means possible. The phenomenon will continue, and there is no plausible remedy in sight, so long as the present crop of politicians are relied on for the solutions. Even if the problem is attended to by some measures that will curtail it, the political class will continue to evade peaceful electoral conduct and devise other means of perpetrating the mayhem in disguise. Hence, this is not a light issue that should be dismissed easily. The study has already established how electoral violence has culminated, in the larger threat of insecurity for the Nigerian state, making it much more difficult to contend with. Therefore, this study argues that practical measures that will compel the eradication of the problem must be looked into.

One of the ways suggested is that domestic civil societies should forge a strong alliances with international civil societies and other world powers to initiate strong sanctions against any politician that is identified with proof as a sponsor of electoral violence. This will deter many of them and gradually will eradicate the problem, because the foreign powers are the destination of their wealth, and the medical care and education of their children. The elites cannot afford to play around with their means of international linkage. Second, a massive and rigorous public enlightenment campaign should be mounted nationwide in local languages. Analysts, experts, academics, and all public influencers should be engaged in sending strong messages against the evil act, to shape the minds of our youth to desist against the evil acts, and to counter them in a civil and legal way. Furthermore, a movement or vanguard should be established by civil societies against electoral violence as a special counter-movement. In relation to the above, community policing activities should be geared towards integrating prevention of electoral violence in our respective communities. While it is difficult and nearly impossible to have substantive laws from policymakers on the radical sanctioning of offenders, stakeholders in the electoral process should not be discouraged from mounting pressure on the National Assembly for the enactment of such laws, notwithstanding the existence of some parts thereof in the 2010 Electoral Act which the INEC is not making much effort to implement. Finally, the offer of loans in international financial institutions should have the attached condition of peaceful electoral conduct if the advanced democratic states are genuinely the global champions and vanguard of democracy. The African Union also should be strengthened with a view to initiating treaties on non-electoral non-violence supported by all member countries.

## Bibliography

Adeniyi, O. (2017). *Against the Run of Play: How an Incumbent President was Defeated in Nigeria*. BookBaby.

Birch, S. (2020). *Electoral Violence, Corruption and Political Order*. Princeton University Press.

Birch, S., Daxecker, U., & Hoglund, K. (2020). Electoral Violence: An Introduction. *Journal of Peace Research, 57*(1), 3–14.

Bratton, M. (2008). Vote Buying and Violence in Nigerian Election Campaigns. *Electoral Studies, 27*(4), 621–632.

Burchard, S. M., & Simati, M. (2019). The Role of the Courts in Mitigating Election Violence in Nigeria. *Review of African Studies, 38*(1), 123–144.

Campbell, J. (2010). *Electoral Violence in Nigeria*. Council on Foreign Relations.

Campbell, J. (2019). *Tracking Election Violence in Nigeria*. Council on Foreign Relations. Retrieved from https://www.cfr.org/blog/tracking-election-violence-nigeria on 25 December 2021.

Collier, P. (2007). *Wars, Guns and Votes: Democracy in Dangerous Places*. Harper.

Collins E-Book. https://doi.org/10.2979/africonfpeacrevi.1.1.161

Delay, J. (2019). *Nigeria: Widespread Violence Ushers in President's New Term Investigate Attacks, Ensure Justice*. Human Rights Watch.

Demarest, L., & Langer, A. (2019). Reporting on Electoral Violence in Nigerian News Media: "Saying It as It Is"? *African Studies Review, 62*(4), 83–109.

Fafchamps, M., & Vicente, P. C. (2013). Political Violence and Social Networks: Experimental Evidence from a Nigerian Election. *Journal of Development Economics, 101*(13), 27–48.

Fjelde, H., & Hoglund, K. (2014). Electoral Institutions and Electoral Violence in Sub-Saharan Africa. *British Journal of Political Science, 46*(1), 297–320.

Friedrich Ebert Stiftung. (2001). *Political and Electoral Violence in East Africa.* Centre for Conflict Research.

Human Rights Watch. (2019). Nigeria: Widespread Violence Ushers in President's New Term. *Investigate Attacks, Ensure Justice.* Human Rights Watch.

Huntington, S. (2004). *The Third Wave: Democratisation in the Late Twentieth Century.* University of Oklahoma Press.

Igwe, P. I., & Amadi, L. (2021). Democracy and Political Violence in Nigeria Since Multi-party Politics in 1999: A Critical Appraisal. *De Gruyter, Open Political Science, 4*(1), 101–119.

Ikelegbe, A., & Garuba, D. (2011). *Youths and Conflicts in West Africa: Regional Threats and Potentials.* ECOWAS.

Kwarkye, S. (2019). *Roots of Nigeria's Election Violence.* Retrieved from https://issafrica.org/iss-today/roots-of-nigerias-election-violence on 25 December 2021.

Le Van, Carl, A. 2015. *Dictators and Democracy in African Development. The Political Economy of Good Governance in Nigeria.* New York: Cambridge University Press.

Mochtak, M. (2018). *Electoral Violence in the Western Balkans: From Voting to Fighting and Back.* Routledge, Taylor & Francis.

Onapajo, H. (2014). Violence and Votes in Nigeria: The Dominance of Incumbents in the Use of Violence to Rig Elections. *Africa Spectrum, 49*(2), 27–59.

Onubogu, O., & Hassan, I. (2018). *The Risk of Election Violence in Nigeria is Not Where You Think Containing Violence at the State Level Will Be Key to a Peaceful Election.* United States Institute for Peace.

Shenga, C., & Pereira, A. (2019). The Effects of Electoral Violence on Electoral Participation in Africa. *Cadernos De Estudos Africanos, 10*(1), 145–165.

Siollun, M. (2021). *What Britain Did to Nigeria: A Brief History of Conquest and Rule.* Hurst Publisher.

Sule, B., Azizuddin, M., Sani, M., & Mat, B. (2017a). Political Behaviour and Voting Pattern in Nigeria's Fourth Republic: The Case of 2015 Presidential Election. *Asia Pacific Journal of Education Arts and Sciences, 4*(4), 1–13.

Sule, B., Sani, M. A. M., & Mat, B. (2017b). Independent National Electoral Commission (INEC) and Campaign Financing Monitoring in Nigeria: The 2015 General Election. *Journal of International Studies, 13*(1), 15–31.

Sule, B., Mohd, M. A., & Mat, B. (2018). Godfatherism and Political Party Financing and Corruption in Nigeria's Fourth Republic: The Case of 2015 General Elections. *GEOGRAFIA Malaysian Journal of Society and Space, 14*(1), 1–14.

Sule, B., & Sambo, U. (2020). The 2019 General Election and the Politics of Inconclusive Election in Nigeria. *Khazanah Sosial, 2*(3), 105–124.

Straus, S., & Taylor, C. (2009). Democratisation and Electoral Violence in Sub-Saharan Africa, 1990–2007. In D. A. Bekoe (Ed.), *Voting in Fear: Electoral Violence in Sub-Saharan Africa* (pp. 23–43). United States Institute of Peace.

Taylor, C. (2018). *Shared Security, Shared Elections: Best Practices for the Prevention of Electoral Violence.* American Friends Service Committee (AFSC).

US International Centre for Electoral Support. (2018). *Preventing Election Violence in Nigeria 2018*. Retrieved from https://www.US+International+Centre+for+Electoral+Support+%282018%29+Preventing+Election+Violence+in+Nigeria+2018 on 25 December 2021.

United State Agency for International Development. (2020). *Nigeria Post-Election Survey*. International Foundation for Electoral System.

United States Institute for Peace. 2020. *Preventing Election Violence*. USIP. www.usip.org

Von Neumann, J., & Morgenstern, O. (1944). *Theory of Games and Economic Behaviour*. Princeton University Press.

Wilkinson, S. I. (2004). *Votes and Violence: Electoral Competition and Ethnic Riots in India*. Cambridge University Press.

# Ungoverned Space and National Security in Nigeria

## Arinze Ngwube

## 1 Introduction

Nigeria has been bedevilled by a myriad of security challenges, including the Boko Haram insurgency, banditry, kidnapping, herder/farmer clashes, and piracy. These insecurities are occurring almost simultaneously with the common shelter for these crimes being the forest—an ungoverned space. Nigeria is blessed with a total land area of 91,077,000 ha (910,770 km$^2$) and a total forest area of 11,089,000 ha (110,890 km$^2$) which amounts to 12.18 per cent forest cover (FAO, 2019). These forests are endowed with multifarious ecosystems and varied biodiversity which should have been utilized to achieve sustainable livelihood, industrial raw materials, and food security, and to reduce poverty and hunger in the land. Nigeria has been split into units or division zones for effective administrative and policing purposes. The implication of this division is that there is no space that is not covered by the country's defense, security, intelligence, and police systems. A total of 774 local governments have been created to ensure even development of their domains. These sections are manned by security, police, and intelligence agencies in the country. The question one asks is: "What are the factors responsible for there to be an abode for criminals and activities that threaten national unity?" The first duty of any government is that of protecting society

A. Ngwube (✉)
Department of Political Science, Federal University, Oye, Nigeria
e-mail: arinze.ngwube@fuoye.edu.ng

from violence and invasion of privacy. When a government loses the capacity for both, anarchy beckons.

The unceasing social injustice and inequitable distribution of the commonwealth has intensified the vexation of insecurity across geopolitical zones. The lives of Nigerians are now at the mercy of criminal syndicates who often provide the option to their victims to either provide ransom or be killed. Insecurity is becoming horrendous, and it has taken on polygonal dimensions, leaving individuals with a perpetual encumbrance. How does the porosity of ungoverned spaces entrench insecurity in Nigeria? To what extent does this relate to insecurity? This chapter is structured as follows. Section 2 conceptualizes the notions of ungoverned space, national security, and violence. Section 3 addresses the theory of ungoverned spaces. Section 4 examines ungoverned spaces as a threat to national security. The last Section 5 concludes the chapter and provides some recommendations.

## 2 Conceptual Clarification

To enhance the understanding of this chapter, it is necessary to put the discourse in a conceptual context to provide a framework for analysis. Thus, we can proceed to clarify the concepts of "ungoverned space," "national security," and "violence".

### Ungoverned Space

Patrick (2010) opines that ungoverned space suggests an area that is experiencing a vacuum in political order and requires either the insertion or the positioning of prior structures of governances. It refers to physical territory and the non-physical spaces in which effective state sovereignty and control is either absent, or exists only partially (Jackson, 1990).

Taylor (2016: 10) provides the following dynamic explanation of ungoverned territories:

> A place where the state or central government is unable or unwilling to extend control effectively govern or influence the local population and where a provincial, local population and where a provincial, local, tribal or effectively govern due to inadequate governance capacity, insufficient political will gaps in legitimacy, the presence of conflict or restrictive norms of behavior. Ungoverned areas should be assumed to include ungoverned, ill-governed contested and explorible areas.

The existing ungoverned environment is driven by incessant conflict in different parts of the country, which in turn makes such spaces more prone to terrorist recruitment. Terrorism, criminal activities, drug trafficking and related activities are the by-products of ungoverned spaces. According to the Rand Corporation (2007), examples of ungoverned spaces with potential for accommodating terrorist organizations may be drawn from eight regions including the East African corridor, West Africa, the Sulawesi-Mindanao Arc, the Colombia-Venezuela border, the Guatemala-Chiapas border, the Pakistan Arabian-Afghanistan border, the North Caucasus, and the Arabian Peninsula. In that particular study, Rabas and Peters (2007) examined ungoverned spaces through two measures: conduciveness to terrorism and governability (Robasa & Peters, 2007). These are consequences of the lack of social amenities and result in insecurity. There exist the Odua People's Congress (OPC), the Movement for the Actualization of Sovereign States of Biafra (MASSOB), and the Northern Arewa Youths, all with access to arms, and the implication for criminality increases the likelihood of terrorist presence. Thus, a local population with allegiance to their tribal and regional groups, having access to arms, could be overrun by criminals and serve as armed recruits.

Ungoverned spaces are described as areas of limited government control or territories of violence and insecurity where states cannot exercise their full sovereignty (Olaniyan & Akindele, 2017). Ungoverned spaces are areas characterized by persistent insurgencies in some parts of Africa. Ungoverned spaces are those stretches of territory in different parts of the country where the presence and influence of government is hardly in evidence. The absence of security agencies poses a challenge. In this sense, contested spaces or spaces of contestation can be considered as an aspect of ungoverned spaces. These spaces are often characterized by limited government presence in terms of inadequate facilities and infrastructure, including security infrastructure. However, most of the border communities are considered too far away from the hinterlands (Raleigh & Dowd, 2013). Moreover, these ungoverned spaces are often considered threats to national security.

According to the above conceptualization, the notion of ungoverned spaces is conceived from two main viewpoints. First, from the perspective of limited government control. Second, from the viewpoint that contested political spaces transform into territories of violence and insecurity. In line with the former, ungoverned spaces are zones that lie beyond the reaches of the central government (Ali, 2017). States are considered ungoverned if they lack strong state control and social practices defy state regulation. This exposes the vulnerability of such areas which are remote and leads to the latter view that opines that the more remote such areas are, the more vulnerable the inhabitants may be to the lure of violent radicalization and extremism. It is interesting to note that terrorist and insurgent groups like Al-shabaab and Boko Haram take advantage of the weakness and limited reach of state institutions in such spaces to recruit and radicalize the local populace.

As indicated earlier, in addition to the classification and assignment of all parts of the country for management by the local government, state government, and federal government, government agencies like the police, the Department of Security Services, and civil defence also have their jurisdiction clearly covering all parts of the country, including these spaces referred to. The reality is that these spaces are still in existence and serve as a breeding ground for criminals and terrorists. The 9/11 Commission Report states that some of the extremist groups bolted to ungoverned spaces, especially those areas with weak government presence, rugged terrain, and low population density, and those which along borders that were prone to informal interaction with the outside world which provided them often with the opportunity of receiving supplies. This has made ungoverned spaces safe havens for terrorists where they can move freely, recruit, train, indoctrinate, radicalize, and plan attacks. These spaces have given room for terrorist groups to derive more gain from their criminal acts. This has serious implications for peace and security in the polity.

The above analysis corresponds to the current picture in Africa where extremist groups and criminal syndicates have taken advantage of ungoverned spaces to recruit adult youths to foster their agenda and expand their power bases. African state governments have given little or no attention to such environments where terrorists are able to be recruited and are able to achieve their goals, and it is, therefore, difficult to win the war on terror via a military response in Nigeria. Ungoverned space has implications for national security in a polity. The next section explains the concept of national security.

## National Security

Security is the management of threats and is seen as the pursuit of freedom from threat. It requires specification of both a threat and a referent object. Threats is the possibility of harm coming to a valued referent object. The concept of security within the national space is defined within the context of national security. National security involves the dynamics and interrelationships between internal security and external security which touches on transnational threats. National security literature and definitions of national security are copious and still growing (Brown, 1977; Buzan, 1983; Mathews, 1989; Mcnamara, 1968; Imobighe, 1998; Nnoli, 2006; Nwolise, 2008;

Oche, 2005; Okodolor, 2004; Pogoson, 2013). The proliferation of definitions of national security is essentially because the process of discursively "securitizing vulnerable" referent objects (i.e. individual, nation-state or the global system) and defining particular risks, is a political one (Weaver, 1995), which usually depends on who is grappling with the subject. It is therefore common to see reference being made to human security, national security, international security, state security, regime security, and corporate security, among other things.

The conception of national security in this chapter identifies with the revisionist thinking on the subject matter (Gambo, 2008; Onuoha, 2007), which sees national security from the point of view of human security. According to Onuoha (2007: 4), human security entails:

> Freedom from actual and potential threats to human life, safety and survival which may arise as a result of human actions or inactions, or from natural disasters such as flood, earthquake, famine, drought, disease and other non-man-made calamitous events resulting in death, human suffering and material damage.

Nwolise (2008) posits that the relevance of national security explains why the government applies measures to make the security sector effective to prevent people from losing confidence in the ability of the state to protect them. Effective national security is, therefore, understood in the context of this writing to mean the ability of the state to protect its citizenry from hunger, poverty, ignorance, disease, and all forms of defencelessness (Okoli, 2012). This entails protecting the citizens from all forms of social, political, ecological, and territorial, as well as cosmic vulnerabilities. This conception of national security marks a radical departure from the orthodox perspective which conceives of national security merely from a defence/military-centric point of view (Alkali, 2003). As relevant and fundamental as the concept of security is to human societies, it has not only defied any consensus but has created a "battleground of ideological contention" (Alkali, 2003). Irrespective of the conception of security, an important point is that it underpins human existence.

Thus, states define security within the context of their core values, interests, culture, prestige, and socio-economic order. Transformations in the global arena have produced certain mutations in the conceptualization of national security: the focus has moved from an emphasis on protecting and maintaining the state to a focus on the well-being of the people (human security). Within this context, therefore, national security is equated with, and denotes, the physical safety of individuals and groups and freedom from threats, anxiety or danger.

Within the standpoint, Wolfers (1962) defines national security as the absence of threats to acquiring values and subjectively, the absence of fear that such values will be attacked. Maier (1990) similarly defines the concept through the lens of national power by noting that national security is best described as a capacity to control those domestic and foreign conditions that the public opinion of a given community believes necessary in enjoying its own autonomy, prosperity, and well-being. Demonstrating the intertwining relationship between internal and external security with the context of national security, Keenan (2007) defines national security as:

> The dynamics of a state's ability and readiness to deal with effectively with external threats caused by rival states and rival organizations and deal effectively with internal threats—caused by parties inside the society, which put at risk the physical existence of the state's population, its identity, its values and its vital interests. (Keenan, 2007)

However, some authorities have attempted to define national security in terms of demographic threats occasioned by epidemics, natural disasters, climate change, and other events causing severe environmental damage and the ability of the state to put in place an effective emergency response plan to swiftly protect it from anarchy. The argument here is that national security is influenced by two important factors. These are internal threats and external threats. Internal security is mainly concerned with internal threats and includes all state actions directed at emplacing, upholding and deploying national laws, strategies, policies, and state law enforcement agencies in the maintenance of peace, law, and order. There are usually several secondary law enforcement agencies that are statutorily empowered in advancing the internal security interests of a nation.

Harold Brown, US Secretary of Defense from 1977 to 1981, examines external threats within the context of national security:

> The ability to preserve the nation's physical integrity and territory; to maintain its economic relations with the rest of the world on reasonable terms; to preserve its nature, institution, and governance from disruption from outside; and to control its borders. (Brown, 1983)

The primary responsibility for guaranteeing external security lies with the military of a nation and where this is undertaken in conjunction with other security agencies, the military will, in an ideal situation, take command and control pre-eminence in such operational relations. In another contribution, Imobighe (2013) argues that the cause of insecurity in Nigeria is closely tied to the attitude of Nigerian leaders to threat assessment. According to him, the threat which are part of the main determinants of defence and national security planning have not been managed in Nigeria and some other African countries. To this end, he further argues that the misplacement of defence and national security efforts and the haphazard treatment of threats which focuses solely on regime perpetuation and how to silence opposition elements are crucial factors responsible for the increasing incidence of insecurity in the country. According to Tsuwa and Okoh (2016) national security is concerned with protecting the people with political conditions given a priority. The protection is aimed at saving the state and citizens from threats. In essence, a state that lacks the capacity to prevent danger to its territorial integrity can hardly guarantee the well-being of its people.

The task of maintaining national security is as much the responsibility of the government as it is of the citizens. For the state to play its role as an impartial restraining force and thus maintain the delicate balance whose upset could trigger insecurity, it ought to be aloof and non-aligned in the resolution of recurrent conflicts of interest within the polity. The office responsible for the coordination, control, and supervision of national security is the National Security Adviser. He represents the president, through the National Security Council, the Joint Intelligence Board (JIB), and the Intelligence Community Committee. The National Security Adviser has the status, and enjoys the privileges of, a federal minister. He advises the president on National Security. He directs the State Security Service on policies approved by the president (Are, 1999a, 1999b). The National Security Adviser is the principal officer of the National Security Council. The National Security Council comprises the President of Nigeria, The Vice President, The Chief of Defence Staff, The Minister of Internal Affairs, The Minister of Defence, The Minister of Foreign Affairs, The Inspector General of Police, and other persons as the president may at his discretion appoint (Are, 1999a, 1999b).

The National Security Council has the power to advise the president on matters relating to public security, including matters relating to any organization or agency established by law for ensuring the security of the Federation (Are, 1999a, 1999b). The State Security Service is in charge of internal security. The National Intelligence Agency provides external intelligence to Nigeria. The armed forces, the police, and para-military organizations have responsibilities for specific aspects of national security. They are tasked through the relevant ministries, service councils, and established chain of command. The next section will focus on violence.

## Violence

A term commonly used during the last decade of crisis in the public and political discourse that indicates the existence of a conflict is the term "violence" used by citizens in order to support the claim that, "What we experience is violence," and used by the media to refer to protests and mobilizations that ended in violent clashes between police and participants. This is based on literature which argues that certain politic-economic measures could be considered as violent mainly because of their effects on a specified population (Bohm, 2018; Cooper & Whyte, 2017; Farmer, 2004). Habermas (2001) asserts that the twentieth century featured "gas chambers, total war, state-sponsored genocide and extermination camps, brainwashing state-security apparatuses, and the panoptic surveillance of entire population." Tilly (2002) charts some outcomes to those events, claiming that altogether about 100 million people died in the twentieth century as a direct result of action by organized military units backed by one government or another. A comparable number of civilians likely died of war-induced disease and other indirect effects.

The World Bank (2011) describes violence as "a primary development challenge of our time". In Africa, certainly violence is more than merely a development issue. It has become the overriding political challenge of the early twenty-first century for much of the continent; violence is, thus, a challenge of a radically different magnitude. It threatens the peace of the polity. There are at least some dimensions to this challenge, in no particular order. One is piracy, especially in the Gulf of Guinea. Apart from threatening the states along these coasts, piracy also endangers some of the busiest maritime routes as well as global energy security. Another is the growing manifestation of violent extremism, with some of it claiming sectarian inspiration in some parts of Nigeria. The full extent of the group behind this and the nature and extent of relationships that underpin their operations is yet to be understood by our policymakers. There is a related challenge of trans-Sahelian mercenaries, and the free flows in Africa are not new. They were known for their involvement in coups such as those in the Comoros and some African civil wars. Violence is an element hitherto found in every human society and is always culturally defined, but the highly heterogenous forms of violence make the phenomenon elusive and hard to define (Kiess, 2016). In Nigeria today, violence presents a monumental and potentially crippling challenge to our polity's future. It threatens the lives and livelihoods of millions of ordinary people and their families. It threatens the future of legitimate and effective government.

The World Health Organization (1996) defines violence as "the intentional use of physical force or power threatened or actual against oneself, another person, or against a group or community, which either results in, or has a high likelihood of resulting in, injury, death, psychological harm, maldevelopment or deprivation." This definition associates intentionality with the committing of the act itself, irrespective of the outcome. Excluded from the definition are unintentional incidents such as most road traffic injuries and burns. The Nigerian state was founded on violence and maintained by colonialism through violent means (Afigbo, 1966: 539–559). Throughout colonial rule, the state was divorced from the people and violence was the major language the government used. As Ake (1996: 22–32) opined, this character of the Nigerian state, even after independence, remained much as it was in the colonial era. The state in Nigeria represented itself as an apparatus of violence, had a narrow social base, and relied for compliance on coercion rather than authority. It is observed that the Nigerian state has become even more removed from the people. The state has become, literally, the property of only the small percentage of the population that controls its apparatuses, and the rest have wallowed in poverty, the levels of which have now risen astronomically.

The vast majority of the people have become removed from the political system and they cannot easily see any tangible benefit accruing to them by virtue of their membership of the state. They see that the state makes demands from the people in form of taxes, fees, and so forth, but has not been able to address the needs of the people or their problems. The state is thus viewed with suspicion by the people, who also see it as a hostage of privileged groups. The groups that are disadvantaged within the political system see the state as partial. They see it as sanctioning a system that guarantees privileges to others but denies the same to them. This feeling has made the relations of the state with the people very antagonistic; this eventually leads to violence.

## 3  Theoretical Framework

This chapter has adopted the failed state theory. The theory flows remotely from the philosophical foundations of social contract theorists, particularly Thomas Hobbes. A study sponsored by the Rand Corporation identified three main variables that describe the extent to which the state has a monopoly on the use of force, the extent to which the state can control its borders and whether the state is subject to external intervention by other states (Robasa & Peters, 2007). Some territories with modern state systems seem to be degenerating into a Hobbesian pre-social and pre-political state of nature where life is solitary, nasty, brutish and short. However, scholars like Whelan (2006), Menkhaus (2010), Lloyd (2016), and Onwuzuruigbo (2020), among others, have not agreed on what exactly constitute ungoverned spaces.

William Zartman and Robert Rotberg see the state as first and foremost a service provider. According to Zartman (1995) a state has collapsed "when the basic functions of the state are no longer performed," and further "a state has collapsed when it is no longer able to provide the services for which it exists." Rotberg (2004) and Howard (2014) writing on failed states define state failure as the inability of states to provide positive political goods to their inhabitants. Both scholars distinguish between a variety of services that states may provide, ranging from security to the rule of law, the protection of property, the right to political participation, provision of infrastructure, and social services such as health and education. These services constitute a hierarchy. Rotberg (2004) argues that provision of security is the most fundamental service and serves as a condition for the provision of all other services.

Rotberg also argues that failure should be seen as a continuum. There is a need to differentiate between states that are strong, weak, failing, failed, or collapsed. Further, a state may possess some of the features of statehood, but not others. It may have a monopoly over the means of violence but be unable to provide infrastructure or maintain the rule of law, or it may have a functioning military but an inefficient bureaucracy. This conception is then used as a benchmark against which given states are measured. However, the subject of discourse fits into the theory. Rotberg and Campbell (2021) opine that if a state's first obligation to those it governs is to provide for their security and maintain a monopoly on the use of violence, then Nigeria has failed; even if some other aspects of the state still function, criminals, separatists and Islamist insurgents increasingly threaten the government's grip or power, as do rampant corruption, economic malaise, and rising poverty. The scholars opine about the long-term impact on the neighbourhood, elaborating on how state failure in Nigeria yet bodes such ill for the sub-region, yet bodes especially ill for the stability and well-being of weak states in Nigeria's vicinity: Burkina Faso, Cameroon, Chad, Ivory Coast, Mali, and Niger.

Nigeria has been ranked on the Fragile States Index. It may interest the reader to note that many of the business elites are doing well, surrounded by an ocean of poverty, collapsing institutions and decaying infrastructures. Our government no longer possesses a monopoly over the use of violence.

Boko Haram, ISWAP (Islamic State West African Province) and the genocidal Fulani militias not only outnumber the Nigeria military, they are also more than a match for them in terms of the quality of their military arsenals. The government cannot fully police our country's borders which leads to the uncontrolled immigration of well-armed terrorist groups. Nigeria is currently the kidnapping capital of the world, in addition to possessing the unenviable title of being the world capital of poverty. More than 24 million children are out of school (UNICEF, 2021). Some 3.5 million Nigerians are living in makeshift IDP (Internal Displaced Poppulation) camps. UNICEF recently announced that 345,000 children had died in the Northeast over the previous 12 years (UNICEF, 2021). Borno governor, Babagana Zulum (2021), announced that more than 450,000 of his people had gone "missing." On a national scale, we are looking at an estimated one million people who have been lost in the unfolding inferno. The economy is in a tailspin with inflation spiralling out of control and the naira on the verge of collapsing. Unemployment currently hovers above 33% with youth unemployment estimated to be above 40% (NBS, 2021).

## 4 Ungoverned Space Constitutes a Threat to National Security in Nigeria

The Nigerian state is thus a system of violence. In this system, violence can emanate from either side: from the people when they feel that they are left out of the scheme of things and can only can call attention to their plight by violence; or from the state state whenever it wants to assert control or project power. It is thus no wonder that incidents of violence pervade parts of the country. Civil unrest has caused massive human and economic costs for the country. Violent incidents have taken place across six geopolitical zones with the highest frequency of incidents recorded in the northern states of Kaduna, Katsina, Zamfara, Borno, Benue, Taraba, Plateau, and Adamawa. The insecurity plaguing Nigeria is rending its social fabric and generating new pressures along standing ethnic, religious, and geopolitical fault lines. The recurrent violence in different parts of the country has led to the destruction of property, agricultural losses, and human rights violations. The proliferation of small arms in Nigeria further contributes to insecurity. A report by the United Nations Regional Centre for Peace and Disarmament in Africa (UNREC) revealed that Nigeria hosts 350 million or 70% of the 500 million illegal arms in West Africa. It has resulted in a large number of internally displaced persons. In contrast to some of the world where natural disasters have led to people's displacement, according to the UNHCR (2020), as of 2019 over 3.3 million Nigerians have been displaced in Northeastern Nigeria alone, not to mention other parts of the country. Similarly, according to the Internally Displaced Monitoring Centre (2020), a total of 2,583,000 people have been displaced internally in Nigeria as of 31st December 2019. Most of the population at the internally displaced persons' camps are women and children. Most of the women are widows and most of the children are orphans (Mohammed, 2018).

It is noteworthy that all the crises and incidences of violence mentioned above lasted for a long time, despite government assurances that that they would be contained within a short time. This only goes to prove that people see the state as partial. It is difficult for the state to successfully mediate conflicts in the country. The people see the state as favouring one side or the other in a conflict, and there is usually deep mistrust between the sides in the conflict. In the end, the government has been left with few options other than force to resolve issues. This is why residues of ill-feeling continue to linger within both sides in a conflict long after the conflict was supposedly resolved. A system of violence exists in Nigeria. Violence is an ever-present reality. Most existing violent situations remain so for a long time, while new ones emerge even before the old ones go away.

Nigeria has been experiencing increasing violent attacks over the years by non-state actors in spaces referred to as ungoverned, owing to the weak presence of formal institutions. From these spaces, terrorists and bandits make videos and coordinate media propaganda. It is of interest to note that they are beyond the reach of security agencies. Nigeria has witnessed frequent attacks from these non-state actors, including terrorists, bandits, kidnappers, and criminal herdsmen. The launch of these attacks is from areas where there is an absence of state capacity. These spaces are beyond the reach of government and thus pose a significant threat to security and stability.

Ungoverned spaces serve as fertile ground where the activities of criminal gangs thrive and the spaces fall within the strategic frontier of security priorities. Examples include the Boko Haram camps in Sambisa Forest, bandit hideouts in the Kwiambana and Ajjah forests in Zamfara, herdsmen camps in Birnin Kogo, forests in Kastina, havens for kidnappers in the Guma forests between Benue and Nassarawa States, and militant camps in the Niger Delta. These places have long existed and have been brought to light owing to security situations (see Fig. 1).

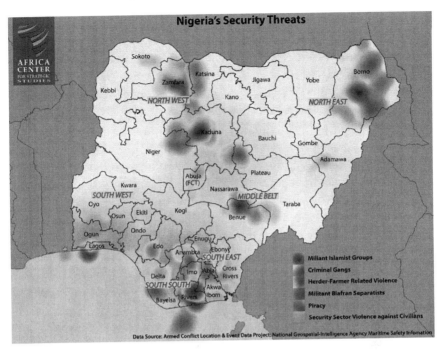

Fig. 1 Nigeria's security threats (*Source* Armed Conflict Location and Event Project 2021)

At the time of writing, it has been two years since the Office of the National Security Adviser (ONSA) and other stakeholders launched the National Security Strategy (NSS) 2019 document. The federal government has yet to bring into implementation the aspect which dwells on addressing insecurity stemming from ungoverned spaces. The 2019 NSS document is reviewed every five years, the last review being in 2014. It has noted ongoing military offensives in the North East and North West leading to the shutting down of telecommunication networks in the region. Other aspects of the NSS document have not been implemented; there are no specific timelines for measures outlined in the document. The document states that ungoverned spaces, especially around our international boundaries, forests and game reserves provide opportunities for criminal networks to fester and generally promote crime. The document further states that ungoverned spaces constitute a critical fragility in Nigeria's national security and are antithetical to the nation's security.

On the subject of securing ungoverned spaces, the document posited that "in order to dominate and protect these ungoverned spaces along our international boundaries we will ensure the state monopoly of force in border and frontier communities by establishing more military units to provide credible presence to support border security operations by other statutory agencies" (National Security Strategy, 2019). The document stated that the Nigerian police would be enabled to strengthen their presence in border communities in conjunction with other statutory security agencies to consolidate law and order. "We will ensure that forests and national game reserves are closely monitored by forest guards to prevent them from becoming safe havens for criminal gangs" (Ibid.) The document goes further, explaining what the government will do regarding development. The government has promised to facilitate basic infrastructural penetration by both public institutions and corporate organizations. The document goes further in explaining how government will support small and medium scale enterprises for the youth in order to reduce crime in the polity.

This has added to the ongoing discourse among scholars on the subject (Olaniyan & Akindele, 2017; Onwuzuruigbo, 2020; Raleigh & Dowd, 2013). The aforementioned spaces lie beyond the control of the centralized state. They are not necessarily governance vacuums. However, conventional state policies distort the way one views these spaces and deny alternative governance structures. Studies at the Centre for Public Authority and International Development (CPAID) (2021) show that all spaces are governed in some form, but not necessarily by formal government institutions, and influence is exerted by different non-state actors to varying degrees.

The ongoing conflicts in Zamfara State in North West Nigeria have been associated with a contest over the illegal extraction of gold deposits (Ogbonnaya, 2020). A huge informal economy of illicit transactions exists in these ungoverned spaces where entities fight for the control of minefields and the exportation of gold internationally. Military action has been the default response to bring these areas back under state control. Such actions, though deemed necessary by many, are insufficient as they have been uninterruptedly resisted and, in some cases, undermined. The growing threat of violent actors raises questions about the wisdom and effectiveness of this approach. This suggests a need to revisit existing responses based on a securitized approach.

It is of interest to note the absence of federal, state, or local government presence in aspects of functional social services. One discovers that citizens in these spaces are left to the forces of nature; little education and enlightenment means a virtual state of nature in which ignorance and superstition hold the people mortal hostages in the absence of constituted authority. They find themselves at the mercy of self-appointed agents filling the gaping vacancy left by command, to humiliate the people into a blind and helpless obedience. The majority of the rural communities, especially on the fringes of the different parts of the country, find themselves in this situation. To citizens in these areas, government is almost a fairytale told by wayfarers from a distant place. This dominance of ungoverned space is greater in states with vast stretches of land and with low levels of urbanization and Western education.

Reports from different parts of the country indicate that forests have become safe havens for the operation of assorted criminal groups (Ajayi, 2021). Kidnappers and abductors take their victims into forest camps where they are held while ransom negotiations proceed by cellphone. This takes place far from the prying eyes of the police and other security operatives. Between 2005 and 2008 the forests in the border areas between Rivers and Abia states were the operational base of kidnappers operating in both states. Similar operations were occurring in the forests in the border areas between Rivers and Imo State, off the Port Harcourt-Owerri highway.

In January 2021, the governor of Ondo State took the decision to evict errant herdsmen from the state's forest reserves. This led to a face-off that spiralled into a North–South war of words, in the entire South West (Kabir, 2021). In Kaduna State there was an ongoing war of nerves between Governor El-Rufai's government and bandits who abducted 39 students from the state forestry school and were still holding them in forests at the time of writing (Olufemi, 2021). Bandits and kidnap rings have entrenched their presence in these forests. The Nigerian military has had the unwholesome task of conducting occasional indiscriminate aerial bombardments to sort out criminal elements, with predictable collateral human losses. Ungoverned spaces are areas and zones in countries and regions which lie beyond the reach of the government. It has been observed that regional security outfits like Amotekun, established to tackle insecurity, are essentially the organized response to the emerging threat emerging from ungoverned spaces. The absence of proper governance in this and similar areas has created concerted intellectual and infrastructural responses aiming at a broad-based national response.

It is expected that the leadership could form a security strategy with a view to proffering modern, research-based and data-driven solutions to what the country is faced with today. On a continental level, the greatest threat to stability in Africa is the increase in transnational terrorist groups and criminals that occupy the ungoverned spaces. Nigeria is suffering from the inability of the government to secure our borders and protect our citizenry. The situation is creating problems not only for Nigeria but also for the sub-region. Parts of northern Nigeria are becoming enclaves of banditry for gangs of cattle rustlers who maraud through largely ungoverned forests. For example, there are reports of illegal gold miners setting up equipped towns inside the bushes, with their own militia for security.

This goes to show that there is a need for the serious interrogation of cattle rustling and ungoverned forest spaces in the north. Nationally, there is poor forest governance, which creates a vacuum of government and its agents. This then emboldens Fulani herders and their cattle to take over these spaces, even in the southern parts of the country, where their activities scare off the landowners and farmers. This has led to clashes among the locals and provided room for kidnappers to use for operational bases. This situation of ever-present violence in Nigeria is due to the role that violence has played in the country's political system. It has served both the state and the people, becoming the tool to force attention to be given to demands.

It may interest the reader to know that the state is not ready to do anything about these demands that brought about the violence in the first place. Instead, the state matches the violence of the people with its own countervi-olence. It is in this way that the Nigerian political system could be described as an equilibrium, of violence. In this equilibrium what the people want from the state is equal to what the state does not want to give them. The violence the state is ready to marshal in defence of its position is, therefore, equal to the violence the people have unleashed in pursuit of their demands. The state of equilibrium would also hold if the violence were to be initiated by the state, in which case, the people would also counter with their own violence.

## 5  Conclusion

This chapter has examined how space has constituted a threat to national security in Nigeria. The relevant agencies, such as the DSS (Department of State Security), DIA (Defence Intelligence Agency), NIA (National Intelligence Agency), and the Nigerian police, who are stakeholders in addressing our national security, have failed in implementing the National Security Strategy document which mentions ungoverned space as a threat to the polity. This is undoubtedly a critical indication concerning ongoing efforts against current security challenges. This has given criminal entities the opportunity to move into ungoverned spaces and to assert their presence. The situation on the ground definitely shows that there is no end to violence in the polity. Both the government and non-state actors continue to claim victories in the field, and no one seems to be on the retreat. The absence of intelligence has also played a role. The lack of appropriate assets to deploy, such as drones and other means of surveillance, constitutes a challenge.

The chapter has also observed with regard to the current security challenges that government has not had a significant impact on the lives of the people at any level. Most of the communities affected by violence also confide that they only see their representatives when they come to campaign. This disclosure indicates that there has been a systematic decline in the presence of government in most communities. This brings to our understanding the consequences of negligence and the deteriorating impact of governance.

## Recommendations

If Nigeria is to have the peace and development in the polity which it desires, this can only be achieved when a vulnerability assessment of the country is conducted. This will identify the crisis-prone and crime-infested areas that require security presence.

There is a need for the restructuring and comprehensive redistribution of security and paramilitary organizations in the country to cover all areas of perceived vulnerability and all gaps and weaknesses in security.

It is important for leadership to realize that ungoverned spaces are linked to failure on the part of government to have an impact on the lives of the people. Government at the local, state, and federal levels should, as a matter of urgency and in a quest for comprehensive development, look at all parts of the country in the provision of infrastructure and development. The security agencies, for their part, should conduct comprehensive intelligence mapping of all parts of the country in the identification of ungoverned spaces, to add security operations.

The security forces should, as a matter of urgency, factor into their operations sustained surveillance and clearance operations on remote and inaccessible areas, especially forests, throughout the country.

## References

Afigbo, A. (1966). A Reassessment of the Historiography of the Colonial Period in West Africa. In A. Ajayi & I. Espie (Eds.), *A Thousand Years of West African History*. Nelson University Press.

Adinoyi, S. (2021). *Zulum: Poor Implementation of Security Strategy Responsible for Insurgents Occupation of Borno Village*. www.thisdaylive.com. Accessed 21 April 2022.

Ajayi, O. (2021). *Banditry: Secure Your Forest Reserves Charges States*. www.vanguardngr.com/2021,19 March Accessed 29 October 2021.

Ake, C. (1996). *Democracy and Development in Africa*. Brookings.

Ali, F. (2017). *Winning Hearts and Minds in Ungoverned Spaces*. UNDP Regional Service Centre.

Alkali, A. R. (2003). *International Relations and Nigeria Foreign Policy* (2nd ed.). North Point Publishers.

Are, L. K. (1999a, June 19–22). *Meeting the Challenges of National Security*. Paper Presented at the National Defense College Abuja.

Are, L. K. (1999b, August 19–22). *Organs and Process of National Security*. Paper presented at the National Defense College.

Bohm, M. L. (2018). *The Crime of Maldevelopment: Economic Deregulation and Violence in the Global South*. Routledge.

Brown, H. (1983). *Thinking About National Security Defense and Foreign Policy in a Dangerous World* (1st edn.). Westview Press.

Brown, L. (1977), Redefining National Security. *World Watch Paper No.14*. World Watch.

Buzan, B. (1983). *People, States and Fear: The National Security Problem in International Relations*. Wheatsheaf Books.

Centre for Public Authority and International Development. (2021). CPAID Report.

Cooper, V., & Whyte, D. (Eds.). (2017). *The Violence of Austerity*. Pluto Press.

Commission on Terrorist Attacks Upon the United States, The 9/11 Commission Report: Final Report of the National Commission on Terrorist Attacks upon the United States (9/11 Report), gov.info, (July 22, 2004).

FAO. (2019). *Nigeria*. www.fao.org. Accessed 27 December 2019.

Farmer, P. (2004). An Anthropology of Structural Violence. *Current Anthropology, 45*(3), 305–325.

Gambo, A. N. (2008). *Conflict in the Niger Delta and National Security in Nigeria*. Mano Expressions.

Habermas, J. (2001). *The Post National Constellation: Political Essays*. Polity.

Howard, T. (2014). *Failed States and the Origins of Violence. A Comparative Analysis of State Failure as a Root Cause of Terrorism and Political Violence*. Routledge.

Imobighe, T. (1998). *The Management of National Security*. Inaugural Lecture, Edo State University.

Imobighe, T. (2013). Dimensions of Threats and National Development Challenges in Nigeria. In O. Mbachu & B.Umar (Eds.), *Internal Security Management in Nigeria: A Study in Terrorism and Counter Terrorism*. Medusa Academic Publishers Limited.

Internally Displaced Monitoring Centre. (2020). *Nigeria: Country Information*. Retrieved 16 May 2020. www.internal.displacement.org/countries/Nigeria

Jackson, R. (1990). *Quasi States: Sovereignty International Relations and the Third World*. Cambridge University Press.

Kabir, A. (2021, May 21). Analysis: How Southern Governors Ban on Open Grazing May Reduce Former-herder Crisis. *Premium Times*.

Keenan, J. (2007). The Banana Theory of Terrorism: Alternatives Truths and the Collapse of the "Second" (Saharan) Front in War on Terror. *Journal of Contemporary Africa Studies, 25*(1), 14–25.

Kiess, J. (2016). *Philosophy and Theology*. Bloomsbury.

Lloyd, R. B. (2016). Ungoverned Spaces and Regional Insecurity: The Case of Mali. *SAIS Review of International Affairs, 36*(1), 131–141.

Maier, C. (1990, June 12). *Peace and Security for the 1990s*. Unpublished Paper for the MacArthur Fellowship Program, Social Science Research Council.

Mathews, J. (1989). Redefining Security. *Foreign Affairs, 68*(2), 162–177.

Mcnamara, R. S. (1968). *The Essence of Security*. Hodder and Stoughton.

Menkhaus, K. (2010). State Failure and Ungoverned Space. *Adelphi Series, 50*(412–413), 171–188.

Mohammed, I. S. (2018). Post Boko Haram Insurgency Nigeria's National Security and Emergent Threats. *Journal of Humanities and Cultural Studies R&D, 3*(2), 1–15.

National Security Agencies Act. (2006). (CAP 278). No 19 of 5 June.

Nigerian Bureau of Statisitcs. (2021). *2021 Annual Report*.

Nigeria National Security Strategy. (2019). Federal Republic of Nigeria.

Nnoli, O. (2006). *National Security in Africa: A Radical Perspective*. PACREP Publishers.

Nwolise, O. B. C. (2008). National Security and Sustainable Democracy. In E. O. Ojo (Ed.) *Challenges of Sustainable Democracy in Nigeria*. John Archers.

Oche, O. (2005). Low Intensity Conflicts, National Security and Democratic Sustenance'. In H.A. Saliu (Ed.), *Nigeria under Democratic Rule 1999–2003*. University of Ibadan.

Ogbonnaya, M. (2020, June 16). *How Illegal Mining is Driving Local Conflicts in Nigeria*. Institute for Security Studies.

Okodolor, C. (2004). National Security and Foreign Policy: Towards a Review of Nigeria's Afro-Centric Policy. *Nigerian Forum, 25*(7–8), 204–223.

Okoli, A. C. (2012). *Emergency Management and Nigeria's National Security: Evaluation NEMA's Role in Oil Pipeline Explosion Disasters in South Eastern Nigeria*. PhD proposal submitted to the Department of Political Science and Defence Studies. Nigerian Defence Academy (NDA), Kaduna.

Olaniyan, R. A & Akindele, R. T. (2017). *Nigeria's Ungoverned Spaces: Studies Insecurity, Terrorism and Governance*. Accessed 15 March 2021 www.thenationolineng.net/studying-nigerias-ungoverned-spaces

Olufemi, A. (2021, November 28). *Horrors On the Plateau: Inside Nigeria's farmer-herder Conflcit*. Al Jazeera. www.aligazeera.com/features/2021/11/28/horrors-on-the-plateau-inside-nigerias-farmer-herders-conflict

Onuoha, F. (2007). *Poverty, Pipeline Vandalization/Explosion and Human Security: Integrating Disaster Management into Poverty Education in Nigeria*. Draft Paper, African Centre for Strategic Research and Studies (ACSRS), National War College Abuja-Nigeria.

Onwuzuruigbo, I. (2020). Enclaves of Banditry: Ungoverned Forest Spaces and Cattle Rustling in Northern Nigeria. *African Studies Review, 20,* 1–24.

Patrick, S. (2010). *Are Ungoverned Spaces a Threat?* Council on Foreign Affairs.

Pogoson, A. (2013). *Nigeria's National Security in an Age of Terrorism.* Gold Press Ltd.

Raleigh, C., & Dowd, C. (2013). Governance and Conflict in the Sahel's Ungoverned Spaces. *Stability: International Journal of Security and Development, 2*(2). https://doi.org/10.5334/sta.bs

Rand Corporation. (2007). *Ungoverned Territories. Understanding and Reducing Terrorism Risks.* Rand Corporation.

Robasa, A., & Peters, J. E. (2007). *Understanding Lack of Governance in Ungoverned Territories: Understanding and Reducing Terrorism Risks.* (Robbas, A, Ed., pp. 1–6).; Rand Corporation.

Rotberg, R., & Campbell, J. (2021). *Nigeria Is a Failed State.* Retrieved 16 December 2020. www.foreignpolicy.com

Rotberg, R. (2004). *When States Fail: Causes and Consequences.* Princeton University Press.

Taylor, A. J. (2016). Thoughts on the Nature and Consequences of Ungoverned Spaces. *SAIS Review of International Affairs, 36*(1), 5–51.

Tsuwa, J., & Okoh, J. O. (2016). Nigeria Prisons Service and Internal Security Management in Nigeria. In J. S. Omotola & I. M. Alumona (Eds.), *The State in Contemporary Nigeria: Issues Perspectives and Challenges.* John Archers (Publishers) Limited.

Tilly, R. C. Violence Terror and Politics as Usual Summer 2002 cited on June 23 2008 *Boston Review.* A Political and Literary Forum. www.bostonreview.net/BR27.3/tilly.htm.l

UNHCR. (2020). *Nigeria Emergency.* Retrieved 16 May 2020. www.unhcr.org/nigeria-emergency.htm

UNICEF. (2021). *The State of the World's Children.* Flagship Report: UNICEF.

United States Department of State Country Reports on Terrorism. (2011). www.stategov/j/ct/ris/crt2011. Accessed 10 April 2021.

Weaver, O. (1995). Securitization and Desecuritization. In R. Lipschutz (Ed.), *On Security.* Columbia University Press.

Whelan, T. (2006). Africa's Ungoverned Space. *Nacao Defesa, 111,* 61–73.

Wolfers, A. (1962). National Security as an Ambiguous Symbol. *Political Science Quarterly, 67*(4), 481–502.

World Bank. (2011). *Conflcit, Security and Development: World Development Report 2011.* World Bank.

WHO Global Consultation on Violence and Health. (1996). *Violence a Public Health Priority.* Geneva World Health Organization. 1996 document WHO/EHA/SPEPOA.

Zartman, W. (1995). *Collapsed States: The Disintegration and Restoration of Legitimate Authority.* Lynne Rienner.

# Children, Youth and Violence

# Trauma, Violence, and Memory in African Child Soldier Memoirs

Stacey Hynd

Our memories filled up too fast with horrors that only human beings are capable of doing. (Keitetsi, 2004: 125)

## 1 Introduction

Children have historically been heavily involved in conflict, as victims, perpetrators, and witnesses, both in Africa and across the world. Global estimates from the 1990s and early 2000s posit that over 300,000 child soldiers were fighting or had recently been demobilized. An estimated 120,000 of those were African, and indeed for most of the 1990s–2000s the iconographic image of "the child soldier" was overwhelmingly African—a small, wild-eyed African boy in ragged clothes, brandishing an AK-47 (CSUCS, 2008). Since the 1990s, the "child soldier crisis" has become a major humanitarian and human rights project, from the United Nations Machel Report in 1996 to the Kony 2012 phenomenon and the #BringBackOurGirls outcry over the 2014 kidnapping of 276 schoolgirls by Boko Haram in Nigeria.

This chapter was originally published as a journal article in Culture, Medicine and Psychiatry https://link.springer.com/article/10.1007/s11013-020-09668-4.

S. Hynd (✉)
Department of Archaeology and History, University of Exeter, Exeter, UK
e-mail: s.hynd@exeter.ac.uk

Dominant humanitarian discourses of child soldiering have framed children's involvement in war as a problem primarily of contemporary, asymmetric, and highly violent warfare, linked to a breakdown of familial and social child protection mechanisms, and driven by forcible recruitment by military commanders. These discourses have tended to reject child agency and accountability, portraying child soldiers as iconic victims of war (see Brett & McCallin, 1996; Machel, 1996). The humanitarian appeal of the African child soldier is rooted in how "the brutal existence of a child soldier dovetails neatly with depictions of Africa both as a place of hell and misery and as a continent that, like a child, can be saved" (Mengestu, 2007). Humanitarian campaigns have highlighted the abduction and forced recruitment of children, depicting child soldiers as brutalized, traumatized victims of adult abuses, whose recruitment violates norms of both war and childhood and whose rescue requires international action (Brett & Specht, 2004). Humanitarian and human rights-based interventions to prevent the recruitment and use of children in armed forces are, however, predicated on a contemporary "transnational politics of age" that enshrines Western-originated, now globalized, norms of childhood as a space of innocence, education, and freedom from labour and sexual activity (Rosen, 2007: 296–298). These norms have been subject to sustained academic critique and are far from reality for many African communities, where local understandings of childhood are based more on social and physical status rather than chronological age and foreground children's capacity to be active social agents and productive members of a household, sometimes highlighting the potentially disruptive liminality of children and their capacity for action and violence rather than any innate state of innocence (James & Prout, 1990; Nieuwenhuys, 2010; Shepler, 2014; Twum-Danso, 2005). The image of the innocent and brutalized child soldier as victim in these contemporary humanitarian campaigns therefore "repeats [a] colonial paternalism where the adult Northerner offers help and knowledge to the infantilized South," positioning non-governmental organizations as better able to provide for the needs of children than their own families and societies, and pathologizing children's agency in socially navigating conflict environments (Burman, 1994: 241; Lee-Koo, 2011: 735; Pupavac, 2001). What both supports and disrupts these humanitarian discourses are the voices and memories of African child soldiers themselves.

When it comes to accessing memories of conflict, the published memoirs of former child soldiers grant international audiences detailed individual insights into African conflicts and societies in a way that has been managed by very few other voices. This chapter suggests that whilst sometimes problematic, these memoirs can be productive tools in researching modern African conflict because of what they reveal about how contemporary humanitarian discourses and ideas of trauma shape the narration of war memories, and for what they reveal about the agency and resilience of former child soldiers and the quotidian realities of conflict. The memoirs analysed herein are the ten most widely available commercially published texts written by former child soldiers who were involved in civil wars across sub-Saharan Africa spanning from the 1980s to the early 2000s. The most famous of the memoirists are Ishmael Beah and Emmanuel Jal. Beah was forcibly recruited into the Sierra Leonean armed forces during that country's civil war and was demobilized into a UNICEF rehabilitation centre in Freetown before relocating to America and writing his memoir, *A Long Way Gone*, which became an acclaimed bestseller and was even sold in Starbucks coffee shops (2008). Beah has since become a UNICEF advocate for war-affected children, and a novelist. Emmanuel Jal was recruited into the Sudanese People's Liberation Army [SPLA], surviving life in Pinyudu refugee camp and several military engagements before being taken to Nairobi by Riek Machar's English wife Emma McCune. A 2008 documentary about his life, *War Child*, was followed by the publication of his memoir (2009). Jal has since gained international renown as a political activist, rap artist, actor, and founder of the charity Gua Africa. This chapter also addresses the experiences of two (South) Sudanese "Lost Boys," Deng Adut and Cola Bilkuei, who moved from being SPLA child soldiers to refugees, before settling in Australia (Adut & Mckelvey, 2016; Bilkuei, 2008 [2013]). Insights into child soldiering in the Democratic Republic of the Congo [DRC], like South Sudan an ongoing zone of child recruitment, are provided by the memoirs of Lucien Badjoko and Junior Nzita Nsuami, two *kadogos* (little soldier; child soldier) who served in the Congo Wars (Badjoko & Clarens, 2005; Nzita Nsuami, 2012 [2016]). Girls constitute an estimated 30% of child soldiers and their voices are well-represented in memoirs (McKay & Mazurana, 2004). China Keitetsi gives the earliest account detailed here, covering her time as one of Yoweri Museveni's *kadogos* in the Ugandan bush war and after Museveni's seizure of power in 1986 (2004). From the Lord's Resistance Army [LRA]'s forced recruitment of children in Northern Uganda, memoirs have been written by Grace Akallo, one of the "Aboke Girls" kidnapped by the LRA in 1996, and by Evelyn Amony, who was abducted as a young girl and forced to become one of Joseph Kony's "bush wives" (Amony & Baines, 2015; McDonnell & Akallo, 2007). Finally, Senait Mehari provides a contested account of her experiences in a disintegrating Eritrean Liberation Front [ELF] unit in the Eritrean independence struggle against Ethiopia (2006).

This chapter will put forward two main strands of argument. First, that the historical significance of child soldier memoirs lies not so much in their relating of empirical facts, which are sometimes disputed, but rather in what can be called their affective truths and what they reveal about children's experiences, and narrations, of war. Second, it argues that former child soldiers engage with, but also subtly challenge, dominant contemporary humanitarian discourses surrounding childhood and warfare to develop a "victim, savage, saviour, campaigner" framework for their narratives. The chapter will open by discussing methodological issues about reading child soldier memoirs historically, before qualitatively analysing the functioning of the affective truths of these texts through their narration of memories of recruitment, indoctrination, combat experience, and their subjects' attempts to rework their identities in a post-conflict environment. It will address notions of "victimhood" and "victimcy" (Utas, 2011) by looking at memoirists' accounts of their ruptured innocence and notions of guilt, and address ideas of the "savage" by exploring how violence is narrated. The chapter will analyse how these child soldier memoirs sit in tension with dominant humanitarian discourses surrounding the—usually white, Western—humanitarian as "saviour" to war-affected children, and how these former child soldiers utilize their stories to position themselves as campaigners for those children still caught in conflict.

This chapter will use the term "child soldier" in line with current United Nations categorization to include any person under eighteen years of age who becomes part of an armed group in any capacity, including as a "bush wife" or conjugal slave (UNICEF, 1997): it should be noted however that the vast majority of child soldiers are teenagers, who see themselves as youths or young adults (Shepler, 2014; Twum-Danso, 2005). Although humanitarian practitioners today prefer the term "child [formerly] associated with armed forces or armed groups" as less potentially stigmatizing, this chapter retains the term "child soldier" as it is the terminology most often adopted by the memoirists themselves. For clarity, the term "memoir" will be used throughout, although some of these texts could also be categorized as auto/biography or life writing. There has been considerable debate over whether notions of post-traumatic stress disorder and biomedical or biopsychosocial framings of "trauma" as formulated in the DSM are properly universal and can, therefore, be applied outside the Western contexts in which they were developed (Honwana, 2006: 150–156; Summerfield, 2000). Memoirs however are not medical texts. This chapter is not so much concerned with whether or not, or to what extent, these former child soldiers are traumatized, but rather with how they recount suffering and deploy discourses of trauma in their narratives. As Kleinman argues, medicalizing political violence removes the human context of trauma as the chief focus for understanding violence, and those who suffer it should be understood as social sufferers rather than just patients or victims (Kleinman, 1988, 1995). Former child soldiers' accounts are products both of their individual experiences and memories, and the cultural and societal contexts in which they have grown up, being shaped by collective memories of conflict and displacement in both local African cultures and the West (Kevers et al., 2016). This chapter posits that the suffering expressed by these memoirists is normative for children who have experienced conflict and fighting, rather than pathological, but that many do narrate behaviours and memories that could be classified as "traumatic." An uncritical application of trauma diagnoses in non-Western societies affected by conflict can relabel social suffering as a pathological condition, creating a form of "psychological imperialism" and stressing victimhood rather than recognizing individual and community resilience (Fassin & Rechtman, 2009; Good & Hilton, 2016: 8; Kevers et al., 2016; Pupavac, 2001). Discourses of trauma can also serve to depoliticize and individualize suffering, and medico-humanitarian interventions to alleviate that suffering, leading to a failure to address the structural roots of violence in a society or the global inequalities and political economies that fuel conflict (Lee-Koo, 2011; Summerfield, 2002). However, the evidence presented by these memoirs suggests that discourses of trauma do hold value for some former child soldiers, either because they feel traumatized by their experiences, and/or they have learned to express themselves within such discourses to better communicate their suffering as a result of their engagement with humanitarian organizations, therapeutic interventions, or commercial publishing (Verma, 2012). There is a need for the scholarly analysis of war memories to break away from a simplistic binary relationship between "trauma" and "resilience" which flattens the complexity of human emotions and experiences. For these memoirists, their post-conflict resilience is enhanced through harnessing their own suffering in an attempt to alleviate or prevent the suffering of other war-affected children. Writing their "trauma" and bearing witness to the horrors of war becomes a coping mechanism for these former child soldiers, a moral act of memory, helping to give post hoc reason to their suffering and to assuage the guilt that some of them seem to carry at having survived where their friends and comrades have not.

## 2    Reading Child Soldier Memoirs into/as History

The sub-genre of the child soldier memoir emerged from a cultural nexus of the 1990s–2000s boom in autobiography and childhood autobiography, the growth of child rights, human rights and liberal humanitarianism, alongside the growing delegitimization of warfare and the development of humanitarian psychiatry, creating what Fassin and Rechtman term a new "moral economy of trauma" (Barnett, 2011; Burman, 1994; Douglas, 2010; Fassin & Rechtman, 2009). Whilst children's experiences and voices have historically been marginalized within collective and public histories of war and politics, these African child soldier memoirs and auto/biographical voices have been, if anything, over-privileged in the creation of globalized, collective memories of contemporary conflict in Africa.

It is striking that child soldier memoirs regarding conflicts that occurred prior to the 1980s, even those written more recently, do not notably employ discourses of trauma, rights, or victimhood. The memories are instead narrated with a focus on the author's resilience and agency in becoming a disciplined soldier despite their suffering, and on making a "good war" for themselves as far as their situation allowed, particularly in Second World War memoirs (Kolk & Mandambwe, 2007). Decolonization-era memoirs tend to pay particular attention to the political mobilization and agency of youth in liberation conflicts (Ferdi, 1981). Some memoirists even write of war as being in part a positive experience, when they moved from being marginalized children to feeling empowered, respected, and part of a community, as in Talent Chioma Mundy-Castle's account of her time as a Biafran child spy during the 1967–1970 Nigerian Civil War (Mundy-Castle, 2012). Contemporary child soldier memoirs, however, display a qualitative shift in their politics of memory which are instead enframed by the dominant victimhood-orientated humanitarian, human rights, and trauma discourses which define contemporary accounts of war and violence (Schaffer & Smith, 2004).

One of the core paradoxes of commercial auto/biography is that the memoirist must be both unique and representative in their experiences (Miller, 2001: 8). These child soldier memoirs are written by exceptional children-turned-adults: exceptional in that they are literate, were personally supported by Western/international humanitarians, and in that they survived and escaped their conflicts. Many left Africa to seek new lives abroad, moving from soldier to refugee or migrant status, bringing a globalized, expatriate perspective to their accounts, and highlighting the tensions between universal and local norms of childhood, particularly in their experiences of coming of age in a wartime environment (Douglas & Poletti, 2016: 100). As Deng Adut writes "[i]n the eyes of my culture, I am still a boy. When I should have been going through the rituals of manhood, I was caught in a vicious war. By the time I was returned to my people, I was very much a Westerner. My feet straddle continents, and also the threshold of manhood"

(Adut & Mckelvey, 2016: loc 77). All the memoirists are writing about childhood wartime experiences through their new perspectives as young adults. Life-cycles are important in the framing of traumatic memories, and these memoirs are very much youth narratives, written by young adults who are seeking to establish their identities, their social status, and to claim a position of power from which their voices can be heard and acknowledged (Clifford, 2017). The normative character and moral economy of the world in which a person grows up and learns to perform their identity shapes the life narratives that they tell—but for those whose lives are disrupted as children, particularly as teenagers whose identities are fluid and liminal, their normative character is affected by both war and peace, by their natal cultures, their militarized identities, and their new post-conflict, often expatriated, lives as activists, writers, and professionals.

The writing in memoirs differs markedly from human rights reports that generally balance empirical data with sentimentalized narratives and affective appeals, combining statistics with excerpted, decontextualized, individual testimony, and striking images (Schaffer & Smith, 2004). All commercially available memoirs are edited and adapted through the publishing process, but many child soldier memoirs are also co-written, mediated testimonies (Douglas & Poletti, 2016: 97–98). Badjoko, Jal, Adut, and Mehari's memoirs were all collaboratively written with Western journalists/authors, the extent of whose input is left unclear. The language varies sharply from Jal and Beah's more poetic, fluid prose, honed by their creative talents as rapper and novelist, respectively, to the more fractured, idiomatic language of Keitetsi. Erin Baines, the American academic who edited from a series of interviews Evelyn Amony's account of her life in the Lord's Resistance Army as one of Joseph Kony's wives, notes that when recollecting traumatic stories Evelyn's narrative became less comprehensible or sounded detached, and Baines therefore deliberately worked towards a written transcription that captured this reaction (2015: xx). Tellingly, the memoirs of Lucien Badjoko, one of Laurent Kabila's *kadogo* in the Democratic Republic of the Congo [DRC], were co-written with a French journalist, Katia Clarens, after she met him in a DDR [disarmament, demobilization, and reintegration] camp and he informed her "I have written a short script of my life if you are interested" (2005: 7).[1] Badjoko here displays a variant of what Utas terms "victimcy tactics": children expressing agency through identifying themselves as powerless victims and appropriating humanitarian tropes to secure funds, resources, or protection (Utas, 2011; Verma, 2012). As Kleinman argues, trauma stories have become a currency that social sufferers of political violence and conflict exchange to claim new status as refugees (Kleinman, 1995: 177–188). Both Cola Bilkuei and Deng Adut, former SPLA child soldiers from South Sudan who relocated to Australia, learned to craft and commoditize their life stories to support themselves as they transitioned from military life to refugee and immigrant status. Bilkuei began to shape his narrative to his audience when moving between East African countries and refugee camps seeking aid, and first wrote his life story to be ranked in order of need by the UNHCR in Kenya in 1996: "I started to think about telling my story to anyone who would listen, hoping they would give me money in exchange. Not for the first or last time, my life story was becoming my meal ticket. It might be odd, for an Australian, to see your life story as your sole economic asset. But for me and other Sudanese who have little else to sell, it was a natural thing to do" (2008 [2013]: 153). Ishmael Beah was sent to the United Nations in New York as a child soldier representative and was there drawn to the woman who would become his adoptive mother, Laura Simms, because "[s]he said she would teach us how to tell our stories in a more compelling way" to engage with international audiences (2008: 196).

When many former child soldiers crafted their texts, they therefore had practice at producing the range of narrative elements that Western readers and editors have come to expect, as well as drawing on oral storytelling traditions from their own cultures (Beah, 2008: 217–218; Moynagh, 2011: 48). Unlike human rights reports or truth commission testimonies which are focused on establishing factual accounts of conflict, memoirs, like child soldier novels, often display a marked ahistoricity, eliding context, time and space, and blurring the boundaries between history, memory, and narrative truth: historical and political context to the conflicts they fight in is replaced by an overarching framework of human rights abuses and humanitarian narratives (Coundouriotis, 2010). The preferred narrative framework is one of innocence disrupted by war, violence, and trauma, then humanitarian salvation and recovery, with a corresponding disavowal of violence. It is perhaps significant that those memoirs which most closely follow this framework, like Beah and Jal's, are those which have become the best-selling and most widely lauded by both public and humanitarian sources. Child soldier memoirs are strongly influenced by humanitarian discourses of child soldiering that code children's involvement in war as an adult-perpetrated human rights abuse caused by social breakdown and hyper-violent, non-rule-bound contemporary conflict, and which reject child agency and culpability (see Machel, 1996). The memoirs, however, both challenge and support these discourses (Mackey, 2013; Mastey, 2018; Schultheis, 2008). Where they primarily challenge those discourses is in the much higher level of agency they accord themselves—however tactical or circumscribed that agency is—and in the significance of that agency to their survival and salvation, rather than expressing a reliance on external, humanitarian rescue (Drumbl, 2012: 98–101; Honwana, 2006: 50–51). Makau Mutua writes that contemporary human rights narratives about Africa routinely follow a framework of "Savage, Victim, Saviour" (Mutua, 2001), detailing violence and establishing victimhood to justify external intervention and rescue. Paraphrasing Mutua, this chapter argues that child soldier memoirs follow instead a framework of "Victim, Savage, Saviour, Campaigner", establishing child soldiers as victims of war and military recruitment, who enact and experience violence before being rescued—or rescuing themselves—and seeking to help prevent others suffering their fate. All of the memoirists now campaign against the use of child soldiers, and many explicitly state that their narratives were written to assist these campaigns and bear witness to the violence committed against child soldiers: as Emmanuel Jal sings in his song *War Child*, "I believe I've survived for a reason, To tell my story, to touch lives" (Jal & Davies, 2009: 257). One of the kidnapped Aboke girls from Northern Uganda, Grace Akallo, rhetorically asks herself why she has survived in the LRA, escaping death in raids, from beatings, and even multiple suicide attempts. She credits God for her survival and eventual escape from captivity but believes that for survival to have a purpose: "Surely there was a reason I had escaped death. Maybe I might help change the ten-year-old war … God if You let me go back … I will fight for the children who become victims in this war. They cannot speak" (McDonnell & Akallo, 2007: 113, 125–126). Akallo developed this theme in her testimonies to the UN Security Council and the US House of Representatives, telling the House that what she had faced during her abduction was "beyond fear" and that she was not there to "evoke emotions without action" but to plead for justice and accountability against those who recruit child soldiers (US House of Representatives, 2008; UN SRSGCAC, 2009). Beah asserts that "my own trauma is a small price to pay to expose what continues to happen to children all over the world" (Beah, 2008: 3). These memoirs are performative of a new form of identity for many former child soldiers: that of the empowered "victim" turned "campaigner." Where possible, these memoirs should be read paratextually within the context of wider humanitarian coverage of child soldiering and the author's own websites, interviews, TED talks, and other cultural productions. Nzita Nsuami's memoir *If My Life as a Child Soldier Could be Told* was presented to the UN mission in the DRC and is prefaced by Leila Zerrougui, Special Representative for the UN Secretary-General for Children and Armed Conflict, who supports Nzita Nsuami in using "his experience for the benefit of many other child soldiers," with proceeds of the memoir going to his organization Paix pour l'enfance (Nzita Nsuami, 2012 [2016], first preface). The memoirists have all been active in campaigning against the recruitment of child soldiers and other related rights abuses. They have worked with groups such as UNICEF, Human Rights Watch, and the Coalition to Stop the Use of Child Soldiers to voice their campaign appeals and spoken about child soldiering at the United Nations, as well as setting up their own organizations, such as Jal's Gua Africa, or working locally with rehabilitation and reintegration projects for former child soldiers and refugees.

## 3  Empirical, Narrative, and Affective Truth in Memoirs

As a body of evidence, child soldier memoirs sit amongst therapeutic writing, testimony, human rights reporting, humanitarian campaigning, coming of age narratives, postcolonial life history, and oral storytelling. As Kate Douglas argues, they are products of, and confrontations with, cultural memory (Douglas, 2010: 20). Historically speaking, their narratives sit between empirical or forensic truths, narrative or personal truths, and what can be called affective truths. The term affective truth is used here to argue that these narratives are specifically crafted to prompt an emotional response or "empathic unsettlement" in their readers through authoritative accounts of the—purported—reality of child soldier experience, and to thereby generate humanitarian sentiments and actions from readers (LaCapra, 2014). This is not to say that this affective truth does not also stem from a genuine emotion that the author needs to process and convey, but rather that in the published memoir this emotion is deployed to convey the veracity of experience and is leveraged to prompt a particular response in the reader.

There are perennial ethical and methodological debates over the "truthfulness" or factual nature of memoirs, particularly regarding accounts like those of Ishmael Beah and Senait Mehari who have come under attack by the media and other former child soldiers in their units for misrepresenting the duration of their involvement for or appropriating others' stories (Sanders, 2011: 206–207). Beah notes of his time in the Sierra Leonean army that "My mind had not only snapped during the first killing, it had also stopped making remorseful records, or so it seemed" but then also recounts his military experiences in great detail with extensive dialogue, asserting he has a photographic memory (Beah, 2008: 122, 51). The historical utility of memoirs is not primarily linked to forensic or empirical truths, establishing the facts of what happened, as is the case with human rights reports. But these texts are not simple narrative truths either, nor just an individual's memories of war. What is most significant is how, and why, former child soldiers feel compelled to relate their memories. Their accounts speak to what Baines terms the "ethical significance" of the events they experienced (Amony & Baines, 2015: xxi). Childhood autobiographies today are commonly marketed according to their political and sociological worth, their virtue signalled in their promise of didacticism and their exposure of social injustices (Douglas, 2010: 61). In African child soldier memoirs, this didacticism and exposure operates through the crafting of an affective truth that is framed by notions of violence, suffering, and trauma, contrasting with the innocence and protection that is assumed to be due to children under universal norms of childhood in contemporary geopolitical frameworks (Burman, 1994; Mastey, 2018). Child soldier narratives and images have become so prominent within contemporary humanitarian iconography precisely because child soldiers violate established generational and moral norms, and complicate notions of child victimhood and apolitical status with the juxtaposition of their imbued innocence and violent action: they are profane figures that disrupt the affective and semiotic apparatus of humanitarian concern (Malkki, 2015: 2, 8). Humanitarian advocacy has to balance highlighting the danger occasioned by (as well as for) child soldiers to raise awareness with establishing that they are still redeemable in order to convince audiences of the efficacy of intervention; a balance the memoirists help establish.

## 4 "Victims" to "Savages": Innocence, Violence, and Narrative Rupture

The memoirs nearly all take on a chronological, broadly *Bildungsroman* structure stretching from childhood innocence to the rupture of their entry into an armed group, through the horrors of war to their escape and salvation, and then their struggles to re-adjust to civilian life and eventual empowerment through their personal success and activism. Some open with a nostalgic account of their childhood and the perceived happiness and security of an idyllic family life, with Grace Akallo recalling "[t]he village I knew as a child was a special place. We children felt loved and taken care of … there was never any news of a child being harmed," cherishing a sense of community and family (McDonnell & Akallo, 2007: 48–49). Others challenge normative, Western assumptions of childhood innocence as a state of "not-knowing" and demonstrate how the conflict had disrupted their domestic security and happiness even before their recruitment by an armed group as they were exposed to fighting through attacks on their villages (Amony & Baines, 2015: 10–13; Beah, 2008). Some memoirists conversely highlight their domestic marginalization and lay blame for their entry into armed groups not just on the soldiers who took them, but also upon their families for failing to protect them. Mehari details the abuse she suffered at the hands of her father, but claims she understands the rationality of his decision to hand her and two sisters over to the ELF to reduce the strain on the family's limited food supplies and prevent them all starving (Mehari, 2006: 53). Keitetsi recalls the domestic abuse that drove her to voluntarily seek enlistment with the NRA, whilst Amony locates her abduction by the LRA within her father's failure to pay her school fees, as she was captured after being sent away from school (Amony & Baines, 2015: 147; Keitetsi, 2004: 52–112).

Humanitarian discourses surrounding child soldiering have focused on forced recruitment and abduction as the primary vectors of recruitment. The 1996 Machel Report for the United Nations, the foundational text for contemporary interventions on child soldier issues, issues a stark denial of voluntary recruitment, asserting that children lack the capacity for such agency: "While young people may appear to choose military service, the choice is not exercised freely," and is instead shaped by external forces (Machel Report, 1996: 17). Certainly a number of these memoirs demonstrate the prevalence of forced recruitment and abduction (Amony & Baines, 2015: 16–18; McDonnell & Akallo, 2007: 93–94; Nzita Nsuami, 2012 [2016]). Bilkuei and Adut were both given up by their families in the face of SPLA coercion as part of village quotas for recruitment, whilst Beah was forced to choose between joining the army at gunpoint or being left without protection or resources (Adut & Mckelvey, 2016; Beah, 2008: 106; Bilkuei, 2008 [2013]: 27–29). However, as recent studies have shown, many children do demonstrate limited, tactical agency comparable to that of adult recruits in their recruitment (Honwana, 2006; ILO, 2003). This is borne out in the accounts of Keitetsi, and of Badjoko who, aged twelve, voluntarily joined the Alliance of Democratic Forces for the Liberation of Congo-Zaire [AFDL] alongside his school friends and recalls how "A fire started burning in my stomach. I think about the films I watch every day on video at home … Schwarzenegger, Norris … I really admire them. I'd like to take up a weapon too … We've got to liberate the country from tyranny" (Badjoko & Clarens, 2005: 18; Keitetsi, 2004: 114).

Most of the memoirs contain a "narrative trajectory of rupture" (and later restoration) in their moral framework, with the moment of entry into an armed group framed as a destructive form of rebirth.[2] New recruits were stripped of their old identities and re-socialized into the cultures and power hierarchies of armed groups, which were often framed as new "family" units to capitalize on juvenile loyalties and disciplinary structures (Dallaire, 2011: 102–104; Nzita Nsuami, 2012 [2016]: III; Wessells, 2006: 57–78). Jal remembers SPLA leader John Garang telling the young recruits at Pinyudu to "[a]lways remember that the gun is your father and your mother now" (2009: 96). Processes of military training, indoctrination, and dehumanization generated the moral rupture necessary to inure children to violence and killing, whilst physical violence hardened their bodies to suffering in preparation for war. Discourses of revenge were potent in generating hatred towards the enemy: "visualize the enemy, the rebels who killed your parents, your family, and those who are responsible for everything that has happened to you" (Beah, 2008: 112). This was sometimes supplemented by calls for regime change, the creation of a better, more equal society—or just personal empowerment and enrichment. Taken together, such processes were often successful in remodelling children into soldiers primed to fight for their new commanders. Badjoko remarks that "I have become someone dangerous and I love it. Yes, I am a killer" and "Power is good. I get a kick from it every day. I like to see people move aside as I go by" (2005: 80). For many teenage boys in particular, violence formed an attractive and accessible pathway to manhood, with militarized hegemonic youth masculinities based on the power and social status garnered through displays of force and the skills, discipline, and knowledge developed to become an effective soldier. As such, despite their post-conflict rejection of violence, former boy soldiers frequently reflect back on their training and early combat experiences with an ambivalent pride. As Jal notes before his first attack "I was a man, not a coward. We had AK-47s. We are brave and strong. We were trained fighters who would win this war" (2009: 101). Activities normatively associated with childhood innocence, like play, surface episodically throughout the memoirs, but usually to highlight the loss or corruption of that innocence (see Mastey, 2017; Stargardt, 2006).

Beah contrasts his happy memories of playing soccer as a boy with the horror of shooting other child soldiers across a soccer pitch, recalling sitting on their corpses to eat their food whilst "blood leaked from the bullet holes in their bodies" (2008: 19). Mehari recalls how "play" became denoted as a juvenile activity that older children avoided to signal their transition to militarized identities and superior "adult" status (2006: 70). Yet not all children were successfully militarized; for some, their identities remained liminal or compartmentalized, struggling alternatively to lose or to retain their civilian identities and moralities. China Keitetsi, a former *kadogo* with

Yoweri Museveni's National Resistance Army [NRA] in Uganda, noted that "I had come so far but I never seemed to harden. It was strange to see most other children having a kind of lust for killing and torturing ... It annoyed me that I always had to feel sorry for others, even the enemy" (Keitetsi, 2004: 134).

## 5 Violence as a Currency of Legitimacy?

Violence was at the core of child soldier experiences, and for boys was central to the development of militarized masculinities. Badjoko extensively details the importance of physical violence, and its emotional impacts, in recasting his identity from civilian to soldier: "I take shape every day. Brutally. The machine guns rattle—I evolve. A friend whose legs are torn off dies in my arms—I grow up. I torture a prisoner—I advance" (2005, Acte 2). Former child soldiers typically narrate their first kill as the defining moment in their transition from civilian to military life. Beah similarly gives a graphic account of being ordered to slit a prisoner's throat as part of a training contest:

> The corporal gave the signal with a pistol shot and I grabbed the man's head and slit his throat in one fluid motion. His Adam's apple made way for the sharp knife and I turned the bayonet on its zigzag edge as I brought it out. His eyes rolled up and they looked me straight in the eye before they suddenly stopped in a frightful glance ... The boys and the other soldiers who were the audience clapped as if I had just fulfilled one of life's greatest achievements (2008: 125).

The narration of such extreme violence serves in these memoirs to highlight the shock of the fall, the rupturing of childhood innocence, indicating the depths of savagery from which these child soldiers need to be recovered. The narrative depiction of killing in modern war memoirs has shifted in line with wider attitudes towards violence and the legitimacy of war, moving from the reticent to the brutally explicit (Bourke, 1999). Soldiers have transformed in popular discourses from "sacrificial victims" to "crazed killers" or, increasingly, to "traumatized veterans" (Cobley, 1994: 91). In African child soldier narratives, they are expected to have been all of the above: child/soldier and savage/victim, highlighting the essential liminality of the child combatant. A new "spectacle of suffering" is driving humanitarian constructions of violence (Foucault, 1975). Victimhood has become commodified and mediated in global discourses (Kleinman, 1995: 188). Violence in these child soldier memoirs, therefore, becomes a currency of legitimacy, a currency that establishes the extremes of suffering caused and endured, extremes which are necessary to build a successful narrative of redemption and humanitarian support and thereby gain traction in a crowded market of victimhood, which is a prerequisite for generating subsequent concern and action (Hynd, 2018). Beah's narratives of excessive violence aim to establish the authenticity of his status as both victim and perpetrator, drawing the reader in as a witness, a necessary step in a cycle of disclosure that constructs an identity in order to better provoke an empathetic response: as readers we will not wish to be a "saviour" if we are not sufficiently horrified by the "savage".

This currency of legitimacy is however a gendered framework: for girl soldiers, their legitimacy and authority as memoirists and spokespersons on child soldier issues is claimed not through killing but through their suffering of violence, particularly sexual violence (Hynd, 2020). However, cultural taboos and silencing around sexual violence shape these narratives: girl soldier memoirs tend to recount their experiences of rape and sexual abuse in a very sparing and matter-of-fact manner; the detail and the emotion is starkly restrained, and the horror remains largely unspoken (Mehari, 2006: 125; McDonnell & Akallo, 2007: 110–112). The narration of trauma is clearly gendered in these accounts. The differently gendered accounts, by male and female memoirists, have a different force of affective truth—the male narratives from what they provide in surfeit, the female from what they suppress and leave implicit.[3]

For many child soldiers, their memories are shaped not just by exceptional moments of violence, but by the quotidian realities of conflict: the daily struggles to survive in harsh environments: Mehari notes that she "could not have cared less who the enemy was. My personal enemies were hunger, thirst, the heat, the rats, the hyenas, the relentless military training and the heavy Kalashnikov that I now had to lug around with me all the time" (2006: 85). This chronic suffering weighed severely on many children. As Cola Bilkuei recalled "I felt like an old man, worn down by the life that had been handed to me" (Bilkuei, 2008 [2013]: 93). The apparent frequency of self-inflicted violence and suicide mentioned in the memoirs is indicative of the emotional distress sustained by many child combatants who were unable to socially navigate the violence that surrounded them (Jal & Lloyd Davies, 2009: 63; Keitetsi, 2004: 2; McDonnell & Akallo, 2007: 125). Whilst some child soldiers regard themselves as powerful actors, others find themselves dehumanized and part of an exploitable infrahumanity, both because they are children and because they feel broken by the violence they had experienced (Mbembe, 2003: 32–34). Bilkuei recalls his fears of becoming dehumanized by his time in Pinyudo, a refugee camp in Ethiopia where many of the SPLA's

"Lost Boys" were held, "I was afraid ... If I stayed there, I knew that the need to survive would turn me into an animal" (Bilkuei, 2008 [2013]: 76). As Keitetsi writes "many acted like robots that only did what our new creators desired. If we were "out of order" we would be sent to the front line to die, sending our memory into oblivion" (2004: 125). Regarding the impact of violence and trauma on memory, most of these memoirs display a particular "acoustic register" which focuses not just on sights, but particularly on sounds and smells (Hunt, 2008). Jal and Beah both talk about the "Pictures. Pictures. In my head" that repeatedly flash through their memories, but Jal also notes that as part of these: "My time at the front line taught me just one new thing about war—the worst is when it is over. As the battle falls silent, only the screams of the injured can be heard, and when the guns stop firing and the smell of smoke fades away, the stench of flesh and blood fills the air" (Jal & Lloyd Davies, 2009: 158, 144). Jal states that he could not eat meat for days after a battle because it reminded him of the smell of burning flesh, whilst another former SPLA *jenajesh* (child soldier) Deng Adut recalls the smell of a battle's aftermath turning his stomach and never really getting his appetite back (Adut & Mckelvey, 2016: loc 1014; Jal & Lloyd Davies, 2009: 158).

## 6  Trauma, Guilt, and Memory

For many child soldiers, avoidance of painful memories and their triggers becomes a pragmatic, culturally appropriate, and often effective coping strategy for the psychological and emotional trauma sustained in conflict, particularly in societies like Sierra Leone where "social forgetting", a collective avoidance of relating memories of social suffering, is the preferred memory practice, rather than truth-telling (Boothby, 2006; Shaw, 2007). Memoirists however forgo that coping strategy when they start to write down their memories and narratives. Contemporary African child soldier memoirs are suffused with discourses of trauma and suffering. It is something of a paradox that theoretical discussions often depict violence and pain as essentially unknowable and unspeakable, but that talking and writing are advocated as therapies to heal the victim/sufferer (Miller, 2001: 6). There is of course a wider philosophical and methodological question as to how, and whether, trauma can be accurately written. As Scarry has argued, pain and violence "unmake[s] the world", whilst Žižek stresses the difference between factual "truth" and "truthfulness" in narrating violence and trauma where the reported content "contaminates" the manner of reporting (Scarry, 1985; Žižek, 2009: 3–4). Despite concerns over its factual accuracy, Mehari's account of her life still provides a useful example of the memoir as therapeutic writing, having been written after six years in therapy: "Now that I have written everything down, I am free" (2006: x). Keitetsi was also advised to write her memoir *Child Soldier* as a form of therapy: "I just wrote for the sake of emptying myself of the stones that I could feel breaking my shoulders. This book has helped me to come to terms with my past and helped me come closer to myself" (2004: ix–x). Most of the former child soldiers cited here seem to have written memoirs at least in part as a way of processing their experiences and coming to terms with themselves. It is worth noting however that the labels "trauma" and "traumatized" are much more frequently applied paratextually in interviews, campaigns, or reviews than in the memoir texts themselves. Ethnographic studies suggest that some former child soldiers learn how to "perform" recovery, adopting learned social scripts and discourses of rehabilitation in order to gain support and community acceptance, which raises questions over the efficacy of therapeutic interventions in rehabilitation programming (Verma, 2012). Concerns regarding the universality of trauma diagnoses and talking therapies have led to the increasing use of more culturally relativistic, psychosocial forms of therapy in rehabilitation programmes for demobilized child soldiers, with a focus on art therapy, dance, sport, and group counselling (Boothby, 2006; Honwana, 2006: 150–156; Shepler, 2014: 67–71).

For many child soldiers, including the memoirists, it was after escape or demobilization, with the resultant dislocation from their militarized lives and survival strategies, that the full impact of their experiences emerged, and memories of violence became overwhelming. After Keitetsi escaped from Uganda to South Africa, the UNHCR sent her to a trauma therapist. She recalls from her sessions that "I was so afraid to remember … I was so overwhelmed by emotions … I lost control of myself and everything erupted in my mind at once, twenty-four hours a day" (2004: 262). Years afterwards, Keitetsi notes "[d]espite this new freedom … I still feel the abuse and humiliation, scars which my body carries still, scars that sometimes make me feel like washing off my skin" (Keitetsi, 2004: xi). This embodiment of pain and violence persists for many. Physical and emotional suffering or trauma informs even the methodology of writing. Beah reveals in a published interview that bookends his memoirs that writing required a "reawakening of happy and painful memories, and a deep exploration of them, regardless of the difficulties, physical, emotional and psychological" (2008: endtext 11). Jal writes in his afterword about how

[i]t has been hard for me to tell my story—even physically painful at times as I've freed memories buried deep inside. Sometimes my nose bled uncontrollably or dreams would trap me until I woke up to see war still flashing before my eyes. (Jal & Lloyd Davies, 2009: 41, 61)

Intrusive recollections continued to affect many of the memoirists after their escape from warzones, with some recollections seemingly linked to residual feelings of guilt. Beah tells of how "I would dream that a faceless gunman had tied me up and begun to slit my throat with the edge of his bayonet. I would feel the pain that the knife inflicted as the man sawed my neck. I'd wake up sweating and throwing punches in the air," recalling earlier descriptions of his own initiation into killing (Beah, 2008: 149).

There is a methodological question as to exactly how useful memoirs are for histories of emotion: do memoirs as ego-documents accurately reveal the feelings and sentiments that the writers experienced during conflict, or are those feelings recast through the process of remembering and relating, with memoirs becoming simply presentist documents? Certainly within these memoirs, former child soldiers' memories will doubtless have been reframed by their post-conflict lives and by humanitarian discourses. However, emotions linked to war experience are often sufficiently profound—fear, guilt, rage, despair, hope—to have been firmly imprinted on an individual's memories. Feelings of guilt are a useful example to highlight here. Moral and legal debates abound over whether or not, or to what extent, child soldiers are culpable for their actions in war: are they victims, perpetrators, or both? (Drumbl, 2012: 102–135). International law and humanitarian actors take the position that child soldiers should not be held accountable for their actions, that they are "deviant products of adult abuse" and lack the requisite legally relevant agency to bear responsibility for crimes they commit (Rosen, 2007: 297). However, child soldiers' narratives frequently repudiate the "legal fiction" of the non-violent child, and former child soldiers themselves contend with feelings of guilt, highlighting the complexity of the relationship between culpability and guilt (Sanders, 2011: 199). Some seem to bear a form of survivor's guilt, their trauma rooted in the "enigma of survival" as their friends suffered and died, before finding a rationale for their survival in their new identities as humanitarian campaigners and activists (Caruth, 1996: 58: McDonnell & Akallo, 2007: 181, 190, 194–195). Others, like Nzita Nsuami, assert a religious basis for their survival and adopt a more explicitly Christian discourse of seeking forgiveness: "I am asking for forgiveness from all those to whom I caused harm with the weapons I was made to carry as a child soldier and may they find my repentance expressed in this piece of writing" (Nzita Nsuami, 2012 [2016]: loc. 37).

The guilt that former child combatants feel for the actions they committed in war is rarely explicitly discussed in the memoirs, but it forms an undercurrent to their narration of the violence they participated in, and the intrusive memories which continue to affect them after demobilization. Struggles with feelings of guilt are more prominent in boy soldiers' memoirs, due to gendered currencies of legitimacy that for males focus on the perpetration of violence and the need to reject such violence in order to claim "civilian" status. Jal notes that "I feel no guilt because I was a child who took part in in killings as the hatred and sorrow built up over years was released in mob violence. I did not kill in cold blood, I killed in war. But that day has tormented me" (2009: 265). For many, violence could be normalized and justified at the time of its enactment as a survival strategy within dangerous warscapes. Deng Adut's most horrified memories centre around the torture, killing, and burning of Didinga tribespeople in retaliation for killing an SPLA soldier. "We had killed these people, but it didn't matter. There was so much death around, it did not matter... We were all dead anyway, I thought. It was just that some of us didn't know it yet" (2016: loc 1014). But when reflecting back upon what Adut terms the "mad morality of childhood" as young adults, wartime actions can be reinterpreted through newly adopted (or recovered) moral registers. Adut recalls the killing of the Didinga tribesmen: "When I was a boy, I had been able to put the visions of their melting faces aside because that atrocity had happened in a time and place of endless violence… I hadn't taken on the weights of those deaths in Sudan, because there was no suggestion that I should feel the shame of their murder". When he moved to Australia and became a lawyer, however, Adut accepted that he had been "involved in an outrage" and suffers recurring nightmares about their killing: "I think perhaps the torture and murder dreams are a reminder that I owe a debt to the world that I can never repay but must forever try to" (2016: loc 2519–2525). If anything, discussions of feelings of guilt and shame seem to be less about an affective truth that aims to generate action from the reader, and more an internal struggle for self-acceptance.

# 7 Saviours and Campaigners: Military Demobilization and Activist Re-mobilization

Despite being written within and broadly in support of contemporary humanitarian discourses against children's participation in war, the memoirs are often critical of humanitarian interventions into African conflicts and the forms of child-saving that have taken place (Douglas & Poletti, 2016: 102–104). Accounts from "Lost Boys" in SPLA and refugee camps in Ethiopia recount in great detail the hardships of life in these camps and the minimal amount of humanitarian aid they actually received. Jal in particular recounts how the SPLA manipulated the *khawajas* (Westerners, aid workers) to secure more supplies, but also later reflects on the structural and racial inequality of global humanitarian actions (Adut with Mckelvey 2016: loc 1393; Jal & Lloyd Davies, 2009: 70–73, 181, 249–252). Jal, Beah, and Adut were all helped to relocate away from warzones by individual Western women, and as such the memoirs promote the importance of the individual—usually white—saviour figure who breaks humanitarian norms of neutrality to care for the child as a surrogate parent or alternative family member, going beyond regulations to find practical ways to support the former child soldier: a potentially empowering affective truth for the reader who sees the difference one person's actions can make. But, for the memoirists, these interventions must be based on children's emotional and material needs, not those of the reader/donor as is common in contemporary humanitarian discourses (see Chouliaraki, 2012). Nearly all of the memoirs express a desire for more, and better, intervention that is responsive to children's varied needs. Tellingly, the memoir that most explicitly draws on humanitarian discourses of trauma, Nzita Nsuami's account of his life in the DRC, does so to assert that existing rehabilitation programmes for child soldiers fail to adequately address children's needs for therapy and counselling and to call for more such resources; a call supported in the foreword by the UN Special Representative on Children in Armed Conflict (Nzita Nsuami, 2012 [2016]: xx). Conversely, Adut makes the point that he wanted strong men whom he could respect and who could provide him with discipline to help him rehabilitate and assimilate to his new life in Australia rather than "well-intentioned, but painfully underprepared therapists" (Adut with Mckelvey, 2016: loc 1618).

The memoirs confirm the importance of gender-sensitive rehabilitation and reintegration, for both male and female soldiers (MacKenzie, 2012; Shepler, 2014). Jal recalls how after he had been taken out of the SPLA by Riek Machar's wife Emma McCune to live with her in Nairobi: "It made me angry when she said [that he was too young to be a soldier]. I wasn't a boy. I was a soldier, and at night my dreams haunted me more than they ever had ... Sometimes Emma would try to cuddle me, but I didn't like it. She was a woman, who should not see my fear" (Jal & Lloyd Davies, 2009: 88). Militarized identities for boy soldiers are strongly linked to wartime ideas of hegemonic masculinity and attaining "adult" status and power, making demobilization a disempowering rupture for many. In Beah's account, being repeatedly told "[i]t is not your fault" by civilian workers in the DDR camp antagonized boys who resented the implied lack of agency, and he only slowly came to adopt the humanitarian perspective of himself as a "victim" (Beah, 2008: 140). Girl soldiers, meanwhile, particularly those who have experienced sexual violence and become mothers, face high risks of family and community rejection, and often require additional healthcare, childcare, and vocational training for self-sufficiency (Amony & Baines, 2015; MacKay & Mazurana, 2004).

The memoirs also complicate humanitarian discourses of salvation in the significance they reveal of children's own agency in exiting armed groups. Seven of the ten memoirists make the decision to escape or demobilize, often at great personal risk. Like many other LRA abductees, Grace Akallo escaped from an LRA camp in Sudan during a battle with Ugandan forces, deciding "it was time to live" and leading other scared and starving children in a trek across dangerous territory back towards Uganda (McDonnell & Akallo, 2007: 126, 140–141, 156–162, 173–181). The fortitude, resilience, and capacity for tactical thought that was crucial to the children's survival as soldiers also helped them exit military life and shaped their post-conflict identities, aiding their determination to become activists and campaigners and help save other war-affected children.

## 8 Conclusion

So, what then do the published memoirs of former child soldiers from various African warzones reveal about the relationship between memory, trauma, and conflict? These memoirs do reveal significant details about what happened in their respective conflicts, especially about the lived realities of war for child combatants, providing a useful corrective to the, often decontextualized, narratives excerpted in news or human rights reporting (Moynagh, 2011: 39). But more significantly, their memoirs are representative of a desire to be "both a model and symbol" of the possibility of rehabilitation and reintegration for other child combatants and war-affected children (Nzita Nsuami,

2012 [2016]: loc. 49, 1028). These memoirs also form part of the authors' post-conflict coping mechanisms to deal with the mental and emotional impacts of their war experiences. For some, the act of writing processes wartime trauma, aiding in the recovery of lost or submerged memories that can bolster the (re-)establishment of their civilian identities. For others, writing memoirs serves to leverage their suffering towards efforts to "save" other war-affected children, bringing post hoc reason to their ordeals and purpose to their survival. These memoirs are products of contemporary global rights agendas and humanitarian discourses (and commercial publishing agendas) but they successfully highlight the interrelation and coincidence of suffering and resilience, trauma, and agency, and how, despite the extremity of some of these memoirists' distress, they have still been able to survive, and move beyond simple narratives of victimhood to play an active role in society and seek to help others. On a final level then, these memoirs are crafted to impart particular affective truths about conflict with the aim of generating empathy and action. The "victim, savage, saviour, campaigner" narrative framework highlights the rupture and recovery in their moral values, drawing the reader in by revealing the physical and psychological horrors of child soldiers' lives in war, which particularly focus on their recruitment, indoctrination, and experiences of violence. The narrative framings of the texts also highlight the role of violence as a gendered currency of legitimacy in humanitarian campaigns and memoirs, and its importance in generating emotional reactions in readers with the hope of thereby boosting engaged activism. Considering current concerns about the rise of "clicktivism," as a result of digital social media-led "post-humanitarian" campaigns like Kony 2012 and #BringBackOurGirls, and how they de-emotionalize humanitarian engagement and perpetuate a political culture of narcissism among Western donor-consumers, limiting effective action, perhaps then the affective truths revealed by these memoirs and the voices of their African authors can, and should, take an increased role in speaking out against the targeting and exploitation of children in war, and other related social ills (Chouliaraki, 2012).

**Acknowledgements** Many thanks to the participants in the 'Children, Politics and Conflict' conference, Exeter, 20–21 October 2017 and the peer reviewers at *Culture, Medicine & Psychiatry*, where this chapter was originally published, for their helpful and constructive feedback. I also wish to thank Ana Antic, Kirrily Pels, and my colleagues Rebecca Williams and Emily Bridger for their valuable suggestions and support.

## Notes

1. There are two versions of Badjoko's memoirs publicly available: the 2005 book and a version available at http://www.grands-reporters.com/J-etais-enfant-soldat.html. All translations mine.
2. Many thanks to Nicholas Stargardt for this point. Notably, in the ongoing trial of Dominic Ongwen, who was abducted as a young boy by the LRA only to become a brigade commander within the group and who is now facing war crimes charges at the International Criminal Court, his defence team is building their case around Ongwen's "arrested childhood," suggesting that his normative moral development was halted at the moment of his abduction and thereby claiming diminished responsibility for his wartime actions. Many thanks to Tim Allen for this information. See International Criminal Court, *The Prosecutor v. Dominic Ongwen*, ICC-02/04–01/15. https://www.icc-cpi.int/uganda/ongwen.
3. Accounts of girls as perpetrators of violence are largely absent from published memoirs and humanitarian discourses, as such accounts challenge both childhood and gender norms.

## References

Adut, D. T., & Mckelvey, B. (2016). *Songs of a War Boy*. Hachette.

Amony, E., & Baines, E. (2015). *I Am Evelyn Amony: Reclaiming My Life from the Lord's Resistance Army*. University of Wisconsin Press.

Badjoko, L., & Clarens, K. (2005). *J'étais enfant soldat*. Plon. http://www.grands-reporters.com/J-etais-enfant-soldat.html. Last accessed 10 December 2017.

Barnett, M. (2011). *Empires of Humanity: Histories of Humanitarianism*. Cornell University Press.

Beah, I. (2008). *A Long Way Gone: Memoirs of a Child Soldier*. Harper Perennial.

Bilkuei, C. (2008 [2013]). *Cola's Journey: From Sudanese Child Soldier to Australian Refugee*. Macmillan.

Brett, R., & McCallin, M. (1996). *Children: The Invisible Soldiers*. Rädda Barnen.

Brett, R., & Specht, I. (2004). *Young Soldiers: Why They Choose to Fight*. Lynne Reinner.

Boothby, N. (2006). What Happens to Child Soldiers When They Grow Up? The Mozambique Case Study. *Intervention, 4*(3), 244–259.

Bourke, J. (1999). *An Intimate History of Killing: Face-to-Face Killing in Twentieth-Century Warfare*. Granta.

Burman, E. (1994). Innocents Abroad: Western Fantasies of Childhood and the Iconography of Emergencies. *Disasters, 18*(3), 238–253.

Caruth, C. (1996). *Unclaimed Experience: Trauma, Narrative and History*. John Hopkins Press.

Chouliaraki, L. (2012). *The Ironic Spectator: Solidarity in the Age of Post-Humanitarianism*. Polity Press.

Clifford, R. (2017). Who Is a Survivor? Child Holocaust Survivors and the Development of a Generational Identity. *Oral History Forum* 37 (1).

Coalition to Stop the Use of Child Soldiers. (2008). *Global Report for 2008*. http://www.childsoldiersglobalreport.org/

Cobley, E. (1994). Violence and Sacrifice in Modern War Narratives. *SubStance, 23*(3), 75–99.

Coundouriotis, E. (2010). The Child Soldier Narrative and the Problem of Arrested Historicization. *Journal of Human Rights, 9*(2), 191–206.

Dallaire, R. (2011). *They Fight Like Soldiers, They Die Like Children*. Arrow.

Douglas, K. (2010). *Contesting Childhood: Autobiography, Trauma and Memory*. Rutgers University Press.

Douglas, K., & Poletti, A. (2016). *Life Narratives and Youth Culture*. Palgrave Macmillan.

Drumbl, M. (2012). *Reimagining Child Soldiers in International Law and Policy*. Oxford University Press.

Fassin, D., & Rechtman, R. (2009). *The Empire of Trauma: An Inquiry into the Condition of Victimhood* (R. Gomme, Trans.). Princeton University Press.

Ferdi, S. (1981). *Un enfant dans la guerre*. Seuil.

Foucault, M. (1975). *Surveiller et Punir: Naissance de la Prison*. Gallimard.

Good, B. J., & Hilton, D. E. (2016). *Culture and PTSD: Trauma in Global and Historical Perspective*. Pennsylvania Press.

Honwana, A. (2006). *Child Soldiers in Africa*. University of Pennsylvania Press.

Hunt, N. R. (2008). An Acoustic Register: Tenacious Images and Congolese Scenes of Rape and Repetition. *Cultural Anthropology, 23*(2), 220–253.

Hynd, S. (2018). I Wasn't a Boy, I Was a Soldier: Militarization and Civilianization in Narratives of Child Soldiers in Africa's Contemporary Conflicts, c.1990–2010. In M. C. Thomas & A. Barrios (Eds.), *The Civilianization of Conflict* (pp. 141–161). Cambridge University Press.

Hynd, S. (2020). In/visible Girls: 'Girl Soldiers', Gender and Humanitarianism in African Conflicts, c.1955–2005 In J. Paulmann, E. Möller, & K. Stornig (Eds.), *Gender and Humanitarianism: (Dis-)Empowering Women and Men in the Twentieth Century*. Palgrave Macmillan.

International Labour Office. (2003). Wounded Childhood: The Use of Children in Armed Conflict in Central Africa.

Jal, E., & Davies, M. L. (2009). *Warchild: A Boy Soldier's Story*. Abacus.

James, A., & Prout, A. (1990). *Constructing and Reconstructing Childhood*. Falmer Press.

Keitetsi, C. (2004). *Child Soldier*. Souvenir Press.

Kevers, R., Robe, P., Derluyn, I., & De Haene, L. (2016). Remembering Collective Violence: Broadening the Notion of Traumatic Memory in Post-Conflict Rehabilitation. *Culture, Medicine and Psychiatry, 40*(4), 620–640.

Kleinman, A. (1988). *The Illness Narratives: Suffering, Healing and the Human Condition*. Basic Books.

Kleinman, A. (1995). *Writing at the Margin: Discourse between Anthropology and Medicine*. University of California Press.

Kolk, M., & Mandambwe, J. E. A. (2007). *Can You Tell Me Why I Went to War? A Story of a Young King's African Rifle*. Kachere Books.

LaCapra, D. (2014). *Writing History, Writing Trauma*. Johns Hopkins University Press.

Lee-Koo, K. (2011). Horror and Hope: (Re-)Presenting Militarised Children in Global North-South Relations. *Third World Quarterly, 32*(4), 725–742.

MacKenzie, M. (2012). *Female Soldiers in Sierra Leone: Sex, Security and Post-Conflict Development*. New York University Press.

Mackey, A. (2013). Troubling Humanitarian Consumption: Reframing Relationality in African Child Soldier Narratives. *Research in African Literatures, 44*(4), 99–122.

Malkki, L. (2015). *The Need to Help: The Domestic Arts of International Humanitarianism*. Duke University Press.

Mastey, D. (2017). The Relative Innocence of Child Soldiers. *The Journal of Commonwealth Literature, 54*, 1–15.

Mastey, D. (2018). Child Soldier Narratives and the Humanitarian Industry. *Genre, 51*(1), 81–103.

Mbembe, A. (2003). Necropolitics. *Public Cultures, 15*(1), 11–40.

McDonnell, F. J. H., & Akallo, G. (2007). *Girl Soldier: A Story of Hope for Northern Uganda's Children*. Chosen Books.

McKay, S., & Mazurana, D. (2004). *Where Are the Girls? Girls in Fighting Forces in Northern Uganda*. Rights & Democracy.

Mehari, S. (2006). *Heart of Fire: From Child Soldier to Soul Singer* (C. Lo, Trans.). Profile Books.

Mengestu, D. (2007). Children of War. *New Statesman*.

Miller, L. (2001). *The Limits of Autobiography: Trauma and Testimony*. Cornell University Press.

Moynagh, M. (2011). Human Rights, Child Soldier Narratives and the Problem of Form. *Research in African Literatures, 42*(2), 39–59.

Mundy-Castle, T. C. (2012). *A Mother's Debt: The True Story of an African Orphan*. Author House.

Mutua, M. (2001). Savages, Victims and Saviors: The Metaphor of Human Rights. *Harvard International Law Journal, 42*(1), 201–246.

Nieuwenhuys, O. (2010). Keep Asking: Why Childhood? Why Children? Why Global? *Childhood, 17*(3), 291–296.

Nzita Nsuami, J. (2012 [2016]). *If My Life as a Child Soldier Could Be Told* (B. Boltz, Trans.). Trauma Healing and Creative Arts Coalition.

Pupavac, V. (2001). Misanthropy without Borders: The International Children's Rights Regime. *Disasters, 25*(2), 95–112.

Rosen, D. M. (2007). Child Soldiers, International Humanitarian Law and the Globalization of Childhood. *American Anthropologist, 109*(2), 296–306.

Sanders, M. (2011). Culpability and Guilt: Child Soldiers in Fiction and Memoir. *Law and Literature, 23*(2), 206–207.

Scarry, E. (1985). *The Body in Pain: The Making and Unmaking of the World.* Oxford University Press.

Schaffer, K., & Smith, S. (2004). *Human Rights and Narrated Lives: The Ethics of Recognition.* Palgrave Macmillan.

Schultheis, A. (2008). African Child Soldiers and Humanitarian Consumption. *Peace Review: A Journal of Social Justice, 20*(1), 31–40.

Shaw, R. (2007). Memory Frictions: Localizing Truth and Reconciliation in Sierra Leone. *International Journal of Transitional Justice, 1*(2), 183–207.

Shepler, S. (2014). *Childhood Deployed: (Re-)Making Child Soldiers in Sierra Leone.* New York University Press.

Stargardt, N. (2006). *Witnesses of War: Children's Lives under the Nazis.* Pimlico.

Summerfield, D. (2000). Childhood, War, Refugeedom and Trauma: Three Core Questions for Mental Health Professionals. *Transcultural Psychiatry, 37*(3), 417–433.

Summerfield, D. (2002). Effects of War: Moral Knowledge, Revenge, Reconciliation, and Medicalised Concepts of Recovery. *British Medical Journal, 325,* 1105–1107.

Twum-Danso, A. (2005). The Political Child. In Angela McIntyre (Ed.), *Invisible Stakeholders: Children and War in Africa* (pp. 7–30). Institute of Security Studies.

UNICEF. (1997). *Cape Town Principles and Best Practice on the Prevention of Recruitment of Children into the Armed Forces and Demobilization and Social Reintegration of Child Soldiers in Africa.*

United Nations. (1996). *Impact of Armed Conflict on Children: Report of the Expert of the Secretary-General, Ms. Graça Machel, A/51/306.*

United Nations Office of the Special Representative of the Secretary-General for Children and Armed Conflict. (2009, April 29). *Grace Akallo at the Security Council.* https://childrenandarmedconflict.un.org/statement/29-apr-2009-grace-akallo-at-the-security-council/

United States of America. (2008, April 8). *Child Soldiers Accountability Act of 2007: Hearing before the Subcommittee of Crime, Terrorism and Homeland Security of the Committee on the Judiciary House of Representatives, 110th Congress, 2nd Session.* https://archive.org/stream/gov.gpo.fdsys.CHRG-110hhrg41697/CHRG-110hhrg41697_djvu.txt

Utas, M. (2011). Victimcy as Social Navigation: From the Toolbox of Liberian Child Soldiers. In A. Özerdem & S. Podder (Eds.), *Child Soldiers: From Recruitment to Reintegration* (pp. 213–228). Palgrave Macmillan.

Verma, C. L. (2012). Truths Out of Place: Homecoming, Intervention, and Story-making in War-Torn Northern Uganda. *Children's Geographies, 10*(4), 441–455.

Wessells, M. (2006). *Child Soldiers: From Violence to Protection.* Harvard University Press.

Žižek, S. (2009). *Violence: Six Sideways Reflections.* Profile Books.

# Africa and Violence: The Metamorphosis and Participation of Child Soldiers in Conflict Zones

Toyin Cotties Adetiba

## 1    Introduction

Africa has continued to experience long and ongoing wars with devastating effects on its socio-economics and on its political systems. In most cases, the conflicts are between different ethnic groups in the same country, with high numbers of casualties among women and children. Armed conflicts in Africa are associated with human suffering, the consequences of which are mainly shouldered by the civilian populace since they are the targets of the warring parties. Lidow (2010) concurred that, regardless of the earlier image painted by Mao Tse-tung that rebels operate to win the hearts and minds of the populace, the fact remains that civilians pay the heaviest costs in conflict zones.

Several postcolonial African states have had a taste of civil wars orchestrated in terms of ethnicity which have directly caused the continent's loss of several millions of its population. Indirectly, the cost of internecine wars in Africa, according to Ghobarah et al. (2003), has resulted to much disease, famine, and economic disruption. Kakhuta-Banda (2014) writes that in dealing with civilian populations in Africa, there are different approaches adopted by different armed groups. In Rwanda and [Northern] Uganda, it

T. C. Adetiba (✉)
University of Zululand, Richards Bay, South Africa
e-mail: adetibat@unizulu.ac.za

© The Author(s), under exclusive license to Springer Nature Switzerland AG 2024
O. B. Mlambo and E. Chitando (eds.), *The Palgrave Handbook of Violence in Africa*, https://doi.org/10.1007/978-3-031-40754-3_20

has taken the form of violent campaigns aimed at ethnic cleansing, displacement, extermination, and the abduction of children while attempting to punch up the ranks and file of government or nonconformist forces.

Debatably, war is one of the most catastrophic events known to humankind, entailing particularly grave consequences for the children. It destroys physically and psychologically; through war, children's dreams are shattered, as it negatively affects their survival, mental development, and well-being. Thus, a child that grows up seeing weapons with flying bullets will believe that there is no better life than the one lived amid conflicts.

Over a period of time, Africa has been faced with a number of armed conflicts, where child soldiers have been recruited into military units, assuming both ancillary and combat roles. Some of the countries where child soldiers have been involved in conflicts include Sierra Leone, Burundi, Liberia, Rwanda, Angola, Uganda, and the Democratic Republic of Congo (DRC), Sudan, the Central African Republic, Mali, Nigeria, and South Sudan.

It is disheartening to state that both government and insurgent groups have become increasingly reliant upon the recruitment of children to help fight their battles. Within the international community, this destructive development has received much attention from political leaders, human rights activists, and other members of the international community. Drawing largely on carefully and relevant published works, this paper evaluates the reasons why armed groups recruit children as fighters, the push and the pull factors in relation to children, and the efforts of the international community at stopping child soldiering, and suggests ways of bringing child soldiering to an end.

## 2 Literature/Theoretical Explanations

Until recently the literature on the use of child soldiers was not abundant, with most of the work on child soldiers being conducted by members of the think-tanks, NGOs, and civil-society communities rather than by academics. Of late, research on the use of children in armed conflict by academics has increased tremendously, involving disciplines such as anthropology and development studies, law, political science, economics, psychology, and sociology, among others.

Article 1 of the United Nations Convention on the Rights of the Child (CRC) defines a child as "every human being below the age of eighteen years". Thus, child soldiering is the:

inclusion or use of any person below the age of eighteen in any kind of regular or irregular force in any capacity including, but not limited to: cooks, porters, messengers, and anyone accompanying such groups other than family members. It includes girls and boys recruited for forced sexual purposes and forced marriage. (UNICEF)

The Child Soldier Prevention Act of 2008 defined child soldiers as persons under the age of 18 who take direct part in hostilities as a member of government armed forces, police, or other security forces; or are compulsorily recruited into the government armed forces, police, or other security forces, including noncombat roles; or are recruited and used in hostilities by non-state armed forces (Congressional Research Service, 2020: 1). Child soldering not only violates Article 1 of the UN Convention, but also constitutes a threat to societal peace, while provoking the growth and building of the present and future agents of political instability.

In Africa, the sanctity of children is expressed in the family, in the community, and in the African Charter on Human and People's Rights (ACHPR). Child soldiering is a direct outcome of political arrogance, the poor management of state resources, the abuse of power, and the collapse of socio-economic structures (Egbe, 2014: 349), thus accounting for prolonged conflicts in such countries as Liberia, Uganda, Democratic Republic of the Congo, Sudan, and Sierra Leone.

Dudenhoefer (2016) points out that about 40% of all child soldiers globally are active on the African continent. Drumbl (2012) agrees that although child soldiering is a global phenomenon, nonetheless many African societies are (currently) experiencing or have experienced conflicts at one time or the other. Hence, Achvarina and Reich (2010) assume that since 1975, Africa has become the epicentre of child soldiering owing to the continent's socio-economic and political breakdown.

Children in some conflicts are deliberately targeted not because they fall in the line of war but because of their potential, representing both innocence and society's future (Majekodunmi, 1999). As they represent prospective leaders, this has made them potent in destabilizing populations. Suffice it to say that when civilians, particularly adults, are killed, children are vulnerable to being enlisted and employed as combatants, human shields, or suicide bombers. Although this tactic is uncommon, it is seen as a convenient method to get children enlisted.

Child Soldiers International (CSI) (2016), quoting from the Paris Principles and Guidelines on Children associated with armed forces or armed groups, states that:

A child associated with an armed force or armed group refers to any person below 18 years of age who is, or who has been, recruited or used by an armed force or armed group in any capacity, including but not limited to children, boys and girls, used as fighters, cooks, porters, spies or for sexual purposes. It does not only refer to a child who is taking, or has taken, a direct part in hostilities.

Thus, a child soldier with an armed force or armed group is an underaged person who is part of any kind of regular or irregular armed force or armed group in any capacity.

Lorey (2001) asserts that child soldiers often include very young children, as young as seven in some situations, as well as older children and teenagers. The upper age of 18 corresponds to the threshold between childhood and adulthood as defined in the Convention on the Rights of the Child. Koning (2019: 8) mentions that the use of children in violent conflict is not just a modern occurrence but has its roots in older warfare, typified by states as central actors and a certain code of conduct, and in new wars. These new wars, which have given rise to the number of children that are engaged in violent conflict in Africa, contrast with the old wars since various non-state actors are engaged, with civilians as the prime target and the distinction between combatant and non-combatant imprecise (Kaldor, 2013).

DiCicco (2009) stresses that children are likely to become child soldiers if they are poor, separated from their families, displaced from their homes, living in a conflict zone or with limited access to education, or persuaded into becoming child soldiers through the idea of national liberation. Absolving them of responsibility for their actions, Kakhuta-Banda (2014) states that child soldiers are victims of armed conflicts rather than perpetrators. Ansell (2005) indicates that in developing countries children are recruited by both government and rebel groups because of their energy, their large numbers, and the easy accessibility of small arms, which are easily carried and operated by these children.

Their recruitment sometimes takes the form of force as in the case of kidnapping, while some children volunteer because of intimidation, fear, and poverty. Some become victims because of the influence of the technological advancement of personal weaponry and the proliferation of small weapons (Stohl et al., 2007). Singer (2006) is of the opinion that technological advancement in relation to the proliferation of small arms has contributed immensely to the transformation of children into human fighting machines and they are just as lethal as adults, which increases the likelihood of child recruitment.

Honwana cited in Haer (2019: 76), contends that based on the socio-economic crises concomitant with globalization, many low-income countries, especially in Africa, have been experiencing unabated and widening inequalities, which strain and weaken the socio-political and economic system. This, no doubt, has negatively impacted the capacity of households, and by extension communities, to nurture and protect children. The result of this is the commodification of children, the revaluation of children which increases the chances of child labour and child soldiering.

Contrary to a number of human rights instruments which seek to enshrine rights and freedoms for all people such as: the Universal Declaration for Human Rights, the 1949 Geneva Convention (Art IV) which protects children from taking part in hostilities, the African Charter on Human and People's Rights, the African Charter on the Rights and Welfare of the Child (Art 15) signed in 1979, and the 1989 UN Convention on the Rights of the Child, which came into force in 1990, and stood against the forceful recruitment of children under the age of 18 (OAU, 1981; Pictett, n.d.; United Nations, 2015a;2015b), the use of child soldiers in many conflicts in Africa has continued unabated.

Theoretically, war and child soldiering constitute a realm of conflict in which the child soldier's (words) and actions occasion a transformation in the mind of a child from a state of innocence to a state of interaction, and counteraction, where the consequences of action taken no longer matter; rather, satisfying the master is what matters. Eisenhardt (1989) contends that the majority of theories relating to child soldiers argue from economic perspectives, and that the numbers of theories that are based on cultural or social perspectives are very limited; thus, adopting agency theory will help us to understand: (1) why children are recruited, (2) why they are coerced, (3) why they volunteer to become child soldiers, and (4) what makes them stay in a rebel group.

Scholars in sociology, accounting, economics, finance, marketing, political science, and organizational behaviour are familiar with agency theory (Festinger, 1957). This theory provides an understanding of the relationship between employer and employee, or principal and agent. In the case of the child soldier, the relationship is between the rebel leader and the child (Eisenhardt, 1989). The central elements of this theory are the concepts of contract/agreement between the principal and an agent, and respect for the promise made. Although agency theory may not be perfectly fit to delineate the relationship between the rebel leader and a child, it provides a way of addressing the four questions asked at the end of the previous paragraph.

Becker (1976) is one of the major proponents of rational choice theory, the theory often used in sociology, microeconomics, and political sciences as a framework to understand and model the socio-economic behaviour of individuals or groups. Central to this theory is the assumption that every individual is at some point disposed to making the optimal decision. However, in the case of child soldiers, this theory will assist us to answer the question of why children are recruited.

Beber and Blattman (2010) hold the view that the conscription of children is the easiest decision to make for rebels because it is easier for armed groups to brainwash, control, and mislead them. In addition, children may be used at a very low cost, and have a high retention rate within the rebel groups, thus making them the core of the armed group's means of sustainability, in comparison with adults.

The African Children's Charter (Art. 22) prohibits all recruitment of children under 18, forced or voluntary, by armed forces and armed groups. Moreover, the Optional Protocol on the Involvement of Children in Armed Conflict prohibits all recruitment of children under 18 by armed groups (Art. 4) and prohibits compulsory conscription of children under 18 by armed forces (Art. 2) but permits voluntary recruitment by States under certain conditions (Art. 3). This means that the boundaries between the various forms of recruitment are distorted, and difficult to challenge (UNICEF, 2021).

If we apply rational choice theory, the creation of conditions where children would become the worse choice for rebel groups is very important, while strengthening the policies against the use of child soldiers and the provision of educational opportunities, and technical training for children in conflict zones would make them less vulnerable to being recruited. In the theory of the economics of labour coercion, Acemoglu and Wolitzky (2011), using the coercive principal agent model, contend that the agent (the child) has no wealth, and the principal (the rebel leader) can reprimand as well as reward the agent. The principal has the option to determine the extent of intimidation or coercion.

The central idea of Acemoglu and Wolitzky's model is that the amount of force exerted by the principal to curtail other options might be unavailable to the agent, thus forcing the agent to accept the terms and conditions the principal has offered, which, if given the opportunity, the agent might have been rejected. Acemoglu and Wolitzky also show that coercion always increases the effort of the agent; hence the sense that force, or the threat of it, plays a central role in convincing the agents to accept the principal's terms.

Hence, the possibility of using actual guns as a threat against the children, and possibly against their relatives, as a means of keeping the agents within the group is increased.

Under what circumstances can child recruitment and coercion be the optimal strategies, according to Beber and Blattman (2010)? Obviously, children will be recruited if they are more effective fighters than supposed. Gutiérrez (2009), though, believes that children lack the resilience to fight. Cohn and Guy (1994), however, argue that there are scattered accounts, which include evidence from rebel officers, that attest to children's bravery, stamina, and stealth. Hence, if children are as effective at fighting as adults, then, given the disproportionate number of young people in poor African countries, we should not be surprised to find a disproportionate number in armed groups. Beber and Blattman (2013) argue that there is evidence against this view in the case of the Lord's Resistance Army (LRA) in Uganda, suggesting that children take longer to train and are less likely to be made fighters, at least until they grow older. Although the theory of the economics of labour coercion provides insights into the use of forced recruitment by armed groups, nonetheless the theory does not address the reasons behind the forced conscription that usually targets the children.

In his proposed theory of a bounded rationality, Simon (1955) states that while planning, every individual is limited by his/her own mental ability and the available information. Therefore, the distance between rationality and behaviour is bridged by the concept of decision. Barros (2010: 457) comments that a choice is a selection of one among numerous possible behaviour alternatives, to be carried out by an individual. Therefore, a decision is a process through which this selection is executed. Barros goes further, saying that rationality is a criterion used in the decision that is theoretically grounded on the presupposition that the agents are intentionally rational. Conscious or not, every behaviour involves a selection with a positive expectation. Hence, De Silva et al. (2001) assert that it is not possible for children to truly realize their actions in war, and, thus, a child who becomes a soldier is unaware of their outside options. This theory might be supported by scholars, particularly those in the field of psychology, who would claim that children have less cognitive ability to understand the world around them, in comparison with adults.

If we take the bounded rationality approach into account, the inability to access education is a more crucial factor affecting child soldier recruitment. If children are not educationally engaged, they would find another activity to secure their economic survival or find something to do with their time, hence their vulnerability to joining an armed group as an alternative economic activity (Brett & Specht, 2004: 126). This means that educational opportunities would increase not only the awareness of the outside options, but also the chances of future employment in the labour market. However, this theory does not explain what makes these children stay in the rebel group.

Festinger in his work *A Theory of Cognitive Dissonance* published in 1957, gives insights into situations in which an individual might hold two conflicting ideas, beliefs, feelings, or values. He proposes that cognitive dissonance can be seen as an antecedent condition which leads to activity oriented toward dissonance reduction, just as hunger leads to activity oriented toward hunger reduction. This means that there is a propensity for an individual to alter one of the conflicting attitudes, or beliefs, to reduce the discomfort and reach the sense of inner balance. Hence, child soldiers are somewhat directly exposed to the situations of cognitive dissonance, where they are coerced to kill.

Hypothetically, the previous beliefs and stance of these children are altered, and they take on a new role as killers and fighters, this being the only means to survive and adapt to their new environment. Reinforced by the rebel groups, Lorey (2001: 5–6), postulates that most of these children lose their sense of identity outside the armed group and its violent value system; they are deprived of the opportunities of normal family life, normal developmental experiences, and educational experiences that their non-soldier peers may have, thus, making the process of the reconciliation and reintegration of the child soldiers into the local community very challenging.

Akerlof and Kranton (2005) express the opinion that it has been long accepted in sociology and psychology that people's notions of how to behave depend on the situation, and researchers discern norms for behaviour by varying aspects of the situation. Peculiar to this is identity as a case. According to the theory of identity (how people feel about themselves, and how those feelings depend upon their actions) and to the economics of organization, changes in agents' identities allow a principal to keep the agents within the organization for longer, to extract higher efforts at a low cost, and to avoid monetary compensations or rewards.

It is, however, interesting to note that the theory of the economics of labour coercion and the theory of identity and the economics of organization have similar implications. In the first case, coercion and a sense of fear were employed to obtain the cooperation of the children while in the group, and lead the children to exercise higher efforts, with nothing to serve as motivational factor or reward. Identity building is aimed at achieving the same results. Arguably, there is no research that shows the prevalence of one theory over the other; thus, what makes children stay in a rebel group, exert higher efforts without being rewarded, or change in their identities is unclear. It is apparent that most of the young soldiers are not forced or coerced into participating in conflict but remain subject to subtle manipulations and pressures that are more difficult to disregard than forced conscription (Isenberg, 1997).

## 3    Violent Conflict in Africa

Sub-Saharan Africa has been inundated by violent conflicts for many decades. The joy and hope that existed when states in Africa finally got freedom from the colonialists has long since faded against a backdrop of incessant violent conflicts, denying the continent a successful movement towards sustainable socio-economic and political development (Clempson, 2012).

To date, many African states are still in a state of internecine war. Many regions are still under arms, and have resorted to the use of force, on the basis that either the people reject the right of the democratically elected government to govern them, or the said democratically elected government has not been able to establish an effective measure of control and some form of protection for the citizens.

Fabricius (2021) observes that, as of 2020, there were still sounds of guns across the continent; particular reference may be made to the Sahel, North-East Nigeria, Somalia, Libya, South Sudan, the Central African Republic (CAR) and the eastern provinces of the Democratic Republic of the Congo (DRC). The situation in northern Mozambique, and the continuous war between the federal government of Ethiopia and its Tigray province are not left out of consideration. The legacies of armed conflict, large youthful populations with associated social dynamics such as unemployment and inequality, instability associated with political transitions and grinding poverty has fired conflict in Africa, in addition to historical grievances, which include the constant mobilization of identity for political and economic participation and influence.

Cilliers (2018: 11) mentions that in addition to some external factors such as a probable downward spiral of the global economy, there are structural relationships that drive violence in Africa, which may largely define the future levels of violence in the continent; these relate to the level of poverty, the style of democratic governance, the regime type, the population age, the recurrence of violence, the effect of an unfriendly and bad neighbourhood, and poor governance.

As mentioned earlier, there are some structural factors that drive conflicts in Africa. Structural violence was first discussed in 1969 by Galtung, cited in

Clempson (2012). He distinguished structural violence from direct personal violence. Galtung believed that structural violence was defined by inequality, most especially when it came to the distribution of socio-economic and political power in a social structure. Høivik (1977) agreed that structural violence connotes the high concentration of things that a society needs to survive, such as access to healthcare and medicine, education, and sufficient levels of food and water, in the hands of a few, particularly those in power. What follows is economic deprivation and underdevelopment, and mass poverty, the result of which is conflict, where certain groups in such a society feel neglected and thus blame other groups within society for their woes.

Rupert (2010) argues that according to Wallerstein's world system theory the global system of states is based on a core/periphery model where the core states (the rich) of the model exploit the periphery (the poor) states, which include those of sub-Saharan Africa, through economic and political marginalization, by offering loans and controlling international institutions. Thus, the rich (core) states, while using the international institutions, control the entire system and thereby force a drop in the standard of living in the countries affected, with reference to sub-Saharan Africa. Consequently, there is the possibility of the occurrence of violent conflict at the level of the peripheral states, and because of high levels of inequality and poverty, the conflicts increase tensions between ethnic groups, hence the vulnerability of children to becoming child soldiers while fighting wars they know nothing about.

Very important in the matter of conflict in Africa is the role played by colonialism. Mamdani (1996) and Laremont (2002) posit that, through the partition of Africa, the Europeans carved up as much territory as they could in order to secure Africa's valuable resources for their industries; they created territorial political units that served their geo-political and geo-economic interests with the arbitrary separation of communities and cultures on one hand, and, on the other hand, the reuniting of old enemies and rivals. Thus, the artificially created borders and the mixing of different nations in Africa has meant that the process of creating efficient and sustainable states (with national identity) in sub-Saharan Africa has led to a lot of instabilities in the continent. To date most conflicts in Africa have been the result of ethnicity, power-sharing and factional contentions. Therefore, the possibility of the occurrence of civil conflict is very high when a state has a several large ethnic groups, but only one group has power.

For example, the Berlin Conference of 1884 ceded Rwanda to the Germans, but in 1916 the Belgians took over. The Belgian colonial government favoured the Tutsi ethnic group (about 14% of the population), in what we can call identity creation, over the Hutu group who accounted for almost

85%. The Germans saw the Tutsi as the colonial ruling class, with greater access to resources, employment, and power. Following Rwanda's independence in 1962, these roles were reversed. Storey (1999) opines that the Hutu group sought revenge against the Tutsi, beginning with a series of persecutions and then marginalizing the Tutsi population in all walks of public life. The Tutsi, in response, formed a rebel army (the Rwandan Patriotic Front) to take control of the country again in 1990, the result of which was a full-blown civil war where child soldiers were fully involved, and a genocide resulting in the deaths of hundreds of thousands of the Rwandese.

Further, Scherrer (2002) argued that similarly the Democratic Republic of Congo has had its share of civil conflict (1997–2003). However, in March 2022, after a decade of dormancy, there has been a resurgence of conflict launched by armed groups in eastern Democratic Republic of Congo, resulting in massive displacement of its populations with over 26.4 million people already in need of humanitarian assistance. Like every other state in Africa, its creation was an entirely artificial one, the colonizer (Belgium) bringing together different ethnic groups to make room for easier administration and the control of the country's rich mineral resources. The legacy of colonialism and the social construction of ethnicity and identity have undoubtedly resulted in many conflicts in Africa. Nigeria, Sierra Leone, Burundi, Uganda, Sudan, Côte d'Ivoire, Burkina Faso, Burundi, Cameroon, the Central African Republic (CAR), Chad, Liberia, Kenya, Mali, Mozambique, Niger, Somalia, South Sudan, Eritrea, and Ethiopia: all these countries have suffered from internal conflicts owing to conflicts, wholly or partially from the colonial legacy.

## 4 Why Become a Child Soldier? The "Push" and "Pull" Factors

Arguably, for a long time peace in Africa has been threatened by armed conflicts. The number and intensity of armed conflicts in Africa has increased owing to terrorist actions, thus leading to an increase in the number of refugees and internally displaced people, with unarmed people bearing the negative consequences of these conflicts. But why are child soldiers recruited? Why and how do children join armed forces and groups?

In the last two decades, armed conflicts in Africa have exposed children to murders, and forced conscription into armed groups. Hermenau et al. (2013) comment that in the eastern provinces of the Democratic Republic of the Congo (DRC), the recruitment of child soldiers is an entrenched feature of the armed conflict in the country. This is corroborated by Dallaire (2011) who argues that more than 50% of the population in many African conflict or post-conflict zones consists of children younger than 18 years old.

This means that one of the reasons why child soldiers are recruited is because they are easily disposable and replaceable, as well as very cheap to maintain. Psychologically, they are more susceptible to control and seem to accept more dangerous tasks without any form of fear than adults, who already have more fully informed personalities (Wessels, 2006). Machel (1996) agrees that this is because children have an underdeveloped sense of death and the inability to assess risks, apart from the supply of light weaponry which leads to the increased use of child soldiers.

Dudenhoefer (2016) offers a succinct argument that children and adolescents' identities are still being formed, and as a result they can be easily influenced and controlled or indoctrinated. Gutiérrez (2006) confirms that children are not full moral personalities yet and, therefore, do not make decisions in the same way as adults; thus, their protection and guidance is tied to their "new adopted mentors". Wessels (2006) expresses the opinion that they can be psychologically manipulated through starvation, indoctrination, beatings, the use of drugs, and sometimes sexual abuse, as they are forced to be compliant to the new standards of child soldiering.

Although "push" factors such as grievances, discrimination, poverty, lack of education, abuse at home, and having no communal identity may drive children away from their known environment, "pull" factors such as seeking security in fighting forces, the provision of food, and sense of belonging and ideology or group identity, as well as economic reasons such as gaining profit may encourage children to join fighting forces (Hauge, 2011). Thus, not all child soldiers are forcibly enlisted to become combatants; sometimes they merely make the decision based on their social, cultural, and economic environment and limited opportunities. Hence, Dudenhoefer (2016) argues that children are often promised some payoff when joining armed forces and groups, which can take the form either of monetary or non-monetary rewards. From a different perspective, becoming a fighter may be an attractive possibility for children and adolescents facing poverty, starvation, unemployment, and ethnic or political persecution. This means that when faced with such problems, children become soft targets, as they may be more willing to fight for honour, for revenge, or as a measure of protection against attacks.

Schauer and Elbert (2010: 319) agree that a child might be told, and believe, that they must stand up against an enemy, who would otherwise kill them or hurt their families. Psychologically, they might believe that they must take the place of a family member, who would otherwise have enlisted but does not have the opportunity to join. It might even be on the basis that a family member has been killed by the enemy, hence the need to avenge what might constitute an emotionally perceived life-threat for the child.

Druba (2002) contends that the conditions of civil war and armed conflict often weaken the capability of poor and vulnerable families and communities at large to protect the younger ones; thus, parents might then be forced to give in to the prevailing influence of militia leaders, often from their own ethnic group. Without any form of prejudice, a number of child victims of social chaos and violence often become orphans or refugees, as a result, they are left alone while struggling to survive uncompromising social, emotional, and economic hardship, which is also a potential "push" factor towards recruitment.

Schauer and Elbert (2010: 319) further argue that children might feel that they must protect themselves, where the official state structure, community, or family has failed, perceiving that they have no choice than to do it believing that it is a way of escape (and survival) from the violence and abuses around them. Schauer and Elbert however, said that in the beginning, those children who have joined armed groups, either voluntarily or by coercion, are often subjected to harsh, life-threatening initiation procedures, such as severe beatings, forcing them to kill, or to threatening rituals, such as tattooing, scarring, spraying with human blood, and forced drug intake. This is done to make them real and fearless combatants.

## 5   Efforts at Stopping Child Soldiering

You may know the beginning of a war, but you cannot predict how it will end. Conflicts may last as long as those involved are still alive, because they may find a way of adding to those conflicts. In all these conflicts, both government forces and rebel groups often rely on the recruitment of children to help fight their battles.

The recruitment and use of children in armed conflict is broadly viewed as a human rights problem, a form of trafficking in persons, among the worst forms of child labour, and a war crime (Congressional Research Service, 2020: 1). Given government obligations to protect children from involvement in armed conflict, there can be no excuse for the armed forces of any country unlawfully using children for military purposes or committing other human rights violations against them. In the light of this, there have been several international initiatives launched to help arrest the problem of child soldiering. However, these efforts have had little or limited success as the recruitment of underage soldiers has continue unabated in many African countries.

The United Nations has identified the conscription and use of child soldiers as among six grave violations affecting children in war (others are killing and maiming of children; sexual violence against children; attacks against schools or hospitals; abduction of children; and denial of humanitarian access for children) and has established numerous monitoring and reporting mechanisms and initiatives to combat this practice (Congressional Research Service, 2020). In 2019 the UN confirmed that over 7,000 children had been recruited and used as soldiers and 90% of cases were attributed to recruitment by non-state actors. Internationally, the United States' efforts to eradicate this phenomenon are guided by the Child Soldiers Prevention Act (CPSA) of 2008, which defines the child soldier under US law and restricts certain security assistance to countries that recruit or use child soldiers, among other provisions. The CSPA of 2018, which became law in January 2019, further strengthened some of the 2008 CSPA's provisions. Earlier, in 1989, the UN General Assembly adopted Resolution 44/25, tagged the Convention on the Rights of the Child. The major goal of this resolution is to protect as well as preserve the fundamental human rights of every child. The convention established the international standard of who a child is. Article 1 of the agreement states that "A child means every human being below eighteen years unless, under the law applicable to the child, majority is attained earlier" (Convention on the Rights of the Child, 1989).

In response to the international condemnation of child soldiering across the globe, the UN General Assembly adopted the Optional Protocol to the Convention on the Rights of the Child on the Involvement of Children in Armed Conflicts (Kalis, 2002), thus prohibiting the recruitment or use of persons under 15 as soldiers and considering it as a war crime under the Rome Statute of the International Criminal Court. In addition, it further prohibits persons under 18 from being compulsorily recruited into state or non-state armed forces or directly engaging in hostilities, but permits voluntary recruitment of persons at least 15 years old (Congressional Research Service, 2020).

There have been several international conferences that address the problem of child soldiers in Africa and around the world. These conferences were held to suggest solutions to the problem of child soldiering. Two of such conferences were the International Conference on War-Affected Children and the Amman Conference on the Use of Children as Soldiers held in Maputo, Mozambique in 1999, inspired by the African Conference on the Use of Child Soldiers. In 2000, the Canadian government and UNICEF hosted the

International Conference on War-Affected Children, aimed at reflecting on efforts to nip in the bud all forms of child suffering, including the use of child soldiers. The Amman, Jordan conference (April 2001) on the Use of Children as Soldiers, urged all nations to sign and ratify the Optional Protocol to the Convention on the Rights of the Child on the Involvement of Children in Armed Conflicts.

To relaunch international mobilization on the plight of children in armed conflicts, France and UNICEF organized a ministerial-level conference on 21 February 2017 in Paris, "Protecting Children from War," where all actors working for the protection of children in armed conflict were brought together. The goals of the conference were: to assess the actions taken since the adoption of the Paris Principles and Commitments in 2007 on child soldiers; to recall the existing normative framework and promote its implementation, and relaunch international mobilization on the plight of children in armed conflicts; and to encourage states that had not yet done so to endorse the Paris Principles and Commitments which set out guidelines to protect children from use and recruitment by armed groups, and to facilitate their release and reintegration into their communities. Although they are not legally binding, they have significant political scope as they reflect the international community's collective commitment to eradicate the recruitment and use of child soldiers. Following this conference, 108 states have endorsed these principles, thus enabling governments, the United Nations and civil society actors to cooperate at the national level and in the field to protect children associated with groups or armed forces.

Since the first Free Children from War Conference in 2007, France has been committed to allowing for the demobilization of 2,000 child soldiers. This commitment is reflected in the areas of the demobilization and reintegration of child soldiers, in partnership with UNICEF, in the CAR, Burundi, Sudan, and the DRC, and of humanitarian assistance for children in armed conflicts in the field of education or access to health care. At the United Nations, France is playing a leading role in mobilizing the international community, in particular the Security Council, which has adopted many resolutions instigated by France to protect child soldiers in armed conflicts (The French Mission, 2017).

Kalis (2002) however argued that, notwithstanding the various efforts to put an end to the scourge of child soldiers in Africa, they have had only limited success, and the problem continues to pose a major challenge for the international community. Owing to conflicting interests, not all states agree with the principles and outcomes of conventions or agreements, and thus they refuse to give their support. Kalis further argued that some states may want to conciliate and get into the good books of the international community but may stand to benefit more by means of using child soldiers in the short term, apart from the problem of enforcement, thus, making it extremely difficult for supporters of a particular agreement to decide what actions to take against those who refuse to comply with its mandates.

To enhance the effectiveness of both existing and possible future initiatives to end the use of child soldiers in Africa, Kalis (2002) and Shanahan (2008) suggested that peace agreements between either nations or governments and insurgent groups should include specific measures through demobilization, and reintegration within the community. Fundamentally, psychosocial reintegration is essential to reintegrating former child soldiers and peacebuilding in the community. Reintegration is done to restore social bonds as far as possible and accept and respect each member in the newly shaped community. Corbin (2008) mentioned that for successful reintegration to take place, reunification with the family and inclusion of ex-child-soldiers in the community must be considered. Betancourt et al. (2010) state that successful reintegration and rehabilitation is hinged on the environment the child is returning to, the social institutions helping with the reintegration and the acceptance of the family and the community, educational and training opportunities aimed at helping to build self-sufficiency, and helping children to have a purpose in their life again while building a new life in their community.

Kalis (2002) further proposed that the global community must make a commitment to ban or limit the sale of weapons to countries where there is conflict along with the potential of using children as soldiers. It has been established that the widespread availability of relatively cheap but deadly small arms in Africa is a major contributor to the problem of child soldiers. In line with this, the CSPA prohibited certain types of US security assistance to countries using children as soldiers. These include licenses for direct commercial sales (DCS) of military equipment; foreign military financing (FMF) for the purchase of defence articles and services, as well as design and construction services; international military education and training (IMET); excess defence articles (EDA); and peacekeeping operations (PKO), all aimed at combating the recruitment or use of children as soldiers (Congressional Research Service, 2020).

At the international level, there should be global support for the fight against the use of children as soldiers. The international community should intensify its efforts on the implementation of the sanctioning of violators and the use of juridical instruments to punish offenders, chief among which is the push for accountability in the form of naming and shaming the perpetrators

(Haer, 2019). This has promoted the establishment of country-specific sanction committees that can establish sanctions against individuals insistent on the use of children in armed conflict. At present, sanction committees have been established in Côte d'Ivoire, the Democratic Republic of the Congo, and Somalia (UN, 2015).

Tynes (2011) adds that the international community has also increasingly concentrated on criminalizing child recruitment. For example, in 2012 (14 March), Thomas Lubanga Dyilo, was found guilty by the ICC of recruiting and enlisting children and actively using them in conflicts (ICC, 2012). The Special Court for Sierra Leone also convicted five individuals for their roles in enlisting children for active participation in conflicts; this included Mr Charles Taylor, former Liberian president.

Haer (2019), however, asks whether, notwithstanding the significant efforts of the international community at stopping child soldiering, state and non-state actors still actively recruit children. Answering this question, Lasley and Thyne (2015) contend that the decision to recruit children as soldiers by rebel groups is the product of rational calculation with a keen eye towards the future. Hence, separatist rebel groups, because of their desire for legitimacy, are likely to avoid the use of children in their struggle to be recognized by the international community.

But Hamberg (2013) holds a different opinion, that the motivations of the Sudan People's Liberation Army/Movement in demobilizing its child soldiers shows the ambiguity in the international measures against the use of child soldiers, arguing that such measures did not play a significant role in the decision to release the children; rather, the objective was to secure support from the US. Haer (2019) believes that, despite the efforts of the international community to stop the recruitment of children as soldiers, some state and non-state actors are still actively recruiting children.

## 6    Conclusion

Although the cruel usage of children in violent conflicts has continued to result in much suffering and devastation for many states in Africa, more than ever before, efforts to stop the violation of the rights of these children are more determined than ever. Constantly, international awareness of the problem and its causes has continued to increase, with a growing consensus that something must be done before it is too late. However, the international community must give its full support to every effort geared towards limiting the transfer of small arms and light weapons to Africa, while preventing the recruitment of children under 18 for military service.

Moreover, if the fragile lives of child soldiers are to be reconstructed, their post-war socio-cultural and economic needs must be a focus of advocacy at all levels. In designing peace accords and Disarmament, Demobilization and Reintegration (DDR) procedures, developing community-based reintegration programmes, and establishing reconstruction goals, possible discrimination must be clearly acknowledged and addressed.

Growing up in an armed group is linked to higher levels of trauma-related disorders, aggressive behaviour, and failed reintegration. In developing holistic approaches to child soldiers' reintegration, McKay (2004) suggested that the physical, psychological, spiritual, and social aspects of their reintegration should be considered within the socio-economic and political contexts in which they live.

To facilitate the positive reconstruction of the lives of these children, people with strong influence in their community, particularly, family members, child-protection workers, and the returnee child soldiers, should all work together. McKay (2004: 28) further elaborates that the goal of this reconstruction and rehabilitation should be to ensure that ex-child-soldiers have meaningful futures, find physical and psycho-social healing after their experiences, and acquire the helpful resources that they need to make a livelihood and view themselves as making a positive contribution to their post-war communities.

## References

Acemoglu, D., & Wolitzky, A. (2011). The Economics of Labour Coercion. *Econometrica, 79*(2), 555–600.

Achvarina, V., & Reich, S. (2010). No Place to Hide: Refugees, Displaced Persons, and Child Soldier Recruits. In S. Gates & S. Reich (Eds.), *Child Soldiers in the Age of Fractured States* (pp. 55–76). University of Pittsburgh Press.

Ansell, N. (2005). *Children, Youth and Development*. Routledge.

Barros, G. (2010). Herbert A. Simon and the Concept of Rationality: Boundaries and Procedures. *Brazilian Journal of Political Economy, 30*(3), 455–472. https://doi.org/10.1590/S0101-31572010000300006

Beber, B., & Blattman, C. (2010). *The Logic of Child Soldiering and Coercion* (Unpublished working paper). Yale University.

Becker, G. (1976). *The Economic Approach to Human Behaviour*. University of Chicago Press.

Betancourt, T. S., Agnew-Blais, J., Gilman, S. E., Williams, D. R., & Ellis, H. (2010). Past Horrors, Present Struggles: The Role of Stigma in the Association Between War Experiences and Psychosocial Adjustment Among Former Child Soldiers in Sierra Leone. *Social Science & Medicine, 70*(1), 17–26.

Brett, R., & Specht, I. (2004). *Young Soldiers: Why They Choose to Fight.* Lynne Rienner Publishers.

Child Soldiers International. (2016). *If I Could Go to School … Education as a Tool to Prevent the Recruitment of Girls and Assist with Their Recovery and Reintegration in Democratic Republic of Congo PEIC.* Accessed November 17, 2021, from https://resourcecentre.savethechildren.net/node/13872/pdf/20161114__if_i_could_go_to_school.pdf

Cilliers, J. (2018). *Violence in Africa: Trends, Drivers and Prospects to 2023.* Institute for Security Studies.

Clempson, R. (2012). *The Primacy of Structural Violence in Sub-Saharan Africa.* Accessed October 17, 2021, from https://www.e-ir.info/2012/02/01/the-primacy-of-structural-violence-in-sub-saharan-africa/

Cohn, I., & Guy, S. G. (1994). *Child Soldiers: The Role of Children in Armed Conflict.* Oxford University Press.

Congressional Research Service. (2020). *Child Soldiers Prevention Act: Security Assistance Restrictions.* Accessed October 30, 2021, from https://sgp.fas.org/crs/misc/IF10901.pdf

Convention on the Rights of the Child. (1989). *United Nations General Assembly Resolution 44/25.* Accessed November 12, 2021, from http://www.unhchr.ch/html/menu3/b/k2crc.htm

Corbin, J. N. (2008). Returning Home: Resettlement of Formerly Abducted Children in Northern Uganda. *Disasters, 32*(2), 316–335. https://doi.org/10.1111/j.1467-7717.2008.01042.x

Dallaire, R. (2011). *They Fight like Soldiers.* Arrow Books.

De Silva, H., Hobbs, C., & Hanks, H. (2001). Conscription of Children in Armed Conflict—A Form of Child Abuse: A Study of 19 Former Child Soldiers. *Child Abuse Review, 10*, 125–134. https://doi.org/10.1002/car.669

DiCicco, L. (2009). *Former Child Soldiers Face Psychological Battle.* Accessed October 17, 2021, from http://www.thestar.com/printArticle/627688

Drumbl, M. A. (2012). *Reimagining Child Soldiers.* Oxford University Press.

Dudenhoefer, A. (2016). *Understanding the Recruitment of Child Soldiers in Africa Accord, Conflict Trends.* Accessed October 28, 2021, from https://www.accord.org.za/conflict-trends/understanding-recruitment-child-soldiers-africa/

Egbe, O. D. J. (2014). Book Review: Civil Wars, Child Soldiers and post-conflict Peacebuilding in West Africa. *Africa Research Review, 8*(2), 343–352.

Eisenhardt, K. M. (1989). Agency Theory: An Assessment and Review. *The Academy of Management Review, 14*(1), 57–67. https://doi.org/10.2307/258191

Fabricius, P. (2021, July 28). Violence in Africa is a Catch-22. Tackling the Political Triggers of Unrest Is More Effective Than Responding to Them Via Intervention or Mediation. *Business Day.* Accessed December 7,

2021, from https://www.businesslive.co.za/bd/opinion/2021-07-28-peter-fabricius-violence-in-africa-is-a-catch-22/

Festinger, L. (1957). *A Theory of Cognitive Dissonance*. Stanford University Press.

Galtung, J. (1969). Violence, Peace, and Peace Research. *Journal of Peace Research*, 6(3), 167–191. https://www.jstor.org/stable/422690

Ghobarah, H., Huth, P., & Russett, B. (2003). Civil Wars Kill and Maim People—Long After the Shooting Stops. *American Political Science Review*, 97, 189–202. https://www.jstor.org/stable/3118203

Gutiérrez, S. F. (2009). Organizing Minors: The Case of Colombia. In S. Gates & S. Reich (Eds.), *Child Soldiers in the Age of Fractured States* (pp. 121–142). University of Pittsburgh Press.

Haer, R. (2019). Children and Armed Conflict: Looking at the Future and Learning from the Past. *Third World Quarterly*, 40(1), 74–91. https://doi.org/10.1080/01436597.2018.1552131

Hamberg, S. (2013). Transitional Advocacy Networks, Rebel Groups, and Demobilization of Child Soldiers in Sudan. In T. J. Checkel (Ed.), *Transnational Dynamics of Civil War* (pp. 149–172). Cambridge University Press.

Hauge, W. (2011). Girl Soldiers in Guatemala. In A. Ozerdem & S. Podder (Eds.), *Child Soldiers: From Recruitment to Reintegration* (pp. 91–103). Palgrave MacMillan.

Hermenau, K., Hecker, T., Maedl, A., Schauer, M., & Elbert, T. (2013). Growing Up in Armed Groups: Trauma and Aggression Among Child Soldiers in DR Congo. *European Journal of Psychotraumatology*, 4(1). https://doi.org/10.3402/ejpt.v4i0.21408

Høivik, T. (1977). The Demography of Structural Violence. *Journal of Peace Research*, 14(1), 59–73.

Honwana, A. (2006). *Child Soldiers in Africa*. University of Pennsylvania Press.

ICC. (2012). *The Prosecutor v. Thomas Lubanga Dyilo. ICC-01/04–01/06. 2012*. Accessed November 30, 2021, from https://www.icc-cpi.int/drc/lubanga

ILO. (2018). *Women and Men in the Informal Sector: A Statistical Picture* (3rd ed.). ILO.

International Rescue Committee. (2023). *Democratic Republic of Congo: Decades-Long Conflicts Escalate*. Accessed May 17, 2023, from https://www.rescue.org/article/democratic-republic-congo-decades-long-conflicts-escalate

Isenberg, D. (1997, July). The Invisible Soldiers: Child Combatants. *The Defense Monitor*, 26(3). Accessed October 17, 2021, from http://www.cdi.org/dm/1997/issue4/

Kakhuta-Banda, F. B. (2014). *The Use of Child Soldiers in African Armed Conflicts: A Comparative Study of Angola and Mozambique*. An Unpublished Master Thesis. University of the Witwatersrand, Johannesburg. South Africa.

Kaldor, M. (2013). *New and Old Wars: Organised Violence in a Global Era*. Wiley.

Kalis, M. (2002). *Child Soldiers in Africa; Solutions to a Complex Dilemma Accord* Accessed October 30, 2021, from https://www.accord.org.za/ajcr-issues/child-soldiers-in-africa/

Koning, M. J. (2019). *Identity and Child Soldiering: A Statistical Analysis on the Influence of Identity on the Use of Child Soldiers by Armed Non-state Actors* (Unpublished Master's Thesis). Radboud University, Nijmegen, The Netherlands.

Laremont, R. R. (2002). *The Causes of War and the Consequences of Peacekeeping in Africa.* Heinemann.

Lasley, T., & Thyne, C. (2015). Secession, Legitimacy, and the Use of Child Soldiers. *Conflict Management and Peace Science, 32*(3), 289–308. https://www.jstor.org/stable/26271390

Lidow, N. (2010). *Rebel Governance and Civilian Abuse: Comparing Liberia's Rebels Using Satellite Data.* Accessed October 17, 2021, from www.sscnet.ucla.edu/polisci/wgape/papers/19_Lidow.pdf

Lorey, M. (2001). *Child Soldiers Care & Protection of Children in Emergencies a Field Guide.* Save the Children Federation, Inc.

Machel, G. (1996). Impact of Armed Conflict on Children. New York: UNICEF. In C. Blattman (Ed.), *The Causes of Child Soldiering: Theory and Evidence from Northern Uganda* (2007). Annual Convention of the International Studies Association.

Mahmood, M. (1996). *Citizen and Subject. Contemporary Africa and The Legacy of Late Colonialism.* Princeton University Press.

Majekodunmi, B. (1999). Protection in Practice: The Protection of children's Rights in Situations of Armed Conflict. *UNICEF Experience in Burundi.* Florence, UNICEF Innocent Research Centre.

McKay, S. (2004). Reconstructing Fragile Lives: Girls' Social Reintegration in Northern Uganda and Sierra Leone. *Gender and Development, 12*(3), 19–30. https://doi.org/10.1080/13552070412331332280

Organization of African Unity. (1981). *African Charter on Human and People's Rights.* Accessed December 2, 2021, from https://www.achpr.org/legalinstruments/detail?id=49

Pictett, J. S. (n.d.). *The Geneva Convention of 12 August 1949, Commentary.* Accessed October 27, 2021, from https://www.loc.gov/rr/frd/Military_Law/pdf/GC_1949-IV.pdf

Rupert, M. (2010). Marxism and Critical Theory. In T. Dunne, M. Kurki, & S. Smith (Eds.), *International Relations Theories. Discipline and Diversity* (pp. 153–171). Oxford University Press.

Schauer, E., & Elbert, T. (2010). The Psychological Impact of Child Soldiering. In E. Martz (Ed.), *Trauma Rehabilitation after War and Conflict: Community and Individual Perspectives* (pp. 311–360). Springer Science + Business Media. https://doi.org/10.1007/978-1-4419-5722-1_14

Scherrer, C. P. (2002). *Genocide and Crisis in Central Africa. Conflict Roots, Mass Violence and Regional War.* Praeger.

Shanahan, F. (2008). Cultural Responses to the Reintegration of Formerly Abducted Girl Soldiers in Northern Uganda. *Psychology & Society, 1*, 1–16.

Simon, H. A. (1955). A Behavioural Model of Rational Choice. *The Quarterly Journal of Economics, 69*(1), 99–118.

Singer, P. W. (2006). *Children at War*. University of California Press.
Stohl, R. J., Schroeder, M., & Smith, D. E. (2007). *The Small Arms Trade: A Beginner's Guide*. Oneworld Publications.
Storey, A. (1999). Economics and Ethnic Conflict: Structural Adjustment in Rwanda. *Development Policy Review, 17*, 43–63.
The French Mission. (2017). *Protecting Children from War Conference: Permanent Mission of France to the United Nations in New York*. Accessed November 16, 2021, from https://onu.delegfrance.org/Protecting-Children-From-War-Conference
Tynes, R. (2011). *Child Soldiers, Armed Conflict, and Tactical Innovations*. Unpublished Master Thesis, State University of New York.
United Nations. (2015a) *Sanctions*. Accessed December 2, 2021, from https://childrenandarmedconflict.un.org/our-work/sanctions/
United Nations. (2015b). *Universal Declaration of Human Rights (UDHR)*. Accessed October 1, 2021 from https://www.un.org/en/udhrbook/pdf/2021,_booklet_en_web.pdf
UNICEF. (2021). Girls Associated with Armed Forces and Armed Groups: Lessons Learnt and Good Practices on Prevention of Recruitment and Use, Release, and Reintegration. Accessed October 12, 2021, from https://alliancecpha.org/en/system/tdf/library/attachments/tn_gaafag_eng.pdf?file=1&type=node&id=41543
Wessels, M. (2006). *Child Soldiers: From Violence to Protection*. Harvard University Press.

# Youth, Violence, and Political Accumulation: Urban Militias in Zimbabwe

Simbarashe Gukurume and Godfrey Maringira

## 1 Introduction

The political survival of the Zimbabwe African National Union-Patriotic Front (ZANU-PF) and more particularly of the late President Robert Mugabe has been centred on a masculine politics of violent political mobilization. This practice has been more pronounced in the urban areas where Mugabe and his ZANU-PF party's political support base had dwindled. The chapter focuses on the voices of those who have been victimized by the youth who represented President Robert Mugabe and his political party: the Zimbabwe African National Union-Patriotic Front (ZANU-PF) in the city of Harare. While studies have revealed how ZANU-PF youth mobilized the rural population through threats and acts of violence, there has been limited attention to the political visibility of the youth who used to unleash violence on behalf of President Robert Mugabe and his political henchman in ZANU-PF. We argue that even though ZANU-PF has continued to lose majority parliamentary and local government elections in Harare and other urban areas, the ZANU-PF youth employ(ed) violent strategies to mobilize people to attend ZANU-PF political meetings in both urban and rural areas. These strategies include forcing urban market stall owners to attend ZANU-PF political

S. Gukurume (✉) · G. Maringira
Sol Plaatje University, Kimberley, South Africa
e-mail: simbarashe.gukurume@spu.ac.za

S. Gukurume
School of Humanities, Department of Social Sciences, Kimberley, South Africa

meetings, to welcome the president from foreign trips, and attend commemoration gatherings such as independence day, heroes' day, and defence forces day. At these gatherings, President Robert Mugabe presented public speeches disparaging the opposition political party, the Movement for Democratic Change led by the late Morgan Tsvangirai. The youth who did violence for ZANU-PF were rewarded with residential stands in the city, allocated market stalls at urban markets, and were given authority to extort both street traders and taxi drivers by forcing them to pay terminus and route fees. However, we assert that, for ZANU-PF, mobilizing youth to engage in acts of political violence was not only transactional but also hard work. Importantly, in this chapter we reveal how neo-patrimonial relationships between President Robert Mugabe and the youth drove the latter to engage in political violence for the benefit of the former. We assert that Mugabe and ZANU-PF's prolonged stay in power should be largely understood within the context of widespread political violence and the establishment of an elaborate patron-client relationship. These transactional relations are characterized by political and socio-economic benefits for the clients and patrons alike. Given the entrenchment of such patronage networks scholars have argued that politically active youth within the ruling party feed into the party's elaborate systems of control, dominance and repression which ultimately reproduces authoritarianism (Oosterom & Gukurume, 2022). In what follows, we detail the complex politics of violence in Zimbabwe by tracing it historically and showing how youth are implicated in this long and protracted legacy of violent authoritarianism.

## 2  The Politics of Violence

Zimbabwe has a long history of violence, and its legacies continue to manifest in current political configurations. Indeed, Zimbabwe gained independence through the violent and bloody struggle of the Rhodesian Bush War which formally ended in 1979 and ushered in independence in 1980. The war was mainly fought by the two armed guerrilla wings: the Zimbabwe African National Liberation Army (ZANLA)—an armed wing of ZANU-PF led by Mugabe—and the Zimbabwe People's Revolutionary Army—an armed wing of the Zimbabwe African People's Union led by the late Joshua Nkomo against Rhodesian forces, mainly the British. Through the Lancaster House negotiations, Zimbabwe was granted independence in 1980. However, gaining independence did not mean or bring an end to political violence. There were internal political clashes between ZANU-PF and ZAPU in the

Matabeleland region. The latter was accused of plotting a coup against Robert Mugabe. This was necessitated by the rise of ZIPRA "dissidents" and the "discovery" of arms caches in Matabeleland. In this regard, Robert Mugabe found a legitimate reason to deploy soldiers under the 5th brigade, a North-Korean-trained brigade, to unleash violence against the "dissidents." However, scholars such as Alexander (1998) argue that the rise of dissidents was a consequence of disgruntlement of former ZIPRA guerrillas who felt that they were mistreated by ZANLA former guerrillas in the new Zimbabwe army military barracks. In addition, their ZAPU political leaders such as Lookout Masuku (former commander of ZIPRA) and Dumiso Dabengwa (former head of ZIPRA intelligence) were arrested and indefinitely detained by the Robert Mugabe regime, only to be later acquitted by the supreme court. However, the deployed soldiers unleashed violence, maimed, and killed more than 20,000 civilians (CCJP, 1997). The massacre was termed *Gukurahundi,* a Shona term which means "the first rains that wash away the chaff" (Alexander, 1998; White, 2007). Under this metaphorical representation, the soldiers were depicted as the rains while the dissidents and by extension the civilians were framed as the chaff that should be washed away through state-sanctioned violence and necropolitics: a scenario which relates to the ways in which political elites and the state has sovereign rights to use violence to kill with impunity and dictate who must live and who must die (Mbembe, 2003). This violence ended after the signing of the unity accord in 1986 between ZANU-PF and ZIPRA, leading to the formation of a unity government.

However, what we emphasize here is that Mugabe and his political party, thrive(d) on violence against their political rivals and the citizens. In the post-2000 elections, ZANU-PF relied heavily on commanding youth to do violence, targeting the main opposition political party the Movement for Democratic Change (MDC) and other percieved critics of the regime (Masunungure, 2011; Sachikonye, 2011). ZANU-PF introduced the National Youth Service programme to indoctrinate youth into "Mugabeism politics" and a very specific and narrow patriotic history (Ranger, 2004), in other words, the politics which celebrated Mugabe as the Alpha and Omega of the past, present, and future of Zimbabwean politics (Tendi, 2008). The trained youth pejoratively known as "green bombers" named after the fatigue uniforms that they wore, were deployed in youth militia bases, especially in the rural areas to perpetrate political violence against the MDC (see Chitukutuku, 2017; Oosterom & Gukurume, 2022). Many of the young people deployed were also heavily involved in the land-reform programme in which they intimidated and brutalized white commercial farmers. Through violence and threats thereof, many white commercial farmers were evicted from their farms. This form of violence was described as *jambanja* meaning "indescribable violence characterized with discordant chaos" (Chaumba et al., 2003).

Political violence was exacerbated by a protracted economic crisis which left thousands of people unemployed and impoverished. Thus, when ZANU-PF deployed the war veterans and youth to perpetrate violence, especially in the 2008 elections, thousands of opposition supporters were displaced and killed. Worse still, the Zimbabwean economy was pronounced dead (*kufa*)due to a world record hyperinflation in 2008 (Gukurume, 2010, 2015; Hanke, 2008). While the economy was dying, new forms of getting by emerged in an economy that only allowed the economic logics of *kukiya-kiya*, and ordinary citizens survived through everyday hustling (Jones, 2010a, b). For some scholars, the logics of survival during the economic comatose was improvisational and mirrored what the locals called *kujingirisa* (Gukurume, 2019). *Kujingirisa* bordered on the margins of legality and in fact some illicit and often illegal ways of making do emerged such as *kubhena mari* (Gukurume, 2015), a scenario where people traded foreign currency at inflated premiums through the Real Time Gross Settlement by manipulating the value inconsistencies between the US dollar and the local currency. Given that the hard USD currency was highly coveted on the parallel street market, informal street forex traders offered more money than the official bank rate which meant that people preferred to sell their forex remittances in the streets and get huge amounts of local currency transferred electronically into their banks for onward usage. In such an economy, the production market was literally dead (*kufa*), and the bulk of foodstuffs were imported from neighbouring countries such as South Africa and Botswana. The crisis worsened to the extent that President Robert Mugabe ordered shops to reduce their prices as a way of combating hyperinflation. The former finance minister during the unity government, Tendai Biti (2007) described such an approach of managing hyperinflation as *ginya-nomics* or use of political power to interfere with the market and determine prices through the use of political force. *Ginya-nomics* combines two Shona and English words: *ginya* means by force, sometime masculine and *-nomics* is derived from eco-nomics. This meant that during this time, the government operated on the logics of a command economy than free market where the invisible hand determines prices at the market. Therefore, this was a combative approach to address economic issues which bedevilled the country. These logics of governance gave birth to what we call a "vampire militarized state" whose sole aim was the reproduction of political power at whatever cost. To sustain its hold on power, a vampire state will use legal and extra-legal means for the purpose of retaining political power (ibid.). A vampire state suck the life-blood out of its own citizens to silence them and exacerbate their vulnerability such that they are solely dependent on the state for everything including survival. It was this form of politics and subsequent economic decay which pushed most of the Zimbabwean youth into informal employment: selling second hand clothing, selling airtime on the streets, as vendors, on the street and at local markets, engaging in creative steel and wood furniture work in self-initiated home industries, and as taxi conductors (*hwindi*) and informal transport drivers in the city (*mushikashika*). These informal entrepreneurial spaces have become fertile ground for rent-seeking and extortionist practices by ZANU-PF aligned youth militias that we focus on in this chapter. We focus on the ways in which ZANU-PF youth appropriated political threats, intimidation, and violence not only for political mobilization and electoral success, but also for extorting rents. ZANU-PF youth were able to do violence due to the support they got from both ZANU-PF politicians and the security apparatus such as the police, military, and the most feared Central Intelligence Organization (CIO). These repressive state apparatus orchestrated disappearances, torture, and killing of government critics including opposition supporters and civil society activists such as Itai Dzamara and Tonderai Ndira among many other activists who were abducted and murdered. In the following section, we first describe the complex process and experience of conducting fieldwork in a context marred and mirrored by political violence, and the fear and mistrust of the other: a context characterized by fear and intolerance of the perceived political Other.

## 3   Researching the Context of Fear

In Zimbabwe like many other African countries, it is a political practice to talk about violence, without asking people about it. Therefore, being in a context where violence is legitimized by the state, asking those who do the work of violence and those who experience it or are victims of such violence, becomes politically sensitive. We began doing this research in the city where our conversations were not necessarily about violence, but about what people do to survive. We interviewed young people in various informal livelihood activities such as carpentry and joinery: making couches, tables, chairs, kitchen units, coffins, window/door frames, electric gates and so forth. We conducted interviews, held conversations, and observed the carpenters' everyday livelihood activities. Spending time in the field with participants enabled us to create and cement rapport. This rapport strengthened our relationship with participants and allowed them to open up and share their stories in detail. Conducting research perceived to be political is a precarious practice in Zimbabwe. Most of our interviews often occurred outside the spaces of work such as markets while some were conducted inside the kombi while drivers are waiting to load and sometimes after work. Informal conversations during the day were particularly intriguing and rich. The public bus terminus was an ethnographically productive space with a myriad actors including petty traders/vendors, touts, conductors, and other people playing games while queueing to get their buses loaded. Popular games included pool table, draughts (*tsoro*), and "slug." During these games people often talked about politics and sport as well as other trending stories in the country or city. We normally joined in these conversations and often squeezed our research questions into the discussions to capture people's experiences and views on pertinent issues related to our study. Our participant observation involved more than just observing and chatting, but also playing the games and boarding the public transport to understand the complex socialities engendered in transit and at various bus stops where rents are sometimes demanded, paid and sometimes evaded creatively.

One of our key informants spoke about the fear of the spies "planted" by the government and how ZANU-PF youth used force to indoctrinate them with political ideologies of seeing those critical to the ZANU-PF government as sell-outs and unpatriotic. He talked about how people feared not only strangers but also their neighbours and how this fear had permeated their daily activities and practices in the markets, at the termini and indeed everywhere including bars and the workplace. The pervasiveness of Mugabe's surveillance system and spying network in various spaces is articulated in detail by scholars (McGregor, 2013; Gukurume, 2019) We present these issues in detail in the following sections.

We conducted in-depth interviews at the Glen View complex, and Mbare public transport terminuses to understand how the extortionist and rent-seeking practices of ZANU-PF linked youths in and around Mbare's economic hubs, such as the local and long-distance public transport terminuses played out in everyday life. For us to understand this better, we decided to hang out with touts (*mahwindi*), kombi operators and other people in Mbare. During our informal conversations with transport operators, we often heard the drivers talking to the conductors about *mari yanamukoma* and *mari yevakomana*. This can be literally translated into 'money for the big brothers' (barons) and 'money for the boys' (touts). For public taxis to operate in Mbare, they had to pay kickbacks to *vakomana* and *vanamukoma* without which they would be violently banished from the strategic routes controlled by the ZANU-PF-linked youths and operatives. *Vakomana* literally means boys but in the context of this study it relates to ordinary touts while *vanamukoma* refers to ZANU-PF-linked cartels including youth and former, as well as serving, military personnel that informally controlled public transport spaces in Mbare and in the city centre. Thus, there is a huge distinction between *Mukoma* and *Vanamukoma*. The latter is characterized by violence and intimidation. While *vanamukoma* sounds respectful, it is "respect" which is derived and earned through violence-making. Vanamukoma can be thought of as the 'Big Man' or barons who indirectly control the public bus termini real and perceived threats of violence. The victim is subordinated and calls the other *vanamukoma*, who is the perpetrator. The name calling, of *vanamukoma* is what Bourdieu (1990) refers to as symbolic violence. Such violence has to do with "power differentials" between different individuals and/or people. Thus, calling the other *vanamukoma* is also ideological violence that accentuates the practices of political domination and surbodination. So, what the concept of *vanamukoma* and the subjectivity of *vanamukoma* does is to reproduce the legitimation of unequal power relations and the use of violence. However, the victims of *vanamukoma* are habituated in the practices of unconsciously and unwillingly to political intimidation. These violent relationships are internalized and accepted, as the norm of visible hierarchies and *Vakomana* often become misrecognised. As such, we argue that the concept of *vanamukoma* is not only violent but it is also characterized by the instrumentalization of violence and threats of violence for capital accumulation, and resource accumulation.

While *vakomana* and their activities were not criticized publicly, in private interviews, many taxi operators bemoaned the extortionist practices of the ZANU-PF youth and revealed that it was killing their business. *Vakomana*, in cahoots with *vanamukoma*, deployed violence and threats of violence to claim strategic spaces for primitive accumulation in and around Mbare. They hijacked council markets, buildings, and open spaces and leased them out to vendors for a fee. These ZANU-PF-linked street operatives are often referred to as space baron mafia due to the logicistics of their operations. *Vakomana* often control public toilets and demand money from potential users, they load the omnibuses and demand some commission. Interestingly, while *vakomana* are often the 'foot-soldiers' of *vanamukoma*, paying *vakomana* does not mean that you have to forego the payment for vanamukoma-both have to be paid and sometimes corrupt council officials and police officials have to be paid as well. The similar kinds of logics are reproduced at urban markets where both *vanamukoma* and *vakomana* are also omnipresent. Interestingly, it was not uncommon to hear the same names of *vanamukoma* getting money from the public transport operators, street traders and at urban markets. As such, *vanamukoma* often become rich through such rent-seeking and extortionist practices while some *vakomana* end up owning their own taxis and omnibuses.

## 4 Mobilization Register as Symbolic Violence

On entering the carpentry complex and the Mbare markets and terminuses in the high-density suburbs where people make furniture, electric gates, door/window frames as well as coffins, we were taken to a main boom gate, which was manned by a number of youths (*vakomana*). We were informed that that for all the furniture that left the market, carpenters had to pay a fee depending on the size of the commodity. The mandatory fee ranged from US$1 to US$10 and went to the ZANU-PF-aligned market committee which is referred to as the main board. Without permission from the main board, it was almost impossible to do research in the market. The main board/market committee also functioned as part of the ZANU-PF district committee structures. Throughout the market there was security, mainly youth who kept an eye on who went in and out of the complex. In our conversation with Tafi, the guy we met first, he explained to us that for them to keep working on the complex, they must keep supporting ZANU-PF or at least show that you are supporting the party (*musangano*). In his words he noted, "We were made to be ZANU-PF, the ZANU-PF youth keeps the register, and that security at the gate is one of them." We asked Tafi whether the register was a physical book; if the ZANU-PF youth have a real book. He responded, "It is a real book, all names of people who work here are in their book, with all our details, phone numbers and our physical addresses." We further asked him what the purpose of the register was. He noted, "If there is a ZANU-PF political rally, if the president is coming from abroad, then we are ordered to go to the airport to welcome him and if any of traders here does not go, then you know the consequences of being beaten up and losing your workspace." We asked who owned the carpentry complex and we were told that although it belonged to the city council, its control and management was under the ZANU-PF committee. He further noted that there were standing orders in the complex: "No one is allowed to talk about politics, especially to praise the opposition party, the MDC. Although there are many vendors who are not necessarily

ZANU-PF supporters, many of them have to pretend to support the party in an attempt to keep their spaces of work.

Our conversations with Tafi reveal several sticking issues about the work of violence by the ZANU-PF youth. The register has a figurative representation of violence. It facilitates the work of violence. For us, the register should be read as a form of symbol of violence. Logging people like Tafi into the register and others who work(ed) on the complex is a form of symbolic violence in practice. This is the ZANU-PF way of controlling people, making them obedient cogs who are made to believe in the patriotic history of the revolutionary party. So, what the register does in the everyday life of people working in the complex is that it disciplines them in the ZANU-PF way. The register becomes a biopolitical technology for discipline and punishment in the complex (see Foucault, 1977). However, the discipline and control are political which are made by and for ZANU-PF. Importantly the register is a "biography," where people's addresses and contact numbers are made known to ZANU-PF. It is a biography of the victims of violence, those who are ordered to go and welcome ZANU-PF officials at Harare airport. What is not clear though is how the register is kept, and at what point the pro-ZANU-PF youth flip through the different names presented in the register. Interestingly, the register is also a record, and an "achievement of violence," in which the victims of violence are tendered. It is important here to note that ZANU-PF survives through intense and deliberate political surveillance and biopolitical practices such as the register. Therefore, through the register, ZANU-PF youth can monitor and control the activities of real and perceived political threats to the ZANU-PF government. The register though at complexes and places like where Tafi works, is part of what Foucault (1977) refers to as "technologies of power," with a particular political "gaze" to discipline and punish dissent into a political line. Consequently, we frame the register as a form of political governmentality through which ZANU-PF preserves its political hegemony and control. Interestingly, in the recent August 2023 elections, ZANU-PF through its affiliate organisation Forever Associates Zimbabwe (FAZ) instrumentalised the register at polling stations to take the biographical information of voters before and after voting: a practice of intimidation that was pronounced at rural polling stations. This shows the centrality of the 'register' as a technology and architecture of control, intimidation and violence.

## 5    Singing Songs, Marching, and Dancing for the Enemy

In the city of Harare where most voters shunned both Mugabe and Mnangagwa's political meetings, ZANU-PF youth resort to the use of violence and coercion to mobilize people for political events. At these events people are expected to choreograph and show political support and allegiance through singing and dancing. Many young men, like Tafi, reiterated what it means to be forced to go and welcome ZANU-PF leaders from foreign trips. To retain their operating space in and around the complex, all carpenters and traders are also forced to attend ZANU-PF political rallies where they dance for a man they do not necessarily support. One of our interlocutors, Tindo, revealed that:

> We are always told when the President is leaving the country, and we know when he is coming back. The ZANU-PF youth tells us all this. We are always told that we have a role to play. When he comes back, we close this complex, and go to sing for him. They think we support ZANU-PF, but we don't.

The idea of making young men sing to welcome both Mugabe and Mnangagwa as well as use violence to mobilize people for rallies and other political activities reveals the ways in which politics is mediated by young people like Tindo who are the party foot soldiers. Strong party youths consider themselves the vanguards of the revolution who are every ready to defend the gains of the liberation revolution. However, these are in their minority and many other youth are forced to do this work for survival and maintaining their space of work. Thus, forcing young men to mobilize political support is a clear testimony of how violence is instrumentalized to prop up ZANU-PF in power and reproduce authoritarianism (Oosterom & Gukurume, 2022). Apart from this, young people have become central in defining politics in the Zimbabwean contested political context. At a time when the opposition political party, the MDC, gained political traction, pro-ZANU-PF youth mobilized people in the city of Harare and from peri-urban and rural areas to embark on a one-million-man march in support of Mugabe's continued stay in power. One of our participants, notes that,

> In the complex where we are working, we were told that we are all going for a one-million-man march to support President Robert Mugabe, and after that we would be addressed by the President. There was no room to ask what we were supporting, or whether it was worth marching. In fact it was not, but we just marched in the streets, singing, praising him and denouncing the MDC.

For the carpenters and vendors, attending these events is not a matter of choice. It is an issue of survival and safeguarding livelihoods and sometimes life. As highlighted above, people do not even dare to ask where they are going and why. They are ordered to attend political events as a prerequisite for keeping their operating space. This manipulation of vendors and carpenters shows the complex nature of the violence encountered by many of our interlocutors. Attending the one-million-man march without consent for some of our participants was a symbolic form of violence. The young men who were targeted were forced to close and leave behind their places of work. They had to pay local transport for themselves to the city, to go and march to show support for President Mugabe. The analytical question here is why do ZANU-PF and its youth force people to embark on a one-million-man march to support President Mugabe staying in power? These actions should be understood within the context of Mugabe's own legitimacy crisis to remain in power through violence and escalating rights abuses. This legitimacy crisis was not only international but also domestic and internal within his own party due to factional struggles. For instance, the war veterans within his party who had supported Mugabe and his *henchmen* ZANU-PF party became fractured along factional lines, and some of them gave public press conferences, withdrawing their support to President Mugabe because he had allegedly moved away from what they thought had been agreed during the liberation struggle—the Mgagao declaration of 1975, in which the military chose a political candidature in ZANU-PF (Mhanda, 2011). These events are fascinating as they provide us with the dynamics of what led to the November 2017 coup which eventually ousted Mugabe from power and brought his deputy Emmerson Mnangagwa to power.

At a time when traditional sources of support for Mugabe were withdrawing their support and allegiance, the youth became the remaining constituency that Mugabe and his henchman sought to mobilize in support of President Mugabe. The factional fights within ZANU-PF over succession battles also intensified and fractured ZANU-PF's support systems. The youth were thus mobilized to instil fear, and to intimidate Mugabe's political opponents within and beyond the party. The youthful constituency provided some semblance of legitimacy for Mugabe's leadership. In fact, a few weeks before the November 2017 coup, youth leaders such as Kudzai Chipanga organised a press conference declaring their support for Mugabe and that they were ready to die defending him even against the military (Al Jazeera, 2017).

The questions around the legitimacy crisis explain why President Mugabe compelled the young people to sing, dance, march, and "praise" him. If legitimacy is about the exercise of authority through voluntary obedience (Weber,

1978), then President Mugabe's acts raise critical questions around illegitimacy. ZANU-PF does not, in any case, act according to the law, but it employs the "legitimate" use of violence rather than legitimacy power. In employing the "monopoly of violence", ZANU-PF uses both the youth and state security agents. But the question is, at what point does ZANU-PF use the youth to do the work of violence, and under what circumstances do the state security agents come in to work for ZANU-PF? While scholars such as Caforio (2007) argue that the sole client for the state is the military, ZANU-PF politicians establish patronage and clientship relations in which young people are rewarded with goods for violence and mobilization. As noted by Tonderai,

> The youth do not work alone, they are well-connected to the CIO (Central Intelligence Organization), the police and the military. You cannot argue with a ZANU-PF youth. If you do, then you are literally passed into the hands of the CIO. The youth work as spies and or informers of CIO. Once the youth label you as anti-President Robert Mugabe, for us who are working in the complex doing the carpentry, you know you are out of the place. So we just try to follow their orders for us to survive.

There is a profound relationship between ZANU-PF youth and the intelligence organization, police, and the military. As such, because of the profound relationship between the youth and state security agents, we argue that the politicization of the former is not possible without the latter. It was revealed to us that the violent youth themselves act as an extension of the army and other state security agents. They share information on and about the perceived enemies of, and threats to, the ZANU-PF government. So, in a sense there is an elaborate militarization of the ZANU-PF youth. We use militarization as both a category of analysis and category of practice. While the former has to do with understanding the relationship between the youth and security agents, the latter has to do with the tactics employed by ZANU-PF youth to instil fear in young men working as informal street entrepreneurs in high-density suburbs such as Mbare and Glen View where this study was conducted. While it is difficult for ZANU-PF to pay the youth with money because of the economic crisis crippling the government, they utilize strategies including offering political and material benefits such as mining claims, residential stands, and political positions. Whether political benefits are not material or vice versa, is another question beyond the purview of this chapter. We reveal how ZANU-PF has been able to politically "reward" the youth through allocation of dubious residential stands at the peripheries of the city and by allowing the youth to engage in extortion activities on taxi terminuses in the city. For instance, in Mbare, ZANU-PF youth construct makeshift structures which they rent out to street vendors, control open spaces and public housing flats such as in Magaba, Matapi, and Matererini. At the peak of political violence in 2008, real and perceived MDC supporters were evicted form markets (Oosterom & Gukurume, 2022), as well as from flats and other spaces that informally generate livelihoods in Mbare (Maringira & Gukurume, 2022).

## 6 Political Benefits: Appeasing Youth

One of the remarkable ways in which ZANU-PF leaders such Mugabe and Mnangagwa have been able to remain in power is the party's ability to transform their political hegemony into a source of opportunities for political clients, in this case unemployed young people. To appease the youth doing the work of violence, ZANU-PF has employed illegal strategies such as politicized housing cooperatives on the peripheries of the city and allowing a consortium of youth to extort taxi drivers in city/high density suburb terminuses as discussed earlier. This "political clientelism," can be read as a form of political patronage in which there is a transactional exchange of socio-economic resources for political support (Chabal & Daloz, 1999; Erdmann & Engel, 2007). In a sense patronage is more concerned with the distribution of favours which bind the patron and the client (Ilkhamov, 2007). In such cases, (political) authority is converted into a private patrimony…where the distinction between the office and the office holder is blurred (Bach, 2011). The allocation of dubious residential stands by ZANU-PF to its youth "employees" of violence is illegal in the sense that it is the prerogative of the city council to allocate stands within its jurisdiction area. Interestingly the Harare city council is a stronghold of, and run by, the voted opposition political party MDC Mayor and councillors, hence they do not easily bend to ZANU-PF political demands to misuse city land. However, to frustrate and sabotage the city council, ZANU-PF has created parallel structures and uses the ministry of local government to impose policies and decisions that undermine the authority of the MDC-led council (Oosterom & Gukurume, 2022).

What is interesting is how ZANU-PF uses state resources such as land to "thank" the youth who do violence work for the party. As such, these practices reveal how state and party are conflated and sometimes collapsed for the benefit of ZANU-PF. One of our participants contends that:

> The ZANU-PF youth are people we know, we have lived with them as our neighbours, but what is surprising is that you will hear them saying 'I have a

residential stand.' They don't work anywhere but now they have a stand. This is work for ZANU-PF, its ZANU-PF pension.

In this regard when people talk about residential stands allocation as pensions for ZANU-PF youth, we can think of what ZANU-PF does as legacies of political violence. The stands, therefore, become symbols and objects of violence, but also, importantly, the stands can be understood as metaphors of the violence. They represent violence, the work of ZANU-PF in retaining and keeping a hold on political power. In our conversation with one of the government officials from the Ministry of Local Government, it was noted that:

> The youth are allocated land directly by the Ministry of local government. So what happens is that the youth leaders either register cooperatives, or land developers. So we give them the land around the city, and they are the ones who will now re-allocate it to their fellow youth as residential stands. However, much of the residential stands is sold by these youth leaders to individuals.

We further asked if it was legal for the Ministry to allocate land to the youth on spaces under the city council's jurisdiction and responsibility. The response was that "whatever the Ministry of local government do, allocating residential stands to the youth, was known to the responsible Minister, who as you know, is ZANU-PF. So the whole issue is politics." Following this, scholars such as McGregor (2013) argue that when ZANU-PF lost local government elections, they turned the city into an object of political struggle, undermining the city council responsibilities to deliver services. There is undoubtedly an existence of two parallel systems of power relationship: the formal and informal politics. While there is decentralization of power to city councils, this system creates systems of patronage politics (ibid). By law the city council is under the jurisdiction of the MDC and for us, therefore, what we see as formal politics. The ZANU-PF way is a kind of "informal politics which invade formal institutions" (Erdmann & Engel, 2007).

This is the politics of the city land, whereby ZANU-PF uses its political power in land allocation to gain political mileage. So, what this means is that even though the opposition political party, the MDC, has the responsibility and authority to allocate residential land to both individuals and land developers, ZANU-PF overrides that legal process. The illegality of land allocation is purposeful as it also legitimizes ZANU-PF's ability to take care of its support base: the youth. While the MDC complains about ZANU-PF's activities in land allocation within the city, the response by ZANU-PF Ministers of local government, including Ignatius Chombo, Saviour Kasukuwere, and July

Moyo, has been repressive. Several Harare mayors have been suspended and dismissed on trumped-up charges by the Minister of local government. The Minister is empowered by and through the local authorities act that allows the Minister to oversee the activities of the mayor and veto decisions made by elected councillors of the city. Even though the new 2013 constitution allows the city council to act independently, there has been a continuation of threats from the Minister of local government. This reveals to us how ZANU-PF acts illegally as a way of threatening those who are perceived as critical to its interests. It is against this background that, in the Zimbabwean context, law and politics become intertwined in complex ways. Critics have accused ZANU-PF of manipulating and weaponizing the judiciary system in dealing with political opponents through elaborate "lawfare." The president's power to appoint judges and other top officials allows them to assert control over the courts. Therefore, ZANU-PF becomes a law unto itself, and it is the politics of controlling such appointments that enables ZANU-PF to punish critics through the legal system. In such a situation, where politics is the law, the ZANU-PF youth support base acts illegally and with impunity. For example, the extortion of taxi drivers in city and high-density suburbs and hijacking of city council buildings by ZANU-PF youth is condoned.

## 7 Extortions as "Protection" Fees

ZANU-PF youth do not only survive on dubious and illegal land allocation in the city, but youth extort money from taxi drivers on city/suburb terminuses. In Mbare, a well-known group of ZANU-PF youth, known as Chipangano, extorted money by threatening taxi drives and traders at markets. The Chipangano youth group was a "political cartel" which took over taxi terminuses/ranks, urban markets, and public housing/flats to claim rents. They pushed out the municipal police and other city council officials who collected the revenues. At their peak they became the de facto city authorities and collected rents from council properties. The "political cartel" was a wider network which controlled much of the city/high-density suburban life, allocating market stalls and deciding who operated in profitable market routes like Mbare (Oosterom & Gukurume, 2022). These are the forms of reciprocities which helped to cement political relationships (Pitcher et al., 2009) and they are part of a repertoire of strategies through which ZANU-PF youth accumulated wealth and sought political obedience from the ordinary population.

In our conversation with one of the drivers, named Sandura, he told us that "you must pay Chipangano youth and that will be 'entry fees' and 'protection fees'". For Tilly (1985), this is a "protection racket," in which state-aligned actors create a threat and ask ordinary citizens to pay for a threat which they have created. In a context which is characterized by political uncertainties, youth lives are politically uncertain. Thus, in such political situations, a client will need the patron to either avoid political misfortunes and or be able to achieve goals which would be impossible to accomplish. (see Erdmann & Engel, 2007). Therefore, the extortionist practices happen even along the road to Mbare and other open spaces. The Mbare route is targeted because it is one of the busiest routes to and from the city. This is so because in Mbare suburb, you will find the biggest farmers' fresh produce market, flea markets, home and light industries and the busiest long-distance bus terminus. Mbare is about 3 km from the city, hence people always travel in between the markets and the city, and this makes it a profitable route. Its profitability makes it a target of the *Chipangano* and other ZANU-PF-aligned vigilante groups. One of our participants who has been a taxi driver along that route told us that "they collect roadworthy fees." This is "roadworthy" for and by the youth. By merely paying the money the taxi qualifies to operate and becomes "roadworthy." The idea of "entry fees" reveals to us how ZANU-PF youth make constituencies within constituencies. By this, we mean that the youth have control over particular "terrains" within the city. These are terrains of fear and intimidation, where power is centred around ZANU-PF. The "entry fees" should not only be understood in terms of monetary value, but what we need to draw from this is the signification of "entry fees." For us these "entry fees" are a metaphor of power, of how ZANU-PF, through its youth, creates spaces of power. This is like "roadworthy fees" which imply to us the ways in which we can begin to understand how violence is demarcated in choices of the perpetrator. Violence is made visible in roads as "roadworthy fees" a political practice which reminds us of how ordinary paths/roads are configured into violent spaces. But whether taxi drivers have ways to resist, or some sense of urgency is quite problematic in a context were violence pervades the ordinary spaces like roads, market stall places, and terminuses. In his response, Gomba, a taxi driver notes that "If you try to resist, they can beat you, they can impound your taxi." Asking why they could not report to the police, the taxi driver responded: "How can you report to the police, when the police itself is Chipangano? The police are also ZANU-PF, so where do you report. You must comply if you want to operate in that route." So there are many interesting issues here: the relationship between the youth and the police reveals how the state, which is ZANU-PF, is closely connected in this organized violence. The police are politicized and act in all kinds of unprofessional ways. It is important, therefore, to note that when the police become Chipangano, it defines the actions of both the youth and ZANU-PF to continue to commit crimes with impunity. For Verheul (2013), the attorney general's office evoked a political register in which the office was politicized to support the activities of ZANU-PF. Following this, the deep relationship between ZANU-PF and the police is political and violent towards ordinary citizens and places.

## 8 Conclusion

The chapter has revealed the ways in which ZANU-PF youth mobilized violence to prop up President Robert Mugabe. We have argued that the relationship between ZANU-PF and its youth is a reciprocal transactional political relationship, one in which President Mugabe employed the youth to do the work of violence, and, in return, political benefits were extended to the youth in different ways: such as access to residential stands, ceded power to extort taxi drivers and informal traders, and impunity and immunity from arrests. The chapter contributes to our understanding of the youth and political power where there is a symbiotic relationship between the two. We assert that authoritarian governments work quite hard to keep themselves in power, especially through the work of violence and eleborate patronage networks especially involving millenials. Violence, therefore, is work, which is characterized by the political elite's power and that of the youth. It is also important to note that although youth are often framed as stuck in waithood, they are not just "waiting" in politics; rather they act in specific ways, including the use violence at the service of political elites. We argue that while young people are often portrayed as perpetrators of violence, they should also be understood as victims of structural and systemic violence which makes it easy for them to be incorporated into the violent political patronage networks that political elites instrumentalise to gain political mileage.

**Funding**: This work was made possible by the Sol Plaatje University MIT Research grant, Grant Number MIT14YR2022.

## Bibliography

Alexander, J. (1998). Dissident Perspectives on Zimbabwe's Post-Independence War, Africa. *Journal of the International Africa Institute, 68*(2), 151–182.

Alexander, J., & McGregor, A. (2004). War Stories: Guerrilla Narratives of Zimbabwe's Liberation War. *History Workshop Journal* (57).

Alexander, J. (2003). 'Squatters', Veterans and the State in Zimbabwe, pp. 83–117. In A. Hammar, B. Raftopoulos, & S. Jensen (Eds.), *Zimbabwe's Unfinished Business: Rethinking Land, State and Nation in the Context of Crisis*. Weaver Press.

Alexander, J. (2013). Militarisation and State Institutions: 'Professionals' and 'Soldiers' Inside the Zimbabwe Prison Service. *Journal of Southern African Studies, 39*(4), 807–828.

Bach, D. C. (2011). Patrimonialism and Neopatrimonialism: Comparative Trajectories and Readings. *Commonwealth & Comparative Politics, 49*(3), 275–294.

Biti, T. (2007). *From "Gonomics" to "Ginyanomics": The Doomed Options of a Dying Dictatorship*. Kubatana.net. http://archive.kubatana.net/html/archive/econ/070712tb.asp?sector=ECON&year=2007&range_start=361.

Brubaker, R. (2012). Categories of Analysis and Categories of Practice: A Note on the Study of Muslims in European Countries of Immigration. *Ethnic and Racial Studies, 36*(1), 1–8.

Brubaker, R., & Cooper, F. (2000). Beyond 'Identity.' *Theory and Society, 29*, 1–47.

Caforio, G. (2007). Introduction: The Interdisciplinary and Cross-National Character of Social Studies on the Military—The Need for Such an Approach. In G. Caforio (Eds.), *Social Sciences and the Military: An Interdisciplinary Overview*. Routledge.

Catholic Commission for Justice and Peace in Zimbabwe—CCJPZ. (1997). *Report on the 1980s Atrocities in Matabeleland and the Midlands*. Legal Resource Foundation.

Catholic Commission for Justice and Peace in Zimbabwe—CCJPZ. (1999). *Breaking the Silence Building True Peace: A Report on the Disturbances in Matabeleland and the Midlands 1980–1988*. Legal Resource Foundation.

Chabal, P., & Daloz, J.-P. (1999). *Africa Works: Disorder as Political Instrument*. James Currey.

Chaumba, J., Scoones, I., & Woolmer, W. (2003). From Jambanja to Planning: The Reassertion of Technocracy in Land Reform in South-Eastern Zimbabwe? *The Journal of Modern African Studies, 41*(4), 533–554.

Chitukutuku, E. (2017). Rebuilding the Liberation War Base: Materiality and Landscapes of Violence in Northern Zimbabwe. *Journal of Eastern African Studies, 11*(1), 133–150.

Erdmann, G., & Engel, U. (2007). Neopatrimonialism Reconsidered: Critical Review and Elaboration of an Elusive Concept. *Commonwealth and Comparative Politics, 45*(1), 95–119.

Foucault, M. (1977). *Discipline and Punish: The Birth of the Prison*. Penguin.

Gibson, D. (2010). Construction of Masculinity, Mental Toughness and the Inexpressibility of Distress Among a Selected Group of South African Veterans of the 'Bush War' in Namibia. *Journal of Psychology in Africa, 20*(4), 613–622.

Gukurume, S. (2010). The Politics of Money Burning and Foreign Currency Exchange in Zimbabwe: A Case Study of Mucheke Residents in Masvingo. *Journal of Sustainable Development in Africa, 12*(6), 62–73.

Gukurume, S. (2015). Livelihood Resilience in a Hyperinflationary Environment: Experiences of People Engaging in Money-burning (kubhena mari) Transactions in Harare, Zimbabwe. *Social Dynamics, 41*(2), 219–234.

Gukurume, S. (2019). Navigating the Crisis: University of Zimbabwe Students' Campus Experiences during Zimbabwe's Multi-layered Crisis, *African Identities, 17*(3–4), 277–297.

Hammar, A. (2005). *Disrupting Democracy? Altering Landscapes of Local Government in Post-2000 Zimbabwe*. Crisis States Development Research Centre, Discussion Paper 9.

Hammar, A. (2008). (2008) In the Name of Sovereignty: Displacement and State Making In Post-Independence Zimbabwe. *Journal of Contemporary African Studies, 26*(4), 417–434.

Hammar, A., & Raftopoulos, B. (2003). Zimbabwe's Unfinished Business: Rethinking Land, State and Nation. In A. Hammar, B. Raftopoulos, & S. Jensen (Eds.), *Zimbabwe's Unfinished Business: Rethinking Land, State and Nation in the Context of Crisis*. Weaver Press.

Hammar, A., McGregor, J., & Landau, L. (2010). Introduction. Displacing Zimbabwe: Crisis and Construction in Southern Africa. *Journal of Southern Africa, 36*(2), 263–283.

Hanke, S. H. (2008). *Rest in Peace Zimbabwe Dollar*. Available on http://www.cato.org/zimbabwe. Accessed 29 June 2013.

Ilkhamov, A. (2007). Neopatrimonialism, Interest Groups and Patronage Networks: The Impasses of the Governance System in Uzbekistan 1. *Central Asian Survey, 26*(1), 65–84.

Jones, J. H. (2010a). Freeze! Movement, Narrative and the Disciplining of Price in Hyperinflationary Zimbabwe. *Social Dynamics, 36*(2), 338–351.

Jones, J. L. (2010b). 'Nothing is Straight in Zimbabwe': The Rise of the *Kukiya-kiya* economy 2000–2008. *Journal of Southern African Studies, 36*(2), 285–299.

Maringira, G., & Gukurume, S. (2022). Youth Political Mobilization: Violence, Intimidation, and Patronage in Zimbabwe. *Political Psychology, 43* (6), 1027–1041.

Masunungure, E. V. (2011). Zimbabwe's Militarised, Electoral Authoritarianism. *Journal of International Affairs, 65*(1), 47–64.

McGregor, J. (2013). Surveillance and the City: Patronage, Power-Sharing and the Politics of Urban Control in Zimbabwe. *Journal Southern African Studies, 39*(4), 783–805.

Mhanda, W. (2011). *Dzino: Memories of a Freedom Fighter*. Weaver Press.

Muzondidya, J. (2009). From Buoyancy to Crisis, 1980–1997. In B. Raftopoulos & A. Mlambo (Eds.), *Becoming Zimbabwe, A History From the Pre-Colonial Period to 2008*. Weaver Press.

Ndlovu-Gatsheni, S. J. (2009). Making Sense of Mugabeism in Local and Global Politics: 'So Blair, Keep your England and Let me Keep my Zimbabwe.' *Third World Quarterly, 30*(6), 1139–1158.

Ndlovu-Gatsheni, S. (2013). The Crisis of Adapting History in Zimbabwe. In L. Raw, & E. Tutan (Eds.), *The Adaptation of History: Essays on Ways of Telling the Past*. McFarland & Co.

Oosterom, M., & Gukurume, S. (2022). Ruling Party Patronage, Brokerage, and Contestations at Urban Markets in Harare. *African Affairs, 121*(484), 371–394.

Phimister, I. (2012). Narratives of Progress: Zimbabwean Historiography and the End of History. *Journal of Contemporary African Studies, 30*(1), 27–34.

Pitcher, A., Moran, M. H., & Johnston, M. (2009). Rethinking Patrimonialism and Neopatrimonialism in Africa. *African Studies Review, 52*(1), 125–156.

Raftopoulos, B. (2003). The State in Crisis: Authoritarian Nationalism, Selective Citizenship and Distortions of Democracy in Zimbabwe. In A. Hammar, B. Raftopoulos, & S. Jensen (Eds.), *Zimbabwe's Unfinished Business: Rethinking Land, State and Nation in the Context of Crisis*. Weaver Press.

Raftopoulos, B. (2009) The Crisis in Zimbabwe, 1998–2008. In B. Raftopoulos, & A. Mlambo (Eds.), *Becoming Zimbabwe, A History from the Pre-Colonial Period to 2008*. Weaver Press.

Ranger, T. (2004). Nationalist Historiography, Patriotic History and the History of the Nation: The Struggle over the Past in Zimbabwe. *Journal of Southern African Studies, 30*(2), 215–234.

Sachikonye, L. (2011). *When a State Turns on its Citizens: 60 Years of Institutionalized Violence in Zimbabwe*. Weaver Press.

Tendi, B. M. (2013). Ideology, Civilian Authority and the Zimbabwean Military. *Journal of Southern African Studies, 39*(4), 829–843.

Tendi, B. M. (2008). Patriotic History and Public Intellectuals Critical of Power. *Journal of Southern African Studies, 34*(2), 379–396.

Tilly, C. (1985). War Making and State Making as Organized Crime, pp. 169–185. In P. Evans, D. Rueschemeyer, & T. Skocpol (Eds.), *Bringing the State Back*. Cambridge University Press.

Torpey, J. (1998). Coming and Going: On the State Monopolization of the Legitimate 'Means of Movement.' *Sociological Theory, 16*(3), 239–259.

Verheul, S. (2013). 'Rebels' and 'Good Boys': Patronage, Intimidation and Resistance in Zimbabwe's Attorney General's Office after 2000. *Journal of Southern African Studies, 39*(4), 765–782.

White, L. (2007). 'Whoever Saw a Country with Four Armies?': The Battle of Bulawayo Revisited. *Journal of Southern African Studies, 33*(3), 619–631.

Weber, M. (1978). *Economy and Society: An Outline of Interpretive Sociology*. University of California Press.

Worby, E. (2003). The End of Modernity in Zimbabwe? Passages from Development to Sovereignty. In A. Hammar, B. Raftopoulos, S. Jensen (Eds.), *Zimbabwe's Unfinished Business: Rethinking Land, State and Nation in the Context of Crisis*. Weaver Press.

# Youth, Proliferation of Small Arms and Light Weapons, and Conflicts in 21st Century Africa

Babayo Sule, Ibrahim Kawuley Mika'il, and Mohammed Kwarah Tal

## 1 Introduction

Youth are the centre stage in societal progress and development in most African countries. The youth is the category of the population which is perceived as working and active in productive ventures (Wells & Montgomery, 2014). In contemporary global configuration, youth are the majority in Africa. Even though the trend and pattern of population distribution differ from one country to another, depending on some indicators such as the level of the economic prosperity, political stability and policy choices, culture, faith, and other considerations, most African states still record a high percentage of youth in population distribution (Office of Juvenile Justice Delinquency and Prevention, 2016). However, even with the blessings and potential of youth as a productive segment in many African countries, the

B. Sule (✉)
Department of International Relations, Federal University of Kashere, Gombe State, Nigeria
e-mail: babayosule@gmail.com

I. K. Mika'il
Department of International Relations, Institute for Transport Technology, Zaria, Kaduna State, Nigeria

M. K. Tal
Department of Political Science, Federal University of Kashere, Gombe State, Nigeria

bulge of youth is a global problem and a phenomenon that is worrisome for handlers of public policy and decision making, if it is not managed carefully (Muncie, 2004).

The population of the world is young. Globally, 42% is under the age of 25 (United Nations, 2015). The trend in sub-Saharan Africa has indicated a skyrocketed youth bulge in recent years of study (Khokhar, 2017). This, however, has not been reported in the same way by the United Nations (United Nations, 2015a). There are 1.2 billion youth between the ages of 15 and 24, which only accounts for 16% of the global population based on the UN's submission (United Nations, 2015: 1). The World Economic Forum in 2017 reported that four in ten people (42%) of the global population were aged under 25. The report further observed that while in other parts of the world the population of the youth is declining, in South East Asia and sub-Saharan Africa, it is rising. The figures above indicate that any policy that fails to take into cognizance the policy preference in favour of youth will be to the detriment of that society or state (Gray, 2018).

Africa is one of the areas that has a prevalence of youth population above all other parts of the world (Fukuda-Parr et al. 2013). The youth bulge in Africa is a concern for global key players because it must be approached in the context of poverty, low economic performance, and poor policies, in addition to misgovernance. The youth bulge in Africa indicates that around 63% of the total population of Africa is below the age of 25 as reported by the US Census Bureau (Mbassi, 2017). It is estimated that there will be 830 million youth in Africa by the year 2050, according to the UNDP (United Nations Development Programme), which is projected as both a promise and a peril depending on the utilization of the most active part of the population in the continent (UNDP, 2018). However, these youth are not utilized positively by the continent in terms of productivity. Weak economic and social policies coupled with unstable politics cause deprivation, impoverishment, and low levels of infrastructure which push the youth into helplessness. This phenomenon subjects the youth to vulnerable situations of violence and conflicts involving small arms and light weapons according to earlier report by UNDP (2006).

Small arms in Africa are increasing because of several factors, including leakage from the legal market to the black market through the Libyan route, where armed conflict is becoming more volatile and pervasive in nature, involving the youthful section of the population. A global report reveals that there are approximately 640 million small arms across the globe and that over 500 million are situated in West Africa, with the largest share of 350 million located in Nigeria alone (Method, 2018; Nwachukwu, 2018). Small arms are usually considered as guns, revolvers, rifles, automatic machine guns, propelled grenades and other related weapons, and these are smuggled into Africa through the black market in most cases (United Nations, 2015b). The African terrain makes the easy passage of illegal weapons sustainable because of porous borders, unmanned seas, poorly guarded coastal lands, and large, borderless jungles that facilitate the smuggling (Yacubu, 2005). Small arms are now manufactured in Africa and that has also been a cause of security threats and conflicts in Africa because restive youth are easily attracted into violent armed groups, courtesy of the accessible skills for the production of local weapons (Nowak & Gsell, 2018).

Africa has been recognized (Boulden, 2013; Francis, 2008; Gebrewold, 2009; Osaghae & Robinson, 2005; Stapleton, 2018) as a conflict zone with a volatile environment because of the involvement of youth in violence and armed conflict (Bello, 2016; Higginson et al., 2016; Ikelegbe & Garuba, 2011; Mutto, 2007; Samuel, 2017; Ukeje, 2012). The jobless youth that were reported by the UNDP in 2018 to have been isolated and deprived of quality education, sound healthcare services delivery, and other indicators of sustainable means of livelihood are easily enticed, or even conscripted, to become child-soldiers involved in gun violence in various parts of Africa. Conflicts are being witnessed in Africa since 1990s in Sierra Leone, Liberia, Rwanda, Congo, Somalia, Algeria, Angola, Sudan, Central African Republic, and recently in Tunisia, Egypt, Nigeria, South Sudan, Cameroon, Niger, Chad and several other parts of Africa (Abbink, 2005; Stapleton, 2018). The youth bulge should not be a curse to Africa but rather a blessing and a comparative cost advantage in the global political economy. This could be the case, if there were appropriate policies, sound economic plans, and a genuine desire for development. This chapter is an analysis and a critical conceptual understanding of the effects of guns and age, with special reference to the youth bulge in Africa, and the influence of the emergence of small arms in fuelling armed group conflicts in Africa.

## 2 The Youth Bulge in Africa: Issues and Perspectives

Africa's young population is growing faster than any other continent in the world, as reported in 2017 (The Commonwealth, 2018). In 2022, 60% of Africa's population were under the age of 25. By 2030, young Africans are anticipated to constitute 42% of the global youth while in the same year, Africa's population is projected to have an outlook of 63% youth within the age range of 15–29 years old (World Economic Forum, 2022). Additionally, Africa has the median age of 19.7 years, representing the youngest population in the world. By 2050, one in three young people globally will live in sub-Saharan Africa (ADF, 2022). The projection is that those within the age range of 0–24 years old will increase by 2050 to nearly 50%. In 2050, the African continent will host the largest youth population which will potentially make it twice the size of the population of youth in South Asia, Southeast Asia, East Asia, and Oceania. The issue with the population bulge in Africa is that, if it is not adequately taken care of, risks may emerge in terms of insecurity, instability, and mass migration (Sow, 2018). The distribution of the youth share of the African population is graphically illustrated in Fig. 1.

The African youth population, which has been estimated to be at 830 million by 2050 (a projected increase of nearly 60%), portends risk for the continent if some indicators are considered. For instance, every 24 hours, nearly 33,000 youths across Africa join the labour market in search of employment and about 60% of them will be joining the ranks of the unemployed. These statistics are not welcomed with enthusiasm in Africa because of frightening impending socio-economic and political crises. For instance, each year, about 10 to 12 million youths enter the labour market but only about 3 million are employed. The World Bank reported that 40% of those who joined armed groups and engaged in conflicts are pushed by unemployment and poverty (ADF, 2022). In 2016, not less than 3,000 deaths were recorded from the migrants who were trying to cross the Mediterranean Sea into Europe in search of better opportunities. In March 2023, it was reported that over 1,143 migrants died crossing from Africa between 2022 to 2023, about 50,000 died in search of greener pastures from 2014 to 2023, and 12,395 were missing in the first quarter of 2023 (IOM, 2023). Moreover, the World Bank reported that more than 40% of those who joined rebel movements in Africa did so due to lack of economic opportunities. The UN's secretary general, Antonio Guterres notes that the frustration generated in the youth population is the major source of their resentment and cause of insecurity in the world. More than half a million African youth migrated to European Union countries between 2013 and 2016. By the first quarter of 2023, about 11 million African migrants were living in Europe and, in 2022 alone, more than 1.5 million departed Africa for Europe, including a significant high number of skilful workers and well-trained experts in various fields of human endeavour (Statista, 2023). Many of Africa's young people remain trapped in poverty that is reflected in multiple dimensions, blighted by poor education, lack of access to quality healthcare, malnutrition, and lack of job opportunities. Between 10 and 12 million people join the African labour

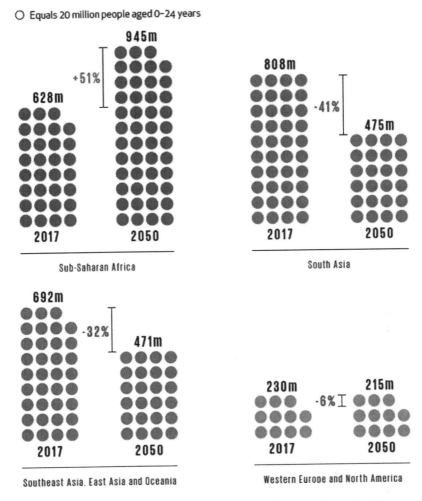

Fig. 1 Youth population increase in Africa (*Source* Sow, Brookings 2018)

force each year, yet the continent creates only 3.7 million jobs annually (Sow, 2018).

According to the US Census Bureau in 2010, 63% of the Africa's overall population was below the age of 25 and by 2022, about 67% is projected to be within the age bracket 15–25 (World Economic Forum, 2022). The average age of the African population is 19. We are talking of over 300 million people that will become 500 million in less than 20 years from now. In sub-Saharan Africa according to the ILO, three in five of the unemployed are youth; and 72% of the youth population live on less than $2 a day. In addition, 10 to 12 million young people join the labour market each year, adding year in year out to the African working poor (Mbassi, 2017). However, Mbassi (2017) concludes his analysis by stating that the youth bulge in Africa is a blessing, and fears should be allayed based on the good news that Africa in the next 30 years will benefit from this demographic explosion, which is within the range of production age, if it is properly utilized.

A study (Feseha, 2018) has established a link between (the) Youth bulge and armed conflict in Africa. This is because youth often play a role in political violence and the presence of a Youth bulge in developing countries is associated with political crisis. The Youth bulge and conflict are seen as causal-effect factors and relationship. For example, youth unemployment in countries like Nigeria and Kenya, which is higher than 20%, is identified as the cause of political violence and armed conflicts and is corroborated by the World Bank report (ADF, 2022) that 40% of youth who were unemployed took part in the rebel movement because of frustration and hopelessness about their future. As indicated above, we should understand that youth bulge is not synonymous with armed violence. A statistical connection cannot be taken as a predicator of war as many countries with youth bulges have not experienced bouts of violent conflict. Malawi, Zambia, and Botswana can be taken as instances where states with a relatively high youth bulge are free from armed conflict. It can also be argued that a youth bulge presents a "demographic window of opportunity" if it is backed by economic opportunities, as in countries like China, South Korea, and Japan. What makes a youth bulge problematic is social policy and economic conditions that are not handled properly, as in the case of some countries like Mali, Nigeria, Niger, Chad, Cameroon, Somalia, Congo, and other sub-Saharan African countries (Feseha, 2018).

## 3 Small Arms in Africa

Small arms and light weapons are traded globally in both legal and illicit modes by state and non-state actors (Blumstein, 2002). These weapons include, among others, guns, pistols, AK 47s, machine guns, automatic guns, rockets, rocket launchers, anti-aircraft guns, grenades, Rocket Propelled Grenades (RPGs), improvised explosive devices (IEDs), and other related weapons, which can be operated by an individual, two persons, or a small group of people (SIPRI Year Book, 2019). The global arms trade is more pronounced in 2018 beyond the past activities and even during the Cold War era. Arms transfers between 2009 and 2013 were 23% higher than in

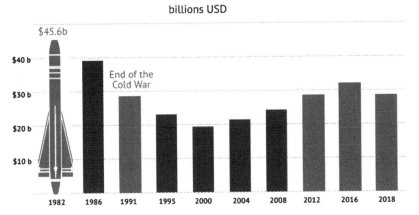

Fig. 2 Total value of global arms trade in USD in 2018 2019 (*Source* SIPRI)

the period between 2004 and 2008. Between 2014 and 2018, arms transfers reached their zenith since the end of the Cold War. SIPRI reported in 2018 that the total global arms trade in 2017 was valued at $95 billion with weapons exports valued at $27.6 billion (Durkin, 2019). Figure 2 illustrated the global trade arms exports in USD in 2018.

The official or legal sale of arms and their trade is complex and difficult to track because sometimes it takes place under covert arrangements because of critical matters of national security (Brown, 2005). The United States and Russia dominate global arms trade deals. According to SIPRI (2019), 202 states, 48 non-state armed groups, and five international organizations were supplied with arms shipments from 2013 to 2018. The United States, Russia, France, Germany, and China are the main global exporters, accounting for 75% of total world exports. The US and Russia alone constitute 57% of the total global share in the arms trade. The five largest global exporters were Saudi Arabia, India, Egypt, Australia and Algeria, all together accounting for 35% of the total global arms import from 2014 to 2018 (Durkin, 2019).

There are efforts to control the global flow of small arms, such as intelligence agencies which provide any relevant information, the Stockholm International Peace Research Institute (SIPRI) which monitors, registers and takes statistics of arms transfer and flow across world countries, the Norwegian Initiative on Small Arms Transfer (NISAT) which tracks governments legal transfer of Small Arms and Light Weapons, and the United Nations Panel of Experts which monitors data and assesses it based on arms transfer under the full or partial UN arms embargo (Freeman, 2018; Holtom & Pavesi, 2018; Stanley, 2018; Wezeman, 2018). Despite all the measures on the ground to protect against the proliferation or illegal transfer of weapons, especially to arms groups, the SIPRI Year Book in 2018 reported that over 42 armed groups continued to receive small arms from the black market. Similarly, the SIPRI (2019) further reported that the illicit arms trade in small arms in parts of Africa, eastern Europe, Asia and South America continues unabated. This has further compounded global security threats where armed militia groups, terrorist groups, political thugs, and armed bandits are easily securing weapons for their crimes from a covert and illicit source.

The proliferation and illegal trafficking of small arms in Africa is more than in any other region of the world because of weak national control, porous national borders, and existing armed conflicts across the continent (Alusala, 2016). After the removal of Muammar Ghaddafi in Libya, a route was smoothly opened up for the illicit flow of small arms in sub-Saharan Africa which has further escalated and aggravated the volatile security region into several armed conflicts (Sen & Kakar, 2017). The trans-Saharan route thus, became the most challenging loophole for arresting the flow and spread of small arms in Africa. Out of the estimated 650 million small arms in Africa, about 540 million are believed to have been present in sub-Saharan Africa with Nigeria having nearly 70% of the total number of weapons (Nowak & Gsell, 2018: 16). With the current socio-economic and political volatility in the region, armed group conflict is inevitable, unless the policymakers take adequate care of the urgent needs and aspirations of the explosive youth population.

These restive youth become vulnerable and easy prey for recruitment into violence and armed groups activities, including terror groups and rebels in Africa. The Al Shabab in Somalia, Al Qaeda in Mali, Boko Haram in Nigeria, Niger, Chad, and Cameroon, as well as Al Qaeda in the Maghreb (AQIM), were all the long-term consequences of the illegal spread of weapons in West Africa coupled with the socio-economic malaise and political imbroglio that have bedevilled the states in the region (Parsons & Johnson, 2014). Crises continue to erupt in various parts of Africa. From ethnic violence and armed conflicts in Rwanda, Sierra Leone, Liberia, Sudan, Central African Republic, Democratic Republic of Congo, Congo Kinshasa, Ethiopia, Kenya, and Nigeria in the 1980s and 1990s, armed group violence led to a new dimension of civil unrest and uprising in the African-Arab world in 2011 in Tunisia, Egypt, and other Middle Eastern Arab countries (McGee et al., 2017). The modern armed group conflict has now became associated with terrorism and armed violence in several parts of the continent, largely because of the existence of small arms (Method, 2018; Nowak & Gsell, 2018). Figure 3 shows routes for the flow of weapons in Africa.

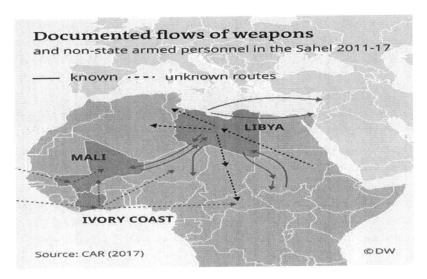

Fig. 3 Flow of weapons in the Sahel 2011–2017 (*Source* DW, 2019)

The menace of weapons, especially SALW, in Africa compelled African leaders to assemble in Johannesburg in South Africa in 2020 and hold a Conference on Silencing the Guns. At the conference, it was resolved that the African Peace and Security Architecture (APSA) and the African Governance Architecture (AGA), which guide member states, as well as the RECs/RMs (Regional Economic Communities/Regional Mechanisms) in their efforts to consolidate governance; prevent, manage and resolve conflicts; and undertake post-conflict stabilization, reconstruction, and development should be fully implemented. It was also agreed that all root causes, triggers and drivers of conflicts should be eradicated, particularly by ending illicit arms/weapons circulation and use; removing socio-economic disparities and the widening inequalities among (our) citizens; and addressing impunity through enhancement of continental, regional, and national institutions. They agreed to redouble efforts to control and curb the illicit flow of arms/weapons into Africa and deploy necessary efforts and resources to prevent and defeat terrorism and violent extremism, as well as transnational organized crime in the continent (African Union, 2020). Apart from blocking the illicit flow of weapons, the African Union (AU) strives to engage the youth in Africa productively through accelerating integration and economic development by establishing organizations which will play a central role in resource mobilization and effective management of the African financial sector (African Union, 2022). However, it seems by 2023, the agenda for silencing the guns was far from being achieved. The escalation of the emergence of armed groups and their activities is increasing instead of minimizing.

## 4 Nature of Conflict in Africa

The existence of a young population in Africa, the failure of the policymakers to engage them productively, and the emergence of SALW have negative repercussions for the peace and security of the continent. This has manifested in the explosion of political violence, ethnic and religious conflicts, terrorism and other related crimes. This section examines this development and the attendant consequences.

In any society, dominant competing interests exist, and once such interests abound, there is a susceptibility to conflict in the scramble towards competition for political power, economic control, and other determinants of social status and influence. The spread of small arms is worrisome when statistics indicate that most of these small arms are possessed illegally by armed groups, terrorists, and ethnic militias (Lott, 2010). In 2016, firearms were used to kill about 210,000 people and 38% of all victims are victims of lethal violence. About 15% of these individuals died in direct conflict, while the majority fell victim to intentional homicide (81%). Latin America and the Caribbean recorded particularly high proportions of firearm deaths in 2016. Firearms were also used in at least half of all lethal violence incidents in several African countries. Benin, Cape Verde, Nigeria, Niger, Cameroon, Mauritania, Senegal, and Togo as well as in Albania, Thailand, and the United States. In countries characterized by the highest levels of lethal violence, 50% of all killings were committed with a firearm, as opposed to about 12% in countries with the lowest rates (Mc Evoy & Hideg, 2017).

In 2016, interpersonal and collective violence claimed the lives of 560,000 people around the world. About 385,000 of them were the victims of intentional homicides from gun possession, 99,000 were casualties of war, and the rest died in unintentional homicides, or due to legal interventions. The ratio of deaths from gun violence is equivalent to 7.50 violent deaths per 100,000 of population. Direct armed conflict resulted in 18% of all violent deaths. Nine countries out of the twenty-three with the highest number of violent deaths in 2016 were affected by armed conflict. In the world, 99,000 people died in armed conflict in 2016. Five of the most violent countries in 2016, with the highest number of violent deaths from the possession of guns, were Syria, El Salvador, Venezuela, Honduras, and Afghanistan. It is believed that if the current rate of violent deaths is not addressed, it will increase the tally from 560,000 in 2016 to 610,000 in 2030. Additionally, more than 1.35 million lives could be saved from violent deaths between 2016 and 2030, particularly if countries pay more attention to the prevention of illegal possession of guns and other small arms (Mc Evoy & Hideg, 2017).

War and conflict in Africa, as elsewhere in the world, have been a historical phenomenon, pervasive and changing with time. During pre-colonial times, African communal societies were engaged in various conflicts, political feuds, violence, slavery, inter-state wars of conquest, and other different forms of conflict (National Association of School Psychologies, 2012). There were wars of colonial conquest in Africa between 1800–1945 in which the dominant colonial powers, or colonial countries, of Britain, France, Germany, Belgium, Netherlands, Italy, Portugal and others scrambled for the control of African economy and politics. Attempts by indigenous Africans at resisting the colonization led to wars of conquest. The possession of superior firepower by the colonial countries succeeded in making them victorious in subjugating the colonized countries. The second stage of armed conflict in Africa was during the First World War (1914–1918) and Second World War (1939–1945) (Stapleton, 2018).

The next stage in the plethora of conflicts in Africa saw the decolonization wars from 1945 to 1990 where colonized African countries fought or struggled for political independence from the European colonizers. Alongside this, in the next stage of conflict, civil wars erupted in Africa post-independence in several African states from 1955 to 2000. The imposition of artificial borders arbitrarily in incipient African states led to the emergence of conflict and civil wars in Congo, Nigeria, Sudan, Ethiopia, Somalia, Rwanda, Liberia, Sierra Leone, Uganda, Burundi, and many others in the 1960s and 1990s. Armed groups and rebels emerged in these countries in succession or power tussles. Additionally, another stage of conflict in Africa, from 1960 to 2000, involved the postcolonial, inter-state conflicts between many African countries. These conflicts include the Egypt-Israeli wars (1956–1973), Libya's conflict with Egypt and the United States (1977–1989), conflicts in the Maghreb: Algeria, Morocco, Mauritania, and Western Sahara (1963–1999), the Ogaden War (1977–1978), the Kagera War (1978–1979), Angola (1975–1989), Mozambique (1975–1993), Chad, Libya, and France (1968–1990), the Christmas War (1985), the Ethiopia-Eritrea War (1998–2000) and the Congo Wars (1996–2002) (Stapleton, 2018). One vital aspect of the conflict in Africa that is not covered in the work of Stapleton (2018) is the armed group conflicts and terrorism in Darfur in Sudan, Somalia, Mali, Central African Republic, Nigeria, Niger, Chad, and Cameroon in the 2000s and beyond which have been devastating and a reminder of how the spread of small arms such as guns have generated security dilemmas in sub-Saharan Africa and beyond. These groups consist of Al Shabab, Boko Haram, Seleka and Anti-Balaka, Janjaweed, Al Qaeda in the Maghreb (AQIM), and ISIS in sub-Saharan Africa.

Peace in most postcolonial African countries has remained a mirage for several decades. Perennial violent armed conflicts, pervasive political instability, deepening economic crises, malnutrition, poverty, and disease, have all contributed in causing armed violence in Africa in various countries and in different dimensions (Francis, 2008). Politically motivated violence is a palpable presence in many African countries. What makes these youths inclined to become absorbed in unwanted political violence are poverty, unemployment, deprivation, ignorance, inequality, misgovernance, and disjointed democratization (Bello, 2016). Ethnicity is also a considerable factor in fuelling armed violence in Africa, and several scholars (Adetoun, 2005; Albert, 2005; Baines, 2005; Bwenge, 2005; Smyth, 2005) have observed that ethnic divisions in several African countries have created ethnic militias and armed groups that wield small arms in unleashing violence and mayhem in their societies.

Africa is characterized by violence from many angles. For many people outside of Africa, the continent conjures up images of perpetual violence seemingly revolving around ethnic or religious identity. Atrocities in Darfur, genocide in Rwanda, clan warfare in Somalia, and the long history of the Tuareg rebellions in Mali support habitual understandings of Africa as the centre stage for insecurity and crisis in the globe (Ascher & Mirovitskaya, 2013). This would not have been possible without the possession of guns and small arms by illegal groups across the continent. Seventy five percent (75%) of armed conflicts across the globe are by non-state actors and are found in the developing world, particularly in recent times, in Africa. Conflicts and civil wars have affected Asian and African societies leading to destruction of basic amenities, creation of wide social chasms, fuelling of immigration, escalating of food insecurity, spreading of disease, and expanding as well as stretching of military expenditure. The conflicts involve both ethnic-based resentments and responses towards marginalization and social inequality (Etefa, 2019).

Political and economic grievances usher in ethnic mobilization. Perhaps Africa is witnessing ethnic conflicts because it is the most ethnically diverse continent of any region in the world (Nasong'o, 2015a). This is evident, given that African states are artificial geographical colonial creations, when one views the postcolonial ethnic conflicts in Rwanda, Nigeria, Kenya and

Ethiopia (Nasong'o, 2015a). Nasong'o (2015b) argued that deep-seated historical and socio-economic grievances are the basis for ethnic conflict in Africa (Nasong'o, 2015b). The ambiguity of soil possession by competing ethnic groups (Singo & Opondo, 2015), battle for hegemony and counter hegemony among various ethnic groups that are co-existing (Jacquemin, 2013) and the search of political identity (Shanguhyia, 2015). Youth are found by several studies (Arnaut, 2005; Burgess, 2005; Dorman, 2005; Jok, 2005; Kagwanja, 2005; Konings, 2005; Last, 2005; Marguerat, 2005; McIntyre, 2005; Nasong'o, 2005c) to be the pivot of ethnic clashes and armed conflict in several African countries.

Most recent armed conflicts have involved regular armies, ethnic militias, political militias, and armed civilians. The presence of organized criminal gangs and non-state armed groups in Central and South America led to political violence and armed conflict in Nicaragua and a humanitarian crisis in Venezuela. In Asia and Oceania, there were seven countries with active armed conflicts in 2018 including Afghanistan, India, Indonesia, Myanmar, Pakistan, the Philippines, and Thailand which cost the lives of 43,000 combatants and civilians. The growing violence in Asia and Oceania are linked with identity politics related to ethnic divisions, religious polarization, and the increasing activities of transnational violent jihadist groups including Islamic State (ISIS) in Afghanistan, China, India, Indonesia, Malaysia, Pakistan, and the Philippines. The only active armed conflict in Europe is that of Ukraine since 2018. There were seven countries in the Middle East and North Africa that were engaged in armed conflict in 2018: Egypt, Iraq, Israel, Libya, Syria, Turkey and Yemen. The major drivers of the conflict consist of regional rivalries, violent jihadist groups, and increasing competition over access to water and the effects of climate change. Sub-Saharan Africa had the highest incidence of countries with active armed group conflicts in 2018 which stood at 11. The conflict affected Burkina Faso, Cameroon, the Central African Republic, the Democratic Republic of Congo, Ethiopia, Mali, Niger, Nigeria, Somalia, South Sudan, and Sudan. The causal factors are identified as extreme poverty, youth bulge, poor governance, economic fragility, ethnicity, election violence, water scarcity, climate change, political motivation, and low levels of resilience. Most of the conflicts took place in the Lake Chad Basin and Sahel areas as a result of violent activities of Islamic groups, armed groups, and criminal organizations (SIPRI Year Book, 2019). The above statistics revealed that the African continent, which has the highest youth population explosion, also recorded a higher level of armed conflict in 2018. There is no better explanation for this correlation than factors that were in the report such as poverty, unemployment, and other socio-economic maladies. This could be interpreted as a danger signal for Africa with a youth bulge and the proliferation of guns or small arms, if adequate social, political, and economic policy measures are not taken rapidly.

The year 2018 witnessed the continued proliferation and expansion of armed group conflicts by youth throughout the Middle East and Africa in Egypt, Iraq, Libya, Syria, Yemen, Nigeria, Somalia, South Sudan, the Central African Republic, the Democratic Republic of Congo, and Afghanistan which was identified as the most lethal area of the armed group conflict. Global security largely deteriorated in Africa, Asia, and South America due to the influence of burgeoning youth populations that were uncatered for, and the existence or spread of small arms possessed by illegal armed groups especially in sub-Saharan Africa where the phenomenon is becoming more rampant than anywhere else in the world. This is because international transfers of small arms have been increasing since 2017 across the globe (SIPRI Year Book, 2018).

Youth and identity politics in Africa are causing violence due to elites' manipulation in the twenty-first century, which has been aided by the possession of guns and the flow of small arms. Weak political institutions are neither a solution nor an alternative to preventing youth armed conflict in the continent (Takeuchi, 2013). Political institutions in Rwanda succeeded in post-conflict peace building, whereas this was not successful in Burundi, for example (Takeuchi, 2013). In Ghana and Cote d' Ivoire, horizontal inequalities, ethnic politics, and violent conflict were recorded as consequences of youth restlessness and the spread of small arms (Langer, 2013). Similar consequences as in Ghana have been recorded in Kenya (Kimenyi, 2013) and in Nigeria (Ukiwo, 2013). This mindset of the youth to exhibit guns and unleash terror in Africa, characterized by Charles Taylor's *Small Boys* (SBU) and *Gronna Boys* in Liberia, Museveni's boy soldiers—*Kidogos*—in Uganda, the "technical" operating *Moryham* youth in Somalia, the lumpen *Rarray Boys* in Sierra Leone, *Bayaye* in Kenya and Uganda, *Manchicha* in Tanzania, *Hittiste* in Algeria, *Tsotsi* in South Africa, and *Area Boys*, *Egbesu Boys* and *Yan Daba* respectively in Lagos, Niger Delta, and Kano in Nigeria, as well as several others across Africa, although the circumstances under which they become active participants in armed conflicts are as varied as the conflicts themselves (Ikelegbe & Garuba, 2011).

It is observed that the escalating insecurity in Africa is the result of armed conflicts and the proliferation of SALW. Hence, several efforts and responses both by governmental and non-governmental agencies are being put in place to counter and reverse the situation. Some African countries have adopted legal frameworks against the proliferation of SALW. For instance, many countries have signed the United Nations Arms Treaty, the UN Protocol Against the Illicit Manufacturing of and Trafficking in Firearms, the United Nations Programme of Action on Small Arms and Light Weapons (UNPOA) 2001, the ECOWAS Moratorium 1998, the ECOWAS Protocol Relating to the Mechanism for Conflict Prevention, Management and Resolution, Peace-Keeping and Security, the Bamako Declaration 2000, and the ECOWAS Convention on Small Arms and Light Weapons and their Ammunition and other Related Materials. Other states that face a high risk of arms proliferation, such as Nigeria, have initiated domestic policies against arms proliferation and violent crimes (Danwanka, 2021). The main challenge for these legal frameworks is effective implementation, monitoring, and response.

The police force is another institution saddled with the task of licensing firearms in African states to check their illicit ownership and excessive spread. Police licensing plays a vital role in arms control in Africa including controlling arms movement, licensing manufacturers, license renewals, revocation of licenses, and control of weapon possession. But licensing faces obstacles due to corruption, internal conflicts in many states, and weak regulations (Dawud & Abdulkadir, 2021). Another agency or body that is instrumental in arms control in Africa apart from the police is civil society. Auwal and Aluigba (2021) report that varied programmes by CSOs (Civil Society Organisations) to counter proliferation of SALW, including UNPOA to prevent, combat and eradicate the illicit trade in small arms and light weapons; the Arms Trade Treaty (ATT), and many others. The actions of civil societies put more pressure on African governments to regulate and increase control of illicit weapons, but the main challenge is lack of capacity and political will to pursue programmes to their logical conclusion.

## 5 Conclusion

The chapter concludes that youth in Africa are neglected by policymakers due to burgeoning corruption, misgovernance, and misplacement of priorities. The youth are, however, experiencing a coincidental bulge in Africa, with around 63% falling within the age category of 18–34 in the midst of this negligence. This condition is exacerbated by contemporary developments in the proliferation of Small Arms and Light Weapons (SALW) across the continent. The chapter reports that the proliferation of SALW is in two stages: the emergence of readily manufactured weapons through illicit routes, black markets, and through local production. Several illegal armed groups have acquired the required skills to manufacture SALW in African countries, making it difficult to tame. The chapter, thus, links the existence of unproductive and underutilized youth in Africa, (the growing populations of youth in particular), and the proliferation of SALW as precursors for conflicts in Africa. The idle youth fall prey to recruitment into non-state criminal armed groups, intra-state factions and rebels, terrorist organizations, ethnic militias, and other illegal armed groups. In addition, the chapter asserts that conflicts have escalated and expanded in Africa after the widespread use of SALW in the twenty-first century. Conflicts are identified in the chapter at different levels, including rebels within a state, civil wars, transnational organized criminal groups, terrorists, bandits, ethnic militias, political gangsters, and inter-state wars. In spite of numerous measures taken by both the United Nations and the African Union, as well as individual states to address the problem of youth and the proliferation of SALW, no strong policies have been designed by African leaders to engage the youth in productive ventures and to block the possession of illicit weapons by youth and non-state groups. The chapter concludes that conflicts in Africa caused by the proliferation of SALW, mostly involving youth, are devastating the political and socio-economic conditions of Africa, and if serious measures are not taken, Africa will continue to suffer insecurity and maldevelopment.

Based on the foregoing, the study recommends some practical policy implications to mitigate the effects of conflicts motivated by youth and the proliferation of SALW. Good governance is the most plausible alternative. African leaders must strive to promote good governance and sound socio-economic policies and increase inclusive political participation to avoid idle youth who can fall prey to recruitment into criminal activities. Multinational joint task forces should be formed regionally and continentally to patrol and water borders from the identified routes that illicit SALW are flowing to Africa. African governments must intensify counterinsurgency and counterterrorism to discourage the resurgence of illicit groups, and to acquire the space to face the business of good governance.

# References

Abbink. (2005). Being Young in Africa: The Politics of Despair and Renewal. In Abbink, J., & Van Kessel, I. (Eds.), *Vanguard or Vandals? Youth, Politics and Conflict in Africa* (pp. 1–36). Tuta Sub Aigede Pallas.

Adetoun, B. A. (2005). The Role and Function of Research in a Divided Society: A Case Study of the Niger Delta Region of Nigeria. In E. Porter, G. Robinson, M.

Smyth, A. Schnabel, & E. Eghosa Osaghae (Eds.), *Researching Conflicts in Africa: Insights and Experiences* (pp. 47–55). United Nations University Press.

ADF. (2022). *Experts Say 'Youth Bulge' Can Promote Security and Prosperity in Africa* (August 23, 2022). Retrieved from https://adf-magazine.com/2022/08/experts-say-youth-bulge-can-promote-security-and-prosperity-in-africa/ on 09 March 2023 at 10: 30 pm.

African Union. (2020). *'Silencing the Guns: Creating Conducive Conditions for Africa's Development': Draft Johannesburg Declaration on Silencing the Guns in Africa*. African Union.

African Union. (2022). *Silencing the Guns 2020: the Framework and Initiative*. African Union.

Albert, I. O. (2005). Applying Social Work Practice to the Study of Ethnic Militias: The Oduduwa People's Congress in Nigeria. In E. Porter, G. Robinson, M. Smyth, A. Schnabel, & E. Eghosa Osaghae (Eds.), *Researching Conflicts in Africa: Insights and Experiences* (pp. 64–89). United Nations University Press.

Alusala, N. (2016). *Lessons from Small Arms and Weapons Control Initiatives in Africa*. BICC Working Paper.

Arnaut, K. (2005). Re-generating the Nation: Youth, Revolution and the Politics of History in Cote d' Ivoire. In Abbink, J. & Van Kessel, I. (Eds.), *Vanguard or Vandals? Youth, Politics and Conflict in Africa* (pp. 110–142). Tuta Sub Aigede Pallas.

Ascher, W., & Mirovitskaya, N. (2013). Development Strategies and the Evolution of Violence in Africa. In W. Ascher & N. Mirovitskaya (Eds.), *The Economic Roots of Conflict and Cooperation in Africa* (pp. 1–34). Palgrave Macmillan.

Auwal, A., & Aluigba, M. T. (2021). Civil Society and Arms Control in Africa. In A. Tar & C. P. Onwurah (Eds.), *The Palgrave Handbook of Small Arms and Conflict in Africa* (pp. 501–516). Palgrave Macmillan.

Baines, E. K. (2005). Gender Research in Violently Divided Societies: Methods and Ethics of 'International' Researchers in Rwanda. In E. Porter, G. Robinson, M. Smyth, A. Schnabel, & E. Eghosa Osaghae (Eds.), *Researching Conflicts in Africa: Insights and Experiences* (pp. 140–155). United Nations University Press.

Bello, U. M. (2016). Political Violence Among Youth Groups in Africa's Budding Democracies—An Explorative Studies of Concepts, Issues and Experience. *Research on Humanities and Social Sciences, 6*(17), 146–153.

Blumstein, A. (2002). Youth, Guns and Violent Crimes. *The Future of Children, 12*(2), 39–54.

Boulden, J. (2013). The United Nations Security Council and Conflict in Africa. In J. Boulden (Ed.), *Responding to Conflict in Africa* (pp. 1–13). Palgrave Macmillan.

Brown, S. (2005). *Understanding Youth & Crime: Listening to Youth?* Open University Press, Mac Graw Hill.

Burgess, G. T. (2005). Imagined Generations: Constructing Youth in Revolutionary Zanzibar. In Abbink, J. & Van Kessel, I. (Eds.), *Vanguard or Vandals? Youth, Politics and Conflict in Africa* (pp. 55–80). Tuta Sub Aigede Pallas.

Bwenge, A. M. (2005). Researching Ethno-Political Conflicts and Violence in the Democratic Republic of Congo. In E. Porter, G. Robinson, M. Smyth, A. Schnabel, & E. Eghosa Osaghae (Eds.), *Researching Conflicts in Africa: Insights and Experiences* (pp. 90–109). United Nations University Press.

Danwanka, A. S. (2021). Legislation, Institution-Building and the Control of Small Arms and Light Weapons in Africa. In A. Tar & C. P. Onwurah (Eds.), *The Palgrave Handbook of Small Arms and Conflict in Africa* (pp. 453–472). Palgrave Macmillan.

Dawud, M. D., & Abdulkadir, T. (2021). Police and the Control of Firearms in Africa. In A. Tar & C. P. Onwurah (Eds.), *The Palgrave Handbook of Small Arms and Conflict in Africa* (pp. 473–500). Palgrave Macmillan.

Dorman, S. R. (2005). Past the Kalashnikov: Youth, Politics and the State in Eritrea. In Abbink, J. & Van Kessel, I. (Eds.), *Vanguard or Vandals? Youth, Politics and Conflict in Africa* (pp. 189–206). Tuta Sub Aigede Pallas.

Durkin, A. (2019). *Global Arms Trade Highest Since End of Cold War*. Hinrich Foundation. Global Trade (September 22nd 2019). Retrieved from https://tradevistas.org/global-arms-trade-highest-since-end-of-cold-war/ on 19 September 2022 at 10: 12 pm.

DW. (2019). *Stemming the Flow of Illicit Arms in Africa*. DW (26-06-2019). Retrieved from Stemming the flow of illicit arms in Africa – DW – 07/26/2019 on 11th October 2023 at 04:07 pm.

Etefa, T. (2019). *The Origin of Ethnic Conflict in Africa: Politics and Violence in Darfur, Oromia, and the Tana Delta*. Palgrave Macmillan.

Feseha, M. (2018). *The Nexus Between Youth Bulge and Armed Conflict*. Africa Portal (9 May 2018). Retrieved From https://www.africaportal.org/features/nexus-between-youth-bulge-and-armed-conflict/ on 19 September 2022 at 10:15 pm.

Francis, D. J. (2008). Introduction: Understanding the Context of Peace and Conflict in Africa. In D. J. Francis (Ed.), *Peace and Conflict in Africa* (Francis, ed., pp. 3–15). Zed Books.

Freeman, S. P. (2018). *How Big is the International Arms Trade*. World Peace Foundation.

Fukuda-Parr, S., Langer, A., & Mine, Y. (2013). Introduction: Disentangling the Linkages Between Horizontal Inequalities and Political Institutions. In Y. Mine, F. Stewart, Fukuda-Parr, & T. Mkandawire (Eds.), *The Palgrave Macmillan Preventing Violent Conflict in Africa: Inequalities, Perceptions and Institutions* (pp. 1–7). Palgrave Macmillan.

Gebrewold, B. (2009). *Anatomy of Violence: Understanding the Systems of Conflict and Violence in Africa*. Ashgate Publishing Company.

Gray, A. (2018). *What You Need to Know About the World Youth in 7 Charts*. World Economic Forum.

Higginson, A., Benier, K., Shendorovich, Y., Bedford, L., Mazerolle, L., & Murray, J. (2016). *Youth Gun Violence and Preventive Measures in Low-Income-Middle Countries: A Systematic Review (Part II)*. International Initiative for Impact Evaluation.

Holtom, P., & Pavesi, I. (2018). *The 2018 Arms Trade Transparency Barometer* (Small Arms Survey, Briefings Paper).

Ikelegbe, A., & Garuba, D. (2011). *Youths and Conflicts in West Africa: Regional Threats and Potentials*. ECOWAS.

IOM. (2023). *Missing Migrants Project*. IOM UN. Retrieved from https://missingmigrants.iom.int/region/africa on 9 March 2023 at 10:43 pm.

Jacquemin, A. C. (2013). Hegemony and Counter-Hegemony: The Root of the Rwandan Genocide. In W. Nasong'o (Ed.), *The Roots of Ethnic Conflicts in Africa: From Grievance to Violence* (pp. 93–124). Palgrave Macmillan.

Jok, M. Jok. (2005). War, Changing Ethnics and the Position of Youth in South Sudan. In J. Abbink & I. Van Kessel (Eds.), *Vanguard or Vandals? Youth, Politics and Conflict in Africa* (pp. 143–160). Tuta Sub Aigede Pallas.

Kagwanja, P. M. (2005). Clash of Generations? Youth Identity, Violence and the Politics of Transition in Kenya, 1997–2002. In J. Abbink & I. Van Kessel (Eds.), *Vanguard or Vandals? Youth, Politics and Conflict in Africa* (pp. 81–109). Tuta Sub Aigede Pallas.

Kimenyi, M. S. (2013). The Politics of Identity: Horizontal Inequalities and Conflict in Kenya. In Y. Mine, F. Stewart, Fukuda-Parr, & Mkandawire, T. (Eds.), *The Palgrave Macmillan Preventing Violent Conflict in Africa: Inequalities, Perceptions and Institutions* (pp. 175–153). Palgrave Macmillan.

Khokhar, T. (2017). *How is the World Youth Population Changing?* World Bank. Retrieved from https://blogs.worldbank.org/opendata/chart-how-worlds-youth-population-changing. The World Bank.

Konings, P. (2005). Anglophone University Students and Anglophone Nationalists Struggles in Cameroon. In J. Abbink, & I. Van Kessel, I. (Eds.), *Vanguard or Vandals? Youth, Politics and Conflict in Africa* (pp. 161–188). Tuta Sub Aigede Pallas.

Langer, A. (2013). Horizontal Inequalities, Ethnic Politics and Violent Conflict: The Contrasting Experiences of Ghana and Cote d'Ivoire. In Y. Mine, F. Stewart, Fukuda-Parr, & Mkandawire, T. (Eds.), *The Palgrave Macmillan Preventing Violent Conflict in Africa: Inequalities, Perceptions and Institutions* (pp. 66–94). Palgrave Macmillan.

Last, M. (2005). Towards a Political History of Youth in Muslim Northern Nigeria, 1750–2000. In J. Abbink & I. Van Kessel (Eds.), *Vanguard or Vandals? Youth, Politics and Conflict in Africa* (pp. 37–54). Tuta Sub Aigede Pallas.

Lott, R. J. (2010). *More Guns, Less Crimes: Understanding Crime and Gun Control Laws*. The University of Chicago Press.

Marguerat, Y. (2005). From Generational Conflict to Renewed Dialogue: Winning the Trust of Street Children in Lome, Togo. In J. Abbink & I. Van Kessel (Eds.), *Vanguard or Vandals? Youth, Politics and Conflict in Africa* (pp. 207–227). Tuta Sub Aigede Pallas.

Mbassi, J. P. E. (2017). *Africa's Youth is an Opportunity to Transform the Continent*. Biz Community. Retrieved from https://www.bizcommunity.com/Article/145/347/165978.html on 19 September 2022 at 11:00 pm.

Mc Evoy, C., & Hideg, G. (2017). *Global Violent Deaths 2017: Time to Decide*. Small Arms Survey.

McGee, T. Z., Logan, K., Samuel, J., & Nunn, T. (2017). A Multivariate Analysis of Gun Violence Urban Youth: The Impact Direct Victimisation, Indirect Victimisation, and Victimisation Among Peers. *Cogent, Social Sciences, 3*, 1328772. https://doi.org/10.1080/23311886.2017.1328772

McIntyre, A. (2005). Children as Conflict Stakeholders: Towards a New Discourse on Young Combatants. In J. Abbink & I. Van Kessel (Eds.), *Vanguard or Vandals? Youth, Politics and Conflict in Africa* (pp. 228–242). Tuta Sub Aigede Pallas.

Method, S. (2018). *Stemming the Tide: African Leadership in Small Arms and Light Weapons Control*. Retrieved from https://oefresearch.org/think-peace/african-small-arms-control on 19 September 2022 at 11:01 pm.

Muncie, J. (2004). *Youth & Crime*. Sage Publications.

Mutto, M. (2007). *The Youth in Africa: A Threat to Security or a Force for Peace?* UNDP.

Nasong'o, W. S. (2015a). From Grievance to Ethnic Mobilisation: An Introduction. In *The Roots of Ethnic Conflicts in Africa: From Grievance to Violence* (pp. 1–10). Palgrave Macmillan.

Nasong'o, W. S. (2015b). Explaining Ethnic Conflicts: Theoretical and Conceptual Perspectives. In W. Nasong'o (Ed.), *The Roots of Ethnic Conflicts in Africa: From Grievance to Violence* (pp. 11–20). Palgrave Macmillan.

Nasong'o, W. S. (2015c). Deep-Seated Historical and Socioeconomic Grievances: The North-South Conflict in Sudan. In W. Nasong'o (Ed.), *The Roots of Ethnic Conflicts in Africa: From Grievance to Violence* (pp. 21–37). Palgrave Macmillan.

National Association of School Psychologies. (2012). *Youth Gun Violence Fact Sheet*. NASP.

Nowak, M., & Gsell, A. (2018). *Handmade and Deadly Craft Production of Small Arms in Nigeria* (Briefing Paper, Small Arms Survey). German Cooperation.

Nwachukwu, C. A. (2018). *Arms Proliferation and Nigeria Customs*. This Day Newspaper. Retrieved from https://www.thisdaylive.com/index.php/2018/09/04/arms-proliferation-and-nigeria-customs/ on 19 September 2022 at 11:11 pm.

Office of Juvenile Justice Delinquency and Prevention, OJJDP. (2016). *Gun Violence and Youth*. US Department of Justice.

Osaghae, E., & Robinson, G. (2005). Introduction. In E. Porter, G. Robinson, M. Smyth, A. Schnabel, & E. Eghosa Osaghae (Eds.), *Researching Conflicts in Africa: Insights and Experiences* (pp. 1–6). United Nations University Press.

Parsons, C., & Johnson, A. (2014). *Young Guns: How Gun Violence is Devastating the Millennial Generation*. Centre for American Progress.

Samuel, O. (2017). Youth Involvement in Political Violence/Thuggery: A Counter Weight to Democratic Development in Africa. *Journal of Political Sciences and Public Affairs, 5*(3), 2–4.

Sen, A., & Kakar, R. (2017, February 20). *Why Are we Failing 75% of the World's Youth at a Time of Unique Opportunity?* The Guardian: Global Development. Retrieved from https://www.theguardian.com/global-development/2017/feb/20/failing-75-per-cent-of-world-youth-unique-opportunity-global-youth-index on 19 September 2022 at 11:20 pm.

Shanguhyia, M. S. (2015). In Search of a Political Identity: The Historical Basis of Zanzibar's Post-Colonial Dilemma. In W. Nasong'o (Ed.), *The Roots of Ethnic Conflicts in Africa: From Grievance to Violence* (pp. 125–154). Palgrave Macmillan.

Singo, M. S., & Opondo, S. O. (2015). Ambiguity of the Soil, Ambiguity of Belonging: Grievance, Resource Avarice, and Conflict in Eastern Democratic Republic of Congo. In W. Nasong'o (Ed.), *The Roots of Ethnic Conflicts in Africa: From Grievance to Violence* (pp. 75–92). Palgrave Macmillan.

SIPRI Year Book. (2018). *Armaments, Disarmament and International Security*. SIPRI.

SIPRI Year Book. (2019). *Armaments, Disarmament and International Security*. SIPRI.

Smyth, M. (2005). Insider-Outsider Issues in Researching Violent and Divided Societies. In E. Porter, G. Robinson, M. Smyth, A. Schnabel, & E. Eghosa Osaghae (Eds.), *Researching Conflicts in Africa: Insights and Experiences* (pp. 9–23). United Nations University Press.

Sow, M. (2018). *Figures of the Week: Africa's Growing Population and Human Capital Investment*. Brookings. Retrieved from https://www.brookings.edu/blog/africa-in-focus/2018/09/20/figures-of-the-week-africas-growing-youth-population-and-human-capital-investments/ on 19 September 2022 at 11:27 pm.

Stanley, A. (2018). *Getting the Youth Bulge Wrong*. Academia, Violence, War. Retrieved from http://politicalviolenceataglance.org/2018/02/15/getting-the-youth-bulge-wrong/ on 19 September 2022 at 11:28 pm.

Stapleton, T. (2018). *Africa: War and Conflict in the Twentieth Century*. Routledge, Taylor & Francis.

Statista. (2022, August 1). *African Migrants Living Outside Africa in 2020, by World Region (in millions)*. Retrieved from https://www.statista.com/statistics/1321673/african-migrants-living-outside-africa-by-region/ on 9 March 2023 at 09:34 pm.

Takeuchi, S. (2013). Twin Countries with Contrasting Institutions: Post-Conflict State Building In Rwanda and Burundi. In Y. Mine, F. Stewart, Fukuda-Parr, & T. Mkandawire (Eds.), *The Palgrave Macmillan Preventing Violent Conflict in Africa: Inequalities, Perceptions and Institutions* (pp. 40–57). Palgrave Macmillan.

The Commonwealth. (2018). *Global Youth Development Index (YDI)*. Retrieved from https://www.thecommonwealth-healthhub.net/global-youth-development-index-ydi/ on 19 September 2022 at 11:31 pm.

Ukeje, C. U. (2012). A Farewell to Innocence? African youth and Violence in the Twenty-First Century. *International Journal of Conflict and Violence, 6*(2), 339–350.

Ukiwo, U. (2013). Managing Horizontal Inequalities and Violent Conflicts in Nigeria. In Y. Mine, F. Stewart, Fukuda-Parr, & T. Mkandawire (Eds.), *The Palgrave Macmillan Preventing Violent Conflict in Africa: Inequalities, Perceptions and Institutions* (pp. 178–205). Palgrave Macmillan.

United Nations Development Programme. (2006). *Youth and Violent Conflict: Society and Development in Progress*. United Nations.

United Nations. (2015a). *Human Cost of Illicit Flow of Small Arms, Light Weapons Stressed in Security Council Debate*. Retrieved from https://www.un.org/press/en/2015/sc11889.doc.htm. On 19 September 2022 at 11: 34 pm.

United Nations. (2015b). *Small Arms in Africa*. United Nations.

United Nations. (2018). *World Youth Report: Youth and the 2030 Agenda for Sustainable Development*. United Nations.

United Nations Development Programme. (2018). *Promise or Peril? Africa's 830 million Youth by 2050*. United Nations.

Wells, K., & Montgomery, H. (2014). Everyday Violence and Social Recognition. In K. Wells, E. Burman, H. Montgomery, & A. Alison Watson (Eds.), *Childhood, Youth and Violence in Global Context* (pp. 1–20). Palgrave Macmillan.

Wezeman, P. D. (2018). *International Arms Flow: Monitoring, Sources and Obstacles*. Netherlands Institute of International Relations.

World Economic Forum. (2022, September 19). *Why Africa's Youth Hold the Key to its Development Potential*. Retrieved from https://www.weforum.org/agenda/2022/09/why-africa-youth-key-development-potential/ on 9 March 2023 at 10:32 pm.

Yacubu, J. G. (2005). Cooperation Among Armed Forces and Security Forces in Combating the Proliferation of Small Arms. In A. Ayissi & I. Sall (Eds.), *Combating the Proliferation of Small Arms and Light Weapons in West Africa* (pp. 55–69). United Nations Institute for Disarmament Research.

# Violence Against Children on the Streets in Sub-Saharan Africa: An Overview

Witness Chikoko

## 1 Introduction and Background

Children are an important asset for any nation (Wakatama, 2007). Children take us into the future (Mushunje, 2006). No children; no future. Children ensure the replacement and growth of families and societies (Mushunje, 2006). The United Nations Convention on the Rights of a Child (UNCRC) (1989), article 19, defines violence against children as including "all forms of physical or mental violence, injury and abuse, neglect or negligent treatment or exploitation, including sexual abuse, while in the care of parents or any legal guardians or any other person who has the care of the child." Violence against children is endemic and its social and economic consequences are far reaching (Arifiani et al., 2019). The UN's World Report on Violence Against Children (2006) observed the paucity of data and statistics on violence against children and recommended increased commitment to improving national data collection and information systems. In order to increase state accountability for violence against children, world agencies such as the United Nations have recommended the elimination of violence against children and women in the Sustainable Development Goals (Arifiani et al., 2019; UN General Assembly, 2015).

W. Chikoko (✉)
Department of Social Work, University of Zimbabwe, Harare, Zimbabwe
e-mail: wchikoko@gmail.com

Although there has been progress in improving the quality of life, the majority of children in Africa face a lot of challenges, violence, and vulnerabilities, among others. Children are at a greater risk of poverty and deprivation, which severely affect their fundamental human rights (United Nations Convention on the Rights of a Child, 1989, Manjengwa et al., 2016). In Africa, there are various categories of children that are vulnerable. These categories include: street children, children involved in child labour, children in rural communities, child soldiers, children with disabilities, children in child-headed households, children in extended family systems, children in step-parent-headed households, children on the move, among others (African Charter on the Rights and Welfare of Children, 1999, United Nations Convention on the Rights of a Child, 1989). This chapter focuses on violence among children in street situations, or street children, using the case of selected African cities, namely, Harare, Lusaka, Nairobi, and Johannesburg, among others.

In order to enable the reader to appreciate the vulnerability to violence of children in street situations in Africa, it is critical to establish the social context of the children. This is due to the fact that violence does not happen in a vacuum. Violence happens in well-defined historical, social, cultural, political, and economic contexts. A deep dive into a description of violence without an overview of the factors that render street children vulnerable to violence runs the risk of missing the enabling variables. Therefore, the first part of the essay provides global data relating to children in street situations in order to highlight the fact that this is a global (and not a peculiarly African) challenge. This is followed by a reflection on the larger African context, after which the chapter summarizes the HIV and AIDS situation that has contributed to the increase in the number of children in street situations in Africa. The ensuing sections explore factors that lead to children getting into street situations in Africa. This background is vital in order for one to understand the multiple forms of violence that some of the children in street situations are exposed to. This is followed by an analysis of the forms of violence, with the conclusion and recommendations bringing the chapter to a close.

## 2 Global Data and Statistics of Children in Street Situations

In order to put the theme of violence and children on the streets in selected cities in Southern and East Africa into its proper context, it is vital to clarify the use of some key concepts. This section seeks to clarify the concept of "children on the streets/street children/children in street situations." The term "street children" is elusive or difficult to define. Skhosana (2013) argues that there is no agreed definition of street children. There have been several debates about the definition of street children for many decades around the world (Skhosana, 2013). Who are these children? Street children are defined as homeless, delinquent, runaways, or abandoned children (Wakatama, 2007). Street children are considered, to stay or live in especially difficult situations (Fernandes & Vaughan, 2008). Scholars such as Lusk (1989) have acknowledged that UNICEF has defined street children in two groups, thus: "children of the streets" and "children on the streets." Skhosana (2013) states that there is another category of street children. Therefore, there are three categories of street children, namely: children of the streets, children on the streets, and children of street families. The distinction has been derived from the experiences of street children in the Latin American continent (Ennew, 1994; Wakatama, 2007). Children "on the streets" refers to those who spend much of their time working in the street environment (Wakatama, 2007). The majority of them return home at the end of each working day (Wakatama, 2007). They still maintain continuing relationships with their families (Swart-Kruger & Donald, 1994; Wakatama, 2007). Some such children supplement family or household income through working on the streets (Wakatama, 2007). They come from very poor backgrounds, and they are responsible for raising income for their families (Wakatama, 2007). On the other hand, children "of the streets" are those who have turned the streets into their homes (Mhizha, 2010; Wakatama, 2007). For them, the streets are intrinsic to their lives. They survive, live, play, sleep, and grow up on the streets (Wakatama, 2007). Such children even lack contact with their families (Wakatama, 2007). The third category of "children of street families" spend most of their nights on the streets, or any other places that are not meant for human habitation, or dangerous places, together with their adult family members and for long periods (Skhosana, 2013). Such children contribute towards family income by generating income on the streets (Skhosana, 2013).

The term "street children" is a social construction (Ennew, 2003; Skhosana, 2013). This social construction reflects society's disapproval of children who are very visible but who are considered as "out of place" (Skhosana, 2013). The term "street children" has been heavily criticized as labelling and stigmatizing (Wargan & Dreshem, 2009). Children in street situations are viewed as delinquent, thus stigmatized and labelled (Skhosana, 2013). The street children themselves dislike or resent the term "street children" (Skhosana, 2013).

There is no exact data or statistics about the populations of children in street situations or street children at the global level (Ndlovu, 2015). However, Kudrati et al. (2008) note that an estimated tens of millions of children are in street situations globally. However, Thomas de Benetiz (2008) and Fernandes and Vaughan (2008) argue that there are between 100 and 150 million street children at the global level. Scholars such as Muchinako et al. (2013) observe that an estimated 250 million children are in street situations. Latin America has an estimate of 40 million street children, with Brazil accounting for 25 million of them (Fernandes & Vaughan, 2008; Ndlovu, 2015). India is estimated to have 18 million children in street situations (Ndlovu, 2015). The population of street children is increasing as a result of modernization, globalization, and urbanization (Kudrati et al., 2008). Despite the dearth of reliable data and statistics on street children at the global level, the problem is huge in many parts of the world (Ndlovu, 2015). Having reflected on the global context, in the following section, the chapter examines the challenge of street children with particular reference to the African context.

## 3 African Data and Statistics of Children in Street Situation

Scholars such as Ndlovu (2015) have observed that the African continent has an estimated 10 million street children. Zimbabwe has more than 12,000 street children, with Harare having an estimated 5,000 (Ndlovu, 2015; UNICEF, 2003). Uganda has an estimated 10,000 street children (Ndlovu, 2015). Zambia has 75 000 street children (Ndlovu, 2015). An estimate of 150,000 children in Ethiopia are in street situations, with Addis Ababa having 60,000 (Ndlovu, 2015). Kenya is estimated to have 250 000 street children, with Nairobi having 60,000 (Ndlovu, 2015).

The advent of colonialism, modernization, and urbanization have had much influence on the way of life among Africans. As a result of colonialism, Christianity has altered the belief systems among Africans (Ndlovu, 2015) Changes in the belief systems have had far reaching consequences on family life (Ndlovu, 2015). The presence of children on the streets demonstrates the breakdown of family systems (Ndlovu, 2015). Within the context of *Ubuntu*, the children belong to the whole clan, society. This is illustrated in the saying that "it takes the whole village to raise a child" (Mugumbate & Chereni, 2019). Family breakdown is demonstrated as the street children were not born in the streets of, say, the Harare Central Business District, Zimbabwe (Ruparanganda, 2008). Therefore, certain difficult questions are always asked about these children. For example, "whose children are these ones?" (Chikoko & Ruparanganda, 2020). Having reviewed the larger African context, the following section of the chapter focuses on the impact of HIV and AIDS.

## 4  Street Children and HIV and AIDS

HIV and AIDS is one of the pandemics that has severely affected street children in sub-Saharan Africa (Dhlembeu & Mayanga, 2006). Sub-Saharan Africa has been the epicentre of HIV and AIDS (Mhizha & Chikoko, 2022). For example, as of 2016, Zimbabwe had a prevalence of 14.6% of the population affected (Mhizha & Chikoko, 2022). Due to the HIV and AIDS, there have been high mortality and low life expectancy rates (Mhizha & Chikoko, 2022). As of 2003, 40,000 children under 15 were newly infected with HIV and AIDS through mother-to-child transmission (Dhlembeu & Mayanga, 2006). HIV and AIDS led to the decline of life expectancy from 61 years in the early 1990s to 35 years by the end of 2004 (Dhlembeu & Mayanga, 2006; Mhizha & Chikoko, 2022). As of 2003, out of the estimated 1.3 million orphans in Zimbabwe, 980,000 were due to HIV and AIDS (Dhlembeu & Mayanga, 2006).

HIV and AIDS has had unprecedented impact on the lives of children in Zambia. In Zambia about 690,000 children were orphaned by HIV and AIDS (Mtonga, 2011). As a result of HIV and AIDS, the orphaned children did not have access to basic needs—rather, their vulnerabilities increased. They became vulnerable to abuse, exploitation, and limited access to education among others (Mtonga, 2011). There has been an increase in child-headed households and street children in Lusaka as a result of HIV and AIDS (Mtonga, 2011).

Studies indicate that, there is a higher prevalence of HIV and AIDS among street children in Johannesburg (Cumber & Tsoka-Gwengweni, 2015). Some of the reasons that account for this high prevalence of HIV among these children include; low condom use, multiple sexual relationships, unprotected sex, transactional sex, and satisfying bodily needs, among others (Cumber & Tsoka-Gwengweni, 2015). The street children suffer from structural violence, where multiple layers of oppression increase their vulnerability to HIV infection.

## 5 Street Children and Social Protection Programmes

One would have expected there to be social protection mechanisms to protect street children from structural and other forms of violence. However, this is not the case. While social protection has been viewed as a core of development policy and practice (Chikoko & Mwapaura, 2023; Roelen & Sabates-Wheeler, 2012), the street children whose well-being is under review have not benefited from it. The domain of social protection comprises: poverty alleviation, reduction and prevention; social compensations; and income distribution (Chikoko & Mwapaura, 2023; Patel, 2015). The term "social protection" is associated with a diversity of strategies such as social assistance, social insurance, and private insurance (Chikoko & Mwapaura, 2023; Patel, 2015). Social protection programmes include safety nets and are broad in scope as well as diverse in practice (Chikoko & Mwapaura, 2023; Devereux, 2006; Devereux & Sabates-Wheeter, 2004). Social protection has also been viewed as an integral part of responding to childhood poverty and vulnerabilities in developing countries (Chikoko & Devereux et al., 2011; Mwapaura, 2023).

The provision of social protection for street children in Uganda has had a number of challenges (Kakuru et al., 2019). Some of the challenges include corruption and the inadequacy of the social protection mechanisms among others (Kakuru et al., 2019). For example, Kakuru et al. (2019) observed that some social protection for street children in Uganda falls short of the key principles of human rights-based approaches to development as cash in kind for children withdrawn from the streets was based on the charity model or approach (Kakuru et al., 2019). In other words, the social protection mechanisms for street children in Uganda were not in line with international best practices (Kakuru et al., 2019).

In addition, limited funding opportunities, incoherent and less coordinated institutional frameworks were some of the challenges that affected the delivery of social protection programmes for street children in Uganda (Kakuru et al., 2019). Kakuru et al. (2019) observed that there were very few meaningful contributions made by the social protection programmes in terms of providing empowerment of the street children of Uganda. The majority of the street children withdrawn from the streets of Kampala, would always find themselves back on the streets, as they were provided with only very limited livelihood opportunities by the social protection mechanisms (Kakuru et al., 2019).

The evidence of the street children of Harare Metropolitan province suggests that there are huge gaps in the provision of government of Zimbabwe-led social protection programmes (Gunhidzirai, 2020). Gunhidzirai (2020) observed that there are a number of government-led social protection programmes in Zimbabwe. These include: child adoption, foster care, the Basic Educational Assistance Module, the National Action Plan for Orphans and Other Vulnerable Children, assisted medical treatment orders, and harmonized social cash transfers, among others (Gunhidzirai, 2020). Gunhidzirai (2020) argues that, to a great extent, the street children of the Harare Metropolitan province not do meaningfully benefit from such social protection programmes. Largely, the social protection programmes in Zimbabwe have been criticized as they do not conform to the key principles of child rights in relation to the street children of the Harare Central Business District (Chikoko & Mwapaura, 2023). In other words, there are huge challenges in child-sensitive social protection programmes among the street children of the Harare Central Business District (Chikoko & Mwapaura, 2023). The challenges include: limited funding opportunities, targeting errors or exclusion issues, and late disbursement of funds (Chikoko & Mwapaura, 2023).

The provision of social protection services among street children in Pretoria, South Africa has also been associated with a number of challenges (Skhosana, 2013). These include: limited numbers of social workers, insufficient collaboration among government departments and civil society organizations, ineffective legal restrictions, brain drain, lack of job satisfaction or low salaries, limited financial and technical resources, corruption, and salary discrepancies between NGOs and government social workers among others (Skhosana, 2013). This lack of social protection in various African countries has increased the vulnerability of street children, pushing them onto the streets. In turn, this has rendered them more susceptible to violence, as is discussed in the later section on "Forms of Violence."

# 6 Reasons for Street Dwelling Among Children in Africa

There are varied and multiple reasons that account for why children continue to live, stay, or work on the streets, thereby increasing their vulnerability to multiple forms of violence. The reasons include: peer pressure, divorce of parents, poverty, collapse of extended family systems, orphanhood, and violence in homes, among others (Nouri & Karimi, 2019). However, Skhosana (2013) argues that reasons why the children live, stay, or work on the streets can be categorized into broader groups, namely, push or pull factors. The push factors include those reasons such as socio-cultural ones such as poverty, family violence, collapse of family structure, and financial problems (Skhosana, 2013). On the other hand, the pull factors include the desire to have freedom, peer pressure, and the need to find a source of livelihood (food and money) (Skhosana, 2013).

## Child Poverty

Aufseeser (2020) observed that there many dimensions of child poverty in relation to children in street situations. Child poverty is evident among street children as they do not have parents to take care of them. Children in street situation have very limited access to basic needs. The street is viewed as a space of vulnerabilities, with children in such spaces considered as poor (Aufseeser, 2020). As a result of poverty, the children in street situations are considered as vulnerable, dependent, and/or complicit in their own poverty (Aufseeser, 2020). However, child poverty is one of the key reasons why children stay on the streets.

In the case of the street children of Harare, scholars such as Mhizha (2010), Ruparanganda (2008), Wakatama (2007) conclude that the majority children decide to stay on the streets as a result of child poverty. Some of the children run away from their families and decide to stay on the streets as a way to make ends meet (Rurevo & Bourdillon, 2003). However, when the children stay on the streets, they become vulnerable as they have limited access to protection, food, shelter, education and health services, among others. The vulnerabilities of street children due to childhood poverty demonstrate violation of national, regional, and international child rights laws, policies, and programmes. Child poverty is in contrast with the "best interests of the child" principle of the ACRWC (1999) and UNCRC (1989).

## Orphanhood

Orphanhood is a situation where a child or children's biological parents are dead. There is single or double orphanhood. Orphanhood has been created by HIV and AIDS and disaster situations, among others. In situations where children do not have anyone else to look after them, some of them resort to staying and working on the streets. This is very common among the children on the streets of Harare, Lusaka, Johannesburg, and Nairobi, among others. With reference to the street children of Harare, Ruparanganda (2008), Wakatama (2007), and Mhizha (2010) observed that a significant number of them were as a result of orphanhood. Mtonga (2011) also observed that some children living and working on the streets of Lusaka, Zambia were as a result of orphanhood. The absence of parents and guardians renders street children prone to different forms of violence.

## Collapse of Extended Family Systems

There has been an erosion of the extended family system in many parts of the world, including sub-Saharan Africa. This has been influenced by the modernization school of thought (Muchinako et al., 2013). With the collapse of extended family systems, a number of children have been left stranded to the extent that they resort to staying and working on the streets (Muchinako et al., 2013).

With the levels of rapid urbanization in the region, more children will reside or work and stay on the streets. The situation is worsened by increasing levels of urban poverty associated with urbanization.

## Peer Pressure

Peer pressure is one of the reasons why some children reside on streets. Peer pressure contributes towards "streethood" among some children in many ways. For example, some street children in Pretoria, South Africa are lured into the streets by their peers and the desire for approval by their friends (Ward & Seager, 2010). The street children are convinced by their friends that there are benefits of staying and/or living on the streets (Ward & Seager, 2010). Some of the benefits are time for leisure, the ability to make their own money and use it on themselves, and freedom, among others (Ward & Seager, 2010).

Similarly, some children reside or stay on the streets of Harare, Zimbabwe as a result of peer pressure (Mhizha, 2010; Ruparanganda, 2008, Wakatama, 2007). The children are convinced by their peers or friends who encourage them to stay or live on the streets (Ruparanganda, 2008). On the streets they enjoy life in the company of their friends and peers (Mhizha, 2010).

## Structure-Related Factors

Structure-related factors also account for street dwelling among children. Some of the structural factors are: economic austerity measures (such as structural adjustment programmes), colonization, and globalization (Muchinako et al., 2013). The majority of cities in sub-Saharan Africa have been severely affected by some of these structural issues that have had unprecedented impact on the growth of children living and working on the streets.

The economic structural adjustments of the 1990s have been associated with children staying on the streets in a number of countries such as Kenya, Zambia, and Zimbabwe. In the case of Harare, Zimbabwe there were more cases of children living, staying, or working on the streets as a result of deepening poverty levels associated with austerity measures of economic structural adjustment policies and programmes (Wakatama, 2007).

The background factors outlined in the preceding sections provide the relevant context for understanding street children's vulnerability to violence. In the following section, the chapter explores the different types of violence that some street children are exposed to. Although these types of types of violence have been isolated for analytical purposes, in real life some children face more than one type in the course of their lives as street children.

## 7  Forms of Violence

### Sexual Violence

Many street children are vulnerable to sexual abuse or exploitation (Fernandes & Vaughan, 2008). Scholars such as Wakatama (2007) note that some street children are sexually active at a much younger age than other adolescents due to the way they must survive on the streets. There are a number of factors that influence the sexual behaviour of street children such as: survival on the streets with limited access to livelihood opportunities, shelter, and clothing, among others (Wakatama, 2007). Substance abuse has influence on the sexual behaviour of these children (Chikoko, 2017). In fact, there is a correlation or intricate relationship between substance abuse and the sexual violence or behaviour of street children (Chikoko, 2017).

Street children in many African cities are faced with sexual abuse, violation, and exploitation. The sexual abuse, violation, and exploitation come in different forms including: transactional sex or commercial sex work, multiple sexual relationships, sodomy, pimping, ritual sex, intergenerational sex, and sexual poaching, among others.

## Commercial Sex

In Bukavu, the street children were involved in sex work through street-based prostitution or picking up clients at bars or night clubs (Shand et al., 2015). The street children of Accra, Ghana practise commercial sex work through picking up clients from bars (Shand et al., 2015). As a result of deepening poverty, some of the street children of the Harare Central Business District engage in commercial sex work as one of their survival strategies (Chikoko, 2014, 2017). The street girls sell sex for survival (Chikoko, 2014, 2017). They sell sex to men from mainstream society and also to fellow street boys (Chikoko, 2014, 2017; Mhizha, 2010; Ruparanganda, 2008).

Shand et al. (2015) observed that some of the street children in Harare were picking up their clients from bars and for pornography filming, among others. Some of the street girls were selling sex at Njanji area and night clubs dotted around the Harare Central Business District, such as Archipelago, and Big Apple among others (Chikoko, 2014, 2017). However, as a result of trading in commercial sex, some of the street girls succumbed to sexually transmitted diseases, including HIV (Wakatama, 2007).

## Intergenerational Sex

Some of the street children of the Harare Central Business District engage in intergenerational sex (Bourdillon, 1991, 1994, 1995; Chikoko, 2017; Mhizha, 2010; Ruparanganda, 2008; Wakatama, 2007). They engage in intergenerational sex with a variety of clients, including those from mainstream society and their counterparts on the streets (Chikoko, 2017). Due to age disparities, most of the girls living on the streets are unable to negotiate for safer sex and endure different forms of abuse.

## Physical Violence

Physical abuse is one of the forms of violence, or exploitation prevalent among the street children of sub-Saharan Africa. The physical abuse comes in different forms or dimensions, such as bullying and corporal punishment, among others. In the case of the street children of Harare, bullying and corporal punishment are serious social problems (Wakatama, 2007).

The street children of Pretoria, South Africa receive corporal punishment from the municipal police (Skhosana, 2013; Ward & Seager, 2010). Similarly, the street children of Harare are victims or survivors of corporal punishment by both municipal police and the Zimbabwe Republic Police (Wakatama, 2007). In some instances, they are severely beaten up by the members of Zimbabwe National Army (Wakatama, 2007).

## Emotional Violence

Many street children are victims or survivors of emotional abuse. The emotional abuse is seen even in the derogatory names that are given to street children. For example, on the streets of Johannesburg, street children are called *malunde* (persons of the street) (Gunhidzirai, 2020). Some of them are also called *malalapipe* (those who sleep in storm water drains) in Johannesburg, South Africa (Swart, 1990; Wakatama, 2007). On the streets of Harare, street children are given all sorts of derogatory names, including *magunduru* (those who sleep anywhere) (Chikoko, 2017). Thus, many street children endure emotional/psychological violence.

## Violence Against the Self: Substance Abuse or Misuse

Makaruse (2010) defines substance abuse as taking too much of a drug, taking a drug too often, or taking drugs or substances for the wrong reasons. Substance abuse or misuse is a common social problem among street children in many parts of the world, including in Africa (Cumber & Tsoka-Gwengweni, 2015; Fernandes & Vaughan, 2008; Gigengack, 2014). Some street children in African cities misuse or abuse a number of psycho-active substances (Cumber & Tsoka-Gwengweni, 2015). The abused or misused psycho-active substances include: cocaine, cigarettes, marijuana, heroin, paint thinners, coca paste, inhalants, and amphetamines, among others (Cumber & Tsoka-Gwengweni, 2015). In a study of three African cities by Shand et al. (2015), street children or youths of Accra abused substances such marijuana (weed), and tramadol (pain killers) among others. The street children in Bukavu, the Democratic Republic of Congo also abused ganga (cannabis), inhaled petrol, and whisky, among others (Shand et al., 2015).

On the streets of Harare Central Business District, the street children also abuse psycho-active substances such as *zed*,[1] *chamba*,[2] *bhurongo*,[3] *dombo*,[4] *chitongo*,[5] and *kachasu*[6] among others (Chikoko, 2017; Shand et al., 2015). In addition, some of the street children of Harare Central Business District abuse aphrodisiac substances (Chikoko, 2014, 2017) including Seven Hours and Sharpshooter, among others (Chikoko, 2017). The street children of Harare Central Business District also abuse or misuse a number of traditional medicines (Chikoko, 2017). These include: *guchu, mudenhatsindi, mudzora, muchemedza mbuya*, and *muvhomora kwayedza*, among others (Chikoko, 2017; Ruparanganda, 2008).

Abuse or misuse of substances is one of the coping mechanisms among street children to help them to overcome struggles (Fernandes & Vaughan, 2008). The majority of street children are victims or survivors of multiple vulnerabilities. Some of their vulnerabilities are associated with deepening poverty, traumatic experiences of abuse and neglect and dropping out of school, among others (Fernandes & Vaughan, 2008). Therefore, one can make the legitimate conclusion that, due to the traumatic experiences of abuse and neglect, some children on the streets engage in violence against the self.

## Access to Food

Many street children in the region have limited access to food. Hunter et al. (2020) noted that some of the street children of Accra, Bukavu, and Harare, scavenged for food in dustbins. As a result of limited access to food, some of the street girls engaged in transactional sex or survival sex (Chikoko, 2014, 2017). The adolescent street girls exchange sex for food with male counterparts on the streets of the Harare Central Business District (Chikoko, 2014, 2017; Mhizha, 2010).

---

[1] *Zed* is strong beer.
[2] *Chamba* is cannabis.
[3] *Bhurongo* is cough syrup.
[4] *Dombo* is crystal methamphetamine.
[5] *Chitongo* is a highly addictive substance.
[6] *Kachasu* is also a highly addictive substance.

Some street children in Pretoria, South Africa also face limited access to food (Skhosana, 2013). The street children scavenge for food in dustbins (Skhosana, 2013). Some of them eat very unclean food which creates diarrhoeal problems, among others (Skhosana, 2013). Hunger is a form of violence that needs to be taken seriously. It is a form of institutionalized violence that many street children endure in different parts of the world, including in Africa.

## Access to Health Services

Evidence suggests that many street children in sub-Saharan Africa have limited access to health services. In a study of street children or youths in Bukavu, Accra and Harare, the researchers discovered cases where street children did not have access to reproductive health services (Hunter et al., 2020). Condoms are a primary method of contraception among street children or youths, however, the use of condoms has been inconsistent because of substance abuse or misuse and inaccessibility, among other factors (Hunter et al., 2020). As a result of the inconsistent use of the condoms, some of the street children succumb to sexually transmitted diseases such as gonorrhoea, HIV, and chlamydia, among others (Hunter et al., 2020).

Ruparanganda (2008) observed that most of the street children of the Harare Central Business District did not access reproductive health services, as they were discriminated against by public hospitals since they were viewed as people of "no fixed abode." As a result of the inaccessibility of the reproductive health services, some of the street girls gave birth on the streets (Ruparanganda, 2008). In addition, as a result of discrimination against the street children of the Harare Central Business District, some of them use *guchu* for treatment of sexually transmitted diseases. Overall, it is clear that many street children in Africa experience structural violence in relation to the health sector (Lee, 2019).

## Limited Access to Livelihood Opportunities

The majority of street children in sub-Saharan Africa have limited livelihood opportunities. As a result, some of them engage in informal and illegal activities. In a study of street children in Bukavu, Harare, and Accra, some of the street children engaged in risky activities so as to raise money for survival (Shand et al., 2015). Shand et al. (2015) observed that the involvement of the street children in illegal and dangerous activities further increased their vulnerability to becoming victims of violence, injury, ill health, and arrest, among others.

Carrying of goods is one of the activities associated with street children or youths of Bukavu, Harare, and Accra (Shand et al., 2015). For example, in Accra, the street children were involved in offloading containers and running errands, among others (Shand et al., 2015). In Bukavu, the street children were also involved in commercial loading and ship unloading, among others (Shand et al., 2015). The street children of Harare were involved in carrying luggage at bus stations, moving furniture, commercial goods, and assisting supermarket customers, among others (Shand et al., 2015).

Vending is one of the activities carried out by street children across many sub-Saharan African cities. For example, in Accra, Ghana, street children are involved in the vending of alcohol, water, fruit, cooked food, candies, airtime, and biscuits, among others (Shand et al., 2015). On the other hand, in Bukavu, street children are involved in the vending of stones, disinfectant, and bicycle renting, among other (Shand et al., 2015).

In Harare, the street children are involved in the vending of a variety of goods (Chikoko, 2017) including: sweets, biscuits, cigarettes, alcohol, fruit, eggs, and music and film CDs, among others (Shand et al., 2015).

Theft is another survival option for some of the street children in sub-Saharan African cities. In Accra, some of the street children were involved in theft through pickpocketing from sex work clients, sale of stolen goods, snatching phones, and internet fraud (Shand et al., 2015). Stealing of car parts and snatching of mobile phones are some common theft methods used by street children in Bukavu (Shand et al., 2015). In Harare, some street children raise money for survival through snatching of mobile phones and jewellery, and stealing from shops, among others (Mhizha, 2010; Shand et al., 2015).

Evidence suggests that the majority of street children do not have access to identity documents such as birth certificates and national identity cards (Wakatama, 2007). Limited access to such important documents further marginalizes these children in terms of educational or job opportunities or benefiting from social protection programmes. Thus, street children experience structural violence that prevents them from enjoying social protection and having access to more viable livelihood options.

## 8 Conclusion

As highlighted above, abuse, or violence, or the exploitation of children in street situations is widespread in most parts of sub-Saharan Africa. The violence has huge implications or consequences on these children in terms of their socio-economic well-being. The violence against street children in sub-Saharan Africa is expressed in many ways, including sexual, physical, or emotional abuse or exploitation. Structural violence also assaults street children in the region. It is also illustrated as the children are vulnerable to disaster situations such as HIV and AIDS and the COVID 19 pandemic, among others. Limited access to basic needs such as food, health services, shelter, educational opportunities, and identity documents also reveal the levels and extent of the vulnerabilities of these children. The violence is in sharp contrast with the principles of international, regional, and national child rights laws, policies, and programmes.

## 9 Recommendations

- Governments and other duty bearers should invest more in technical and/or financial resources to address or reduce violence against street children.
- There should be full implementation of child rights laws, policies, and programmes targeting street children in major cities and towns in sub-Saharan Africa.
- Government and other key stakeholders should implement social protection programmes for street children. Social protection mechanisms could include harmonized social cash transfer programmes, among others,
- There is a need to build community-based structures on child protection in emergencies targeting children in street situations.

## Bibliography

African Union. (1999). *African Charter on the Rights and Welfare of Children* (unpublished).

Arifiani, S. D., Handayani, S. A., Baumont, M., Benmouna, C., & Kusumanunrum, S. (2019). Assessing Large Scale Violence Against Children Surveys in Selected South East Asian Countries: A Scoping Review. *Child Abuse and Neglect, 93*, 149–161.

Aufseeser, D. (2020). Towards a Relational Understanding of Child Poverty: Care and Adverse Inclusion Among Street Affiliated Children in Peru. *Geoforum, 114*, 10–18.

Bourdillon, M. F. C. (1991). *Poor, Harassed but Very Much Alive: An Account of Street People and Their Organisation*. Mambo Press.

Bourdillon, M. F. C. (1994). Street Children in Harare. *Africa Insight, 64*(4), 516–532.

Bourdillon, M. F. C. (1995). The Children on our Streets. *Child Care Worker, 13*(3), 12–13.

Chikoko, W. (2014). Commercial 'Sex Work' and Substance Abuse Among Adolescent Street Children of Harare Central Business District. *Journal of Social Development in Africa, 29*(2), 57–80.

Chikoko, W. (2017). *Substance Abuse Among Street Children of Harare: A Case of Harare Central Business District* (unpublished D. Phil Thesis). Department of Social Work, University of Zimbabwe, Harare.

Chikoko, W., & Ruparanganda, W. (2020). *Ubuntu* or *Hunhu* Perspective in Understanding Substance Abuse and Sexual Behaviours of Street Children of Harare Central Business District, Zimbabwe. *African Journal of Social Work, 10*(1) (Special issue on *Ubuntu* Social Work), 69–72.

Chikoko, W., & Mwapaura, K. (2023). Challenges and Opportunities for Child Sensitive Social Protection Programmes in Zimbabwe. *Journal of Social Development in Africa, 38*(1), 12–20.

Cumber, S. N., & Tsoka-Gwengweni, J. M. (2015). The Health of Street Children in Africa: A Literature Review. *Journal of Public Health, 6*, 566. https://doi.org/10.4081/jphia.2015.566

Devereux, S. (2006). *Social Protection Mechanisms in Southern Africa* (Institute of Development Studies, Working Paper). University of Sussex, United Kingdom.

Devereux, S., & Sabates-Wheeter, R. (2004). *Transformative Social Protection* (IDS Working Paper 232). Institute of Development Studies, University of Sussex, United Kingdom.

Devereux, S., McGregor, J. A., & Sabates-Wheeler, R. (2011). Introduction: Social Protection for Social Justice. *IDS Bulletin, 42*(6), 1–9.

Dhlembeu, N., & Mayanga, N. (2006). Responding to the Orphans and Other Vulnerable Children's Crisis: Development of the Zimbabwe National Plan of Action. *Journal of Social Development in Africa, 21*(1), 35–49.

Ennew, J. (1994). *Street and Working Children: A Guide to Planning*. Save the Children.

Ennew, J. (2003). *Working with street children: Exploring ways for ADB assistance*. Regional and Sustainable Development Department, ADB.

Gigengack, R. (2014). The *chemo* and the *mona*: Inhalants, Devolution and Street Youth in Mexico City. *International Journal of Drug Policy, 25*, 61–70.

Fernandes, G. T., & Vaughan, M. G. (2008). Brazilian Street Children. *International Social Work, 51*(02), 669–681.

Gunhidzirai, C. (2020). *The Perceptions of Government Social Protection Programmes in Mitigating the Challenges Faced by Street Children in Harare Metropolitan Province in Zimbabwe* (unpublished D. Phil Thesis). Department of Social Work/Development, Faculty of Social Sciences and Humanities, University of Fort Hare, South Africa.

Hunter, J., van Blerck, L., & Shand, W. (2020). The Influence of Peer Relationship on Young People's Sexual Health in Sub Saharan African Street Context. *Social Science & Medicine, 288*, 113285. https://doi.org/10.1016/j.socscimed.2020.113285

Kudrati, M., Plummer, M. L., & Yousif, N. D. E. H. (2008). Children of the *sug*: A Study of the Day Lives of Street Children in Khartoum, Sudan with Intervention Recommendations. *Child Abuse and Neglect, 32*, 439–448.

Kakuru, R., Rukooko, A. B., & Tusabe, G. (2019). Social Protection Mechanism for Children Living on the Streets: Perspectives from Uganda. *Journal of African Studies and Development, 11*(1), 1–11.

Lee, B. X. (2019). *Violence: An Interdisciplinary Approach to Causes, Consequences, and Cures*. Wiley Blackwell.

Lusk, M. W. (1989). Street Programmes in Latin America. *Journal of Sociology and Social Welfare, 16*(1), 55–77.

Makaruse, T. (2010). *Substance Abuse Among School Children: A Case Study of Pafiwa High School in Mutasa* (unpublished MSW dissertation). School of Social Work, University of Zimbabwe, Harare.

Manjengwa, J., Matema, C., Tirivanhu, D., & Tizora, R. (2016). Deprivation Among Children Living and Working on the Streets of Harare. *Development Southern Africa, 33*(1), 53–66.

Mhizha, S. (2010). *The Self-Image of Adolescent Street Children in Harare* (unpublished M. Phil Thesis). Department of Psychology, University of Zimbabwe, Harare.

Mhizha, S., & Chikoko, W. (2022). Oliver Mtukudzi and the Call for the Reconstruction of the Lives of Orphans and Children on the Streets. In E. Chitando, P. Mateveke, M. Nyakudya, & B. Chinouriri (Eds.), *The Life and Music of Oliver Mtukudzi: Reconstruction and Identity*. Palgrave Macmillan.

Muchinako, G. A., Chikwaiwa, B. K., & Nyanguru, A. (2013). Children Living and or Working on the Streets in Harare: Issues and Challenges. *Journal of Social Development in Africa, 28*(2), 98–112.

Mugumbate, J. R., & Chereni, A. (2019). Using African *Ubuntu* Theory in Social Work with Children in Zimbabwe. *African Journal of Social Work, 9*, 27–34.

Mushunje, M. T. (2006). Child Protection in Zimbabwe: Yesterday, Today and Tomorrow. *Journal of Social Development in Africa, 21*(1), 12–34.

Mtonga. J. (2011). *On and Off the Streets: Children Moving Between Institutional Care and Survival on the Streets* (unpublished Master of Philosophy Degree (Childhood Studies)). Norwegian University of Science and Technology, Faculty of Social Sciences and Technology Management, Norwegian Centre for Child Research.

Ndlovu, I. (2015). *Life Experiences of Street Children in Bulawayo: Implications for Policy and Practice* (unpublished DPhil Thesis). Faculty of Health and Social Care, The Open University, United Kingdom.

Nouri, A., & Karimi, Y. (2019). A Phenomenological Study on the Meaning of Educational Justice for Street Children. *Education Citizenship and Social Justice, 14*(1), 57–67.

Patel, L. (2015). *Social Welfare and Social Development*. Oxford University Press Southern Africa (PVT) Ltd.

Roelen, K., & Sabates-Wheeler, R. (2012). A child sensitive approach to social protection: Seeing practical and strategic needs. *Journal of Poverty and Social Justice, 20*(03), 291–306.

Ruparanganda, W. (2008). *The Sexual Behaviour Patterns of Street Youth of Harare, Zimbabwe, in the Era of the HIV and AIDS Pandemic* (unpublished DPhil Thesis). Sociology Department, University of Zimbabwe, Harare.

Rurevo, R., & Bourdillon, M. F. C. (2003). Girls: The Less Visible Street Children of Zimbabwe. *Children, Youth and Environment, 13*(1), 1–20.

Shand, W., van Blerk, L., & Hunter, J. (2015). Economic practices of Africa street youth: The democratic republic of Congo, Ghana and Zimbabwe. In T. Abebe, & J. Waters (Eds.), *Labouring and learning Geographies of children and young people*, Singapore, Springer.

Skhosana R. M. (2013). *Social Welfare Services Rendered to Street Children in Pretoria: Perspectives of Service Providers* (unpublished Master of Arts in Social Sciences (Social Work)), University of South Africa, South Africa.

Swart J. (1990). *Malunde: The Street Children of Hillbrow*. Witwatersrand University Press.

Swart-Kruger, J., & Donald, D. (1994). Children of the South African Streets. In A. Dawes, & D. Donald (Eds.), *Childhood and Adversity: Psychological Perspectives from South African Research*, 14–20.

Thomas de Bnetiz, S. (2008). *State of the World's Street children: Violence*. Consortium for street children.

United Nations. (1989). *The United Nations Convention on the Rights of a Child* (unpublished).

United Nations. (2006). *World Report on Violence Against Children* (unpublished).

Wakatama, M. (2007). *The Situation of Street Children on Zimbabwe: A Violation of the United Nations Convention on the Rights of the Child (1989)* (unpublished D.Phil Thesis). School of Social Work, University of Leicester, United Kingdom.

Ward, C. L., & Seager, J. R. (2010). South African Street Children: A Survey and Recommendations for Services. *Development Southern Africa, 27*(1), 85–100.

Wargan, K., & Dresham, L. (2009). *Don't Call me a Street Child: Estimation and Characteristics of Urban Street Children in Georgia* (Save the Children Act Research Report).

# Violence Against Disabled Children in Botswana

Thabile Anita Samboma

## 1   Introduction

Violence against children is a multifaceted problem; it cuts across culture, class, education, ability, income, and ethnic origin. Violence exists in every country of the world, therefore, it can occur against any child. Children with Disabilities (CwD) are at greater risk in comparison with non-disabled peers (Sullivan, 2009). Evidence from a systematic review found that children with disabilities experience violence four times more frequently than non-disabled children in high-income countries (Jones et al., 2012). According to Grech and Soldatic (2016) this systematic review noted the lack of systematically collected data from low and middle-income countries (LMICs), pointing to an underrepresentation of the issue of violence against children with disabilities in LMICs on the agendas of governments and researchers. Furthermore, children with disabilities are more vulnerable to all forms of violence because of the entrenched social and structural discrimination against them. Collins (2020) stated that the majority of children with disability face significant barriers, as some live in relative isolation and are invisible to society, often kept indoors and out of sight. Thus, they have less interaction with peers or anyone in whom they could confide. Stigma surrounding disability can result

T. A. Samboma (✉)
Botswana Institute for Development Policy Analysis (BIDPA), Gaborone, Botswana
e-mail: sambomat@bidpa.bw

in their needs and rights being dismissed by communities, authorities, and families (US Department of Justice, 2010).

People living with disabilities (PWDs) constitute a significant portion of the population worldwide, yet they remain one of the most marginalized and vulnerable populations. Children with disabilities (CwDs) make up around 150 million of the billion people with disabilities in the world. Sub-Saharan African countries have a large number of CwDs who have limited access to healthcare and rehabilitation care. This, combined with chronic poverty, low education, and inadequately trained healthcare professionals, substantially lowers these children's quality of life (Adugna et al., 2020). Nonetheless, it is difficult to obtain accurate data on the number of people with disabilities worldwide because approaches to measuring disability vary across countries and according to the purpose and application of the data (Disability & Human Rights, 2014). A study by the World Bank estimated that there are approximately 600 million people living with disabilities across the world. This number is expected to increase owing to changing global dynamics such as an increase in both population ageing and violent conflict, both of which are highly correlated with disability incidence (Kangere, 2003).

In order to fight violence against CwD, it is of paramount importance that this chapter seeks to understand the violence that occurs against children with disabilities and the challenges that children with disability encounter. This is an essential first step in developing effective prevention programmes to guarantee the rights of children.

After this introduction, the chapter briefly defines some words used. This is then followed by some brief background on Botswana and its position in relation to international treaties and the Sustainable Development Goals (SDGs). It then provides an overview of government structures, institutions, and other components and their approaches to disability and the challenges encountered by children living with disability, and finally it provides a conclusion and recommendations.

## 2   Conceptual Definitions

The chapter applies terminology from international conventions and standard definitions. In order to better place the chapter, in terms of its use of language and applied principles, the terminology is first described here:

- In this study "violence" is defined broadly as any act or threat of sexual, physical, or psychological abuse, neglect, or maltreatment (Njelesani et al., 2018).
- "Violence against children" has been defined by the World Health Organization (WHO) as the intentional use of physical force or power, threatened or actual, against a child, by an individual or group, that either results in, or has a high likelihood of resulting in, actual or potential harm to the child's health, survival, development or dignity (Krug, 2002).
- Violence against children includes all forms of violence against people under 18 years old, whether perpetrated by parents or other caregivers, peers, romantic partners, or strangers (WHO, 2021).
- "Discrimination on the basis of disability" means any distinction, exclusion or restriction on the basis of disability which has the purpose or effect of impairing or nullifying the recognition, enjoyment or exercise, on an equal basis with others, of all human rights and fundamental freedoms in the political, economic, social, cultural, civil, or any other field (UN, 2014).
- A "child" is any person who is 18 years or younger (Government of Botswana, 2009).
- "Disability" includes a physical impairment such as mobility, hearing, visual, and language difficulties, and developmental delays which affect a person's behaviour, emotional expression, and learning abilities. It includes mild to severe disabilities, from cerebral palsy, paralysis, and amputation, to blindness, deafness, autism, and dyslexia (Better Care Network, 2018).

## 3   The Context of Botswana

Botswana is a landlocked country located in Southern Africa. It is bordered by South Africa to the south and southeast, Namibia to the west and north, and Zimbabwe to the northeast. The country has approximately 2.3 million people. It is considered to be is one of the most sparsely populated nations in the world. Of the total population, adolescents aged between 10 and 19 years constitute 22%, making Botswana a young majority nation (UNICEF, 2022). Around 10% of the population lives in the capital and largest city, Gaborone. Botswana gained its independence from British colonial rule in 1966. Since then, it has maintained a strong tradition of stable representative democracy, with a consistent record of uninterrupted democratic elections, nor has there been any civil strife. However, in spite of all this, not enough attention has been paid to the marginalized in society.

Botswana used to be one of the poorest countries in the world. However, the country has since transformed itself into one of the fastest growing economies in the world. Botswana is an upper-middle-income country that has witnessed rapid economic growth for most of its post-independence period since 1966 (Lekobane & Seleka, 2017). Its high gross national income (by some estimates the fourth-largest in Africa) gives the country a modest standard of living and the highest Human Development Index of continental sub-Saharan Africa. However, Botswana is currently one of the most unequal countries globally, having the ninth highest Gini coefficient, indicating the degree of inequality of incomes, according to the most recent UNDP report (2021). Both theoretical and empirical studies have shown the negative effect of inequality on long-run growth, poverty reduction, and social and political stability. Botswana is a member of the African Union, the Southern African Development Community, the Commonwealth of Nations, and the United Nations.

In 2011 the Population and Housing Census indicated that there were about 59,103 people with disabilities in Botswana, which is 2.92% of the total population of 2,024,904. The highest proportion of disabled persons was found in Gantsi (4.4%), followed by Southern district (3.7%), Kgalagadi (3.7%) and North-West district with 3.6%. Unfortunately, obtaining data on a large scale on people living with disability is a challenge; hence, we rely on the Population and Housing Census, which inadequately serves to inform certain issues relating to disability.

## 4 Violence Against Children with Disability (CwD) in Botswana

Botswana is a middle-income country with high levels of violence against women and girls. The 2018 Relationship Study indicates that 67% of women in Botswana have experienced some form of violence in their lifetime, including both partner and non-partner violence (UNFPA, 2018). Botswana is rated the second-highest country in the world in the area for numbers of rape cases at 92.9 per 100,000 citizens. Although the statistics are disheartening, the number of cases of violence against children living with disability is unknown, especially sexual abuse, because police records are not yet disaggregated.

Botswana is a signatory to Agenda 2030. The elimination of violence against children is called for in several targets of the 2030 Agenda for Sustainable Development but most explicitly in Target 16.2: "to end abuse, exploitation, trafficking and all forms of violence against and torture of children." According to Haslam (2015) the Sustainable Development Goals (SDGs) are a powerful tool that people with disabilities can use, nation by nation, to argue for their inclusion. Botswana also adheres to the principle of "Leave No One Behind," and to the principles of human rights, gender equality, and women's empowerment.

The "**Leave No One Behind**" principle adopts a strong people-centred focus based on a clear identification of population groups that have been left furthest behind. The "Leave No One Behind" principle also reaffirms the responsibilities of all states to "respect, protect and promote human rights, without distinction of any kind as to race, colour, sex, language, religion, political or other opinions, national and social origin, property, birth, disability or other status." This principle includes the recognition of individual rights to enjoy social protection, economic opportunity, access to essential services, participation in decision-making processes and a response to sudden shocks and changes in the needs of vulnerable populations.

**Human rights, gender equality and women's empowerment** principles focus on promoting international human rights principles and applying a human-rights-based approach in the analysis, planning, implementation, and monitoring of all SDGs and targets. This approach is adopted in order to effectively address the root causes of poverty, inequality, and discrimination and to ensure that development is more equitable, sustainable, participatory, and accountable to people. These principle also mainstream a gendered perspective in order to transform discriminatory social institutions, recognizing that discrimination can be embedded in laws, cultural norms, and community practices.

## 5 Institutional Frameworks

There are a number of institutions who are legally mandated to deal with children with disability and child violence. Some of the mandated professionals are designated in the Children's Act of 2009. Several blueprints such as Vision 2036 and NDP 11 also refer to disability issues and highlight the importance of inclusion. Recently, a commission was set up to review Botswana's constitution and the commission has recommended that Section 15 of the constitution should be amended to include intersex and disability as grounds for non-discrimination, and that the rights of persons with disabilities should be enshrined in the constitution. The following are some of the institutions mandated to look at issues relating to children with disabilities.

## The Ministry of State President: The Coordinating Office for People with Disabilities

The Government of Botswana created the Coordinating Office for People with Disabilities in the Office of the President in 2010, recognizing the importance of the issue of disability and coordination of the whole government. The Coordinating Office for People with Disabilities is the secretariat for the National Coordinating Committee on Disability (NCCD) which provides oversight of disability policy in Botswana. The coordination role has since been transferred to the Ministry for Presidential Affairs Governance and Public Administration to accord disability the impetus it deserves as a cross-cutting issue. Its location in the Office of the President has given the Coordinating Office for People with Disabilities a high profile, as well as a degree of political legitimacy. In 2020 Botswana established the first National Human Rights Coordinating Committee (NHRCC) consisting of government, business, and civic society. Botswana has newly established the Human Rights unit. The mandate of this unit is to ensure there is implementation of human rights in Botswana and ensure that no one is left behind.

## The National Policy on Care of People with Disabilities in 1996 (NPCPD)

Botswana developed the Policy on Care of People with Disabilities in 1996 as a comprehensive document for guiding service delivery to people with disabilities at the national level. Initially, the coordination role for disability was given to the Ministry of Health (MoH) which had the sole role and mandate for dealing with issues relating to disability. Thus, there were misunderstandings that seemed to suggest that disability was a health issue, hence, the belief that the medical model of rehabilitation was the right approach to follow at that time. Furthermore, Omotoye (2018) argued that the implementation of the NPCPD has been slow and ineffective, especially in improving the lives of people with disabilities. The new reviewed policy aims to embrace the principles of the Conventions on the Rights of People with Disabilities adopted by the United Nations in 2006. The policy is currently under review mainly to address coordination and alignment to the appropriate service providers. Regrettably, although the reviewed policy was to be enacted before the end of the financial year 2015/16, five years down the line, in 2022 it has yet to be enacted.

## The Ministry of Local Government and Rural Development (MLGRD)

The Ministry of Local Government and Rural Development (MLGRD) has the mandate for the provision of social protection services among other things. The Department of Social Protection has the responsibility for administering the Disability Cash Transfer Programme. The programme is coordinated by district commissioners with District Disability Committees assisting in identifying eligible individuals. Through the Department of Social Protection councils/local authorities do offer transport to school for some disabled children.

## 6 Non-Governmental Organizations

Non-Governmental Organizations offer childcare and protection services to children with disabilities and victims of violence. Childcare and protection services in Botswana are widely delivered by the following non-governmental organizations:

**The Botswana Council for the Disabled (BCD)** was registered in 1980. The BCD is an umbrella body for NGOs providing services to persons with disabilities in Botswana. It coordinates the operation of member NGOs which are involved in rehabilitation, education, vocational training, and skills training for people with disabilities. It is also involved in advocacy work and has been very vocal in agitating for both a revised national policy on people with disabilities and in demanding specific legislation to deal with PWDs.

**ChildLine**, provides both emergency and longer-term counselling and support services, as well as services to support child victims through the court process, if cases go to court. Some services have been specifically established to provide services established for child victims of sexual assault while others are specifically for disabled children.

**The Botswana Society for the Deaf (BSTS)** is a non-profit organization mandated to empower and promote the interests and welfare of the deaf in Botswana. They advocate for the rights of the deaf population in Botswana, educate and empower the socially and economically disadvantaged, and provide facilities for use by deaf individuals.

**Pudulogong Rehabilitation and Development Centre** is a charitable non-profit organization, which came into being in 1982 to support visually impaired people in the country who had nowhere to go owing to the lack of suitable skills for employment. It is the first institution of its kind in the country, as the educational system formerly did not have provisions for disabled persons. The Centre has now taken on a new face and has diversified from handicraft skills to a Vocational Training Programme. It provides job opportunities after training and also aims to help trainees to be self-sustainable and less dependent.

## 7 International Conventions

Violence against children with disabilities is multifaceted and a cross-cutting issue for two major United Nations (UN) conventions and their respective committees. This section provides an overview of the Convention on the Rights of Persons with Disabilities (CRPD) and the Convention on the Rights of the Child (UNCRC).

### The Convention on the Rights of Persons with Disabilities (CRPD)

The CRPD is an international human rights convention which sets out the fundamental human rights of people with disability. On 12 August 2021, the United Nations office issued a notification (Ref: C.N.216. 2021.TREATIES-IV.15) communicating Botswana's accession to the Convention on the Rights of Persons with Disabilities (CRPD) with effect from 11 August 2021. The ratification of the convention gives the government of Botswana an opportunity to develop national legal frameworks for disability rights, guided by the norms contained in the CRPD (Southern Africa Litigation Centre, 2021).

The purpose of the United Nations Convention on the Rights of Persons with Disabilities (CRPD) is to promote, protect, and ensure the full and equal enjoyment of all human rights and fundamental freedoms by all persons with disabilities, and to promote respect for their inherent dignity. It is made up of two documents: the Convention on the Rights of Persons with Disabilities, which contains the main human rights provisions expressed as a series of articles, and the Optional Protocol to the Convention on the Rights of Persons with Disabilities (UN, 2006).

## The United Nation Convention on the Rights of the Child (UNCRC)

The United Nation Convention on the Rights of the Child, adopted in 1989, and the UN Convention on the Rights of Persons with Disabilities (CRPD), adopted in 2006, mutually reinforce each other to provide protection against violence aimed at children with disabilities. The rights and principles contained in the CRC, such as the rights to education, health, recreation, and participation, apply to all children, including those with disabilities. This general convention on children also contains specific guarantees for children with disabilities. Additionally, the CRPD, a general convention on persons with disabilities, contains specific guarantees for children. Given that one relates to the specificities of children and the other to the specificities of living with a disability, both conventions are essential to ensuring that children with disabilities are protected from violence (EU, 2015).

## 8 Violence Against Children with Disabilities in Botswana

### Corporal Punishment

Corporal punishment is a disciplinary method in which a supervising adult deliberately inflicts pain upon a child in response to a child's unacceptable behaviour and/or inappropriate language (AACAP, 2014). Excessive corporal punishment is a violation of children's rights to respect for physical integrity and human dignity, health, development, education, and freedom from torture and other cruel, inhumane or degrading treatment or punishment.

In Botswana, corporal punishment is practised at homes; hence, it is not surprising that it is still a norm even in schools. For most Batswana, the idiom "spare the rod and spoil the child" is a truism that should be practised in order to instil discipline in children. In fact, the practice is so prevalent that even the country's laws recognize it as a form of punishment for people who commit minor offences. Mosikare (2020) stated that, past and former students in all basic education public schools in Botswana will attest to having been caned at some point in their journey of education. Many of the disabled children in Botswana have been exposed to this system, which not only inflicts pain but can also inspire fear.

## Use of Vulgar Language and Derogatory Names

Many disabled people live in isolation and shame behind closed doors because of their condition. Some suffer additional emotional pain which arises from being treated as a curse or embarrassment for the family. It is common for children with disability to be called derogatory names such as "*segole*" loosely meaning "one with disability," or "*setsenwa*," one with madness. Some parents still have a habit of referring to children with derogatory names and they seem not to care at all. Many people still link disability with superstition and revenge for the commission of crimes. The resultant attitudes then force the disabled to hide and shy away from seeking help even when it is available. Back in the old days it was very common that upon the arrival of visitors a child living with disability was taken far away where no one would see them, and they would not interact with people. A teacher in Gaborone had the following to say:

> In some of our schools there are children who are loosely termed as 'slow learners'. Slow learners typically don't have a disability, even though they need extra support. Cognitive abilities are too high for these learners to be considered for an Intellectual Disability. However, the abilities are usually too low to be considered for a Learning Disability. Because these take time and a series of assessment we do get students who are very slow in writing, who struggle to pronounce words. Such students are often subjected to both emotional and physical abuse in schools where they find themselves on the receiving end of corporal punishment and called derogatory or deforming names such as 'sematla...ledela' meaning 'idiot'. Such words are painful to children, and they have far reaching consequences as they tend to kill children's confidence."

## Sexual Abuse

All children are vulnerable to sexual abuse; however, literature shows women and girls with disabilities are even more vulnerable to all forms of violence, including physical, emotional, economic, structural, and sexual violence, in comparison with those without disabilities (Dunkle et al., 2018). According to Kvam (2005), literature shows that this vulnerability is fuelled by double discrimination based on disability and its intersection with negative gendered norms and attitudes. The 2014 Gap report stated that societies where gender inequality and violence against women are endemic, women and girls with disabilities are, therefore, even more likely to experience violence. Already Botswana is rated second-highest in the world for numbers of rape cases and the nation is troubled by cases of gender-based violence where children are sexually abused. Communities see the teenage pregnancies of children living with disabilities, yet their perpetrators are either hardly brought to justice or get off scot-free. Apart from the causing of sexual harassment and violence, child marriages and forced marriages are a concern. This has been a major problem in Botswana during the COVID-19 home confinement. Below are some of the harsh realities that children with disability encounter on a daily basis.

> Girls with visual impairments don't know where to run to for protection when approached by predators. I've heard stories of blind girls who unsuspectingly walk on the street and ask for directions and someone says, 'I'll help you, I'll guide you,' and they are led into places where they are raped. (Resident of Gaborone City)
>
> Young boys living with disabilities are usually molested and abused by older men and women in the society and their problems are hardly known. This could be because communities don't know much about children with disability and how to deal with them. For girls it may be easy to know when they have been sexually abused when we see them pregnant, but boys, it is so difficult. Even when there is a change of behaviour in a boy child it is usually dismissed, while in actual fact, emotionally, there is a battle they are going through. (Social worker)
>
> Sometimes the people living with disabilities are hesitant to report to the police out of fear of stigma and possible communication barrier. This compels them to continue staying with the perpetrator who continues with the violence because there is no sign-language access to where they would report. I therefore appeal to the law enforcers across Botswana to be at their best in the matter of models suitable for communication with the disabled persons. (Member of Botswana Society For The Deaf (BSFTD))

## Child Labour

Children with disabilities also face economic and social hardships as they are vulnerable to being forced into child labour and are more likely to face the threats of violence, neglect, and abuse. Too many children acquire physical, cognitive, and emotional disabilities from child labour, and too many children already with disabilities continue to be recruited into it. These violations of human rights often involve the worst forms of child labour, such as hazardous work, bonded labour, and child trafficking, and can lead to serious injury, sexual exploitation, and death.

A social worker in Gaborone stated that:

Societal attitudes and perceptions and culture have made it in such a way that a child with disability is not important and does not matter. That is why there are cases where some are taken from their families to go and work at the farms where no one will see them or consider their work load.

## 9   Factors Contributing to Violence Against Children with Disability in Botswana

### Lack of Children's Voices

Botswana is a signatory to a children's convention, the UHCRC, which emphasizes that the views of children need to be given due weight in decisions affecting their lives. Children's rights are rarely acknowledged by adult duty-bearers. In African culture, when there is a gathering, children are not supposed to talk when elders talk; it is actually something of a taboo for children to express themselves. It is this kind of culture that breeds a hostile environment towards children with disability, making them even more vulnerable to abuse.

### Lack of Human Capacity/Public Education

The child protection system comprises police officers, social workers, health officers, and community leaders who lack the skills to interact with the disabled. For instance, the police and social workers are incognizant of deaf culture and are unable to communicate with deaf persons. Services rendered by the child protection system are not inclusive, as it seems they cater for people who are able-bodied only. There is also the problem of inaccessible information as some forms of communication like posters and graphics do not cater for those who have visibility challenges.

### Societal Perceptions and Attitudes

Sadly, there is a common and disturbing attitude that society holds about people with disabilities, a false belief that the dreams, aspirations, and desires of an "able-bodied" person change the minute they become sick or disabled. Our society devalues a person with a disability and assumes that they could not possibly want the same things as an able-bodied person. Society's intolerance of difference and lack of understanding about disability may lead to disabled children being considered less than human and not worthy of care. They may be seen as having no feelings, and therefore as suffering no emotional consequences after being abused or neglected.

## Structural Barriers

Children with disability encounter structural barriers in accessing education, employment, health services, social events, and leisure pursuits which are inherent in the service facilities in Botswana. Infrastructure such as buildings and transport are not user-friendly for the disabled. In some instances, a child reporting their problem sometimes lacks privacy because wheelchairs cannot be brought into offices; thus, they will have to narrate their concerns in the open, outside the building. It is difficult for children with disability to use public transport and, moreover, it is expensive for their caregivers to hire private cars.

## Gaps in the Legislature

The law does not favour children with disability, in most instances. They are required to provide proof of accusations and identify perpetrators, describing what they looked like and the items of clothing they were wearing. This is a hindrance to justice. Furnishing such proof is difficult as some of the victims are blind or partially blind or deaf and cannot identify these perpetrators, therefore, perpetrators get away with crimes as they do not get convicted. Mentally ill or intellectually challenged people often face challenges as they are not believed owing to their mental state.

## Lack of Data on Violence against CwD

Data on violence against children with disabilities is scarce. This could be for several reasons. First, data in child protection systems such as the police is not disaggregated. For instance, if there is a case of sexual violence against a child with disability it is grouped with cases involving the able-bodied. Second, institutions are working in "silos" and this affects the quality of the data as there is inconsistency. Third, because of communication barriers, some cases of violence never reach the right officers such as the police. To a large degree people with disability are rarely actively involved in the process of research on disability, and mostly participate passively.

# 10 Conclusion and Recommendations

This chapter looked at the violence that occurs against children with disabilities and the challenges that children with disability encounter. The chapter has noted several challenges. Although the government recognizes children with disability, not much has been done to support them. For instance, the constitution of Botswana is silent on people living with disability; the policy is still pending enactment. Furthermore, challenges such as inaccessible buildings, transport, attitudes and perception, stigma, and the poor coordination of institutions are an obstacle to CwD. There is scarcity of data about those living with disability. This chapter proposes some recommendations for implementation with a view to putting them into operation.

The government should be inclusive and, thus, reinforce children's visibility in policymaking and programmes. Children with disability should be given a national platform where they can be involved in decision making, especially on matters that affect them.

There is a need to build the capacity of children with disability to prevent, identify, and manage violence. The government of Botswana should invest in empowerment-focused approaches that direct substantial resources towards: (1) providing individuals with disabilities with the information and tools that they need to prevent and stop abuse; (2) linking them with support from peers, advocates, and professionals that they can trust to assist them; and (3) proactively communicating that persons with disabilities have a right to be safe, that experiencing violence or abuse is neither their fault nor a sign of incompetence, and that they can manage abuse in their lives by trusting themselves and using their tools and means of support.

The government should deploy skilled staff across the child protection system so that children with disability do not struggle when they have compelling matters that need to be attended to at various places such as hospitals, police-stations, and social welfare offices and so forth.

Promoting awareness of the rights of children with disabilities is the responsibility of disability service organizations who should raise public awareness of the rights of disabled children and challenge stereotypes and misinformation about disability. In this process it is critical that disabled children represent themselves in all matters that concern them. Therefore, it is necessary to adopt an inclusive approach. There is a need for the collaboration of various sectors and entities to offer public education on how society should interact with children with various disabilities. Public education is critical as it is likely to minimize negative attitudes, negative perceptions, and stigma.

Structural access barriers could be addressed through the implementation of system-wide policies. It is important to highlight that information on the rights of PWDs is embedded in policy documents which are inaccessible to most persons, therefore, all relevant documents should be made available in all accessible formats in order to cater for people living with disability. In addition, infrastructure should be user-friendly and accessible to everyone.

A coordinated multi-sectoral approach needs to be adopted to support the government in generating disaggregated data and evidence on the well-being of children, specifically children living with disability. The availability of data is essential in order to achieve greater national commitment to children with disabilities. Sound data provides the foundation for the establishment of sound policies, strategic plans, and effective services and support.

# Bibliography

AACAP. (2014). *Corporal Punishment in Schools*. https://www.aacap.org/AACAP/Policy_Statements/1988/Corporal_Punishment_in_Schools.aspx. Accessed 14 May 2023.

ACPF. (2011). *Children with Disabilities in South Africa: The Hidden Reality*. The African Child Policy Forum. http://uhambofoundation.org.za/new_wp/wp-content/uploads/2016/06/2011-ACPF-Children-with-disabilities-in-South-Africa-The-hidden-reality.pdf

Adugna, M. B., Nabbouh, F., Shehata, S., Ghahari, S. (2020). Barriers and Facilitators to Healthcare Access for Children with Disabilities in Low and Middle Income Sub-Saharan African Countries: A Scoping Review. *BMC Health Services Research, 20*, 15. https://doi.org/10.1186/s12913-019-4822-6. https://bmchealthservres.biomedcentral.com/articles/10.1186/s12913-019-4822-6

Better Care Network. (2018). *Children with Disabilities*. https://bettercarenetwork.org/library/particular-threats-to-childrens-care-and-protection/children-with-disabilities. Accessed 15 June 2022.

Collins, O. (2020). Violence Against Children with Special Needs: Types, Causes and Health Consequences. *International Journal of Health and Pharmaceutical Research, 5*(3), 1–6.

Disability and Human Rights. (2014). https://www.hhrguide.org/2014/03/21/disability-and-human-rights/. May 2015, 2023.

Dunkle, K., Van der Heijden, I., Stern, E., & Chirwa, E. (2018). Disability and Violence Against Women and Girls. *Global Programme. July 2018 Brief*, London. pp. 1–6.

European Union. (2015). *Violence against Children with Disabilities: Legislation, Policies and Programmes in the EU*. Publications Office of the European Union.

Government of Botswana. (2009). *Children's Act*.

Grech, S., & Soldatic, K. (2016). *Disability in the Global South*. Springer.

Haslam, D. (2015). A Massive Step Forward and a Wakeup Call to Include People with Disabilities. *The Huffington Post*. http://www.huffingtonpost.co.uk/dominic-haslam/a-massive-step-forward-people-with-disabilities_b_7941638.html. Accessed 17 May 2023.

Jones, L., Bellis, M. A., Wood, S., Hughes, K., McCoy, E., Eckley, L., & Officer, A. (2012). Prevalence and Risk of Violence Against Children with Disabilities: A Systematic Review and Meta-Analysis of Observational Studies. *Lancet, 380*(9845), 899–907.

Kangere, M. (2003). *A Paper Presented at an Expert Meeting for Inclusion of Disability in Dutch Development Co-operation Policy and Practice*. The Hague.

Krug, E. G. (2002). *World Report on Violence and Health*. World Health Organisation.

Kvam, M. H. (2005). Experiences of Childhood Sexual Abuse Among Visually Impaired Adults in Norway: Prevalence and Characteristics. *Journal of Visual Impairment & Blindness, 99*(1), 241–251.

Lekobane, K. R., & Seleka, T. B. (2017). Determinants of Household Welfare and Poverty in Botswana, 2002/2003 and 2009/2010. *Journal of Poverty, 21*(1), 42–60.

Mosikare, L. (2020). *Schools Spare the Cane*. https://www.mmegi.bw/ampArticle/188712. Accessed 14 May 2023.

Njelesani, J., Hashemi, G., Cameron, C., et al. (2018). From the Day They are Born: A Qualitative Study Exploring Violence Against Children with Disabilities in West Africa. *BMC Public Health, 18*, 153.

Omotoye, M. (2018). *Public Policy Implementation Prospects and Challenges in Botswana: Case of the National Policy on Care for People with Disabilities* (Working Paper No. 49). Botswana Institute for Development Policy Analysis (BIDPA), Gaborone.

Southern Africa Litigation Centre. (2021). *Ratification of the Convention on the Rights of Persons with Disabilities in Botswana*. https://www.southernafricalitigationcentre.org/2021/08/16/ratification-of-the-convention-on-the-rights-of-persons-with-disabilities-in-botswana/. Accessed 27 May 2023.

Sullivan, P. M. (2009). Violence Exposure Among Children with Disabilities. *Clinical Child and Family Psychology Review, 12*, 196–216.

WHO. (2021). *Corporal Punishment and Health*. https://www.who.int/news-room/fact-sheets/detail/corporal-punishment-and-health. Accessed 14 May 2023.

UN. (2006). *Convention on the Rights of Persons with Disabilities (CRPD)* https://humanrights.gov.au/our-work/disability-rights/united-nations-convention-rights-persons-disabilities-uncrpd. Accessed 27 May 2023.

UN. (2014). *The Convention on the Rights of Persons with Disability: Training Guide* (No. 19). United Nations Human Rights Commissioners Office.

UNDP. (2021). *Inequality in Botswana: An Analysis of The Drivers and District-level Mapping of Selected Dimensions of Inequality*. Gaborone, Botswana.

UNFPA. (2018). *The Botswana National Relationship Study*. Gaborone, Botswana.

US Department of Justice. (2010). *Justice Department's 2010 ADA Standards For Accessible Design Into Effect*. No. 12–328.

# Nature, Religion and Cultural Violence in Africa

# Violence against Nature in African Traditional Thought and Practice

Obert Bernard Mlambo and Kudzanai Melody Mlambo

African traditional thought and beliefs do not permit the treatment of nature (flora and fauna) as mere things or commodities. It has been argued that, in general, Shona environmental taboos transcend simple prohibitions relating to certain sacred sites, plants and nonhuman animal species, pools, rivers, and so on, and that they enforce a desirable and sustainable use of the environment (Gelfand, 1979). In this regard, Gelfand has reiterated that a critical study of avoidance rules entails that correct behaviour and attitude to the environment is emphasized. Thus, traditional beliefs, taboos, and sacred places allow analysis of such practices and beliefs as means of preventing environmental degradation. This chapter, while not denying that there is some validity to this conception, acknowledges African beliefs and practices that are not so friendly to the environment, and departs from an overly one-sided and romantic view of the role of African traditional beliefs and myths in shaping attitudes to nature. While we agree that myths are tools through which people think—templates for conceptual thought about the universe and the environment—we argue that there is a difference between cultural thinking and critical thinking (see McClymont, 2018). Myths and

O. B. Mlambo (✉)
Classical Studies Section, School of Languages and Literatures, Rhodes University, Makhanda, South Africa
e-mail: obertmlambo@gmail.com

K. M. Mlambo
TH KÖLN, Köln, Germany

traditional beliefs are interpretive templates which provide a framework for making sense of cultural worldviews and processes. Mythology and traditional beliefs are part of culture and involve cultural thinking (McClymont, 2018), whereby one imbibes beliefs from the air one breathes or the surrounding culture and not through critical reasoning. Cultural reason exists in primal and ancient cultures generally and even in modern contexts when one accepts belief uncritically (McClymont, 2018). The mythical worldview has reference points in tradition and everyday life, but excites wonder and reverence, and not always critical reflexivity. The violence against nature that we examine in this chapter exposes the differences between cultural reasoning and critical thinking. Violent actions against nature committed in certain cultural processes betray cultural reasoning as opposed to critical thinking. We therefore critique the benefits of African traditional beliefs and myths in preserving the environment, exploring how such practices are in some respects violent towards the natural environment and to human beings.

We seek to demonstrate the violent tendencies against nature implicit and explicit within traditional African attitudes towards nature. Such attitudes to nature are not static; they have changed and still change as the African life-milieu has changed and continues to change. We thus acknowledge that attitudes to nature must be contextualized in relation to their various milieus, and their meanings also change according to their milieu. Likewise, the sacred (involving deities and rituals) is experienced in relation to its various milieus. African society, like every other society, has evolved from the milieu of nature, through the milieu of society, to the milieu of technology (see Ellul's theory of the three milieus (Ellul, 1989: 89–140). The dominant power of a milieu assumes one of three forms: nature, society, or technology (Stivers, 1993: 510). In traditional African settings, the power of nature continues to determine human-animal/plant relations, even in the era of technology (see McClymont & Mlambo, 2016). A milieu, as defined by Stivers (1993: 509) "is an environment, at once both material and symbolic, in which humans face their most formidable problems and from which they derive the means of survival and the meaning of life." The African traditional lifestyle and belief system have persisted in the milieu of technology in such a way that it is worthwhile framing the African's relationship with nature in terms of the concept of violence.

Stivers has argued that every milieu has a principle by which it experiences renewal. Nature experiences renewal through the feast, society through sacrifice, and technology through consumption (Stivers, 1993: 509). Drawing upon this formulation of the renewal of milieus, we examine how in African culture, for example, the idea of feasts and sacrifice may violate nature, at least through the lens of modern perspectives on violence to nature. Mbiti has observed that the African is notoriously religious: "Wherever the African is, there is his religion: he takes it to the fields where he is sowing or harvesting a new crop. ... [I]f he is a politician he takes it to the house of parliament" (Mbiti, 1969: 1). Religion, Mbiti states, is by far the richest part of the African heritage found in all areas of human life. The African has not been changed entirely by technological ways of living. He has not abandoned his religion, as he still looks towards nature for reified religious symbols which he appropriates in ritual practices, involving feasts and sacrifices. As Stivers (1993: 511) notes, myth and ritual, as they are known to us, come from societies already in the milieu of society or in transition to it. The African is, thus, existing in the milieu of society where myths and ritual are a common feature. For Mbiti (1969: 167) religion for Africans is more than anything else; it is religion which colours their understanding of the universe and their empirical participation in that universe, making life a profoundly religious phenomenon. We therefore locate the African as simultaneously living in the three milieus of nature, society, and technology.

We are cognizant of the conceptual and practical challenges inherent in the traditional understanding of the African's relations with nature. For traditional Africans, there seems to have been no sense of moral good and evil in the milieu of nature, where evil was experienced in the form of misfortune such as disease, famine, suffering, and death, as "moments of the cosmic totality"(see Eliade, cited in Stivers, 1993: 512). One particular conceptual challenge is that the African, for example, does not think it an unlawful form of violence to kill a goat for ritual purposes, nor does he/she think it violence to put a spell onto a chicken or a goat and drive them away from human custody, to cause them to roam freely in landscapes that are not their natural habitats (see Mlambo and Chitando, forthcoming). A second challenge involves the use of the concept of violence in explaining attitudes to nature within African traditional culture, which has not developed the concept of animal rights (see Horsthemke, 2015). We ascribe the lack of a conception of unlawful violence to animals to the mythical belief system of African traditional society. Stivers (1993: 508) argued that religious myths, by their nature, conceal the act of murder as scapegoating; instead they represent the murdered as fully deserving to be killed. Simultaneously, however, the ritual victim is sacralized and transformed into a deity who now can be made to work for the benefit of society (ibid.). We shall demonstrate how a similar logic of violence operates in an African context.

To make a case for our appropriation of the concept of violence in the present task, we draw upon Girard's theory of the scapegoat to frame our argument, which relates to the case of the African's ritual killing of animals and fellow humans. The latter are killed for possessing some physical features of difference that are deemed inauspicious for the prosperity and well-being of the community, while the former are killed for sacrificial purposes. We thus particularly seek to explore the logic of ritual violence against animals and crops, and also instances of violence against people with albinism, individuals with a physical or mental disability, twins, triplets, or quadruplets that have been recorded in some parts of Africa. Girard argued that ritual scapegoating, sacrifice, and rites of all sorts have their origin in an act of killing (Stivers, 1993: 507–508). Members of a society are united by their consensus to kill a scapegoat for the good of the entire community.

Stivers (1993: 507) has the following to say about Girard's theory:

> The first stereotype is that of the crisis. Some event perceived as momentous, externally or internally provoked causes people to act increasingly similarly, such as hoarding food during the time of famine...The second stereotype is about the "crime" that precipitated the homogeneity of behavior, the loss of social differences...The third stereotype concerns universal signs for the choice of the scapegoat. The victims are always those who are different, whether ethnically, culturally, or physically; the differences must be readily observable...The victim is ultimately condemned for not being different in a manner appropriate to cultural assumptions.

Before exploring violent acts against nature framed in terms of Girard's scapegoat theory, we start by examining Shona names that capture violent images of violence against nature. We analyse a number of Shona names that are pregnant with environmental meaning and connotation. The names also refer to or relate to crops, wild birds, or animals. We start off with the name *chimedzanemburungwe* (one who swallows a fruit together with its seeds). The word *mburungwe* means "seed," and *chimedza* means one who "swallows." The whole word is a demonstration of cultural knowledge regarding the importance of seeds as guarantee of the propagation of the plant species. Implied by the name, is knowledge that seed must not be destroyed, but spared for future cultivation. Thus, the word *chimedzanemburungwe* is used to describe a person who destroys everything—someone who leaves nothing standing for the future. This name was used to describe individuals with such destructive tendencies in society. Similarly, the word, *marambatemwa* (holy groves) indicates forests that cannot be cleared. Trees in such forests, literally, as the meaning of the Shona implies, "refuse to be cut down." The word, so to speak, attributes agency to the trees of the forest and instructs society not to think of cutting down such trees, because the sacred trees would not permit anyone to cut them down. That such forests existed is a clear indication that such prohibitions were made to protect the forests from human action. Indeed, human settlements may be made by encroaching into forests. Such forests got cleared to pave the way for human settlements. Cultural wisdom developed myths that would not allow clearing of certain forests, by giving agency to trees in such forests, representing them as trees that defied the axe. That we have forests that were given such names as *marambatemwa* or *kumazivandadzoka* (dangerous forests or mountains not to be ventured into by humans) which demonstrate that traditional thought inscribed some prohibitions and, as it were, put up a "No Through Road" sign to curb violent human exploitation of the environment. Such prohibitive measures speak of existing struggles against violence towards nature in African communities. That trees, unintelligent objects, were given agency to stop humans from cutting them down shows in itself that human agents could not win the war alone. Such prohibitive names given to forests were efforts to repulse bad human action and behaviour.

A similar understanding of violent human action against nature is captured in descriptions of Zimbabwe's violent land redistribution programme instigated by Zimbabwe's guerrilla war veterans, that reached boiling levels between 1998–2008. Field work conducted by one of the writers of this chapter revealed how Zimbabwe's liberation war veterans were referred to in some places by the moniker *zvimedzanemburungwe* (this is the plural of the word *chimedzamburungwe* mentioned earlier). This nickname was given by the farm workers of former white farmers, whose harvest and fruit trees were plundered by the war veterans. Orange plantations and sugar estates, for example, were harvested with reckless abandon (see Buckle, 2001, 2002; Barker, 2001, 2007). The name *zvimedzanemburungwe* was often used together with the word *vanarandazha* meaning "plunderers" or *vanakadyakwande* lit. "people who eat a lot without getting nourished" which were used to describe the veterans' limitless appetite for expropriation, not only of land but anything they found on farms, although they lacked the aptitude for farming. The last-mentioned word was also used to mock the war veterans for expropriating farms, yet failing to become rich, always depending on government handouts for survival. The liberation war veterans were in some places called *vanamupisasango,* or arsonists. This was in reference to acts of arson on white-owned farms by war veterans and their supporters. The same were also mockingly called *Nzvoveramukobodo* a word used to describe one who destroys things noisily and carelessly! The word captures the absence of peace and tranquillity that characterized farms formerly owned by whites. During the violent expropriations, the noise of gunshots, swearing, and the hurling of insults as war veterans plundered many farms was common. There was yet another word, *Vanamavhunga*, used to describe violent activity by liberation war veterans on the farms that they occupied. The word has a double meaning. Literally, it describes violence among plants in a field, where parasitic plants tend to dwarf smaller and weaker ones, in the process depriving smaller crops of sunshine, air, and nutrients. In the context of the liberation war veterans, their violent activities and behaviour were seen as disruption of normal phenomena, or disruption of normal life on the farms through macho and dominating behaviour.

Some names reveal an awareness of violence against nature among the Shona people, in the process, describing the violation of the environment by social miscreants. The name *Mungoshi*, from the verb *kungosha* (to defecate), for example, means someone who defecates in inappropriate places, someone who contaminates the environment with their faeces. Such violators of nature are also branded *varoyi* (witches), who do not act in accordance with the protective moral environmental code enshrined in African traditional thought and spirituality (see Daneel, 1987). The code, it must be stated, is not a written code, but an oral one, as enshrined in what the community elders execrate as good and what they denounce as evil and harmful to the environment. The word *muroyi* (witch) conveys the act of causing spiritual trouble. Thus, those who defile the environment are also perceived as violators of the spiritual order of cosmos. Societal miscreants who violate the environment are also referred to as *nhundiramutsime* (a name describing someone who urinates in a well or any fresh water body). The same characters are also labelled *maboorangoma* (literally those who pierce the drum to spoil the dance party), or *mharadzi* (destroyers).

It is an important cultural tenet among the Shona people that land (including everything therein) should belong to the living, the unborn, and the dead. It is for this reason that among the Shona no one has liberty to gather wild fruits wastefully, wantonly cut down trees, hunt certain animals, or pollute certain water bodies in areas or places regarded as sacred. It is true that Shona religious beliefs play an integral role in determining positive values and attitudes towards the environment and are a crucial component of any efficacious environmental policy among communities (see Schofeleers, 1978). Yet we should not over-romanticize this aspect of African tradition and ignore the other side of the coin. At the practical level, there is a descriptive language that captures acts of violence against nature. A violent method of harvesting fruits from a tree is succinctly called *kukwazha* (purging). The violent clearing of trees is known as *kukuhuna* (deforestation). *Mutemarege wembada* is also a loaded adverb, that describes a violent and unsparing way of extracting resources, as does a leopard when killing its prey. The foregoing define crime and catalogue behaviour characteristic of violent and harmful actions against the environmental common good. The ancient Greek philosophy of Aristotle had a more or less similar understanding of violations committed against nature by humans. He developed the concept of "natural" and "violent" in which violence was generally understood as causing something to act against nature (Aristotle *Metaphysics* Book 5 1015a). Africans traditionally believed in a world in which ancestors were present in nature. The humans existing on earth were expected to be in solidarity with all creation, and with the ancestors through the tribal elders' rules that prohibited tree felling in the traditional holy groves (*marambatemwa*) of the ancestors (Daneel, 1987: 69).

Ancestral spirits were, therefore, part of nature, hence the need to reverence the earth. Ecological violence was therefore, perpetrated against nature when people neglected contour ridges, practised riverbank cultivation, permitted overgrazing of pastures, and felled trees without planting any in return, which caused soil erosion. Such activities violated the good earth by taking it for granted and exploiting it without nurturing or reverencing it (Daneel 1987: 67). Such violence against the earth is evidenced by "barren, denuded plains, erosion gullies, unprotected riverbanks and clouds of wind-eroded dust" (Daneel, 1987: 67). That human actions against nature are understood as violence in the context of African traditional thought is evidenced by the stigmatization of offences which cause firewood shortage, soil erosion, poor crops, and the absence of wildlife as forms of wizardry—the gravest of all sins, threatening not only human survival but all other forms of life (ibid.).

## 1 Ngozi and Violence against Animals

In the African belief system of dealing with issues of restorative justice and healing, animals and plants play a central role. Theoretically, injuries can be the result of many causes. What is more, some injuries are not physical, but psychological and spiritual. There is a Shona proverb: *mushonga wengozi kuiripa* (The remedy for a vengeful spirit lies in paying for damages inflicted against the victim). A person might have been killed, and the murderer would be expected to placate the spirit of his/her victim. In dealing with the avenging *ngozi* spirit of a victim of murder, the cure can be prescribed in form of handing over a female child from one family to another. A child represents hope, future, joy, and posterity. The violence comes in the decision to single out that which stands for hope in a family, to hand over the child to another family as compensation for a murder committed by a relative. There is a sacrificial element in using a girl child to pay the debt of those who committed the crime. The girl child stands as a banished victim. Once something is banished, it is exposed to violent elements, and as such she ceases to enjoy the care and protection of her former parents. Psychological violence also may affect the child as she may suffer from loneliness and the feeling of being unwanted. The mother of the child is also violated. Society made her to give birth to a child that she will not raise—giving birth in order to make payment to the *ngozi*.

There was in African traditional belief systems some collective violence, carried out as a mechanism that created myths, in which a significant cause was always sought at the level of social relations where a human scapegoat was identified as a victim. Twins or people with albinism were usually identified as scapegoats. A twin or albino might be deemed the unique cause of a plague, drought, or misfortune in a family or community, in which case the drought or plague became theirs to dispose of through their deaths. The remedy for the misfortune lay in banishing them from society or disposing of them at birth. Such violent disposal of twins and people with albinism involved projection on to them, in Girardian fashion, the paranoid suspicion of the community suffering from a drought or plague. Thus twins or people with albinism or even children born with deformities were disposed of, as the extermination of too unacceptably different individuals for the sake of community cohesion accounted for the logic of violence against individuals.

Sometimes belief in *ngozi* (an aggrieved spirit of a murdered person or someone who has been the victim of a grave injustice prior to death): see above and also (Gelfand, 1959: 153; Daneel, 1971: 133–140), led to violent action against both animals and humans. The *ngozi* spirit in customary law and traditional religion wreaks havoc in the offender's family through illness and death. The *ngozi* spirit has a legitimate claim to full compensation in the form of up to ten sacrificial beasts called *mitumbu* (literally "corpses" or "bodies," since they pay for the corpse of the deceased) (Daneel, 1987: 84). In some cases the offender's relatives also provide the *ngozi* with a young wife, who must sweep and tend the small hut specifically erected for her disgruntled "spirit-husband."

In Girardian terms, violence is sacred, as it is the source of the order and unity of society against the scapegoat (Girard, 1987: 32). Acts of murder are kept alive not only in myths, but are systematically repeated in ritual, in which the re-enactment is often an enactment of murder, where sometimes there may be a substitution for the ritual victim—animals or crops may become symbolic surrogates (Stivers, 1993: 508).

Religious phenomena, Girard (1987: 37) argues, are often characterized by a double transference: aggressive transference and reconciliatory transference. The latter transference sacralizes the victim, but is easily forgotten or lost, as humans are capable of hating their victims and as a result not sacralizing them (Girard, 1987: 37). The murder of albinos for ritual purposes expresses this logic in an African context, where the murdered albino is used as magic to cause good fortune. There is, however, an element of veneration of the murdered victim, as their spirit is regarded as something that can cause good fortune for a successful business venture. Outside the context of albinos, in some cases, rituals involve killing one's own mother, sister, or brother, whose death is believed to cause success in one's business enterprise.

## 2   Traditional Medicine

The process of making herbal medicine involved *kupurura mashizha emuti*, the violent reaping of leaves from a herb or shrub. Some medicines are produced from tree bark removed from a tree trunk, leaving the tree without both the inner bark and the outer bark.

In traditional custom, when people harvest honey from a tree, the tree whose trunk will be sheltering the bees is cut down to the ground. When people extract the honey, fire is used to smoke out the bees in the process. Sometimes as many as ten buckets of honey are extracted during winter season. The whole idea of harvesting honeycombs can seem cruel, as all year round the bees would have gone into the flowers looking for nectar to make honey which they would feed on during the cold season when they could not fly out of the hive. By a cruel irony that is precisely the time when people go out to harvest the honey, at a time when the bees have no other source of food. This means a great number of bees die. Nine buckets of honey means that several generations of bees would die, as this could have fed the bees for three or more years.

## 3   African Agrarian Thought: Violence against Nature in African Wisdom Literature

African traditional agrarian thought articulates the relation of agriculture and society. It interrogates practices and systems that have a negative bearing to the environment. It explores areas where environmental and/or agricultural science do not link up with human interests.

African agrarian philosophy and history, as contained in proverbs and wisdom literature, provide insights relevant to the topical issue of Zimbabwe's land reform, giving a critically nuanced and balanced view of the costs and benefits of violent land redistribution processes. If the land reform had been pursued without violence, and arson and the destruction of the environment and property, how might society have turned out? What would our agricultural economy likely to have been like? African agrarian thought thus offers some intelligent reflection on land use and the risks of Zimbabwe's current civilization. Agrarian philosophy allows for approaches to agricultural thinking that involve an agrarian land ethic, which evaluates, utilitarian, ecological, and egalitarian approaches to land utilization.

The adage *nhaka haigobgwi* (inheritance should not be sold) is a violent dictum in the context of the African struggles with colonial domination. The adage shows what is not accepted when it comes to the African heritage. It draws the line between friend and enemy. The dictum was and still is used to refer to the violence suffered by Africans when their land was taken by the colonial government. The violence that the African used to reclaim their land is also reflected in the adage. The adage itself is violent. It is a warning posed against fellow Zimbabweans not to support imperialism in any form, as that is deemed an act of giving away one's heritage. The adage is ancient, yet still applied in the postcolonial agrarian contexts of the violent land expropriation that has taken place in Zimbabwe since 1998.

Another aspect of violence has to do with the concept of property in an African context. Prosperity and happiness require the ownership of property. But there is the question of whether we should conceive property or land as privately owned or commonly owned. The African concept of communalism perceives land as communally owned. The Communist thinker Karl Marx believed that ultimately the means of production should be commonly owned. But the biblical concept of "Thou shalt not steal" presupposes the existence of private property (Rommen, 1998: 59). The issue of private versus common ownership remains a hot issue in modern Zimbabwe, when we consider the issue of land titles versus leases, and also when we look at belief in the free market, which emphasizes private property, and belief in a command economy which ultimately treats the means of production as socially owned (McClymont n.d). There are also the issues of justice, contracts, labour issues, exploitation, corruption, and so on which are relevant to farmers and farm workers of all sorts. In Zimbabwe the issue of land reform has been crucial, and there have been people who view it positively as the reclamation of land from the whites, and negatively, linking it with the destruction of the agricultural industry in Zimbabwe.

While we are on the topic of food insecurity, we may note that beggars in Shona communities, while begging for food, always perform a song and dance in which hunger is depicted as thorny and painful—a razor that cuts to pieces one's internal organs. One such song goes: "*Zhara chinangunangu chinangunangu. Zhara chinangunangu. Mudumbu mune reza, mune reza, mudumbu mune reza* (Hunger can prick like thorns, can prick like thorns. In my stomach there is a razor. In my stomach there is a razor). This song demonstrates the link between violence and food shortage.

While in modern times Africans may suffer food shortage, in more ancient times they were vulnerable to the violence of nature itself. The following two proverbs demonstrate an awareness of violence in nature among Africans:

*Chiripo chinenge chariuraya zizi, harifi nemhepo* (There is something that kills the owl; it does not die from the wind). *Charova sei chando chakwidza hamba mumuti?* (How is it that cold weather has come forcibly, that caused a tortoise to climb into a tree?)

People in Africa were aware that in their environment there were sometimes very chilly nights and violently strong winds. This demonstrates that they were aware that nature was violent on its own. The proverbs also suggest that Africans in ancient times were also at the mercy of the extremes of the environment such as the cold and the wind, to which we may add the scorching sun, and flooding among others. We need to remember that Africans formerly lived in caves and later on in huts made from poles and mud. These structures did not always provide adequate protection against nature. Therefore, such proverbs show that they were sometimes vulnerable to the environment.

## 4  Traditional Hunting Practices

Africans in pre-colonial times not only suffered from the violence of nature but were also able to inflict violence on nature itself in their turn, by hunting animals. Yet hunting in traditional times was not conceptually regarded as unlawful violence. Traditionally and religiously these animals were believed to have been provided by the ancestors. For example, finding an animal to hunt, birds to shoot, and even picking mushrooms along one's path were seen as blessings from the ancestors. Hunting enabled humans to survive. They obtained meat and hides for clothes. Thus, hunting was a necessary means for survival. There are totemic clans deemed traditionally to be blessed by the ancestors as great hunters.

In practice, some animals die or break their hooves and disappear without human agency. However, where animals are killed, there is terror in the mind and body of animals. Some animals could be scared as a result of hunting activities and stray into territories that were not their original habitat where they were killed by other animals. Those Africans who killed animals that had strayed in this way did not see it as violence. When fishing, they could catch a frog and smash it against the rock screaming: "*Ndabata ngoro!*" (I caught something useless). At other times they would be angry if they missed their prey and would say: "*Masango matema!*" These words mean literally "black veldt" and allude to the failure by the hunters to find an animal in the course of hunting.

Starting a fire was and is a method of hunting used in most African societies. This method of starting a veldt fire drives animals in the direction where hunters lie in wait expecting to make a kill. The fires often grow uncontrollably huge and have caused huge damage to forests, in the process killing birds, reptiles, and insects. The Shona people have a proverb which was developed from a hunting context: *Tsuro haiponi rutsva kaviri* (A rabbit cannot escape an inferno twice). The proverb boasts that a rabbit may escape a veldt fire, but only once. That the proverb mentions the persistence in occurrence of veldt fires is an indication that they were a frequent phenomenon. There is yet another proverb whose setting and context is from a hunting scene. The proverb goes: *Ateya mariva murutsva haachatyi kusviba magaro* (He who sets up mousetraps in the ashes will not be afraid to dirty their buttocks dirty). This proverb refers to the practice of trapping mice, which could be an unsavoury dirtying process when forests got destroyed by man-made fires. This is an indication that forest fires were such a common feature that a *rutsva* developed to describe the state of charred matter in forests.

The former proverb also describes the merciless attitude of the hunter. In many cases, hunters would insult their prey and mercilessly beat it with hunting clubs: *Waiti wakangwara, nhasi ndakubata! Nhasi sadza rinonduiona!* (This animal thought it was clever, today I caught it! Today I will eat plenty of sadza! So, even after the animal was caught, it was subjected to further violence. This explains the meaning of the proverb *Nzwira pamuviri tsvimbo yarova dapi* (You must hit the big rat until it feels the pain before its death)— The proverb was used in some kind of ritual celebration, when after catching one's animal, the hunter would insult it and hit it up with his club—a violent practice of killing the prey and venting his anger on it after spending the whole day in the scorching sun, running hard, and even getting injured while hunting. Hunters, therefore, used to kill for practice.

The African hunter's violent disposition to animals can be demonstrated more palpably as represented in some African proverbs. *Tsuro haiponi rutsva kaviri* (A hare cannot escape veld fires twice). There was the assumption that the rabbit or hare that escaped, next time, the hunter will get it without fail. There was, therefore, no need to give up or to be merciful the next time they caught their prey.

Another proverb goes thus: *Ateya mariva murutsva haachatyi kusviba magaro*. African people actually praised each other for showing bravery during hunting. One would be looked down upon if they exhibited cowardice. The proverb also shows violent images of arson and veld fires. In this proverb we see wild animals and forests being destroyed by fire. The proverb implies that forests are torched by human beings or by natural causes and animals die as a result.

The two proverbs show that Africans are aware of the violence that visits nature from time to time and from different directions. They are aware that forests or bushes were constantly gutted by fire. The phenomenon of *rutsva* was constant. The burning of bushes was a constant phenomenon in their lives.

We may here reflect on an African proverb, which reveals a lot about African home economics and its impact on the environment. Analysis of this proverb helps us connect domestic economy and the wider kind of economy and shows how agriculture is related to people's responsibilities as citizens. In fact the proverb exposes human actions past and present that can amount to violence against nature. We need to remind ourselves that economics is an issue that is linked to property, and also the land. It involves not only proper management of the household or family but property. There is a link between what we normally think of as economics and what has been traditionally called "home economics" involving cooking and household management as the proverb demonstrates.

The proverb goes: *Akanga nyimo ave ngarara* (One who dares to roast round nuts is a societal rebel.) Roasted round nuts were a delicacy snack in the African family. If a child stole them, he was deemed a rebellious child, as the act of stealing round nuts would mean there was no looking forward to the following planting season. The cultural logic implied in this proverb is that seed must be preserved. The practice of eating seed was a kind of violence against nature as this deprived the fields of the new green crop. The community from which this proverb came depended on farming. Farming was the only way they met half way with nature in order to be productive. By putting seed to soil, they were communicating with nature so that the seed would multiply, so that they would have enough for eating and for trade. If the seed was roasted and eaten there would be nothing to bring them together with nature. The link between mankind and nature was the seed, so when the seed was destroyed, people would just sit around when the rain came. The act of eating seed was similar to the crime of cutting down forests. It distanced Africans from communing with nature. The proverb above shows how African agrarian thought articulated wasteful habits in African households, and also represents humans as drivers of food insecurity. African agrarian thought is, therefore, an important source for ideas on human habits and activities at a household level and their harmful and violent implications on the environment.

What is more, most hunting traps are made from bark fibre (bark with the hard outer cover removed). The process of extracting bark fibre from trees was itself environmentally unfriendly.

Another hunting method involved playing drums in the forest as a strategy to scare animals out of their habitat, so that dogs could be unleashed on them. This hunting method violates the ecosystem. Wild animals in their dens are startled to leave their habitat. Wild birds are also affected as they are suddenly startled into flying away. Singing birds are all of a sudden scared away by the hunters. The more frequently this method was used, the more it scared the birds away. It is one characteristic feature of brooding birds to abandon their nests at the slightest disturbance. Imagine a case where a huge forest of three hectares is burnt— it would need a whole new season for birds to lay eggs again. Some animals like foxes and their young and snakes were killed in forest fires.

There was and still is a traditional method of catching fish using a poisonous substance called *rudu* in Shona, made from the leaves of a certain tree. The substance is thrown into the river and causes fish to get drowsy and to float helplessly on top of the water. Many fish are caught using this method, so that some pools end up without fish altogether.

*Kuchera hunza*, was another method of hunting. A whole herd of buffaloes would be driven into a pit, where both young and small animals would be killed indiscriminately.

The digging up of mice was another cruel method of hunting. The method involved blocking underground holes in order to make sure no single mouse escaped. Through this method, sacks and buckets were filled with mice.

## 5   Cultural Practices

This brings us to the issue of cultural practices, from which we can deduce the meaning of cultural discourses, vocabulary and action (see Rouse, 2007). Social practices derive from customs, beliefs, and symbols, among others. (Schatzki, 2006: 12). Practices, it has been argued, are always embodied. It has been demonstrated by Clifford Geertz (1973) that culture is a matter of publicly observable symbols and rituals and the organization of discourses and practices. Drawing on this, we explore how Shona cultural practices and discourses are productive of a violent disposition towards nature.

A village man in his late 50s, interviewed by one of the authors of this chapter, recalled how his grandfather would disparage him for moving about in the village without a club or any form of weapon as a man (Interview with Mr X: 24 December 2021). Hunting was a practice which society regarded as a manly practice. A real man would not go about without a weapon. Carrying a weapon was seen as a marker of masculinity. "*Uri munhu wemurume wekupi unofamba usina tsvimbo? Ko ukasangana nemhembwe yakakuvara gumbo kana yakabereka unoita sei?* (What kind of man are you, walking around without a club? If you meet an antelope with an injured leg, or one suckling, what are you going to do)? (Ibid.). Boys were chastised for walking without a weapon. There was also a traditional practice that encouraged young children to be violent towards creatures. Kids would be trained to catch locusts to pluck off their legs and wings. A kid who found a bird's nest and caught the bird was usually told by parents to put back the nest in its place, in order that he could also catch the partner of the bird he would have caught earlier. There was no sense in sparing the other bird which survived the first raid.

Our informant's grandfather's remarks that a man must always bear a weapon when journeying, in case he comes across a wounded antelope shows that there was no sense of sparing the wounded antelope. This belief contradicted the celebrated values of Ubuntu, which would seem to demand that a wounded animal or a suckling animal must not be killed.

There is a Shona proverb which celebrates easy chances: "*Mudzimu waro bonga kuwana huku dzichirwa*" (A jackal is lucky to find chickens fighting). Traditional African culture celebrates taking advantage over nature. Easy chances are celebrated where a man is supposed to grab his lordship over nature. If he fails to do that he may as well die. It is natural to kill and eat what comes one's way. To this effect there is another proverb: "*Garwe haridyi chebamba, charo chinoza neronga*" (A crocodile does not struggle for food; it survives through what comes to its habitat, the river). It is natural in traditional Shona culture to eat what comes one's way. There was also a common saying among very recent generations of people now in their 40s and 50s, according to the old man who granted the interview that was quoted above. He remembered as he grew up how they would say: "*Ndakasangana nechimusikana chiya, ishiri yakatyoka bapiro. Hazvina kunditorera nguva kurara naye!*" (I came across that girl, she was a bird with broken wings. It took me no time at all to sleep with her). In this day and age, one would rush to the vet with an injured animal. This does not happen in traditional Shona society. Shona tradition believes that animals do not have an immortal soul.

A careless attitude to nature may also be manifested in the burial of the dead. In Shona culture, after burying a corpse, a tree is cut (which is called in Shona *chizhuzhu*) and placed on the soil mount. All graves in grave yards are marked that way. In general, every grave claimed its tree. In places where there are generally no trees, they use stone boulders hewn from river beds and found in mountains and other places, where these stones hold soils together. This removal of stones has caused environmental degradation due to soil erosion and the siltation of rivers.

Nature is further damaged under modern African village conditions, in which big trees are felled to manufacture the wheels of scotch carts or sledges. Africans are imitating cars in order to manufacture something that may assist them in loading their harvest. This desire to be modern comes at the expense of a large number of trees of various species. One can also mention brick laying in rural communities, where the desire to be modern has led many to dig ditches to obtain the soil used to make bricks for the construction of houses.

## 6   Conclusion

This chapter has demonstrated that African traditional beliefs are not what they seem. A romanticized view of such beliefs ought to be challenged as there is more harm than good in certain attitudes to nature exhibited in behaviours framed by notions of African belief systems. We have demonstrated the violent tendencies against plants and animals within traditional African attitudes towards nature. African societies, it has been noted, are not static. They have drastically changed. The African life-milieu has continued and continues to change. It is therefore important to contextualize the African's attitudes to nature in relation to various social milieus. Africa has evolved from the milieu of nature, through the milieu of society to the milieu of technology. Although in traditional African settings, the power of nature can be seen somewhat to continue to determine human-animal/plant relations, even in the era of technology, attitudes to nature have seen a major shift towards an attitude of ambivalence and disdain to traditional values and belief systems that govern human-animal/plant relations.

## Bibliography

Barker, J. (2007). *Paradise Plundered: The Story of a Zimbabwean Farm.* Jim Barker.
Buckle, C. (2001). *African Tears: The Zimbabwe Land Invasions.* Covos Day.
Buckle, C. (2002). *Beyond Tears: Zimbabwe's Tragedy.* Jonathan Ball.
Daneel, M. L. (1971). Shona Independent Churches and Ancestor Worship. In D. B Barrett, *African Initiatives in Religion*, (pp.161–170). East African Publishing House.
Daneel, M. L. (1987). *Quest for Belonging: Introduction to a Study of African Independent Churches.* Mambo Press.
Eliade, M. (1969). *The Quest.* University of Chicago Press.
Ellul, J. (1989). *What I Believe.* Trans. Geoffrey Bromiley. Grand Rapids, Michigan: Eerdman.
Geertz, C. (1973). *The Interpretation of Cultures.* Basic Books.
Gelfand, M. (1959). *Shona Ritual, with Special Reference to The Chaminuka Cult.*
Gelfand, M. (1979). *Growing up in a Shona Society: From Birth to Marriage.* Mambo Press.
Girard, R. (1987). *Things Hidden Since the Foundation of the World.* Trans. Stephen Bann and Michael Metteer. Stanford University Press.
Girard, R. (1989). *The Scapegoat.* Yvonne Freccero. Trans. Baltimore: The John Hopkins. University Press.
Horsthemke, K. (2015). *Animals and African Ethics.* Palgrave MacMillan.
Mbiti, J. S. (1969). *Africa Religions and Philosophy.* Heinemann Education Books Ltd.
McClymont, J. D. (2018). "Some Misconceptions about Culture: Views from a Zimbabwean Classical Thinker." In F. Mangena & J. D. McClymont (Eds.), *Philosophy, Race and Multiculturalism in Southern Africa*, (pp. 233–250). (The Council for Research in Values and Philosophy).
McClymont, J. D., & Mlambo. O. B. (2016). "African Values in a Modern City: Threats and Benefits." In Magosvongwe, R., O. B. Mlambo, & E. Ndlovu. (Eds.), *Africa's Intangible Heritage and Land: Emerging Perspectives*, (pp. 112–120). University of Zimbabwe Publications.
John, D. MClymont. (n.d.). *Handout 5: Ecotheology, Land and Empire.*
Chitando, E., & Mlambo, O. B. (forthcoming). *Cursed goats in the urban landscapes of Zimbabwe: Exploring African Religious Thought, Spirituality and Development.*
Rommen, H. A. (1998). *The Natural Law.* Liberty Fund Inc. Available online at http://ollresources.s3.amazonaws.com/titles/676/0017_Bk.pdf.

Rouse, J. (2007). "Practice Theory." *Division I Faculty Publications*. 43. https://wesscholar.wesleyan.edu/div1facpubs/43 Accessed 15 March 2020.

Schatzki, T. R. (2006). Introduction: Practice Theory. In T. R. Schatzki, K. K. Cetina, & E. von Savigny (Eds.), *The Practice Turn in Contemporary Theory*, (pp. 10–23). Routledge.

Schoffeleers, J. M. (Ed.). (1978). *Guardians of the Land: Essays on Central African Territorial Cults*. Mambo Press.

Stivers, R. (1993). The Festival in Light of the Theory of the Three Milieus: A Critique of Girard's Theory of Ritual Scapegoating. *Journal of the American Academy of Religion, 61*(3/Autumn), 505–538.

Taringa, N. (2006). How Environmental is African Traditional Religion? *Exchange, 35*(2), 191–214.

# Yearning for Old Time Religion in the Face of Globalization? Interpreting Fundamentalisms and Violent Extremism in Africa

Ezra Chitando

## 1 Introduction

Literature on religion and violence continues to expand (see e.g. Armstrong, 2014; Avalos, 2005; Bartov & Mack, 2001; Cavanaugh, 2009; Kaplan, 2015). Scholars remain preoccupied with unravelling the interface between religion and violence. Can religion, often presented as the highest form of moral accomplishment, be associated with violence, often presented as the lowest form of character failure? Does religion cause violence, or do conflict entrepreneurs in various contexts only appropriate and deploy religion to meet their (non-religious) goals? These questions have been applied to the African context, with scholars interrogating the extent to which religion is implicated in violence in Africa (see e.g. Alao, 2022; Kitts, 2016). In this chapter, I argue that although the violence that is associated with religion cannot and should not be reduced to religion, it would be disingenuous of us as researchers and activists to completely delink religion and violence. This is for two main reasons. First, there are some religious actors who consciously, deliberately, clearly, and unambiguously reference and link their violent actions to religion. Given the phenomenology of religion's emphasis on upholding the point of view of the believer (see e.g. Cox, 1992 and Chitando, 2005), it is strategic to appreciate some religious actors' insistence

E. Chitando (✉)
Department of Philosophy, Religion and Ethics, University of Zimbabwe, Harare, Zimbabwe
e-mail: chitsa21@yahoo.com

that they are motivated by religious convictions when engaging in violence. Second, reflecting on the possible relationship between religion and violence does not necessarily suggest ruling out the (potentially greater) impact of non-religious factors in violence associated with religion. Thus, in this chapter I maintain that globalization might be a helpful concept when reflecting on fundamentalisms and violent extremism in Africa.

Although the chapter suggests a connection between the more recent phenomena of globalization and fundamentalisms and violent extremism, it is vital to acknowledge that the continent of Africa has never been closed and out of bounds to the rest of humanity. History confirms that Africans have always interfaced with people from other continents. Across the different historical epochs, Africans have enjoyed trade relations with individuals and groups from other parts of the world. Within the specific area of religion, African Traditional Religions constitute the "initial, original, aboriginal religion" (Idowu, 1973) which was handed down from one generation to another. However, this religion was not characterized by fundamentalism or narrow interpretations of reality. African Traditional Religions were always open to new revelations and embraced new ideas and objects. The absence of missionary elders to propagate African Traditional Religions (Okeke et al., 2017: 2) generally made them more or less tolerant and open. However, the arrival of missionary religions that made (and still make) absolute truth claims laid the foundation for fundamentalisms and violent extremism in Africa. In particular, militant versions of Christianity and Islam demonized African Traditional Religions and insisted on only one way to salvation. The era of globalization has generated and entrenched fundamentalisms in Africa, although many Africans are resisting these rigid, violent, and extremist versions of reality.

Globalization has contributed to uncertainty in contemporary African lives as it has joined forces with other challenges that threaten human flourishing on the continent, including catastrophes and insecurity (Abrahamsen, 2013). Whereas religion seeks to provide its adherents with a sense of belonging and rootedness, globalization brings these into serious question. Globalization does not brook any rivals and presents itself as irresistible. It seeks to drag everyone, kicking and screaming, into Euro-American value systems, while rubbishing the cherished values and traditions of others. Further, it has brought all the established truths of religion under scrutiny, offering as it does alternative ways of being. According to Stuart Bate (2000: 45–46), "The certainty of the 'authority' of modern Western culture has been replaced by the uncertainty of the present age where 'authority' is increasingly questioned and also diffused to many competing centres". In the quest to recover 'certainty' and 'authority,' fundamentalisms and violent extremism are generated and entrenched. This has led some to commit religion-related armed conflict or terrorism. Others have engaged in sectarian violence, harassment over attire, killing religious competitors over assumed disrespect, and other violent acts.

This chapter contends that fundamentalisms and violent extremism in Africa are inspired by the quest to recover some mythical "old time religion" on the part of some of the followers of missionary religions such as Christianity and Islam, as well as African Traditional Religions (although the greater focus is on the first two). It argues that this search for "old time religion" that is supposedly characterized by certainty and clearly articulated boundaries between "insiders" and "outsiders" is at the heart of fundamentalisms and violent extremism in Africa. The chapter maintains that instead of rushing to seek to "overcome" fundamentalisms and violent extremism, there is a need to appreciate the factors that drive them, particularly the force of globalization. Further, the chapter argues that Africa is not a hapless victim of globalization, but that it is always negotiating with globalization. In the first section, the chapter summarizes the impact of globalization on religion in Africa. In the second part, the chapter highlights the religious responses to globalization through the emergence and intensification of fundamentalisms and violent extremism. In the third section, the chapter explores the African religious response to fundamentalisms. A concluding section brings the chapter to a close.

## 2 "Swamped and Alarmed by New Ideas and Experiences"? African Religions and Globalization

A longer narrative is required to do justice to Africa's (largely violent) encounter with globalization in general, and African religion's interface with globalization. Admittedly, there is no unanimity over the heuristic value of the term globalization and its implications for Africa (Cooper, 2001). However, globalization, understood as "a process that encompasses the causes, course, and consequences of transnational and transcultural integration of human and non-human activities" (Al-Rodhan, 2006: 5), has had a very direct impact on Africa in many ways. The continuous movement of people, ideas, and objects in different directions has affected Africa/ns in different ways. The impact has been both positive and negative, although most African intellectuals and activists place emphasis on the latter. In this regard, globalization itself is experienced as a violent process that dislocates indigenous Africans.

The main critique of globalization and its encounter with, and impact on, Africa is that it tends to be one-sided, arrogant, and injurious to the well-being of Africans. In almost all cases, globalization seeks to impose "global" ideas, cultures, and practices on the rest of the world. However, it emerges that in most instances, the "global" culture is in fact, very specifically Global North culture. The "rest" of the world is expected to fit into this model. In terms of economics, the rest of the Global South is meant to consume products from the Global North, while the latter benefits from its wanton exploitation of resources from other parts of the world. In relation to religion, globalization has been experienced mostly as imposing particular versions of religion as normative, while condemning others as fundamentalisms, reactionary, or conservative. Writing with particular reference to African Traditional Religions, Kasongo makes the following submission:

> However, when an incoming culture (in this case civilization/modernism) seeks to totally replace the existing cultural value, it causes social frustration and generates maladjustment of group members to this new system which leads to the "demise" of the traditional society. New behaviors that meet the new cultural values are persuasively created as they collision with the existing values. Like [a] volcano, this confrontational situation steers and spirals social conflicts. If the African's system of modernity does not include its traditional system of socialization, civilization as we know will always be a failure. (Kasongo, 2010: 315–316)

Although Africa is home to a multiplicity of religions (Platvoet, 1996), this chapter shall concentrate on the two dominant missionary religions, namely, Christianity and Islam (with African Traditional/Indigenous Religions being always behind, beneath, and even ahead of these). While some African intellectuals and nationalist scholars would categorize these two as "foreign," the argument has been made that these religions have been in Africa for so long that they now qualify to be classified as "African" religions (Mbiti, 1996). Although one is aware that these two religions are characterized by internal diversity, the chapter will adopt a more general approach when analysing the impact of globalization on African religions. Our initial focus shall be on Christianity, before moving on to Islam. Agbiji and Swart (2015: 3) maintain that "Whilst the African traditional religious heritage remains a potent force that—on a subconscious level—still influences the values, identity and outlook of Africans, Christianity and Islam have become major sources of influence in African society."

Christianity itself was a globalizing religion from the onset (Müller, 2011). From its origins, Christianity sought to be a religion that would spill "to the ends of the earth." Missionary Christianity was arrogant, regarding itself as the one and only way to salvation. It demonized and dismissed African Traditional/Indigenous Religions and refused to enter into dialogue with indigenous spirituality. Missionary Christianity, however, provided its followers with certainty as it drew its boundaries with precision. It was clear on what belonging to a church entailed, distinguishing between "the saved" and the "heathen." However, with globalization gaining momentum, the distinctions have become blurred. New forms of Christianity have emerged that have sought to reinforce hybridity by combining Christianity with African Traditional/Indigenous Religions. Such appropriations have occurred from both the side of Christianity and of African Traditional/Indigenous Religions. Globalization has facilitated the rapid flow of people and ideas between Africa and other parts of the world, enabling new forms of religious expression. Thus, "increasing contact between Christians around the world sparks reflection on identity. Christians see ways in which they differ (ethnicity, language, denomination) as well as ways in which they are the same (practice, core theology, creeds)" (Johnson, 2010: 166).

For many African Christians, globalization has brought them into contact with new and contradictory versions of Christianity. Unlike the (presumably) "safe and secure" faith that was handed down to them by successive generations of Christians, the new faith they now encounter is "de-rooted, floating and tentative." As the chapter shall illustrate further below, the issue of homosexuality, for example, highlights the tension that globalization brings to many African believers. Where previously there were clear and unambiguous values, suddenly globalization avails new and vexing values. As Kaoma (2014) indicates, the contestation over homosexuality in African Christianity is predominantly a reaction to globalization. The violence of globalization is experienced in that it is imposed and, while it is supposed to increase options to others, it quickly mutates into being the only option!

Alongside Christianity, Islam is one of the major religions of Africa. Like Christianity, Islam has an uneasy relationship with globalization. On the one hand, Islam attacks globalization as deepening global economic inequality. On the other hand, although ideologically Islam (like some versions of Christianity) presents globalization as a negative force, it is helpful to acknowledge the close relationship between globalization and the rapid conversion to Islam that is currently underway. Processes such as the annual pilgrimage to Mecca

(Hajj), for example, have been made easier by globalization. However, this has brought with it specific challenges, such as the high number of vulnerable pilgrims who feel compelled to undertake the once-in-a-lifetime journey to the holy city of Mecca in Saudi Arabia. Commercial interests have overtaken spiritual, health, and safety considerations. Thus:

> In this environment, internationalizing the Hajj may no longer be enough even if the Saudis once again come to view it as a necessary evil. The reformist momentum is shifting steadily from trying to fine-tune the Hajj to reimagining it altogether. Instead of seeing the Hajj merely as an annual religious festival, Muslims increasingly regard it as a permanent worldwide network of trade, migration, and political competition—a multifunctional and hierarchical system riddled with injustices and abuses that no state or coalition can address independently.
>
> Perceptions of the Hajj as a global nexus of labor, goods, and power are widespread not only in the Middle East, but particularly in the Asian and African countries that have contributed the greatest number of workers to Saudi Arabia and its neighbors while suffering the highest casualties in repeated pilgrimage disasters. Demands for holistic reform of the Hajj are bound to soar as the Islamic world absorbs the stunning details of multi-year death rolls recently made public by whistle blowers in the Saudi Ministry of Health. (Bianchi, 2017: 3)

As the above example illustrates, an age-old Muslim practice such as the pilgrimage to Mecca, is caught up in the intricacies of globalization. However, as with their Christian counterparts, African Muslims have experienced globalization principally through the identity question that it poses. The interaction with the outside world, particular through images beamed by the media, has introduced new questions for African Muslims. Even as the religious ideology proclaims that all Muslims are part of one, undivided Muslim family (the ummah), other identity issues such as race, ethnicity, class, gender, disability, and others emerge as real challenges. It is in this context that fundamentalisms have emerged.

## 3 "Gimme Old Time Religion!"[1] Christian and Muslim Fundamentalisms and Violent Extremism in Africa as the Search for Certitude in the Face of Globalization

It might appear odd that, thus far, the chapter has not articulated its operational definition of fundamentalisms and violent extremism, despite having used the terms already. This is part of a deliberate strategy, as it is often helpful to define concepts in those sections where the concepts will be deployed to a greater extent. Like globalization, fundamentalism is a term that is widely used, yet it defies simple definitions. Instead of being consumed by the exercise of defining, the chapter adopts an open/working definition of the phenomenon. This is due to the fact that a final/exhaustive/comprehensive definition of fundamentalism is unlikely to be propagated. Thus, the chapter understands fundamentalism as the conviction that there are certain basic beliefs and practices (fundamentals) that should not be tampered with in order for a religion to remain authentic and meaningful in the eyes of the adherent(s). Very helpful theoretical work has been undertaken by, among others, Emerson and Hartman (2006) and the multiple volumes by the Chicago Fundamentalism Project by Martin E. Martey and R. Scott Appleby. It will not be possible to review the major relevant works herein due to considerations of space. However, it is important to distinguish fundamentalisms from religious extremism, terrorism, or violence. These concepts are often (wrongly) used interchangeably. For example, Odhiambo (2014) uses the terms together, thereby suggesting that religious fundamentalism gravitates (naturally?) towards terrorism. Unfortunately, this is a problematic assumption and insinuation. Fundamentalisms can lead to terrorism. However, fundamentalisms can also be non-violent. Violent extremism is a concept that is closely related to fundamentalism. Thus:

> Search for Common Ground defines violent extremism as the choice individuals make to use or support violence to advance a cause based on exclusionary group identities. The particular identity of the perpetrator of violence does not determine what constitutes violent extremism, nor does the nature of the ideology, even if that ideology may be considered radical by many. Rather, violent extremism relates to an individual or group's violent advancement of an exclusionary ideology, which seeks to eliminate the 'other' group, culture, or identity. (Search for Common Ground, 2017: 4)

---

[1] From an old Christian hymn.

Before proceeding to a discussion of how African Christian and Muslim fundamentalisms and violent extremism have emerged in response to globalization, it is vital to acknowledge that African Traditional/Indigenous Religions are not immune to fundamentalism and violent extremism. Any religion that has a basic set of beliefs and practices that it seeks to protect as foundational is susceptible to fundamentalism, and potentially, violent extremism. In fact, there may be a need to divest the term fundamentalism of its negative connotation. Fundamentalism, in and of itself, is not bad or threatening. What is potentially threatening is when a particular group insists that the fundamentals must be protected by any means necessary, including the use of violence and terror.

The encounter with globalization has forced many Africans to adopt fundamentalist positions. Writing from within the context of South Africa, Sakuba refutes the idea that African Traditional Religions are incapable of fundamentalism. He argues as follows, regarding the spaces for fundamentalism:

> The third platform is newspapers, especially the comments page. African traditionalists with fundamentalistic personalities use these spaces very creatively. On trains, people become engaged in heated debates about a number of issues. Some debates continue for a week or a month until something new comes up. Behind these debates are current issues such as gay and lesbians, same-sex-marriage, the ban on corporal punishment in schools, teenage pregnancy and many more. If one listens to these debates it is quite easy to see who is a fundamentalist and who is not. What is also interesting about these debates is that African traditional fundamentalists get an opportunity to share a stage with African Christian fundamentalists. (Sakuba, 2008: 393)

Why have some African Traditionalists, African Christians, and African Muslims taken up fundamentalisms and resorted to violent extremism? As the previous sections have highlighted, globalization has brought up the identity question to the fore. As they encounter new issues and themes, traditional/old/established religious ideas and positions are being brought into serious question. In other instances, these established religious dogmas are even being brought into disrepute, or disparaged. This generates uncertainty and loss of confidence. Fundamentalisms become a very attractive option as they bring with them a sense of boundary, certainty, and fixation. Fundamentalisms offer an anchor and support to some Africans as they wrestle with the incessant flow of people, ideas, objects, and images. In a rapidly changing world, religious fundamentalisms constitute a "place of quiet rest" where believers feel protected and reassured that the centre still holds.

Religious fundamentalisms and violent extremism in Africa are, for the most part, a direct response to the experience of globalization as a violent threat. When globalization razes "established" truths to the ground, some believers are forced to retreat to the "safe spaces" of fundamentalisms. This is because fundamentalisms are not given to ambiguity, ambivalence, and tentativeness. No. They draw sacred rings around "old time religion." They stubbornly claim that they are built on eternal, unchanging and unchangeable divine truths. All other ground might be shifting sand, but on these (clearly identified) fundamentals, they stand. They shall not be moved. They shall not budge. The winds of globalization shall leave the believers as they found them initially: standing firm on the revealed truth.

Globalization, with its emphasis on choice and particularly freedom in relation to sexual expression, causes extreme anxiety among many Africans. In particular, the debate over homosexuality and the conservative stance adopted by many religious leaders (Chitando & Van Klinken, 2016), brings the tension to the fore. Some African Traditionalists, African Christians, and African Muslims feel that their religions and ancestral heritage are under an incessant onslaught. They feel that they need to defend these from hostile forces. Some are willing to use violence to resist globalization, resulting in the emergence of extremist groups that espouse a religious agenda. It is, therefore, not surprising that studies on the path to extremism identify the need to defend one's own religion as a major factor (UNDP, 2017: 47).

The effect of globalization on the religious scene in Africa has been to bring "same" and "other" together. Those who have faithfully followed the injunctions of their religions and have worked for their own salvation "in fear and trembling" (Philippians 2: 12) are suddenly confronted by those for whom faith is of no consequence. The boundaries that were set so carefully and patiently are quickly overrun by new information, principles, and rights. When African representatives of their respective religions try to challenge emerging trends that jettison beliefs and practices that have been handed down from generation to generation, they are dismissed as relics from a long-gone era. This leads to profound soul searching that results in some finding answers and meaning in fundamentalisms and violent extremism. Kanu (2017: 102) makes the following observation, Although each person is an individual substance, globalization brings persons together from different backgrounds—social, cultural, economic, religious, educational, racial etc., to relate with the [an]other. At this point of encounter, the self gets in contact with the other, the different, the dissimilar, the distinct to which the self must relate.

## 4 "It Has Been Revealed to Us": Sacred Texts, Prophets and Charismatic Leaders in African Christianity and African Islam's Confrontation with Globalization

Principally, globalization forces some African Christians and African Muslims (and also African Traditionalists) to seek recourse to their sacred texts (and ancestral pronouncements). Thus, the revealed "Word of God," namely the sacred text, is invoked to settle contemporary arguments. All answers to the present predicament are to be found in the past! To go forward is to go back! Are we debating the status of women, a question brought about by globalization? What does the Bible say? What does the Quran say? What does "our culture" proclaim? Are we wondering whether or not homosexuals must be accorded space in our communities? What does the Bible say? What does the Quran say? What did our ancestors declare? Do we intend to introduce comprehensive sexuality education in our schools, including primary schools? What has God said in His (fundamentalists insist on the male identity of God) Word (the Bible and the Quran)? How have we "always" handled issues of human sexuality in our communities?

It is clear that for most fundamentalists, the sacred texts of Christianity and Islam already contain the correct and unfailing answers to contemporary ethical challenges. Further, these sacred texts are infallible, and the revelation contained therein does not require any interpretation. Those who suggest that the Bible could be "re-written," as Zimbabwe's former president and leading theologian, Canaan Banana tried to do (Mukonyora et al., 1993) are deemed as representing the devil. Any effort to contextualize and interpret the Quran from the point of view of liberation theology, such as the one by the South African Muslim, Farid Esack (1997) is dismissed as heretical.

The sacred texts of the Bible and the Quran are deployed by some fundamentalist African Christians and Muslims as ultra-defensive systems to protect themselves against the forces of globalization. These two texts become the bulwark to defend them against a "wicked and permissive generation" that accommodates everything. The sacred texts are approached from a fundamentalist perspective. Indeed, it is difficult to make any reference to fundamentalism without making reference to how those who subscribe to this worldview read sacred texts. Fundamentalism contends that the sacred text is unambiguous in its proclamation and that it has direct relevance/application to contemporary ethical dilemmas.

Alongside sacred texts being deployed to mitigate the impact of globalization and to give a sense of certainty to African Christians and Muslims, the emergence of prophetic and charismatic figures who call upon society to recover "old time religion" is a significant factor. In both African Christianity and Islam, predominantly young male charismatic figures have appeared on the religious scene to challenge globalization and to reassure their communities that the "eternal truths" of their religions are still safe and relevant. Although they might use some of the products of globalization, such as media technologies, they are essentially its dissenters. They do not subscribe to the process of globalization, and they seek to provide security to their communities, even as they might threaten the security of others in the process.

The prophets and charismatic figures in African Christianity and Islam seek to rally their communities against the onslaught of globalization. They reassure them that modernity and its pleasures will not erase the revelations from the long past. However, they also challenge concessions and transformation relating to gender and the place of women in society. For the most part, they insist on women upholding "traditional" gender roles. Unfortunately, most of these gender roles seek to entrench the restriction of women to the domestic sphere. Most of the prophets and charismatic figures contend that globalization is introducing "unacceptable" gender norms and values. Thus:

> the increased globalisation of social, political and economic practices has led not only to increased interaction (for example, transnational networks and global governance) across countries and regions, but also to a (re-)surgence of various and contentious streams of religiously defined fundamentalisms, partly in response to the perceived threat of an increasingly complex globalised world and to the spread of putatively alien values, aimed at the establishment of a different set of socio-cultural values and socio-political systems. (Deris & Fleschenberg, 2010: 10)

Sacred texts, prophetic and charismatic figures are among the arsenal deployed by African Christianity and African Islam (as well as African Traditional/Indigenous Religions) to reassure these communities of their survival and flourishing in the face of globalization. Through the idiom of revelation, both from the long past and ongoing, they embolden individuals and communities to face the world with confidence. They are joined in this exercise by some African intellectuals who also adopt fundamentalist positions in their engagement with globalization. Although they may not speak the language of having received revelation, they are keen to demonstrate the importance of African identity, pride, and dignity in the wake of globalization. Their ideologies and theories are designed to reassure Africans of their integrity. Space considerations prevent a detailed discussion of this theme.

However, the quest to recover the African origins of Christianity or participation of Africans in the Bible (Adamo, 2001) and the role of Africans in Islam (Chande, 2012) represent this trend. It is built on the desire to counter the violence of globalization by recovering and deploying African identity.

## 5   Taming Globalization and Making It Work for Africans and Their Religions

From the foregoing, one would be forgiven for concluding that African religions have had no fighting chance in the face of globalization. It would appear that they have all been forced to concede to the violence of globalization. It would seem that they can only resort to fundamentalism and violent extremism. However, fundamentalism is not a positive or popular term in the study of religion or in society. It carries a negative connotation. Thus, any scholars of religion, moderate religious leaders, and members of the public are convinced that fundamentalism is wrong, fundamentally. For example, David Chidester, who has devoted a lot of effort towards clarifying religion in South Africa, argues that fundamentalism must be resisted. He writes, "we must be worried about religious fundamentalism because it violates the moral order of modernity by its irrational violence and intolerance, its puritanical mores and patriarchal gender discrimination, which deploy premodern religious impulses to challenge modern social formations" (Chidester, 2008: 350).

Chidester's argument has been taken up by a number of other scholars. For example, Hadsell and Stückelberger (2009) have edited a volume on how to overcome fundamentalism. While this chapter concedes that the violence that has been unleashed as some religious groups and individuals have grappled with the violence of globalization threatens the health, well-being and development prospects of the Africans, it also argues that we need to invest more in efforts that clarify how fundamentalism and violent extremism emerge in the first instance. As this chapter has highlighted, globalization has been a major factor in the rise of fundamentalisms and violent extremism. In this, however, it remains important to acknowledge that Africans have not been hapless onlookers and victims of globalization. Neither has violence been their only option. Ukah (2012: 504) argues that "Africa has redefined and re-imagined the globalization paradigm to suit its specific conditions, requirements, and predicaments."

Nonetheless, due to the fact that the theme of how Africa has negotiated globalization and fundamentalism requires a longer narrative, in this section the chapter shall only highlight some of the main themes that need elaboration in a separate reflection. First, some African Christians in particular have utilized the opportunities availed by globalization to take their versions of Christianity to Europe and North America. They regard this as a "reverse mission." To this extent, therefore, Africans are Africanizing globalization. In this way, they have sought to take the sting out of the violence of globalization.

Second, many African Christians and African Muslims are appropriating the media technologies brought about by globalization to put across their own agendas and preach peace and prosperity. Thus, as noted above, Africans have not been hapless consumers of religious ideologies brought about by globalization. Rather, some Africans, particularly young people, have been actively involved in the very process of globalization itself. Through media technologies, many young African Christians and African Muslims are defying narratives of lack of sophistication. Instead, they are presenting very vibrant and assertive images of their communities of faith and of themselves, thereby resisting the images of doom and destruction.

Third, some African Christians and Muslims have appropriated globalization to facilitate interfaith solidarity. This defies the dominant narrative of internecine religious conflicts in Africa that is beamed by global media networks. Indeed, when one consumes global media, one gets the impression that, for example, African Christians and African Muslims are locked in mortal combat in every part of the continent. In reality, however, globalization has also facilitated harmonious interactions across the different faith communities. To say this is not to whitewash the serious tensions and violence that are experienced in some places. However, globalization has not just brought out differences and tensions, but also appreciation of shared values. Thus:

> The phenomenon of globalisation of religion has made it easier to transfer the all-embracing message of any religion all over the world. As a result, societies are becoming less exclusive and more multi-religious. Social reality forces world religious communities to get rid of their exclusive attitudes and to develop some universal orientations, which should be more accommodating to the other. In these conditions, various forms of interreligious dialogue shall have crucial importance. Thus interreligious dialogue will be fruitful as people of different religions and faith encounter each other in an atmosphere of freedom and openness for each partner to listen and understand each other. (Oluganji, 2013: 38)

Although Oluganji is using the future tense in the citation above, it is reassuring to observe that interreligious dialogue is a reality in many parts of the continent. This dialogue takes place at different levels and is accomplished in different ways. It goes a long way in preventing violence and planting and nurturing the seeds of peace and development. The most important factor is that there are notable attempts to overcome fundamentalisms and promote more peaceful models of interaction across the religious divide in many parts of Africa. Therefore, the insistence on making violent extremism the defining feature of religion in Africa must be critiqued.

## 6 Conclusion

Globalization has had a notable impact on religion in Africa. This chapter has paid particular attention to the cultural dimension of globalization, examining its role in religious fundamentalism and violent extremism in African Christianity and African Islam (and African Traditional/Indigenous Religions). The chapter has argued that globalization destabilizes notions of truth and certainty in received beliefs and practices. This generates anxiety on the part of believers. Fundamentalisms and violent extremism emerge to reassure believers that they can resist the forces of globalization. They also equip them to develop a sense of identity and confidence to face the rapidly changing world. For a significant number, it has been a call to arms and violent acts to recover "old time religion," religious certainty, and security. However, the chapter also maintains that globalization has not been unchallenged in its encounter with Africa/ns. It has illustrated how some African Christians and Muslims have utilized globalization to achieve their set religious objectives, particularly in relation to overcoming violence and promoting peace and integration. Adopting a critical approach to the study of religion and violence in Africa, this chapter has utilized the concept of globalization to highlight the complexity that accompanies the interface between the two concepts. Further reflections are required in order to generate African traditions in the understanding of religion and violence.

## Bibliography

Abrahamsen, R. (Ed.). (2013). *Conflict & Security in Africa.* James Currey.

Adamo, D. T. (2001). *Africa and Africans in the Old Testament.* Wipf and Stock.

Agbiji, O. M., & Swart, I. (2015). Religion and Social Transformation in Africa: A Critical and Appreciative Perspective. *Scriptura, 114*(1), 1–20.

Alao, A. (2022). *Rage and Carnage in the Name of God: Religious Violence in Nigeria XE Nigeria.* Duke University Press.

Al-Rodhan, N. R. F. (2006). *Definitions of Globalization: A Comprehensive Overview and a Proposed Definition.* http://citeseerx.ist.psu.edu/viewdoc/download?doi=10.1.1.472.4772&rep=rep1&type=pdf. Accessed 25 July 2018.

Armstrong, K. (2014). *Fields of Blood: Religion and the History of Violence.* Alfred A. Knopf.

Avalos, H. (2005). *Fighting Words: The Origins of Religious Violence.* Prometheus Books.

Bartov, O., & Mack, P. (Eds.). (2001). *In God's Name: Genocide and Religion in the Twentieth Century.* Berghahan Books.

Bate, S. C. (2000). Matthew 10: A Mission Mandate for the Global Context. In T. Okure (Ed.), *To Cast Fire upon the Earth: Bible and Mission Collaborating in Today's Multicultural Global Context.* Cluster.

Bianchi, R. R. (2017). Reimagining the Hajj. *Social Sciences, 6*(2), 36. https://doi.org/10.3390/socsci6020036

Cavanaugh, W. (2009). *The Myth of Religious Violence: Secular Ideology and the Roots of Modern Conflict.* Oxford University Press.

Chande, A. (2012). Islam and Qur'anic Figures in Africa: Prophets, Sages and Disciples. *Mathal, 2*(1), Article 1. https://doi.org/10.17077/2168-538X.1025

Chidester, D. (2008). Religious Fundamentalism in South Africa. *Scriptura, 99,* 350–367.

Chitando, E. (2005). Phenomenology of Religion and the Study of African Traditional Religion. *Method and Theory in the Study of Religion, 17*(4), 299–316.

Chitando, E., & Van Klinken, A. (Eds.). (2016). *Christianity and Controversies over Homosexuality in Contemporary Africa.* Routledge.

Cooper, F. (2001). What is the Concept of Globalization Good For? An African Historian's Perspective. *African Affairs, 100*(399), 189–213.

Cox, J. L. (1992). *Expressing the Sacred: An Introduction to the Phenomenology of Religion.* University of Zimbabwe Publications.

Derichs, C., & Andrea, F. (2010). Religious Fundamentalisms and their Gendered Impacts in Asia. In C. Derichs, & A. Fleschenberg (Eds.), *Religious Fundamentalisms and their Gendered Impacts in Asia. Berlin*: Friedrich-Ebert-Stiftung Department for Asia and the Pacific.

Emmerson, M. O., & Hartman, D. (2006). The Rise of Religious Fundamentalism. *Annual Review of Sociology, 32,* 127–144.

Esack, F. (1997). *Quran, Liberation and Pluralism: An Islamic Perspective of Inter-Religious Solidarity Against Oppression.* Oneworld Publications.

Hadsell, H., & Christoph, S. (Eds.). (2009). *Overcoming Fundamentalism: Ethical Responses from Five Continents.* Globethics.net.

Idowu, E. B. (1973). *African Traditional Religion: A Definition.* SCM Press.

Kanu, I. A. (2017). African Philosophy, Globalization and the Priority of 'Otherness.' *Igwebuike: An African Journal of Arts and Humanities, 3*(5), 92–109.

Kaoma, K. (2014). The Paradox and Tension of Moral Claims: Evangelical Christianity, the Politicization and Globalization of Sexual Politics in Sub-Saharan Africa. *Critical Research on Religion, 2*(3). https://doi.org/10.1177/2050303214552571.

Kaplan, J. (2015). *Radical Religion and Violence: Theory and Case Studies*. Routledge.

Kasongo, A. (2010). Impact of Globalization on Traditional African Religion and Cultural Conflict. *Journal of Alternative Perspectives in the Social Sciences, 2*(1), 309–322.

Kitts, M. (2016). Whose "Religion" and Whose "Violence"? Definition and Diversity in African Studies: Introduction to the Special Issue on Religion and Violence. *Journal of Religion and Violence, 4*(1), 3–14.

Johnson, T. M. (2010). Globalization, Christian Identity, and Frontier Missions. *International Journal of Frontier Missiology, 27*(4), 164–169.

Mbiti, J. S. (1996). Challenges facing religious education and research in Africa: The case of dialogue between Christianity and African Religion. *Religion and Theology, 3*(2), 170–179.

Mukonyora, I., et al. (Eds.). (1993). *Rewriting the Bible: The Real Issues: Perspectives from within Biblical and Religious Studies in Zimbabwe*. Mambo Press.

Müller, R. (2011). Christianity and Globalisation: An Alternative Ethical Response. *HTS Teologiese Studies/ Theological Studies, 67*(3), Art. #963, 7 pages. https://doi.org/10.4102/hts.v67i3.963

Odhiambo, E. O. S. (2014). Religious Fundamentalism and Terrorism. *Journal of Global Peace and Conflict, 2*(1), 187–205.

Okeke, C. O. et al. (2017). Conflicts between African Traditional Religion and Christianity in Eastern Nigeria: The Igbo Example. *SAGE Open* April–June, 1–10.

Olagunju, O. (2013). Globalization and Inter-Religious Dialogue in African Cultural Context. *Journal of Studies in Social Sciences, 2*(1), 31–52.

Platvoet, J. G. (1996). The Religions of African in their Historical Order. In J. Platvoet, J. Cox & J. Olupona (eds.), *The Study of Religions in Africa: Past, Present and Prospects* (pp. 46–102). Roots and Branches.

Powers, P. (2021). *Religion and Violence: A Religious Studies Approach*. Routledge.

Sakuba, X. (2008). 'Fundamentalism in African Traditional Religion': A Reflection on Some Points for Consideration. *Scriptura, 99*, 388–403.

Search for Common Ground. (2017). *Transforming Violent Extremism: A Peacebuilder's Guide*. https://www.sfcg.org/wp-content/uploads/2017/04/Transforming-Violent-Extremism-V2-August-2017.pdf Accessed 11 July 2023.

Ukah, A. (2012). Religion and Globalization. In E.K. Bongmba (Ed.), *The Wiley-Blackwell Companion to African Religions*. Blackwell Publishing Ltd.

UNDP. (2017). *Journey to Extremism in Africa: Drivers, Incentives, and the Tipping Point for Recruitment*. United Nations Development Programme Regional Bureau for Africa.

# In God's Name: Violent Extremism in North East Nigeria

Jacinta Chiamaka Nwaka

## 1   Introduction

With the expansion of violent extremist acts of terror in the last two decades, and their apparent entanglement with religion, the role of religious actors and faith communities in countering violent extremism has been emphasized (Mandaville & Nozell, 2017). Consequently the countering of terrorism/violent extremism has become the focus of the foreign policies of many countries, especially in the West, reflecting the taking of measures for the effective engagement of religious actors, ideas, and institutions. While the former president of the United States, George Bush, set the process in motion in 2001 with the establishment of a team on faith-sector engagement in the White House, and the creation of an office at the United States Agency for International Development to deal with religion in international development (US Department of State and USAID, 2016), President Obama formalized and institutionalized these efforts by taking further bold steps that finally saw the establishment of the Office of Religion and Global Affairs at the Department of State (Hayward, 2012). But religion will become a solution only if its role in violent extremism is ascertained. Presently, there remains a heated debate on the role of religion in this regard. Maintaining that an

J. C. Nwaka (✉)
University of Benin, Benin, Nigeria
e-mail: jacinta.nwaka@uniben.edu

Department of History and International Studies, University of Benin, Benin City, Nigeria appeal to religion alone is out of the question in explaining the root of violent extremism and terrorist acts, Armstrong (2014) emphasizes underlying societal factors such as political and socio-economic issues. On the other hand, Juergensmeyer (2001) underscores religion as a motivation for extremist acts of terror. Hence, foregrounding religion may appear an antidote to terrorism and other extremist acts of violence. Although currently, there seems to be a shift towards the acceptance of a complex web of underlying factors including religion (Blinken, 2016), the degree to which religion is a factor in violent extremism has yet to yield guidance for policy-making (Mandaville & Nozell, 2017). Indeed, understanding religion in violent extremism is not a matter of trying to establish whether religion is the cause or not, but rather establishing, to use the Wilton (2016: 3) statement, "the interplay between religion and widely varying local and contextual factors such as state violence, corruption, certain kinds of socio-economic deprivation, localized conflict, youth disaffection and identity crisis."

Relying on data from media reports, official documents, oral sources, and extant literature, this chapter interrogates in relation to socio-economic variables the religious motivation of Boko Haram, a violent extremist group that visibly began its violent acts of terror in the North East zone of Nigeria in 2009. To an average Nigerian, Boko Haram is a terrorist Islamist group that aims at using violence to Islamize the entire country. Even at the professional level of policy-making and analysis, some Nigerian experts cannot help viewing the group as a violent extremist group with the ulterior motive of Islamization. Boko Haram operates mainly in Muslim enclaves in Nigeria, with its attacks directed against both Muslims and non-Muslims. Its casualties to date, no doubt, remain mostly Muslims. Though pockets of evidence on forceful recruitment exist, winning adherents to the group is largely dependent on overt and covert appeals (Anonymous Informant, personal communication, June 7, 2021). How does one explain these complexities? To what extent is religion the motivating factor for violent extremism in the North East zone of Nigeria? What is the relationship between religion and other identifiable variables (in this study, socio-economic variables)?

## 2   Islam and Violent Extremism

Extremism, as projected by Berger (2017), is the belief that an in-group success or survival is dependent or inseparable from negative acts against an out-group. Such negative acts may include discriminatory behaviours, verbal attacks, suppression, or violence. When such extreme belief in harmful acts involves violence against an out-group, it becomes violent extremism. In other words, violent extremism is the assumption that an in-group success or survival is dependent on the use of violence against an out-group. Violence in this context may be subjective or termed "defensive," or else pre-emptive or offensive; the central point is that it is not conditional. The in-group survival is inseparably dependent on it. Despite Irm Haleen's (2020) postulation that there is nothing uniquely Islamic about violent extremism, most terrorist attacks, including devastating ones in recent times, have been carried out in the name of Islam. Is Islam inseparable from violence?

Three outstanding pillars upon which connections between Islam and violent extremist acts are often made are analysed in this section as a framework for my analysis of Boko Haram in the North East of Nigeria. The first entry point is that Islam is believed to be a religion that emphasizes the concept of a "holy war" (Jihad) against non-Muslims (infidels) with the ultimate aim of their conversion to the Islamic religion. In contrast to mainstream Muslims, who project Jihad as the sixth pillar of Islam (the other five pillars being the confession of faith (*shahadah*), almsgiving, prayer, fasting and the Hajj or pilgrimage to Mecca), radical Muslims see Jihad as the root and anchor of Islam—a divinely ordained and revealed instrument for winning the entire human race to God. In this sense, Jihad becomes a divinely sanctioned violent means to force unbelievers to either believe or be rooted out of the web of God's people. Among the verses of the Islamic holy book often cited in support of offensive Jihad against the people of other faith are the following:

> *Kill them (non-Muslims) whenever you may come* upon them, and capture them and besiege them and lie in wait for them in each and every ambush. (Al-Taubah—the Immunity 9.5).
>
> And fight against them until there is no longer disorder rooted in rebellion against God and the religion. (Al-Baqarah, The Cow, 2: 193)

While at war, the Quran enjoins the Muslims to kill their enemy:

> Kill them wherever you come upon them, and drive them out from where they drove you out; kill them; such is the recompense of unbelievers. (Al-Baqarah, The Cow, 2: 191)

These verses do receive interpretations implying the explicit permission of God to wage war against non-believers beyond self-defence. The fact is that they are often lifted and interpreted out of context by the fundamentalists (Camur, 2019). The first one above, for example, was meant for people of other faiths who violated their agreement with Muslims, perhaps in an Islamic state. It can be inferred from the verse that Islamic traditions approve of the existence of Muslims and non-Muslims together on the basis of bonds and agreements. That same verse, in its later part, equally enjoins Muslims to treat such people with compassion and allow them their freedom if they honour the treaties. Indeed, taking a verse out of its setting or a few wordings from a verse, Camur (2019) argues, will invariably generate incorrect conclusions. The same Islamic corpus that seems to have given approval for the use of violence against non-believers in the name of God contains a certain number of peaceful revelations and teachings that reflect Prophet Mohammed's dispositions towards peaceful relations with non-Muslims. For example, after migrating from Mecca to Medina, the Prophet enjoined his followers thus:

> Do not argue with those who were given the book save in the best way, unless it be those of them given to wrong doing. Say: We believe in what has been sent down to us and what was sent down to you, and your God and our God is one and the same. We are Muslims wholly submitted to hi. Al-Ankabut, The Spider, 29: 46)
>
> Call to the way of your Lord with wisdom and fair preaching, and argue with them in a way that is better. (Al-Nahl, The Bee, 16: 125)

Even when war was for the first time allowed, it is evident in the Quran that it was geared towards self-defence:

> Fight in the way of Allah, those who fight you, but transgress not the limits. Allah likes not the transgressors. (Al-Baqarah, The Cow, 2: 190).
>
> And if they incline to peace, you (also) incline to it, and (put your) trust in Allah. (Al-Anfal, The Spoils of War, 8: 61)

The polytheists were considered unjust and enemies of the Muslims by the Prophet, not because they were unbelievers but because they persecuted and drove the Muslims out of Mecca. Thus, the Quran speaks of:

> those who have been driven from their home land against all right, for no other reason than that they say; 'Our Lord is Allah.' (Al-Haj, The Pilgrimage, 22: 40)

These persons must fight to defend and take back their land. Virtually all the battles of Prophet Mohammed in the early days—the Battle of Badr (624 CE), the Battle of Uhud (625CE) and the Battle of the Trench (627CE) were defensive battles (Camur, 2019). Arguably, Islam from the beginning seeks a stable environment of justice and freedom that promotes both the spiritual and temporal well-being of Muslims. It abhors any form of unreasonable violence.

But for the propagators of offensive Jihad, the peaceful content of the Islamic tradition is related to earlier revelations which were later replaced by more belligerent ones. Yet, logically and humanly speaking, one might argue that the earlier revelations are likely to be closer to the truth and less distorted than later ones, which may be subject to the manipulative tendencies of humans for various reasons. According to Dogan (2018), radical extremist groups in Muslim majority communities had, in the seventh century, interpreted the Quran and the traditions of the Prophet in very extreme way in their bid to justify violence beyond what was stipulated. Armstrong (2014: 304) equally traces the genesis of offensive Jihad after the seventh century. In trying to establish that "the problem lies not in the multifaceted activities that we call 'religion', but in the violence embedded in our human nature and the nature of the state," she identifies the dilemma among Muslims from the eighth century when Mohammed Idris al-Shaffi supported offensive war between Muslims and non-Muslims in contrast to other Islamic leaders—Abu Hanifa an-Numan Ibn Thabit, Malik Ibn Anas, and Amad Ibn Hanbal—who were in favour of defensive war. The violence which came after the early Islamic period was, in her view, political, economic, and social violence anchored on religion. Political leaders, she maintains, used Islam and Islamic leaders to justify their violence for mundane reasons (Armstrong, 2014). In his study of central Nigeria, Anes (1934) observes that unlike the earlier jihadists who had a good dose of religious puritanical tendencies as their objective in northern Nigeria, the later flag bearers of Danfodio's Jihad to the Middle Belt were largely motivated by economic and political gains. Hence, the argument in support of offensive Jihad on grounds that its revelations came later to replace what was earlier and perhaps originally revealed to the prophet is unconvincing. Retaining the two revelations simultaneously, on the other hand, is contradictory.

As far as the concept of Jihad is concerned, Yaman (cited in Camur, 2019: 2) has pointed to a shift from its original meaning—"struggle" or "striving"—to a holy war in order to legitimize violence. Islam differentiates between the lesser (external) Jihad, which is the struggle with the enemy on the battlefield, and the greater (internal) Jihad, that entails a battle with oneself to curtail those human desires that push against the dictates of Islam. The Prophet Mohammed was noted to have remarked before his followers after returning from a war: "You have arrived with an excellent arrival; you have come from the Lesser Jihad to the Greater Jihad—the striving of a servant (of Allah) against his desires" (Bar, 2004: 32). In other words, the internal Jihad is a private struggle against all the cravings that are forbidden in Islam, while the external Jihad is a military, violent, and collective struggle against an enemy who fails to live in peace with Muslims (Topaloglu, 1993: 532). While the concept of Jihad as a holy war has held sway among the majority of Muslims, the divinely ordained war is expected to be in consonance with the basic tenets of Islamic religion encapsulated in the Quran and the traditions of the Prophet. From the above expositions, the only ground upon which violence is approved in Islam is the self-defence of a Muslim community, or a Muslim state (in this case to protect it or to re-conquer a Muslim territory earlier subdued). According to Bar (2004:32), Islamic law stipulates that when it comes to defensive Jihad to liberate an Islamic territory from occupation, "a woman needs not ask permission of her husband, nor a child of his parents nor a slave of his master." Thus, external jihad is a collective responsibility while internal Jihad is a personal duty.

Fundamentalism is another outstanding pillar through which violent extremism is linked to Islam. In a broad sense, fundamentalism is the strict adherence to an ideology, and particularly a belief system (religious ideology). Religious fundamentalism, according to Altemeyer and Humerberger (1992: 121), is:

> the belief that there is one set of religious teachings that contain the fundamental basic, intrinsic, essential, inerrant truth about humanity and deity; that this essential truth is fundamentally opposed by forces of evil which must be vigorously fought; that this truth must be followed today according to the fundamental, unchangeable practices of the past; and that those who believe and follow these fundamental teachings have a special relationship with the deity

Simply put, fundamentalism in a religious context is an extreme view of the superiority of one religion over another. A fundamentalist Islamic approach to one's individual belief system is more of a personal affair, an individual difference variable which appeals more to the internal (greater) Jihad. It is a desire for personal revival and commitment to the principles of Islamic religion, which ordinarily should appeal to peaceful and democratic means for its extension beyond the realm of personal sanctification. However, Islamic fundamentalists have increasingly been associated with violence since the 1980s. The decline of the Ottoman Empire and the imperial domination of the twentieth century generated a revival of anti-Western sentiments, manifesting in a new commitment to stricter adherence to Islamic laws. Believing that liberal adherence underlies the decline of a once-flourishing civilization

(Abi-Hashem, 2004), some clerics advocate stricter adherence to the Islamic code as a way of restoring the superiority of Islam (Ahmad, 1999). As a result of the above, radicalized Muslims, both the "born again" Muslims who adopt stricter interpretation of religious identity and converts from other faith or non-faith backgrounds referred to by Francis and Knott (2017) as "new Muslims," are seen as militant in their extreme view and understanding of the principles of Islamic religion, exhibiting tendencies to foist on the public their interpretations of Islamic injunctions and teachings (Wright, 2016). It is in this sense that the theological basis for radicalization has been underscored (Gartenstein-Ross & Grossman, 2009; Pech & Slade, 2006; Rausch, 2015). Gartenstein-Ross and Grossman (2009) identified six stages in the steps towards religiously-framed extremism that justified the basis for the use of violence: according Islam a legalistic interpretation; believing only a selective and ideological group of religious authorities; perceiving the West and Islam as incompatible; having low tolerance for perceived religious deviance; attempting to impose religious belief on others; and the expression of radical political views.

A few posers may assist to emphasize a dilemma here. First, if strict adherence to the Islamic codes is the underlying cause of violent extremism, why are radicalized fundamentalist groups in other areas not violent? Second, if fundamentalism is rooted in the drive to uphold and promote the core principles and values of Islam, why must the focus be on the belligerent aspect of those principles which are contentious? The Quran contains a certain number of peaceful injunctions derived from the Prophet's revelations. Rothschild et al. (2009) have argued that the fundamentalists' anti-Western teachings can be attenuated if fundamentalists are exposed to the compassionate values embedded in Islam. Third, if the aim of the extremists is to do away with or suppress Western civilization, why are extremist acts of terror more concentrated on Muslim states? Of the total of 70,767 terrorist attacks between 2011 and 2016, 60,320 (85%) took place in Muslim-dominated states (Cordesman, 2017). Indeed, one would have expected Iraq, Syria, and Afghanistan, with the obvious presence of Western countries partnering with Muslim governments, to account for the greater number of terrorist attacks during this period. Yet only 21,113 (37%) occurred in these countries (Cordesmann, 2017). Moreover, the vast majority of Muslims do not accept the fundamentalists' extreme acts of violence as rooted in Islam. Indeed, one may incline to the conclusion of Cordesman (2017: 2) that "most fundamentalist extremist groups are simply minority Muslims seeking power primarily in their own areas of operation and whose primary victims are fellow Muslims." This echoes Armstrong's (2014) view that the belligerent content of the Islamic corpus is emphasized largely for motives beyond religion.

A more intersectional analysis, diluting the theologically-based ideology of violence in relation to violent extremism, has also emerged. In trying to analyse the conceptualization of the radicalization of violence from 2004, Kundnani (2012) identifies a nuanced theory that links religion to violence not on the basis of religious beliefs themselves, but rather on the basis of the interdependence of religion, emotion, identity, and group dynamics. Religion is seen as an extreme response to "a cognitive opening," an "identity crisis," or a bonding mechanism (Kundnani, 2012: 14). An alternative perspective was proffered by Hellyer and Grossman (2019) who maintained that radicalization did not spring from religious beliefs, but rather found expression through their frame. In other words, rather than seeing religion at the root of violence, we should see radicalization as seeking expression through religion. This echoes Roy's (2017: 136) postulation that we are faced with not so much the "radicalization of Islam" but rather the "Islamization of radicalism." The central point in the nuanced perspective is the rejection of religion as the root or predominant cause of violent extremism; rather religion produces its effects in association with other variables, which arguably may be more pronounced when cases of violent extremism are subjected to critical scrutiny.

A third entry point from which insight on the relationship between Islam and violent extremism could be gained is the notion that Islam is inseparable from politics. Islam, from the viewpoint of the Political Islam theory, is a cultural, religious, and political system (March, 2015):

> Islam is a cultural, religious and political system, only the political system is of interest to 'kafir' (non-Muslim) since it determines how we are defined and treated. The Islamic political system is contained in the Quran, the Hadith and his biography, the Sira. (Political Islam n.d.)

If Islam is a way of life with cultural, religious, and political components that make up a whole, the implication is that it is different from a common Western concept of religion, whereby religion may be defined as a relationship between God and humans according to a particular belief system, upheld by its adherents to govern their conduct in line with a certain morality supported by rituals such as prayers, processions and so forth (Tarlow, 2018). Religion in this context is a category of faith that is by definition private and personal. Islam as a way of life described above appears not to fit into this Christianized concept which is taken to be a universal underpinning of religion. While there is no doubt that Islam has a faith component that is meant to uplift its practitioners at a personal and private level, Islam is not reducible to the individualized religion familiar in a Christian context, but rather encompasses other components that tend to qualify it more as a public religion of law and culture. Though the political component, no doubt, is the most needed for the maintenance of the whole, its religious dimension remains a most useful instrument in the struggle for the survival of Islam for a number of reasons. First, religion connotes a sense of sacredness and, thus, is inclined to give approval to actions carried out in the name of God. Attributing divinity to one's act not only renders it unquestionable, but also shields such action from criticisms (Tarlow, 2018). Second, religion is associated with external symbols and rituals that help to sharpen the in-group versus out-group divide. Ginges et al., (2009: 226), referring to what they call "coalitional commitment," postulate that engagement with activities such as prayers, rituals, and fasting, among others, related to one's religion tends to increase in-group cooperation and commitment to the group's members. Through parochial altruism, such collective actions may generate support for hostility against an out-group. Arguably, hostility in this context may be more intense when the out-group is perceived as evil and the architect of an unpleasant situation in which the in-group sees itself a victim. Third, as a free-floating phenomenon, religion can be manipulated for desired goals. Though this is applicable to non-Islamic religions, the appeal to religion for mobilization and manipulation for violence tends to be more potent in Islamic religion (Wright, 2016). Drawing on the expositions above, we may say that a threat to the political or more external components of Islam is tantamount to a threat to its theological component. While the use of religion for the advancement of the political component of Islam as whole may not be pronounced in a Muslim-dominated Islamic state, in a country such as Nigeria, with what seems to be a near-balanced equalization in religious composition, the volatility of religion is not far from its function in the service of politics.

## 3   The Boko Haram Phenomenon

Derived from the combination of the Hausa word *boko* (book) and the Arabic word *haram* (forbidden), the words *Boko Haram*, literally translated, mean that the book is forbidden. There are two possible interpretations of the phrase: that Western education is a sin, and that Western civilization is forbidden. According to one of Boko Haram's members, "While the first (in error) gives the impression that we are opposed to formal education coming from the West…which is not true, the second affirms our belief in the supremacy of Islamic culture, for culture is broader, it includes education but not determined by Western education" (cited in Onuoha, 2012: 2). Though Boko Haram is the most popular name by which the sect is known, it has adopted the name of Jama'atu Ahli s-Sunnah lid-Da'wati wal-Jihad (People Committed to the Propagation of the Prophet's Teachings and Jihad) (Walker, 2012). From its officially adopted position, the group could be said to be strongly against Western traditions and cultures, which are believed to be in opposition to Islamic values, customs and beliefs. There seems to be a near-consensus about the origin of the group around 1995. Until the year 2002, it was basically a non-violent fundamentalist group committed to social programmes geared towards youth empowerment.

Led by Ustaz Mohammed Yusuf, the group visibly began its acts of insurgency in Nigeria in 2003 when it attacked the village of Kanama in Yobe, killing about 30 persons. Other attacks were recorded in areas such as Dambo, Gwoza, Bama, and Geldam in the North East. Attacks at this early stage were mostly directed at the state security outpost stations, perhaps to obtain weapons for further destabilization (Cook, 2011). While these earlier confrontations may all together be regarded as the acts of its budding stage, Boko Haram became a full-blown insurgency group in Nigeria in 2009 following its violent clash with the Bauchi State Security Agency entrusted with the task of enforcing a newly introduced law, which required motorcyclists to wear clash helmets. The refusal of members of the sect to abide by this rule bred a violent scenario that witnessed the killing of 17 members of the group by the government security agency (Bakare et al., 2009). Ransacking the sect's hideout in Bauchi, security agents found the group was in possessions of materials for making explosives—a development that led to the intensification of the crackdown by the state law enforcement agents. In response, Boko Haram engaged in reprisal attacks that left about 1,000 persons dead. Included in those who lost their lives in the clash was Yusuf (Bakare et al., 2009). Consequently, the group retreated and remained inactive until the following year, when, in a video clip, the second-in-command, Abubakar Shekau, declared his intention as the new leader of the group to avenge the death of Yusuf and other members. From 2010, Boko Haram began to use various strategies—suicide bombing, abduction, petrol bombing, armed assault and so on—to unleash violence on Nigerians and the Nigerian state. The police and the UN's headquarters in Abuja, for example, were bombed in June and August 2011 respectively. While the attack on the police headquarters was in line with the group's acts of terror since 2003, the bombing of the UN building which claimed about 23 lives reflected the pattern of global terrorist organizations such as Al-Qaeda and

Al-Shabaab. Thus, a possible link between Boko Haram and these groups was not ruled out completely, even though evidence of such linkage was not visible (Camphell, 2013).

Between 2011 and 2015, the scale and scope of Boko Haram terror attacks increased tremendously, with a consistent string of assassination campaigns, suicide bombings, and mass attacks against civilians and security forces. More than 20,000 lives were reportedly lost to this insurgent group between 2014 and 2015, making it one of the deadliest terrorist groups in Africa (Allen, 2019). In a sequel to the declaration of the Islamic States in Iraq and Syria, Boko Haram declared its allegiance to the new states and followed suit with intense pressure on Nigeria and its neighbouring states of Cameroon, Niger, and Chad for territorial control. Apparent pressure for a territorial claim produced a combined military operation from these four countries (Joint Task Force) which, in addition to the war efforts of civilian militia groups, yielded the desired result when the group lost almost all its territories in the space of five months (Allen, 2016)—hence, the popular statement of the Nigerian Government in 2015 that Boko Haram has been "technically defeated" (BBC News, 24 Dec. 2015).

Yet, while its activities declined from 2016 to 2018, from late 2018 the group's attacks were on the rise once again. Unlike the period when attacks were directed against both civilians and security forces, the new wave of attacks witnessed what seemed to be a shift in strategy: targeting state facilities (state security forces) and civilians who collaborated with them (ICG, 2019). In 2018, for example, about 450 members of the Nigerian security forces lost their lives in counter-insurgency against the group; the number nearly doubled in 2019, with 750 state security casualties occurring (ICG, 2019). The shift in strategy is credited to a splinter group, the Islamic State of West Africa (ISWA) led by Abu Musa al-Barnawi.

## 4   Motivations for Violent Extremism in the North East

### Religious Motivation

Explanations for violent extremism in the North East of Nigeria have been approached from various angles, among which are pull and push factors, pre-conditions and triggers, religious and non-religious. In drawing deeper inferences from what is visible from official documents, media reports, oral sources, and extant literature, to uncover the underlying motivations for violent extremist acts in the region, this section adopts a framework which attends to religious and non-religious (socio-economic) factors. Generally speaking, Boko Haram is seen as an Islamist extremist group that is committed to a struggle towards the imposition of radical interpretation of Islam on Nigerians, using violence. The religious interpretation of the sect is anchored on three main points.

The first stems from the ideology of the group. Boko Haram ideology, as Forest (2012) observes, seems to be deeply embedded in Islamism. Some expressions of the group members capture what may be assumed to be strong affirmation of this deep rootedness. In one of his preachings, Yusuf was said to have remarked: "Our land was an Islamic State before the colonial masters turned it to a 'kafir' (infidel) land. The current system is contrary to true Islamic beliefs" (Salkida, 2009: 2). The sect attributes importance to a verse in the Quran which states that anyone who is not governed by what Allah has revealed is among the transgressors. Boko Haram stands out as a puritanical movement that is geared towards reviving Islamic traditions and principles that were obviously affected by the forces of modernity. This view is affirmed by Last (cited in Forest, 2012) who had earlier observed that a sense of uneasiness and insecurity about the future of Islam in northern Nigeria, especially with the fading influence of religious leaders like the Sultan of Sokoto, characterized all Muslim communities in the region. A central point in Boko Haram's ideology seems to be a resentment of this Western domination of Islamic values and the push for a new status quo that will be anchored either on an ideal past or a new future embedded in Islamic law (Sharia). Drawing on the Quran, albeit erroneously, Boko Haram perceives violence as a legitimate weapon to bring about this desired change. Since the ideology of a group is a very crucial element in any decision to join a terrorist organization and to perpetrate acts of terror (Thurston, 2011), Boko Haram, having projected its ideology as a divine mandate involving a struggle between good and evil, light and darkness, and true believers and infidels/apostates, tends to bear a compelling appearance of legitimacy that exerts influence beyond its own members.

In the second place, Boko Haram is seen as a variant of the Islamic fundamentalist movements that have gained much ground in Nigeria since the 1980s. The first among them was Maitatsine, an Islamist militant group led by a young Islamic preacher, Muhammadu Marwa, from Cameroon. Like Boko Haram, Maitatsine aggressively preached against Western influence on Islam, declining acceptance of the legitimacy of secular authority over Muslim communities, of the Nigerian constitution, and of democratic practices. Like Boko Haram, Maitatsine members saw themselves as true Muslims with a mandate to fight against the infidels and apostates, so as to promote the cause of Islam. Its violence spread from Kano, where it started, to some other northern states before it was finally dealt a severe blow by the Nigerian military. In addition to Maitatsine was the Islamic Movement of Nigeria, led by an Islamic cleric El-Zakzaki. Though relatively less violent, the group, which was prominent in the 1980s and 1990s, holds a fundamentalist ideology that is similar to that of Boko Haram. Other Islamic fundamentalist groups that were not so prominent emerged before the era of Boko Haram, calling for Islamic revival. Thus, Boko Haram had its precursors in these earlier Islamist extremist groups that were not averse to violence.

Lastly, Boko Haram is linked to other Islamist extremist groups outside Nigeria, such as Al-Qaeda, and especially its affiliate in the Islamic Maghreb (AOIM), and Al-Shabaab. Although the linkage was doubted in its earlier days (BBC News, 6 Oct. 2009), developments from 2010 have strongly pointed to that connection. A statement from the sect following the bombing of the UN building in 2011 alluded to the linkage:

> All over the world, the UN is a global partner in the oppression of believers. We are at war against infidels. In Nigeria, the Federal Government tries to perpetuate the agenda of the UN... We have told everyone that the UN is the bastion of the global oppression of Muslims all over the world. (Vanguard News 28 Aug. 2011: 2)

As early as 2011, a spokesman of the sect, Abul Qaga, made a statement supporting the link between Al-Qaeda and Boko Haram: "It is true that we have link with Al-Qaeda. They assist us and we assist them" (Vanguard 24 Nov. 2011: 1). Another statement credited to another spokesman of the sect announced the return of sect members from Somalia where they went for military training: "We want to make it known that our Jihadists have arrived in Nigeria from Somalia where they have received real training on warfare from our brethren who made that country ungovernable" (IPT News 6 June 2011). Also, General Carter Ham of the United States once noted that information was abundant with regard to Boko Haram's contact with Al-Qaeda in the Islamic Maghreb (AOIM) and Al-Shabaab in Somalia. What constituted a worry to the US then, according to him, was "a clearly stated intent by Boko Haram and al Qaeda in the Islamic Maghreb to coordinate and synchronize their efforts" (*Time* Magazine, 2011: 4). Since 2012, evidence of such linkage with external extremist Islamist groups is no longer in doubt. While such networking may reflect a need for military and other training, weapon acquisition and financing, the fact that Boko Haram is a radical Sunni Islamist sect operating largely in communities of moderate Muslims (Sufi) in Nigeria implies that the group may incline to the stance of Sunni extremist groups outside Nigeria. The point being emphasized is that Boko Haram's gravitation towards other Islamist extremist and terrorist groups points to its religious undertone. In summary, the sect's theologically woven ideology, the existence of Islamist fundamentalist groups as its precursors, and the linkage to other Islamist extremist and terror groups together form the pillar upon which the religious motivation for violent extremism in the North East can be anchored.

## Non-Religious (Socio-economic)

> The dragon's teeth of terror are planted in the fertile soil of…poverty, and the war on terror will not be won until we have come to grip with the problem of poverty and thus the source of discontent. (Wolfensohn, cited in Krueger, 2008: 12)

The above statement represents one of the cornerstones upon which the non-religious explanation of violent extremism is founded. Referring to the underlying cause of Boko Haram, the former US President, Bill Clinton remarked: "Poverty remained the primary driver for the attacks by the Boko Haram and needed to be addressed by strong local and federal government programs" (Premium Times, 2013: 1). Similarly, the former US Under-Secretary for Africa, Mr Johnnie Carson, was said to have argued that Nigeria could only come out of the trap of Boko Haram, if its government decided to address the extreme poverty in the northern region of Nigeria (Ogbozor, 2016: 16). In addition to these views of policy-makers and administrators, official data affirm the poor state of Nigeria, particularly in the North East, during the early phase of insurgency in the area.

Nigeria is the sixth largest producer of oil globally, but the wealth accruing from its black gold ends up in the hands of a few, leaving the majority of its citizens poor and deprived. The Evans School of Policy Analysis and Research Group (EPAR) pointed to the growth of the economy of Nigerian in 2014 and an apparent decline in the standard of living at the same time (EPAR, 2014). According to the BBC report of National Bureau of Statistics (NBS) in 2010, 60.9% of Nigerians live in abject poverty (BBC News, 2012). The North East zone of Nigeria is the most affected in this regard. Data from the National Bureau of Statistics in 2010 shows that the area had the highest poverty rate of 64.8%, followed by the North West with 62.2%, while the lowest poverty rates of 31.2% and 40.2% were recorded in the South East and South West respectively (NBS, 2010). Before this period, the poverty index

Table 1 Poverty index of Nigeria (CBN, 2006)

| No | States | Percentage of poverty |
|---|---|---|
| 1 | Jigawa | 95 |
| 2 | Kebbi | 89.7 |
| 3 | Adamawa | 71.7 |
| 4 | Bauchi | 86.3 |
| 5 | Yobe | 83.3 |
| 6 | Sokoto | 76.8 |
| 7 | Gombe | 77 |
| 8 | Kwara | 85.2 |
| 9 | Zamfara | 80.9 |
| 10 | Kogi | 88.8 |

in Nigeria at the budding stage of Boko Haram revealed that the top five poorest states were all in the north (UNDP, 2009). This affirms the earlier report of the Central Bank of Nigeria in 2006, indicating that the top ten poorest states in Nigeria were from the north (CBN, 2006) (Table 1).

According to the 2012 Global Security Briefing of the Oxford Research Group, Borno State, where Boko Haram originated, had 83% of its young people designated as illiterate, while 48.5% of the children did not go to school (Rogers, 2012). Statistics further show that the entire North East had the highest rate of unemployment. From 2008–2009, the rate of unemployment in the area stood at 38.0 above the national average of 21.7 (NBS, 2011).

Theories on basic need and relative deprivation are among the most highly represented in tracing the underlying socio-economic current behind Boko Haram. Scholarly research traces the root of the precarious socio-economic conditions to a number of anomalies in the Nigerian system—corruption, the subversion of prevailing democratic norms through the subtle suppression of the independence of the legislature and the judiciary, ethnicism, nepotism and partisanship—all of which not only detract from the legitimacy of the Nigerian state, but also account for its failing status (Agbiboa, 2013a; Ngwa, 2020; Ogbozor, 2016; Maiangwa et al., 2012). Aggrieved and disheartened by the inability of the state to perform its function *vis-à-vis* the economic and social wellbeing of its citizens, the most affected consciously and unconsciously tend to withdraw their allegiance from the state, transferring their loyalty to groups that appear to possess what it takes to address their grievances, irrespective of the means used. The scenario is aptly captured by Adibe (2012).

the Nigerian State…is regarded as the enemy, not just by Boko Haram, but by several Nigerians and groups, each attacking it with as much ferocity as Boko Haram's bombs, using, whatever means they have at their disposal: politicians entrusted to protect our patrimony steal the country blind, law enforcement officers see or hear no evil at a slight inducement, government workers drag their feet and refused to give their best while revelling a moon lightening, organized labour, including university lecturers go on indefinite strikes on a whim while journalists accept "'brown envelopes" to turn truth on its head or become uncritical champions of a selected anti-Nigerian state identity. What all these groups have in common with Boko Haram is that they believe that the premise on which they act is justifiable, and that the Nigerian State is unfair to them, if not an outright enemy

Echoes from administrators and policy makers, statistics from national bureau and other agencies, and scholarly research all have their point of convergence in identifying socio-economic deprivations and the orchestrated grievances as the bedrock of violent extremism in the North East.

## The Meeting Point of Religious and Non-Religious Factors

Despite what appears to be the religious basis of Boko Haram, there is a near-consensus among scholars about the role of religion as a fault-line for group mobilization for violence (Agbiboa, 2013a; Agbiboa, 2013b; Ochogwu & Okechukwu n.d). In comparison with other major religions, Islam seems to be more susceptible to religious appeal. Kressel (2007) who observes that Islamist extremist groups are far more frequent and dangerous today than other fundamentalist groups found in other major religions. The seeking of a foundation for violence exclusively in the belligerent content of the Islamic corpus is not only simplistic but unconvincing, as was shown above; neither does fundamentalism provide strong grounds for violence, since there are many religious fundamentalist groups who are not inclined to violence. If one appeals to a third point of connection which presents Islam, as a whole, endowed with various vital components, the political wing seems the most vital aspect that ensures the maintenance and survival of the whole in a hegemonic manner. With the development of the modern state system, the acquisition of power and authority for territorial control shed much of its primordial content in favour of increased contestation in a democratic setting around the globe. Threatened by the new reality, the importance of the religious component of Islam became more evident. In a symbiotic relationship, religion and politics became two bedfellows committed to the survival of each other.

Before the imposition of colonial rule, Muslims in northern Nigeria enjoyed considerable power, perhaps more so than other groups in other parts of present-day Nigeria. With colonial rule, the influence of Islamic emirates in the region not only waned, but the limitation of Western education and its civilizing influence in southern Nigeria created a north–south dichotomy in which the north remained backward and underdeveloped in comparison with the south. On the eve of independence, the southern nationalists' potential, given their exposure, seemed to have tilted the balance of power towards the south. The northern Muslim political elites appealed to religion in their contest for power, arguing for the implementation of Sharia law. A compromise was later arrived at in which the ruling class shelved religion for political reasons, without meaning to tamper with the role it was beginning to play in the politics of the nation (Nwaka & Nwaokocha, 2017). The Sharia question resurfaced in 1979, as another opportunity for political re-arrangement on a level playing field was approaching. Standing on an earlier position taken, that Sharia in law "was the goal and that anything else could only be a temporary compromise" (Kenny, 1996: 347), the political elites from the north staged a walk-out from the Constitutional Conference of 1979 following the rejection of Sharia law by the Constitutional Drafting Committee. Although the walkout and the violence it engendered in the north did not lead to the adoption of Sharia law in the Nigerian constitution, the victory of Shehu Shagari, a northern Muslim, seemed to have calmed the heat of the period. The Nigerian political centre from 1979 to 1999 was dominated by northern Muslims of both military and civilian stock. Hence, the emergence of Olusegun Obasanjo, a southern Christian, as the president of Nigeria in 1999 with a possibility of eight years in office was an obvious threat to the northern Muslim ruling class. Given the political climate in Nigeria at that time, it was almost impossible to contemplate a relatively stable Nigeria without a southern president. Consequently, religion was once again invoked.

With all the tensions injected into the polity, 12 northern states including Borno, the home of Boko Haram, adopted Sharia law between 1999 and 2000, establishing a group called Hizbah to enforce the Islamic code. Indeed, many northern elites (especially from the core north) were embittered by the emergence of Obasanjo. The imposition of Sharia was therefore a response to what they might have termed an "ugly" development. Sharia, it could be argued, was a move to destabilize the government and possibly create an opportunity for its replacement. Its connection to the analysis of violent extremism in this chapter can be understood from two dimensions. First, with the emergence of a southern Christian as president of Nigeria, frustrated and poor masses of the north, angry at the corrupt predatory Nigerian state that was perceived as the architect of their situation, expected worse. Recourse to theological foundations offered a sense of hope, both here and hereafter. In this context, resistance through an extremist group ideology that appeared to hold a glimmer of hope became irresistible. Second, following the adoption of Sharia, local politicians who, as Maier (2000) observes, lacked the political clout to win elections in their localities used religion (Sharia law) as a tool to gather support from a frustrated and helpless populace with promises of a better future. When these figures were unable to fulfil their promises after occupying the corridors of powers, grievances from the discontented and disaffected populace heightened, as the latter categorized the former as part of the problem. This turned out to be a very good opportunity for an extremist group to employ similar methods in the search for political power. There seems to be an agreement on the emergence before 1999 of Boko Haram as a non-violent Islamist extremist group with a commitment towards improving the status of the poor youth in Borno State. It was purported to have been used by the former governor of Borno State, Alhaji Modu Shariff, to secure a governorship position in 1999 (Omipidan, 2009). Yet having been denied the expected reward, the leader of the group, feeling disappointed and abandoned, was said to have turned his talent for sermonizing against Borno State, casting aspersions on it as an apostate and corrupt entity (Omipidan, 2009). Yusuf's seditious preaching might have generated the antagonistic feelings that led to his being banned from the Indimi mosque in Maiduguri (Camphell, 2014), and hence his migration from Maiduguri to a village in Yobe State known as Kanama, where he set up an Islamic community to be governed by Sharia law.

In addition to this, some disaffected Nigerian politicians of northern stock seem to have lent their support to the group, especially with the emergence of President Jonathan. Boko Haram recorded the heights of its acts of terror since 2012 in the first tenure of Jonathan's administration. President Jonathan in 2012 affirmed this, noting that sympathizers of the group had infiltrated his government as members of the legislature, executive, and judiciary (Premium Times, 2012). A one-time Commissioner of Religious Affairs in Borno State, Alhaji Boji, was said to have been a prominent financier of the group before his death at the hands of security personnel (Olojo, 2013). According to Ngwa (2020), a key spokesman of the group revealed that the former governors of Kano and Bauchi, Ibrahim Shekarau and Issa Yuguda respectively, had made a monthly payment to the group. The argument here is that violence associated with Boko Haram is rooted in and nurtured by the unquenchable desire to maintain political control at the national and local levels in Nigeria. Coinciding with the rise of global terrorism, Boko Haram acquired a "moral" and financial base that enabled it to expand beyond the control of its nurturers.

Although more of a quest for territorial control, with religion indisputably at its service, the ideology of the sect is in resonance with widespread discontentment orchestrated by socio-economic deprivation in the North East of Nigeria. An ideology, Forest (2012) argues, remains unpopular unless it resonates with the socio-economic and political context of the people whose support its owners seek. In the early days of its existence, the sect gained support mostly from unemployed youth between 16 and 40 years old, and poor families (Anonymous Informant, personal communication, 29 Sept. 2020). Ahmed Salkida's interview (cited in Olojo, 2013) with the leader of the group before his death revealed that Yusuf attributed the numerical strength of the group mostly to school dropouts, unemployed youth, and low-income civil servants. As part of its foundational principles, the sect ran social programmes in its early years, through which it provided employment opportunities for impoverished indigenous youth from the area (Anonymous Informant, personal communication, 17 Sept. 2020). By representing the Nigerian state and its government at all levels as a monster preying on its people, the ideology of the group, supported by its social services, became compelling to an illiterate and vulnerable population. Its theological basis not only certified the authenticity and mission of the sect in the corrupt and predatory context of Nigeria, but also seems to have sanctified in the minds of the people whatever means were deemed appropriate by the sect to end what was perceived as evil. As the group expanded its base and perfected its terror tactics, confidence in its potential to actualize its perceived mission increased, drawing both active and surreptitious supporters to the sect. Arguably, violent extremism in the North East is driven not simply by the socio-economic circumstances of the region but by the development in such a precarious condition of a compelling ideology that is in resonance with the yearnings of the masses. In other words, any other group with such an ideology (religious or otherwise) in a similar situation would have sailed through.

An interesting dynamic in the analysis of the interplay of religion and socio-economic drivers of the sect is further visible in the war economy of the region. There is no gainsaying that a huge chunk of oil and gas resources is annually channelled to the North East to promote the government counter-insurgency campaigns. Motivations for joining Boko Haram have in recent times been linked more to economic gains than was hitherto the case. 65% of the respondents in a recently conducted study identified financial reasons as the basis for joining Boko Haram (Ewi & Swiifu, 2017). Possibly motivated by a desire to gain from the resources pumped into the region, as well as take control of the informal trade route of the Lake Chad and Sahel region, the sect has redirected its activities away from "internal conflict of political opportunism cloaked in radical Islamist ideology to a more regionalized intervention" (Omenma, 2019: 183). In this new wave, the space has not only expanded for many more actors, but opportunities for enrichment include the taking of kickbacks by politicians, relating to military procurement, as well as skimming from soldiers salaries and, on the part of soldiers themselves, extortion from traders, producers, aid workers and even the vulnerable in camps in the form of so-called "protection" money. We may also mention the charging of exorbitant fees to escort traders and others through dangerous zones (Freeman, 2019: 4). The presence of international aid organizations has further enlivened opportunities for these fortune-seekers, creating a space for what Senator Sani (quoted in Freeman, 2019: 5) calls "humanitarian entrepreneurs."

The new dynamics reflect the demography of Boko Haram membership. Prior to 2014, the sect was largely dominated by poor and unemployed youth who were influenced to a marked degree by the ideology of the group. Currently, enticing opportunities for enrichment have significantly altered this demographic pattern. The membership of Boko Haram presently includes a good number of professionals —politicians, lecturers, lawyers, engineers, parliamentarians, bankers, traders, military men, police, and personnel from paramilitary agencies (Anonymous informant, personal communication, 2020). Interestingly, the North East has emerged from being one of the poorest enclaves in Nigeria to one of the fastest growing markets thriving on insecurity (Freeman, 2019). Minshi (2018) notes that a unique economy comprised of private security contractors dependent on a level of insecurity for their survival has developed in the region. By implication, as many people, especially politicians, make their fortunes from insecurity in the North East, the incentive to put an end to it dwindles. The war economy has not only become a hindrance to an end or reduction in violence caused by Boko Haram, but arguably has further obscured the religious basis of violent extremism in the North East.

## 5   Conclusion

Contestations for power, especially in relation to territorial control, are generally associated with violence, which, more often than not, manifests in varied forms—political, religious, socio-economic and so on. Given Nigeria's ethno-religious composition and its political history, we may say that religious violence is among the variables that have historically defined its political landscape. Thus, the emergence of an Islamist extremist group in the second half of the last decade of the twentieth century and its utilization for political struggle by some northern political elites in an era of re-democratization, when it was crystal clear that religion (Sharia) was at the service of politics in Nigeria, has set the background for violent extremism in the North East. Having been exposed to the potency of religious instrumentation, Yusuf and his group Boko Haram have employed a similar strategy to what Omenma calls "political opportunism" (Omenma, 2019: 4) to seek territorial space, declaring Borno an apostate and corrupt state in need of "true" Sharia. Following news of the terrorist attack on the US on September 11 2001, the sect became emboldened in its drive to create an Islamic state in Nigeria.

Thus my first submission is that Boko Haram is a politically driven movement anchored on religion. The symbiotic relationship between the religious and political components of Islam and the peculiarity of the Nigeria's historical context make religious instrumentation most tenable.

Yet, though rooted in a political agenda, violent extremism in the region was driven in its early days not so much by its roots as by the socio-economic realities of the North East which were in resonance with the ideology of the group. An ideology, religious or otherwise, that promises a better life to a poor and disaffected populace is, arguably, irresistible. The theological dimension of the sect's ideology, and especially the double assurance of a better reward here and hereafter (including the promise of a paradise with virgins) makes it compelling for a teeming populace of poor, illiterate, and uninformed northerners. Any potent means in a "divinely ordained" struggle is automatically approved by them.

My second submission is that the socio-economic situation in the North East was one of the potent drivers and sustainers of the conflict, mostly in its early days. Though the resonance of this situation with the ideology of the sect created a possibility for violence that seems to be plausibly informed by religion, the ultimate basis of the violence was ignorance and frustration and not the faith content of Islam. Any other powerful and compelling ideology, religious or non-religious, arguably would have generated, to a very large extent, a similar response from the populace.

Finally, I submit that, with the new complication introduced by the region's war economy in the last couple of years, insecurity appears to have completely lost its theological investiture. Hence, Boko Haram can currently be said to be religious only in name.

From the submissions made, it could be argued that the solution to violent extremism in the north lies not so much in dealing with root causes as in addressing the drivers and sustainers of the conflict. Indeed, not all conflicts can be rooted out. Given Nigeria's context and global trends, an end to the sect of Boko Haram, or the prevention of the emergence of a similar group may not be feasible. Nevertheless, starving the group of its drivers/sustainers may bring about a considerable reduction in the violence and insecurity engendered by its activities.

## Bibliography

Abi-Hashem, N. (2004). Peace and War in the Middle East: A Psychopolitical and Socio-Cultural Perspective. In F. M. Moghaddan & A. J. Marsella (Eds.), *Understanding Terrorism: Psychosocial Roots, Consequences and Interventions* (pp. 69–89). American Psychological Association.

Adibe, J. (2012). *Boko Haram: Symptom of Crisis in Our Nation-building Project.* http://dailytrust.com.ng/index.php?option=com

Agbiboa, D. E. (2013a). Why Boko Haram Exists: The Relative Deprivation Perspective. *African Conflict and Peacebuilding Review, 3*(1), 144–157.

_____. (2013b). Boko Haram, Religious Violence and the Crisis of National Identity in Nigeria: Towards a Non-Killing Approach. *Journal of Development Societies,* 29. http://jds.sagepub.com/content/29/4/379

_____. (2015). The Social Dynamics of Nigeria's Boko Haram Insurgency: Fresh Insight from the Social Identity Theory. *Center for Effective Global Action.* http://www.cega.berkley.edu-assets/miscellanous_files/110

Ahmad, K. A. S. (1999). Islam. The Essentials. In K. Ahmad. Leicester (Ed.), *Islam: Its Meaning and Message.* The Islamic Foundation.

Allen, N. (2019, December 24). How Boko Haram has Regained the Initiative and What Nigeria Should Do to Stop it, Commentary. *Texas National Security Review.* https://warontherocks.com/2019/12/how-boko-haram-has-regained-the-initiative-and-what-nigeria-should-do-to-stop-it/

Allen, N. (2016, September, 22). Charting Boko Haram Rapid Decline, Commentary. *Texas National Security Review.* www.warontherocks.com/2016/09/charting-boko-haram-rapid-decline.accessed12th

Altemeyer, B., & Hunsberger, B. F. (1992). Authoritarianism, Religious Fundamentalism, Quest and Prejudices. *International Journal for the Psychology of Religion, 2,* 118–133.

Anes, C. G. (1934) *Gazetteers of the Northern Provinces of Nigeria, Vol. IV The Highland Chieftaincies*. Frank Cass.

Armstrong, K. (2014). *Fields of Blood: Religion and the History of Violence*. Penguin Random House.

Bar, S. (2004). The Religious Sources of Islamic Terrorism. *Policy Review, 25*, 27–37.

Bakare, W., Demola, A., & Hamed, S. (2009, July 31). Islamic Militant Leader Killed—Borno Government. *The Punch*.

British Broadcasting Corporation (BBC) News. (2015, December 24). *Nigeria Boko Haram: Militants "Technically Defeated." Buhari*. BBC: See British Broadcasting Corporation.

_____. (2009, August 4). *Is al Qaeda Working in Nigeria?* https://news.bbc.co.uk/2/hi/Africa/8182289.stm.

_____. (2012, February 13). *Nigerians Living in Poverty Rise to Nearly $61*. https://www.bbc.com/news//world-africa-17015873

Berger. J. M. (2017). Extremist Construction of Identity: How Escalating Demands for Legitimacy Shape and Define In-group Out-group Dynamics. *International Center for Counter-Terrorism Studies, The Hague, 8*(7).

Berger, J. M. (2018). *Extremism*. MIT Press.

Blinken, A. (2016). *New Frame work for Countering Violent Extremism*. Remarks at the Brookings Institution. https://2009-2017.state.gov/s/d/2016d/252547.htm.

Campbell, J. (2013, October 1). *Should US Fear Boko Haram*. CNN. https://www.cfr.org/blog/should-united-states-fear-boko-haram

Campbell, J. (2014). *Boko Haram: Origins, Challenges and Responses*. NOREF Policy Brief

Camur, A. (2019). *Three Theorists on Religious Violence in an Islamic Context: Karem Armstrong, Mark Juergensmeyer and William Cavanaugh*, (Graduate Thesis and Dissertation). https://schoarcommons.usf.edu/etd/7756

Central Bank of Nigeria (CBN). (2006). *First Quarter Economic Report*. Central Bank of Nigeria.

Cook, D. (2011). The Rise of Boko Haram in Nigeria. *CTC Sentinel, 4*(9). www.ctc.usma.edu/the-rise-of-boko-haram-in-nigeria

Cordesman, A. (2017). *Islam and the Patterns in Terrorism and Violent Extremism*. Working Draft, Centre for Strategic and International Studies. https://www.csis.org/analysis/islam-and-patterns-terrorism-and-violent-extremism.

Department of State and USAID Joint Structure on Countering Violent Extremism. (2016). https://pdf.usaid.gov/pdf_doc/PBAAE503.P4

Dogan, R. (2018). *Terrorism and Violence in Islamic History and Theological Responses to the Argument of Terrorists*. Nova Science Publisher.

Evans School of Policy Analysis and Research Group (EPAR). (2014). *Economic Growth and Poverty in Nigeria: Part 2 of 2*. https://www.epar.evans/uw.edu/blog/economic-growthpoverty-nigeria-part 2–2

Ewi, M., & Swiifu, U. (2017). Money Talks: A Key reason Youths Join Boko Haram. Institute for Security Studies. https://frantic.s3-eu-west-1.amonnaws.com/kua-peacemakers/2016/07/Money-talks-A-key-reason-youth-join-Boko-Haram.pdf.

Forest, J. (2012). *Confronting the Terrorism of Boko Haram in Nigeria. Joint Special Operations University (JSOU)*, Report, 12–13 May.

Francis, M., & Kim, K. (2017). *Islam: Conversion. Lancaster UK: Center for Research and Evidence on Security*. https://crestresearch.ac-uk/resources/islam-conversion.

Freeman, C. (2019, July 28). *Spoils of War: The conflict with the Boko Haram Insurgency has Raged for a Decade—Is the War Economy Too Lucrative for Peace to Prevail?* Tortoise Media. https://members.tortoisemedia.com/2019/07/28/boko-haram/content.html.

Gartenstein-Ross, D., & Grossman, L. (2009) *Homegrown Terrorists in the US and UK: An Empirical Examination of the Radicalization Process*. Foundation for Defence and Democracies

Ginges, J., Hansen, I., & Norenzayan, A. (2009). Religion and Support for Suicide Attacks. *Psychological Science, 20*(2), 224–230.

Harleem, I. (2020). *The Essence of Islamist Extremism*. Routledge.

Hayward, S. (2012). *Religion and Peacebuilding*, Special Report No. 313. USIP. www.usip.org/sites/defang/files/SR313pdf.

Hellyer, H. A. & Michele, G. (2019). *A Framework for Understanding The Relationship Between Radicalization of Religion and Violence*. Technical Report (Global Governance Programme) GREASE Concept Papers, Religion, Diversity and Radicalization. https://www.grease-eui.eu/wp-content/uploads/site/8/2019/05/GREASE_01.2_hellyer.

International Crisis Group (ICG). (2019, May 16). *Facing the Challenges of the Islamic State in West Africa Province, Report, 273*. https://www.crisisgroup.org/africa/west-africa/nigeria/273-facing-challenge-islamic-state-west-africa-province.

Investigative Project on Terrorism (IPT). (2011, June 16). *News*. Al Qaeda Training Reaches Nigerian Islamists. https://www.investigativeproject.org/2981/al-qaida-training-reaches-nigerian-islamists.

Juergenmeyer, M. (2001). *Terror in the Mind of God: The Global Rise of Religious Violence*. University of California Press.

Kenny, J. (1996). Sharia and Christianity in Nigeria: Islam and a Secular State. *Religion in Africa, 26*(4), 38–364.

Kressel, N. J. (2007). *The Danger of Religious Extremism*. Amherst, Prometheus Book.

Krueger, A. B. (2008). *What Makes a Terrorist: Economics and the Root of Terrorism*. Princeton University Press.

Kundnani, A. (2012). Radicalization: The Journey of A Concept. *Race and Class, 54*(2), 325–347.

Maiangwa, B., Okeke, U. U., Whetto, A., & Onapajo, H. (2012). "Baptism of Fire": Boko Haram and the Reign of Terror in Nigeria. *Africa Today, 59*(2), 40–57.

Maier, K. (2000). *This House Has Fallen: Nigeria in Crisis*. Penguin Book.

Mandaville, P., & Nozell, M. (2017). *Engaging Religion and Religious Actors in Countering Violent Extremism*. Special Report 413. USIP.

March, A. F. (2015). Political Islam: Theory. *Annual Review of Political Science, 18*, 103–123.

Munshi, N. (2018). Groups Adapt to Insurgency to Tap Nigerian Growth. *Financial Times*. https://www.ft.com/content/b45be464_r940-11w8-ar46-2022a0b02a6c.

National Bureau of Statistics (NBS). (2010). *Nigeria's Poverty Profile*. https://www.tuchivers.org/tucpublication/nigeria/poverty/profile2010.

_____. (2011). *Statistical News: Labour Force Statistics No. 476*. NBS Publication

NBS: See National Bureau of Statistics.

Ngwa, N. R. (2020). Drivers of Political Radicalization and De-radicalization of Terrorism in Northern Nigeria. *International Journal of Politics and Security, 2*(3), 1–33.

Nwaka, J. C., & Nwaokocha, O. A. (2017). Compromise Without Consensus: The Shadow of Sharia Over Nigeria's Democracy. *Journal of History and International Studies, 2*(2), 88–107.

Ochogwu, J. P., & Maximilian, U. O. (n.d.). Countering Violent Extremism in the North East: A Transgenerational Approach. *Nigerian Journal of Administrative and Political Studies, 5*(1), 113–124. https://bsum.edu.ng/journals/njaps/v5n1/files/file8.pdf.

Ogbozor, E. (2016). Causes and Consequences of Violent Extremism in North East Nigeria. *Working Paper, Household in Conflict Network, Institute of Development Studies*, University of Sussex. https://www.hicn.org/wp-content/uploads/sites/10/2012/06/HiCN-WP-227.pdf

Okeke, U. U., & Benjamine, M. (2012). Boko Haram Terrorism in Nigeria: Causal Factors and Central Problematic. *African Renaissance, 9*(1), 91–118.

Olojo, A. (2013). Nigeria's Troubled North: Interrogating the Drivers of Public Support for Boko Haram. *International Centre for Counter-Terrorism Studies- The Hague, 4*(7). https://www.icct.nl/publication/nigerias-troubled-north-interrogationg-the-drivers--of-public-support-for-boko-haram

Omipidan, I. (2009, August 2). Why North is on Fire. *Sunday Sun*.

Omenma, J. T. (2019). Untold Story of Boko Haram Insurgency: The Lake Chad Oil and Gas Connection. *Politics and Religious Journal, 13*(1), 180–213. https://doi.org/10.1017/S1755048319000166

Onuoha, F. C. (2012). Boko Haram: Nigeria XE "Nigeria"'s Extremist Islamic Sect. *Al Jazeera Center for Studies, 29*, 1–6.

Pech, R. J., & Slade, H. W. (2006). Religious Fundamentalism and Terrorism: Why Do They Do It and What Do They Want? *Foresight, 8*(1), 8–20.

Political Islam. (n.d.). https://www.politicalislam.com

Premium Times. (2013, February 27). Bill Clinton Counters Jonathan, Insists Poverty Behind Boko Haram, Ansaru Insurgency. https://www.premiumtimesng.com/news/122116-bill-clinton-counters-jonathan-insists-poverty-behind-boko-haram-ansaru-insurgency.html?tztc=1

_____. (2012, January 8). Boko Haram has Infiltrated my Government, Says Jonathan. https://www.premiumtimesng.com/news/3360-boko-haram-has-infiltrated-my-government-says-jonathan.html

Rausch, C. C. (2015). Fundamentalism and Terrorism. *Journal of Terrorism Research, 6*(2), 28–35. https://www.hicn.org/wp-content/uploads/sites/10/2012/06/HiCN-WP-227.pdf

Rogers, P. (2012, 30 April). Nigeria: The Generic Context of Boko Haram Violence. *Global Security Briefing*. Oxford Research Group. https://www.files.ethz.ch-isn/143259/712-04pdf.

Rothschild, Z. K., Abdollahi, A., & Pyszczynski, T. (2009). Does Peace Have a Prayer? The Effect of Mortality Salience, Compassionate Values and Religious Fundamentalism on Hostility Towards Out-Group. *Journal of Experimental Social Psychology, 45*(4), 816–827.

Roy, O. (2017). *Jihad and Death: The Global Appeal of Islamic State*. Oxford University Press.

Salkida, A. (2009, July 27). Sect Leader Vows Revenge. *Daily Trust*.

Tarlow, P. (2018). Then Interaction of Religion and Terrorism. *International Journal of Safety and Security in Tourism/Hospitality*. https://www.palermo.edu/Archivos_content/2017/Economicas/journal-tourism/edicion16/PAPER-2.pdf.

Time Magazine. (2011, August 31). *Nigeria's Boko Haram: Al Qaeda's New Friend in Africa?* https://content.time.com/time/world/article/0,8599,2091137,00.html

Thurston, A. (2011, September 1). *Threats of Militancy in Nigeria: Commentary for Carnegie Endowment for International Peace*. https://carnegie-mec.org/2011/09/01/threat-of-militancy-in-nigeria-pub-45463

Topaloglu, B. (1993). Jihad. *TDV Encyclopedia of Islam, 7*, 531–534.

United Nations Development Programme (UNDP). (2009). *Human Development Report 2008–2009*. Abuja, UNDP. UNDP: See United Nations Development Programme.

Vanguard News. (2011a, August 17). *Why We Attacked UN Building—Boko Haram*. https://www.vanguardngr.com/2011/08/breaking-news-boko-haram-claims-responsibility-for-un-house-suicide-bombing/

———. (2011b, November 24). *Al Qaeda Assist Us and We Assist them: Boko Haram Spokesman*. https://www.vanguardng.com/2011/11/al-assist-us-and-we-assist-them-boko-haram-spokesman.

Walker, A. (2012, June). *Who is Boko Haram? USIP*, Special Report 308. https://www.usip.org/sites/default/files/SR308.pdf.

Wilton, P. (2016, April). *Statement: Religion, Radicalization and Countering Violent Extremism*. www.wiltonpark.org.uk/wp-content/uploads/statement-on-religion-radicalization-and-countering-violent-extremism.pdf.

Wright, J. D. (2016). Why is Contemporary Religious Terrorism Predominantly Linked to Islam? Four Possible Psychosocial Factors. *Perspectives on Terrorism, 10*(1), 19–31.

# Beyond Ethnicity: Reflections on the History and Politics of Violence in Uganda

Evarist Ngabirano

## 1  Introduction

Recent incidents of violence in Uganda received significant global attention and concern as events that reproduce Uganda's past in the present. The first and most recent bloodbath was the killing of close to 60 people on the streets of Kampala in the process of suppressing the demonstrations that followed the arrest of the leading opposition leader in the 2020/2021 general elections in Uganda. The opposition leader was mainly supported by the majority of people of his ethnicity; the Baganda of the central region. The second incidence of political violence happened in 2016 when the militia of the Bakonzo ethnicity and government security forces clashed, leading to the killing of close to five security officers and more than 100 people who occupied the king's palace. A similar clash happened in 2014 and government forces killed close to 100 people of the Bakonzo ethnic militia in Bundibugyo district.

The explanations given by conventional historians focus on African agency as opposed to the historical and political contexts of Uganda as a postcolonial state. The claim here is that postcolonial ethnic mobilization/nationalism in East Africa received inspiration from native intellectuals and politicians like Isaya Mukirane, the father of the current king of the Bakonzo, and

E. Ngabirano (✉)
Faculty of Humanities and Social Sciences, Mountains of the Moon University, Fort Portal, Uganda
e-mail: engabirano@mmu.ac.ug

© The Author(s), under exclusive license to Springer Nature Switzerland AG 2024
O. B. Mlambo and E. Chitando (eds.), *The Palgrave Handbook of Violence in Africa*,
https://doi.org/10.1007/978-3-031-40754-3_28

that these leaders mobilized their people along ethnic lines and wrote self-interested history books to validate and authenticate their leadership positions and inspire future generations. The argument here is that successive postcolonial heads of states have exacerbated the problem through patronage politics. That is how the creation of kingdoms and districts along ethnic lines, which are sources of violence in Uganda, is explained. In response, this study deploys historical and political science approaches to demonstrate how the pervasive postcolonial ethnic nationalism/mobilization in Uganda was derivative of the colonial mode of governance.

The past matters today and continues to define the future. This chapter reflects on the history and politics of political violence in Uganda. It is about the past, the present, and future. The core focus in this reflection is the question of agency. So far the literature on Uganda overwhelmingly emphasizes individual agency as opposed to institutions of governance. The idea here is that the political elites in Uganda have been, and continue to be, self-interested. In this case, leaders like King Edward Mutesa II, Milton Obote, Idi Amin, Yusufu K. Lule, Godfrey Binaisa, Paul Muwanga, and even Yoweri Museven, the contemporary president of Uganda, have acted and continue to act with self-interest.

At the dawn of independence, the Uganda People's Congress (UPC)-Kabaka Yekka alliance that brought the king, Edward Mutesa II into politics was a product of Baganda and Milton Obote's self-interest. This self-interest is also manifested in the abrogation of the independence constitution, abolition of the kingdoms, the violent military attack on the king's palace, and the subsequent escape into exile by the king. The politics that propelled Obote into power and sustained him there in the 1960s were stained with blood, all to serve personal interest in staying in power.

In the early 1970s, non-political leaders like Idi Amin, also in the grip of self-interest, hatched a plan to overthrow the government, which happened in 1971. Driven by self-interest, Amin became the number one dictator of the world, executing anyone with a dissenting voice. The first victims were the Luo who were ethnically kin to Obote, his predecessor. This implies that Amin had to cleanse the army of the Lango and Acholi (Luo) replacing them with the Kakwa, his fellow tribesmen. Almost all other ethnic groups in Uganda became victims of Amin's terror attacks and murders. It is estimated that about 500,000 people died in his regime, which lasted eight years.

The 1979 liberation war from neighbouring Tanzania and the political formations that accompanied it were also entangled in self-interested political and/or military intrigues, which led to the failure of the Uganda National Liberation Front (UNLF) umbrella regime. For instance, Yusufu K. Lule, the first president of the regime was accused of being a self-interested leader in his choice of ministers, the majority of whom were of his ethnicity, the Baganda. He was replaced by Godfrey L. Binaisa who was deposed by a military commission on the selfish motives of Obote and his supporters. Out of self-interested motives, Obote and his supporters rigged the 1980 elections and masterminded the killings of opposition leaders; something that triggered another liberation war led by Yoweri Museven, the current president of Uganda. The liberation war which lasted for five years was horrible and involved everyone, men, women, and children in all walks of life. It is estimated that between 300,000 to 500,000 people could have perished in this struggle across the country.

While Museven is celebrated for waging a war against the self-interested politics of the 1970s and 1980s, several scholars have accused him of patronage politics associated with his long stay in power. Moreover, his takeover of power in 1986 did not immediately pacify the country. The north, which had for a long time dominated the army under successive regimes, including those of Obote and Tito Okello Lutwa, went on the offensive, first under Alice Lakwena of the Holy Spirit Movement (HSM), and later under Joseph Kony of the Lord's Resistance Army (LRA). This war went on for 20 years devastating the northern part of the country. This chapter focuses on the following debates: history, politics, and agency; patronage politics; and inclusion and exclusion debates.

## 2  History, Politics, and Agency

Uganda has had a violent history that has attracted the attention of academic debate. A brief look at Uganda's history indicates that the country has never had a peaceful transition of power from one head of state to the next. The lines along which the divisions are drawn to justify ethnic violence are several, and the contestation is mainly concerning rights of access to political power, land, and other resources. At the national level, lines have been drawn between Northerners and Southerners, Baganda and the rest of Ugandans, and the main religious groups, namely: Muslims, Anglicans, and Catholics.

The first set of scholarly literature attributes ethnic violence in Uganda to culture. The argument of culture has been discredited in academic debate. I, however, deploy it here mainly to articulate my point of view, specifically, that the problem of ethnic violence has not been sufficiently historicized. The idea stressed in the argument of culture is that Ugandans are just violent. They have been fighting for so long that they have fallen in love with it. It is part of their culture. This group of literature makes no attempt to historicize. The agency emphasized here is ethnicity and religion, and nothing more. To open up this debate, I single out Roland A. Atkinson (1994) whose view is that Uganda's recent and distant pasts do relate perfectly. So, he explains how "many of the events and relationships characteristic of Uganda's recent history-including politics and political violence-have been intimately bound up with Uganda's perceptions of their societal and ethnic identity" (Ronald R. Atkinson, 1994). So, the idea here is that Ugandans know themselves as belonging to ethnicities and this, in itself, leads them into violent confrontations. Atkinson, therefore, believes that representation of identity in the colonial and postcolonial periods, however distorted, has not been "plucked from the air or created out of nothingness" (Ronald R. Atkinson, 1994). Justus Mugaju and Oloka Onyango (2001) believe that the use of force was an intrinsic characteristic of the Ugandan population. Thus "the war tradition from the colonial autocrats to the postcolonial warlords has been more internalized in Uganda's political culture and psyche than the ballot tradition" (Justus Mugaju & Oloka Onyango, 2001: 4). So, in this regard, ethnicity is distinct and antagonistic. There is no need to historicize or politicize it. People fight just because they are different in ethnicity and religion.

Dan M. Mudoola (1993) attempted to historicize, and established that, in serving their own interests, colonial officials and postcolonial leaders manipulated ethnic and religious identities. He underscored the socio-economic inequalities associated with the unequal access to political power and other resources to explain the ethnic and religious antagonism in Uganda. As a solution, he suggested that resources including political power should be distributed on the basis of ethnicity and religion (Mudoola, 1993: 107–108). In the same way, Kasozi (1994) interpreted Uganda's political instabilities through the lenses of socio-economic inequalities. The socio- economic disparities that Kasozi is concerned with here are the country's resources, which are unfairly distributed among different religions, ethnic groups, regions, classes, and genders. But Kasozi focuses more on the unfairness between "Asians" and "Africans"; "North" and "South"; Buganda and the rest; and rural and urban (Kasozi, 1994: 7–8). Like Mudoola, Kasozi suggests a deliberate equitable distribution of the country's resources to these groups.

Several Ugandan scholars have focused on individual agency to explain the post-independence politics of ethnicity. The first scholar is Samwiri Karugire (1996) who analyses the causes of political instabilities in Uganda and concludes that the problem has been one of leadership. In this view, it was postcolonial leaders who failed to solve the problems they inherited from colonialism, which included ethnicity. Instead of resolving ethnic divisions created by colonialism, postcolonial leaders exploited them to entrench themselves in political power (Samwiri Karugire, 1996: 4–5). However, Karugire puts the blame mainly on presidents, Idi Amini and Milton Obote.

Yoweri K. Museveni (1992) appears to be more sensitive to the socio-economic concerns and believes that they would polarize society along ethnic and religious lines if there were no good leadership. He, however, believes that leaders can overcome ethnicity and sectarianism because these are caused by a failure to identify the real interests of the people. To him the real interests of the people are built on modernization. The leadership, therefore, must help people to overcome primitive ways to embrace modern agriculture built on technology and large-scale production. He believes that the ideology of the Movement System was the best because it shunned tribalism and religious divisions (Museveni, 1992). Kasozi (1994) considers the postcolonial leadership crisis as secondary to the socio-economic inequalities and ethnicity but Karugire and Museveni think otherwise although the two disagree on the role of the economy. However, all have failed to do justice to the historicity of violence in Uganda. Karugire (1996: 4–5) laments that colonialists were able to rule for seventy years in peace while postcolonial leadership led the country into violence in a short span.

Shifting away from the question of leadership, scholarly literatures have focused on systems of governance. The argument here is that the political party system was a breeding ground of religious, ethnic, and regional cleavages. The main protagonists of the argument include Dan Mudoola and Tarsis Kabwegyere. Their argument is that political parties manipulated religion and ethnicity to capture and maintain power. Dan Mudoola (1993: 89) for instance explains how "major political parties—the Uganda People's Congress (UPC) and the Democratic Party (DP) regarded the ethno-political arena as one of their major constituencies." The implicaton is that the politics leading to the election of the president clearly demonstrated that the institution was regarded as a national institution for bargaining among ethnic groups (Mudoola, 1993: 89). Tarsis B. Kabwegyere (1974) explains how kingdom districts dominated these politics at the dawn of independence to the extent that the president had to be elected from among the rulers of the kingdoms. These literatures present the multi-party system of governance as responsible for the political instabilities in Uganda but do not bother to question what turned tribes into political identities or what made the kingdom districts from which heads of states were to be drawn so special.

In this same debate about governance systems, a body of literature has argued that even the movement governance system deployed religion and ethnicity to consolidate itself in power. I identify Nelson Kasfir (1976) and

Aili Mari Tripp (2010) as key proponents of this argument. Kasfir (1976), for instance, argues that the movement system began radically by empowering Ugandans but, over the years, it has been used to enhance its own legitimation and deepen its position of power rather than to extend the frontiers of democracy. He believes that the aim of those who support the movement system have been reduced to self-perpetuation and entrenchment (Kasfir, 1976). Aili Mari Tripp (2010) likens Ugandan politics to hybrid regimes that are fraught with contradictions: "Their leaders adopt the trappings of democracy, yet they prevent democracy—sometimes through patronage and largess, other times through violence and regression for the sole purpose of remaining in power" (Tripp, 2010: 1).

There is a diversified body of literature that advances the view that colonial legacy accounts for the pervasive ethnic patriotism in East Africa and Uganda in particular. The idea here is that the reproduction of ethnic politics in the post-independence period can best be described as derivative. Notwithstanding the validity of this argument, a noticeable body of literature cautions that the emphasis placed on colonial legacy could be exaggerated and simplistic. As an example, this group of literature cites African-led activism and self-interested politics in the late colonial and early post-independence periods. Evarist Ngabirano (2021) critiques this argument in his article entitled "Beyond Local Government Reforms: A Case Study of Toro and Kigezi Districts in the Politics of Postcolonial Uganda." Carol Summers (2014: 21–35, 22), for instance, argues that the Baganda of Uganda were patriots who understood power in terms of its relationship with the land and the tribe. That is how the activism of the 1950s in Bugada that advanced the cause for the return of the Kabaka was understood and explained by scholars.

The body of literature that builds on this idea of African agency is significant. The first set focuses on the role of indigenous intellectuals. The argument advanced here is that colonialism did a good job by introducing local council government reforms after the end of World War II. The idea here is that the introduction of these local councils before independence affectively brought indirect rule politics to a close end (Cooper, 2009). Thus, the colonial regime had succeeded in imposing "strict limits" on ethnic governments established in the early period of colonial rule (Peterson, 2009: 154). The implication here is that the ethnic nationalism that happened in the 1950s onwards can only be explained from the angle of African agency outside the colonial mode of governance. It is in this context that the 1953 pro-monarchy activism advancing the cause for the Kabaka's return from exile is explained (Summers, 2014: 22). Moreover, the literature also advances it to justify a wave of post-independence federal demands elsewhere in Uganda.

For instance, Peterson (2009: 174) claims that this discourse of monarchical nationalism in Buganda gave colonial Uganda's other monarchies a path to follow. Furthermore, Peterson (2009) argues that post-independence leaders and intellectuals like Isaya Mukirane were inspired by Buganda to lead a rebellion on the basis of ethnicity. On this basis all community leaders were branded "ethnic patriots" to place emphasis on African agency in this project of "ethnic patriotism." To these actors Jonathan Glassman (2011: 6–7) attributed the rise of racial thought in colonial Zanzibar. However, Yahya Sseremba (2019: 311–328) makes an important point when he argues that the agency of native actors should be analysed from the context of the circumstances within which colonialism made ethnicity the basis for political inclusion.

In his recent publication, Sseremba (2019: 311–328) argued that the initiative of African indigenous intellectuals in presenting their societies as "tribes" is not an independent initiative but rather something that developed out of circumstances within which the colonialists made ethnicity the basis for qualifying for land and other rights. It is these circumstances along which groups of people mobilized their societies as distinct "tribes" to convince the modern state that they met the requirements for being natives with rights over land and political power (Sseremba, 2019). In this way Sseremba (2019) claims to go beyond the critics of scholars who advance the agency of colonialism. While these critics focused on how individual agency shaped their own societies, he analyses how they were shaped by the circumstances in which the modern state privileged ethnicity. My argument here is that Sseremba (2019) also did not historicize sufficiently because he ignored the agency of ethnographers like Tom Stacey who took a leading role in the projects of indigenous intellectuals. I claim that indigenous intellectuals were not in most cases self-interested, and I give Paulo Ngologoza of Kigezi as an example. I argue that "Ngologoza derived inspiration from a multiplicity of sources including pre-colonial, colonial and the socio-economic aspirations of his society, Kigezi to think in terms of residence as opposed to his ethnicity, the Bakiga" (Ngabirano, 2021: 5).

The second body of literature that emphasizes native agency focuses on the *longue durée*. Here the agency of colonialism is recognized in addition to insisting that the pre-colonial past needs to be examined to unearth processes that explain contemporary politics of ethnicity in governance. Paul Nugent (2008: 922), for instance, believes that colonialism was significant but insists that it was not the first historical moment to determine the way Africans related to their neighbours. The implication here is that colonialism had antecedents upon which it was able to build the project of ethnic-based governance. There is a significant debate here advanced by Leroy Vail (1989) and others who suggest that ethnic patriotism was a colonial creation. Vail (1989) for instance thought that colonialism crafted tribes into being and they were, therefore, never organic to the African way of life. Terence Ranger (1989) gave the example of the Manyika ethnic consciousness, concluding that it was an invention of missionaries in Zimbabwe.

However, Thomas Spears (2003: 3–27) argued against the idea of colonial invention, which he claims is often overstated. In his view, colonialism did not have sufficient power and ability to manipulate African institutions such as ethnicity to rule Africa. The implication here is that ethnic institutions of governance were negotiated pre-colonial practices. In response to this claim, it has been clarified in the literature how ethnicity and traditions existed in the pre-colonial time but how these were multiple, competing, and constantly changing. However, in a self-interested manner, colonialism singled out several of these for their administrative practice, setting a stage for derivative responses similar to that of Bakonzo and Bamba in Toro.

A significant body of literature attests to the above colonial practice in several parts of Africa. When Yususfu Bala Usman (2006: 43–45) identified this practice, he insisted on studying the formation and transformation of communities of the area as a historical process. For instance, he argued that it made sense to treat the Fulani as a territorial group of people as opposed to treating them as an ethnic category with land and political rights. Mahmood Mamdani (2009: 93) identified the category "Arab" and argued that colonialism compressed "varied identities of multiple histories into one single identity—a uniform Arab identity—by legal and administrative fiat, complemented by history writing. Sseremba (2019) recognizes that this freezing of hitherto complex identities in several parts of Africa is what happened in Western Uganda. However, this applies to Toro and Ankole as opposed to Kigezi of Southwestern Uganda. On meeting resistance from the colonized, colonial officials recognized that Kigezi was multi-ethnic. In addition to this colonial approach, the pre-colonial and the socio-economic aspirations of the people inspired indigenous leaders like Ngologoza to focus on developing a residence-based narrative and mode of mobilization in Kigezi.

## 3    Politics of Patronage Debate in Museveni's Uganda

The current president of Uganda, Yoweri Museven recognizes the multi-ethnic identity of Uganda and works to ensure that their political representation and other privileges are met. This is manifested in the ways in which the president appoints ministers in his government, recognizes kingdoms and creates new districts along ethnic divides. However, while recognizing and creating kingdoms on demand, Museveni has obstinately rejected calls for the restoration of the kingdom in his territory of residence, Ankole, on the same basis of ethnic diversity. Museveni here no doubt represents a post-independent leader that is not self-interested. However, several political scholars have criticized him of patronage politics.

The idea of politics of patronage suggests that the current head of state is responsible for the ethnic violence and all other forms of insecurities associated with ethnic manoeuvres. Joshua Rubongoya (2007) begins this argument with the claim that the current president thrives on neo-patrimonial legitimacy, which involves the award of personal favours in the form of patronage, which has aggravated the problem of ethnic antagonism. For example, the idea is that Museveni has, in his politics of patronage, created kingdoms even where they previously never existed in order to gain popular support. This has been a major finding in the work of Anna Reuss and Kristoff Titeca (2017: 131–141) who examined how Museveni created kingdoms in the Rwenzori to gain much-needed support from the well-known opposition stronghold districts, such as Kasese, but ended up aggravating divisions that sparked off the most recent bloodbath in the region. Elliot Green (2010: 94) claims that the creation of new districts as a new way of obtaining regime supporters enhanced ethnic conflicts. The other way of winning regime support that Museveni has deployed according to Clair Medard and Valerie Golaz (2013: 555–556) is by instigating claims of autochthony. They claim that Museveni does this by identifying with minorities like the Banyala in Buganda and championing peasant land rights among the landless majorities.

I want to advance two key points to explain my position in regard to this debate. I emphasize that the agency to create kingdoms and districts was from society and not from the head of state. The argument here is not whether a given set of demands is from society but whether it can be, or is, integrated into a colonial project. As already noted, the ability to do the latter makes indirect rule a successful political project. To illustrate my claim, let me focus on the project of the current head of state. First, President Yoweri Museven's political project was at the beginning not self-interested because the Resistance Councils (RC) that were set up as administrative units repudiated indirect rule with its focus on residence.

Second, Museveni's political project shifted to methods of indirect rule after the introduction of the multi-party constitution. All of a sudden, the agency of society became all-important to Museveni because he needed popular support to win in multi-party competitive politics. Most importantly, I want to emphasize that the agency of society has been reproduced historically and sustained in the imagination of the colonized. The indirect rule that happened after independence did not, therefore, require local agents of British rule but rather the imagination and institutions that were shaped by colonial rule.

## 4      Politics of Inclusion and Exclusion Debate

There is a constant call for equal ethnic representation in administrative units of modern states. Sseremba (2019), however, claims that the call for the three-tribe solution in Toro of Western Uganda was the beginning of the continuous reproduction of tribalism. That instead, the people of Kasese, one of the districts that split from Toro proposed a political identity based on residence as opposed to the ethnic identities that make up the district. This chapter reinforces this idea but also seeks to refine it because it underscores the idea of homogeneity of residence. The point here is that ethnic identities were colonial political categories and not culturally distinct. The thrust of this idea is to question the dominant claim in the existing literature on Uganda that suggests equal distribution of the "national cake" as a solution to postcolonial ethnic antagonism in Uganda (Sseremba, 2019). My claim is that, even if ethnic identities were constituted political categories as opposed to cultural, they have become undeniable parts of postcolonial politics as they make up the heterogeneity of residence that we call districts. This calls for a political solution that takes into account the existence of these identities. But I further claim that even the call for recognition of the ethnic heterogeneity does not guarantee coexistence because it is tantamount to a demand for reform within indirect rule, calling for its consistent application. I compare two multi-ethnic districts of Toro and Kigezi and draw lessons from other countries including Ghana and Tanzania to demonstrate a more successful inclusive mode of governance in a modern state.

In the late 1950s and early 1960s Africa was finally emerging from colonial rule. Uganda gained independence in 1962 and adopted a federal constitution, which had been agreed upon the previous year at the London Conference. The Uganda People's Congress (UPC) and Kabaka Yekka (KY) party had emerged as victors in the 1962 general election to form a government in which Milton Obote, the leader of UPC, became the Prime Minister with executive powers. Obote received the instruments of power from the British on Independence Day while Kabaka Edward Mutesa II was to be sworn in as the first president in 1963. Subsequently the non-kingdom districts like Kigezi were arranging to elect constitutional heads who would be legible for election as presidents under the federal constitution of Uganda. Kigezi, whose multi-ethnic identity was based on residence as opposed to tribe, elected John Bikangaga, a Mukiga, as a constitutional head for the district. My claim is that the election of a Mukiga as a constitutional head of a multi-tribal district of Kigezi is remarkable because the Bakiga, like the Bakonzo of Toro, never had a lineage of leadership. I argue that these sorts of politics were only possible in Kigezi as opposed to Toro where only one tribe, the Batoro, were officially recognized. While it was possible for a Mukiga to become a constitutional head of Kigezi in the early 1960s, in Toro even the position of the prime minister was reserved for *Batoro Nyakabara* (real Batoro). The idea here is that the king descended from the royal family and selected his assistants from the royal lineage of the Batoro. Unlike Kigezi where a king was elected, in Toro kingship was inherited. Thus far, the post-independence politics of Kigezi were democratic and inclusive while those of Toro were undemocratic and exclusive. Moreover, I claim that the inclusive politics of Kigezi stem from the fact that the intellectual and political work of Bakiga leaders went beyond ethnic patriotism. The idea here is that leaders like Ngologoza wrote "Kigezi and its People" that inspired the development of a residence-based identity known as the *Banyakigezi* as opposed to ethnic identities.

To pursue a nationalist project, Obote realized the importance of residence and its heterogeneity. The overriding idea behind this realization was that national unity was key to furthering national interests. To achieve this, every effort was to be made to replace ethnic interests with national ones. In mid-1960, for instance, Obote sent the Bakonzo leaders to Kigezi to consult with Bikangaga who is reported to have advised them to abandon the secessionist project because Uganda was about to be declared a republic and the kingdoms abolished. Indeed this came to pass in 1967. In the early 1970s, Kigezi elders would write a memorandum to the then president, Idi Amin, expressing national interests. Kingship or traditional institutions, they argued, were "tribal institutions, which were mainly responsible for disunity of Ugandans as they instilled tribal misunderstandings, mistrust and hatred in society." As a consequence, they asserted "many people owed allegiance to tribal governments more than their nation, Uganda yet for the people of Kigezi national interests must of necessity override local interests" (Dornbos, 2001: 135). This expression of nationalism is remarkable in the sense that it sought to demolish the political structures that perpetuated colonialism into the postcolonial and as such it sought to detribalize and/or to decolonize.

I now examine the path taken by nationalists to decolonize the African continent in order to explain the residence-based politics in Kigezi as opposed to ethnic/ancestry politics in Toro. Following the model of European nationalism, many post-independence states sought to develop national cultures associated with language and ideology. Tanzania for instance enforced Swahili as a national language and adopted a socialist political ideology. This could pass for a nationalism that enforces uniformity/homogeneity similar to the colonial order enforced on Toro. But Swahili, unlike Rutoro, was not ethnic and socialism was thought to be African by nature. I want to relate socialism ideology with Kigezi's inter-ethnic politics that identified with residence as opposed to tribe. To demonstrate these links I revisit Julius Nyerere who wrote: "We in Africa have no need of being converted to socialism than we have of being 'taught' democracy. Both are rooted in our past—in traditional society which produced us" (1979: 12). This train of thought makes Nyerere a believer in a humanism based on a socialist attitude of the mind traced from the tribal days, which gave every individual the security that comes with belonging to a wide extended family. I deduce in this idea a claim that I have articulated before about Kigezi's identity that was multi-ethnic and geographical. While recognizing the need to modernize the traditional structures to make Tanzanians meet new aspirations for a higher standard of living, he acknowledged the need to preserve such African heritage within the wider society of the nation, but which must extend beyond the tribe, the community, the nation, the continent, and the whole society of humankind (Nyerere, 1979: 12). Several other nationalists built on this same idea and organized their politics along these lines. Obote for instance developed a common man's charter in which he proposed a move to the left (socialism). This policy document that was never implemented stated:

> We reject both in theory and practice that Uganda as a whole or any part of it should be the domain of any person, of feudalism, of capitalism, of vested interests of one kind or another, of foreign influence or of foreigners. We further reject exploitation of material and human resources for the benefit of a few. (KabDA Box 996 Visitors-General Vol. 7 file, The Common Man's Charter)

The overriding idea behind this trend of politics was to totally demolish the inequalities associated with legacies of colonial institutions. Even if kingdoms were abolished in 1967, privileges associated with them remained pervasive. For instance the colonial order that privileged Batoro identity over Bakonzo and Bamba continued to be discriminative in terms of access to political power, land, and other resources.

I interacted with Michael A. Tagoe (interview 2019, Accra, Ghana) and read the literature of Kwame Nkrumah to get the story of nationalism in Ghana and found remarkable similarities in the way nationalists organized their politics. Tagoe is a provost at the College of Education, University of Ghana. I met him at Peduase Valley Resort, at the Next Generation Social Sciences in Africa 2019 Fellows Workshop hosted by University of Ghana, Accra. Like Nyerere and Obote, Nkrumah articulated socialist ideas. Nkurumah (1964: 78) believed that the principles that informed capitalism were "in conflict with the socialist egalitarianism of the traditional African society." To overcome the clutches of colonial institutions that enforced capitalism, Nkrumah (1964: 79) proposed a philosophy of consciencism whose "basis was in materialism." In order to emancipate the African continent, Nkrumah believed in the emancipation of man first. To achieve this, he outlined two objectives: "first the restitution of the egalitarianism of human society, and second, the logistic mobilization of all our resources towards the attainment of that restitution" (Nkrumah, 1964: 78). Unlike Obote's common man's charter, which was never, implemented, Nkrumah's "avoidance of discrimination act" made significant political impact on Ghana (Tagoe interview 2019, Accra, Ghana). The key reforms associated with this act focus on building the multi-ethnic political identity that was based on residence in Ghana, as opposed to ethnicity. The idea behind this form of politics was the principle of equal access to political power and other resources by all ethnic identities in Ghana.

To avoid discrimination, the state provides funding to all cultural institutions and appoints ministers on a tribal and regional basis (Asante & Gyimah-Boadi, 2020). The idea here is to distribute the national cake equally. It is important to note that "inequality and ethno-regional rivalry may cause tensions but they have not erupted in violent conflict largely because successive Ghanaian governments have adopted practices of symbolic distribution, representativeness and inclusion" (Asante & Gyimah-Boadi, 2020). My claim is that this Ghanian account exemplifies a political solution to postcolonial politics of ethnicity but does not necessarily lead to detribalization and/or decolonization of politics. Rather, I claim that this way of organizing politics projects a consistent way of reproducing indirect rule. I propose that a conscious development of identity based on residence as opposed to ethnicity would go a long way to detribalize and decolonize politics. I found this consciousness in the intellectual and political work of African leaders like Ngologoza of Kigezi who wrote *Kigezi and Its People* to inspire the young generation develop a residence-based identity as opposed to tribe. I relate this to the Tanzanian model of identity that emphasized one cultural identity for Tanzania as opposed to the Ghanian that recognized cultural heterogeneity.

Sseremba (2019) makes an important claim in asserting that the three-tribe solution in Toro and the idea of sharing the 'national cake' equally was a prelude to ethnic patriotism in Uganda and Toro in particular but offered no political solution. In suggesting this, he assumed that ethnic heterogeneity was a colonial project in Africa as opposed to being in the nature of African society. My claim is that, though ethnicity became a political project for colonial administration, it was only a product of a continuing process; old and new in a simultaneous way, grounded in the past and perpetually in the making. Moreover, as Bruce Berman (1998: 305–341) says colonialism was really allied to 'local big men'. The problem arises when a nation is equated with ethnicity that has authentic culture as the case was in the project of enforcing homogeneity on Toro. That is what Mamdani referred to as tribalism that may be a prelude to genocide. That is what is implied in Samola Machel's well-known call: "for the nation to live, the tribe must die" (Mamdani, 1996: 135, Albie & Welch, 1990: 2). Thus, my claim is that recognizing that residence is heterogeneous ethnically and organizing its politics in a way that ensures equal access to political power and resources is a political but not a proper way of resolving conflict in Africa because it falls short of detribalizing and decolonizing postcolonial politics. To reiterate my claim, I want to emphasize that detribalization and decolonization will happen only if there is a conscious development of a residence-based identity as espoused in the intellectual and political works of Nyerere on Tanzania and Ngologoza on Kigezi. In these politics that emphasize uniformity of the culture of residence, the outcome is that the differences between majority and minority groups is not cultural but political. The idea here is that everyone's identity is included in the same culture of residence. The point I want to make here is that people's cultural identity matters to them more than politics because culture gives belonging while politics does not. That is why it is wrong to transform culture into a political mobilization tool. As long as people feel that they belong to the culture of residence, its politics does not matter.

## 5    Conclusion

The politics of postcolonial Uganda have largely been divisive along ethnicity and religious lines. A wide range of scholarly literature focus on individual agency and politics of patronage to explain the recurrence of political violence that is ethnically based. A close study reveals that almost all post-independence leaders in Uganda acted in many ways that reflected self-interested politics based on ethnicity and religion. However, this inclination can only be understood in the historical and political circumstances within which they were born and reproduced. Thus, an examination of the pre-colonial and colonial modes of governance and the postcolonial socio-economic aspirations becomes relevant in understanding why community leaders acted with self-interest. The idea that Museveni, the current president of Uganda has exacerbated ethnic politics through patronage should also be understood in the circumstances within which it is being deployed. In the first decades, his government set up Resistance Council administrative units that were residence-based and carried no self-interested politics but when political parties were introduced, the presidency, which largely depends on popular support, gave in to the derivative demands from the masses. My analysis is that recognizing the multiple identities imbedded in residence and ensuring equal representation is a political but not a proper way of resolving conflict in a modern state like Uganda. Borrowing from the example of Tanzania, I claim that there must be a conscious development of a residence-based identity, which leads to cultural uniformity. In such a polity, the difference between majority and minority groups will not be cultural but political. I claim that this will overcome violence because everyone's identity is included in the same culture of residence.

## Bibliography

Albie, S., & Gita, H. W. (1990). *Liberating the Law, Creating Popular Justice in Mozambique.* Zed books.

Asante, R., & Gyimah-Boadi, E. (2020). "Ethnic Structure, Inequality and Governance of the Public Sector in Ghana," United Nations Research Institute for Social Development (UNRISD). (2004) http://www.unrisd.org/80256B3C005BCCF9/(httpAuxPages)/8509496C0F316AB1C1256ED900466964/$file/Asante%20(small).pdf, accessed on 12 January.

Atkinson, R. (1994). *The Roots of Ethnicity: The Origins of Acholi of Uganda Before 1800.* University of Pennsylvania Press.

Berman, J. B. (1998). Ethnicity, Patronage and the African State: The Politics of Uncivil Nationalism. *African Affairs, 97*, 305–341.

Cooper, F. (2009). *Africa Since 1940: The Past of the Present*. Cambridge University Press.

Glassman, J. (2011). *War of Words, War of Stones: Racial thought and Violence in Colonial Zanzibar*. Indiana University Press.

Green, E. (2010). Patronage, District Creation and Reform in Uganda. *Studies in Comparative International Development, 45*(1), 94.

Doornbos, R. M. (2001). *The Ankole Kingship Controversy: Regalia Galore Revisited*. Fountain publishers.

Kabwegyere, B. T. (1974). *The Politics of State Formation: The Nature and Effect of Colonialism in Uganda, Nairobi, Dar es salaam*. East African Literature Bureau.

Kasfir, N. (1976). *The Shrinking of Political Arena: Participation of Ethnicity in African Politics: A Case Study of Uganda*. University of California Press.

Kasozi, A. B. K. (1994). *The Social Origin of Violence in Uganda*. McGill Queen's University Press.

Karugire, R. S. (1996). *Roots of Instability in Uganda*. Fountain Publishers.

Mamdani, M. (1996). *Citizen and Subject: Contemporary Africa and the Legacy of Late Colonialism*. Princeton University Press.

Mamdani, M. (2009). *Saviors and Sarvivors: Darfur*. Panteon Books.

Medard, C., & Golaz, V. (2013). Creating Dependency, Land and Gift Giving Practices in Uganda. *Journal of East African Studies, 7*(3), 549–568.

Mugaju, J., & Oloka-Oyango, J. (Eds.). (2001). *No-party Democracy in Uganda: Myths and Realities*. Fountain Publishers.

Mudoola, M. D. (1993). *Religion, Ethnicity and Politics in Uganda*. Fountain Publishers.

Museveni, K. Y. (1992). *What is Africa's Problem?* NRM Publications.

Ngabirano, E. (2021, December). "Beyond Local Government Reforms: A Case Study of Toro and Kigezi Districts in the Politics of Postcolonial Uganda" *Nationalism and Ethnic Politics*. https://doi.org/10.1080/13537113.2021.1990704

Nkrumah, K. (1964). *Consciencism: The Philosophy and Ideology for Decolonization and Development with Particular Reference to the African Revolution*. Heinemann.

Nugent, P. (2008). "Putting the History back into Ethnicity, Enslavement, Religion, and Cultural Brokerage in the Construction of Mandinka/Jola and Ewe/Agotime identities in West Africa c.1650–1930" *Comparative Studies in Society and History, 50*(4).

Nyerere, K. J. (1979). *Ujamaa: Essays on Socialism*. Oxford University Press.

Peterson, D. (2009). "States of Mind: Political History and the Rwenzururu Kingdom in Western Uganda" In D. Peterson, & G. Macola (Eds.), *Recasting the Past: History Writing and Political Work in Modern Africa*, Ohio University Press.

Ranger, T. (1989). "Missionaries, Migrants and the Manyika: The Invention of Ethnicity in Zimbabwe" In L. Vail (Ed.), *The Creation of Tribalism in South Africa*. James Currey, University of California Press.

Reuss, A., & Titeca, K. (2017). Beyond Ethnicity: The Violence in Western Uganda and Rwenzori's 99 Problems. *Review of African Political Economy, 44*(151), 131–141. https://doi.org/10.1080/03056244.2016.1270928

Rubongoya, J. (2007). *Regime Hegemony in Museveni's Uganda: Pax Musevenica*. Palgrave Macmillan.

Spears, T. (2003). Neo-Traditionalism and the Limits of Invention in British Colonial Africa. *The Journal of African History, 44*(1), 3–27.

Sseremba, Y. (2019). The Making and Remaking of "Native Tribes" in Uganda's Toro Kingdom. *Nationalism and Ethnic Politics, 25*(3), 311–328.

Summers, C. (2014). Local Critiques of Global Development: Patriotism in Late Colonial Buganda. *International Journal of African Historical Studies, 47*(1), 21–35.

Tripp, A. M. (2010). *Museveni's Uganda: Paradoxes of Power in a Hybrid Regime*. Lynne Rienner Publishers.

Usman, Y. B. (2006). *Beyond Fairly Tales*, Abdullahi Smith, Center for Historical Research.

Vail, L. (Ed.). (1989). *The Creation of Tribalism in South Africa, James Currey*. University of California Press.

# The Intersectionality Between Violence and Poverty in Africa: Sketching the Prevalence of Various Forms of Violence in South Africa

Rabson Hove

## 1    Introduction

Violence in Africa and South Africa in particular is a lived phenomenon. Africa is born out of the shackles of colonialism and the wars of resistance and independence. On the one hand, colonialists used violence as a tool of oppression, while on the other the oppressed used violence as a means to gain independence during colonialism. Like most other countries in Africa, South Africa experienced colonial oppression and violence under apartheid. It also fought for independence, but violence has been perpetuated as part of popular culture. It has become a way of resolving problems and an element of survival skills. Violence in South Africa ranges from political violence to farm attacks, taxi-violence, domestic violence, gender-based violence, and xenophobic violence. These forms of violence are exacerbated by poverty, or are a result of poverty generated by the apartheid context. The forms of violence escalate every day. The alarming rate of violence leaves citizens feeling unsafe even when they are in their own homes. This makes it difficult to prevent or mitigate violence in South Africa.

It would be difficult to talk of violence in South Africa without linking it to poverty. Owing to the historical apartheid system, poverty is so widespread that other people choose violence to earn a living. This chapter seeks to discuss the prevalence of violence in South Africa. It will explore the possible

---

R. Hove (✉)
University of South Africa, Pretoria, South Africa
e-mail: hover@unisa.ac.za

linkage between different forms of violence and poverty as the source or effect of violence.

## 2   Violence and Poverty as Reminiscent of the Apartheid System

The political history of apartheid in South Africa is inherently intertwined with social disorganization, hatred, fear, and mistrust. Breetzke (2010: 447) rightly observed that "no other country in the world has endured such a direct and sustained attack on the social fabric of its society through state laws and policies aimed at enforcing and accentuating spatio-social segmentation." The systemic social disorganization and division is a creation of the system of governance, of education, and of economic and social separation of people. The government of apartheid was predominantly white, creating laws that segregated Africans in the education system. The Bantu Education Act of 1953 left the education system racially divided with "certain subjects such as mathematics being excluded from the curriculum in Black schools" (Breetzke, 2010: 448). These, and other, apartheid policies disempowered Black South African society and "left most Black youths and youths of colour socially and economically marginalised" (Bezuidenhout, 2003: 4). According to Allen (2018: 3):

> The nation of South Africa is no exception of countries that continue to deal with the negative consequences of oppression that originate from a coercive and segregated history. Different forms of oppression that currently function in the nation center around the violent and turbulent history of colonialism, slavery, forced black labour, and institutionalized segregation during Apartheid, all of which were based upon intersecting racial, ethnic, and classist lines. The traumatic and lasting effects of intersectional oppression in South Africa remain evident, seen in the high rates of poverty along racial lines, a massive inequality gap, continued community racial segregation, and gender violence.

Violence ranges from domestic violence to gender-based violence, housebreaking, robberies, political violence, and xenophobia. These forms of violence may at times be mutually inclusive and characterized by verbal abuse, pain infliction, and murder (Pillay, 2008b; Stone, 2006). One may argue that violence in South Africa is the result of apartheid which caused many citizens to be dispossessed, marginalized, brutally wounded, and murdered. Such activities kill people's consciences and cause them to undermine the sacredness of human life.

Among other issues, crime is caused by high levels of poverty among South Africans in general and the Black community in particular. Collins (2013) observed that violence in South Africa is the result of social stressors such as poverty and overcrowding among township communities. In these crowded communities most people are unemployed because the apartheid system historically segregated these communities from the mainstream education and economy. Breetzke (2010: 448) observed that "Black youths were not only marginalized by these policies but were perennially exposed to crime and violence within their segregated communities. Levels of crime in the formerly segregated Black residential areas, known as townships of apartheid South Africa were notoriously high." In these townships and informal settlements, violent crimes such as robbery, housebreaking, murder, and rape are closely associated with alcohol and substance abuse (Pillay, 2008a, 2008b). The violent crimes in South African townships, urban centres, and on freeways also involve "gang violence, taxi violence and cash-in-transit robberies" (Clack & Minnaar, 2018: 104).

> Poor workers cannot claim their rights and neither can they report abuse and poor working conditions in companies and farms. These cases are rarely reported to the police largely because of fear of intimidation or dismissal and/or eviction (of their whole family) from the farm where they are employed—a result many farm workers simply cannot contemplate given their precarious economic existence (low wages and long working hours) and widespread poverty in rural areas of South Africa.

The violent abuse and killings of farm workers by farmers, who perpetuate apartheid and human rights violations, are underreported or ignored. These forms of violent attacks are typically a hangover from the apartheid system when there was white farmer superiority over the poor black farm worker.

In most cases a farm attack is characterized by physical assaults on the farm's occupants with the intention of achieving a particular goal (Swart, 2003). Clack and Minnaar (2018: 104) maintain that "the so-called 'farm attacks' most often result in robbery, assault, physical injuries and sometimes death (murder)." Those who attack and kill farmers seem to be avenging historical dispossession and acquiring economic resources for personal and family survival. Akinola (2020: 65) posits that "Apartheid South Africa was noted for historical land dispossession, domination by the white group and disempowerment of the black population." Addressing "the land-related structural and physical violence" in South Africa is proving to be difficult for the post-apartheid governments (Akinola, 2020). Whether or not it is viewed as a crime, it is still violence against farm owners who are believed to be beneficiaries of apartheid political and economic system that has dispossessed other sections of South African society. The issue of historical land inequality and the current desire for land redistribution are some of the causes of farm attacks and murders (Jeffrey, 2015; Obeng-Odoom, 2012). Akinola (2020: 83) posits that:

> Farm conflict is the consequence of decades of un-addressed land inequality in the country, and particularly in the farm. It is reaction against oppressions in the farm. It is the height of an expression of consistent abuse of the rights of farm workers or labour tenants. Violence should be condemned in all ramifications in the farm, but we all know why it happens.

The high incidence of violent crime in South Africa is a key indicator of a number of socio-political elements that have long-term effects on democratic processes, economic growth, and social cohesion (Pillay, 2008b: 142). Violence is evidently shown by the rise in the statistics reporting violent crimes in South Africa. Below are the statistics released by the police minister, Bheki Cele, in February 2023.

> At the release of the crime stats for Q3 2022, Cele said that 7,555 murders were recorded during the period—marking a 10% increase year on year (y-o-y). Sexual offences also increased by 9.6%—rising from 14,188 to 15,545. Rape (9.8%), sexual assault (4.1%) and attempted sexual offences (45.6%) also increased. Common robbery (21.2%), common assault (12.0%), assault with the intent to inflict grievous bodily harm (8.7%), and robbery with aggravated circumstances (10.8%) all increased y-o-y. Overall, the total number of contact crimes increased by 19,067 (11.6%) from Q3 2021 to Q3 2022. (Business Tech, 17 February 2023)

The statistics give us a rough picture of the increase in violent crimes in South Africa. At the presentation of the above statistics of violent crime, "Police Minister Bheki Cele said that the statistics don't paint an overall positive picture of the crime situation in South Africa" (Business Tech, 2023). Stone (2006: 7) rightly argued that, "In sum, the distinctive feature of crime in South Africa is its violence rather than its volume." May be mistakenly entered at times but do not usually lie on a large scale? Violence is a pandemic that the government law enforcement agents and community do not have solutions for right now.

## 3    Political Violence: A Tool for Fighting Poverty

Another instance of violence continuing to be used in political conflict is political killings. The history of colonization and apartheid in South Africa has created a situation where violence has been central to social interactions and disputes (Vetten & Ratele, 2013). Even though the political change that ended apartheid may have reduced the level of violence in the nation at the time, violence has continued to escalate to this day. Since apartheid ended, most political killings have been connected with regional political rivalry and have ties to organized crime, particularly in the taxi business (Bruce, 2014). Only when the murder is as the result of a political objective is it referred to as a political killing. Bruce (2014: 2) maintains that "Unless the motive becomes clear (for instance through information revealed at a trial) it would be more accurate to refer to killings of political office bearers or party members as 'suspected' or 'possible' political killings." Political violence has been on the rise since the time of apartheid and continues in the new dispensations of the post-apartheid era. Hlongwane (2022) admits that efforts to curb political violence are failing. Mbhanyele (2022), Bruce (2014), and Hlongwane (2022) agree that political killings happen across the country but are concentrated in Mpumalanga and KwaZulu Natal Province. According to Jeffery (2015) more than 15,000 civilians were killed shortly after 1994, the most of whom, if not all, were black people who died in inter-party violence. The fatality rate between 1985 and 1989 was close to 1000 per year; between 1990 and 1994, it increased to 3,400 per year. Focusing on KwaZulu-Natal province alone, Bruce (2013: 15) affirms that:

> Combining these figures results in an estimated total of 107 deaths in political killings in the period from 2003 to 2013. It may be noted that the NFP figure of 22 killings between early 2011 and July 2012 and the ANC figure of 38 killings over 2011 and 2012 (to September) appear to imply that over 50% of this figure is accounted for by the period of 21 months from January 2011 to September 2012, suggesting that in this period political killings once again reached a rate of intensity comparable to that experienced in KwaZulu-Natal in the late 1990s.

He further advances that killings have been a constant feature of political life in South Africa for most of the time since 1994, mostly in KwaZulu-Natal but also in Mpumalanga (Bruce, 2013). In the North-West in recent years, political killings have also emerged as a major problem. In the North-West, murders have included those of ANC regional secretary Obuti Chika in December 2012 and anti-corruption whistleblower and Rustenburg councillor Moss Phakoe in March 2009. Ten of the victims, including six politicians and three prominent government officials were from Mpumalanga (Bruce, 2014: 3). Although three provinces seem to be at the top of the list, the above information demonstrates that political violence and killings vary from province to province, are on the rise, and have a significant impact on the country's political landscape.

As discussed earlier, political killings are as a result of inter- and intra party violence. However, post-apartheid political killings have primarily been connected with regional political disputes and have ties to criminal organizations, particularly in the taxi sector (Bruce, 2013). It is not easy to clearly identify motives for the killings, whether they are political or related to business/economics. Reasons for political violence include political rivalry, political intolerance, factionalism, corruption, competition for limited resources, and the availability of illegal firearms (Hlongwane, 2022; Isike, 2019; Krelekrele, 2018).

In Africa, and South Africa in particular, politics has become a lucrative business and career. Those in political positions have more access to economic resources and easily escape from the cycle of poverty (De Haas, 2020). For that reason, the young and the old jostle for political positions in political parties and government, hence the rise of political rivalries which result in political violence and killings. According to Bruce (2013) political positions provide the advantage to those in power of giving their relatives access to business and employment opportunities. Those in government and top political positions have influence on employment and government tenders. Bruce (2013) posits that localized political contestation is likely to continue to be marked by highly inflamed political disputes since political office holds such great value in most of poorer South Africa. Hamber (1998: 2) states that political violence is contingent on a range of factors: "These can include the relative political, social and ideological strengths of opposing political groups, and the functionality of violence to these groups." For Bonnin (2004: 1), the 1980s saw "violent political struggles between supporters of the United Democratic Front (UDF) on the one hand and the Inkatha Freedom Party (IFP) on the other." During election season, political intolerance between political parties is common, and KZN has not been an exception (Nomarwayi et al., 2020). Hlongwane (2022) avers that competition for positions among political parties and within political parties result in the manipulation of votes. Manipulation of votes is coupled with killings to eliminate those who create competition for those influential positions. Bruce (2013) rightly observes that political killings also occur in other situations, such as conflicts between groups of supporters of opposing political parties, resulting in massacres.

Political corruption through manipulation of votes leads to economic corruption, by allowing access to state resources (Hlongwane, 2022; Nomarwayi et al., 2020). For Nomarwayi et al. (2020) most of the political killings are motivated by long-standing conflicts and contentiousness over political power, which, among other things, ensures or guarantees access to financial security and advantages through state resources at local government level. Nomarwayi et al. (2020: 8) argue that:

> Since 1994, political elites connected to the ANC have been contesting for power to amass state resources at local government level through projects or tender system. As a result, this contestation of political power led to the killings of councillors and mayors at local government level. This is because these incumbents are closer or perceived as the key players in the distribution of resources through political networks. The reality of the situation is that through these political networks, factions have emerged creating looters versus losers scenario at all costs.

The government resources are ill-gotten and abused to enrich a few political leaders and their cronies. "Access to networks that include people who are willing to carry out such killings may be one condition that enables such violence to flourish" (Bruce, 2013: 22). Krelekrele (2018) argues that there is a blurred line between those who are killed for political rivalry and those who are killed for access to economic resources. Isike (2019) also submits that political killings are a result of corruption, factionalism, and competition. Political killings are meant to eliminate competition over resources and access to economic opportunities and these emanate from disputes and the politics of preference within the ruling party, the ANC. Among Within the ruling party's officials, it has become a tendency that local government resources are distributed for self-enrichment (Atkinson, 2007; Mle & Maclean, 2011). Already the process is corrupt and unethical. Some political leaders have lost their lives when they have sought to fight corruption. James Nkambule, a former ANC Youth League leader and COPE member, was assassinated in October 2010 as a result of raising concerns about corruption connected with the construction of the Mbombela World Cup stadium (Bruce, 2013: 16). The impediment to curbing corruption by the government is violence unleashed by those within the political ranks and the government who benefit from it. Whistle-blowers are at risk because those in power are involved.

## 4   Taxi Violence: Competition to Fight Poverty

One of the most common scenes of violence in South Africa is in the taxi transport industry. This violence has been closely connected with political violence since it involves government or political leaders competing to climb the economic ladder and escape from poverty. Ngubane et al. (2020: 84) argue that "The root of taxi violence and the reasons for its persistence are located in the unresolved socio-economic conditions in South Africa." The apartheid system had a history of segregating the Black taxi-transport business in favour of the popular rail and bus transport systems owned by the government and white business companies (Gwilliam, 2003). Therefore, violence in this sector is as the result of competition, corruption, and jealousy in the post-apartheid era.

One of the major causes of persistent taxi violence in South Africa is the competition for major lucrative routes. "The competition for the control and domination of routes in the industry often results in an upsurge in violent occurrences, especially gun-related murders" (Ngubane et al., 2020: 84). Violence is caused by taxi owners and drivers who seek to eradicate competition by assassinating those who are a threat to their business (Gwilliam, 2003; Ngubane et al., 2020). The desire for busy routes causes the poaching of passengers which results in drivers, taxi owners, and associations becoming involved in serious conflicts as those on specific routes fight to control their territory. Ngubane et al. (2020: 100) suggest that the excessive competition and conflict between rival taxi owners and associations could be resolved by putting in places clear policies on route allocations and punishing those who breach the principles.

Lucrative routes are central to successful taxi operations; hence, some taxi owners and government officials engage in corruption in the process of route allocation. Ngubane et al. (2020: 96) observe that:

> Corrupt and dishonest owners that fight over routes perpetrate taxi violence. Corrupt transport department officials may allocate one route to two different taxi associations without negotiations for joint ventures, which naturally results in oversaturation of routes, conflict and bloody clashes.

These shenanigans create jealousy, as some will be successful while others suffer from business failures, resulting in violence (Breetzke, 2010). As a way of doing away with such competition, "some of the people in the association hire hitmen to kill drivers who are contesting with them for the same route" (Khosa, 2001). While taxi-related violence occurs in different forms, hitmen, frequently referred to as *izinkabi* (plural) or *inkabi* (singular), are hired by taxi bosses to eliminate rivals in the industry (Ngubane et al., 2020). The hitmen are hired from remote rural areas such as such as eMsinga, Mbumbulu, and kwaMaphumulo in Kwazulu-Natal and from neighbouring countries to make it difficult for that person to be apprehended (Dugard, 2001; Ngubane et al., 2020). Molefe (2016) posits that taxi violence not only affect the owners, associations, and drivers but also members of the public who happen to be passengers and passers-by. Others are killed while commuting; yet others are mistakenly shot when the violence occurs.

According to the conflict theory, violence is frequently caused by the nation's general lack of economic prospects which results in the impoverishment of the citizens. One may argue that taxi violence is not an end in itself but a result of poverty and the long history of marginalization in the mainstream economy of those who dominate this sector.

## 5  Violence on the Farms: A War of Poverty

Besides violence in the poor township and people in the informal settlements, there is another form of violence called farm attacks or murders. On the one hand farm attacks are instituted by farmers abusing the poor farm workers, while on the other hand farmers are attacked by their workers or outsiders with an intention of killing livestock or getting away with some cash from the farm. Clack and Minnaar (2018: 108) critically observed that:

> Poor workers cannot claim their rights and neither can they report abuse and poor working conditions in companies and farms. These cases are rarely reported to the police largely because of fear of intimidation or dismissal and/ or eviction (of their whole family) from the farm where they are employed—as a result many farm workers simply cannot contemplate given their precarious economic existence (low wages and long working hours) and widespread poverty in rural areas of South Africa.

The violent abuse and killings of farm workers by the farmers who perpetuate apartheid and human rights violation are underreported or ignored. These forms of violence attacks are typically a hangover of apartheid system when there is white farmer superiority over the poor black farm worker. In most cases a farm attack is characterized by physical assaults to the farm's occupants with the intention of achieving a particular goal (Swart, 2003). Clack and Minnaar (2018: 104) maintain that "the so-called 'farm attacks', most often result in robbery, assault, physical injuries and sometimes death (murder)".

Those who attack and kill farmers seem to be avenging historical dispossession and acquiring economic resources for personal and family survival. Akinola (2020: 65) posits that "Apartheid South Africa was noted for historical land dispossession, domination by the white group and disempowerment of the black population". Addressing "the land-related structural and physical violence" in South Africa is proving to be difficult for the post-apartheid government (Akinola, 2020). Whether or not it is viewed as a crime, it is violence against farm owners who are believed to be beneficiaries of apartheid political and economic system that have dispossessed the other sections of South African society. The issue of historical land inequality and the current desire for land redistribution are some of the consequences of farm attacks and murders (Jeffrey, 2015; Obeng-Odoom, 2012). Akinola (2020: 83) also posits that

> Farm conflict is the consequence of decades of un-addressed land inequality in the country, and particularly in the farms. It is reaction against oppressions in the farm. It is the height of an expression of consistent abuse of the rights of farm workers or labour tenants. Violence should be condemned in all ramifications in the farms, but we all know why it happens.

Apartheid has created the wider economic gap that remains a cause of violent conflict in the farms. The land inequality leads those without land to seek illegal means to compensate themselves through farm murder and robberies.

## 6 The Role of Poverty in Domestic and Gender-Based Violence

Like many other forms of violence in South Africa, domestic and gender-based violence (GBV) are a common feature. Collins (2013) argues that using violence is believed to be a valuable and effective tool to control interpersonal interactions. I have decided to connect domestic and gender-based violence, with the understanding that domestic violence happens in household and families, while GBV may happen outside a family set-up. Domestic violence can be categorized into numerous types, including assault, rape, pointing a gun, intimidation, murder, stalking, harassment, property destruction, emotional, physical, sexual, and financial abuse (Stanley et al., 2012). Domestic violence is committed by an intimate partner in a marriage relationship or a family member. Gender-based violence involves intimate partner violence, sexual harassment, workplace harassment, and femicide (Willman & Corman, 2013). As indicated above, GBV can fall under the heading domestic violence depending on the relationship between the victim and the perpetrator. Causes of domestic violence include "Jealousy, low self-esteem, strong emotions, inferiority complex, excessive use of alcohol and drug abuse amongst others" (Buntin, 2015). The perpetrator might have low self-esteem and seek to control the other owing to debts and loss of employment (Buntin, 2015; Gluck, 2019).

In GBV men and women are both victims and perpetrators. However, due to patriarchal stereotypes GBV is generally thought to be violence against women (Thobejane & Luthada, 2019). The major causes of GBV are personality disorders which cause aggression against men or women (Ademiluka, 2018). One of the biggest societal problems in the world today is gender-based violence (GBV), with one in three women experiencing non-partner sexual or physical violence in their lifetimes (World Health Organization, 2021). Kim et al. (2007: 1798) found that "among those reporting ever having experienced such violence, 71.3% had experienced physical violence alone, and 19.1% had experienced both physical and sexual violence. Only 9.6% reported sexual violence alone." Violence against women is usually guided by patriarchal mindsets of undermining women as second-class citizens, and this is reinforced by culture and religion. Ademiluka (2018) also argues that traditionally, in the public arena and governance, African women are viewed as insignificant others who have limited roles to play in society. Consequently, men in general, and particularly in South Africa, have a culture of dominating and even abusing women. Tran (2022: 13) submits that "Throughout South Africa, discursive violence against women makes them among the most burdened and silenced." Stories concerning femicide and sexual assault elicit varied reactions of astonishment and horror (van Niekerk & Boonzaier, 2019). Violence against women involves all forms of abuse inflicted by husbands on their wives and boyfriends on their girlfriends (Ademiluka, 2018; Collins, 2013). Such violence is used as a form of control, discipline, and punishment and includes a combination of physical, sexual, rape, emotional and psychological, socio-economic or financial violence, and femicide (Olalere, 2022; Willman & Corman, 2013). The cause of violence is often the socio-economic situation, when there is a lack of provisions (poverty).

Although violence is commonly known to be against women, gender-based violence against men is also a widespread phenomenon but very few people talk about it, including the victims (Allen, 2018; Thobejane & Luthada, 2019). Ademiluka (2018) puts it succinctly when he says there is sufficient proof that women can commit sex crimes against men. Fapohunda et al. (2021: 659) also noted that another study indicated that of 100 male victims of domestic abuse—despite the fact that they were the obvious victims—many believed that the police discriminated against them, with a fifth being detained. In such circumstances men suffer in silence due to the patriarchal system that shames a man if he reports any form of abuse from a woman.

Thobejane and Luthada (2019: 13) further advance that:

> Other forms of men-battering include: slapping; pouring hot water when asleep or pouring hot water over an innocent man; chopping man's genitals; verbal insults; insults before children; slashing; pouring petrol over him and setting him on fire; whips; throwing chairs, benches, stools, utensils and other objects in the house at the man, especially after serious disagreements in the house.

Usually, physical, economic, and financial abuse from women is frequently experienced by African men who fail to support their families as expected in African culture (Thobejane & Luthada, 2019). They can suffer from economic power domination from women. It should be noted that despite the fact that women also commit various forms of violence against men, women are more severely affected by gender violence than males. "The nexus between poverty and unemployment creates jealousy and guilty consciences to the poor and causes them to be violent against those who are employed and successful in business (Breetzke, 2010: 450). Domestic violence and gender-based violence are not just forms of violence but they are as a result of the socio-economic situations of the perpetrators and victims. As van Niekerk and Boonzaier (2019: 31) succinctly put it, explaining the situation of women working on farms:

> The position of women farm workers is especially oppressive and treacherous as they are paid less than their male counterparts and face greater levels of insecurity through lack of permanent employment as well as through being placed in positions of dependence on partners who may be abusive. Migrant women farm labourers are seldom granted residence rights, although these may be granted to men labourers.

Men and women with little or no access to economic means such as job and business opportunities tend to suffer economic domination and financial abuse from their counterparts. Andresen (2006) cites economic deprivation, in the form of unemployment, as the greatest predictor of crime rates. This results in violence forcing the other to submit for economic survival (Collins, 2013). Sometimes the abuse ends up in the brutal deaths from shootings, arson, or suicide of both victims and perpetrators.

## 7 Xenophobic Violence in South Africa

Andile Mngxitama (2008) defines xenophobia as the hatred of foreigners. Xenophobia leads to branding and labelling foreigners as an illegal, unwanted individuals who unduly deprive citizens of their services and opportunities. Whether this is true or not, Gelb (2008) interprets the xenophobic manifestation of hatred for those who are considered to be better off, and especially those of foreign descent. Tevera (2013) submits that some more radical assessments have attributed xenophobic attacks to problems with service delivery in many urban areas as well as rising levels of poverty and unemployment in recent years, which have led to locals' frustrations and their use of foreign migrants as scapegoats. Xenophobia predominantly occurs in townships and informal settlements because millions of newcomers to the townships come to compete with impoverished, unskilled South Africans for employment prospects, unlike the skilled and educated African migrants who land in middle-class South African suburbs (Abdi, 2011; Misago et al., 2009). However, Duponchel gives a unique explanation citing the involvement of the rich in the violent attacks of the foreigners. According to Duponchel (2013: 9) "Xenophobic violence can be seen as a competition between the richest and the poorest. The poorest are manipulated by the elite to turn against outsiders the elite itself created so that the richest can retain power and wealth." In the South African context, xenophobia mostly targets foreigners from African countries.

A diversified and active African diaspora, comprising communities of Zimbabweans, Batswana, Basotho, Swazi, Somalis, Nigerians, Senegalese, and Congolese, has emerged as a result of the post-apartheid labour recruiting boom in South Africa (Tevera, 2013). Duponchel (2013) argues that the outbreak of xenophobic violence in South Africa is exacerbated by an influx of neighbouring Zimbabweans increasing competition for scarce resources. The influx of African immigrants is developing into a dynamic, multicultural set-up, which is dominated by a fast-expanding, informal street-trading sector where local and international traders frequently compete, but also cooperate (Tevera, 2013). The causes of xenophobic violence include, among other issues: poverty, crime, unemployment, rising inflation, competition for business, and poor service delivery (Abdi, 2011; Crush et al., 2018; DHA, 2008; Pillay, 2008a, 2008b; Robins, 2009). Abdi (2011: 698) avers that:

> South African-born interviewees cited the now common grievances against newcomers and migrants, claiming that they contribute to crime, sexually exploit local women, displace South African workers by accepting lower wages and undermine the labour unions. However, the most commonly recurring

theme had to do with migrants driving locally owned shops out of business and setting up unfair competition.

For some observers, this violence had been a long time coming, as township residents had been living in a socio-economic pressure-cooker (Robins, 2009). Crush et al. (2018) also highlighted that, due to violence directed at migrants, between mid-2009 and late 2010, there were at least 20 fatalities, 200 foreign-owned businesses were plundered, and more than 4,000 people were evacuated, and in 2012 almost 250 major injuries and 140 fatalities took place. Generally speaking, this type of xenophobic violence has been most prevalent in the Western Cape and Gauteng (Crush et al., 2018: 23). Tevera (2013: 17) also noted that:

> A case in point is Alexandra whose 350,000 residents experience high levels of unemployment, poor accommodation, inadequate infrastructural services, systemic exclusion and deprivation. Here, unemployment and infrastructural challenges are decisive determinants in the reproduction of poverty and deprivation that in turn have generated conditions that are conducive to the emergence of conflict or violence. In Alexandra, as in many former African townships, residents often struggle violently for access to basic infrastructural services, such as decent toilets, clean water and electricity.

Poverty and unemployment are the primary drivers of division between locals and foreigners and fuel xenophobic violence. Above all, poverty is the central cause of violence against foreigners. Xenophobic violence has led to the destruction and loss of property, displacement, injury, and loss of life.

## 8   Closing Recommendations

Violence is an inherited and abiding behaviour that kills the conscience of the offender, who tends to undermine, marginalize, and objectify the victims in order to abuse or murder them. Political violence has remained a challenge throughout South Africa. There is a need for political education promoting political tolerance to reduce political violence. Political diversity must be celebrated for the sake of community and nation building. Any form of corruption should not be tolerated among members of political parties members of political parties with the aim of preventing access to or abusing local and national government resources.

Taxi violence can only be reduced by police deployment to hot spots of violence. There is a need for government intervention in regulating the taxi industry. Those who are involved in corruption of route allocation should be strictly dealt with so that taxi violence and murder is limited. Education on business ethics, fair competition, and customer care needs to be reinforced among taxi owners, associations, and drivers. All interventions should be aimed at the reduction of violence and the promotion of economic growth (Hinsberger et al., 2016).

Land and economic inequalities should be addressed with haste so that those who do not have land will benefit from land redistribution. Perpetrators of violence and abuse on farms and in farming communities need to face the full might of the law. Strict laws for gun possession should be implemented to curb farm robberies, attacks, and killings. Progress should begin with addressing wages and the general working conditions of farm workers. This will correct the inequalities between male and female workers and, hence, prevent violence between men and women and the generally the killing on the farm of either workers or farmers.

Kim et al. (2007) argue that gender inequality manifests itself explicitly in violence against women, which is also increasingly acknowledged as a major risk factor for a variety of adverse economic development consequences. Since poverty leads to suffering, domestic, and gender-based violence, the government needs to create a conducive environment for job creation and provision of some economic opportunities especially for the youth. The question of the abuse of men and women by their partners would in this way be reduced. According to qualitative data, a decrease in violence is brought about by a number of actions that empower women to question the legitimacy of such behaviour, to demand and receive better treatment from partners, and to bring to an end violent relationships (Kim et al., 2007: 1798). The impact of poverty, unemployment, and violent crimes illustrates the importance of addressing these issues in South Africa (Breetzke, 2010). The reduction of poverty lowers the vulnerability of both men and women to violence in its various forms.

Xenophobia has resulted in the displacement of many, and the deaths of migrants and thousands of South Africans that have drawn global attention (Abdi, 2011). "Violence had high economic and social costs due to the destruction of properties and the dislocation of some urban communities" (Tevera, 2013: 19). To curb violence the government and the local communities need to work on the lack of integration of non-nationals into local communities to reduce xenophobic attitudes and resentment towards foreign nationals. Any strategy to promote tolerance and coexistence should be combined with initiatives to address the issues of poverty and employment.

This will facilitate integration between locals and foreigners, cooperation, and the appreciation of diversity.

## 9 Conclusion

Apartheid has had a bearing on many forms of violence across South African society. It has led to poverty and deprivation, especially for the majority of the people living in townships and informal settlements. Its educational, economic, and political policies have led to a separation and marginalization that have disadvantaged the Black majority. A culture of violence that grew out of apartheid is continuously showing itself in the post-apartheid era. This chapter has discussed the role of apartheid in perpetuating poverty and violence. It has further argued that political violence, domestic violence, farm attacks, taxi violence, and xenophobia are motivated by poverty. Every section of the chapter has discussed the causes and nature of violence. Even though there are many causes of violence in South Africa, poverty is a primary source of violence, as people use violence as a means to ensure social, political, and economic survival. The chapter gives some recommendations that could empower people, families, and communities to avert violence in South Africa.

## References

Abdi, C. M. (2011). Moving Beyond Xenophobia: Structural Violence, Conflict and Encounters with the 'Other' Africans. *Development Southern Africa, 28*(5), 691–704.

Ademiluka, S. O. (2018). Patriarchy and Women Abuse: Perspectives from Ancient Israel and Africa. *Old Testament Essays, 31*(2), 339–362.

Akinola, A. O. (2020). Farm Attacks or 'White Genocide'? Interrogating the Unresolved Land Question in South Africa. *African Journal on Conflict Resolution, 20*(2), 65–91.

Allen, S. (2018). *The Importance of an Intersectional Approach to Gender-Based Violence in South Africa.* https://pdxscholar.library.pdx.edu/cgi/viewcontent.cgi?article=1632&context=honorstheses. Accessed on 5 July 2023.

Andresen, M. A. (2006). Crime Measures and the Spatial Analysis of Criminal Activity. *British Journal of Criminology, 46*, 258–285.

Atkinson, D. (2007). *Taking to the Streets: Has Developmental Local Government Failed in South Africa?* (pp. 53–77). State of the Nation.

Bezuidenhout, C. (2003). Introduction and Terminology Dilemma. In C. Bezuidenhout & S. Joubert (Eds.), *Child and Youth Misbehaviour in South Africa: A Holistic View* (pp. 1–11). Van Schaiks.

Bonnin, D. (2004). *Understanding the Legacies of Political Violence: An Examination of Political Conflict in Mpumalanga Township, KwaZulu-Natal, South Africa* (Crisis States Programme: Working Papers Series No. 1).

Breetzke, G. D. (2010). Modeling Violent Crime Rates: A Test of Social Disorganization in the City of Tshwane, South Africa. *Journal of Criminal Justice, 38*(4), 446–452.

Bruce, D. (2013). A Provincial Concern? Political Killings in South Africa. *South African Crime Quarterly, 45*, 13–24.

Bruce, D. (2014). *Political Killings in South Africa The Ultimate Intimidation.* Institute for Security Studies.

Buntin, J. T. (2015). Intimate Partner Violence. *International Encyclopedia of the Social & Behavioral Sciences: Second Edition*, 685–688. https://doi.org/10.1016/B978-0-08-097086-8.35026-7

Business Tech. (2023, February 17). *Violent Crime in South Africa Is Getting Worse—Here Are All the Latest Stats.* Business Tech. https://businesstech.co.za/news/lifestyle/665791/violent-crime-in-south-africa-is-getting-worse-here-are-all-the-latest-stats/. Accessed on 4 July 2023.

Clack, W., & Minnaar, A. (2018). Rural Crime in South Africa: An Exploratory Review of 'Farm Attacks' and Stocktheft as the Primary Crimes in Rural Areas. *Acta Criminologica: African Journal of Criminology & Victimology, 31*(1), 103–135.

Collins, A. (2013). Violence Is Not a Crime—The Impact of 'Acceptable' Violence on South African Society. *SA Crime Quarterly, 43*, 29–37.

Crush, J., Tawodzera, G., Chikanda, A., Ramachandran, S., & Tevera, D. S. (2018). *Migrants in Countries in Crisis: South Africa Case Study: The Double Crisis–Mass Migration from Zimbabwe and Xenophobic Violence in South Africa.* International Centre for Migration Policy Development.

de Haas, M. (2020, January 21). South Africa Fails to Get to the Bottom of Killings in KwaZulu-Natal. *The Conversation.* https://theconversation.com/south-africa-fails-to-get-to-the-bottom-of-killings-in-kwazulu-natal-128167. Accessed on 6 July 2023.

DHA. (2008). *Annual Report for 2007–2008: Building the New Home Affairs.* Pretoria.

Dugard, J. (2001). *From Low-Intensity War to Mafia War: Taxi Violence in South Africa, 1987–2000* (Vol. 4). Centre for the Study of Violence and Reconciliation.

Duponchel, M. (2013). *Who's the Alien? Xenophobia in Post-apartheid South Africa (No. 2013/003)* (WIDER Working Paper).

Fapohunda, T., Masiagwala, P., Stiegler, N., & Bouchard, J. P. (2021). Intimate Partner and Domestic Violence in South Africa. In *Annales Médico-psychologiques, revue psychiatrique, 179*(7), 653–661.

Gelb, S. (2008). Behind Xenophobia in South Africa—Poverty or Inequality? In S. Hassim, T. Kupe, & E. Worby (Eds.), *Go Home or Die Here: Violence, Xenophobia and the Reinvention of Differences in South Africa*. Wits University Press.

Gluck, S. (2019). *Effect of Domestic Violence, Domestic Abuse on Women and Children*. Healthy Place. https://www.healthyplace.com/abuse/domestic-violence/effects-of-domestic-violence-domestic-abuse-on-women-and-children

Gwilliam, K. (2003). Urban Transport in Developing Countries. *Transport Reviews, 23*(2), 197–216.

Hamber, B. (1998). Violence and the Transition in South Africa. In Bornman, E., Van Eden, R., & Wentzel, M. (Eds.), *Violence in South Africa* (pp. 349–370). Human Science Research Council.

Hinsberger, M., Sommer, J., Kaminer, D., Holtzhausen, L., Weierstall, R., Seedat, S., & Elbert, T. (2016). Perpetuating the Cycle of Violence in South African Low-Income Communities: Attraction to Violence in Young Men Exposed to Continuous Threat. *European Journal of Psychotraumatology, 7*(1), 290–299.

Hlongwane, P. (2022). Political Killings in South Africa: A Political Conundrum? *International Conference on Public Administration and Development Alternatives (IPADA)*.

Isike, C. (2019, May 12). Factionalism and Corruption Could Kill the ANC—Unless It Kills Both First. *The Conversation*. https://theconversation.com/factionalism-and-corruption-could-kill-the-anc-unless-it-kills-both-first-116924. Accessed 5 July 2023.

Jeffrey, A. (2015, February 6). Unintended Consequences of ANC Land Proposals. *Fin24*. https://www.fin24.com/BizNews/Unintended-consequences-of-ANCLand-Proposals-20150206. Accessed 5 July 2023.

Khosa, M. M. (2001). *Empowerment Through Economic Transformation*. HSRC.

Kim, J. C., Watts, C. H., Hargreaves, J. R., Ndhlovu, L. X., Phetla, G., Morison, L. A., Buaza, J., Porter, J. D., & Pronyk, P. (2007). Understanding the Impact of a Microfinance-Based Intervention on Women's Empowerment and the Reduction of Intimate Partner Violence in South Africa. *American Journal of Public Health, 97*(10), 1794–1802.

Krelekrele, T. (2018). Briefing Paper 469: Political Violence in KwaZulu-Natal. *South African Catholic Bishops' Conference*. Parliamentary Liaison Office.

Mbhanyele, S. (2022, March 14). What Drives South Africa's Political Violence? *Mail and Guardian*. http://mg.co.za/opinion/2022-03-14-what-drives-south-africas-political-violence/. Accessed 5 July 2023.

Misago, J. P., Landau, L. B., & Monson, T. (2009). *Towards Tolerance, Law, and Dignity: Addressing Violence Against Foreign Nationals in South Africa*. International Organisation for Migration and Forced Migration Studies Programme. University of the Witwatersrand.

Mle, T. R., & Maclean, S. (2011). Ethics, Integrity and Good Governance: The Case of South Africa's Local Sphere of Government. *Journal of Public Administration, 46*(4), 1364–1383.

Mngxitama, A. (2008). *We Are Not All Like That: The Monster Bares Its Fangs.* http://www.blacklooks.org/2008/06/we_are_not_all_like_that_the_monster_bares_its_fangs. Accessed 3 July 2023.

Molefe, I. N. (2016). *The Policing of Taxi Violence in Stanger Area* (Masters dissertation). https://uir.unisa.ac.za/bitstream/handle/10500/22198/dissertation_molefe_in.pdf?sequence=1&is. Accessed 5 July 2023.

Ngubane, L., Mkhize, S., & Olofinbiyi, S. A. (2020). Taxi Violence in South Africa: Insight from Mpumalanga Township, Kwazulu-Natal Province, South Africa. *African Journal of Peace and Conflict Studies, 9*(3), 81–104.

Nomarwayi, T., Breakfast, N. B., Bradshaw, G., & Dlamini, S. (2020). Political Killings in the Post-Apartheid South Africa: A Political and Criminological Perspective in Kwazulu-Natal Province, 1994–2019. *Gender and Behaviour, 18*(1), 15006–15016.

Obeng-Odoom, F. (2012). Land Reforms in Africa: Theory, Practice, and Outcome. *Habitat International, 36*, 161–170.

Olalere, F. E. (2022). Gender-Based Violence: An Exploration of Its Forms, Concepts and Causes in South Africa. *Proceedings–Kuala Lumpur International Communication, Education, Language and Social Sciences* (pp. 75–84).

Pillay, D. (2008a). Relative Deprivation, Social Instability and Cultures of Entitlements. In S. Hassim, T. Kupe, & E. Worby (Eds.), *Go Home or Die Here: Violence, Xenophobia and the Reinvention of Differences in South Africa.* Wits University Press.

Pillay, S. (2008b). Crime, Community and the Governance of Violence in Post-Apartheid South Africa. *Politikon, 35*(2), 141–158.

Robins, S. (2009). Humanitarian Aid Beyond 'Bare Survival': Social Movement Responses to Xenophobic Violence in South Africa. *American Ethnologist, 36*(4), 637–650.

Stanley, N., Graham-Kevan, N., & Borthwick, R. (2012). Fathers and Domestic Violence: Building Motivation for Change through Perpetrator Programmes. *Child Abuse Review, 21*, 264–274. https://doi.org/10.1002/car.2222

Stone, C. (2006). *Crime, Justice, and Growth in South Africa: Toward a Plausible Contribution from Criminal Justice to Economic Growth* (John F. Kennedy School of Government Working Paper No. RWP06-038). Center for International Development Working Paper, 131.

Swart, D. (2003). Farm Attacks in South Africa—Incidence and Explanation. *Acta Criminologica: Southern African Journal of Criminology, 16*(1), 40–45.

Tevera, D. (2013). African Migrants, Xenophobia and Urban Violence in Post-apartheid South Africa. *Iternation Special Edition, 7*, 9–26.

Thobejane, T. D., & Luthada, V. (2019). An Investigation into the Trend of Domestic Violence on Men: The Case of South Africa. *OIDA International Journal of Sustainable Development, 12*(3), 11–18.

Tran, D. (2022). Realities Beyond Reporting: Women Environmental Defenders in South Africa. *Feminist Media Studies, 23*(5), 2152–2169.

van Niekerk, T. J., & Boonzaier, F. A. (2019). An Intersectional Analysis of Responses to Intimate Partner Violence in Two Marginalised South African Communities. *International Journal of Child, Youth and Family Studies, 10*(1), 26–48.

Vetten, L., & Ratele, K. (2013). Men and Violence. *Agenda: Empowering Women for Gender Equity, 27*(1), 4–11. https://doi.org/10.1080/10130950.2013.813769.

WHO. (2021). *Violence Against Women*. https://www.who.int/news-room/fact-sheets/detail/violenceagainst-women. Accessed on 8 July 2023.

Willman, A. M., & Corman, C. (2013). *Sexual and Gender-Based Violence: What Is The World Bank Doing and What Have We Learned, a Strategic Review*. http://hdl.handle.net/10986/16733. Accessed on 5 July 2023.

# Violence Against Nature in Africa: A Historical Assessment

Marlino Eugénio Mubai

## 1   Introduction

As the nations of the world disagree on the achievements of the 27th United Nations Climate Change Conference, more commonly referred to as COP27 held in Sharm El-Sheik, Egypt from 6 to 18 November, 2022, African countries are engaged in a parallel and sometimes contradictory agenda of publicizing their natural resources for national and foreign investors. Global industrial powers, and emerging ones such as China and India, are engaged in a fierce competition to control access to African raw materials. In ways that resemble the nineteenth century scramble for Africa, African leaders are special guests at summits such as the EU - Africa; US and Africa; Japan and Africa; China and Africa; India and Africa; and Russia and Africa, to mention but few. Generally, in these economic summits Africa is begging for Foreign Direct Investment in exchange for its natural endowments. Meanwhile, across the continent, civil society organizations and indigenous people's organizations are sending alarming signals about the status of natural resource depletion, unsustainable extraction practices, and violence against civilians and environmental activists. "Moreover, because natural resources are the ultimate source of all the energy and goods consumed and thrown away, their extraction harms the environment not only at the point of extraction but globally as well" (Downey et al., 2010: 420). Bearing this context in mind,

M. E. Mubai (✉)
Department of History, Eduardo Mondlane University, Maputo, Mozambique
e-mail: mmubai@icloud.com; marlino.mubai@uem.mz

this chapter looks at the violent nature of human interaction with nature from pre-colonial times to the present. It aims to demonstrate that the peripheral position of Africa in the world economy as a source of cheap raw materials results in acts that can be categorized as violence against nature. It draws on extensive literature works by environmental historians, political ecologists, literature scholars, law scholars, human rights organizations, indigenous people, and eco-socialist scholars, to define and describe the diverse manifestations of violence against nature in Africa. The chapter begins with a brief discussion of the concept of violence against nature and, following a historical chronology, it traces the various manifestations and consequences of violence against nature in Africa. It ends with some concluding remarks with a focus on the effects of violence against nature on socio-ecological systems amid global warming and climate change.

## 2 Violence Against Nature: Towards a Working Concept

Before engaging in the definition of violence against nature, one must define nature. According to the Merriam Webster Online Dictionary, nature refers to: "the physical world and everything in it such as plants, animals, mountains, oceans, stars, etc. that is not made by people" (https://www.merriam-webster.com/dictionary/nature. Accessed 15 November 2021). The Oxford Reference Online Dictionary defines nature along the same lines, highlighting that it refers to "the phenomena of the physical world collectively, including plants, animals, the landscape, and other features and products of the earth, as opposed to humans or human creations" (https://www.oxfordreference.com/view/10.1093/acref/9780198609810.001.0001/acref-9780198609810-e-4825. Accessed 15 November 2021). When it comes to the interaction of humans with nature, the latter is confused with environment, thus there is a need to define "environment." The Merriam Webster Online Dictionary defines 'environment' "as (i) the circumstances, objects, or conditions by which one is surrounded; (ii) the complex of physical, chemical, and biotic factors (such as climate, soil, and living things) that act upon an organism or an ecological community and ultimately determine its form of survival; (iii) the aggregate of social and cultural conditions that influence the life of an individual or community" (https://www.merriam-webster.com/dictionary/environment). The Oxford Online Dictionary defines "environment" as (i) the conditions that affect the behaviour and development of someone or something; the physical conditions that someone or something exists in; (ii) "the natural world in which people, animals and plants live" (https://www.oxfordlearnersdictionaries.com/definition/american_english/environment. Accessed 7 May 2023).

These definitions show that the meaning of nature and "environment" overlap. This explains why in scholarly definition, violence against nature is presented as environmental violence (Barca, 2014; Lee, 2016). For Lee, environmental violence has many interpretations. Lee limits the discussion of environmental "violence to":

> (a) the violence between people(s) over natural resources; (b) environmental policies that can be violent against people; (c) the secondary violence from the natural world as a result of human degradation of the earth; and (d) direct damage to the environment by humans that threatens their own survival. (Lee, 2016: 106)

Barca departs from the Persistent Organic Pollutants (POP) to define "environmental violence as violent acts perpetrated against non-human nature with the aim of (re)producing oppressive social relations and political control" (Barca, 2014: 3). Barca provides empirical evidence of environmental violence from different fields of enquiry, including:

- the works of environmental historians who are concerned with connections between war and environmental devastation;
- political ecologists who focus on the analysis of the production of violent environments though social conflict, accumulation by dispossession, corporate/state recourse to violence and terror in political discourse;
- scholars' insights from indigenous, postcolonial, feminist, and cultural minority writers looking at the harm done by "development" to their land and people;
- law scholars studying ecocide theory focusing on the destruction or widespread contamination of habitats as crime against humanity;
- human rights organizations focusing on the assassination of environmental activists who oppose the plunder of the natural resources of the developing world;
- indigenous people who look at environmental violence as the severe and ongoing harm caused by environmental toxins to indigenous women, girls, unborn generations and indigenous people as a whole; and
- eco-socialists who assert that the capitalist system is built upon interconnected exploitation of (and thus violence against) both human and non-human nature. (Barca, 2014: 3–4)

The linkage between capitalism and violence against both human and non-human nature is also referred to as "ecological imperialism," a term popularized by environmental historian Alfred Crosby (1986) in his ecocentric interconnectivity argument (Esparza, 2021: 353). Crosby explains the success of European imperialism as the result of "portmanteau ecologies or biota," a term he coined to refer to a collection of biotic agents (European animals, viruses, plants, etc.) that were specially evolved on the European continent. He explains that these organisms adapted well to the new environments they were taken to by colonization. He goes on to assert that by this biotic success, Europeans were extraordinarily gifted and successful in their colonial effort (Crosby, 1986: 7). It is important to observe that behind what Crosby calls the success of the colonial effort lies a mantle of destruction of natural ecologies. Because of this, ecological imperialism continues to attract scholarly discussion. Frame (2014) sees the neoliberal policies that swept through the developing world in the 1980s as a historically distinct moment of ecological imperialism. On the basis of a case study in Tanzania, Frame argues that "the foreign investment regimes since Africa's colonial era reproduce neocolonial situation whereby African political economic structures are subjugated for the metabolic needs of core economies, in a manner amenable to the ever-expanding needs of capital accumulation" (Frame, 2014). The linkage of foreign direct investment to ecological imperialism is also defended by Ayelazuno and Mawuko-Yevugah (2019) who, on the basis of a study of large-scale mining in Ghana, come to the conclusion that "the mining-FDI is essentially ecological imperialism, wreaking havoc on the ecosystem of mining communities whose livelihood strategies are in conflict with the accumulation and political interests of foreign mining companies and the Ghanaian political class respectively" (Ayelazuno & Mawuko-Yevugah, 2019: 243). They come close to defining ecological imperialism as a form of violence against nature when they state that "human beings are part and parcel of the ecology; they have a symbiotic relationship with the non-human components of the ecology, therefore any intrusion into this relationship constitutes one dimension of destruction of the ecology" (Ayelazuno & Mawuko-Yevugah, 2019: 251). Ecological imperialism may also be considered as environmental colonialism. In this point of view, violence against nature is expressed by the promotion of African landscapes as areas of conservation, thus displacing native groups from their historic homeland, leaving them worse off economically and in some cases in dire poverty (Nelson, 2003: 67). Very often, these conservation movements use religious and moral vocabulary, such as saving the world from rape and pillage, building cathedrals in the wildness, creating a new "Noah's'

'Ark," but they mask intrusion or violence against African environments. As Nelson explains, the Edenic depiction of Africa excludes Africans from their environments and masks violence towards human beings who are also part of nature (Nelson, 2003: 67). Murphy (2009) argues that the relationship between environment and colonialism is important for understanding contemporary imperialisms. He goes on to argue that colonialism has had devastating consequences for indigenous people and nature around the world. He gives examples of the alienation of people from their land and resources, the implanting of settlements in distant territories, the commodification of nature and the exploitation of commodities frontiers (Murphy, 2009).

The discussion of the working definition of violence against nature, shows that nature is not explicitly mentioned in the literature. It requires a reading between the lines to observe that nature is often conceived in terms of environment and ecology. Consequently, the understanding of violence against nature requires familiarization with concepts such as ecological imperialism, environmental imperialism, environmental colonialism, ecocide and environmentalism at large. A common aspect of the way scholars address human-nature relations is the acknowledgement of unequal power relations and the commodification of nature. Thus, for the purposes of this chapter, the study of violence against nature considers people as part of natural ecology. In this approach, violence against nature is conceived in line with Lee (2016) who brings together the violence between people(s) over natural resources, the environmental policies that can be violent against people, the secondary violence from the natural world as a result of human degradation of the earth, the direct damage to the environment by humans that threatens their own survival, and climate change. This broad concept has the advantage of considering human beings as part and parcel of the environment, possessing a symbiotic relationship with the non-human components of the ecology. Following Crosby's (1986) intrinsic approach, humans are seen as having an impact upon nature and, in its own way, nature has an impact upon people (Esparza, 2021: 259). Thus, the following section provides examples of how nature has been subject to violence in Africa and what this has meant in terms of sustainability.

## 3  Nature as the Object of Violence in Africa, from 1885 to the 1980s

In his popular textbook entitled *Africans: A History of a Continent*, environmental historian John Illife states that the "chief contribution of Africans to global history was their capacity to colonize an especially hostile region of the world on behalf of the entire human race" (Illife, 2007: 1). Illife provides examples of how early inhabitants of the African continent transformed the environment and, in the process, were transformed by it. Illife's statement reminds us that long before European expansion in the late fifteenth century and colonial domination in the late nineteenth century, the ecologies of Africa were subject to transformation to meet the needs of their inhabitants. It also takes us back to the biblical commands to subdue the earth and to have dominion over it (Genesis 1:28). Without taking for granted human-nature interactions before colonization, this section pays particular attention to the period of European colonial domination because of the magnitude of violence against nature in this period. It keeps in mind that there are no fixed dates that mark the beginning and the end of colonial period. However, for the purpose of this study, the working period of colonial domination is 1885 to 1980. Keeping in mind that the dates of colonial occupation varied according to the type of resistance against occupation, this study considers the Conference of Berlin of 1884/1885 as a major indication of colonial domination because of the way colonial powers mobilized their resources towards effective occupation of African land and human beings.[1] The end of colonial period is a fluid moment in African history. While many African countries obtained their independence in the 1960s, in southern Africa colonial domination lasted until 1990 with Namibia's independence (Meredith, 2011; Young, 2012). Nevertheless, given the specificity of South African and Namibian colonialism, this chapter takes the independence of Zimbabwe on 18 April 1980, as the working date for the end of the European colonial era on African soil.

This section departs from the assumption that from the late nineteenth century to the present the history of Africa is dominated by selective narratives of violence related to warfare. In academic and popular literature, African countries are described as failed states experiencing unprecedented levels of violence. Very often, this violence is associated with a natural resource curse whereby the abundance of natural resources triggers violence (Homer-Dixon et al., 1993: 38–45). As Malaquias (2001) puts it in the case of the

---

[1] This chronology conflicts with nationalist discourse pointing to 500 years of colonial domination.

Angolan Civil War, the availability of significant oil and diamonds perpetuated the conflict (Malaquias, 2001: 534). Yet in Angola, Frynas and Wood (1999) observe that "mineral wealth has not only fuelled Angola's war but has also intimately shaped the contours of the conflict" (Frynas & Wood, 1999). What these narratives miss is that both nature and men are victims of violence. Thus, reducing violence to the military conflicts that have plagued the African continent since colonial times fails to capture the centrality of nature to human history and represents a reductionist approach to violence in Africa. As the seminal work of environmental historian Kjekshus puts it, "ecological impacts of colonization in East Africa exceeded slave-raiding and intertribal warfare" (Kjekshus, 1977: 81). On the basis of examples from different regions of the continent, this section shows that nature suffers violence and humans are both actors and victims of such violence.

Following the so-called European discoveries of the late fifteenth century which resulted in the integration of Africa into the global trade triangle expressed by the Atlantic Slave Trade, the last quarter of the nineteenth century witnessed what is conventionally known as the scramble for Africa. Driven by the Industrial Revolution that saw improvements in navigation technology, weaponry, and manufacture, European nations, led by the British, the French, the Portuguese, Germans and Belgians, saw in Africa a new frontier to acquire the much-needed raw materials to supply their booming industry. They also needed markets for manufactured products, and Africa appeared to be the right place owing to its proximity to European industrial centres and its rich and vast natural resource endowment. To access these resources, Europeans used various strategies, including religious indoctrination, negotiations, and above all military violence. In this period, Africa experienced the hardship of warfare waged with new military technology, paving the way for long cycles of violence that ended up dominating the narratives of African history. What is often overlooked in these narratives is that the wars of colonial occupation created havoc in both human and local environments.

Following the defeat of African states, the map of the continent was redrawn, separating people and environments. Under the mantra of the modernization enterprise, Africa witnessed unprecedented levels of expropriation of land, water, and other natural resources and the destitution of millions of Africans and their descendants. The division of African territories into settler and exploitation colonies expressed the exploitative nature of colonization. Countries with large reserves of minerals, including the modern-day Democratic Republic of Congo, South Africa, Ghana, Sierra Leone, and Zambia, to mention but five, were subject to intense mineral exploitation without respecting local environments. Water streams were polluted, and large expanses of land were left with deep holes, endangering local ecologies (Fayiga et al., 2018; Leuenberger et al., 2021; Ochieng et al., 2010; Vicente, 2000). In addition to pollution, violence against nature in colonial Africa included occupational diseases, particularly tuberculosis and other respiratory illnesses. Millions of underpaid mine workers without appropriate healthcare and retirement insurance transferred the burden of occupational disease to their home villages (Basu et al., 2009; Stuckler et al., 2010).

In addition to the extraction of natural resources through mining, African environments were subject to transformation through agriculture. In settler colonies such as South Africa, Zimbabwe, Namibia, Kenya, Mozambique, and Angola, native people were evicted from their fertile agricultural land to make room for the commercial cultivation of monocultures. As Crosby (1986) has argued, the introduction of new crops dramatically affected local crops. Miracle (1965) observes that crops such as millet, which easily adapted to the local microclimate, were replaced with maize, which requires more water and is less resistant to drought. Intensive use of monocultures such as sisal and cotton depleted soils, reducing their productivity (Sabea, 2008: 432). Although it is not publicized, colonial agriculture introduced chemical fertilizers which had a negative impact on water streams and wildlife in a similar way to what was depicted in Rachel Carson's book *Silent Spring* in the United States (Carson, 2002). The creation of informal settlements for cheap labour comprising people who had been evicted from their lands, contributed to the degradation of soil (Koning & Smalling, 2005: 3–11, Pile, 1996: 60).

Colonization brought investment in transportation systems, to evacuate the resources extracted from Africa to Europe and other global markets. On the basis of early industrialization technology, the construction of railways, airstrips, roads, water and dry ports required intensive labour which, in many territories such in the modern-day DRC, Mozambique, and Angola, took the form of forced labour resembling slavery. Lots of ink has been used to describe the inhumane work conditions of forced labour, but little has been said about the impact of this on humankind as part of the local ecology. Though the use of rudimentary technology and structural violence, large hectares of forests were depleted to give way to new roads and railways (Kwashirai, 2006: 552; Rudel & Roper, 1997: 53–65). These new transportation corridors crossed unique ecosystems, exposing wild animals to violence and extinction. The cutting of trees for timber endangered many species of plants, while the construction of bridges exposed fish to the greed of men and to the poisonous and polluting effects of construction chemicals.

The exploitation of African natural resources required electricity. This led to the construction of large hydropower dams, which affected local ecosystems dramatically. The Zambezi River is paradigmatic in the ways it was transformed to accommodate large dams such as Kariba in modern-day Zambia-Zimbabwe and Cahora (formerly Cabora) Bassa in modern-day Mozambique. In the latter, the dam was also conceived as a weapon to counter the liberation movement fighters. Without taking for granted the contribution of dams to economic development, one must recognize that these projects perpetrated and continue to perpetrate violence against people and ecologies. As Allen and Barbara Isaacman observed in their prize-winning book on the Cahora Bassa Dam, for the local people who cyclically suffer cyclical inundations and for the fish populations and other aquatic life, the construction of Cahora Bassa Dam did not bring the much-anticipated benefits (Isaacman & Isaacman, 2016).

The colonial enterprise also saw Africa as a playground where European elites toured to shoot game for recreational purposes. Despite the coincidence of colonial enterprise with the conservation movement, African wildlife continued to suffer violence which transformed local ecologies (Mandala, 2015; Prendergast & Adams, 2003; Steinhart, 1989). Even the affirmation of the conservation movement and subsequent transformations of large extensions of land into natural game reserves and national parks was done in ways that perpetuated violence against nature. As many scholars have indicated, colonial attempts to preserve African wildlife separated people from local ecologies and prioritized the conservation of nature over human livelihoods. Driven by images of a pristine Africa, which reminded a degenerated Europe of its past, environmentalists rallied for the conservation of what they saw as the last spot of genuine contact with nature. To achieve this goal, they evicted populations that had established symbiotic relationships with local ecologies, rendering them vulnerable to poverty (Colua et al., 2021). Thus, even the idea of the conservation of natural resources masked subtle forms of violence against nature.

Violence against nature is also manifested in the way people work the land. Colonial administrations across African blamed slash-and-burn agricultural practices for environmental degradation. Some scholars (Giblin, 1992; Kjekshus, 1977) warn us to take these colonial discourses with a grain of salt. Nevertheless, when we look at nature in its totality, from the celebrated African "Big Five" to the birds, bush rats, squirrels, bees, and grasshoppers, to mention but a few wild animals, slash-and-burn agricultural practices have been indeed a form of violence against nature.

Overgrazing has been another form of violence against nature. The way colonial authorities in territories such as South Africa, Namibia, Zimbabwe, and Kenya treated local pastoralist groups was markedly a form of violence against people, cattle and natural resources. In fact, the struggle over the control of the best land for grazing resulted in violence between European settlers and African pastoralist groups (Anderson & Grove, 1987: 111; Galaty & Wood, 1999; Wiles et al., 2005). Moreover, the eviction of Africans from their traditional lands to make room for the European dairy industry is, in its own right, a form of violence against nature which is often overlooked because of a non-human-centric analysis of nature.

## 4 Nature as the Object of Violence in Africa, 1980s–Present

The 1960s inaugurated what historian Crawford Young called the moment of euphoria in African history (Young, 2012). In this period, over a dozen African states obtained their independence from colonial domination. Despite some variations in mobilization and strategies of fighting, land, and other natural resources were at the centre of political mobilization against colonial occupation. In territories such as Kenya, Zimbabwe, Namibia, and South Africa, the struggle was markedly in the name of recovering ancestral land. (Barry, 2002; Bundy, 1984; Kiljunen, 1980; Molapo, 2014; Moyo, 1994). As David Anderson (2005) highlights in the case of Kenya, the Kikuyu Mau Mau were, above all, fighting for their land. In Zimbabwe Jocelyn Alexander (2007) and Lan (1985) highlight the way the ZANLA guerrilla fighters mobilized over land and other natural resources. Given this historical background, for millions of people who had lost their lands owing to colonial discriminatory policies, independence brought the hope of environmental justice. Some scholars have observed that Africans came close to satisfying their aspirations through policies of nationalization and expropriation of land without compensation, but it did not take long before the former colonial masters reversed the situation through the policies of structural adjustment and their prescription of the privatization of land and other natural resources (Demissie, 2016; Evers et al., 2013). The nationalistic policies enacted in the first years of independence may have lessened the human dimension of violence against nature, but the reliance on extractive industry to sustain ambitious development programmes continued to expose nature to the unsustainable practices of natural resource exploitation.

An overview of the major exports of postcolonial states shows that African raw materials continued to dominate national economies. In many cases, the method of extraction of these resources resembled colonial methods. The copper industry in Zambia and the Democratic Republic of Congo, it has provoked serious environmental problems in those countries. Similar situations occurred with gold mines in Ghana, iron ore and diamonds in Sierra Leonne and Liberia, crude oil in Nigeria, and small-scale gold mining in Mozambique, Zimbabwe, and Tanzania (Alberdi & Barroso, 2021; Boas & Jennings, 2007; Ebiede, 2011). Along with the mining industry, violence in Africa has been manifested by the way African governments with the connivance of international capital have been engaged in the felling of trees. All over sub-Saharan Africa, indigenous endemic species of hardwood which took hundreds of years to grow are cut down and exported to international markets without creating direct benefits for local people (Santos, 2009). This constitutes a form of violence against both trees and the local people.

The depletion of forests destabilizes local ecosystems, as men equipped with saws penetrate deep into the forest which constitutes the habitat of diverse wildlife. In fact, wild animals are particularly targeted for commercial purposes in ways that call to mind the practices of colonial times. As has been argued earlier in this chapter, the introduction of national parks designed to give privileges to wildlife instead of people constitutes a form of violence. Moreover, the restrictive measures introduced by conservationists in Africa made room for diverse forms of resistance which translated into widespread violence against nature as defined in this chapter. Deprived of their traditional sources of subsistence and facing a lack of job opportunities, African youth have engaged in the poaching of animals with high commercial value, including elephants, rhinoceroses, lions, and pangolins (Lunstrum & Givá, 2020). It is to be feared that the rapacious nature of this hunting brought some species of animals into near extinction threatening the stability of local ecosystems. Thus, poverty brought about by failed economic policies has pushed some segments of the population to engage in acts of brutality against animals. In southern Africa images of dead rhinos and elephants with their tusks removed are symbols of human cruelty against wildlife (Pavid, 2021). These images are used to justify tough measures against poaching, but they overlook a real dimension of the problem by silencing stories of less popular animals, including antelopes, gazelles, rabbits, and monkeys.

Moreover, during the Mozambican civil war, that lasted for 16 years and coincided with prolonged cycles of droughts, the military used automatic rifles to hunt for food (Mubai, 2015). The location of the major military camps of the guerrilla fighters inside national parks sheds light on the level of violence perpetrated against wildlife. In addition to hunting to feed thousands of guerrilla fighters and populations under their control, the transformation of forests into a battleground (McNeely, 2003) has had profound impacts which are not yet fully understood.

Thus, poaching and warfare are forms of violence against nature, but state policies to curtail poaching are also responsible for violence against nature, as broadly defined in this chapter. Examples from Mozambique, South Africa, and Botswana show that the new millennium has witnessed the toughening of measures against poachers. For example, in Botswana the government has issued a law that allows police to shoot to kill all people involved in poaching (Mogomotsi & Madigele, 2017). Evidence from the Limpopo National Park communities in Mozambique show that many young men suspected of poaching have been killed in both the Limpopo and Kruger National Parks (Witter & Satterfield, 2019). In this case, violence against nature is manifested by the abuse of the state military apparatus to protect wildlife. State violence against nature at large is also manifested by the way governments are silencing environmental defenders. According to Butt et al. (2019) between 2002 and 2017, 1,558 people in 50 countries were killed for defending their environments and lands (Butt et al., 2019: 242). The killing of environmental defenders is violence against nature because it silences important environmental issues, undermines international conventions such as the Convention on Biological Diversity, and limits efforts to meet the United Nations Sustainable Development Goals (Butt et al., 2019: 746).

The hunting of big mammals with commercial value overshadows the violence against small wildlife. In many African rural communities hunting is a rite of passage and is responsible for the diet of local communities. Historically, this hunting for subsistence has relied on traps and bows, which are believed to cause little damage to the ecosystems. However, in recent times, the demand for bush meat in cities has transformed the hunting of these species into mass killing for commercial purposes (Batumike et al., 2020). Traps and bows have been replaced by automatic rifles, causing havoc in the wild (Braga-Pereira et al., 2020). In countries such as Ghana and the Democratic Republic of Congo it is reported that hunting for commercial purposes is leading to the decline of wildlife, particularly tropical vertebrates (Brashares et al., 2004).

In addition to wildlife, Africa is also endowed with rivers, lakes, and oceans, which are home to diverse wildlife. Human intrusion to these ecosystems is also responsible for the disturbance of ecological relationships. As happens inland, marine and aquatic resources are subject to overexploitation and toxic pollution. For example, artisanal and large-scale fishing is responsible for the depletion of fish across African coastal communities. Studies conducted in Kenya, Tanzania, and Mozambique show that artisanal fishermen report the reduction of catches. They attribute the reason for this reduction to the use of inappropriate fishing arts like the use of mosquito nets to fish. As happens inland, water resources are also subject to state regulations through the establishment of marine protected areas. In Mozambique, important fishing communities such as Inhaca, Bazaruto, and Quirimbas have seen their native areas transformed into National Parks and Reserves (Tinley et al., 1976). While these initiatives help in protecting endangered species, in some cases they are conducted in a brutal way against people who are wrongly placed as in separation from their ecosystems. According to Benjaminsen and Bryceson (2012), "wildlife and marine conservation in Tanzania lead to forms of "green" or "blue" grabbing' which translates into dispossession of local people's land and resources, sometimes involving violence" (Benjaminsen & Bryceson, 2012: 336). Testimonies of fishermen in Tanzania and Zimbabwe report that authorities use violence against fishermen and destroy their fishing equipment (Benjaminsen & Bryceson, 2012). Thus, the end of colonization in Africa was not translated into effective peace and environmental justice. In fact, most of the colonial policies that saw people as separated from nature have been continued by postcolonial governments. Whenever the government has had to decide between protecting wildlife or people, it has been inclined to protect wildlife by introducing policies that have turned out to be violent against people (Mace, 2014).

Considering that violence against nature is also manifested through violence among people over natural resources, and secondary violence in the natural world as a result of the human degradation of the earth, postcolonial Africa has many examples of this dimension of violence against nature. Across Africa, brutal civil wars have been associated with the control of natural resources; thus, as Downey et al. (2010) put it, "military, police, mercenary, and rebel forces play a role in harming the environment" (Downey et al., 2010: 419). They proceed to argue that military activity may be a key driver for environmental degradation, because military equipment, military bases, weapons production and disposal, and war all produce severe environmental degradation (Downey et al., 2010: 419). They conclude that "armed violence plays a critical role in facilitating natural resources extraction, without which ecological unequal exchange could not occur and much of environmental degradation would not occur" (Downey et al., 2010: 437). In the Mozambican civil war, the location of military bases was strategically determined by the natural form of water sources and wildlife (Mubai, 2015: 74). In the Great Lakes region, "the headquarters of several tropical forests World Heritage sites in DRC were taken over by the military, including Virunga National Park, Kahuzi-Biega National Park, and the Okapi Wildlife Reserve" (McNeely, 2003: 146). In Angola, UNITA, the Angolan rebel movement, sustained its guerrillas with diamond mining (Power, 2001: 490). According to Malaquias, as of 2001, Angola rebels were still able to mine diamonds worth US$120–300 million (Malaquias, 2001: 525). The civil wars in Liberia and Sierra Leonne in the late 1980s and early 1990s were over the control of natural resources (Alao, 2007; Ross, 2004a, 2004b). Similarly, the wars of succession in Sudan, Ethiopia and the DRC were also about the control of strategic natural resources (Le Billon, 2001; Sefa-Nyarko, 2016; Simpson, 2014). However, the literature is silent about the significance of these wars for local ecosystems. Little is said about the use of forced labour in the extraction of resources and the lack of environmental awareness on the part of the warlords. Considering that wars bring chaos it is unlikely that the mining operations that take place in conflict zones will respect local environments. Consequently, mining operations in conflict zones, have been responsible for the pollution of rivers and the endangerment of endemic species (Banza, 2009; Bethany et al., 2018; Brauer, 2011; Nkuba et al., 2019).

One of the features of the wars that have affected postcolonial Africa is the displacement of people from their native lands. People, as part of nature, are forced to abandon their ancestral lands and to live as displaced people or refugees. Very often, people find refuge in urban centres which lack the adequate social and economic infrastructure to cater for a large number of displaced people. Lacking appropriate urban planning, many displaced people settle in areas prone to natural disasters. For example, a great part of internally displaced people of the Mozambican civil war who settled in Maputo city occupied areas prone to flooding and soil erosion. Consequently, in 2000, when the city was devasted by one of the worst floods in living memory, the majority of victims were internally displaced people (Christie & Hanlon, 2001). Because they built their settlements near natural watercourses, they interfered in local ecosystems. In Maputo Bay, Mozambique, the destruction of mangroves and other coastal habitats as the result of a proliferation of badly planned or unplanned settlements and infrastructure as well as pollution from various local and remote sources, including domestic and industrial waste water, shipping, and nitrate and pesticide contamination from agriculture has led to the reduction of fish populations (de Boer, 2002; Nhantumbo & Gaile, 2020; Rosendo et al., 2014). Similar examples are found in Sierra Leone and Angola where displaced people have occupied land not suitable for habitation, thus becoming vulnerable to mudslides (Musoke et al., 2019; Redshaw et al., 2019).

Like other parts of the world, Africa is witnessing the human degradation of the earth resulting in secondary violence from the natural world. Climate change is often associated with the degradation of the earth which has an impact on social-ecological systems which might be "experienced through both changes in mean conditions such as temperature, sea-level, and annual precipitation over long-time scales, but also through increases in the intensity and in some cases frequency of floods, droughts, storms and cyclones, fires, heatwaves, and epidemics" (Barnett & Adger, 2007: 640). Despite evidence showing that the Africa contribution to global warming and consequently to the degradation of the earth is minor, Africa is more vulnerable to violence from the natural world (Wisner et al., 2004). In North East Nigeria,

> environmental scarcity occasioned by lowering amount of rainfall has caused tremendous damage to human life through incessant conflict in the quest for scramble and domination of scarce existing land resources. Rivers have almost dried up and vegetation scanty and bare in many instances. This affects agricultural activity and animal husbandry resulting in conflict. (Obiocha, 2008: 222)

In fact, one of the major obstacles to African development is the occurrence of extreme natural disasters, including cyclones, floods, violent storms, droughts, and hurricanes which are believed to result from global warming. For example, from 1965 to 1998 there were twelve major floods, nine major droughts, and four major cyclone disasters in Mozambique. Four major droughts and famines between 1980 and 1992 caused an estimated 100,000 deaths (Wiles et al., 2005: 5). The new millennium began with the great floods of 2000, and Cyclones Idai, Kenneth and Freddy are the latest examples of Mozambique's vulnerability to natural disasters in the new millennia (Palinkas, 2020).

Mozambique's vulnerability is the consequence of people's dependency on climate-sensitive forms of natural capital (Barnett & Adger, 2007: 641). Like Mozambique, Zimbabwe, South Africa, and Tanzania have also witnessed the increase of extreme secondary violence from the natural world (Nhamo & Chikodzi, 2021: 62). These extreme natural events are often measured by their impact on human settlements and the economic infrastructure, but their impact goes beyond that. Floods transport plastics and other polluting substances into the seas and rivers, causing negative impacts which are yet to be fully assessed. Rivers, which constitute the major sources of drinking water for the people, are polluted giving rise to problems of public health. A study conducted in Accra, Ghana, shows an increase in water contamination resulting from both human mismanagement of waste and from floods (Karley, 2009). Natural disasters such as droughts and floods have a direct impact on agricultural production, which constitutes the basis for the subsistence of the majority of the African population. If one considers that the lack of food is a form of violence and can trigger violence over the access to the small quantities available, these natural phenomena represent the manifestation of violence from and towards nature. In fact, a study on climate change and collective violence concluded that climate change is a risk-multiplier that increases the risk of collective violence due to already existing causative factors. It goes on to explain that within low-income countries, climate change often exacerbates socioeconomic disparities, making the poor poorer and those who are vulnerable more vulnerable (Levy et al., 2017: 251). Barnett and Adger (2007) argue that "climate change increasingly undermines human security by reducing access to, and the quality of, natural resources that are important to sustain livelihoods." They also aver that "in certain circumstances direct and indirect impacts of climate change on human security may increase the risk of violent conflict" (Barnett & Adger, 2007: 640).

## 5 Conclusion

Keeping in mind the symbiotic relationship between humans and nature, this chapter looked at violence against nature in Africa from the colonial period to the present. It also kept in mind the overlapping meaning of nature and environment, so as to broaden the understanding of violence against nature in Africa. By defining violence towards nature in terms of violence among people over natural resources, environmental policies that can be violent against people, secondary violence from the natural world as a result of human degradation of the earth, direct damage to the environment by humans that threatens their own survival, and climate change, the chapter highlighted the centrality of the natural environment in African historical processes. A reading between the lines reveals that nature is often conceived in terms of environment and ecology. Consequently, the understanding of violence against nature requires familiarization with concepts such ecological imperialism, environmental imperialism, environmental colonialism, ecocide, and environmentalism at large. Looking at violence through these lenses brings in humans as part of nature; thus, all forms of violence among people over natural resources is also violence against nature. Ironically, by acting as both the agents and objects of violence against nature, humans cause the degradation of the earth and end up threatening their own survival by contributing to climate change. A look at the history of Africa from the late nineteenth century shows that the history of Africa has been punctuated by violence against nature. This violence is manifested by the way in which colonial powers, international corporations, and postcolonial governments have defined Africa as the home of cheap raw materials to supply industrial centres in the northern hemisphere. In the process, African natural resources, including wildlife, water streams, fish populations, forests, soils, and, above all, humans have been subject to concealed violence.

# Bibliography

Adams, W. M., & Hutton, J. (2007). People, Parks and Poverty: Political Ecology and Biodiversity Conservation. *Conservation and Society, 5*(2), 147–183.

Alao, A. (2007). *Natural Resources and Conflict in Africa: The Tragedy of Endowment*. University of Rochester Press.

Alberdi, J., & Barroso, M. (2021). Exploring Emerging Violence in Times of Transnational Extractivism in Cabo Delgado. *Global Society, 35*(2), 229–246.

Alexander, J. (2007). The Historiography of Land in Zimbabwe: Strengths, Silences, and Questions. *Safundi: The Journal of South African and American Studies, 8*(2), 183–198.

Anderson, D. (2005). *Histories of the Hanged: Britain's Dirty War in Kenya and the End of Empire*. Weidenfeld & Nicolson.

Anderson, D., & Grove, R. (1987). *Conservation in Africa: Peoples Policies and Practice*. Cambridge University Press.

Ayelazuno, J. A., & Mawuko-Yevugah, L. (2019). Large Scale Mining and Ecological Imperialism in Ghana. *Journal of Political Ecology, 26*, 243–262.

Banza, C. L. N. (2009). High Human Exposure to Cobalt and Other Metals in Katanga, a Mining Area of the Democratic Republic of Congo. *Environmental Research, 109*(6), 745–752.

Barca, S. (2014). Telling the Right Story: Environmental Violence and Liberation Narratives. *Environment and History, 20*, 535–446.

Barnett, J., & Adger, W. N. (2007). Climate Change, Human Security and Violent Conflict. *Political Geography, 26*, 639–655.

Barry, S. (2002). Debating the Land Question in Africa. *Comparative Studies in Society and History, 44*(4), 638–668.

Basu, S., Stuckler, D., Gonsalves, G., & Lurie, M. (2009). The Production of Consumption: Addressing the Impact of Mineral Mining on Tuberculosis in

Southern Africa. *Globalization and Health,* 5(11). https://doi.org/10.1186/1744-8603-5-11
Batumike, R., Imani, G., Urom, C., & Cuni-Sanchez, A. (2020). Bushmeat Hunting Around Lomami National Park, Democratic Republic of the Congo. *Oryx, 55*(3), 421–431.
Benjaminsen, T. A., & Bryceson, I. (2012). Conservation, Green/Blue Grabbing and Accumulation by Dispossession in Tanzania. *The Journal of Peasant Studies, 39*(2), 335–355.
Bethany, B., Sheehan, S., & Yong, J. L. (2018). *Cultures of the World: Angola.* Marshall Cavendish.
Boas, M., & Jennings, K. M. (2007). Failed States' and 'State Failure': Threats or Opportunities? *Globalizations, 4*(4), 475–485.
Braga-Pereira, F., Bogoni, J. A., & Alves, R. R. N. (2020). From Spears to Automatic Rifles: The Shift in Hunting Techniques as a Mammal Depletion Driver During The Angolan Civil War. *Biological Conservation, 249,* 108744. https://doi.org/10.1016/j.biocon.2020.108744
Brashares, J. S., Arcese, P., Sam, M. K., Coppolillo, P. B., Sinclair, A. R. E., & Balmford, A. (2004). Bushmeat Hunting, Wildlife Declines, and Fish Supply in West Africa. *Science, 306*(5659), 1180–1183.
Brauer, J. (2011). *War and Nature: The Environmental Consequences of War in Globalized World.* AltaMira Press.
Bundy, C. (1984). Land and Liberation: The South African National Liberation Movements and the Agrarian Question, 1920s–1960s. *Review of African Political Economy, 29,* 14–29.
Butt, N., Lembrick, F., Menton, M., & Renwick, A. (2019). The Supply Chain of Violence. *Nature Sustainability, 2,* 242–247.
Carson, R. (2002). *Silent Spring.* Houghton Mifflin.
Christie, F., & Hanlon, J. (2001). *Mozambique and the Great Flood of 2000.* James Currey.
Chung, F. (2006). *Re-living the Second Chimurenga: Memories from Zimbabwe's Liberation Struggle.* The Nordic Africa Institute.
Colua, E. O., Otsuki, K., & Mubai, M. E. (2021). Tackling Challenges for Co-management of Natural Resources: The Community Council in Limpopo National Park, Mozambique. *Development in Practice.* https://doi.org/10.1080/09614524.2021.1898547
Crosby, A. (1986). *Ecological Imperialism: The Biological Expansion of Europe 900–1900.* Cambridge University Press.
De Boer, W. F. (2002). The Rise and Fall of the Mangrove in Maputo Bay, Mozambique. *Wetlands Ecology and Management, 10,* 313–322.
Demissie, F. (Ed.). (2016). *Land Grabbing in Africa: The Race for Africa's Farmland.* Routledge.
Downey, L., Bonds, E., & Clark, K. (2010). Natural Resource Extraction, Armed Violence, and Environmental Degradation. *Organization & Environment, 23*(4), 417–445.

Ebiede, T. M. (2011). Conflict Drivers: Environmental Degradation and Corruption in the Niger Delta Region. *African Conflict & Peacebuilding Review, 1*(1), 139–151.

Esparza, J. (2021). A Natural Arch: Ecological Imperialism and the "Crosby Effect". In American Environmental History. *History in the Making, 14*(14), 235–264.

Evers, S. J. T. M., Seagle, C., & Krijtenburg, F. (2013). *Africa for Sale? Positioning the State, Land and Society in Foreign Large-Scale Land Acquisition in Africa*. Brill.

Fayiga, A. O., Ipinmoroti, M. O., & Chirenje, T. (2018). Environmental Pollution in Africa. *Environment Development Sustainability, 20*, 41–73.

Frame, M. (2014). *The Foreign Investment in African Resources: The Ecological Aspect to Imperialism and Unequal Exchange* (Ph.D. Dissertation). University of Denver.

Frynas, J. G., & Wood, G. (1999). Oil and War in Angola. *Review of African Political Economy, 90*, 987–606.

Galaty, J. G., & Wood, G. (1999). Grounding Pastoralists: Law, Politics, and Dispossession in East Africa. *Nomadic Peoples, 3*(2), 56–73.

Giblin, J. L. (1992). *The Politics of Environmental Control in Northeastern Tanzania, 1860–1940*. University of Pennsylvania Press.

Holy Bible. 2011. *New International Version (NIV)*. Genesis 1:28. Biblica.

Homer-Dixon, T. F., Boutwell, J. H., & Rathjens, G. W. (1993). Environmental Change and Violent Conflict: Growing Scarcities of Renewable Sources Can Contribute to Social Instability and Civil Strife. *Scientific American, 268*(2), 38–45.

https://www.merriam-webster.com/dictionary/environment. Accessed 15 November 2021.

https://www.merriam-webster.com/dictionary/nature. Accessed 15 November 2021.

https://www.oxfordlearnersdictionaries.com/definition/american_english/environment. Accessed 15 November 2021.

https://www.oxfordreference.com/view/https://www.oxfordreference.com/view/10.1093/acref/9780198609810.001.0001/acref-9780198609810-e-4825. Accessed 15 November 2021.

Illife, J. (2007). *Africans: The History of a Continent*. Cambridge University Press.

Isaacman, A. F., & Isaacman, B. S. (2016). *Barragens, deslocamento e ilusão de desenvolvimento: Cahora Bassa e seus legados em Moçambique, 1965–2007*. Imprensa Universitária.

Karley, N. K. (2009). Flooding and Physical Planning in Urban Areas in West Africa: Situational Analysis of Accra, Ghana. *Theoretical and Empirical Researches in Urban Management, 4*(4), 25–41.

Kiljunen, K. (1980). Namibia: The Ideology of National Liberation. *Bulletin, 11*(4), 65–71.

Kjekshus, H. (1977). *Ecology Control and Economic Development in East African History: The Case Study of Tanganyika, 1850–1950*. University of California Press.

Koning, N., & Smalling, E. (2005). Environmental Crisis or the 'Lie of the Land'? the Debate on Soil Degradation in Africa. *Land Use Policy, 22*, 3–11.

Kwashirai, V. C. (2006). Dilemmas in Conservationism in Colonial Zimbabwe, 1890–1930. *Conservation and Society, 4*(4), 541–561.

Lan, D. (1985). *Guns and Rain: Guerrillas and Spirit Mediums in Zimbabwe*. James Currey.

Le Billon, P. (2001). The Political Ecology of War: Natural Resources and Armed c=Conflicts. *Political Geography, 20*(5), 561–584.

Lee, B. X. (2016). Causes and Cures VIII: Environmental Violence. *Aggression and Violent Behavior, 30*, 105–109.

Leuenberger, A., Cambaco, O., Zabré, H. R., Lyatuu, I., Utzinger, J., Munguambe, K., Marten, S., & Winkler, M. S. (2021). It's Like We Are Living in a Different World: Health Inequality in Communities Surrounding Industrial Mining Sites in Burkina Faso, Mozambique and Tanzania. *International Journal of Environmental Research Public Health, 18*. https://doi.org/10.3390/ijerph182111015

Levy, B. S., Sidel, V. W., & Patz, J. A. (2017). Climate Change and Collective Violence. *Annual Review of Public Health*. https://doi.org/10.1146/annurev-publhealth-031816-044232

Lunstrum, E., & Givá, N. (2020). What Drives Commercial Poaching? From Poverty to Economic Inequality. *Biological Conservation, 245*, 108505. https://doi.org/10.1016/j.biocon.2020.108505

Lunstrum, E., Givá, N., Massé, F., Mate, F., & José, P. L. (2021). The Rhino Horn Trade and Radical Inequality as Environmental Conflict. *The Journal Peasant Studies*. https://doi.org/10.1080/03066150.2021.1961130

Mace, G. M. (2014). Whose Conservation. *Science, 345*(6204), 1558–1560.

Malaquias, A. (2001). Making War and Lots of Money: The Political Economy of Protracted Conflict in Angola. *Review of African Political Economy, 28*(90), 521–536.

Mandala, V. R. (2015). The Raj and the Paradoxes of Wildlife Conservation: British Attitude and Expediencies. *The Historical Journal, 58*(1), 75–110.

Masalu, D. C. P. (2000). Coastal and Marine Resources Use Conflicts and Sustainable Development in Tanzania. *Ocean and Coastal Management, 43*(6), 475–494.

McGregor, J. (2008). Patrolling Kariba's Waters: State Authority, Fishing and the Border Economy. *Journal of Southern African Studies, 32*(4), 861–879.

McNeely, J. A. (2003). Conserving Forests Biodiversity in Times of Violent Conflict. *Oryx, 37*(2), 142–152.

Meredith, M. (2011). *The State of Africa: A History of the Continent Since Independence*. Simon and Schuster.

Miracle, M. P. (1965). The Introduction and Spread of Maize in Africa. *Journal of African History, 6*(1), 39–55.

Mogomotsi, G. E. J., & Madigele, P. K. (2017). Live by the Gun, Die by the Gun: Botswana's 'Shoot-to-Kill' Policy as an Anti-Poaching Strategy. *SA Crime Quarterly, 60*, 51–59.

Molapo, R. (2014). Voices of Liberation: Songs and the Liberation Struggle in South Africa. *Mediterranean Journal of Social Sciences, 5*(27), 985–990.

Moyo, S. (1994). *The Land Question in Zimbabwe*. SAPES Trust.

Mubai, M. E. (2015). *Making War on Forest and Village: Southern Mozambique during the Sixteen-Year Conflict, 1976–1992* (Ph.D. Thesis). University of Iowa.

Murphy, J. (2009). *Environment and Imperialism: Why Colonialism Still Matters* (Sustainability Research Institute Papers). University of Leeds.

Musoke, R., Chimbaru, A., Jambai, A., Njuguna, C., Kayita, J., Bunn, J., Latt, A., Yao, M., Yoti, Z., & Yahaya, A. (2019). A Public Health Response to a Mudslide in Freetown, Sierra Leone, 2017: Lessons Learnt. *Disaster Medicine and Public Health Preparedness, 14*(2), 256–264.

Nelson, R. (2003). Environmental Colonialism: 'Saving' Africa from Africans. *The Independent Review, 8*(1), 65–86.

Nhamo, G., & Chikodzi, D. (Ed.). (2021). *Cyclones in Southern Africa, Vol 3: Implications for Sustainable Development Goals*. Springer.

Nhantumbo, E., & Gaile, B. (2020). *Shallow Water Shrimp Fishery in Mozambique: Who Benefits from Fiscal Reform?* (IIED Working Paper).

Nkuba, B., Bervoets, L., & Greenen, S. (2019). Invisible and Ignored? Local Perspectives on Mercury in Congolese Gold Mining. *Journal of Cleaner Production, 221*, 795–804.

Obiocha, E. E. (2008). Climate Change, Population Drift and Violent Conflict over Land Resources in Northeastern Nigeria. *Journal of Human Ecology, 23*(4), 311–324.

Ochieng, G. M., Seanego, E. S., & Nkwonta, O. I. (2010). Impacts of Mining on Water Resources in Africa: A Review. *Scientific Research Essays, 5*(22), 3351–3357.

Palinkas, L. A. (2020). *Global Climate Change, Population Displacement, and Public Health: The Next Wave of Migration*. Springer.

Pavid, K. (2021). *Wildlife Photographer of the Year: The Brutal Reality of Rhino Poaching*. https://www.nhm.ac.uk/discover/the-brutal-reality-of-rhino-poaching.html. Accessed 22 December.

Pile, K. (1996). Soil Erosion and People's Perceptions in Rural Community in Kwazulu-Natal South Africa. *GeoJournal, 39*(1), 59–64.

Power, M. (2001). Patrimonialism and Petro-Diamond Capitalism: Peace, Geopolitics and the Economics of the War in Angola. *Review of African Political Economy, 28*(90), 489–502.

Prendergast, D. K., & Adams, W. M. (2003). Colonial Wildlife Conservation and the Origins of the Society for the Preservation of the Wild Fauna of the Empire (1903–1914). *Oryx, 37*(2), 251–260.

Redshaw, P., Boon, D., Campbell, G., Willis, M., Mattai, J., Free, M., Jordan, C., Kemp, S. J., Morley, A., & Thomas, M. (2019). The 2017 Regent Landslide, Freetown Peninsula, Sierra Leone. *Quarterly Journal of Engineering and Hydrology, 52*, 435–444.

Ripple, W. J., Abernethy, K., Betts, M. G., Chapron, G., Dirzo, R., Galetti, M., Levi, T., Lindsey, P. A., MacDonald, D. W., Machovina, B., Newsome,

T. M., Peres, C. A., Wallach, A. D., Wolf, C., & Young, H. (2016). Bushmeat Hunting and Extinction Risk to the World's Mammals. *Royal Society Open Science, 3*(160498), 160498. https://doi.org/10.1098/rsos.160498

Rosendo, S., Celliers, L., & Mechisso, M. (2014). Management of Maputo Bay. In S. Bandeira & J. Paula (Eds.), *The Maputo Bay Ecosystem* (pp. 399–418). WIOMSA, Zanzibar Town.

Ross, M. L. (2004a). How Do Natural Resources Influence Civil War? Evidence from Thirteen Cases. *International Organization, 58*(1), 35–67.

Ross, M. L. (2004b). What Do We Know About Natural Resources and Civil War? *Journal of Peace Research, 41*(3), 337–356.

Rudel, T., & Roper, J. (1997). The Paths to Rain Forest Destruction: Crossnational Patterns of Tropical Deforestation, 1975–1990. *World Development, 25*(1), 53–65.

Sabea, H. (2008). Mastering the Landscape? Sisal Plantations, Land, and Labor in Tanga Region, 1893–1980s. *International Journal of African Historical Studies, 41*(3), 411–432.

Santos, J. R. M. (2009). *Degradação ambiental na África Subsahariana: Modelos explicativos para os principais problemas*. Universidade de Lisboa.

Sefa-Nyarko, C. (2016). Civil War in South Sudan: Is It a Reflection of Historical Secessionist and Natural Resources Wars in Greater Sudan? *African Security, 9*(3), 188–220.

Silvester, J. G. (1993). *Black Pastoralists, White Farmers: The Dynamics of Land Dispossession and Labour Recruitment in Southern Namibia, 1915–195* (Ph.D. Thesis). University of London.

Simpson, B. (2014). The Biafran Secession and the Limits of Self-Determination. *Journal of Genocide Research, 6*(2/3), 337–354.

Steinhart, E. I. (1989). Hunters, Poachers and Gamekeepers: Towards a Social History of Hunting in Colonial Kenya. *The Journal of African History, 30*(2), 247–264.

Stuckler, D., Basu, S., & McKee, M. (2010). Governance of Mining, HIV and Tuberculosis in Southern Africa. *Global Health Governance, 4*(1), 1–13.

Tinley, K. L., Rosinha, A. J., Lobão, J. L. P., & Dutton, T. P. (1976). Wildlife and Wild Places in Mozambique. *Oryx, 13*(4), 344–350. https://doi.org/10.1017/S00 3060530001406X

Vicente, E. M. (2000). *Impact of Alluvial Gold Mining on Surface Water Quality in the Revue Basin-Manica District, Mozambique* (MSc Thesis). University of Kwazulu-Natal.

Wiles, P., Silvester, K., & Fidalgo, L. (2005). *Disaster Risk Management Working Paper Series No. 12: Learning Lessons from Disaster Recovery: The Case of Mozambique*. The World Bank.

Wisner, B., Blaikie, P., Cannon, T., & Davis, I. (2004). *At Risk: Natural Hazards*. Routledge.

Witter, R., & Satterfield, T. (2019). Rhino Poaching and the 'Slow Violence' of the Conservation-Related Resettlement in Mozambique's Limpopo National Park. *Geoforum, 101*, 275–284.

Young, C. (2012). *Africa and the Diaspora: Postcolonial State in Africa: Fifty Years of Independence, 1960–2010*. University of Wisconsin Press.

# Xenophobia, Afrophobia, or Promoting Xenophilia? Semantic Explorations of Violence and Criminality in South Africa

Martin Mujinga

## 1 Introduction

The organized stoning, killings, maiming, and burning alive of individuals, looting of shops, and destruction of the property of foreigners have, of late, characterized the attitude of some South Africans towards immigrants from within the African continent (Kumalo & Mujinga, 2017: 47). One of the justifications for attacking immigrants is the claim that South Africa has a history of violence that has been exacerbated since 2000 (Myambo, 2019). The targeted populace is mostly black Africans, whom South Africans call *makwerekwere*,[1] and nationals from Bangladesh and Pakistan. Brutal killings and dispersions of immigrants in South Africa intensified in 2008, 2015, and 2019. These acts left scholars grappling with the proper term to give to the phenomenon. On the one hand, academics refer to the attacks as expressions of xenophobia and Afrophobia. On the other hand, some South African politicians reluctantly call them acts of criminality. This violence is distinctive and decisive because it only affects African foreign nationals and no European or Indian is attacked (Essa & Patel, 2015).

---

[1] When South Africans could not comprehend the language of the foreigners, they derogatorily called them *Makwerekwere* (Bridger, 2015).

M. Mujinga (✉)
Research Institute for Theology and Religion, University of South Africa, Pretoria, South Africa
e-mail: martinmujinga@gmail.com

© The Author(s), under exclusive license to Springer Nature Switzerland AG 2024
O. B. Mlambo and E. Chitando (eds.), *The Palgrave Handbook of Violence in Africa*, https://doi.org/10.1007/978-3-031-40754-3_31

The reasons for the attacks on foreign nationals have been intensively investigated by scholars such as (Crush & Ramachandran, 2009; Essa & Patel, 2015; Landau, 2018; Tshabalala, 2015). These scholars generally agree to name these attacks as xenophobia and/or Afrophobia. However, this chapter challenges the use of xenophobia and Afrophobia as concepts to justify the acts of violent criminality conducted by some black South Africans in disguise. This chapter proposes to call the attacks acts of criminality rather than xenophobia and/or Afrophobia. The justifications for reaching this conclusion are as follows: first, the South African constitution has no room for racialism, division, or violence. As such, the acts of violence and criminality are portraying a country that has lost its constitutional mandate and historical memory. Second, by behaving criminally, some black South Africans are fighting against the values of Black consciousness which was their tool of emancipation during apartheid. Third, the research agrees with the position of some South African politicians that the attacks are acts of criminality.

## 2 Research Methodology

This chapter utilized the desk research methodology. Desk research gives the researcher information that he/she may never have the resources to generate him/herself (Cameron, 2018). In desk research, data types are vast in their availability, and they include libraries and the internet (Haradhan, 2018: 1). Four reasons governed the decision to employ desk research for this chapter. First, the research was undertaken in Zimbabwe whereas the area of research is South Africa, which makes it difficult to do an empirical study that requires one to be in the area of research. This detachment of the area of study from the researcher would not allow for primary sources to be gathered. Consequently, desk research proved to be a strategic methodology. Second, this is not an empirical study where primary sources are used but it is an analysis of already gathered data. Third, most of the research on xenophobia/Afrophobia is on electronic sources, including both verbal and written material. Fourth, desk research saves time and resources and is also effective as the researcher uses already analysed data (Cameron, 2018).

Although the methodology is helpful, Cameron (2018) cautions that the researcher must reach a full understanding of how the analysed data was collected because most of the data could be biased. To emphasize rigour and validity, the researcher was conscious of analysing the data not as a victim, a victor, or a survivor but as an independent researcher. In order to understand the justification of xenophobia/Afrophobia in South Africa, it is important to direct the readers to a brief history of violence in South Africa.

## 3 A Brief History of Violence Against African Migrants in South Africa

While there were incidents of violence against Blacks from outside South Africa, after the majority rule in 1994 the incidences of xenophobia increased (Gumede, 2018; Neocosmos, 2010). For example, immigrants from Malawi, Zimbabwe, and Mozambique living in the Alexandra Township were physically assaulted over a period of several weeks in January 1995 (South Africa History Online, n.d.). Armed gangs identified suspected undocumented migrants and forced them to march to the police station in an attempt to "clean" the township of foreigners. The campaign, known as *buyelekhaya* (go back home), blamed foreigners for crime, unemployment, and sexual attacks (Nahla, 2008). In September 1998, a Mozambican national and two Senegalese were thrown out of a moving train. The assault was carried out by a group of people returning from a rally that blamed foreigners for unemployment, crime, and the spread of HIV and AIDS (Nahla, 2008). Some South Africans associated African migrants with the negative stereotype of being from less "developed" countries. In October 2001, residents of the Zandspruit informal settlement gave Zimbabwean citizens ten days to leave the area. When the foreigners failed to leave voluntarily, they were forcefully evicted, and their shacks were looted and burnt down. These Zimbabweans were accused of being employed whilst locals remained jobless (Independent Online, 2008).

Attacks on foreign nationals increased remarkably in late 2007 and many foreigners were attacked between January and May 2008. The most severe incident occurred on 8 January 2008 when two Somali shop owners were murdered in the Eastern Cape (Independent Online, 2008). In March 2008 seven people were killed, including Zimbabweans, Pakistanis, and a Somali national after their shops and shacks were set alight in Atteridgeville near Pretoria (Independent Online, 2008). According to Nyamnjoh (2014: 398), between 2000 and March 2008, about 67 people died in what were identified as xenophobic attacks. In May 2008, 64 people died in a wave of anti-immigrant violence in the Alexandra township of Johannesburg before spreading to other parts of Gauteng. In these attacks, hundreds were injured and maimed, and thousands were displaced (Landau, 2018: 18; Tafira, 2018: 15). Of those killed, 21 were South African citizens but the attacks were attributed to xenophobia (Bridger, 2015). This contradiction of attacking fellow South Africans and calling the attacks xenophobia justifies criminality under the camouflage of xenophobia/Afrophobia.

The nationwide attacks resumed in April 2015. There was an upsurge in xenophobic attacks throughout the country, starting in Durban. The (now late) Zulu King Goodwill Zwelithini was accused of fuelling the attacks. He said in his address, "I request the South African government to help us clean our land of 'lice'. We need to remove all itching bedbugs and lay them in the sun. We request that all foreigners take their baggage and be sent back" (Zwelithini, 2015). This speech led to the displacement of over 6,000 immigrants. 3,000 shops in KwaZulu Natal were looted and seven people were killed. Among those killed were Ethiopian, Mozambican, Bangladeshi, Zimbabwean, and three South African citizens (Kumalo & Mujinga, 2017: 50). The attacks continued in Johannesburg, Eastern Cape, and other parts of the country. At higher learning institutions, the attacks coincided with student protests and slogans like #FeesMustFall which were chanted by violent students who were also destroying property. The attacks continued, with some taxi drivers transporting looters for free (Naicker, 2016).

In a 2017 press conference, the then deputy police minister Bongani Mkongi (cited by Chigumadzi [2019]) stated that: "It is dangerous that the city's suburb of Hillbrow was made up of 80% foreign nationals. One day the whole of South Africa could become foreign and a future president could be a foreigner." The video capturing this speech went viral in March 2019, resulting in African migrants in KwaZulu-Natal being attacked. In November 2018, the minister of health, Aaron Motsoaledi (also cited by Chigumadzi [2019]) mentioned that South Africa needed to re-examine its immigration policies, saying "Our hospitals are full, we cannot control them… [Migrants] are causing overcrowding."

In 2019, riots started again in Durban. Businesses owned by foreign nationals were attacked by over 100 people, resulting in more than 50 people seeking shelter at a local police station and mosque. These riots claimed the lives of three people (Chigumadzi, 2019). Some African countries whose citizens were attacked blamed President Cyril Ramaphosa as the perpetrator. During his campaign for the 2019 general election ANC rally, President Ramaphosa said: "Everyone just arrives in our townships and rural areas and sets up businesses without licenses and permits. We are going to bring this to an end. And those who are operating illegally, wherever they come from, must now know" (Ramaphosa, 2019). In the same address, the president also committed himself to cracking down on undocumented foreigners involved in criminal activities (SABC, 2019).

The anti-immigrant campaign was also fuelled by other political leaders such as Mmusi Maimane, who was the leader of the opposition Democratic Alliance, and Mosia Lekota of Congress of the People. The two political leaders claimed that foreigners were flooding the country and undermining its security and prosperity (Chigumadzi, 2019). In all these xenophobic/Afrophobic statements, only the Economic Freedom Fighters (EFF) spoke against the attack of foreigners. Its leader, Julius Malema, challenged his compatriots by announcing as follows, "We call on our fellow South Africans to stop violence against other poor people in our communities. Xenophobic violence will never resolve the problems our country faces because they were never caused by foreign nationals in the first place" (Malema, 2019). The attack of foreigners continued again on 1 September 2019 in Jeppestown and Johannesburg Central Business District, with riots and looting of shops owned by foreign nationals (Ferial, 2019). Thousands of migrants were displaced and 12 people were killed—ten South Africans and two Zimbabweans amid mass plundering and destruction of foreign-owned homes, property, and businesses (Dahir, 2019).

The September 2019 the attack on Africans and Asians had a negative impact on South Africa in particular. Some African countries responded negatively, and some South African businesses outside South Africa were affected. In Nigeria and Zambia, some South African businesses such as Pick 'n' Pay, Shoprite, and MTN were looted and the South African embassy in Lagos had to close down (Sibeko, 2019). In Zimbabwe, South African president Cyril Ramaphosa was booed at the funeral of former president Robert G. Mugabe. Moreover, soccer matches between South African national team Bafana-Bafana and Zambia and Madagascar respectively were also cancelled (Sibeko, 2019).

In response to this negative publicity, first, President Ramaphosa had to apologize to Zimbabweans before he gave his tribute to Mugabe during the funeral. Second, envoys were sent to discuss the violence against foreigners of African origin and also offer the country's apology (Chigumadzi, 2019). The history of South Africa's violence against foreigners and the actions of President Ramaphosa as both the "perpetrator" and "apologizer" raises a number of questions such as: Is South Africa in agreement that some of its black citizens act in criminal ways? If not, why are some scholars naming the phenomenon as xenophobia or Afrophobia, while some politicians are saying these are violent criminal activities? If yes, are xenophobia and Afrophobia being used as just semantic tools to explain the criminal activities of some of the black South Africans? A semantic reflection on xenophobia and Afrophobia will help us understand whether the attacks are xenophobia, Afrophobia, or if they are acts of criminality.

## 4 Unpacking Xenophobia and Afrophobia in the South African Context

Some scholars have generally accepted xenophobia and Afrophobia as appropriate terms to describe the attacks of immigrants in South Africa, as argued earlier (see also Crush & Pandelton, 2004; Crush & Ramachandran, 2009; Essa & Patel, 2015; Landau, 2018; Tshabalala, 2015; Tshaka, 2016). This chapter argues that the attacks are neither xenophobia nor Afrophobia, but they are acts of violent criminality by some black South Africans. In order to reach this conclusion, the chapter starts by examining the definitions of xenophobia and Afrophobia.

Whitehead (2012) avers that the terms we use do not have one correct meaning, but they mean different things to different people at different times. Words come into existence to express thoughts by a group of people that share them at a point in time. For example, xenophobia and Afrophobia are used as semantic resources to express the brutal attacks on foreigners in South Africa. For Whitehead (2012), words might be shared with other subject fields, but quite often the definitions for these shared terms are different. Moreover, those in specific subject fields create new, distinct terms used to describe the same concept as other terms found in other subject fields. As such, we end up with the same words—different definitions or same definitions (Whitehead, 2012). This is why it is important to engage xenophobia and Afrophobia before we conclude that the attacks of foreigners are acts of criminality.

## 5 Definition and Interpretation of Xenophobia

According to Crush and Ramachandran (2009: 4), "the word xenophobia has Greek origins, *xenophobes*. *Xenos* means foreign while *Phobos* refers to fear." The Webster's New Encyclopedic Dictionary (1996: 1205), mentions that "xenophobia means fear and hatred of strangers or foreigners or anything strange or foreign." In the South African context, xenophobia entails a massive dislike of foreigners. This is mainly experienced by black foreigners, including refugee children who are hated and accused of exacerbating the country's socio-economic problems (Crush & Pandelton, 2004: 1). The hatred of foreigners by some South Africans is attributed to the fear of loss of social status and identity; a threat perceived or real, to citizens' economic success; a way of reassuring the national self and its boundaries in times of national crisis; a feeling of superiority and poor intercultural information (Mogekwu, 2005).

The definition of xenophobia as provided above is not limited to pigmentation, but it expresses the hatred of any stranger or foreigner. In this regard, the use of the term xenophobia to refer to the attack of foreigners is problematic. The first scholar who refutes the use of xenophobia to refer to the attack of foreigners is Rothney Tshaka. According to Tshaka (2016), "if foreigners were the main target, those who are anti-foreigner would no doubt have sought out all foreigners and made it known that they are not welcome in South Africa." Unfortunately, the attacks are selective because whites from Europe and America, by virtue of their skin, are seen as contributing to the economy, while black Africans are seen as destroying the economy (Tshaka, 2016). Given this scenario, Tshaka prefers to use the term Afrophobia to describe the selective attack of foreigners.

The second scholar who denies the attacks as xenophobia is Wahbie Long (2015: 510). Long argues that:

> [T]he facts seem to indicate that South Africa is one of the more violent places on earth. We have been and continue to be a country with significant levels of political violence, criminal violence, and domestic violence and now, we are witnessing violence against fellow Africans. While many have termed this 'xenophobia', a more accurate term may well be 'Afrophobia'.

Long (2015) prefers to use Afrophobia arguing that some of those involved in the killings have a history of antisocial behaviour that leads them to attack fellow Africans. Long agrees with Tshaka because the violence that he describes is mostly experienced by black Africans and white foreigners are hardly touched by this form of violence.

The third disputation of the use of xenophobia comes from Kenneth Tafira (2018), although he differs with Tshaka (2016) and Long (2015). Tafira equates xenophobia to racism because racism is not only pinned on skin colour (2018: 15). Tafira stresses that the 2008 and 2015 attacks in South Africa were by blacks on blacks because the black African foreigners were deemed socially and culturally inferior. The cultural differences were enunciated by dissimilates in nationality, language, dress, customs, social and territorial origin, speech patterns, and accent (Tafira, 2018: 15). Steve Biko (cited in Ferm [1984: 65]) defines racism as the feeling of superiority by the whites and the inferiority of the blacks during apartheid. Allan

Boesak (also cited in Ferm [1984: 67]) asserted that racism was a demonic, pseudo-religious ideology practised by the minority rule during apartheid. Moreover, Parratt (2000: 59) states that "Racism is the domination of one racial group by the other." Going by these three definitions and interpretations of racism, Tafira's claim of equating xenophobia to racism is somehow misleading. Ilevbare and Adesanya (2008) separate xenophobia from racism, arguing that someone of a different race does not necessarily have to be of a different nationality. The two scholars note that, in various contexts, xenophobia and racism are used interchangeably, although they can have wholly different meanings. Xenophobia is based on various aspects, while racism is based solely on race and ancestry only (Ilevbare & Adesanya, 2008).

The fourth challenge of relating the attacks to xenophobia was put forward by Sibusiso Tshabalala (2015). Tshabalala mentions that at the heart of South Africa's complex problem with xenophobia is the loaded meaning of the term "foreigner." Pejoratively, the term "foreigner" in South Africa usually refers to African and Asian nationals (Tshabalala, 2015). However, "other" foreigners, particularly those from Europe and America, go unnoticed. They are often lumped in with tourists, or even better, referred to as "expats" (Tshabalala, 2015). Based on this point, the use of xenophobic attacks is selective because some sections of the population of foreigners are not included, which is the same point raised by Tshaka (2016).

Myambo (2019) stresses that, in South Africa, whiteness or lightness often denotes power and prestige, while dark skin is often used as a way to identify foreigners during xenophobic attacks. Tshabalala (2015) cautions that the fluidity of the term xenophobia justifies the reason why the South African government is hesitant to call the attacks xenophobic. Myambo strongly argues the moment scholars continue to claim that the attack on foreigners in South Africa is an expression of xenophobia, we will have continuous challenges. The first challenge relates to the selective application of the attacks where whites from Europe and America are not attacked. Second, during the attacks, some South Africans are also killed. For example, in September 2019, ten South Africans were killed, compared to two Zimbabweans. An analysis of the meaning and application of xenophobia in South Africa makes the term inappropriate. Another term is, therefore, necessary.

## 6   Understanding Afrophobia in the Context of the Attack of Foreigners in South Africa

The weaknesses of xenophobia, as noted above, draws us to interrogate "Afrophobia," a term which some scholars are also using to describe the attacks on foreigners. According to the Online Dictionary,[2] Afrophobia is the noun that refers to the fear, hate, or dislike of Black Africans and Black African descendants. The Thesaurus Online Dictionary[3] also defines Afrophobia as a term used to refer to a range of negative attitudes and feelings towards black people or people of African descent around the world. The two definitions emphasize "black" and "Africa," thereby making Afrophobia different from xenophobia which generalizes the hate to all foreigners regardless of colour or creed. According to Tshaka (2016), the term Afrophobia became popular after the 2008 outbreaks of violence in South Africa against other Africans. In present-day South Africa, Afrophobia is a manifestation of distrust and envy towards black foreigners, seen as a threat because they can "slip undetected into the black communities and, thus, potentially steal the jobs and women of the indigenous black South African men" (Tshaka, 2016). Locals who have been disappointed by the South African liberation project take this distrust to justify their antagonism towards other African nationals.

The first challenge of adopting Afrophobia has been raised by Tshabalala (2015), who reiterates that while we can ascribe the attacks to sentiments of Afrophobia, we must be willing to agree that the attacks are fuelled by a sense of hatred, dislike, and fear of foreigners and that is xenophobia. This analysis takes us back to the problem of who is black, who is a foreigner, and who is an African. The fact that other foreign nationals from Pakistan and Bangladesh have been profiled in this wave of attacks dismisses the use of the term Afrophobia because they are neither black nor African, but they are Asians. Although Pakistanis and Bangladeshis and other whites have light pigmentation, however, Asians are treated as criminals while Europeans and Americans are seen as benefactors and potential employers.

Second, the attack of the immigrants in South Africa and the sparing of the whites from Europe and the Americas is neither xenophobia nor Afrophobia but xenophilia which is a war of pigmentation where white is superior and black is inferior. Xenophilia means affection for unknown foreign objects, manners, cultures, or people (Myambo, 2019). For Myambo

---

[2] https://www.yourdictionary.com/afrophobia.
[3] http://www.red-network.eu/?i=red-network.en.thesaurus.1.

(2019), xenophilia is applied when a migrant benefits from positive stereotypes of being wealthier, fairer, or coming from a "developed" country. This is in contrast to the converse, namely, that being darker, poorer, and coming from an "inferior" country can factor into xenophobia (Myambo, 2019). The application of Afrophobia to refer to the attack of foreigners is equally deceptive. It is against this background that this chapter proposes the attacks as acts of criminality. This seeks to rescue those scholars who are struggling to name the phenomenon as it is, thereby resorting to semantics. Before we pursue "criminality," as a new term that explains the attacks, we start by drawing attention to South Africa's visible and long-standing currency that make the country unique, namely, South Africa's constitution, "rainbowism," and Ubuntu philosophy. This is due to the fact that if South Africa would uphold the Ubuntu philosophy, it would minimize the acts of violent criminality that the chapter has described in the preceding sections.

## 7 Criminality Camouflaged by Semantic Twists

In the foregoing sections, it was argued that neither xenophobia nor Afrophobia can best describe the attacks on black Africans from other African countries in South Africa, but they are acts of criminality. This section aims to justify the proposal of acts of criminality as a reality in South Africa. According to a Pew Research poll conducted in 2018, 62% of South Africans viewed immigrants as being a burden on society by taking jobs and social benefits. The same research also found that 61% of South Africans thought that immigrants were more responsible for crime (Budiman, 2019). The conclusions of Pew Research are pointers to the possibility of criminality by some black South Africans in attacking immigrants "claiming their jobs and social benefits" (Budiman, 2019). Moreover, the attack on Africans by some black South Africans are acts of criminality hiding behind foreigners and some politicians were instigating the attacks (Charman & Piper, 2012: 81).

Former presidents Thabo Mbeki and Jacob Zuma confirmed that the attacks were neither xenophobic nor Afrophobia but acts of criminality. After the 2008 attacks, Mbeki (cited in Essa and Patel [2015]) reiterated that: "those who wanted to use the term xenophobia were trying to explain the naked criminality in the garb of xenophobia" (see also Tagwirei, 2019). The same statement was also uttered by President Zuma (cited in Gqirana [2015]). Zuma confirmed that:

> [T]he word xenophobia should not be used excessively because it would give the impression that most South Africans were xenophobic, yet they are not. No one can say South Africans attack foreigners only. We have a history that these things happen. There is violence here that nobody has forgotten. Political violence here you could not say was xenophobic. (Gqirana, 2015)

Zuma further stated: "at some point, I was giving an example, I was explaining to someone who was researching to say that research was not accurate to say the majority of South Africans are xenophobic. We are not!" (Gqirana, 2015). In his further disagreement with the use of the term xenophobia, Zuma went on to say:

> [W]hat I was saying is you cannot interpret when people are fighting from that simple logic, for example in Johannesburg you know at times the entire Soweto was fighting the majority were Zulus, and you could not say that was xenophobic. Some of these things were manipulated by those who were in charge at the time. But there was a lot of violence in KwaZulu-Natal amongst Zulus, would you say they were xenophobic? No. There is a minority, and we will deal with that. The incident in Alexandra where a Mozambican Emmanuel Sithole, was brutally stabbed in pictures published on the front page of the Sunday Times, was 'purely criminal' but because it happened at the time of the xenophobic attacks, it is now said this is how we kill people in South Africa. No! (Gqirana, 2015)

From the statements by Mbeki and Zuma, it might be argued that xenophobia or Afrophobia are being used excessively, and yet the truth is South Africa has a history of violence and some individuals act criminally. Landau (2018) confirms that the government continues to sideline xenophobic violence the same way it does violence affecting South African communities. The government has neutralized anti-outsider violence by blaming it variously on criminality or the natural resentment of South Africans towards those whom they perceive as stealing opportunities from them.

## 8 Findings of the Study and Proposals to Move from Criminality to Xenophilia

Although xenophobia and Afrophobia were regarded as problematic concepts that could disguise criminality by some black South Africans, the country can still rebuild itself from criminality to xenophilia where humanity will be treated with respect. To move from criminality to xenophilia, South Africa has to realize that it lost its visible and long-standing ideological currency resulting in losing its historical memory. South Africa was among the last African countries to gain its political independence. During apartheid, the country received a lot of support from other African countries (Tagwirei, 2019; South Africa History Online, n.d.). Muzengeza (2015) feels that xenophobia or Afrophobia in South Africa, is just the convenient amnesia of the country.

It is a fact that most of the immigrants in South Africa are not there by choice, but some are running away from their challenged and challenging economies, as well as social and political unrest. As such, a number of them will be illegal migrants, while others would be refugees among the poor in South Africa's urban townships. These people who will be seeking refuge in the fellow another African country find themselves as victims largely from local mobs of young, unemployed, black South Africans within the communities they live.

The need for hospitality to fellow Africans was emphasized by President Cyril Ramaphosa. During his televised address after the attacks in September 2019, the president called for an end to the attacks. He reiterated that South Africa is not the only country that is "home" to millions of foreigners, but other countries are "homes" to many African immigrants (eNCA, 2019). President Ramaphosa also appealed to South Africans not to express their anger to foreigners because criminality, whether by immigrants or locals, is not an excuse for the attacks (eNCA, 2019).

This chapter argues that the criminality that is camouflaged in the attack on African migrants defeats the legacy of Black consciousness. During apartheid, some black South African scholars argued for a Black God (Tutu, 1998: 59). During apartheid black people were treated as subhuman and Black consciousness was an emancipation tool for people who suffered social injustice every day. Black consciousness gave birth to Black theology, which had a preferential option for the poor blacks whose lives were dominated by suffering (Chitando, 2009: 94). Given that the attacks of foreigners proves the point raised by Chitando (2009) that, for some, Black theology lost its mandate the moment South Africa became independent. The political independence of the black majority wrong-footed Black theology in South Africa (Chitando, 2009: 96). Since 1994, publications on Black theology slowed down and the leading voices like Frank Chikane, Desmond Tutu, Alan Boesak, Simon Maimela, and Mokgethi Mothlabi were muted because the enemy was no longer on the throne (Chitando, 2009: 96). For some, it can be argued that the victim moved from the rough seat of the oppressed and sat on the high seat of the victor and oppressor. As such, the ill-treatment of black Africans is a form of revenge by the survivors of oppression performed criminally.

The attack on black Africans in South Africa can also be answered by Frantz Fanon (1963: 52) who maintains that:

> [W]hen oppression is over; the colonised man will first manifest his aggressiveness which has been deposited in his bones against his own people. This is the period when [they] beat each other up, and the police and magistrates do not know which way to turn when faced with the astonishing waves of crime.

From the argument by Fanon, it is clear that the cruelty and brutality that was bequeathed to some black South Africans is manifesting in the anger they are emptying onto fellow Africans because these Africans are now vulnerable and defenceless (see e.g. Bascom, 2009).

## 9 Conclusion

The attacks, beatings, maiming, killings, and displacements of black Africans in South Africa are due to various factors. These include speeches by the community and political leaders, claims of the abuse of the rights of the citizens, the alleged criminality of the foreigners, and poor service delivery. The activities became rampant in 2000 and the worst years have been 2008, 2015, 2019, and 2021. However, scholars, the media, and politicians have been grappling with the proper name to give to the phenomenon. Xenophobia has been the most common label, however, an interrogation of the concept shows that it is inadequate since it entails hate of foreigners, and yet some whites from Europe and America are not hated, but loved [xenophilia]. Afrophobia has also been proposed by a number of scholars but the problem with the word is that even some nationalities from Asia have been attacked, rendering Afrophobia an equally challenging term.

This chapter concludes that the attack on the black Africans is a loss of historical memory by some South Africans since Africa stood by them during their struggle against apartheid. In addition, the attacks are a fight against South Africa's constitution, which is inclusive. Moreover, the nation is also defeating its "rainbowism" philosophy where every South African, regardless of colour or creed, has the same rights in the motherland. Likewise, the Ubuntu philosophy (Gathogo, 2008; Mbaya, 2010) and the values of Black consciousness, have also been demeaned by the sporadic attacks on foreigners through criminal means. Violent criminality by some black South Africans on black Africans who have come from outside South Africa needs to be named for what it is. This will enable various stakeholders to devise more effective strategies to overcome violence and recover peace, while working towards integration and prosperity in South Africa and beyond.

# References

Bascom, L. C. (2009). *Voices of the African American Experience*. Greenwood Press.

Bridger, E. (2015). *Xenophobia in South Africa: Historical Legacies of Exclusion and Violence*. Viewed 3 March 2020 from https://imperialglobalexeter.com/2015/05/06/xenophobia-in-south-africa-historical-legacies-of-exclusion-and-violence/

Budiman, T. C. (2019). *In South Africa, Racial Divisions and Pessimism About Democracy Loom Over Elections*. Pew Research Center. Viewed 3 March 2020. https://www.pewresearch.org/fact-tank/2019/05/03/in-south-africa-racial-divisions-and-pessimism-over-democracy-loom-over-elections/

Cameron, S. (2018). *What Are the Advantages and Disadvantages of Secondary Research?* Viewed 9 April 2020. https://bizfluent.com/info-8205583-advantages-disadvantages-secondary-research.html

Charman, A., & Piper, L. (2012). Xenophobia, Criminality, and Violent Entrepreneurship: Violence Against Somali Shopkeepers in Delft South Cape Town, South Africa. *South African Review of Sociology, 43*(3), 81–105. https://doi.org/10.1080/21528586.2012.727550

Chigumadzi, P. (2019). *Afrophobia Is Growing in South Africa. Why? Its Leaders Are Feeding It*. Viewed 15 December 2019. https://africanarguments.org/2019/10/08/afrophobia-is-growing-in-south-africa-why-its-leaders-are-feeding-it/

Chitando, E. (2009). *Troubled But Not Destroyed: African Theology in Dialogue with HIV and AIDS*. World Council of Churches.

Crush, J., & Pandelton, W. (2004). *Regionalizing Xenophobia? Citizen Attitudes to Immigration and Refugee Policy in Southern Africa*. Idasa.

Crush, J., & Ramachandran, S. (2009). *Xenophobia, International Migration and Human Development* (Human Development Research Paper 47). Cape Town.

Dahir, A. L. (2019). *These Charts Show Migrants Aren't South Africa's Biggest Problem*. Viewed 12 April 2020. https://qz.com/africa/1705349/-these-charts-show-migrants-aren'-tSouth-Africa's-biggest-problem/

eNCA. (2019). *President Cyril Ramaphosa Speaks Out Against Xenophobic Attacks*. Viewed 12 April 2020. https://www.youtube.com/watch?v=ECz3_PGiImA

Essa, A., & Patel, K. (2015). *Foreigners in S Africa Fearful After Xenophobic Attacks*. Al Jazeera. Viewed 12 April 2020. https://www.aljazeera.com/news/2015/4/2/foreigners-in-s-africa-fearful-after-xenophobic-attacks

Fanon, F. (1963). *The Wretched of the Earth*. Grove.

Ferial, H. (2019, September 3). Battlefield Jozi: City in Lockdown as Looters Target Migrant-Rich Areas Across, Johannesburg and East Rand. *Daily Maverick*.

Ferm, D. W. (1984). *Third World Theologians: An Introductory Survey*. Orbis Books.

Gathogo, J. (2008). African Philosophy as Expressed in the Concept of Hospitality and Ubuntu. *Journal of Theology of South Africa, 130*, 39–53.

Gqirana, T. (2015). *Zuma, South Africans Are Not Generally Xenophobic and Must Promote Social Cohesion*. Viewed 11 July 2023, from https://mg.co.za/article/2015-04-16-zuma-do-not-turn-xenophobia-into-a-political-football/

Gumede, W. (2018). *SA Has a History of Violence from Days of Colonialism, Apartheid*. Viewed 28 March 2020. https://www.iol.co.za/pretoria-news/sa-has-history-of-violence-from-days-of-colonialism-apartheid-william-gumede-17600721

Haradhan, K. M. (2018). Qualitative Research Methodology in Social Sciences and Related Subjects, Qualitative Research Methodology in Social Sciences and Related Subjects. *Journal of Economic Development Environment and People, 7*(1), 23–48. https://doi.org/10.26458/jedep.v7i1.571

Ilevbare, F. A., & Adesanya, A. A. (2008). Away with Xenophobia and Lessons for the Sustenance of Brotherhood for Africa Development. *Xenophobia: Contemporary Issues in Psychology*, 6 (Special Issue), *16*(3), 199–206. https://doi.org/10.4314/ifep.v16i3.23788

Independent Online. (2008). *Raging Mob Evicts Zimbabweans*. Burns Homes. Viewed 12 April 2020. https://www.iol.co.za/news/south-africa/raging-mob-evicts-zimbabweans-burns-homes-75597

Kumalo, S. R., & Mujinga, M. (2017). God's Hospitality Is for All: An Afro-Theological Perspective on State and Migration in South Africa. In N. Blader & K. H. Kjellin (Eds.), *Mending the World? Possibilities and Obstacles for Religion, Church and Theology* (pp. 47–61). Pickwick Publications.

Landau, L. B. (Ed.). (2018). *Exorcising the Demons within Xenophobia: Violence and Statecraft in Contemporary South Africa*. United Nations University Press.

Long, W. (2015). Anger and Afrophobia in South Africa. *South African Medical Journal, 105*(7), 510. https://doi.org/10.7196/SAMJnew.7968

Malema, J. (2019). *Julius Malema on Xenophobic Attacks on Nigerians in South Africa*. YouTube. Viewed 23 May 2020. https://www.theelephant.info/videos/2019/09/10/julius-malema-on-xenophobic-attacks-on-nigerians-in-south-africa/

Mbaya, H. (2010). Social Capital and the Imperatives of the Concept and Life of Ubuntu in South Africa. *Scriptura, 104*, 367–376.

Mogekwu, M. (2005). African Union: Xenophobia as poor intercultural communication. *Ecquid Novi: African Journalism Studies, 26*(1), 5–20.

Muzengeza, W. (2015, April 22). Xenophobia or Afrophobia in South Africa: It Is Just Convenient Amnesia. *Pambazuka News*.

Myambo, M. T. (2019). *Being Darker Makes Being a Migrant Much Harder*. Viewed 12 April 2020. https://theconversation.com/being-darker-makes-being-a-migrant-much-harder

Nahla, V. (2008). *Creating the Nation: The Rise of Violent Xenophobia in the New South Africa*. Centre for the Study of Violence and Reconciliation.

Naicker, C. (2016). The Languages of Xenophobia in Post-Apartheid South Africa: Reviewing Migrancy, Foreignness, and Solidarity. *Agenda: Feminist Magazine*

Neocosmos, M. (2010). *From "Foreign Natives" to "Native Foreigners": Explaining Xenophobia in Post-Apartheid South Africa*. CODESRIA.

Nyamnjoh, F. B. (2014). Exorcising the Demons Within Xenophobia, Violence, and Statecraft in Contemporary South Africa. *Journal of Contemporary African Studies, 32*(3), 397–401.

Parratt, J. (2000). *A Guide to Doing Theology*. SPCK.

Ramaphosa, C. (2019, March 27). *ANC 2019 Elections Rally Address*. Unpublished Speech.

SABC News. (2019, March 27). Scores of Foreign Nationals Attacked in Durban. *SABC News*.

Sibeko, S. (2019). *South Africa Acknowledges "Afrophobia" Partly to Blame for Violence Against Foreigners*. Viewed 14 December 2020. https://af.reuters.com/article/top News/idAFKCN1VQ0Y9-OZATP

Sonke Gender Justice. (n.d.). Challenging xenophobia through keeping leaders accountable for inciting hate. Policy Development & Advocacy. https://genderjustice.org.za/project/policy-development-advocacy/challenging-xenophobia-keeping-leadersaccountable-inciting-hate/

South Africa History Online. (n.d.). *South Africa's Foreign Relations During Apartheid*. Viewed 14 December 2020. https://www.sahistory.org.za/article/south-africas-foreign-relations-during-apartheid-1948

Tafira, K. (2018). *Xenophobia in South Africa: A Brief Summary*. Palgrave Macmillan.

Tagwirei, C. (2019, September 14). *A New Word Is Needed for Xenophobia, But It's Not Criminality*. Viewed 15 April 2020. https://www.businesslive.co.za/bd/opinion/2019-09-14-a-new-word-is-needed-for-xenophobia-but-its-not-cr

Tshabalala, S. (2015). *Why Black South Africans Are Attacking Foreign Africans But Not Foreign Whites*. Viewed 15 April 2020. https://qz.com/384041/why-black-south-africans-are-only-attacking-foreign-africans-but-not-foreign-whites/

Tshaka, R. (2016). *Afrophobia Versus Xenophobia in South Africa*. Viewed 15 April 2020. https://www.unisa.ac.za/sites/corporate/default/News-&-Media/Articles/Afrophobia-versus-xenophobia-in-South-Africa

Tutu, D. N. (1998). *The Works of Desmond Tutu*. Hodder and Stoughton.

Webster's New Encyclopedic Dictionary. (1996). Webster's New Encyclopedic Dictionary.

Whitehead, G. (2012). *The Importance of Proper Definition*. Viewed 9 April 2020. https://piadvice.wordpress.com/2012/06/13/the-importance-of-proper-definition/

Zuma, J. (2015). *President's Freedom Day Speech*. Pretoria—Union Building. Viewed 9 April 2020. https://www.gov.za/speeches/president-jacob-zuma-freedom-day-celebrations-27-apr-2015-0000

Zwelithini, G. (2015, March 21). *Speech at Pongola*. Unpublished Speech. Viewed 9 April 2020.

# Enchanted Worldviews and Violence Against Persons with Albinism in Sub-Saharan Africa

Francis Benyah

## 1 Introduction

Albinism is a medical condition which refers to the deficiency of melanin[1] pigmentation or inherited disorder or abnormalities of melanin synthesis (Oetting et al., 1996: 330). Individuals who are affected by the medical condition are referred to as albinos. The condition is very visible in affected individuals and mostly manifests in the skin colour, eyes, and hair of affected individuals. Despite growing awareness of albinism as a global public health issue (Hong et al., 2006), individuals affected with the condition suffer from multiple forms of treatment that affect their social positioning and mobility in most parts of Africa south of the Sahara (Aborisade, 2021; Tambala-Kaliati et al., 2021). This is due, in part, to the ways in which the disease condition is entangled in myths and traditional African ontologies that promote an understanding and belief that albinos are non-humans (Bradbury-Jones et al., 2018; Imafidon, 2017, 2019; Machoko, 2013). Indeed, historically, the view that albinos are non-humans has existed for a long time in Africa and the Ancient Mediterranean World spanning over centuries or millennia

---

[1] Melanin is the substance that gives a person his or her skin colour. Persons with albinism have low amount of melanin or no melanin in their bodies making them look white in black population. The amount of melanin also determines how their bodies look.

F. Benyah (✉)
Åbo Akademi University, Turku, Finland
e-mail: fbenyah87@gmail.com

© The Author(s), under exclusive license to Springer Nature Switzerland AG 2024
O. B. Mlambo and E. Chitando (eds.), *The Palgrave Handbook of Violence in Africa*,
https://doi.org/10.1007/978-3-031-40754-3_32

(Hilton, 2021). What is disturbing, however, is the recent reported killings of albinos in various parts of Africa, especially in Tanzania, Senegal, Malawi, Uganda, etc.[2]

Reportedly, this violence has been motivated by the belief that albino body parts contain rare sacred qualities that make them potent for sacrifices and rituals involving the slaying of humans (Benyah, 2017, 2023; Bradbury-Jones et al., 2018; Hilton, 2021). In countries such as Tanzania, Malawi, Senegal, and so on, reports are rife of businessmen, politicians, and ritualists harvesting albino body parts for rituals to win political power, and for use in potions for medicine and to bring about breakthrough in business (Gifford, 2015; Mire, 2017). Indeed, Paul Gifford (2015) has written about the awareness of the violence against albinos among politicians in the West African country of Senegal. In referring to a debate or discussion that took place in the parliament of Senegal after their elections in 2012, Gifford (2015) observes that no one could challenge a comment on such dastardly and invidious acts on albinos on the floor of parliament in Senegal. He notes that, prior to the 2012 general elections in Senegal, reports of mysterious deaths were associated with ritual sacrifices to win political power, and albinos were the main targets of the ritual murderers. Gifford asserts:

> After the elections, in the Legislative Assembly a deputy shouted across to the benches of the previous government: "Since you have lost power, albinos have found peace and we no longer find human remains in the streets." Nobody asked: What was he saying? What did that mean? Everyone knows full well. (Gifford, 2015: 15)

Persons living with albinism have thus become the targets of politicians who seek to win or hold on to power. They have also become economically viable resources for rituals in the mining industries and for bringing about breakthroughs in other life pursuits (Brilliant, 2015).

Such attacks on albinos have generated interest in the global media and spurred academic research in the fields of anthropology, religion, health, philosophy, education, and human rights that examines the motivations behind the attacks on albinos (Brilliant, 2015; Hong et al., 2006; Lund & Taylor, 2008). Despite the growing interest in the subject of albinism, very

---

[2] Several YouTube videos and newspaper reports make evident the personal experiences of individuals with albinism. See this link, https://www.youtube.com/watch?v=BVAyFlVw_e8 for the Al Jazeera documentary titled "Africa Investigates – The Spell of the Albino" by a Tanzanian journalist, Richard Mgamba. See also the United Nations report "Deadly Hunt: Albinos in Tanzania", https://www.youtube.com/watch?v=zd7RRr5Eubg. In these videos, albinos recount their experiences of being chased by unknown assailants, with some showing their body parts maimed.

little is known about the ways that African cosmogony underpins the violence against albinos. In fact, the issue of albinism, until recently, had not received any major attention in academic literature. Ways in which the African ontological framework grounds albinism as an alterity, and its corollary, violent practices, remain underdeveloped.

In this chapter, I argue that the violence, injustice, and inhumane treatment perpetrated against persons with albinism can be understood or influenced by the enchanted worldviews of the African. Thus, I locate violence against persons with albinism within the context of the religio-cultural and magical beliefs that are prevalent in most African societies.

In terms of organization, I first present a theoretical perspective on enchanted cosmology. Second, I show how the social construction of albinism as otherness or alterity influences attacks on affected individuals. In the third section, I present empirical cases of violence against persons with albinism. The fourth section present the social and psychological effects of violence against persons with albinism, and, finally, I conclude.

## 2 Africa and the Enchanted Cosmos

The view that Africa is an enchanted continent is well established in the literature (Assimeng, 1989; Balcomb, 2019; Ellis & Ter Haar, 2004; Mbiti, 1992). Specifically, I use the tern enchanted worldview to refer to a society or community where belief in the world of spirits, demons, and moral forces is highly pervasive (Taylor, 2007). Thus, enchantment or enchanted notion in the context of this discussion refers to the sustained belief that the universe or one's environment is not only composed of the physical creatures or things seen around oneself but there also exist unseen spirit beings which can be appropriated either for good or ill depending on one's motives and needs (Gifford, 2015). I shall return later in this section to discuss the harnessing or appropriation of spirit forces for one's benefit (either good or bad) and why it is important for the discussion.

In the enchanted world, there is no demarcation or boundary between the physical and the metaphysical. Both worlds interpenetrate each other and are influenced by the actions of their members. Balcomb argues that an important feature of an enchanted world "is an apparent absence of boundary between personal agency and impersonal force, between mind and meaning, between individual and community, between person and world, and between experience and belief" (see Balcomb, 2019: 237). In such a universe, it is believed that some powers lurk behind almost everything, including living and non-living objects or organisms, and mysterious forces are at work either for good or evil. Scott William Hoefle in his article "Enchanted (and Disenchanted) Amazonia" captures this succinctly:

> In enchanted-vitalist worldviews, Nature is not divided into material-physical and spiritual-metaphysical, or organic-vital and inorganic-nonvital, phenomena. Not just humans, fauna and flora are living organisms, but land, water and even rocks can be considered living entities, possessing similar vital attributes. Consequently, humans are not beings apart, but rather are intimately tied to a holistic earth whose vitality must be actively conserved. In addition, the natural, social and spiritual spheres are interrelated and not considered to be worlds apart. Nature is animated with spiritual entities with which humans must interact in a reciprocal way, and contact with the ancestors is not severed by death. (Hoefle, 2009: 109)

Hoefle's description of an enchanted worldview fits the context I deal with in this chapter. For most Africans there is no demarcation between the physical and the spiritual. These two streams or spheres interpenetrate each other. The observation made by Imasogie (1983: 75) that "for Africans, there is no solid line of demarcation between the sacred and the secular because the spiritual interpenetrates this [material or physical] world" is not an overstatement. Indeed, the conscious need among Africans for more potent powers to neutralize and ultimately ward off supernatural evil realities is an indication of the ubiquitous nature of the belief in both the physical and spiritual and their symbiotic relationship. It shows the intense nature of the physical and the spiritual world for Africans and the attempts that are made by religious adherents to harness the benefits thereof.

Many Africans hold the strong belief that the world is full of divinities, spirits, demons, and their human allies in the forms of witches and wizards (Imasogie, 1983). Such beliefs are mostly sustained by basic tenets of African Traditional Religion such as belief in God, divinities, spirits, ancestors, and magic and medicine (Idowu, 1973). Contemporary forms of Christianity, such as Pentecostalism and their constant attacks on and attempts to demonize African Traditional Religion, and reveal the secret of the occult world, also continue to reinforce sustained belief in such supernatural entities (Meyer, 1999; Robbins, 2003). Other factors that influence belief in supernatural entities include the magical, healing, and ritual aspects of some religious practices (Graveling, 2010). Josephson-Storm (2017) has noted that studies in the Global South have pointed out not only traditional but also modern forms of magic that include Internet-based virtual Haitian Voodoo, Vietnamese divinities that are appeased with cans of Coke and Pepsi, faith-healing and notorious pairs of demonically possessed underpants in Ghana.

All these phenomena, to an extent, reveal the enchanted imagination in the Global South, especially among Africans. Indeed, the African way of life, and beliefs, traditions, customs, and cultural ceremonies such as funerals and ritual practices, are evidence of the sustained belief in the supernatural in the natural order of things (Graveling, 2010). The resilient nature of religion in the public sphere in most African states clearly demonstrates the pervasiveness of religion in ways unanticipated by theories of modernity and the locus of disenchantment (Josephson-Storm, 2017; Obadare, 2018; Yelle & Trein, 2022). In many African societies, such beliefs have been shown to be pervasive even in the face of current developments in science and technology and the modernization of African cultures and societies through engagement with external cultural forces (Gyekye, 2013).

The belief in the existence of supernatural beings, both good and bad, in the mind of the African makes Africans susceptible to and haunted by a sense that the spirit world could affect their lives and everyday experiences. As a result, this religious imagination shapes lives and the attitudes of everyday experience. Thus, in the enchanted world, humans feel vulnerable to evil spiritual forces and cosmic powers, and therefore feel the need for protection (Atiemo, 2017). The malevolent spirits that are believed to be part of the universe are assumed or believed to be responsible for life's debilitating issues. These forces are also believed to be the cause of human failures, as they are believed to make people dysfunctional in areas of life such as education, marriage, business, jobs, among others (Acolatse, 2018; Asamoah-Gyadu, 2008).

These feelings of vulnerability, unsafeness, insecurity, and volatility on the part of humans in an enchanted society are what Charles Taylor, in his book *A Secular Age,* describes as the "porous self" (Taylor, 2007). In his article, "The Porous Self and the Buffered Self," Balcomb (2019) uses Taylor's typology to explain how the concept of the porous self is immanent in contemporary Africa and commensurate with theological formulations on the continent. Balcomb explains that "the porous self is profoundly vulnerable to the surrounding world" (Balcomb, 2019: 238). That is, in the context of the enchanted (also described as the porous self), humans feel vulnerable to the thoughts and feelings of others who might want to harm them. Human beings in this environment are also "vulnerable to the forces attached to the meanings of things that you [or they] have limited or control over; are vulnerable to possession by the spiritual beings that roam the cosmos; vulnerable to substances that are charged with causal forces" (Balcomb, 2019: 238).

This vulnerability, Taylor (2007: 37) argues, "extends to more than just spirits which are malevolent…it goes beyond them to things which have no wills, but are nevertheless redolent with evil meanings." Balcomb (2019) raises the issue of Taylor's negligence to the fact that the porous self is not always negative, as Taylor seems to suggest. On the contrary, Balcomb highlights the sense of insecurity that lies at the intersection of the two worlds—the self and the spiritual world—and posits that this sense of insecurity or vulnerability is to be seen "in the special gift of the spirit medium who is able to be possessed by spirits with specific personal identities in order to gain special knowledge or insight into specific issues that are related to the material world" (Balcomb, 2019: 238).

Although Balcomb (2019) may be right in his argument, especially when one considers the role of spirit mediums in relation to indigenous cults or shrines, I disagree with him to a large extent. This is because such mediums, as we will see later in the context of this discussion, are sometimes a negative phenomenon. For instance, such spirit mediums and the insecurity that is associated with them has in some instances led to the perpetration of violence and heinous crimes against certain individuals and groups of people (an example is the case of persons living with albinism as I discuss in this chapter).

Similarly, in his recent book *African Philosophy and Otherness of Albinism: White Skin, Black Race*, Elvis Imafidon (2019) presents a convincing but ambiguous argument on the role African ontologies play in providing grounds for the maltreatment of albinos in most African societies. The ambiguity in his argument lies in his attempt to exonerate traditional African ontologies and their attendant beliefs and practices as a basis for discrimination and violence against albinos, even though he admits, in another part of his argument, that African traditions indeed supply the grounds for ill-treatment of albinos. A finding from a recent report by the Ghana Association of Persons with Albinism (GAPA), reveals that the ritual banishment of persons with albinism is influenced by the spiritual beliefs of the communities that are involved in the practice (GAPA, 2019). According to the report, the origin of the practice of ritual banishment of persons with albinism in communities such as *Kwahu Burukuwa* and *Akwamufie*, all in the Eastern Region of Ghana, could be traced to belief in local deities namely *Abena Oku* and *Tutu Abu*, who are believed to have disdain for the acceptance of persons with albinism. Because of the belief that these local deities have a dislike for people with albinism, individuals with the condition are not welcomed or allowed to stay in these communities, as well as in other communities with similar beliefs and customs. In other words, it is a taboo for albinos to live in such communities in Ghana (GAPA, 2019).

Albino body parts are sought out because those who are responsible for such acts, or their perpetrators, have supposedly been told by a spiritualist or a witch-doctor, through a spirit medium, that sacrificing an albino body part could bring them good fortune in the pursuit of their life-goals, be they a breakthrough in business, ascending to political office, or healing a chronic ailment, among others (Clarke & Beale, 2018; Gifford, 2015). In this case, the porous self and one's vulnerability produce negative energies that induce negative actions against another human being. The need for protection and the warding off of evil spirits in an enchanted society thus makes albinos susceptible to attacks for rituals involving human slaughter. This is also congruent with the fact that an enchanted universe may have an animate existence where sacrifices have proportionate outcomes and causal influence. In the next section, I discuss how the otherness of albinism in the African context makes people believe that albinos carry a rare sacred quality that makes them potent for ritual sacrifices, a violent act which has been decried by many as inhumane.

## 3 The Socially Constructed Otherness of Albinism and Related Violence

In the previous section, I laid a foundation for the understanding of why persons living with albinism are susceptible or prone to attacks in their environment, especially in some societies in Africa. My argument stood on the point that the enchanted worldview of the African and the vulnerability conditioned by their symbiotic relationship within the cosmic struggle may motivate the violence encountered by persons living with albinism. I do not seek to argue that African Traditional Religion and its belief systems are inevitably linked to the violence perpetrated on albinos, but rather that individual feelings of vulnerability within the cosmic struggle, the need for protection, and the quest for success and prosperity in a bad economic situation may furnish the basis upon which such attacks are perpetrated on affected victims. In other words, albinos bear the brunt of the dissatisfaction of individuals who become disenchanted with their socio-economic conditions and who place their hope in the realm of the supernatural as a safeguard and a means for prospering.

From the Christian side, Päivi Hasu (2012) has highlighted how the expansion of Pentecostalism and the revival of occult beliefs and practices have been occasioned by economic transformation and the neoliberal economy. For Hasu (2012), the penchant for economic wealth and success can be linked to the spiritual worldviews that often motivate and inspire people to action against the demonic forces of witchcraft that prevent people from obtaining their God-desired success. Indeed, Comaroff and Comaroff (2001), have pointed out the parallel relationship between occult economies, the use of magical means for material ends, and new religious movements across the globe. According to Comaroff and Comaroff (2001), the aforementioned economies have two dimensions. Firstly, there is the material aspect created by the need to produce wealth or account for its acquisition by appealing to techniques that resist explanation in the conventional mode of practical reason. Second, there is an ethical dimension grounded in the moral discourses engendered by the production of value through magical means (Comaroff & Comaroff, 2001; see also Hasu, 2006). The argument here is that enchanted worldviews are produced by underlying religious beliefs and ideas which inform "the ways economic circumstances are perceived, interpreted and acted upon in specific social and historical contexts" (Hasu, 2006: 679). Such actions may inculcate or produce certain religious rituals or sacrifices which are sometimes violent in nature (Hoskins, 1993).

In this section, my aim is to expand the argument by explaining how the socially constructed notions of albinism in most African communities account in multiple ways for their otherness, that is, the way they are viewed, and how such views or perceptions, contribute to the violence against them. In doing so, I approach the discussion in this section from three viewpoints. First, I highlight some historical accounts of how albinism was perceived or constructed. Second, I will continue the discussion on the historical trajectory of the sacredness and alterity of albinism and show how it still exists today in contemporary African societies. Third, I will present ways in which these socially constructed narratives fuel violent acts against albinos.

As I have already mentioned, while albinism can be explained medically, the condition is however shrouded in superstitious narratives and myths in most African communities. The supernatural explanations and myths have, over time, overshadowed the scientific basis of the genetic disorder. Imafidon (2019) argues that the pervasive nature of traditional African worldviews contributes to the persistence of superstitious views of albinism. He writes that "albinism is socially and culturally represented as an unwelcome abnormality or difference" and not only "abnormal but repugnant" (Imafidon, 2019: 19). What is evident, however, is that such constructed notions or views about albinism are not recent. Evidence in the literature suggest that such notions existed even in ancient societies (Hilton, 2021; Kromberg, 2018). Writing on the historical antecedents of some of these notions, Kromberg mentions that the report by Pearson et al. (1911–1913), which he collected from several parts of the world in the seventeenth century, gives a very chilling account of how persons with albinism were treated as mascots carrying a sacred quality.

In Africa, albinism was, and still is, construed as a disorder that is unnatural, tainted, and a distinguishing mark that suggests a deviation from the normal. Following this is the belief that albinos are sacred beings who possess some rare qualities that make them somewhat sacred, and different from any other "normal" human being. The concept of "othering" as a social category is defined as "the process through which a dominant group defines into existence a subordinate group" and "this is done through the invention of categories and labels, and ideas about what characterizes people belonging to these categories" (Khan et al., 2015: 29). Reportedly, in Malawi, "name-calling such as 'mizukwa' (ghosts), 'napweri' (tomato with white spots) and 'mzungu osauka' (poor white person)" has been cited in connection with some of the labels used in referring to persons with albinism (Likumbo et al., 2021: 8; see also Baker et al., 2010; Cruz-Inigo et al., 2011). In Tanzania, terms such as *zeru* (ghost) are used of albinos and in Zimbabwe *sope*, which means "inhabited by evil spirits," also applies to persons with albinism (Aborisade, 2021). In South Africa, there are social tags such as *inkawu* (monkey) and *isishawa,* which means "curse" (Aborisade, 2021). Among the Ashanti of Ghana, *ofri* or *ofridjato* is a derisive term for a person with albinism. The term means "scorched or marked person" (Benyah, 2017). In Anlo-Ewe, in the Volta Region of Ghana, *gesoshi* refers to the supernatural and means an incomplete being, and a*gbelimoryevu* refers to a plant.

Significantly, "othering" also occurs when "when a person, group or category is treated as an 'object' by another group. This 'objectification' allows actors to break the moral rules of social relationships" (Khan et al., 2015: 29). This concept of otherness ties in with the argument made by Imafidon (2017), that one of the reasons why albinos encounter social stigma and other forms of violence can be clarified using Jürgen Habermas' ethical and moral views.[3] Commenting on Habermas' ethical point of view from within an African philosophical framework, Imafidon (2017: 164), postulates that

---

[3] Habermas ethical view popularly referred to as Discourse Ethics (DE) articulates a view that a norm is right if and only if it is accepted by all participants in discourse without any form of coercion. In other words, an action could be justified if that action is seen right or there are no dissenting views about it within community. Such norms functions within an ideal conditions of justification.

"the ethics of solidarity also informs the basis for the justification within the African worldview for the established alterity and, by implication, stigmatization of persons with albinism." From this standpoint, he argues that such ideology promotes harmony between social groups but disallows anything that is seen or viewed as a threat to social integration. In this sense, albinism, which is seen as a manifestation of immoral, evil, ancestral, or divine displeasure at the living for some transgression, is discarded or removed to avert any negative consequences.

Indeed, "evidence from multiple disciplines suggest that societies have devalued, marginalized or otherwise excluded certain members from their ranks throughout history and across the globe" (Wesselmann et al., 2019: 1). Some of these incidents have led to a whole group of people or an entire race being subjected to maltreatment, brutalities and killings, discrimination, and isolation. To a large extent, these atrocities are oftentimes influenced by both religious and secular ideologies. In her inaugural address as the External Professor of Religion, Human Rights and Social Change at the Institute of Social Studies in The Hague, Netherlands, titled "Rats, Cockroaches and People Like Us," Gerrie ter Haar (2000: 17) stressed how "both religious and secular ideologies tend to ascribe evil notably to those who are not considered people like us." She argued that "both types of ideology have shown a capacity to destroy the lives of others by placing them outside the category of humans." She emphasized the fact that, despite the difference in approach on occasions when these instances may happen, one cannot ignore the fact that "some form of disqualification as a person" does occur. Ter Haar (2000) indicates for example, how during "the Second World War, whole groups were described as not fully human, not 'people like us'" (Ter Haar, 2000: 18). She notes further that "Anti-Arab pogroms in 1950s Algeria were known to French settlers as 'ratonnades' or 'rat-hunts'" and "in preparation for the 1994 genocide in Rwanda, the organs of state and mass communication consistently conveyed the message that part of the population were actually cockroaches" (Ter Haar, 2000: 18).

A reference could also be made to the Dutch Reformed Church and the apartheid regime in South Africa, where Christian political theologies became a basis for political rulership without democratic legitimacy. As Leatt (2017: 27) puts it, there was a "subordination of black interests to white rule by instrumentalizing traditional leadership, customary law, Christianity, violence and duplicitous forms of legality" for political dominance by claiming South Africa, for instance, as a Christian country ruled by Christian values. This saw a particular group being humiliated and injustices meted out to them, a situation which led to both economic, cultural, and social exclusion (see also Khan et al., 2015).

Albinism is greeted with resentment in most African communities (Benyah, 2017). The prejudice and violence meted out to persons living with albinism is influenced by the belief that albino bodies contain a rare sacred quality. There is no doubt that the strong belief in the sacred quality of albinos and the assumed magical powers inherent in their bodies underpin the violent acts perpetrated against them. The belief that albino body contains magical powers is co-terminous with the idea of the white body having magical prowess which was promoted during the colonial era. According to Mire (2017), Dyer has asserted that in the age of Western colonialism claims that the white European body had "special and unique power" and possessed "enterprise" existed (Dyer 1997, cited in Mire, 2017: 133). In an unexpected turn of events, it seems also that some African witch doctors are making similar claims in view of the white bodies of African albinos (Mire, 2017).

Historical records indicate that in the sixteenth and seventeenth centuries various attempts were made by American colonial masters and slave owners to theorize on and expound the otherness of albinism and reduce those with the condition to non-humans (Mire, 2017). These attempts were made not only to reduce albino bodies to non-humans, but also because American slave masters and racial scientists saw the whiteness of the African slave bodies or what they called the "White Negro" as a revolutionary attempt that could end the very enterprise of slavery (Mire, 2017). Mire uses Nietzsche's concept of "willful forgetting" as a metaphor and critically examines how the historically grounded Western cultural production of "othering" was used to categorize persons who exhibited skin whitening, vitiligo, and albinism as alien, and suppressed their dominance as a group that potentially threatened to erode white supremacy or "challenge the socially constructed racial purity of whiteness" and the enterprise of slavery (Mire, 2017: 126). Mire (2017) discusses how, during the period of colonization and enlightenment, an American slave-owning colonist and racial theorist, Thomas Jefferson, politicized the whiteness of African slaves as a form of abnormality and sought to disqualify albinism as a condition that could not be produced sexually. She quotes Martin (2002) as saying that:

> In order to mitigate this threat to the order of nature and society, Jefferson attempts to stabilize the revolutionary potential of the white Negro body by effacing the distinction between it and the body of the albino and reinforcing the difference between African and Anglo-Saxon skin. He describes the color of the albino as 'a pallid cadaverous white, untinged with red,' reducing the albino, through this description, beyond the position of an analysable living

object of natural history to that of a dissectible corpse, apparently devoid of the warming and to a small extent, humanizing blood that marks proper whiteness of skin. (Martin 2002, cited in Mire, 2017: 131)

According to Mire (2017: 131), "the medicalisation of the interracial reproduction of whiteness was designed to remove moral responsibility from white masters" who took sexual advantage of their female slave subjects. American racial scientists sought to completely exclude people who suffered from albinism as a potential group that threatened racial purity and continued dominance. In this case, the skin colour became a marker of exposure to social stresses and as a criterion for social classification (Gravlee et al., 2005). Thus, "the failure to contain the alien, in this case the African slave with the white skin, indicates the extent to which violence could be unleashed to contain, isolate and ultimately eradicate otherness" (Mire, 2017: 133).

## 4   Reported Cases of Violence Against Persons with Albinism in Tanzania and Ghana

In this section, I present reported cases of violence against albinos in Tanzania and Ghana. Although there are reported cases of violence against albinos in other countries, I use these two countries as a reference point for the purpose of this discussion.

A video documentary uploaded in the United Nations YouTube account titled "Deadly Hunt: Albinos in Tanzania"[4] shows a precarious situation of violence against albinos and rumours about their supposedly magical powers and their deadly consequences. The documentary begins with a reporter stating that in Tanzania "albinos have long suffered discrimination" and have begun experiencing terror connected to their reputation as individuals with magical powers which has deadly consequences for their well-being. A voiceover continues the narration and mentions that in a remote district in northern Tanzania, a 28-year-old woman (an image of the woman is shown) was attacked and brutally assaulted by a group of men with sharp objects. The documentary shows the image of the 28-year-old woman with dismembered hands being fed by the mother. The loss of her two hands has made

---

[4] https://www.youtube.com/watch?v=zd7RRr5Eubg&t=113s (accessed on 20th November 2022). Apart from this, there are multiple YouTube videos and documentaries showing killing and manhunts for albino body parts. A search term "albino killings in Africa" on YouTube will display most of these videos.

her incapable of performing any basic household duties for herself and her three-year-old son. The reporter continues to relate how the woman walks to a room and is assisted by another woman to put on a prosthetic arm to aid in her household chores. The reporter continues the narration and states that "[she] is a victim of a brutal assault targeted at her because she is an albino." The voiceover mentions that attacks such as this have been multiplying in the village and other surrounding communities and towns.

The voiceover continues and Peter Ash, a Canadian businessman, is interviewed. Ash is an albino himself. According to him, he read about the attacks on albinos and has been crying himself to sleep after reading about the attacks. The interview continues, and Ash states that he could not believe children and women were chopped up for their body parts and used in potions. In the course of the interview, terrifying images of supposedly harvested body parts are shown in the video. Ash continues to express his views about the attacks on albinos and says that the violence has nothing to do with poverty but rather is influenced by witchcraft beliefs and evil intentions as well as discrimination.

The voiceover continues the narration and mentions that in the Mwanza region around Lake Victoria in Northern Tanzania, "more than 50 albinos have been murdered" within two years. The voiceover mentions that "the attacks are spurred by rumours that potions made from albinos' blood, skin and body parts can bring wealth and good fortune." An image of two men with a bowl beside them is shown; they are gathering something from the ground, traces of blood are shown on the ground. The items gathered are supposedly the body parts of albinos gathered by body harvesters. The voiceover mentions an albino woman Mariam (whose hands have been chopped off by body harvesters) was several months pregnant when a group of men accosted and attacked her at night. Mariam is interviewed in her local dialect and the voiceover translates as follows: "The leader had a machete, a torch and a bottle. He started to cut me up. He totally cut off this arm and gave it to the man with him. I was slaughtered like a goat."

Mariam's sister narrated the horror and traumatic experience Mariam had to go through after the attack on her. According to her, Mariam bled profusely, and it took them about ten hours to get her to a nearby hospital. The voiceover mentions that Mariam's sister believes it is a miracle her sister is alive. The voiceover mentions that the baby Mariam was carrying in her womb died. Aside from the case of Mariam, the documentary mentions that there are several reported cases of the killing of albinos in Tanzania.

In Ghana, and other West African countries such as Nigeria, albinos reportedly face similar cases of abuse. In Ghana, for instance, report is rife that politicians also sacrifice albino body parts to improve their political fortune.[5] There are reports that also indicate that some communities in Ghana sacrifice albino body parts to boost their farm yield. In 2015, for example, an albino was reported to have claimed that some indigenes of his community in the Bono East Region of Ghana sacrificed albinos, which they believed would result in a bumper harvest for the community. He claimed:

> I saw a lot of people coming to the house. I heard them saying that we thank God, this year the harvest will be very plentiful, this year will have a lot of harvesting, anytime we have an albino to sacrifice to the gods, we get a lot of harvest that year. We thank God we have had one and this one is very energetic and very healthy.[6]

Indeed, other reports also suggest that albinos are the preferred candidates for rituals involving human slaughter at gold mines (Brilliant, 2015). According to reports, they are believed to carry some supernatural qualities that help to attract lots of gold when they are sacrificed at mining sites (Bryceson et al., 2010). The stories of sacrificing albinos go beyond the limits of farmers and gold miners and include others such as politicians, footballers, and businessmen. Politicians reportedly use albino body parts to increase their chances of winning political power, and businessmen use them for protecting themselves against evil powers and bringing good fortune and good lack to their business or trade (Baker et al., 2010; Gifford, 2015).

In Ghana, the report by the GAPA (2019), revealed that three communities, namely Abease, Bukuruwa, and Akwamufie, had customary practices that deemed the presence of albinos taboo, or prevented them from residing, in any of the above-mentioned communities. These customary practices, according to GAPA, are connected to the existence of gods or deities in the community. Other reports indicate that, in the past, albinos were deemed suitable for treatment as sacrificial lambs who were believed to be a good omen, or used for ritual cleansing purposes (Affram et al., 2019). In other communities, especially in Atebubu, there are reports that suggest children born with albinism are sometimes killed at birth.

These reported cases, as well as possible unreported cases, point significantly to the danger and violence albinos encounter in their lives in various parts of Africa. What is of interest in the context of this discussion is the enchanted views which influence such heinous crimes and violence against

---

[5] https://www.ghanaweb.com/GhanaHomePage/features/Albinos-Blood-Hands-of-Some-Politician-179011 (see this report by the Ghanaweb, accessed on 15 February 2023).

[6] Unwanted: How albinos are killed for rituals in Ghana, retrieved from https://www.myjoyonline.com/unwanted-how-albinos-are-killed-for-rituals-in-ghana/ (accessed on 10 March 2023).

albinos. Clearly, some religious belief system and/or quest for power, dominance, and wealth are among the motivations for the killing of albinos. Such magico-religious practices produce an underlying motivation for the sacrifice and violent acts against albinos.

## 5 The Social and Psychological Effects of Violence Against Persons with Albinism

In this section, I present the social and psychological effect of violence against persons with albinism. In many ways, one cannot deny the fact that the cases reported above have social and psychological implications for the victims of such attacks. In the first part of this section, I take a look at the social implications of violence towards albinos. In the second part, I examine the psychological effect or implication of violent action against albinos.

To begin with, constant attacks on albinos increase their isolation and hinder them from full participation in community social events and other activities such as education. Owing to the societal stigma, discrimination, and violence which they face, individuals with albinism are not able to realize their full potential by participating freely in social events at certain places and in certain communities in Ghana. Previous reports suggest that in a community in the Eastern Region of Ghana, an albino was asked to hide himself in a car at a funeral he attended, to prevent his being censured by community leaders. Such community censures prevent albinos from enjoying free movement as individuals with human respect and dignity.

Social support is a basic human need (Chang & Schaller, 2000), that every individual in society requires to achieve their potential. Lack of social support results in the inability to generate the self-confidence and social capital needed for personal advancement in different areas of life. Social support is aimed at producing a verbal and non-verbal communication between a receiver and a recipient that helps an individual to minimize uncertainty regarding a distressing situation (Albrecht & Adelman, 1987). The ability to reduce or minimize uncertainty heightens the perception that the individual has control over his or her life experiences making the individual feel protected in a vulnerable situation or circumstance. The denial of social support for persons living with albinism causes them to lack the ability to deal and cope with life-stresses because the provision of resources, both psychological and material, are not derived from their social networks (Cohen, 2004). This situation also affects their overall well-being.

Moreover, the seeking out of the body parts of albinos induces considerable fear, and places them in an unsafe situation and in a position of insecurity. For instance, prior to the 2016 elections in Ghana, there were reports that some politicians were hatching plans to sacrifice an albino to help them win political power. These reports, which were circulated on various media platforms, cautioned albinos to be careful about their public movements, and advised them to stay indoors if they had no serious or important business that required them to go out.[7] Alternatively, they were advised to go to places of interest in the company of other people. In Tanzania, reports suggest that, in early 2009, the government, through the police chief, provided several hundreds of albinos with cell phones with a direct line to the police. The phones were to be used to call the police for assistance if they realized they were being tracked by body-harvesters (Gifford, 2015). These reports, among many others, provide significant evidence of the fear and insecurity persons with albinism have to undergo to protect and safeguard themselves from people who commit acts of violence against their personhood.

In addition, the view that albinos are mascots bearing potential powers makes them seem less human in their societies or communities. One important point mentioned in the previous discussion is that the violence perpetrated against albinos is based on the belief that their bodies carry a sacred quality that makes them potent for sacrifices. This notion about the personhood of individuals with albinism makes them less human, and this affects their social position and well-being. In effect, albinos are not regarded as humans with dignity and respect, and they face multiple forms of discrimination, rejection, and social stigma. The violence carried out as a result of this view about their personhood also has the consequence of pushing them to the margins of society. Although one can argue that some individuals with albinism have been able to break down these negative social barriers and attain certain life-goals for themselves and their families, such achievements, nevertheless, are not free from challenges. Despite the fact that this would be statistically difficult to prove, it can be suggested that it is only a small number of persons with albinism who have been able to break down the negative social barriers and associated challenges and succeed with their life-goals and dreams.

The violent acts inflicted on persons with albinism can result in Post-Traumatic Stress Disorder (PTSD), which is a mental health condition often triggered by a frightening, terrifying, or stressful event. A person with PTSD relives the event through flashbacks and nightmares, and very often

---

[7] See the report by Nana Kofi Amankwah 2010, https://www.ghanaweb.com/GhanaHomePage/features/Albinos-Blood-Hands-of-Some-Politician-179011 (accessed on 6 March 2023).

develops feelings of isolation and petulance that may affect their day-to-day life. One of the key causes of PTSD is violent personal assault. An act of violence perpetrated on persons with albinism such as the one encountered by Mariam in Tanzania is a compelling example of a personal assault that could result in her experiencing PTSD. For instance, in the report, Mariam's sister mentioned the ordeal Mariam had to go through after the incident. The type of traumatic injury or assault experienced by Mariam is notably one of the events that is most likely to cause PTSD. According to Charuvasta and Cloitre (2008), though not all traumas are equal in the risk of subsequent PTSD, traumas instigated by fellow human beings are the ones most likely to lead to PTSD. According to them, this corroborates the characterization of PTSD in the Diagnostic and Statistical Manual of Mental Disorders that suggests that PTSD may be more severe or long lasting if the stressor is of "human design" or origin (Charuvasta & Cloitre, 2008). Indeed, the kind of atrocities and violence encountered by persons with albinism increase the risk of PTSD. Not only that, but such traumatic experience can also potentially affect their mental condition and consequently their social mobility and well-being. This is because the terror that is associated with the violent act can affect their ability to "form cooperative social networks based on trust and norms of behavior" (Charuvasta & Cloitre, 2008: 4). Thus, they can appear disinterested or detached as they make an effort to let go of or not think about painful experiences in order to suppress the memory of these experiences. The violent experiences encountered can affect their ability to maintain relationships with family and friends, and their readiness to work and perform their daily activities. It is important to note that these behaviours are part of mental illness.

Finally, stigma can also induce stress that can have a lasting effect on the mental condition of persons living with albinism. Previous studies have shown that persons living with albinism run the risk of developing mental health problems due, in part, to stigma, discrimination, and marginalization (Affram et al., 2019). Stigma can result in feelings of shame, hopelessness, and isolation. It can also make a person lose self-confidence or lower their self-esteem. This can lead the individual to lose hope of overcoming their situation or illness or being able to achieve their life-dreams or goals. These experiences can have a lasting psychological or mental effect on the person and thereby affect their overall well-being. Previous reports on the experiences of persons with albinism suggest that most of them are ridiculed and tagged with derogatory names that cast a slur on their personhood. Such verbal abuse has the tendency of inducing psychological distress which can potentially affect their mental well-being.

## 6   Conclusion

This chapter has discussed the violence perpetrated against persons with albinism in Africa by using examples from Tanzania and Ghana. The central argument made in this chapter is that the enchanted worldview of the African and the vulnerability that comes with the African idea of the spirit world provides a breeding ground for violence against albinos. Furthermore, the quest for success and accumulation of wealth which is often influenced by occult and magical beliefs (associated with this spiritual worldview) may underpin violence against albinos in Africa. The question remains of how such beliefs and their associated practices can be altered in dealing with such vices. While religion and/or the notion of a spirit world may not in itself be a negative phenomenon, the downside of such beliefs and practices needs to be discussed and addressed in the discourse on religion and society.

The chapter has also highlighted the socially constructed notions of albinism in most African communities, and how these account, in multiple ways for the explanation of their "otherness," that is, the way they are perceived, and, consequently, the violence perpetrated against them. This is seen in the ways they are constantly being hunted by body-harvesters for dubious motives and for the purpose of so-called spiritual breakthroughs in healing, business, and politics.

In consequence, violence towards albinos also has implications for their mental well-being. The chapter also brought to the fore some of the psychological implications of violence against albinos. Indeed, there is a strong nexus between stigma and symptoms of depression and anxiety, which, if not handled properly can have the long-term effect of producing low self-esteem for individuals with albinism. Not least of their concerns is the PTSD that also comes with the assaults they encounter.

I recommend further studies in the future to explore the psychological and mental health implications of violence against albinos, and how this affects well-being, and social integration.

## Bibliography

Aborisade, R. A. (2021). "Why Always Me?": Childhood Experiences of Family Violence and Prejudicial Treatment Against People Living with Albinism in Nigeria. *Journal of Family Violence, 36*, 1081–1094. https://doi.org/10.1007/s10896-021-00264-7

Acolatse, E. E. (2018). *Powers, Principalities, and the Spirit: Biblical Realism in Africa and the West*. Wm. B. Eerdmans Publishing.

Affram, A. A., Teye-Kwadjo, E., & Gyasi-Gyamerah, A. A. (2019). Influence of Social Stigma on Subjective Well-Being of Persons with Albinism in Ghana. *Journal of Community & Applied Social Psychology, 29*(4), 323–335.

Albrecht, T. L., & Adelman, M. B. (1987). *Communicating Social Support*. Sage.

Asamoah-Gyadu, J. K. (2008). Conquering Satan, Demons, Principalities, and Powers: Ghanaian Traditional and Christian Perspectives on Religion, Evil, and Deliverance. In N. Doom-Harder & L. Minnema (Eds.), *Coping with Evil in Religion and Culture: Case Studies* (pp. 85–105). Brill.

Assimeng, M. (1989). *Religion and Social Change in West Africa*. Ghana Universities Press.

Atiemo, A. O. (2017). In Need of a New Lens: An African Christian Scholar's Religious Critique of Western European Attitudes Toward Religion and Development in Africa. *Religion and Theology, 24*(3–4), 250–273.

Baker, C., Lund, P., Nyathi, R., et al. (2010). The Myths Surrounding People with Albinism in South Africa and Zimbabwe. *Journal of African Cultural Studies, 22*(2), 169–181. http://www.jstor.org/stable/41428130

Balcomb, A. O. (2019). The Porous Self and the Buffered Self: The Relevance of Charles Taylor's Characterisations for the African Context. *Religion and Theology, 26*(3–4), 233–254.

Benyah, F. (2017). Equally Able, Differently Looking: Discrimination and Physical Violence Against Persons with Albinism in Ghana. *Journal for the Study of Religion, 30*(1), 161–188.

Benyah, F. E. K. (2023). Are Albinos People Like Us? Albinism and Social Exclusion in Sub-Saharan Africa. In A. A. Aminkeng, M. Kwanzema, M. Meijer, & F. E. K. (Eds.), *Contemporary Discourses in Social Exclusion* (pp. 143–170). Palgrave Macmillan.

Bradbury-Jones, C., Ogik, P., Betts, J., et al. (2018). Beliefs About People with Albinism in Uganda: A Qualitative Study Using the Common-sense Model. *PLOS One, 13*(10). https://doi.org/10.1371/journal.pone.0205774

Brilliant, M. H. (2015). Albinism in Africa: A Medical and Social Emergency. *International Health, 7*(4), 223–225.

Bryceson, D. F., Jønsson, J. B., & Sherrington, R. (2010). Miners' Magic: Artisanal Mining, the Albino Fetish and Murder in Tanzania. *The Journal of Modern African Studies, 48*(3), 353–382. http://www.jstor.org/stable/40864761

Chang, S. C. H., & Schaller, J. (2000). Perspectives of Adolescents with Visual Impairments on Social Support from their Parents. *Journal of Visual Impairment & Blindness, 94*(2), 69–84. https://doi.org/10.1177/0145482X0009400202

Charuvasta, A., & Cloitre, M. (2008). Social Bonds and Post-traumatic Stress Disorder. *Annual Review of Psychology, 59*, 301–328. https://doi.org/10.1146%2Fannurev.psych.58.110405.085650.

Clarke, S., & Beale, J. (2018). Albinism and Social Marginalization. In J. Kromberg & M. Prashiela (Eds.), *Albinism in Africa: Historical, Geographic, Medical, Genetic, and Psychosocial Aspects* (pp. 257–270). Academic Press.

Cohen, S. (2004). Social Relationships and Health. *American Psychologist, 59*(8), 676–684. https://psycnet.apa.org/doi/10.1037/0003-066X.59.8.676

Comaroff, J., & Comaroff, J. (2001). Millenial Capitalism: First Thoughts on a Second Coming. In J. Comaroff & J. Comaroff (Eds.), *Millenial Capitalism and the Culture of Neoliberalism* (pp. 1–56). Duke.

Cruz-Inigo, A., Ladizinski, B., & Sethi, A. (2011). Albinism in Africa: Stigma, Slaughter and Awareness Campaigns. *Dermatologic Clinic, 29*(1), 79–87. https://doi.org/10.1016/j.det.2010.08.015

Ellis, S., & Ter Haar, G. (2004). *Worlds of Power: Religious Thought and Political Practice in Africa.* Oxford University Press.

GAPA. (2019). *Ritual Banishment and Stigmatization of Persons with Albinism in Ghana: A Contextual Analysis Report.* https://africaalbinismnetwork.org/resource-country/ghana/. Accessed on 3 March 2023.

Gifford, P. (2015). *Christianity, Development and Modernity in Africa.* Hurst & Company.

Graveling, E. (2010). West Africa. In R. D. Hecht & V. F. Biondo (Eds.), *Religion and Everyday Life and Culture* (pp. 205–231). Praeger.

Gravlee, C. C., Dressler, W. W., & Bernard, H. R. (2005). Skin Color, Social Classification, and Blood Pressure in Southeastern Puerto Rico. *American Journal of Public Health, 95*(12), 2191–2197.

Gyekye, K. (2013). *Philosophy, Culture and Vision: African Perspectives.* Sub-Saharan Publishers.

Hasu, P. (2006). World Bank & Heavenly Bank in Poverty & Prosperity: The Case of Tanzania Faith Gospel. *Review of African Political Economy, 33*(110), 670–692.

Hasu, P. (2012). Prosperity Gospels and Enchanted Worldviews: Two Responses to Socio-Economic Transformation in Tanzanian Pentecostal Christianity. In D. Freeman (Ed.), *Pentecostalism and Development: Churches, NGOs and Social Change in Africa* (pp. 67–86). Palgrave Macmillan.

Hilton, J. L. (2021). Albinism in the Ancient Mediterranean World. *Journal for the Study of Religion, 34*(1), 1–28.

Hoefle, S. W. (2009). Enchanted (and Disenchanted) Amazônia: Environmental Ethics and Cultural Identity in Northern Brazil. *Ethics Place and Environment (Ethics, Place & Environment (Merged with Philosophy and Geography)), 12*(1), 107–130.

Hong, E. S., Zeeb, H., & Repacholi, M. H. (2006) Albinism in Africa as a Public Health Issue. *BMC Public Health,* 6. https://doi.org/10.1186/1471-2458-6-212

Hoskins, J. (1993). Violence, Sacrifice, and Divination: Giving and Taking Life in Eastern Indonesia. *American Ethnologist, 20*(1), 159–178.

Idowu, E. B. (1973). *African Traditional Religion: A Definition.* SCM Press Ltd.

Imafidon, E. (2017). Dealing with the Other Between the Ethical and the Moral: Albinism on the African Continent. *Theoretical Medicine and Bioethics, 38*(2), 163–177.

Imafidon, E. (2019). *African Philosophy and the Otherness of Albinism: White Skin, Black Race.* Routledge.

Imasogie, O. (1983). *Guidelines for Christian Theology in Africa*. African Christian Press.

Josephson-Storm, J. A. (2017). *The Myth of Disenchantment: Magic, Modernity, and the Birth of the Human Sciences*. The University of Chicago Press.

Khan, S., Combaz, E., & McAslan, F. E. (2015). *Social Exclusion: Topic Guide* (Revised ed.). GSDRC, University of Birmingham.

Kromberg, J. G. R. (2018). Introduction and Historical Background. In K. Jennifer & P. Manga (Eds.), *Albinism in Africa: Historical, Geographic, Medical, Genetic, and Psychosocial Aspect* (pp. 1–25). Academic Press.

Leatt, A. D. (2017). *The State of Secularism: Religion, Tradition and Democracy in South Africa*. Wits University Press.

Likumbo, N., De Villers, T., & Kyriacos, U. (2021). Malawian Mothers' Experience of Ran Children Living with Albinism: A Qualitative Descriptive Study. *African Journal of Disability, 10*, 1–11. https://doi.org/10.4102%2Fajod.v10i0.693

Lund, P. M., & Taylor, J. S. (2008). Lack of Adequate Sun Protection for Children with Oculocutaneous Albinism in South Africa. *BMC Public Health, 8*. https://doi.org/10.1186/1471-2458-8-225

Machoko, C. G. (2013). Albinism: A Life of Ambiguity—A Zimbabwean Experience. *African Identities, 11*(3), 318–333. https://doi.org/10.1080/14725843.2013.838896

Mbiti, J. S. (1992). *African Religions and Philosophy* (Rev ed.). Heinemann.

Meyer, B. (1999). *Translating the Devil: Religion and Modernity Among the Ewe in Ghana*. Edinburgh University Press

Mire, A. (2017). Otherness and Stigmatized Whiteness: Skin Whitening, Vitiligo and Albinism. In L. Bernhard (Ed.), *Anthropology and Alterity: Responding to the Other* (pp. 124–147). Routledge.

Obadare, E. (2018). *Pentecostal Republic: Religion and the Struggle for State Power in Nigeria*. Zed Books.

Oetting, W. S., Brilliant, M. H., & King, A. R. (1996). The Clinical Spectrum of Albinism in Humans. *Molecular Medicine Today, 2*(8), 330–335. https://doi.org/10.1016/1357-4310(96)81798-9

Robbins, J. (2003). On the Paradoxes of Global Pentecostalism and the Perils of Continuity Thinking. *Religion, 33*(3), 221–231. https://doi.org/10.1016/S0048-721X(03)00055-1

Tambala-Kaliati, T., Adomako, E. B., & Frimpong-Manso, K. (2021). Living with Albinism in an African Community: Exploring the Challenges of Persons with Albinism in Lilongwe District, Malawi. *Heliyon, 7*(5). https://doi.org/10.1016/j.heliyon.2021.e07034

Taylor, C. (2007). *A Secular Age*. Harvard University Press.

Ter Haar, G. (2000). *Rats, Cockroaches and People Like Us: Views on Humanity and Human Rights*. Institute of Social Studies.

Wesselmann, D. E., Michels, C., & Slaughter, A. (2019). Understanding Common and Diverse Forms of Social Exclusion. In S. C. Rudert, R. Greifeneder, & K. D.

Williams (Eds.), *Current Directions in Ostracism, Social Exclusion, and Rejection Research* (pp. 1–17). Routledge.

Yelle, R. A., & Trein, L. (Eds.). (2022). *Narratives of Disenchantment and Secularization: Critiquing Max Weber's Idea of Modernity*. Bloomsbury.

# Violence Against Persons with Albinism in Malawi

Jones Hamburu Mawerenga

## 1 Introduction

This chapter discusses the phenomenon of violence against Persons with Albinism (PWAs) in Malawi. The aim of the chapter is to highlight the horrendous acts of debilitating violence perpetrated against PWAs in Malawi.

Violence against PWAs in Malawi is driven by superstitious beliefs and it manifests in various forms such as verbal abuse, defilement, rape, abductions, body mutilations, and killings. The situation has worsened to include exhumations of the remains of PWAs in order to extract their bones for ritual purposes (Chamayere, 2020).

Herein lies the knowledge gap to be filled by this chapter. The existing knowledge gap is reflected by the following sections of the chapter: (1) general discussion about albinism in Malawi; (2) the myths and superstitious beliefs concerning albinism in Africa; (3) verbal abuse against PWAs in Africa; (4) abduction, attacks, and killings of PWAs in Malawi; (5) exhumations of the remains of PWAs; and (6) Malawi's Constitution and the albinism discourse in the country.

---

J. H. Mawerenga (✉)
University of Malawi, Zomba, Malawi
e-mail: jmawerenga@unima.ac.mw

© The Author(s), under exclusive license to Springer Nature Switzerland AG 2024
O. B. Mlambo and E. Chitando (eds.), *The Palgrave Handbook of Violence in Africa*,
https://doi.org/10.1007/978-3-031-40754-3_33

## 2   General Discussions of Albinism in Malawi

Hong et al. (2006: 212) note that the word "albinism" etymologically comes from the Latin word "albus" meaning white. Oetting et al. (1996: 330) intimate that albinism refers to a group of inherited genetic disorders in which a person has partial or complete loss of the pigmentation (melanin) which is responsible for the colouring of the skin, eyes, and hair.

Lynch et al. (2014: 216) write that people with albinism have different levels of melanin, which cause variations in skin colour, hair colour, and eye movements. The disease begins at birth and lasts for the rest of a person's life. PWAs are predisposed to at least two lifelong physical and health problems: vision impairment and skin damage from ultraviolet light, which can lead to skin cancer. This genetic disorder can be passed down from either parent and is difficult to prevent, particularly if both parents are unaware of their family history. If both parents have albinism or bear the gene, their children are more likely to be born with it. Poverty, the lack of sunscreen lotions, the lack of hats with larger brims, the lack of clothing which almost covers the entire body, the lack of sunglasses, and the lack of access to adequate healthcare can aggravate health issues associated with albinism.

Mártinez-García and Montoliu (2013: 319) explain that there are several types of albinism characterized by different gene defects. They include: Oculocutaneous albinism (OCA), Ocular Albinism (OA), Hermansky-Pudlak Syndrome, Chediak-Higashi Syndrome, and Griscelli Syndrome.

Amnesty International (2016: 1) reports that Malawi has an estimated population of approximately 10,000 PWAs. However, the 2018 Malawi Housing and Population Census (MHPC) Comprehensive Report, which the National Statistical Office (NSO) released in June 2019, indicated that Malawi has 134,636 PWAs,[1] representing 0.8% of the country's population (Sangala, 2019: 1).

The MHPC found that out of the total population of persons with albinism, 65,366 are male while 69,270 are female. In the Northern Region, there are 17,165 while 58,509 are in the Central Region and 58,962 live in the Southern Region. Persons with albinism living in urban areas are 17,156 while 117,480 live in rural areas (Sangala, 2019: 1).

---

[1] Patricia Lund, a scholar who has researched on the topic of albinism in Malawi and other parts of the world, has expressed doubts concerning the validity and reliability of the MHPC findings regarding the number of persons with albinism in the country. Instead, she argues that the number of people with albinism in Malawi should be approximately 10,000. Communication between Dr. Patricia Lund and Dr. Jones Mawerenga during the writing of a collaborative article on "We are humans, Just Like You: Albinism in Malawi – Implications for security," 2021.

The 2016 Amnesty International report on violence and discrimination against persons with albinism in Malawi made the following observations:

> Since November 2014, Malawi has seen a sharp increase in human rights abuses against people with albinism, including abductions, killings and grave robberies by individuals and criminal gangs. At least 18 people have been killed and at least five have been abducted and remain missing. According to the Malawi Police Service, at least 69 cases involving crimes related to people with albinism have been reported since November 2014. (Amnesty International, 2016: 1)

A non-governmental organization, Under the Same Sun (UTSS), and the UN Human Rights Council (UNHRC) have gathered data which demonstrates an escalation of violence against PWAs in Malawi in recent years. UTSS records 56 cases of violence against PWAs, including 18 killings, 25 survivors, 5 missing persons and 7 grave robberies (UTSS, 2021). The UNHRC records over 150 cases of killings, attacks, and other human rights violations against PWAs reported in Malawi since 2014 (UNHRC, 2019: 1).

Deprose Muchena, Amnesty International's Director for East and Southern Africa, lamented the killing of Ian Muhamba, a 20-year-old man with albinism, who was reported missing on 23 July 2021 in Blantyre and whose mutilated body was discovered on 14 August 2021 at Kachere township. He said:

> This brutal murder is the latest reminder that Malawi remains a dangerous place for persons with albinism. The Malawian government must protect this vulnerable group from murder, abduction and persecution, in a context where perpetrators are rarely held to account. (Amnesty International, 2021)

In an interview with Africa Renewal, Miss Ikponwosa Ero, the United Nations independent expert on the rights of persons with albinism, described the situation of people with albinism in Africa as a tragedy. She referred to the 7,000–10,000 people living with albinism in Malawi and thousands of others in Tanzania, Mozambique, and other African countries as "an endangered people" facing a "risk of extinction if nothing is done" (*Africa Renewal*, 2017: 1).

Having presented a general discussion of albinism in Malawi, I now proceed to deal with the myths and superstitious beliefs concerning albinism in Africa.

## 3 Myths and Superstitious Beliefs Concerning Albinism in Africa

Culpepper (2000) defines a myth as an unusual traditional story of ostensibly historical events that serves to unfold part of the worldview of a people or explain a practice, belief, or natural phenomenon. Baker et al. (2010: 169) observe that myths concerning albinism are widespread in Africa.

Lund and Gaigher (2002: 365) argue that albinism in Africa is portrayed as a condition which is deeply immersed in myths and superstition, resulting in the stigmatization and rejection of the affected people. Baker (2008: 113) argues that the negative portrayal of albinism in Africa contributes to an overt discrimination that results from a fundamental failure in understanding the condition. Benyah (2017: 161) argues that myths and misconceptions about albinism serve as a linchpin for the unleashing of violence against PWAs in Africa.

Cimpric (2010) evaluates the commodification and monetization of PWAs body parts whose "magical and mystical" values are prized on the occult market. Trade in their body parts is associated with the "occult economy." In this chapter, "occult economy" refers to the use of magic in order to gratify money-oriented passions. The use of these magical techniques defies the principles of science and is inexplicable in any conventional way.

Cimpric (2010) argues that the ritual murder and raping of PWAs is believed to influence the surreptitious factors of economic growth, the accumulation of wealth and good health. Burke (2013: 57) insinuates that the violence unleashed against PWAs in Africa is due to increased social inequalities, especially poverty and unemployment. Machoko (2013: 320) intimates that some Africans believe that poverty, unemployment, and sickness could be solved on the occult market by the supposedly magical powers of the body parts of PWAs.

Possi and Milinga (2018: 83) suggest that the albinism discourse should prioritize in its agenda the bullying of children with albinism owing to the visible difference of their skin colour. Taylor et al. (2019: 13) hint that the problem is heightened in sub-Saharan Africa where witchcraft-related beliefs have fuelled the attack, mutilation, and killing of people with albinism, as some people believe that their body parts bring good luck. Franklin et al. (2018: 3) propound that children are a special target for this type of violence because the innocence of the victim is deemed to increase the potency of the amulets and charms. Ojilere and Saleh (2019: 147) submit that young girls with albinism are also victims of defilement and rape owing to the unsubstantiated belief that having sexual intercourse with them can cure HIV/AIDS.

Inexorably, the ongoing violence, stigma, and discrimination against PWAs precipitate the conditions of violence, consequently endangering their lives and having an impact on their mental health and psycho-social well-being (Aquaron et al., 2009; Braathen & Ingstad, 2006; Hong et al., 2006; Thuku, 2011).

Myths and superstitious beliefs regarding albinism are also responsible for infanticide. For instance, in rural areas of Zimbabwe and Venda in RSA, babies with albinism have been killed at birth (Baker et al., 2010: 172–173). Machoko (2013: 318) explains that in traditional Zimbabwean societies, babies with albinism have been ritually killed in at least four ways: through exposure to harsh climatic and environmental conditions, by suffocation, by being buried alive, and by being murdered.

Cruz-Inigo et al. (2011: 79) lists at least 15 common myths and misconceptions regarding albinism in sub-Saharan Africa: (1) weaving the hair of people with albinism into a net improves the chances of catching fish; (2) the body parts of people with albinism worn as amulets bring good luck, fortune, and health; (3) the body parts of people with albinism are a necessary ingredient for witchdoctor potions; (4) people with albinism have magical superpowers and can cure diseases; (5) intercourse with a lady with albinism will cure HIV/AIDS; (6) spitting on a person with albinism prevents the condition in one's family; (7) the mother of a child with albinism was laughed at by a person with albinism during pregnancy; (8) albinism is caused by a missing top layer of the skin; (9) people with albinism and their mothers are possessed by evil spirits; (10) the devil stole the original child and replaced it with a person with albinism; (11) albinism is very contagious and spreads through touching; (12) people with albinism are indwelt by the ghosts of European colonists; (13) people with albinism have low brain capacity and cannot function at the same level as others; (14) the mother of a person with albinism was impregnated by a white man; and (15) albinism is a curse from the gods or from dead ancestors, and as a result, being in contact with a person with albinism will bring bad luck, sickness or even death.

Lynch et al. (2014: 216) indicate that myths alleging that PWAs are not of this world are prevalent in Malawi. It is commonly believed that people with albinism are not fully part of the world of the living but are ghosts (*Mzukwa*). It is also believed that "if you laugh at a *Nyau* (a member of a secret society of the Chewa people in Malawi who often wear masks and perform dances called *Gule Wamkulu*) you will have a baby with albinism." Van Breugel (2001: 126) indicates that the association of albinism and *Nyau* or *Gule Wamkulu* has a specific religious significance: namely, it is the symbolic representation of the invisible spirit world. The *Nyau* dancers are identified with the spirits (*mizimu*) to such an extent that many of their customs appear to be part of this process of identification. They have to undergo a transformation like a deceased person whose body is symbolically characterized by reversals. Hence, persons with albinism are not considered to be proper human beings but ghosts (*mzukwa*) who are reincarnated spirits of the dead in a bodily form.

Baker (2007) asserts that the notion that people with albinism do not fully belong to the world of the living is supported by the "death myth." Lund and Gaigher (2002: 365) maintain that the "death myth" claims that people with albinism do not die a natural death but simply go into the bush and disappear. This belief is commonly heard in South Africa. Participants in a study on albinism in Malawi also expressed the belief that people with albinism do not die a natural death, but just disappear and, more specifically, die or disappear before they reach the age of 40.

Tambala-Kaliati et al. (2021: e07034) explain four superstitious beliefs about albinism held in Malawi. First, PWAs thought that their condition was caused by their mothers' anaemia during pregnancy. Second, some PWAs claimed that their illnesses were caused by their mothers' blood transfusions during childbirth. Third, since the majority of women with albinism, were born after their parents had given birth to other children who did not have albinism, they were persuaded that their older siblings cleansed their mother's womb, causing the PWAs to be born with thinner, paler skin. Fourth, some people with albinism believe that their mothers were cursed as a result of jealousy and envy in their families.

People with albinism are also identified with water spirits (*njuzu*) in Zimbabwe, the Western Democratic Republic of Congo (DRC), and in Central African Republic (CAR) (Cimpric, 2010; Machoko, 2013). Cimpric (2010) explains that the birth of a person with albinism was believed to be the result of a woman having sexual intercourse with a water spirit. Consequently, this prompted fishermen to use the hair of PWAs to attract fish in Lake Victoria.

Myths and superstitious beliefs concerning albinism in Africa have several implications. First, they lead to socially constructed discrimination which greatly compromises the quality of life of people with albinism (Hong et al., 2006: 2). Second, mothers of children with albinism are stigmatized and suffer psychological distress (Hong et al., 2006: 2). Third, the social construction of albinism based on African myths affects PWAs and their families biologically, medically, socially, psychologically, and economically (Hong et al., 2006: 2). Fourth, black mothers of babies with albinism are unhappy for both the child and themselves and have to endure ridicule from society (Kromberg et al., 1987: 911). Fifth, children with albinism experience bullying at school and in most cases fail to access special needs education, and this negatively affects their academic success (Baker et al., 2010: 169). Sixth, criminals have been targeting PWAs for their body parts which are believed to have some magical powers with the potential to bring good fortune (Mswela, 2017: 1). Seventh, women with the condition of albinism are often the targets of sexual violence because of the myth which claims that sexual intercourse with a woman or a girl with albinism can cure HIV/AIDS (Duri & Makama, 2018: 77).

Having presented a discussion on myths and superstitious beliefs concerning albinism in Africa, I now proceed to consider verbal abuse against PWAs in Africa.

## 4    Verbal Abuse Against Persons with Albinism in Africa

Verbal abuse is another form of violence perpetrated against PWAs in Africa. Ramanathan and Makoni (2007) elucidate that language provides the basis for constructing social ideas and discourses on disability and albinism in Africa.

Brocco (2015: 1143) draws out several implications of the use of language for PWAs in Africa. First, labels for PWAs demonstrate that individuals with albinism are perceived as different by other community members, and they also reveal the assignment of social significance attached to that difference (Green et al., 2005: 201). Therefore, the examination of the onomastic performatives associated with albinism in Africa enables us to understand how the notions of normalcy and difference are produced (McPherron & Ramanathan, 2011: 2). Second, language and labelling for PWAs constitutes proof of their social positioning in African societies (Avoke, 2002: 769). Third, discriminatory language used to describe PWAs has the potential to influence various forms of exclusion and marginalization in society (Singal, 2010: 415).

Kadenge et al. (2014: 1230) contend that the use of derogatory language in describing albinism provides the grounds for further prejudice and social rejection of persons with albinism. For instance, in Zimbabwe, persons with albinism are called *sope*, which suggests that they are inhabited by evil spirits. Kuster (2000: 40–41) mentions that in Tanzania, PWAs are also ridiculed and called *nguruwe*, which means "pig" or *zeru-zeru*, which means "ghost." In Malawi, they are called *mzukwa* which means "ghost," and *mzungu*, which means a "white person." Kromberg (1992: 159) postulates that the difference in skin-colour of persons with albinism in comparison with normally pigmented family members and the rest of the black community leads to the formulation of pejorative language.

Chunga (2020: 12) reports that in Malawi, PWAs endure verbal abuse, name-calling and insults emanating from myths and superstitious beliefs about their condition. Amnesty International (2016: 1) insinuates that PWAs are treated like sub-human beings and are subjected to a range of descriptions that are largely disparaging. For instance, they are often referred to as "yellow man" or *Zigoma*, after the late Jeffrey Zigoma, who was a famous gospel musician with the condition of albinism. Some have been called *mzungu osauka* (poor white person) and *mzungudala* (fake white person). Women with albinism are called *machilitso* (cure), referring to the belief that having sex with a person with albinism can cure HIV/AIDS. Another abusive term is *napweri* which likens people with albinism to a tomato affected by leaf-spots which gives it white patches, or dry pigeon peas, for when they are dry they are kind of brownish. Chamayere (2020: 11) states that *nyau likobiri* is another insulting name for a person with albinism in Malawi, and it suggests the monetary value associated with the PWAs body parts.

Amnesty International (2016: 1) recounts the commodification and monetization of PWAs in Malawi as being associated with sneering terms such as "money", "deal" or "millions." These reproachful terms imply that PWAs could be sold in order to make money. For example, an activist with albinism said that he was told by a neighbour that he was "money" and that if the neighbour found a "market" he would sell members of his family, who all have albinism, to buyers of body parts.

Brocco (2015: 1144) argues that name-calling and insults have a damaging psycho-social impact on the lives of PWAs in at least two ways. First, PWAs are dehumanized, and this can lead to their withdrawal from society and suffering loss of self-confidence and self-esteem (Tambala-Kaliati et al., 2021: e07034). Second, these pejorative names are embedded in myths and superstitious beliefs surrounding the condition of albinism and affect various spheres of the lives of PWAs for example, education, employment, marriage and children, safety and security, and generally their daily life (Baker et al., 2010: 173).

In Malawi, the despicable naming associated with the condition of albinism has contributed to a sharp increase in superstition-driven attacks against persons with albinism in the form of abductions, body mutilations, killings and grave robberies. Therefore, the chapter argues that the depreciatory naming of the condition of albinism in Malawi has very negative connotations, consequently, perpetuating violence and discrimination against persons with albinism in the country (Chikwamba, 2013).

Having presented a discussion on the verbal abuse against PWAs in Malawi, I now proceed to present a discussion on the abduction, attack, and killing of PWAs in Malawi.

## 5 Abduction, Attack, and Killing of PWAs in Malawi

This chapter argues that the aforementioned myths and superstitious beliefs about albinism and the negative type of language used to describe the phenomenon of albinism generally contribute to violence against PWAs in Malawi.

Therefore, in this section of the chapter, I will present a discussion of incidents of the violent abductions, attacks, and killings of PWAs in Malawi.

### 11-Year-Old Boy with Albinism Attacked in Karonga District

Kumwenda (2015: 1) relates that an eleven-year-old boy with albinism, whose identity was not disclosed, survived an abduction at Ipyana, in Karonga district, on 4 September 2015. Two men abducted him and tried to cut off a throat and right arm.

Kumwenda (2015: 1) says that Enock Livason, a Karonga police spokesperson, said that they had arrested two suspects: Fiskani Mtambo (35) from Mukwavi Village, Traditional Authority (T/A) Mwenewenya in Chitipa, and Sam Wamisi Kaumba (32) from Cheyama Village, T/A Kyungu in Karonga. The two suspects are reported to have deceived the boy into accompanying them to a nearby market to collect a chicken which his mother had bought. However, when they got to Ipyana, they dragged the boy to a nearby forest and started cutting off his throat and right arm. Fortunately, some people in the surrounding area heard the boy's cries for help and they quickly rushed to the forest to rescue him. His two attackers managed to escape from the crime scene but were arrested later on the same day.

## Alfred Chigalu Attacked in Phalombe District

Nkawihe (2015: 1) reports that Alfred Chigalu, a 17-year-old boy with albinism, was brutally attacked in Mnasi Village, Traditional Authority Mkhumba, in Phalombe district, on 29 November 2015. He sustained deep stab wounds on his head, on both arms, and on the upper part of his left leg.

According to Augustus Nkhwazi, a police publicist, Alfred was attacked during the night at 11 pm while he was sleeping at his home. Unidentified criminals carrying *phanga* knives, broke into his house and started hacking him. But he cried out loudly for help and his neighbours quickly rushed to rescue him (Nkawihe, 2015: 1).

Nkawihe (2015: 1) narrates that police officers who arrived at the scene found Chigalu in a pool of blood since he was bleeding profusely. They quickly rushed him to Phalombe Health Centre, where, upon arrival, he was referred to the Holy Family Mission Hospital where he received treatment.

## A Thug Chopped Off Tafwauli Ngoma's Toes

Mkandawire (2019: 11) relates that on 15 February 2020, an unidentified criminal chopped off two toes from Miss Tafwauli Ngoma, a 92-year-old woman with albinism at Kapopo Mhlanga Village, T/A M'mbelwa, in Mzimba district.

Mkandawire (2019: 11) records that Tafwauli Ngoma met her fate when she was making fire in her kitchen at around 5 pm at her home. The assailant came in, asking for fire to light his cigarette. Then, he suddenly produced an axe, grabbed the woman and hacked off her right big toe and left little left toes before fleeing, leaving her in a pool of blood.

Mkandawire (2019: 11) explains that Tafwauli's daughter and grandson who both lived with her, had at the time of the attack, gone to Kapopo Trading Centre to buy some groceries. It was later, after the daughter and grandson had returned from the market, that they found her in agony and profusely bleeding. They rushed with her to Mzimba Police Station to report the crime incident before taking her to Mzimba District Hospital for treatment.

## MacDonald Masambuka

Mwiba (2018: 1) writes that MacDonald Masambuka, a 22-year-old man with albinism, was found brutally murdered after he went missing on 9

February 2018 at Duwamakawa village, in the area of Traditional Authority Nkoola in Machinga district.

Boaz (2018: 3) states that a Mr. Charles Yohane, one of the suspects in MacDonald's murder case, had conspired with MacDonald's elder brother, Cassim Masambuka, that they should trick MacDonald into going to Chikweo Trading Centre, on Friday which was a market day. Thus, the three, MacDonald Masambuka, Alfred Yohane, and Cassim Masambuka, rode their bicycles to Chikweo. But when they were passing a graveyard, Alfred and Cassim stopped and started beating MacDonald. Then suddenly gangsters who were hiding in the graveyard, rushed to the scene and also joined in beating MacDonald. When they saw that they were failing to overpower MacDonald and kill him, they decided to leave him. But Cassim, MacDonald's brother, warned them that if they made the mistake of leaving him alive, he was going to report them to the police, and they would be arrested. So, they all resolved to make sure that they killed him and harvested his bones which they would purportedly sell for K40 million.

Boaz (2018: 3) comments that after a protracted fight against MacDonald, the gangsters succeeded in killing him. Then, they cut off both his arms and legs and handed them over to a medical officer, Lumbani Kamanga, who doused them with petrol and set them on fire to enable the easy removal of the flesh and the harvesting of the bones.

Chitsulo (2018: 1) reports that the Malawi police found the body of late MacDonald Masambuka on 1 April 2018 buried within the district. His body was properly laid to rest on 2 April 2018 with some body parts missing.

Kumbani (2018: 1) articulates that the police arrested Reverend Father Thomas Muhosha, a Catholic priest, of Mulombozi Parish, Zomba Diocese, in Zomba district, on 16 April 2018, in connection with the murder of MacDonald Masambuka.

Kumbani (2018: 1) affirms that Lumbani Kamanga, a medical officer, was also arrested by police in connection with the murder of McDonald Masambuka. Kumwenda (2018: 1) declares that Chikondi Chileka, a police officer, was also arrested on suspicion of being involved in MacDonald Masambuka's murder.

Baker et al. (2021: 57) draws some safety and security implications for the albinism discourse in Malawi. For instance, questions are being raised concerning the underground networks and markets that promote the sale of PWA's body parts in Malawi. Mswela (2019: 3) argues that the involvement of a religious leader, a police officer, a medical doctor, and a family member in the murder of MacDonald Masambuka is intriguing as it raises ethical, safety and security and human rights implications.

Having dealt with the abductions, attacks, and killings of PWAs in Malawi, I now proceed to present a discussion of the exhumations of the remains of PWAs in Malawi.

## 6  Exhumations of the Remains of People with Albinism in Malawi

This chapter observes that violence against PWAs in Malawi is perpetrated against them during their lifetime and even when they are dead and buried, by tampering with their graves, and exhuming their bones, as outlined below.

### Luka Kondwani Banda's Body Exhumed in Mzimba District

Unknown criminals exhumed the body of Luka Kondwani Banda, a boy with albinism, who died on 14 May 2016 in Mzimba district (Malenga, 2016: 1).

Luka Banda died, aged 17, after a long illness and was buried on 15 May 2016 in Mponda-Mvula Village in the district. His grave was found tampered with by unknown criminals on Sunday, 29 May 2016, according to a report from the village leaders (Malenga, 2016: 1).

According to the Mzimba police, they visited the crime scene, and discovered that both arms of the corpse had been removed (Malenga, 2016: 1).

### The Grave of a Boy with Albinism Exhumed in Neno District

In June 2016, the grave of an 11-year-old boy with albinism who died in 2008 was exhumed by unknown criminals in Kalinde Village in Traditional Authority (T/A) Mlauli in Neno District (Malikwa, 2016: 1).

According to Raphael Kaliati, Neno Police Station spokesperson, there was a funeral in the village, and when people went to the graveyard to dig a grave, they noticed that another grave had been tampered with. The undertakers then reported this to the village headman Kalinde who referred the matter to the police (Malikwa, 2016: 1).

The police then visited the crime scene and ordered the removal of the remaining soil. This is when they found that all the bones of the deceased had been exhumed except for a few bones from the back and the upper jaws.

According to a police statement, they suspected that this criminal incident occurred between the months of April and May 2016 (Malikwa, 2016: 1).

## Stelia Bello's Body Exhumed in Thyolo District

In May 2016, Elida Bello of Byson Village, T/A Kapichi, Thyolo district, reported to police that criminals had disinterred the bones of her late younger sister, Stelia Bello, from her grave. The deceased was a person with albinism and had died in 1984 (Malawi 24, 2017: 1).

According to a police report, people from Byson Village who live around the graveyard saw something unusual inside the graveyard as they were passing by. The villagers informed the village headman, who went to the graveyard and found that the grave of the late Stelia Bello had been disturbed. The village headman later informed the relatives, who referred the matter to the police (Malawi 24, 2017: 1).

Thereafter, the police, accompanied by Medical Officers from Khonjeni Health Centre, went to the crime scene where they found that some bones had been removed from the dead body. The police then launched a manhunt for the criminals who had exhumed the bones of Stelia Bello from her grave (Malawi 24, 2017: 1).

## Chosadziwa Kaunda's Body Exhumed in Mulanje District

Chosadziwa Kaunda, a 16-year-old girl with albinism, died of natural causes in 2016. Her remains were entombed at Chibade Village, T/A Njema, in the Mulanje district (*Nyasa Times*, 2017: 1).

On 30 May 2017, Ireen Moses, the mother of the deceased, was notified by village headman Chibade that unknown thugs had tampered with her daughter's concrete tomb, resulting in exhumation of Chosadziwa's body (*Nyasa Times*, 2017: 1).

Three suspects, Thomas Ndini, Enock Banda, and Jonas Ogara, connived to exhume the deceased body of Chosadziwa Kaunda from her grave and steal her bones. The three were charged and convicted for unlawfully exhuming a human corpse, contrary to Sections 131 (b) and 404 of Malawi's Penal Code (*Nyasa Times*, 2017: 1).

Village headman Chibade then ordered his subjects to rebury Chosadziwa's empty coffin after a search of her body in the surrounding areas proved futile (*Nyasa Times*, 2017: 1).

Having presented a discussion on the exhumations of the remains of the persons with albinism, I now make a presentation on Malawi's Constitution and the albinism discourse.

## 7 Malawi's Constitution and the Albinism Discourse

This section of the chapter presents a discussion on the compliance of the national legal framework in Malawi with international standards of human rights. It examines the national laws protecting the rights of persons with albinism in the country. Specifically, it highlights the constitutional provisions on the relevant rights accorded to persons with albinism. Further, it discusses the penal provisions that can be used to prosecute and punish perpetrators of the abductions, attacks, killings, and exhumations of the remains of PWA's (Kapindu, 2016).

Gumboh (2012: 295) argues that the Bill of Rights contained in Chapter IV of the Constitution of Malawi guarantees the protection of a wide range of rights, that is, civil, political, economic, social, and cultural rights which are supposed to be enjoyed by all people without distinction (Chirwa, 2005: 207).

Erasmus (2006: 28) articulates that the Bill of Rights in the constitution of Malawi has at least five implications. Firstly, it stipulates essential conditions in the state affecting human beings. It is, therefore, based on fundamental values such as human dignity and protection against abuse of power. Secondly, it is a means to promote democracy. Thirdly, it is part of a supreme and justiciable Constitution. Fourthly, the courts ultimately interpret the provisions in the Bill of Rights and the constitution generally. That is the final stage in the process of giving effect to human rights. However, the Courts cannot do it alone. All branches of government are bound by the Constitution. When the judicial process is invoked, it mostly means that somewhere a human right has been violated. Fifth, the Bill of Rights is frequently a source of constitutional litigation.

Section 15 (1) of Malawi's Constitution is a preamble for the provisions concerning the protection of human rights and freedoms. It states that

> the human rights and freedoms enshrined in this Chapter (4) shall be respected and upheld by the executive, legislature and judiciary and all organs of the Government and its agencies and, where applicable to them, by all natural and legal persons in Malawi and shall be enforceable in the manner prescribed in this Chapter. (Constitution of the Republic of Malawi, 1994)

Section 20(1) of the Constitution prohibits discrimination in the enjoyment of human rights. It states:

> Discrimination of persons in any form is prohibited and all persons are, under any law, guaranteed equal and effective protection against discrimination on grounds of race, colour, sex, language, religion, political or other opinion, nationality, ethnic or social origin, disability, property, birth or other status. (Constitution of Malawi)

Therefore, any form of discrimination against PWAs in Malawi is both illegal and unconstitutional.

The Bill of Rights gives prominence to the right to life under Section 16 of the Constitution. There is no derogation, restriction or limitation with regard to the right to life [Section 44(1) (a)]. The Constitution also guarantees the right to personal liberty (Section 18). Section 19(1) states that "The dignity of all persons shall be inviolable" (Constitution of the Republic of Malawi, 1994). Thus, the killing of persons with albinism in Malawi serves as a blatant violation of the Constitution.

The nature of the violent abductions, attacks, and subsequent killings of persons with albinism in Malawi clearly violates the constitutional provision in Section 13(3). It states that: "No person shall be subject to torture of any kind or cruel, inhuman or degrading treatment or punishment" (Constitution of the Republic of Malawi, 1994).

Malawi's Constitution recognizes the need to pass specific legislation to address inequalities in society and the need to recognize criminal liability for discriminatory practices. Section 20(2) states: "Legislation may be passed addressing inequalities in society and prohibiting discriminatory practices and the propagation of such practices and may render such practices criminally punishable by the courts" (Constitution of the Republic of Malawi, 1994). Kapindu (2016) argues that it is in line with this provision, that parliament introduced the Penal Code (Amendment) Act, Bill No. 28 of 2016 to respond to the rising crimes against persons with albinism in the country.

Malawi's Constitution also provides for the right to education. For instance, Section 25(1) states: "All persons are entitled to education." Section 25(2) states: "Primary education shall consist of at least five years of education. (Constitution of the Republic of Malawi, 1994). Therefore, the current situation whereby students with albinism are dropping out of school for fear of their safety, deprives them of the rights in this provision.

Section 30 (1) of the Constitution provides for the right to development. It states: "All persons and peoples have a right to development and therefore to the enjoyment of economic, social, cultural and political development and women, children and the disabled in particular shall be given special consideration in the application of this right." Section 30(2): "The State shall take all necessary measures for the realization of the right to development. Such measures shall include, amongst other things, equality of opportunity for all in their access to basic resources, education, health services, food, shelter, employment and infrastructure" (Constitution of the Republic of Malawi, 1994). This necessitates action on behalf of persons with albinism in order to ensure that they have a meaningful participation in the socio-economic, and political development of the nation.

Kapindu (2016) observes that in 2012, the Parliament of Malawi adopted the Disability Act (Act No. 8 of 2012) which aims at equalizing opportunities for persons with disabilities through the promotion and protection of their rights. The Act creates various offences relating to unfair discrimination against persons with disabilities, including persons with albinism.

Kapindu (2016) argues that the Penal Code [Chapter 7:01] of Malawi provides for a wide range of crimes under which the perpetrators of violence and other crimes against people with albinism can effectively be charged and ensure the administration of justice. For instance: Section 131A: Trespassing on Burial Places for Extraction or Exhumation; Section 131B: Unlawful Exhumation of Human Corpse; Section 131C: Causing Exhumation and Extraction; Section 209: Murder; Section 223: Attempt to Murder; Section 224A: Possession, Selling or Buying of human Corpse or Tissue; Section 224B: Conspiracy or Causing another to Harm a Person with Disability; Section 224C: Aggravating Circumstances; Section 260: Kidnapping; Section 16: Prohibiting of Sale of Body or Tissue; Section 78: Child Abduction; and Section 79: Child Trafficking.

Malawi's Constitution is very progressive in stipulating various provisions which protect the human rights and freedoms of all people. Hence, PWAs are entitled to the enjoyment of all the rights and freedoms enshrined in the Constitution.

## 8 Conclusion

This chapter has exposed the gruesome violence against PWAs in Malawi, including verbal abuse, abductions, attacks, torture, killings, body mutilations, and exhumation of their remains from their graves. These violent crimes are tantamount to gross human rights violations which, if not stopped, could lead to the extinction of PWAs in the country.

Therefore, this chapter argues that the ongoing violence against PWAs in Malawi must be stopped as a matter of compelling urgency. The following steps are necessary in curbing the tide of violence against PWAs in Malawi.

First, the Government should ensure that adequate financial resources are made available to fully implement the National Action Plan on Persons with Albinism. This point was reiterated on the International Albinism Day 2019, by the former National Coordinator of the Association of Persons with Albinism in Malawi (APAM), Overstone Kondowe, who called for action:

> We are human beings too and have an equal right to be included in society and live in safety. The National Action Plan on Persons with Albinism in Malawi is designed to deliver this in all areas of life including education, employment and safety, but policies mean little if they are not delivered. We need to see concrete actions and plans being implemented. (Baker et al., 2021: 78)

Second, the key to ending these abhorrent crimes lies in the identification and addressing of the root causes of discrimination and violence against PWAs (Salewi, 2011). Benyah (2017: 161) identifies religious, socio-cultural, economic, and political causes of discrimination and violence against PWAs in Africa.

Third, awareness must be raised, and action taken on multiple levels by individuals, the community, albinism associations, civil society, the media, and the international community in enhancing the understanding of albinism, challenging the negative beliefs associated with albinism, and changing societal attitudes (Baker et al., 2021: 74).

Fourth, to effect long-term change, the government of Malawi and the international community must adopt a coordinated collaborative stance in improving the well-being of PWAs, encompassing education, healthcare, monitoring and reporting, policing, and the criminal justice system (Baker et al., 2021: 74).

## Bibliography

Allen, K. (2011). The Human Rights Case of Persons with Albinism in Uganda. *Undergraduate Journal of Global Citizenship, 1*(1), 1.

Aquaron, R., Djatou, M., & Kamdem, L. (2009). Sociocultural Aspects of Albinism in Sub-Saharan Africa: Mutilations and Ritual Murders Committed in East Africa (Burundi and Tanzania). *Medecine tropicale: revue du Corps de sante colonial, 69*(5), 449–453.

Avoke, M. (2002). Models of Disability in the Labelling and Attitudinal Discourse in Ghana. *Disability & Society, 17*(7), 769–777.

Baker, C. (2007). *Crossing Places: New Research in African Studies*. Newcastle.

Baker, C. (2008). Writing Over the Illness: The Symbolic Representation of Albinism. In *Social Studies of Health, Illness and Disease* (pp. 113–127). Brill.

Baker, C., Lund, P., Massah, B., & Mawerenga, J. (2021). We Are Human, Just Like You: Albinism in Malawi—Implications for Security. *Journal of Humanities, 29*(1), 57–84.

Baker, C., Lund, P., Taylor, J., & Nyathi, R. (2010). The Myths Surrounding People with Albinism in South Africa and Zimbabwe. *Journal of African Cultural Studies, 22*(2), 169–181.

Benyah, F. (2017). Equally Able, Differently Looking: Discrimination and Physical Violence Against Persons with Albinism in Ghana. *Journal for the Study of Religion, 30*(1), 161–188.

Braathen, S. H., & Ingstad, B. (2006). Albinism in Malawi: Knowledge and Beliefs from an African Setting. *Disability & Society, 21*(6), 599–611.

Brocco, G. (2015). Labeling Albinism: Language and Discourse Surrounding People with Albinism in Tanzania. *Disability & Society, 30*(8), 1143–1157.

Burke, J. (2013). Media Framing of Violence Against Tanzanians with Albinism in the Great Lakes Region: A Matter of Culture, Crime, Poverty and Human Rights. *The Australasian Review of African Studies, 34*(2), 57–77.

Chamayere, M. (2020). *Albinism in Malawi: An Evaluation of Theological and Human Rights Interventions* (Dissertation). University of Malawi.

Chikwamba, G. (2013). *An Investigation into the Coping Mechanism of People with Albinism. A Case Study of Zimbabwe Albino Association* (Dissertation). Bindura University of Science and Education.

Chirwa, D. M. (2005). A Full Loaf Is Better Than Half: The Constitutional Protection of Economic, Social and Cultural Rights in Malawi. *Journal of African Law, 49*(2), 207–241.

Chunga, P. (2020). *An Investigation of Discrimination Faced by People with Albinism and Their Coping Mechanisms in Malawi* (Dissertation). University of Malawi.

Cimpric, A. (2010). *Children Accused of Witchcraft: An Anthropological Study of Contemporary Practices in Africa* [Les enfants accusés de sorcellerie: etude anthropologique des pratiques contemporaines relatives aux enfants en Afrique].

Cruz-Inigo, A. E., Ladizinski, B., & Sethi, A. (2011). Albinism in Africa: Stigma, Slaughter and Awareness Campaigns. *Dermatologic Clinics, 29*(1), 79–87.

Culpepper, J. C. (2000). Merriam-Webster Online: The Language Center. *Electronic Resources Review, 4*(1/2), 9–11.

Duri, F. P. T., & Makama, A. (2018). Disabilities and Human Insecurities: Women and Oculocutaneous Albinism in Post-colonial Zimbabwe. In *Rethinking Securities in an Emergent Technoscientific New World Order: Retracing the Contours for Africa's Hi-jacked Futures* (p. 77). Langaa RPCIG.

Erasmus, G. (2006). *The Bill of Rights: Human Rights Under the Malawi Constitution*. Constitution Review Conference, Capital Hotel, Lilongwe, pp. 28–31.

Franklin, A., Lund, P., Bradbury-Jones, C., & Taylor, J. (2018). Children with Albinism in African Regions: Their Rights to 'Being' and 'Doing.' *BMC International Health and Human Rights, 18*(1), 1–8.

Green, S., Davis, C., Karshmer, E., Marsh, P., & Straight, B. (2005). Living Stigma: The Impact of Labeling, Stereotyping, Separation, Status Loss, and Discrimination in the Lives of Individuals with Disabilities and Their Families. *Sociological Inquiry, 75*(2), 197–215.

Gumboh, E. (2012). Human Rights Under the Malawian Constitution, DM Chirwa: Recent Publications. *African Human Rights Law Journal, 12*(1), 295–300.

Hong, E. S., Zeeb, H., & Repacholi, M. H. (2006). Albinism in Africa as a Public Health Issue. *BMC Public Health, 6*(1), 1–7.

Kadenge, M., Mabugu, P. R., Chivero, E., & Chiwara, R. (2014). Anthroponyms of Albinos Among the Shona People of Zimbabwe. *Mediterranean Journal of Social Sciences, 5*(27 P3), 1230.

Kapindu, R. E. (2016). *Handbook for Investigators, Prosecutors and Magistrates concerning Offences Against Persons with Albinism*. Ministry of Justice and Constitutional Affairs, Lilongwe.

Kromberg, J. (1992). Albinism in the South African Negro. IV: Attitudes and The Death Myth. *Birth Defects Original Article Series, 28*(1), 159–166.

Kromberg, J. G., Zwane, E. M., & Jenkins, T. (1987). The Response of Black Mothers to the Birth of an Albino Infant. *American Journal of Diseases of Children, 141*(8), 911–916.

Kuster, R. (2000). White Skin, Black Souls. *New African, 382*, 40–41.

Lund, P. M., & Gaigher, R. (2002). A Health Intervention Programme for Children with Albinism at a Special School in South Africa. *Health Education Research, 17*(3), 365–372.

Lynch, P., Lund, P., & Massah, B. (2014). Identifying Strategies to Enhance the Educational Inclusion of Visually Impaired Children with Albinism in Malawi. *International Journal of Educational Development, 39*, 216–224.

Machoko, C. G. (2013). Albinism: A Life of Ambiguity—A Zimbabwean Experience. *African Identities, 11*(3), 318–333.

Mártinez-García, M., & Montoliu, L. (2013). Albinism in Europe. *The Journal of Dermatology, 40*(5), 319–324.

McPherron, P., & Ramanathan, V. (2011). Language, Body, and Health: An Introduction. In *Language, Body, and Health* (pp. 1–11). De Gruyter.

Mkandawire, M. (2019). *Deconstructing the Myth of Albinism in Malawi* (Doctoral Assignment). Malawi Assemblies of God University.

Mswela, M. (2017). Violent Attacks Against Persons with Albinism in South Africa: A Human Rights Perspective. *African Human Rights Law Journal, 17*(1), 114–133.

Mswela, M. (2019). Tagging and Tracking of Persons with Albinism: A Reflection of Some Critical Human Rights and Ethical Issues Arising from the Use of the Global Positioning System (GPS) as Part of a Solution to Cracking Down on

Violent Crimes Against Persons with Albinism. *PER: Potchefstroomse Elektroniese Regsblad, 22*(1), 1–27.

Mwiba, D. M. (2018, June). Medicine Killings, Abduction of People with Albinism, Wealth and Prosperity in North Malawi: A Historical Assessment. *Proceedings of the African Futures Conference, 2*(1), 170–171.

Oetting, W. S., Brilliant, M. H., & King, R. A. (1996). The Clinical Spectrum of Albinism in Humans. *Molecular Medicine Today, 2*(8), 330–335.

Ojilere, A., & Saleh, M. M. (2019). Violation of Dignity and Life: Challenges and Prospects for Women and Girls with Albinism in Sub-Saharan Africa. *Journal of Human Rights and Social Work, 4*(3), 147–155.

Possi, M. K., & Milinga, J. R. (2018). Perceptions on People with Albinism in Urban Tanzania: Implications for Social Inclusion. *Journal of Advocacy, Research and Education, 5*, 81–92.

Ramanathan, V. (2009). *Bodies and Language*. Multilingual Matters.

Ramanathan, V., & Makoni, S. (2007). Bringing the body back: The (mis) languaging of bodies in bio-medical, societal and poststructuralist discourses on diabetes and epilepsy. *Critical Inquiry in Language Studies, 4*(4), 283–306.

Salewi, D. H. (2011). *The Killing of Persons with Albinism in Tanzania: A Social-Legal Inquiry* (Dissertation). University of Pretoria.

Singal, N. (2010). Doing Disability Research in a Southern Context: Challenges and Possibilities. *Disability & Society, 25*(4), 415–426.

Tambala-Kaliati, T., Adomako, E. B., & Frimpong-Manso, K. (2021). Living with Albinism in an African Community: Exploring the Challenges of Persons with Albinism in Lilongwe District, Malawi. *Heliyon, 7*(5), e07034.

Taylor, J., Bradbury-Jones, C., & Lund, P. (2019). Witchcraft-Related Abuse and Murder of Children with Albinism in Sub-Saharan Africa: A Conceptual Review. *Child Abuse Review, 28*(1), 13–26.

Thuku, M. (2011). Myths, *Discrimination, and the Call for Special Rights for Persons with Albinism in Sub-Saharan Africa*. Amnesty International Editorial Review on Special Programme on Africa.

van Breugel, J. W. M. (2001). *Chewa Traditional Religion*. Kachere.

## Online Publications

*Africa Renewal*. (2017). Ending Albino Persecution in Africa. https://www.un.org/africarenewal/magazine/december-2017-march-2018/ending-albino-persecution-africa. Accessed 7 July 2021.

Amnesty International Report. 2016/17-Malawi. (2016). *We Are Not Animals to Be Hunted or Sold*. https://www.amnesty.org/en/documents/afr36/4126/2016/en/. Accessed 10 July 2021.

Boaz, B. (2018, February 3). Mmene adafera Masambuka: Anathira Petulo thupi lake nkuliotcha. *Mkwaso Newspaper*, Vol. 271. http://www.montfortmedia. Accessed 12 July 2021.

Chitsulo, L. (2018). *Missing Person with Albinism Found Murdered.* https://www.mwnation.com. Accessed 12 July 2021.

Kumbani, P. (2018). *Priest Arrested Over Albino Killings.* https://www.mwnation.com. Accessed 12 July 2021.

Kumwenda, T. (2015). *Malawi: Albino Attacks Resurfaces, Body Parts Found in Mchinji as Abducted Karonga Boy's Throat Cut.* https://www.nyasatimes.com. Accessed 12 July 2021.

Kumwenda, T. (2018). *Malawi Police Officer Arrested for Albino Abduction in Machinga: Masambuka's Body Found Buried in a Garden.* https://www.nyasatimes.com. Accessed 12 July 2021.

Malawi Government. (1994). *Constitution of Malawi.* https://www.malawi.gov.mw/index.php/resources/documents/constitution-of-the-republic-of-malawi. Accessed 13 July 2021.

Malawi Population and Housing Census Report. (2018). http://populationmalawi.org/wp1/wp-content/uploads/2019/10/2018-Malawi-Population-and-Housing-Census-Main-Report-1.pdf. Accessed 7 July 2021.

Malawi 24. (2017). *Bones of an Albino Exhumed from the Grave.* https://malawi24.com/2017/05/29/malawi-albino-attacks-bones-person-albinism-stolen-grave/. Accessed 9 July 2021.

Malenga, B. (2016). *Albino's Body Exhumed from the Grave.* https://malawi24.com/2016/05/30/just-albinos-body-exhumed-grave/. Accessed 5 July 2021.

Malikwa, M. (2016). *Albino Grave Exhumed in Neno.* https://mwnation.com/albino-grave-exhumed-in-neno/. Accessed 5 July 2021.

Muchena, D. (2021). *People with Albinism in Urgent Need of Protection.* https://www.amnesty.org/en/latest/news/2021/08/malawi-people-with-albinism-in-urgent-need-of-protection-after-horrific-killing/. Accessed 7 July 2021.

Nkawihe, M. (2015). *Malawi: Albino Attacks Continue in Malawi, 17-Year-Old Hacked in Phalombe.* https://www.nyasatimes.com. Accessed 12 July 2021.

*Nyasa Times.* (2017). Court Convicts Three Men for Exhuming Albino Corpse. https://www.nyasatimes.com/malawi-court-convicts-3-men-exhuming-albino-corpse-witchcraft-rituals/. Accessed 8 July 2021.

Sangala, T. (2019). *Population of People with Albinism Hits 134000.* https://times.mw/population-of-people-with-albinism-hits-134000/. Accessed 5 July 2021.

United Nations High Commissioner for Human Rights. (2013). *Persons with Albinism.* https://www.ohchr.org/files/Issues/Albinism. Accessed 7 July 2021.

UNHRC. (2019). *Malawi: UN Experts Urge Action Over Albinism 'Atrocities' in Runup to Elections.* https://reliefweb.int/report/malawi/malawi-un-experts-urge-action-over-albinism-atrocities-run-elections. Accessed 4 July 2021.

Under the Same Sun. (2021). *Attacks Against Albinos in Africa.* https://www.underthesamesun.com. Accessed 7 July 2021.

# Globalization, Islamic Fundamentalism and Violence Through the Youth in Kenya

Susan M. Kilonzo

## 1 Introduction

Globalization is a process that can be linked to social and economic relationships and networks organized on a local and/or national levels. It also connects social and economic relationships and networks on a wider scale at the regional and global levels. Through the use of technology, globalization makes economic, political, and cultural exchanges possible. Communication, too, is eased. These issues enable globalization processes to provide a considerable amount of influence on fundamentalism since the world has shrunk into a global village—with distance decreased and borders erased. Obadale (n.d.) explains that among many facets, globalization is characterized by expansion of technology, liberalization of cross-border trade and resource movements, increased global competition, and expanded cross-national interactions, among others. Subsequently, I pick on three broad aspects: (1) instantaneous communications; (2) economic mobility; and (3) diminished significance of national boundaries, among the many aspects of globalization, to discuss how these have facilitated Islamic fundamentalism. Islam and Islamic fundamentalism are two different issues. While Islam is a religion based on the teachings of the Prophet Muhammad, and the holy Qur'an, Islamic fundamentalism is a political and religious ideology that seeks to return to what its adherents see as the "fundamental" principles of Islam,

S. M. Kilonzo (✉)
Maseno University, Maseno, Kenya
e-mail: skilonzo@maseno.ac.ke

as they interpret them. This can sometimes involve a strict and literal interpretation of Islamic texts, and the rejection of modern secular values and practices. Islamic fundamentalism is, therefore, associated with extremist and violent actions, such as terrorism.

There is no doubt that religion influences the development of individuals, societies and nations. Mtata (2012) explains that religious authority can have tremendous influence on how the youth think about life and how they live. Religious institutions such as churches or mosques are structured to allow communities to raise legitimate questions and expectations. But religion has also been used as a tool of war. Wars and crusades have been waged in the name of religion, as have persecutions and torture (Batson, 1993: 4). Recently, with the ease with which people, information and economies flow, courtesy of globalization, the factors conducive to and responsible for a quick spread of religious ideologies have been hastened. Religion is an identity indicator, which has the potential to promote peacebuilding or foster conflict (Kristian & Røislien, 2008). The ability to gather is, for instance, evidenced in the acts of radicalization and terrorism. More often than not, and throughout history, religion has been blamed for violence. However, several scholars argue that religion itself is not responsible for violence, but rather people use religion as a tool to justify violence (Appleby, 2000; Chitando & Tarusarira, 2019; Juergensmeyer, 2000).

Scholars point out that religion is a complex and multifaceted phenomenon that can be interpreted and practised in different ways (Juergensmeyer, 2000). While some people use religion to promote peace and tolerance, others use it to justify violence and aggression. Religion is, therefore, not inherently violent, but rather its interpretation and application can lead to violence. Studies have shown that violence associated with religion is often a result of social and political factors rather than religious beliefs (Appleby, 2000). For instance, conflicts between religious groups may be fuelled by economic, political, or ethnic tensions rather than differences in religious doctrine. This implies that in some instances, religion can be used to legitimize violence, but it is often the underlying social and political factors that are the root causes of conflict. Further, research suggests that religious violence is often carried out by individuals or groups who are motivated by political or economic objectives rather than religious zeal (Bloom, 2012). These actors use religion to mobilize support for their cause and justify their actions, but their ultimate goal is not necessarily religious in nature. Religion, therefore, is not the primary cause of the violence, but rather a tool that is used to achieve other goals.

Although Islam is not responsible for fundamentalism and violence, as people use religion as a tool to justify their actions (Esposito, 1998; Mahmood, 2005), it has been frequently associated with fundamentalism and violence. The multiple interpretations within the religion (Esposito, 1998) allows for extremist perspectives that may translate to fundamentalist beliefs that ultimately propagate violent activities. While some Muslims interpret Islam in a peaceful and tolerant manner, others may interpret it in a more fundamentalist and militant way. Further, political and social factors are often the underlying causes of violence associated with Islam (Mahmood, 2005). For instance, conflicts between Muslims and non-Muslims may be fuelled by political or economic tensions (Wiktorowicz, 2004) rather than differences in religious doctrine. In the end, this is just the use of religion to legitimize violence in order to address underlying social and political factors that are the root causes of conflict. Islam, therefore, is not the primary cause of fundamentalism and violence, but rather a tool that is used to achieve other goals.

Islamic fundamentalism has been a growing concern in Kenya due to the rise of Islamist militant groups like Al Shabaab (Nyangau & Kabue, 2019). One of the contributing factors to the rise of Islamic fundamentalism in Kenya is the marginalization of the Muslim community. According to a report by the International Crisis Group, Muslims in Kenya are disproportionately affected by poverty and discrimination (International Crisis Group, 2019). This has led to a sense of alienation and resentment, which has been exploited by Islamist groups to recruit new members. Furthermore, the influence of external actors has contributed to the spread of Islamic fundamentalism in Kenya. Al Shabaab, for example, has been able to establish a presence in Kenya due to its proximity to Somalia, where the group is based (Horn, 2018). The group recruits Kenyan Muslims by framing their struggle as a defence of Islam against the Western-backed government in Somalia. The Kenyan government has been accused of targeting Muslims and using excessive force in its efforts to combat terrorism (Kamau, 2019), leading to a further sense of alienation and resentment among the Muslim community.

The literature is keen on the dynamics of radicalization processes resulting from this sense of alienation, and the challenges that face the Muslim community especially. Mwalimu (2021) for example shows that youth and Islamic radicalization been a growing concern in Kenya especially with the rise of Islamist militant groups like Al Shabaab. One of the factors that contribute to the radicalization of youth in Islamic fundamentalism is the lack of education and employment opportunities (Githuku, 2019). Young people in Kenya face high rates of unemployment, and many are unable to access quality education. This creates a sense of hopelessness and makes them vulnerable to extremist ideologies. Further, social networks and peer pressure are contributing factors to youth involvement in Islamic fundamentalism (Odongo & Ogola, 2017). Young people in Kenya often join extremist groups due to the influence of their friends or family members who are already involved in such groups, and in a way, they are in search of sense of belonging and acceptance that comes with being part of a group. It is also important to note that not all youth who are involved in Islamic fundamentalism are driven by the same factors. Some are motivated by a desire to defend their religion or community, while others are attracted to the idea of violence and radicalism (Mwalimu, 2021). The broader factors that facilitate this kind of involvement, such as those resulting from globalization, are therefore key, and this forms the focus of this chapter.

The chapter examines the role of communication, economic mobility and the diminished significance of national/geographical boundaries in radicalizing the youth in Kenya. The chapter shows that the combination of ease of communication, widespread unemployment, and the porousness of the Kenya-Somalia border make it easy for Al Shabaab Islamists to operate terror cells across the two countries. These cells are used to both recruit desperate unemployed youths and launch devastating terrorist attacks such as the Westgate Mall attack in Kenya and sustained bombing of targets in the Somali capital of Mogadishu. The chapter, therefore, juxtaposes the role played by fundamentalism in radicalization and the enabling environment as provided by globalization.

## 2  Operational Definitions of Key Concepts

### Fundamentalism

Fundamentalism is the literal interpretation of and adherence to religious doctrines. In most literature, it is used synonymously with religious extremism. Fundamentalism has its origin in Christianity, but has become a phenomenon of all religions, especially Islam. Islamic fundamentalists, also called Islamists, regard themselves as the true followers of the Qur'an and Hadith (practices and traditions) as taught by the Prophet Muhammad. These Islamists view the terror that they wreak on others as justifiable jihadist acts against the non-believers. This understanding of fundamentalism has been termed as political Islam and is characterized by the formation of groups that propagate extreme ideologies of the religion. Islamic fundamentalism is a term used to describe the conservative and literalist interpretation of Islamic scripture and values. It often entails a rejection of Western cultural and political influence and a desire to establish an Islamic state or society based on Sharia law. The term is often used interchangeably with Islamic extremism or radicalism (Kepel, 1993). The roots of Islamic fundamentalism as Roy (2013) shows, can be traced back to the late nineteenth century, with the emergence of movements such as the Muslim Brotherhood in Egypt and the Deobandi movement in India. These movements sought to restore Islamic values and traditions in response to what they saw as the corrupting influence of Western colonialism and modernity.

Islamic fundamentalism gained momentum in the twentieth century, particularly after the Iranian Revolution in 1979, which saw the establishment of an Islamic Republic. The rise of extremist groups such as Al Qaeda and ISIS in the twenty-first century further underscored the influence and impact of Islamic fundamentalism (Grinin, 2019). In Africa, such groups include the Muslim Brotherhood in Egypt, Renaissance Party in Tunisia, Boko Haram in West Africa (mostly Nigeria), and Al Shabaab in Somalia, among others (Engineer, 1984; Kilonzo, 2020).

## Radicalization

Radicalization is the beginning of the process of fundamentalism, which culminates, especially in political Islam, in violent extremism.

The Media Council of Kenya (2016: 2) explains that:

> Radicalization as the process through which an individual or groups of individuals are transformed by an ideology or belief system shifting mind-sets away from the mainstream… [I]t helps fulfil a sense of meaning, belonging, acceptance, purpose, value, having special power, dignity and respect as well as being a defender of a religion, race, tribe, political thinking or a cause. When the process leads to violence, then it is referred to as Radicalization into Violent Extremism (RVE) process.

The term "radicalization" encompasses a wide range of concepts—from being used as a tool to recruit the marginalized, to embodying a dangerous path towards violent actions (Jirires, 2016). Onuoha (2014) explains that the concept of radicalization as having gained significant currency among government officials, media practitioners, scholars, and security officials in discourses on terrorism and violent extremism, especially since the terrorist attacks of 11 September 2001 (Onuoha, 2014: 2). As Onuoha argues, radicalization begins with changes in self-identification due to grievances. A grievance is then understood to create the sense of alienation or disenchantment that provides a cognitive opening for radicalization. A radical ideology—an extreme set of ideas—then provides the individual with a new outlook and explanation for the world in which they find themselves. Individuals become mobilized as they slowly integrate into a community of other like-minded people (Onuoha, 2014: 2), and extremist or violent activities result (CLEEN, 2014). This then is termed as the darker side of social capital (also see Shore 2008). The masses join forces for negative activities whose resultant effects harm rather than build.

Having looked at the meaning and application of the term radicalization, an understanding of a brief history of the process in Kenya is imperative. In Kenya, radicalization can be traced to the 1970s with the return of young Muslim elites who had acquired their Islamic education in Saudi Arabia and Pakistan (International Crisis Group, 2012: 5; Thordsen, 2009: 53). The young elites were acquainted with *Wahhabism* during their studies and as such they embarked on a mission to disseminate similar ideas through madrassas (Chande, 2000: 351). Recently, there has been a marked increase in the number of youths drawn to Al Shabaab extremism as evidenced by rising recruitments and terrorist attacks in various parts of Kenya and re-emergence of radical groups such as the Mombasa Republican Council (MRC). Moreover, controversial preachers have used literal translations of the Qur'an and Hadith to reach out to more youth to join the Jihad in Somalia. Most of the recruits are unemployed youths, who are made vulnerable to the forces of radicalism and criminality due to the feelings of real and perceived marginalization, which result in a sense of hopelessness, identity crisis, and feelings of being excluded from national resources. Consequently, radicalization should be viewed as an interactive process between the individual and external influences—terrorist groups and recruiters—as well as the actions of public authorities, especially the State (GOK, 2015; Kilonzo, 2020). Most of these youths join the Al Shabaab, which has roots in Somalia, from the international terror group Al Qaeda, but has since spread across a number of East African countries including Kenya, Uganda, Tanzania, and South Sudan. The section below gives a brief overview of Al Shabaab activities in Kenya with most of those involved in the execution of violence being the youth.

## 3  Al Shabaab Factor in Kenya

Al Shabaab appeared on the scene at a time when Somalia was on the verge of forming a stable government. Jones et al. (2016) detail the historical origins and the phases of growth of the group. They indicate, "Al Shabaab's ideological origins can be traced to the 1960s, when *Salafi* and *Wahhabi* networks from Saudi Arabia and Egypt were first introduced into Somalia, challenging the Sufi Koranic supporters who had historically dominated" (p. 9). According to Ibrahim (2010), the present Al Shabaab broke out from the militant wing of the pre-2008 Council of Islamic Courts (CIC) without long-term local or global strategies. They emerged from two previous Somali Islamist groups—the Islamic Union and the Islamic Courts Union (ICU). Their clear break from ICU happened during the Djibouti peace deal negotiations between the Transitional Federal Government (TFG) and the ICU. They refused to join in the negotiations, declaring the peace deal as a betrayal. The initial strategy of the group was to transform and change Somalia Sunni community into more radical *Wahhabi/Salafi* followers.[1] Other scholars indicate that Al Shabaab is an offshoot of the Jihadist organization Al Qaeda whose aim is to fight Western interests and establish Islamic states globally (Marchal, 2009).

Al Shabaab's terrorist attacks gained notoriety in Kenya in 2011 with kidnappings for ransom and other unprovoked attacks on civilian and military targets (Owen, 2012). In October 2011, the Government deployed the Kenya Defence Force (KDF) in southern Somalia in an effort to stem the spate of attacks launched from there. The terror group vowed revenge on Kenya, which they accused of being a puppet of the West (Hansen, 2013: 130; Magak & Omwalo, 2014; Mwakimako & Willis, 2016). This has been shown not to be the only reason for increased attacks by the group on Kenyan soil. In one study, Cannon and Pkalya (2017: 1) argue that, Al Shabaab targets Kenya more than other frontline states because of the opportunity spaces linked to Kenya's international status and visibility, its relatively free and independent media that widely publicizes terrorist attacks, a highly developed and lucrative tourist sector that provides soft targets, the comparatively high number of Kenyan foreign fighters within the group's ranks, the presence of terror cells in Kenya, expanding democratic space, and high levels of corruption. Between October 2012 and September 2013, there were 13

---

[1] Rabasa (2009) explains that the growth of radical Islam in East Africa in recent decades has manifested itself in the spread of *Salafi* and *Wahhabi* ideologies, which has put pressure on traditional and Sufi practices, and in the emergence of extremist and terrorist groups influenced by these ideologies.

Al Shabaab terrorist attacks on Kenya, resulting in more than 100 deaths in various parts of the country (Botha, 2013; Magak & Omwalo, 2014). These attacks targeted business premises, pubs, restaurants, public transport vehicles, markets, and churches.

Magak and Omwalo (2014: 50–55) detail the attacks in villages/farms, shopping malls, and churches and provide statistics for the same as they attempt to show how the Somali identity factor has been affected by the Al Shabaab attacks. One widely covered attack was the 21 September 2013 Westgate Mall in Nairobi, which saw the death of 67 people of different nationalities (Magak & Omwalo, 2014: 54). An analysis provided on Al Shabaab's terror activities by Gartenstein-Ross and Appel (2014) indicates that, although scholarly works have depicted the Westgate Mall attack by the Al Shabaab as a sign of fear and desperation of a group that is suffering from internal power struggle, the group's ability to conduct well-organized lethal attacks has not in any way significantly declined.

The Somali identity in Kenya has been discussed widely. Magak and Omwalo (2014) expound on how this identity has been associated with Al Shabaab. However, the literature indicates that Al Shabaab radicalization has moved beyond ethnic Somalis to recruit non-ethnic Somalis globally, especially in Kenya. Shauri and Wanjala (2017: 147) allude to the unchecked religious teachings and practices as continuous indoctrination in places of worship, aimed at radicalizing Muslim youths. What the existing literature does not show is how globalization has played a role in the radicalization processes.

## 4  Al Shabaab, Globalization, and Radicalization in Kenya

Globalization is a perfect vehicle for radicalization as it fosters interaction and integration among individuals and states internationally. Aspects of globalization such as communication technology, and cross-border social and economic relationships and networks, (Cuterera, 2012; Obadale, n.d) provide effective pathways for youth Islamist radicalization and engagement with extremist movements in Kenya, such as Al Shabaab, which are known to receive funding from various sources, including foreign terrorist organizations, local sympathizers, and illicit activities such as smuggling and piracy. For example, Al Shabaab has been involved in the smuggling of charcoal, sugar, and other commodities from Somalia into Kenya, generating millions of dollars in revenue. Additionally, piracy off the coast of Somalia has provided a significant source of funding for Al Shabaab and other extremist groups. Efforts to combat the funding of extremist movements in Kenya include increasing surveillance of financial transactions, cracking down on illicit activities such as smuggling and piracy, and working with international partners to disrupt funding networks. However, these efforts are complicated by the complex nature of these networks and the difficulty in identifying and disrupting them. All these engagements, whether by the radical groups or the government, are an indication that within a global village, the environment for radicalization, terrorism, but also control of the same, is made easier. The section below expounds on how communication, economic mobility and fluidity of national borders have facilitated radicalization and therewith, fundamentalism.

## Communication and Radicalization

Technological advancement has made communication faster, cheaper, and accessible to many. The diverse modes of communication services have hastened the ease with which populations are able to receive and pass on information. The social media platforms, mobile telephony, and transportation means are now, more than ever, advanced. This revolution in technology and communication is affecting virtually all the fields of human life. The ubiquitous social media has availed user-friendly and cost-effective means of communication even to the not-so-rich populations (Jeppesen, 2016; Magak et al., 2013). There are all manner of offers for mobile and Internet subscribers to access their desired means of communication. Moreover, as Jirires (2016) argues, the open Internet space (dark web), has been a perfect breeding ground for (religious) extremism. The dark web, which has a vast terrorism database, provides a fertile radicalization ground for Islamic fundamentalists; a place where they can carry out their nefarious activities anonymously. Subsequently, media, whether mainstream or alternative/social, has shaped perceptions, beliefs, and values among young people in Kenya. It can contribute to youth radicalization (Mugo & Mberia, 2017; Ngunjiri, 2016).

Ngunjiri (2016) shows that media communication can reinforce stereotypes and negative perceptions of certain groups, which can contribute to feelings of marginalization and exclusion among young people. This is also aligned to the fact that media can be used to spread conspiracy theories and misinformation, which can fuel resentment and anger among young people (Mugo & Mberia, 2017). This misinformation can create a sense of injustice and lead to fertile ground for radicalization, as young people seek to identify with groups that offer a sense of belonging and purpose.

Any misfits within a given society, especially youth, in search of social accommodation, can easily find extremist information on different communication platforms such as mobile telephones and the Internet. The explosion of social media, which are widely used by the youth, has therefore been a boon for fundamentalist radicalization. The youth constitute about one-third of Kenya's population of 45 million. Most of these youth are unemployed: a fact that makes them vulnerable to radicalizing ideological messages that promise them economic benefits (Botha, 2013).

Botha (2013) says that peer influence plays a big role in radicalization. She reveals that 38% of youth in Mombasa who joined Al Shabaab were introduced by their friends. This introduction may be through the spreading of extremist ideologies to recruit vulnerable young people (Mugo & Mberia, 2017). For instance, extremist groups may use social media platforms to disseminate propaganda that promotes violence and encourages young people to join their cause. Social media platforms such as Facebook, Twitter, and WhatsApp have been used to spread extremist ideologies, particularly among vulnerable youth populations, by creating echo chambers, where young people are exposed only to like-minded individuals and viewpoints (Macharia & Gathogo, 2020).

Bakker (2006) argues that the role of family and family ties is crucial for investigation of approaches to radicalization. Social affiliation, the most crucial factor in this process, plays a role in radicalization that results in violence. Subsequently, at a time where family and parenting roles seem to have been replaced and/or greatly influenced by technological advancement, peer relations are deemed valuable by the youth. These relations are strengthened by the easy access to mobile telephony and the Internet, that allow for extremist groups to spread their messages and recruit vulnerable individuals (Macharia & Gathogo, 2020; Muema, 2019).

There are also indications of home-based terrorism activities that scholarly research has termed as terror cells (Cannon & Pkalya, 2017: 8–9). The effectiveness of these terror cells implies the effective use of modern communication technology. This is a challenge that the Kenya government has been grappling with for a long time, with limited success. Some of the most horrendous incidents like the Westgate Mall and Mpeketoni attacks that killed 67 and 65 people respectively (Magak & Omwalo, 2014), seem to have happened without any foresight by the security forces in the country. The Garissa University College attack in 2015 where Al Shabaab took students hostage (Torbjörnsson, 2016), killing 148 people, caught the security forces unaware.[2] How then, one would ask, are such massacres executed, if not through the help of communication technology?

## Diminished Significance of National Borders and Radicalization

Diminished borders refer to the breaking down of physical, cultural, and linguistic barriers that previously separated people and communities (Wambugu & Nyabuto, 2019). The changing terrain of communication and technological advancement has almost completely dissolved physical national and international borders. Information, goods, and services are able to cross borders physically and virtually without enormous challenges. For physical porosity of borders, there has to be lack of effective border controls, which enables the free movement of people and goods across national boundaries. The instability and conflict in neighbouring countries such as Somalia, Ethiopia, and South Sudan have also contributed to the porous borders situation in Kenya (Wachira & Ng'ang'a, 2020; Wambua & Mburu, 2019). Diminished borders are also as a result of technological advancement, and especially the rise of social media and other forms of technology that facilitate virtual movement of ideas, goods and services. Nyambura and Mwema (2018) argue that the internet and social media have significantly reduced physical, cultural, and linguistic barriers that previously separated people and communities. This, in turn, has made it easier for extremist groups to spread their messages and recruit vulnerable youth populations. The study also found that the anonymity of social media had made it easier for young people to access extremist content without fear of being identified. These processes have created new opportunities for youth radicalization (Nyambura & Mwema, 2018; Wambugu & Nyabuto, 2019), facilitating the spread of extremist ideologies and the recruitment of vulnerable youth populations (Wachira & Ng'ang'a, 2020; Wambua & Mburu, 2019). The porous borders, therefore, enable extremist groups to cross into Kenya and recruit vulnerable youth populations, as it is difficult for security agencies to identify and prevent the movement of extremist groups across borders. This creates a sense of lawlessness that makes it easier for extremist groups to operate (Wachira & Ng'ang'a, 2020).

---

[2] See "Garissa University College Attack in Kenya: What Happened?". *BBC News*, June 19th 2019. Garissa University College Attack in Kenya: What Happened?—BBC News. Accessed 8 March 2023.

The International Crisis Group (ICG) (2012: 1) explains that the militant Al Shabaab movement has built a cross-border presence and a clandestine support network among Muslim populations in Kenya's north-eastern, coastal, and Nairobi regions and is trying to radicalize and recruit youth from these areas, often capitalizing on longstanding grievances against the central government. The availability of mediascape, including WhatsApp, Facebook, YouTube, LinkedIn, and Instagram, among others, is a favourable means through which the physical borders are dissolved to facilitate growth of the group's terror cells in Kenya. According to Cannon and Pkalya (2017: 8–9):

> With a relatively high number of recruits, Al Shabaab has been able to establish networks and cells of home-grown extremists that are assessed to be behind at least some of the terrorist attacks in Kenya. Four of the five Garissa University College attackers were Kenyans, for example. Two of the four Westgate Mall attackers were Somali refugees who had grown up in Kenya. The high number of Kenyan returnees from Somalia, as Al Shabaab trainees or otherwise—estimated to be more than 700—is further evidence that Al Shabaab chooses to attack Kenya on account of its relative ease as a target and the opportunities it provides.

This is an indication of not just how the nationals of the two countries are able to easily cross border but also how advancement in communication technology facilitates terror activities. Within this loop, money and arms are able to circulate easily for the radicalized groups to achieve their objectives. In addition, the economic movement of goods and services across polarized borders has also meant availability of arms. Rabasa (2009) asserts that there is a covert arms market in the Eastleigh, a trading hub located to the east of Nairobi. She adds that these arms are also brought to airfields and trafficked in north-western Kenya.

The long and porous Kenya-Somalia border, that is impossible to police effectively, helps the violent activities of As Shabaab fundamentalists. While citing Human Rights Watch (2002), Rabasa (2009: 20) explains that:

> State presence in border areas is marginal throughout East Africa, reflecting a general inability of the governments to police the outer reaches of their territories. Kenya's border with Somalia, for instance, is porous and in large part arid and thinly populated, largely by ethnic Somalis. Although there are nominal customs checkpoints at the main Kenyan entry points, the rest of the border is rarely patrolled and there are many smuggling routes.

Somalis, including refugees and Al Shabaab militants, enter Kenya mainly through the north-eastern part; a border region between the two countries. Indeed, northern Kenya hosts two large refugee camps—Kakuma and Dadaaab Refugee Camps. Although regulations for registering refugees in the country are clear, the porous Kenya-Somalia border allows easy access into Kenya, where corrupt Kenya government officials give the refugees Kenyan identity cards.[3] With these porous borders, it is easy to move the radicalized youth across the borders into Somalia for training. In addition, small arms flow across unchecked, creating a cycle of demand that fuels violent extremism and armed criminality (ICG, 2012: 1). Botha (2013) explains that since Somalia has suffered various forms of conflict that have affected its socio-economic state, the ground has become fertile for recruiting and training the youth for religious extremism. The country, therefore, provides a safe haven for training camps and other opportunities for extremists to organize.

## Economic Mobility and Radicalization

Economic mobility refers to the ability of individuals to move up the economic ladder and improve their standard of living (Njeru & Kaburu, 2019). It is also seen as opportunities availed by globalization that allow for goods and services to move freely from one place to the other. Mutahi and Mutuku (2018) and Njeru and Kaburu (2019) show that young people who lack economic opportunities are more likely to become radicalized. These studies also show that extremist groups exploit the economic frustration of young people by offering them financial incentives in exchange for their participation in extremist activities. Globalization has facilitated the movement of goods and services across borders. Besides the transfer of physical goods and services, there are now virtual markets and virtual trade. Money and services can cross borders through the airspaces for transfer provided by financial institutions and mobile telephony money exchange services. In Kenya, mobile money transfer services, including *Mpesa*, Airtel Money, *M-Shwari*, *MCHANGA*, and Equitel Money among others, have meant that the access to goods and services is not dictated by physical proximity.

The phenomenal growth of Somali-owned businesses in Kenya's commercial towns and urban centres is based on family relations and friends. In Nairobi for instance, most of the Somali business people are concentrated in Eastleigh, nicknamed "Little Mogadishu," a trading hub located to the

---
[3] www.bbc.com/news/world-africa-20819462, accessed 3 May 2018.

east of Nairobi. By September 2012, Eastleigh accounted for 25% of the total Nairobi City Council's tax revenue.[4] Somalis are very communal, with close-knit social systems. Their religious, social, cultural, and economic ties hold them together. They, therefore, tend to live together, especially in Kenya where they are not the majority. In most Kenyan towns and cities, they have established businesses in the same streets, most of which have been dubbed "Garissa Lodges," Garissa being one of the major towns in the Somali-dominated north-eastern Kenya. This has facilitated an avenue for the radical *imams* to use their family ties and businesses to target the youth for radicalization. Mostly, the youth are brainwashed with promises of economic support through these ties. They are then transported across the porous border into "lawless" Somalia, where the radicals have established bases for training, and are able to receive financial support from their support agencies, like Al Qaeda and family support systems in Kenya and other countries to sustain their activities.

While citing Salih (2004), Rabasa (2009) argues that:

> Islamic charities have played an important role in the spread of radical Islam in East Africa. There are, of course, different categories of Islamic NGOs. Some provide relief and humanitarian assistance. Others are engaged in long-term development activities. Some are involved in *da'wa* (literally, "the call," Islamic missionary activity). And yet others have been used as vehicles to spread political Islam or to support militant groups. (p. 41)

With regard to radicalization and funding, Moller (2006: 18–19) says that whereas Islamic communities in Kenya have until recently been predominantly Sufi and generally peaceful, Islamic reform movements may be gaining ground, most of them related to *Salafism* and especially *Wahhabism*.[5] The factors highlighted as having facilitated these are presence of Islamic NGOs and charities partly financed by Saudi Arabia and other Gulf states, (believed to be propagating Islamic radicalism and even sponsoring terrorism), the construction of mosques and *madrasas* funded by the same Arab countries teaching *Wahhabism* and Arab sponsorship for study visits to Saudi Arabia where the students are exposed to radical Islamism. Indeed, the ICG (2002) argues that some charities proselytize and promote an Arab-Islamist

---

[4] www.bbc.com/news/world-africa-11962254, accessed 3rd May 2018.

[5] Rabasa (2009) explains that the growth of radical Islam in East Africa in recent decades has manifested itself in the spread of Salafi and Wahhabi ideologies, which has put pressure on traditional and Sufi practices, and in the emergence of extremist and terrorist groups influenced by these ideologies.

curriculum, engage in political activism and advocate Somalia's transformation into a strict Islamic state. With the fruits of globalization, through scholarships and funded project activities, this curriculum easily crosses borders to targeted communities. Under the cover of these charitable activities, the Islamists are able to target the marginalized youth who are desperate to get help. As the ICG (2012) and Botha (2013) argue, a history of insurgency, misrule, and repression, chronic poverty, massive youth unemployment, high population growth, insecurity, poor infrastructure, and lack of basic services, have combined to produce some of the Kenya's bleakest socio-economic and political conditions.

In the year 2014, a number of Muslim clerics who were specifically associated with radicalizing the youth in Mombasa were said to have been assassinated by unknown men, though word around the streets was that the killings were orchestrated by the police. Radical Islamist Sheikh Sharif Abubakar, alias Makaburi, was killed on April 1, 2014. He had denied a direct role in radical preaching using recorded tapes, face-to-face meetings and printed materials that were confiscated by the police. He, however, seemed to use disaffected youth and is quoted as having said: "The youth are disgruntled and fed up with the leadership of people who are concerned only with their economic interests." These youths were ideologically the orphans of Sheikh Aboud Rogo, the radical Islamist and suspected Al Shabaab mastermind who was killed in Mombasa by "unknown men" on August 27, 2012.[6]

## 5 Tripartite Contribution Towards Fundamentalism

As the discussion above shows, the three facets of globalization: communication and technology, diminished borders, and economic mobility, amalgamate in many ways than they disengage, so that the totality of the three contributes to the use of religion as a tool for expression and assertion of extremist views. They accelerate Islamic fundamentalism. There is considerable literature on the resultant effects of extreme violent activities, an indication that, if globalization is fashionable, then this can only be true of some aspects and fields and not others. Diminished significance of borders, improved communication technology, and economic mobility are, in our case, contributing negatively towards the fight on religious extremism. Communication has played a significant role in the rise of fundamentalism,

---

[6] https://www.standardmedia.co.ke/article/2000141747/why-mosques-at-kenya-s-coast-have-turned-into-hotbeds-of-islamic-radicalism, accessed 20th July 2018.

especially given the advent of the internet and social media platforms, and this also influences the aspect of physical borders as extremist groups can communicate with their followers without necessarily having to physically cross geographical locations. This allows them to spread their ideologies. According to Joffé, social media has facilitated the growth of fundamentalism as it enables extremist groups to communicate with their followers, recruit new members, and radicalize them (Joffé, 2017) through proxy. Subsequently, social media platforms such as Twitter and Facebook have enabled extremist groups to easily reach a global audience and recruit new members (Al-Rawi & Lewis, 2018). The anonymity provided by these platforms has made it easier for extremist groups to spread their message without fear of detection (Anderlini & Davies, 2017). As a result, fundamentalist ideologies have been able to penetrate different societies and cultures, leading to the radicalization of individuals. The anonymity provided by these platforms has allowed extremist groups to propagate their ideologies, making it difficult for authorities to track them.

The recruitment through these forms of social media are largely, but not exclusively, targeted towards economically disadvantaged youth. This category of persons are more likely to be drawn to extremist ideologies as they seek to find meaning and purpose in life (Krueger, 2017). Combined, communication technologies and economic mobility have therefore contributed to the rise of fundamentalism. According to Ali and Fathi (2018), the lack of economic opportunities and social mobility have led to the growth of fundamentalist ideologies in the Middle East and North Africa. The inability of governments to address economic inequality has left many young people feeling disillusioned with the political system, making them susceptible to extremist ideologies. Additionally, extremist groups often provide economic incentives, such as employment opportunities or financial support, which makes them appealing to vulnerable individuals.

The detrimental effect of these two combined aspects is further exacerbated by the notion of diminished borders that allow for free movement of people and goods across borders. This means that extremist groups can spread their ideologies across different regions. Extremist groups often take advantage of the porous borders to move their operatives and propaganda materials across different regions (Barakat, 2017). This has led to an increase in cross-border attacks, making it difficult for authorities to combat the growth of fundamentalism.

A few strategies are therefore needed if an effort is to be made in countering fundamentalism. First, it is important to understand the nature and impact of the different factors of globalization and the degree to which they vary or interact. This kind of analysis is important in helping map out the possible ways through which the channels of radicalization, fuelled by radicalization, can be put under check. Further, there is a need for the Kenyan and other African governments to tap into the three highlighted aspects of globalization wisely, as synergies for networking and empowering the youth, so that religious fundamentalisms, and specifically radicalization and violence, can be significantly reduced. Second, religion in Africa and other developing countries can be used as a means to provide the basic frame of reference. Mtata (2012) argues that, positively viewed, religion and other secular avenues can be used to address youth's underlying social, economic, and political factors that contribute to the radicalization of youth. This can be achieved through education, youth-empowerment programmes, and the promotion of inclusive governance and socio-economic development (Lual, 2019).

The third approach may be the need to strengthen community resilience by fostering interfaith dialogue, promoting social cohesion, and encouraging community-led initiatives that counter extremist narratives. This involves working with local religious and community leaders to develop and implement effective prevention strategies (Hussain, 2017). Additionally, as Ndiku (2019) argues, law enforcement and security agencies should adopt a community-oriented policing approach, which involves building trust and cooperation between law enforcement agencies and the community. This approach can help identify and prevent radicalization before it leads to violent extremism. Finally, for the overall good of the continent, there is a need for regional cooperation and collaboration as an essential approach in addressing the transnational nature of radicalization. This includes sharing intelligence, exchanging best practices, and developing joint initiatives to address the threat of violent extremism in the region (Abdi, 2017).

## 6 Conclusion

This chapter argues that the widespread use of social media platforms such as Facebook, Twitter, and WhatsApp has enabled extremist groups to spread their ideologies to a broader audience. This is especially complicated by the ability of the extremist groups to have anonymous accounts that allow the groups to recruit and radicalize young people through extremist propaganda materials online, without betting nubbed. This has facilitated the growth of extremist networks in Kenya and beyond. This aspect of technology also partly speaks to diminished borders since goods and services need not physically cross borders. The diminished borders are also enabled by virtual communication that facilitates an easier way of recruiting and planning for execution of terror activities. Subsequently, the goods, services, operatives and propaganda material find their way across different regions. The porous border between Kenya and Somalia, for instance, has facilitated the movement of extremists and their materials across the border, leading to an increase in terrorist attacks (Smith & Bwana, 2017).

This chapter took a narrow perspective in understanding how communication and technology, economic mobility, and diminished significance of borders contribute towards radicalization and, in the end, towards fundamentalism and violence. From the discussions, religion has been used to recruit and mobilize the youth for terror activities. This chapter calls for a reversed approach by religious leaders who are in positions of authority to use the same facets of globalization to turn things around. As appears from the chapter's discussions, it is possible to view religion as a promoter of violence or dismiss it as irrelevant to development objectives. It is also possible to pay attention to the extremist beliefs and actions of a minority, rather than the ways religion guides and inspires the majority for good (Jafari, 2007: 111–112). If this happens, and as Jafari (2007) warns, we risk misunderstanding the local (and global) dynamics of fundamentalism and simultaneously overlook globalization as a potent resource for addressing the issue. Religion, with its unmatched authority among many communities in every region of the world, carries within it a diverse set of traditions and methodologies that, together with the fruits of globalization discussed in this chapter, can promote peace, development, and specifically youth empowerment. Scholars are called upon to explore possible models that would turn things round. This would ensure that scholars contribute meaningfully towards addressing the felt needs of their communities and nations.

# References

Abdi, A. (2017). Regional Cooperation in Countering Violent Extremism in the Horn of Africa. *African Security Review, 26*(3), 234–245.

Al-Rawi, A., & Lewis, J. (2018). The Social Media Battlefield: Countering Islamist Extremist Narratives Online. *Studies in Conflict & Terrorism, 41*(2), 117–135.

Ali, M., & Fathi, M. (2018). *The Economic Roots of Political Islam: Evidence from the Arab World* (Economic Research Forum, Working Paper No. 1244).

Anderlini, S. N., & Davies, M. L. (2017). Countering Violent Extremism (CVE) Through Women's Rights and Empowerment: Lessons from Kenya. *International Centre for Counter-Terrorism, 8*, 1–16.

Appleby, R. S. (2000). *The Ambivalence of the Sacred: Religion, Violence, and Reconciliation*. Rowman & Littlefield.

Bakker, E. (2006). *Jihadi Terrorists in Europe: Their Characteristics and the Circumstances in Which They Joined the Jihad. An Exploratory Study*. Clignendael.

Barakat, S. (2017). The Geography of Jihadism in Africa. *Stability: International Journal of Security and Development, 6*(1), 1–12.

Batson, D. (1993). *Religion and the Individual: A Socio-Psychological Perspective*. New York University Press.

Bloom, M. (2012). Religion and Violence: A Dialectical Engagement Through the Insights of Girard and Weber. *Journal of Religion and Violence, 1*(1), 67–87.

Botha, A. (2013). *Assessing the Vulnerability of Kenyan Youth to Radicalism and Extremism* (pp. 1–28). Institute for Security Studies, Paper 245.

Cannon, B. J., & Pkalya, D. R. (2017). Why al Shabaab Attacks Kenya: Questioning the Narrative Paradigm. *Terrorism and Political Violence*. https://doi.org/10.1080/09546553.2017.1290607.

Chande, A. (2000). Radicalism and Reform in East Africa. In N. Levtzion & R. L. Pouwels (Eds.), *Islam in Africa* (pp. 349–369). Ohio University Press.

Chitando, E., & Tarusarira, J. (Eds.). (2019). *Religion and Human Security in Africa*. Taylor & Francis Group, Routledge.

CLEEN. (2014). *Youths, Radicalization and Affiliation with Insurgent Groups in Northern Nigeria*. CLEEN Foundation. Justice Sector Reform. 978-978-51062-8-2.

Cuterera, S. (2012). Globalization: Definitions, Processes and Concepts. *Revista Română de Statistică—Supliment Trim, IV*, 137–146.

Engineer, A. A. (1984). Islamic Fundamentalism and the Muslim World. In A. A. Engineer (Ed.), *Islam and Revolution* (pp. 1–12). Ajanta Publications.

Esposito, J. L. (1998). Islam and Violence. In J. L. Esposito (Ed.), *The Oxford History of Islam* (pp. 645–692). Oxford University Press.

Gartenstein-Ross, D., & Appel, H. (2014, April 3). Al Shabaab's Insurgency in Somalia: A Databased Snapshot, *Georgetown Journal of International Affairs*. http://journal.georgetown.edu/alShabaabs-insurgency-in-somalia-a-data-based-snapshot/. Accessed 23 February 2023.

Githuku, A. N. (2019). Unemployment and Radicalization of Youth in Kenya: The Case of Mombasa County. *Journal of Politics and Society, 26*(1), 78–96.

GOK. (2015). *Strengthen Community's Capacity against Radicalization and Violent Extremism in Kenya*. Project Document. GOK and UNDP.

Grinin, L., & Korotayev, A. (2019). Islamism and its Role in Modern Islamic Societies. In *Islamism, Arab Spring, and the Future of Democracy*. Perspectives on Development in the Middle East and North Africa (MENA) Region. Springer. https://doi.org/10.1007/978-3-319-91077-2_3.

Harpviken, K., & Røislien, H. (2008). Faithful Brokers? Potentials and Pitfalls of Religion in Peacemaking. *Conflict Resolution Quarterly, 25*(3), 351–373.

Hansen, J. S. (2013). *Al-Shabaab in Somalia: The History and Ideology of a Militant Islamist Group, 2005–2012*. Hurst & Company.

Horn, P. (2018). Kenya and al Shabaab: Beyond Military Engagement. *African Affairs, 117*(468), 688–710. https://doi.org/10.1093/afraf/ady014.

Human Rights Watch. (2002, May). *Playing with Fire: Weapons Proliferation, Political Violence, and Human Rights in Kenya.*

Hussain, A. (2017). Countering Violent Extremism in Africa: An Overview of the Challenges and Opportunities. *Institute for Security Studies*, 1–11.

Ibrahim, M. (2010). *The Al Shabaab Myth: Notoriety Not Popularity.* NCEIS Research Papers Vol.3 (5). National Centre of Excellence For Islamic Studies. University of Melbourne.

International Crisis Group (ICG). (2002). Somalia: Countering Terrorism in a Failed State, Nairobi/Brussels, ICG Africa Report No. 45.

International Crisis Group (ICG). (2012). Kenya Somali Islamist Radicalization. Africa Briefing N°85, Nairobi/Brussels, 25 January 2012.

International Crisis Group (ICG). (2019). *Kenya's Resilience to Al Shabaab's Regional Designs.* https://www.crisisgroup.org/africa/horn-africa/kenya/kenyas-resilience-alShabaabs-regional-designs.

Jafari, S. (2007). Local Religious Peacemakers: An Untapped Resource in US Foreign Policy. *Journal of International Affairs, 61*(1), 111–130.

Jeppesen, S. (2016). Understanding Alternative Media Power: Mapping Content and Practice to Theory, Ideology, and Political Action. *Democratic Communiqué, 27*, 54–77.

Jirires, T. I. (2016). Online Radicalization vs. In-Person Radicalization: Is There a Difference? *Journal for Deradicalization, 6*, 206–230.

Joffé, G. (2017). Terrorism and Social Media: What Is the Link? *Journal of Terrorism Research, 8*(2), 1–10.

Jones, S., Liepman, A., & Chandler, N. (2016). *Counterterrorism and Counterinsurgency in Somalia: Assessing the Campaign Against Al Shabaab.* RAND Corporation.

Juergensmeyer, M. (2000). *Terror in the Mind of God: The Global Rise of Religious Violence.* University of California Press.

Kamau, J. (2019). Kenya: Anti-Terror Police Accused of Abuse. *Al Jazeera.* https://www.aljazeera.com/news/2019/11/28/kenya-anti-terror-police-accused-of-abuse.

Kepel, G. (1993). *Muslim Extremism in Egypt: The Prophet and the Pharaoh* (2nd ed.). University of California Press.

Kilonzo, S. (2020). Religion, Youth and Development in Africa. In E. Chitando, M. R. Gunda, & L. Togarasei (Eds.), *Religion and Development in Africa* (pp. 103–123). University of Bamberg Press.

Krueger, A. B. (2017). *What Makes a Terrorist: Economics and the Roots of Terrorism.* Princeton University Press.

Lual, D. K. (2019). The Role of Education in Preventing Youth Radicalisation in Africa. *The Journal of Pan African Studies, 12*(2), 217–228.

Macharia, K., & Gathogo, J. (2020). The Role of Social Media in Radicalisation of Youth in Kenya. *International Journal of Social Science and Humanities Research, 8*(2), 1–10.

Magak, K., & Omwalo, B. (2014). The Children of Sisyphus: The Somali Ethnic Identity Factor in Kenya's Peace and Security. *Journal of International Politics and Development, 12*(2), 47–62.

Magak, K., Kilonzo, S., & Ogembo, J. (2013). Indigenous Language FM Stations as Community Development Media: The Case of Radio Lake Victoria. In A. Ojebode (Ed.), *Community Media for Development and Participation: Experiences, Thoughts and Forethoughts* (pp. 114–136). John Archers Publishers.

Mahmood, S. (2005). *Politics of Piety: The Islamic Revival and the Feminist Subject.* Princeton University Press.

Marchal, R. (2009). A Tentative Assessment of the Somali Harakat Al-Shabaab. *Journal of Eastern African Studies, 3*(3), 381–404.

Media Council of Kenya. (2016). *A Handbook on Reporting Terrorism.* International Media Support and Media Council of Kenya.

Moller, B. (2006). *Political Islam in Kenya* (DIIS Working Paper no. 2006/22).

Mtata, K. (2012). Religion and Development: Friends or Foes? In K. Mtata (Ed.), *Religion: Help or Hindrance to Development.* Proceedings from a Conference held in Eberhard Hitzler, 21–25 October 2012. Lutheran World Federation Documentation 58. Liepzig: Lutheran World Federation.

Muema, J. (2019). Social Media and Youth Radicalisation in Kenya. *International Journal of Scientific and Research Publications, 9*(2), 300–304.

Mugo, M. N., & Mberia, H. K. (2017). The Role of Media in Radicalization and Violent Extremism: A Review of Literature. *Journal of Communication and Media Studies, 9*(3), 33–47.

Mutahi, P. N., & Mutuku, J. M. (2018). Economic Mobility and Youth Radicalization in Kenya. *Journal of Development and Agricultural Economics, 10*(4), 109–117.

Mwakimako, H., & Willis, J. (2016). Islam and Democracy: Debating Electoral Involvement on the Kenya Coast. *Islamic Africa, 7*(1), 19–43. https://doi.org/10.1163/21540993-00701001.

Mwalimu, N. (2021). Youth Radicalization and Extremist Violence in Kenya: A Review of Literature. *Journal of Terrorism Research, 12*(2), 1–14. https://doi.org/10.15664/jtr.1723.

Ndiku, J. (2019). Community Policing and Countering Violent Extremism: Experiences from Kenya. In *Countering Violent Extremism in Africa* (pp. 73–85). Palgrave Macmillan.

Ngunjiri, J. (2016). Media and Radicalization of Young People in Kenya: A Case Study of the Coastal Region. *Journal of African Media Studies, 8*(1), 33–47.

Njeru, A. W., & Kaburu, J. K. (2019). Economic Mobility and Youth Radicalization in Kenya. *International Journal of Economics, Commerce and Management, 7*(11), 1–12.

Nyambura, J. K., & Mwema, M. (2018). Diminished Borders and Youth Radicalization in Kenya. *Journal of Media and Communication Studies, 10*(2), 20–28.

Nyangau, W. M., & Kabue, S. K. (2019). The Role of Poverty in Radicalization Among the Muslim Youth in Kenya. *Journal of Poverty, Investment and Development, 47,* 25–34. https://doi.org/10.7176/JPID/47-03.

Odongo, D. S., & Ogola, G. O. (2017). Examining the Causes of Youth Involvement in Terrorism and Radicalization in Kenya. *Journal of Terrorism Research, 8*(1), 1–13. https://doi.org/10.15664/Jtr.1219.

Onuoha, F. (2014). Why do Youth Join Boko Haram? *United States Institute of Peace Special Report.* No. 348. USIP.

Owen, F. (2012). Somalia: Little Hope for Peace. *Centre for Security Studies Analysis in Security Policy.* No. 119. September 2012. ETH, Zurich.

Rabasa, A. (2009). *Radical Islam in East Africa for United States Air Force.* RAND Corporation.

Roy, O. (2013). *Holy Ignorance: When Religion and Culture Part Ways.* Oxford University Press.

Shauri, H., & Wanjala, S. (2017) Radicalization and Violent Extremism at the Coast of Kenya: "Powerful Voices of Coexistence, Are They Being Heard?" In N. Kimani & I. Cege (Eds.), *Meeting of Cultures at the Kenyan Coast* (pp. 145–154). Twaweza Communications.

Smith, D. J., & Bwana, C. (2017). Countering Radicalisation in the Horn of Africa: A Kenyan Case Study. *Terrorism and Political Violence, 29*(3), 442–463.

Thordsen, S. (2009). *New Muslim Activism in Kenya.* MA dissertation in Political Science, Aarhus University. http://www.specialer.sam.au.dk/.

Torbjörnsson, D., & Jonsson, M. (2016). Containment or Contagion? Countering al Shabaab Efforts to Sow Discord in Kenya. *Studies in African Security.* FOI Memo 5742, Project number A16104. https://www.foi.se/download/18.7fd35d 7f166c56ebe0bbdf9/1542369068783/Containment-or-Contagion_FOIMemo-5742.pdf.

Wachira, G. K., & Ng'ang'a, S. K. (2020). Porous Borders and Youth Radicalization in Kenya. *International Journal of Humanities and Social Science Research, 9*(1), 1–12.

Wambua, J. K., & Mburu, P. M. (2019). Porous Borders and Youth Radicalization in Kenya. *International Journal of Social Sciences and Humanities Research, 7*(1), 1–10.

Wambugu, S. K., & Nyabuto, D. K. (2019). Social Media and Youth Radicalization in Kenya. *International Journal of Humanities and Social Science Research, 8*(1), 1–9.

Wiktorowicz, Q. (2004). Islamic Activism and Social Movement Theory: A New Direction for Research. In D. A. Snow, S. A. Soule, & H. Kriesi (Eds.), *The Blackwell Companion to Social Movements* (pp. 295–323). Blackwell.